THE AMERICAN REVOLUTION
1773–1776

THE AMERICAN REVOLUTION

WRITINGS FROM THE PAMPHLET DEBATE

II: 1773–1776

Gordon S. Wood, *editor*

THE LIBRARY OF AMERICA

Visit our website at www.loa.org.

This paper meets the requirements of
ANSI/NISO Z39.48–1992 (Permanence of Paper).

Distributed to the trade in the United States
by Penguin Random House Inc.
and in Canada by Penguin Random House Canada Ltd.

Library of Congress Control Number: 2014946652
ISBN 978–1–59853–378–1

973.3

First Printing
The Library of America—266

Manufactured in the United States of America

The American Revolution:
Writings from the Pamphlet Debate 1773–1776
is kept in print by a gift from

SIDNEY AND RUTH LAPIDUS

to the Guardians of American Letters Fund,
established by The Library of America
to ensure that every volume in the series
will be permanently available.

The American Revolution:
Writings from the Pamphlet Debate 1773–1776
is published with support from

THE BODMAN FOUNDATION

Contents

Preface

"What do we Mean by the Revolution? The War? That was no part of the Revolution. It was only an Effect and Consequence of it. The Revolution was in the Minds of the People, and this was effected, from 1760 to 1775, in the course of fifteen Years before a drop of blood was drawn at Lexington. The Records of thirteen Legislatures, the Pamphlets, Newspapers in all the Colonies, ought to be consulted, during that Period to ascertain the Steps by which the public Opinion was enlightened and informed concerning the Authority of Parliament over the Colonies."
—John Adams to Thomas Jefferson, 1815

British imperial reforms undertaken in the 1760s sparked one of the most consequential constitutional debates in Western history. Taken up between American colonists and Britons and among the colonists themselves, this debate was carried on largely in pamphlets—inexpensive booklets ranging in length from five thousand to twenty-five thousand words and printed on anywhere from ten to a hundred pages. Easy and cheap to manufacture, these pamphlets were ideal for rapid exchanges of arguments and counter-arguments. Pamphlets concerned with the American controversy from both sides of the Atlantic number well over a thousand, and they cover all of the significant issues of politics—the nature of power, liberty, representation, rights, constitutions, the division of authority between different spheres of government, and sovereignty. This Library of America volume, the second of a two-volume set, presents the most interesting and important of these works, with a preference in selection for pamphlets directly in dialogue with one another. By the time the debate traced here was over, the first British Empire was in tatters, and Americans had not only clarified their understanding of the limits of public power, they had prepared the way for their grand experiment in republican self-government and constitution-making.

Introduction

The Peace of Paris of 1763 ending the Seven Years War made Great Britain the greatest power in the world. France, Britain's principal enemy, had been humbled, her authority totally expelled from the North American continent. But victory had been costly and Britain's national debt was staggering. Tens of thousands of native peoples in the west and over seventy thousand French subjects now had to be dealt with. At the same time the jerry-built imperial structure that had developed over a century and a half had to be reformed. Who was to pay for the administration of this newly enlarged empire and the peacetime army required to maintain order among its discordant parts? After years of war, English taxpayers were already overburdened. Since the results of the war greatly benefited the crown's North American subjects, British officials naturally looked to them for new revenues.

The result was a series of British administrative and legislative actions that would collectively assume for Americans the character of a conspiracy against their traditional rights. To prevent costly clashes with the Indians in the west, white settlers somehow had to be kept from encroaching on native lands. The first measure therefore was a royal proclamation in 1763 forbidding American colonists from moving westward across a line crudely drawn along the Appalachians. This act of crown prerogative was followed by a succession of parliamentary acts that increasingly inflamed colonial opinion. The Sugar Act of 1764 transformed the Molasses Act of 1733, which had sought only to regulate the flow of trade, into a revenue-raising measure. The British government recognized that the colonial customs system—so notoriously corrupt and ineffective that it failed to collect enough revenue even to cover the cost of its operation—had to be overhauled if it was to be productive of both proceeds and good order. So the Sugar Act also placed new regulatory burdens on colonial commerce, including the expanded use of writs of assistance (or search warrants) and the establishment of a vice-admiralty court in Halifax, Nova Scotia, which required no jury trials for enforcement. Under pressure from colonial merchants holding depreciated paper money that could not be used to pay their creditors in Britain, Parliament in 1764 also passed a Currency Act prohibiting colonial assemblies from making paper money legal tender; this had the effect of seriously restraining the colonists' trade with one another. In 1765 the Quartering Act set down regulations requiring the housing and provisioning of British troops in America.

While these actions, engineered by George Grenville, the British prime minister, provoked protests in most of the colonies, American opposition to them was nothing compared to the firestorm ignited by Parliament's passage of the Stamp Act in the spring of 1765. This act levied a tax on legal documents, newspapers, and nearly every form of paper used in the colonies. Suddenly, the issue was no longer the commercial fairness of Britain's attempts to remodel its empire. It had become a matter of constitutional principle, one that struck at the heart of the colonists' relationship with the mother country.

Newspapers and pamphlets, the number and like of which had never appeared in America before, exploded in anger. Mobs in the thirteen colonies forced the stamp agents to resign, preventing the issuance of any stamps in all but one. (Before resigning, the stamp agent in Georgia did manage to distribute some stamps to customs officials who briefly used them in Savannah, infuriating colonists there and elsewhere.) In October 1765 thirty-seven delegates from nine colonies met in New York in the Stamp Act Congress and drew up a set of formal declarations denying Parliament's right to tax Americans. "It is inseparably essential to the Freedom of a People, and the undoubted Right of *Englishmen*," the Congress declared, "that no Taxes be imposed on them, but with their own Consent, given personally, or by their Representatives." And since "the People of these Colonies are not, and from their local Circumstances cannot be, Represented in the House of Commons in *Great-Britain*," they could be taxed only by persons known and chosen by themselves, who served in their respective legislatures. Although the colonists sometimes stumbled and fumbled in the pamphlet debate triggered by the imperial reforms, especially as they sought to explain why they accepted Parliament's authority in some areas but not in others, they never deviated from this essential point.

Under pressure from colonial boycotts of British goods, the British government, now headed by the Rockingham Whigs, retreated and on February 21, 1766, repealed the Stamp Act, an extraordinary action that rankled many Englishmen for whom Parliament's authority was sacrosanct. As a face-saving measure Parliament simultaneously passed the Declaratory Act, affirming its authority to make laws for the colonies "in all cases whatsoever." Though most Americans rejoiced at the repeal of the hated Stamp Act, here was the seed of future conflict.

The colonists groped to understand and explain their position in the empire. They knew, as the Stamp Act Congress admitted, that they owed "all due Subordination to that August Body, the Parliament of *Great-Britain*." But for them this "due subordination" meant allowing Parliament only to regulate their trade, not to tax them. This in turn raised the question of whether duties levied on imports into the colonies should be considered trade regulations or taxes. Some Americans, including Benjamin Franklin, had hinted during the debate over the Stamp Act that while colonists would rightfully object to "internal" taxes, like the stamp duty, they might be reconciled to "external" taxes in the form of customs duties. In 1767 Charles Townshend, the chancellor of the Exchequer, seized upon this suggestion by placing duties on colonial imports, including glass, paper, and tea. Inspired by influential pamphlets like John Dickinson's *Letters from a Farmer in Pennsylvania*, however, most Americans repudiated the distinction and made clear their opposition to all parliamentary taxes.

Enforcement of the Townshend duties and the new administrative reforms accompanying the duties—which included the establishment of a new American Board of Customs Commissioners, unwisely situated in Boston—soon proved impossible. As they had with the Stamp Act, colonists again organized nonimportation agreements to bring pressure to bear on British merchants and manufacturers, and through them, on Parliament itself. And if informal, voluntary boycotts weren't sufficient, mobs arose everywhere to intimidate those who violated the nonimportation agreements. Importers in Boston who refused to sign the agreements had the signs, doors, and windows of their businesses smeared with "every kind of Filth," sometimes labeled "Hillsborough paint," in honor of Lord Hillsborough, the much hated secretary of the American Department.

In time it became clear that the financial returns to the British government from the customs reforms were not worth the costs. By 1770 less than £21,000 had been collected from the Townshend duties, while the loss to British business because of American nonimportation movements in 1769 alone was put at £700,000. It was therefore not surprising that the British government abandoned the hope of securing revenue from the duties and labeled the Townshend program, in Lord Hillsborough's words, "contrary to the true principles of Commerce."

Thus by the end of the 1760s British plans for reforming the empire were in shambles. Sending troops in October 1768 to quell the disorder in Massachusetts was the ultimate symptom of the ineffectiveness of the British government's authority, and many Britons knew it. The use of force, it was argued in Parliament and even in the administration itself, only destroyed the goodwill on which the colonists' relation to the mother country must ultimately rest. Many British ministers remained confused and uncertain. "There is the most urgent reason to do what is right, and immediately," wrote secretary at war Lord Barrington to Governor Bernard in 1767, "but what is that right, & who is to do it?"

Only in March 1770, after years of instability in the British government, did George III finally find a minister whom he liked and who had the confidence of a majority in the House of Commons. The earl of Guilford, better known by his courtesy title, Lord North, became head of the Treasury and prime minister of His Majesty's government—an office he would retain until he lost the confidence of the House of Commons in 1782 following news of the British defeat at Yorktown. In 1770 he knew that Parliament would have to retreat once more and repeal the Townshend duties. Only the duty on tea was retained, to serve, as Lord North said, "as a mark of the supremacy of Parliament, and an efficient declaration of their right to govern the Colonies."

During the next two years the imperial controversy seemed to subside, but the issues aroused earlier lay just below the surface. Despite the repeal of nearly all the customs duties, illegal trade and customs racketeering persisted—resulting in numerous conflicts between royal officials and smugglers. The most notorious incident occurred in Rhode Island, where defiance of the Navigation Acts seemed to be a way of life. In June 1772 a British naval schooner, the *Gaspee*, ran aground while searching for smugglers in Narragansett Bay. A group of Providence men boarded the ship at night, overpowered its crew, wounded its captain, and set it afire. Harassing and intimidating customs officials was one thing; attacking His Majesty's warship was quite another. A furious British government sent a special investigatory commission to the colony with the authority to send all persons charged back to England for trial, but it could not find anyone to testify. Alarmed by the British claim that suspected colonists would be brought back to England for prosecution, the Virginia House of Burgesses called for the establishment of intercolonial committees of correspondence. Since Virginia was by far the richest and most populous of all the colonies, any American resistance movement would need its participation.

It was Massachusetts, however, that remained the center of action. Outraged by the news that the Crown would now use the customs revenues to pay the salaries of the justices of the Superior Court in the colony, Boston, under the leadership of Samuel Adams, in November 1772 formed a committee of correspondence that drew up a list of grievances and colonial rights. These included protests against the Declaratory Act, the appointment of new customs officials, and the introduction of fleets and armies into the colonies. Mindful that their seventeenth-century ancestors had fled from the cruel persecutions of the prelates of the Church of England, the Bostonians also expressed concern over "the various attempts which have been and are now making to establish an American Episcopate." This "Boston Pamphlet," as it was called, was sent to the towns of the colony, where it was enthusiastically received; within months more than half had formed their own committees of correspondence in support of Boston's action. By 1773 Massachusetts was primed to resist whatever move the British government might next decide to make.

It did not have long to wait. That same year Parliament passed the Tea Act, designed to bail out a financially beleaguered East India Company. The measure allowed the company to sell its tea directly to the colonies through its own agents. This would mean that the company's product, even with payment of the tea duty, would be cheaper than smuggled Dutch tea, which, it was estimated, constituted five-sixths of all the tea consumed in America. Since the price of tea paid by colonial consumers would in fact be lowered, North and his ministry did not anticipate any popular reaction in America to this latest measure.

They could not have been more mistaken. Organized opposition began in New York and soon spread to the other ports. When tea ships in Boston were prevented from unloading their cargoes, Massachusetts Governor Thomas Hutchinson, whose two sons were among the few merchants granted a monopoly to sell the tea, refused to let the ships leave without being unloaded and the duty paid. In response, on December 16, 1773, a group of patriots disguised as Mohawk Indians dumped about £10,000 worth of tea into Boston Harbor. "This is the most magnificent Movement of all," exulted John Adams. "This Destruction of the Tea is so bold, so daring, so firm, intrepid and inflexible, and it must have so important Consequences, and so lasting, that I cant but consider it as an Epocha in History."

Adams was not exaggerating. The Boston Tea Party set in motion the chain of actions that led to out-and-out fighting and ultimately to the end of the first British Empire. To British officials in London it was the final outrage. The government became convinced that it had too long appeased the colonies. Under threat of mobs and boycotts Parliament had repealed the Stamp Act and then the Townshend duties, acquiescing to the point where its authority in America now seemed to carry no weight at all. It was high time, Lord North declared in the House of Commons, to show the colonists "that we are in earnest and that we will proceed with firmness and vigour."

In 1774 overwhelming majorities in Parliament passed a succession of laws that came to be known as the Coercive Acts—soon labeled the Intolerable Acts in America. The British government assumed that Massachusetts was the center of the disturbances in the colonies and that isolating and punishing it would undermine resistance elsewhere. The first act closed the port of Boston until the tea was paid for. The second altered the Massachusetts charter and reorganized its government: members of the Council, or upper house, were now to be appointed by the royal governor instead of being elected by the legislature as they had been in the past; town meetings were restricted; and the governor's power of appointing judges and sheriffs was strengthened. The third act allowed royal officials who had been charged with capital offenses to be tried in England or in another colony to avoid hostile juries. The fourth gave the governor power to take over private buildings for the quartering of troops. At the same time Thomas Gage, commander in chief of the British army in America, replaced Thomas Hutchinson as governor.

Coinciding with this punishment of Massachusetts was Parliament's passage of the Quebec Act of 1774. The result of a decade-long attempt to organize the former French territory in Canada, the act granted to the French inhabitants of Quebec the right to their customary civil law and to the practice of their Roman Catholic religion. Although by eighteenth-century standards the act was remarkably liberal and enlightened, Puritan New Englanders could only regard it as "dangerous to an extreme degree to the protestant religion and to the civil rights and liberties of all America." So much was eighteenth-century Englishness identified with Protestantism that most colonists considered this act in support of "popery" to be just another one of the Intolerable Acts designed to punish them.

If conceived as a means of isolating Massachusetts from the other colonies, the Coercive Acts had precisely the opposite effect. Many Americans, especially those in the important colony of Virginia, had been stunned by the Boston Tea Party's destruction of private property, which seemed to them an excessively violent reaction to the Tea Act. But the British response changed minds overnight. If the Ministry could do what it did to Massachusetts, Americans everywhere concluded, it could do the same to any of the colonies. The time for coordinated action had come.

The pamphlet debate traced in these volumes led British and American writers to examine and clarify their differing experiences of the empire, and in so doing it exposed divergent perspectives that were to prove irreconcilable. Although it had begun with the clash between the concepts of virtual and actual representation, the debate soon turned into an argument over the proper division of power within the empire; it would end, as the pages that follow demonstrate, as a struggle over sovereignty, that is, where final, supreme, indivisible power in the empire lay. This last issue was one that words alone could not resolve.

Gordon S. Wood

The Speeches of His Excellency Governor Hutchinson, to the General Assembly of the Massachusetts-Bay. At a Session Begun and Held on the Sixth of January, 1773. With the Answers of His Majesty's Council and the House of Representatives Respectively. Boston, 1773.

Thomas Hutchinson was the last civilian governor of the Massachusetts Bay Colony, succeeding Francis Bernard on August 2, 1769. Before being elevated to the colony's highest office, he had been the speaker of the Massachusetts House of Representatives, councilor, lieutenant governor, and chief justice. He was well-educated, enlightened (in the 1750s he had supported the French Acadian refugees who were expelled from Nova Scotia), and the most accomplished historian in eighteenth-century America, author of a three-volume *History of the Province of Massachusets-Bay*. But during the imperial crisis of the 1760s and early 1770s he was incapable of comprehending the powerful popular forces at work in the Bay Colony. He would end his long and illustrious career in Massachusetts politics as one of the most hated men in America.

So inflammatory did Governor Hutchinson believe the "Boston Pamphlet" to be that he knew he must respond. In January 1773 he called the Massachusetts legislature together for an emergency session, and over the course of a three-month period he debated with it the nature of the English constitution. He made the same essential point about the sovereignty of Parliament that William Knox had in his influential 1769 pamphlet, *The Controversy between Great Britain and her Colonies Reviewed*. "I know of no Line," Hutchinson told the legislature, "that can be drawn between the supreme Authority of Parliament and the total Independence of the Colonies: It is impossible there should be two independent Legislatures in one and the same State." Hutchinson assumed, of course, that no right thinking Whig would ever want to be outside the protection of Parliament.

In its response, the Council (the upper house of the legislature) avoided the stark alternatives the governor had laid down and sought instead to find some limits on Parliament's authority. But the House of Representatives willingly accepted the governor's logic. In remarks prepared with the assistance of nonmember John Adams, the House declared, "If there be no such Line, the Consequence is, either that the Colonies are the Vassals of the Parliament, or, that they are totally

Independent. As it cannot be supposed to have been the Intention of the Parties in the Compact, that we should be reduced to a State of Vassallage, the Conclusion is, that it was their Sense, that we were thus Independent." Since, as the governor had said, two independent legislatures in the same state were impossible, the House reasoned that colonies had to be "distinct States from the Mother Country," united and connected only through the king "in one Head and common Sovereign."

To make its case that Massachusetts was tied solely to the Crown, the House drew on the seventeenth-century history of the colony advanced by Edward Bancroft in his 1769 *Remarks*. This was the "anonimous Pamphlet" by which, Hutchinson chided the representatives in his first response to the House, "I fear you have too easily been mislead."

THE
SPEECHES

OF

His Excellency Governor HUTCHINSON,

TO THE

GENERAL ASSEMBLY

OF THE MASSACHUSETTS-BAY.

At a Session begun and held on the Sixth
of *January*, 1773.

WITH THE

ANSWERS

OF

His MAJESTY'S COUNCIL

AND THE

HOUSE OF REPRESENTATIVES
RESPECTIVELY.

[*Publish'd by Order of the House.*]

BOSTON; NEW-ENGLAND:

PRINTED BY EDES AND GILL, PRINTERS TO THE
HONORABLE HOUSE OF REPRESENTATIVES.
M,DCC,LXXIII.

Speeches, &c.

Gentlemen of the Council, and,
   Gentlemen of the House of Representatives.

I HAVE nothing in special Command from his Majesty to lay before you at this Time; I have general Instructions to recommend to you, at all Times, such Measures as may tend to promote that Peace and Order upon which your own Happiness and Prosperity as well as his Majesty's Service very much depend. That the Government is at present in a disturbed and disordered State is a Truth too evident to be denied. The Cause of this Disorder appears to me equally evident. I wish I may be able to make it appear so to you, for then I may not doubt that you will agree with me in the proper Measures for the Removal of it. I have pleased myself, for several Years past, with Hopes that the Cause would cease of itself and the Effect with it, but I am disappointed, and I may not any longer, consistent with my Duty to the King and my Regard to the Interest of the Province, delay communicating my Sentiments to you upon a Matter of so great Importance. I shall be explicit and treat the Subject without Reserve. I hope you will receive what I have to say upon it with Candor, and, if you shall not agree in Sentiments with me, I promise you, with Candor likewise, to receive and consider what you may offer in Answer.

When our Predecessors first took Possession of this Plantation or Colony, under a Grant and Charter from the Crown of England, it was their Sense, and it was the Sense of the Kingdom, that they were to remain subject to the supreme Authority of Parliament. This appears from the Charter itself and from other irresistable Evidence. This supreme Authority has, from Time to Time, been exercised by Parliament and submitted to by the Colony, and hath been, in the most express Terms, acknowledged by the Legislature and, except about the Time of the Anarchy and Confusion in England which preceeded the Restoration of King Charles the Second, I have not discovered that it has been called in Question even by private or particular Persons until within seven or eight Years last past. Our Provincial or Local Laws have, in numerous Instances, had Relation to Acts of Parliament made to respect the Plantations in general and this Colony in particular, and in our Executive Courts both Juries and Judges have, to all Intents and Purposes, considered such Acts as Part of our Rule of Law. Such a Constitution, in a Plantation, is not peculiar to England but agrees with the Principles of the most celebrated Writers upon the Law of Nations that "when a Nation takes Possession of a distant Country and settles there, that Country, though separated from the principal Establishment or Mother Country, naturally becomes a Part of the State equally with its ancient Possessions."

So much however of the Spirit of Liberty breathes thro' all Parts of the English Constitution, that although from the Nature of Government there must be one supreme Authority over the whole, yet this Constitution will admit of subordinate Powers with legislative and executive Authority, greater or less according to local and other Circumstances. Thus we see a Variety of Corporations formed within the Kingdom with Powers to make and execute such Bylaws as are for their immediate Use and Benefit, the Members of such Corporations still remaining subject to the general Laws of the Kingdom. We see also Governments established in the Plantations which, from their separate and remote Situation, require more general and extensive Powers of Legislation within themselves than those formed within the Kingdom, but subject nevertheless, to all such Laws of the Kingdom as immediately respect them or are designed to extend to them, and accordingly we in this Province have, from the first Settlement of it, been left to the Exercise of our legislative and executive Powers, Parliament occasionally though rarely, interposing as in its Wisdom has been judged necessary.

Under this Constitution, for more than One Hundred Years, the Laws both of the supreme and subordinate Authority were in general, duly executed, Offenders against them have been brought to condign Punishment, Peace and Order have been maintained and the People of this Province have experienced as largely the Advantages of Government, as, perhaps, any People upon the Globe, and they have from Time to Time in the most public Manner expressed their Sense of it and, once in every Year, have offered up their united Thanksgivings to God for the Enjoyment of these Privileges and, as often, their united Prayers for the Continuance of them.

At Length the Constitution has been called in Question and the Authority of the Parliament of Great-Britain to make and establish Laws for the Inhabitants of this Province has been, by many, denied. What was, at first, whispered with Caution, was soon after openly asserted in Print and, of late, a Number of Inhabitants in several of the principal Towns in the Province, have assembled together in their respective Towns and, having assumed the Name of legal Town Meetings, have passed Resolves which they have ordered to be placed upon their Town Records, and caused to be printed & published in Pamphlets and News-Papers. I am sorry that it is thus become impossible to conceal what I could wish had never been made public. I will not particularize these Resolves or Votes and shall only observe to you, in general, that some of them deny the supreme Authority of Parliament, and so are repugnant to the Principles of the Constitution, and that others speak of this supreme Authority, of which the King is a constituent Part and to every Act of which his Assent is necessary, in such Terms as have a direct Tendency to alienate the Affections of the People from their Sovereign who has ever been most tender of their Rights, and whose Person, Crown and Dignity we are under every possible Obligation to defend and support. In consequence of these Resolves, Committees of Correspondence are formed, in several of those Towns, to maintain the Principles upon which they are founded.

I know of no Arguments, founded in Reason, which will be sufficient to support these Principles or to justify the Measures taken in Consequence of them. It has been urged, that the sole Power of making Laws is granted by Charter to a Legislature established in the Province, consisting of the King by his Representative the Governor, the Council and the House of Representatives—that by this Charter there are likewise granted or assured to the Inhabitants of the Province all the Liberties and Immunities of free and natural Subjects, to all Intents Constructions and Purposes whatsoever, as if they had been born within the Realm of England—that it is Part of the Liberties of English Subjects, which has its Foundation in Nature, to be governed by Laws made by their Consent in Person or by their Representative—that the Subjects in this Province are not and cannot be Represented in the Parliament of Great-Britain and, consequently, the Acts of Parliament cannot be binding upon them.

I do not find, Gentlemen, in the Charter such an Expression as *sole* Power or any Words which import it. The General Court has, by Charter, *full* Power to make such Laws as are not repugnant to the Laws of England. A favourable Construction has been put upon this Clause when it has been allowed to intend such Laws of England only as are expresly declared to respect us. Surely then this is by Charter a Reserve of Power and Authority to Parliament to bind us by such Laws, at least, as are made expresly to refer to us and consequently, is a Limitation of the Power given to the General Court. Nor can it be contended that by the Liberties of free and natural Subjects is to be understood an Exemption from Acts of Parliament because not represented there, seeing it is provided, by the same Charter, that such Acts shall be in Force; and if they that make the Objection to such Acts will read the Charter with Attention, they must be convinced that this Grant of Liberties and Immunities is nothing more than a Declaration and Assurance on the Part of the Crown that the Place to which their Predecessors were about to remove was and would be considered as Part of the Dominions of the Crown of England, and therefore that the Subjects of the Crown so removing, and those born there or in their Passage thither or in their Passage from thence, would not become Aliens but would throughout all Parts of the English Dominions, wherever they might happen to be, as well as within the Colony, retain the Liberties and Immunities of free and natural Subjects, their Removal from or not being born within the Realm notwithstanding. If the Plantations be Part of the Dominions of the Crown, this Clause in the Charter does not confer or reserve any Liberties but what would have been enjoyed without it and what the Inhabitants of every other Colony do enjoy where they are without a Charter. If the Plantations are not the Dominions of the Crown will not all that are born here be considered as born out of the Ligeance of the King of England, and whenever they go into any Part of the Dominions will they not be deemed Aliens to all Intents and Purposes, this Grant in the Charter notwithstanding?

They who claim Exemption from Acts of Parliament by Virtue of their Rights as Englishmen, should consider that it is impossible the Rights of English Subjects should be the same, in every Respect, in all Parts of the Dominions. It is one of their Rights as English Subjects to be governed by Laws made by Persons in whose Election they have, from Time to Time, a Voice—They remove from the Kingdom where, perhaps, they were in the full Exercise of this Right to the Plantations where it cannot be exercised or where the Exercise of it would be of no Benefit to them. Does it follow that the Government, by their Removal from one Part of the Dominions to another, loses it's Authority over that Part to which they remove, and that they are freed from the Subjection they were under before; or do they expect that Government should relinquish its Authority because they cannot enjoy this particular Right? Will it not rather be said that, by this their voluntary Removal, they have relinquished for a Time at least, one of the Rights of an English Subject which they might if they pleased have continued to enjoy and may again enjoy whensoever they will return to the Place where it can be exercised?

They who claim Exemption, as Part of their Rights by Nature, should consider that every Restraint which Men are laid under by a State of Government is a Privation of Part of their natural Rights, and of all the different Forms of Government which exist, there can be no two of them in which the Departure from Natural Rights is exactly the same. Even in Case of Representation by Election, do they not give up Part of their natural Rights when they consent to be represented by such Person as shall be chosen by the Majority of the Electors, although their own Voices may be for some other Person? And is it not contrary to their natural Rights to be obliged to submit to a Representative for seven Years, or even one Year, after they are dissatisfied with his Conduct, although they gave their Voices for him when he was elected? This must therefore be considered as an Objection against a State of Government rather than against any particular Form.

If what I have said shall not be sufficient to satisfy such as object to the Supreme Authority of Parliament over the Plantations, there may something further be added to induce them to an Acknowledgment of it which I think will well deserve their Consideration. I know of no Line that can be drawn between the supreme Authority of Parliament and the total Independence of the Colonies: It is impossible there should be two independent Legislatures in one and the same State, for although there may be but one Head, the King, yet the two Legislative Bodies will make two Governments as distinct as the Kingdoms of England and Scotland before the Union. If we might be suffered to be altogether independent of Great-Britain, could we have any Claim to the Protection of that Government of which we are no longer a Part? Without this Protection should we not become the Prey of one or the other Powers of Europe, such as should first seize upon us? Is there any Thing which we have more Reason to dread than Independence? I hope it will never be our Misfortune to know by Experience the Difference between the Liberties of an English Colonist and those of the Spanish, French or Dutch.

If then the Supremacy of Parliament over the whole British Dominions shall no longer be denied, it will follow that the *meer* Exercise of its Authority can be no Matter of Grievance. If it has been or shall be exercised in such Way and Manner as shall appear to be grievous, still this cannot be sufficient Grounds for immediately denying or renouncing the Authority or refusing to submit to it. The Acts and Doings of Authority in the most perfect Form of Government will not always be thought just and equitable by all the Parts of which it consists, but it is the greatest Absurdity to admit the several Parts to be at Liberty to obey or disobey according as the Acts of such Authority may be approved or disapproved of by them, for this necessarily works a Dissolution of the Government. The Manner then of obtaining Redress must be by Representations and Endeavours, in such Ways and Forms as the established Rules of the Constitution prescribe or allow in order to make any Matters alledged to be Grievances appear to be really such; but I conceive it is rather the *meer* Exercise of this Authority which is complained of as a Grievance, than any heavy Burdens which have been bro't upon the People by Means of it.

As Contentment and Order were the happy Effects of a Constitution strengthened by universal Assent and Approbation, so Discontent and Disorder are now the deplorable Effects of a Constitution enfeebled by Contest and Opposition. Besides Divisions and Animosities which disturb the Peace of Towns and Families, the Law in some important Cases cannot have its Course,—Offenders ordered by Advice of His Majesty's Council to be prosecuted, escape with Impunity and are supported and encouraged to go on offending,—the Authority of Government is bro't into Contempt, and there are but small Remains of that Subordination which was once very conspicuous in this Colony, and which is essential to a well-regulated State.

When the Bands of Government are thus weakened, it certainly behoves those with whom the Powers of Government are intrusted to omit nothing which may tend to strengthen them.

I have disclosed my Sentiments to you without Reserve. Let me intreat you to consider them calmly and not to be too sudden in your Determination. If my Principles of Government are right let us adhere to them. With the same Principles our Ancestors were easy and happy for a long Course of Years together, and I know of no Reason to doubt of your being equally easy & happy. The People, influenced by you will forsake their unconstitutional Principles and desist from their Irregularities which are the Consequence of them, they will be convinced that every Thing which is valuable to them depend upon their Connexion with their Parent State, that this Connexion cannot be continued in any other Way than such as will also continue their Dependance upon the supreme Authority of the British Dominions, and that, notwithstanding this Dependance, they will enjoy as great a Proportion of those Rights to which they have a Claim by Nature or as Englishmen as can be enjoyed by a Plantation or Colony.

If I am wrong in my Principles of Government or in the Inferences which I have drawn from them, I wish to be convinced of my Error. Independence I may not allow myself to think that you can possibly have in Contemplation. If you can conceive of any other constitutional Dependance than what I have mentioned, if you are of Opinion that upon any other Principles our Connexion with the State from which we sprang can be continued, communicate your Sentiments to me with the same Freedom and Unreservedness as I have communicated mine to you.

I have no Desire, Gentlemen, by any Thing I have said to preclude you from seeking Relief, in a constitutional Way, in any Cases in which you have heretofore or may hereafter suppose that you are aggrieved and, although I should not concur with you in Sentiment, I will, notwithstanding, do nothing to lessen the Weight which your Representations may deserve. I have laid before you what I think are the Principles of your Constitution: If you do not agree with me I wish to know your Objections: They may be convincing to me, or I may be able to satisfy you of the Insufficiency of them: In either Case I hope, we shall put an End to those Irregularities, which ever will be the Portion of a Government where the Supreme Authority is controverted, and introduce that Tranquility which seems to have taken Place in most of the Colonies upon the Continent.

The ordinary Business of the Session I will not now particularly point out to you. To the enacting of any new Laws which may be necessary for the more equal and effectual Distribution of Justice, or for giving further Encouragement to our Merchandize, Fishery, and Agriculture, which through the Divine Favour are already in a very flourishing State, or for promoting any Measures which may conduce to the general Good of the Province I will readily give my Assent or Concurrence.

Council Chamber   T. HUTCHINSON.
6 January, 1773.

ON *the 25th of* January William Brattle, Harrison Gray, James Pitts, James Humphrey, *and* Benjamin Greenleaf, *Esquires, a Committee of his Majesty's Council, waited on the Governor with an Answer to the foregoing* SPEECH, *viz.*

May it please your Excellency,
THE Board have considered your Excellency's Speech to both Houses with the Attention due to the Subject of it; and we

hope with the Candour you are pleased to recommend to them.

We thank you for the Promise, that "if we shall not agree with you in Sentiments, you will with Candour likewise, receive and consider what we may offer in Answer."

Your Speech informs the two Houses that this Government is at present in a disturbed and disordered State; that the Cause of this Disorder is the unconstitutional Principles adopted by the People in questioning the Supreme Authority of Parliament; and that the proper Measure for removing the Disorder must be the substituting contrary Principles.

Our Opinion on these Heads, as well as on some others proper to be noticed, will be obvious in the Course of the following Observations.

With regard to the present disordered State of the Government, it can have no Reference to Tumults or Riots: from which this Government is as free as any other whatever. If your Excellency meant only that the Province is discontented, and in a State of Uneasiness, we should intirely agree with you; but you will permit us to say we are not so well agreed in the Cause of it. The Uneasiness, which was a general one throughout the Colonies, began when you inform us the Authority of Parliament was first called in Question, viz. about seven or eight Years ago. Your mentioning that particular Time might have suggested to your Excellency the true Cause of the Origin and Continuance of that Uneasiness.

At that Time the Stamp-Act, then lately made, began to operate: Which with some preceeding and succeeding Acts of Parliament, subjecting the Colonies to Taxes without their Consent, was the original Cause of all the Uneasiness that has happened since; and has occasioned also an Enquiry into the Nature and Extent of the Authority by which they were made. The late Town-Meetings in several Towns are Instances of both. These are mentioned by your Excellency in Proof of a disordered State: But tho' we do not approve some of their Resolves, we think they had a clear Right to instruct their Representatives on any Subject they apprehended to be of sufficient Importance to require it: which necessarily implies a previous Consideration of, and Expression of their Minds on, that Subject: however mistaken they may be concerning it.

When a Community, great or small, think their Rights and Privileges infringed, they will express their Uneasiness in a Variety of Ways: some of which may be highly improper, and criminal. So far as any of an attrocious Nature have taken Place, we would express our Abhorrence of them: and as we have always done hitherto, we shall continue to do, every Thing in our Power to discourage and suppress them. But it is in vain to hope that this can be done effectually so long as the Cause of the Uneasiness, which occasioned them, exists.

Your Excellency will perceive that the Cause you assign is by us supposed to be an Effect derived from the original Cause abovementioned: the Removal of which will remove its Effects.

To obtain this Removal, we agree with you in the Method pointed out in your Speech, where you say, "the Manner of obtaining Redress must be by Representations and Endeavours in such Ways and Forms as the Constitution allows, in order to make any Matters alledged to be Grievances appear to be really such." This Method has been pursued repeatedly. Petitions to Parliament have gone from the Colonies, and from this Colony in particular; but without Success. Some of them, in a former Ministry, were previously shewn to the Minister, who (as we have been informed) advised the Agents to postpone presenting them to the House of Commons 'till the first reading of the Bill they refer'd to: when being presented, a Rule of the House against receiving Petitions on Money Bills was urged for the rejecting of them, and they were rejected accordingly: And other Petitions for want of Formality, or whatever was the Reason, have had the same Fate. This we mention, not by Way of Censure on that honourable House, but in some Measure to account for the Conduct of those Persons, who despairing of Redress in a constitutional Way, have denied the just Authority of Parliament: concerning which we shall now give our own Sentiments, intermixt with Observations on those of your Excellency.

You are pleased to observe, that "when our Predecessors first took Possession of this Colony, under a Grant and Charter from the Crown of England, it was their Sense, and it was the Sense of the Kingdom, that they were to remain Subject to the Supreme Authority of Parliament." And to prove that Subjection the greater Part of your Speech is employed.

In order to a right Conception of this Matter, it is necessary to guard against any improper Idea of the term *Supreme* Authority. In your Idea of it your Excellency seems to include *unlimited* Authority: for you are pleased to say, you "know of no Line that can be drawn between the Supreme Authority of Parliament and the total Independence of the Colonies:" But if no such Line can be drawn a Denial of that Authority in any Instance whatever implies and amounts to a Declaration of total Independence. But if Supreme Authority includes unlimited Authority, the Subjects of it are emphatically Slaves: and equally so whether residing in the Colonies or Great-Britain. And indeed in this Respect all the Nations on Earth, among whom Government exists in any of its Forms, would be alike conditioned: excepting so far as the mere Grace and Favor of their Governors might make a Difference; "for from the Nature of Government there must be, as your Excellency has observed, one Supreme Authority over the whole."

We cannot think, "that when our Predecessors first took Possession of this Colony it was their Sense, or the Sense of the Kingdom, that they were to remain Subject to the Supreme Authority of Parliament" in this Idea of it. Nor can we find that this appears from the Charter; or that such Authority has ever been exercised by Parliament, submitted to by the Colony, or acknowledged by the Legislature.

Supreme or unlimited Authority can with Fitness belong only to the Sovereign of the Universe: And that Fitness is derived from the Perfection of his Nature.—To such Authority, directed by infinite Wisdom & infinite Goodness, is due both active and passive Obedience: Which, as it constitutes the Happiness of rational Creatures, should with Chearfulness and from Choice be unlimitedly paid by them.—But with Truth this can be said of no other Authority whatever. If then from the Nature and End of Government, the supreme Authority of every Government is limited, the Supreme Authority of Parliament must be limited; and the Enquiry will be what are the Limits of that Authority with Regard to this Colony?—To fix them with Precision, to determine the exact Lines of Right and Wrong in this Case, as in some others, is difficult; and we have not the Presumption to attempt it. But we humbly hope, that as we are personally and relatively, in our private and public Capacities, for ourselves, for the whole Province, and for all Posterity, so deeply interested in this important Subject, it will not be deemed Arrogance to give some general Sentiments upon it, especially as your Excellency's Speech has made it absolutely necessary.

For this Purpose we shall recur to those Records that contain the main Principles on which the English Constitution is founded; and from them make such Extracts as are pertinent to the Subject.

Magna Charta declares, "that no Aid shall be imposed in the Kingdom, unless by the Common Council of the Kingdom, except to redeem the King's Person, &c". And that "all Cities, Boroughs, Towns and Ports shall have their Liberties and free Customs; and shall have the Common Council of the Kingdom concerning the Assessment of their Aids, except in the Cases aforesaid."

The Statute of the 34th of Edward I, de tallagio non concedendo, declares "that no Tallage or Aid should be laid or levied by the King or his Heirs in the Realm, without the Good Will and Assent of the Arch Bishops, Bishops, Earls, Barons, Knights, Burgesses, and other the Freemen of the Commonalty of this Realm."

A Statute of the 25 Ed. 3, enacts "that from thenceforth no Person shall be compelled to make any Loans to the King against his Will, because such Loans were against Reason and the Franchise of the Land."

The Petition of Rights in the 3d of Charles 1st, in which are cited the two foregoing Statutes, declares that by those "Statutes, and other good Laws and Statutes of the Realm, his Majesty's Subjects inherited this Freedom, that they should not be compelled to contribute to any Tax, Tallage, Aid, or other like Charge, not sett by common Consent of Parliament." And the Statute of the I. of William 3d, for declaring the Rights and Liberties of the Subject and setling the Succession of the Crown declares, "That the levying of Money for or to the Use of the Crown, by Pretence of Prerogative without Grant of Parliament, for longer Time, or in any other Manner than the same is or shall be granted, is illegal."

From these Authorities it appears an essential Part of the English Constitution, that no Tallage or Aid or Tax shall be laid or levied "without the Good Will and Assent of the Free-men of the Commonalty of the Realm." If this could be done without their Assent, their Property would be in the highest Degree precarious: or rather they could not with Fitness be said to have any Property at all. At best they would be only the Holders of it for the Use of the Crown; and the Crown be in Fact the real Proprietor. This would be Vassallage in the extreme; from which the generous Nature of Englishmen has been so abhorrent, that they have bled with Freedom in the Defence of this Part of their Constitution, which has preserved them from it: and influenced by the same Generosity, they can never view with Disapprobation any lawful Measures taken by us for the Defence of our Constitution, which intitles us to the same Rights and Privileges with themselves.

These were derived to us from Common Law, which is the Inheritance of all his Majesty's Subjects; have been recognized by Acts of Parliament; and confirmed by the Province Charter, which established its Constitution; and which Charter has been recognized by Act of Parliament also. This Act was made in the second Year of his late Majesty GEO. II, for the better Preservation of his Majesty's Woods in America: in which is recited the Clause of the said Charter reserving for the Use of the Royal Navy all Trees suitable for Masts: and on this Charter is grounded the succeeding enacting Clause of the Act. And thus is the Charter implicitly confirmed by Act of Parliament.

From all which it appears, that the Inhabitants of this Colony are clearly intitled to All the Rights and Privileges of free and natural Subjects: which certainly must include that most essential one, that no Aid or Taxes be levied on them without their own Consent, signified by their Representatives. But from the Clause in the Charter relative to the Power granted to the General Court to make Laws, not repugnant to the Laws of England, your Excellency draws this Inference, that "surely this is by Charter a Reserve of Power and Authority to Parliament to bind us by such Laws, at least, as are made expressly to refer to us, and consequently is a Limitation of the Power given to the General Court."—If it be allowed that by that Clause there was a Reserve of Power to Parliament to bind the Province, it was only by such Laws as were in Being at the Time the Charter was granted: for by the Charter there is nothing appears to make it refer to any Parliamentary Laws, that should be afterwards made, and therefore it will not support your Excellency's Inference.

The Grant of Power to the General Court to make Laws runs thus,—"full Power and Authority, from Time to Time, to make, ordain and establish all Manner of wholesome and reasonable Orders, Laws, Statutes and Ordinances, Directions and Instructions, either with Penalties or without (so as the same be not repugnant or contrary to the Laws of this our Realm of England) as they shall judge to be for the Good and Welfare of our said Province," &c.—We humbly think an Inference very different from your Excellency's, and a very just one too, may be drawn from this Clause, if Attention be given to the Description of the Orders and Laws that were to be made.—They were to be wholesome, reasonable and for the Good and Welfare of the Province, and in order that they might be so, it is provided that they be "not repugnant or contrary to the Laws of the Realm," that were then in being: by which Proviso, all the Liberties and Immunities of free and natural Subjects within the Realm were more effectually secured to the Inhabitants of the Province agreeable to another Clause in the Charter, whereby those Liberties and Immunities are expressly granted to them: and accordingly the Power of the General Court is so far limited, that they shall not make Orders and Laws to take away or diminish those Liberties and Immunities.

This Construction appears to us a just one, and perhaps may appear so to your Excellency if you will please to consider, that by another Part of the Charter effectual Care was taken for preventing the General Assembly passing of Orders and Laws repugnant to, or that in any Way might militate with Acts of Parliament then or since made, or that might be exceptionable in any other Respect whatever: for the Charter reserves to his Majesty the Appointment of the Governor, whose Assent is necessary in the passing of all Orders and Laws: after which they are to be sent to England for the Royal Approbation or Disallowance: by which double Controul effectual Care is taken to prevent the Establishment of any improper Orders or Laws whatever.—Besides, your Excellency is sensible that "Letters Patent must be construed one Part with another, and all the Parts of them together," so as to make the whole harmonize and agree. But your Excellency's Construction of the Paragraph impowering the General Court to make Orders and Laws, does by no means harmonize and agree with the Paragraph granting Liberties and Immunities; and therefore we humbly conceive is not to be admitted: Whereas on the other Construction there is a perfect Harmony and Agreement between them. But supposing your Excellency's Inference just, that by the said former Paragraph (considered by itself) are reserved to Parliament Power and Authority to bind us by Laws made expressly to refer to us. Does it consist with Justice and Equity that it should be considered apart, and urged against the People of this Province with all its Force and without Limitation, and at the same Time the other Paragraph which they thought secured to them the essential Rights and Privileges of free and natural Subjects be rendered of no Validity? If the former Paragraph (in this supposed case) be binding on this People, the latter must be binding on the Crown, which thereby became Guarantee of those Rights and Privileges. Or it must be supposed that one Party is held by a Compact, and the other not: Which Supposition is against Reason and against Law; and therefore destroys the Foundation of the Inference. However, supposing it well founded, it would not from thence follow, that the Charter intended such Laws as should subject the Inhabitants of the Province to Taxes without their Consent: For (as appears above) it grants to them all the Rights and Liberties of free and natural Subjects: Of which one of the most essential is a Freedom from all Taxes not consented to by themselves.—Nor could the Parties, either Grantor or Grantees, intend such Laws. The Royal Grantor could not, because his Grant contradicts such Intention; and because it is inconsistent with every Idea of Royalty and royal Wisdom, to grant what it does not intend to grant. And it will be readily allowed that the Grantees could not intend such Laws, not only on account of their Inconsistency with the Grant, but because their Acceptance of a Charter, subjecting them to such Laws, would be voluntary Slavery.

Your Excellency next observes, "that it cannot be contended that by the Liberties of free and natural Subjects is to be understood an Exemption from Acts of Parliament, because not represented there, seeing it is provided by the same Charter, that such Acts shall be in Force."—If the Observations we have made above, and our Reasoning on them be Just, it will appear that no such Provision is made in the Charter, and therefore that the Deductions and Inferences derived from the Supposition of such Provision, are not well founded. And with Respect to Representation in Parliament, as it is one of the essential Liberties of free and natural Subjects, and properly makes those who enjoy it liable to Parliamentary Acts, so in Reference to the Inhabitants of this Province, who are intitled to all the Liberties of such Subjects, the Impossibility of their being duely represented in Parliament, does clearly exempt them from all such Acts at least, as have been or shall be made by Parliament to Tax them: Representation and Taxation being in our Opinion constitutionally inseperable.

"This Grant of Liberties and Immunities, your Excellency informs us, is nothing more than a Declaration and Assurance on the Part of the Crown, that the Place to which our Predecessors were about to remove, was and would be considered as Part of the Dominions of the Crown, and therefore that the Subjects so removing would not become Aliens, but would both without and within the Colony retain the Liberties and Immunities of free and natural Subjects."

The Dominion of the Crown over this Country before the Arrival of our Predecessors was meerly ideal. Their Removal hither realized that Dominion, and has made the Country valuable both to the Crown and Nation, without any Cost to either of them from that Time to this. Even in the most distressed State of our Predecessors, when they expected to be destroyed by a general Conspiracy and Incursion of the Indian Natives, they had no Assistance from them. This Grant then of Liberties, which is the only Consideration they received from the Crown for so valuable an Acquisition to it, instead of being violated by military Power, or explained away by nice Inferences and Distinctions, ought in Justice, and with a generous Openness and Freedom, to be acknowledged by every Minister of the Crown, and preserved sacred from every Species of Violation.

"If the Plantation be Part of the Dominions of the Crown this Clause in the Charter (granting Liberties and Immunities) does not, your Excellency observes, confer or reserve any Liberties but what would have been enjoyed without it; and what the Inhabitants of every other Colony do enjoy, where they are without a Charter."—Although the Colonies considered as Part of the Dominions of the Crown are intitled to equal Liberties, the Inhabitants of this Colony think it a Happiness, that those Liberties are confirmed and secured to them by a Charter; whereby the Honour and Faith of the Crown are pledged, that those Liberties shall not be violated. And for Protection in them we humbly look up to his present Majesty, our rightful and lawful Sovereign, as Children to a Father, able and disposed to assist and relieve them; humbly imploring his Majesty, that his Subjects of this Province, ever faithful and loyal, and ever accounted such till the Stamp-Act existed, and who in the late War, and upon all other Occasions, have demonstrated that Faithfulness and Loyalty by their vigorous and unexampled Exertions in his Service, may have their Grievances redressed, and be restored to their just Rights.

Your Excellency next observes "that it is impossible the Rights of English Subjects should be the same in every Respect, in all Parts of the Dominions," and Instances in the Right of being "governed by Laws made by Persons, in whose Election they have a Voice." When "they remove from the Kingdom to the Plantations where it cannot be enjoyed," you ask, "will it not be said, that by this their voluntary Removal, they have relinquished, for a Time at least, one of the Rights of an English Subject, which they might if they pleased, have continued to enjoy, and may again enjoy whensoever they will return to the Place where it can be exercised."

When English Subjects remove from the Kingdom to the Plantations with their Properties, they not only relinquish that Right *de facto*, but it ought to cease in the Kingdom *de jure*. But it does not from thence follow, that they relinquish that Right, in Reference to the Plantation or Colony to which they remove. On the contrary, being become Inhabitants of that Colony, and qualified according to the Laws of it, they can exercise that Right equally with the other Inhabitants of it. And this Right, on like Conditions, will travel with them through all the Colonies, wherein a Legislature, similar to that of the Kingdom, is established. And therefore in this Respect, and we suppose in all other essential Respects, it is not impossible the Rights of English Subjects should be the same "in all Parts of the Dominions" under a like Form of Legislature.

This Right of Representation is so essential and indispensible in Regard of all Laws for levying Taxes, that a People under any Form of Government destitute of it, is destitute of Freedom—of that Degree of Freedom, for the Preservation of which, Government was instituted; and without which, Government degenerates to Despotism. It cannot therefore be given up, or taken away, without making a Breach on the essential Rights of Nature.

But your Excellency is pleased to say, that they "who claim Exemption as Part of their Rights by Nature, should consider that every Restraint which Men are laid under by a State of Government, is a Privation of Part of their natural Rights. Even in Case of Representation by Election, do they not give up Part of their natural Rights, when they consent to be represented by such Persons as shall be chosen by the Majority of the Electors, although their own Voices may be for some other Person? And is it not contrary to their natural Rights to be obliged to submit to a Representative for seven Years, or even one Year, after they are dissatisfied with his Conduct, although they gave their Voices for him, when he was elected? This must therefore be considered as an Objection against a State of Government rather than against any particular Form."

Your Excellency's Premises are true, but we do not think your Conclusion follows from them. It is true, that every Restraint of Government is a Privation of natural Right: and the two Cases you have been pleased to mention, may be Instances of that Privation. But as they arise from the Nature of Society and Government; and as Government is necessary to secure other natural Rights infinitely more valuable, they cannot therefore be considered as an Objection either "against a State of Government" or "against any particular Form of it."

Life, Liberty, Property, and the Disposal of that Property with our own Consent, are natural Rights. Will any one put the other in Competition with these, or infer that because those other must be given up in a State of Government, these must be given up also? The Preservation of these Rights is the great End of Government: but is it probable they will be effectually secured by a Government, which the Proprietors of them have no Part in the Direction of, and over which they have no Power or Influence whatever? Hence is deducible, Representation: which being necessary to preserve these invaluable Rights of Nature, is itself, for that Reason, a natural Right, coinciding with, and running into, that great Law of Nature, Self-Preservation.

Thus have we considered the most material Parts of your Speech, and agreeable to your Desire disclosed to you our Sentiments on the Subject of it.

"Independence, as your Excellency rightly judged, we have not in Contemplation." We cannot however adopt "your Principles of Government," or acquiesce in all the Inferences you have drawn from them.

We have the highest Respect for that august Body the Parliament, and do not presume to prescribe the exact Limits of its Authority, yet with the Deference that is due to it, we are humbly of Opinion, that as all human Authority in the Nature of it, is and ought to be limited, it cannot constitutionally extend, for the Reasons we have above suggested, to the levying of Taxes in any Form, on his Majesty's Subjects of this Province.

In such Principles as these "our Predecessors were easy and happy:" and in the due Operation of such, their Descendants the present Inhabitants of this Province have been easy and happy: but they are not so now. Their Uneasiness and Unhappiness are derived from Acts of Parliament, and Regulations of Government, that lately and within a few Years past have been made. And this Uneasiness and Unhappiness, both in the Cause and Effects of them, though your Excellency *seems* and can only seem, to be of a different Opinion, have extended and continue to extend to all the Colonies throughout the Continent.

It would give us the highest Satisfaction to see Happiness and Tranquility restored to the Colonies; and especially to see between Great-Britain and them an Union established on such an equitable Basis as neither of them shall ever wish to destroy. We humbly supplicate the Sovereign Arbiter and Superintendent of human Affairs for these happy Events.

———————

AND on the 26th of January *the House of Representatives sent up to his Excellency their Answer, by Mr.* Adams, *Mr.* Hancock, *Mr.* Bacon, *Col.* Bowers, *Major* Hawley, *Capt.* Derby, *Mr.* Phillips, *Col.* Thayer, *and Col.* Stockbridge.

May it please your Excellency,

YOUR Excellency's Speech to the General Assembly at the Opening of this Session, has been read with great Attention in this House.

We fully agree with your Excellency, that our own Happiness as well as his Majesty's Service, very much depends upon Peace and Order; and we shall at all Times take such Measures as are consistent with our Constitution and the Rights of the People to promote and maintain them. That the Government at present is in a very disturbed State is apparent! But we cannot ascribe it to the People's having adopted unconstitutional Principles, which seems to be the Cause assigned for it by your Excellency. It appears to us to have been occasioned rather, by the British House of Commons assuming and exercising a Power inconsistent with the Freedom of the Constitution, to give and grant the Property of the Colonists, and appropriate the same without their Consent.

It is needless for us to enquire what were the Principles that induced the Councils of the Nation to so new and unprecedented a Measure. But when the Parliament by an Act of their own expresly declared, that the King, Lords and Commons of the Nation "have, ever had, and of Right ought to have full Power and Authority to make Laws and Statutes of sufficient Force and Validity to bind the Colonies and People of America, Subjects of the Crown of Great-Britain, in all Cases whatever," and in Consequence hereof another Revenue Act was made, the Minds of the People were filled with Anxiety, and they were justly alarmed with Apprehensions of the total Extinction of their Liberties.

The Result of the free Enquiries of many Persons into the Right of the Parliament to exercise such a Power over the Colonies, seems in your Excellency's Opinion, to be the Cause of what you are pleased to call the present "disturbed State of the Government;" upon which you "may not any longer consistent with your Duty to the King, and your Regard to the Interest of the Province, delay communicating your Sentiments." But that the Principles adopted in Consequence hereof, are unconstitutional, is a Subject of Enquiry. We know of no such Disorders arising therefrom as are mentioned by your Excellency. If Grand Jurors have not on their Oaths found such Offences, as your Excellency with the Advice of his Majesty's Council have *ordered* to be prosecuted, it is to be presumed they have followed the Dictates of good Conscience. *They* are the constitutional Judges of these Matters; and it is not to be supposed, that moved from corrupt Principles, they have suffered Offenders to escape a Prosecution, and thus supported and encouraged them to go on offending. If any Part of Authority, shall in an unconstitutional Manner, interpose in any Matter, it will be no wonder if it be brought into Contempt; to the lessening or confounding of that Subordination which is necessary to a well regulated State. Your Excellency's Representation that the Bands of Government are weakened, we humbly conceive to be without good Grounds; though we must own the heavy Burthens unconstitutionally brought upon the People have been and still are universally and very justly complained of as a Grievance.

You are pleased to say, that "when our Predecessors first took Possession of this Plantation or Colony, under a Grant and Charter from the Crown of England, it was their Sense, and it was the Sense of the Kingdom, that they were to remain subject to the Supreme Authority of Parliament;" whereby we understand your Excellency to mean in the Sense of the Declaratory Act of Parliament aforementioned, in all Cases whatever. And indeed it is difficult, if possible, to draw a Line of Distinction between the universal Authority of Parliament over the Colonies, and no Authority at all. It is therefore necessary for us to enquire how it appears, for your Excellency has not shown it to us, that when or at the Time that our Predecessors took Possession of this Plantation or Colony, under a Grant and Charter from the Crown of England, it was *their Sense*, and the Sense of the *Kingdom*, that they were to remain subject to the Supreme Authority of Parliament. In making this Enquiry, we shall, according to your Excellency's Recommendation, treat the Subject with Calmness and Candor, and also with a due Regard to Truth.

Previous to a direct Consideration of the Charter granted to this Province or Colony, and the better to elucidate the true Sense and Meaning of it, we would take a View of the State of the English North American Continent at the Time when and after Possession was first taken of any Part of it, by the Europeans. It was then possessed by Heathen and Barbarous People, who had nevertheless all that Right to the Soil and Sovereignty in and over the Lands they possessed, which God had originally given to Man. Whether their being Heathen, inferred any Right or Authority to Christian Princes, a Right which had long been assumed by the Pope, to dispose of their Lands to others, we will leave to your Excellency or any one of Understanding and impartial Judgment to consider. It is certain they had in no other Sense forfeited them to any Power in Europe. Should the Doctrine be admitted that Discovery of Lands owned and possessed by Pagan People, gives to any Christian Prince a Right and Title to the Dominion and Property, still it is vested in the Crown alone. It was an Acquisition of Foreign Territory, not annexed to the Realm of England and therefore at the absolute Disposal of the Crown. For we take it to be a settled Point, that the King has a constitutional Prerogative to dispose of and alienate any Part of his Territories not annexed to the Realm. In the exercise of this Prerogative, Queen Elizabeth granted the first American Charter; and claiming a Right by Virtue of Discovery, then supposed to be valid, to the Lands which are now possessed by the Colony of Virginia, she conveyed to Sir Walter Rawleigh, the Property, Dominion and Sovereignty thereof, to be held of the Crown by Homage, and a certain Render, without any Reservation to herself of any Share in the Legislative and Executive Authority. After the Attainder of Sir Walter, King James the First created two Virginia Companies, to be governed each by Laws transmitted to them by his Majesty, and not by the Parliament, with Power to establish and cause to be made a Coin to pass current among them; and vested with all Liberties, Franchises and Immunities within any of his other Dominions, to all Intents and Purposes, as if they had been abiding, and born *within the Realm.* A Declaration similar to this is contained in the first Charter of this Colony, and in those of other American Colonies; which shows that the Colonies were not intended or considered to be within the Realm of England, though within the Allegiance of the English Crown. After this, another Charter was granted by the same King James, to the Treasurer and Company of Virginia, vesting them with full Power and Authority, to make, ordain and establish all Manner of Orders, Laws, Directions, Instructions, Forms and Ceremonies of Government and Magistracy, fit and necessary, and the same to abrogate, &c. without any Reservation for securing their Subjection to the Parliament and future Laws of England. A third Charter was afterwards granted by the same King to the Treasurer and Company of Virginia, vesting them with Power and Authority to make Laws, with an Addition of this Clause, "so always that the same be not contrary to the Laws and Statutes of this our Realm of England." The same Clause was afterwards copied into the Charter of this and other Colonies, with certain Variations, such as that these Laws should be "consonant to Reason," "not repugnant to the Laws of England," "as nearly as conveniently may be to the Laws, Statutes and Rights of England," &c. These Modes of Expression convey the same Meaning, and serve to show an Intention that the Laws of the Colonies should be as much as possible, conformant in the Spirit of them to the Principles and fundamental Laws of the English Constitution, its Rights and Statutes then in Being; and by no Means to bind the Colonies to a Subjection to the Supreme Authority of the English Parliament. And that this is the true Intention, we think it further evident from this Consideration, that no Acts of any Colony Legislative, are ever brought into Parliament for Inspection there, though the Laws made in some of them, like the Acts of the British Parliament are laid before the King for his Assent or Disallowance.

We have brought the first American Charters into View, and the State of the Country when they were granted, to show that the Right of disposing of the Lands was in the Opinion of those Times vested solely in the Crown—that the several Charters conveyed to the Grantees, who should settle upon the Territories therein granted, all the Powers necessary to constitute them free and distinct States—and that the fundamental Laws of the English Constitution should be the certain and established Rule of Legislation, to which the Laws to be made in the several Colonies were to be as nearly as conveniently might be, conformable or similar; which was the true Intent and Import of the Words, "not repugnant to the Laws of England," "consonant to Reason," and other variant Expressions in the different Charters. And we would add, that the King in some of the Charters reserves the Right to judge of the Consonance and Similarity of their Laws with the English Constitution to himself, and not to the Parliament; and in Consequence thereof to affirm, or within a limited Time, disallow them.

These Charters, as well as that afterwards granted to Lord Baltimore, and other Charters, are repugnant to the Idea of Parliamentary Authority: And to suppose a Parliamentary Authority over the Colonies under such Charters, would necessarily induce that Solecism in Politics *Imperium in Imperio*. And the King's repeatedly exercising the Prerogative of disposing of the American Territory by such Charters, together with the Silence of the Nation thereupon, is an Evidence that it was an acknowledged Prerogative.

But further to show the Sense of the English Crown and Nation that the American Colonists and our Predecessors in particular, when they first took Possession of this Country by a Grant and Charter from the Crown, did not remain subject to the Supreme Authority of Parliament, we beg Leave to observe; that when a Bill was offered by the two Houses of Parliament to King Charles the First, granting to the Subjects of England the free Liberty of Fishing on the Coast of America, he refused his Royal Assent, declaring as a Reason, that "the Colonies were *without the Realm and Jurisdiction of Parliament.*"

In like Manner, his Predecessor James the First, had before declared upon a similar Occasion, that "America *was not annexed to the Realm*, and it was not fitting that Parliament should make Laws for those Countries." This Reason was, not secretly, but openly declared in Parliament. If then the Colonies were not annexed to the Realm, at the Time when their Charters were granted, they never could be afterwards, without their own special Consent, which has never since been had, or even asked. If they are not now annexed to the Realm, they are not a Part of the Kingdom, and consequently not subject to the Legislative Authority of the Kingdom. For no

Country, by the Common Law was subject to the Laws or to the Parliament, but the Realm of England.

We would if your Excellency pleases, subjoin an Instance of Conduct in King Charles the Second, singular indeed, but important to our Purpose; who, in 1679, framed an Act for a permanent Revenue for the Support of Virginia, and sent it there by Lord Colpepper, the Governor of that Colony; which was afterwards passed into a Law, and *"Enacted by the King's most excellent Majesty, by and with the Consent of the General Assembly of Virginia."* If the King had judged that Colony to be a Part of the Realm, he would not, nor could he consistently with Magna Charta, have placed himself at the Head of, and joined with any Legislative Body in making a Law to Tax the People there, other than the Lords and Commons of England.

Having taken a View of the several Charters of the first Colony in America, if we look into the old Charter of this Colony, we shall find it to be grounded on the same Principle: That the Right of disposing the Territory granted therein was vested in the Crown, as being that Christian Sovereign who first discovered it, when in the Possession of Heathen; and that it was considered as being not within the Realm, but only within the Fee and Seignory of the King. As therefore it was without the Realm of England, must not the King, if he had designed that the Parliament should have had any Authority over it, have made a special Reservation for that Purpose? which was not done.

Your Excellency says, it appears from the Charter itself, to have been the Sense of our Predecessors who first took Possession of this Plantation or Colony, that they were to remain subject to the Authority of Parliament. You have not been pleased to point out to us how this appears from the Charter, unless it be in the Observation you make on the above-mentioned Clause, viz. "That a favourable Construction has been put upon this Clause, when it has been allowed to intend such Laws of England only as are expresly made to respect us," which you say "is by Charter a Reserve of Power and Authority to Parliament to bind us by such Laws at least as are made expresly to refer to us, and consequently is a Limitation of the

Power given to the General Court." But we would still recur
to the Charter itself, and ask your Excellency, How this appears
from thence to have been the Sense of our Predecessors? Is any
Reservation of Power and Authority to Parliament thus to
bind us, expressed or implied in the Charter? It is evident, that
King Charles the first, the very Prince who granted it, as well
as his Predecessor, had no such Idea of the supreme Authority
of Parliament over the Colony, from their Declarations before
recited. Your Excellency will then allow us further to ask, by
what Authority in Reason or Equity the Parliament can enforce
a Construction so *unfavourable* to us. *Quod ab initio injustum
est, nullum potest habere juris effectum,* said *Grotius.* Which
with Submission to your Excellency may be rendered thus,
*Whatever is originally in its Nature wrong, can never be sancti-
fied or made right by Repetition and Use.*

In solemn Agreements subsequent Restrictions ought never
to be allowed. The celebrated Author whom your Excellency
has quoted, tells us that "neither the one or the other of the
interested or contracting Powers hath a right to interpret at
Pleasure." This we mention to show, even upon a Supposition
that the Parliament had been a Party to the Contract, the In-
validity of any of its subsequent Acts, to explain any Clause in
the Charter; more especially to restrict or make void any
Clause granted therein to the General Court. An Agreement
ought to be interpreted "in such a Manner as that it may have
its Effect:" But if your Excellency's Interpretation of this Clause
is just, "that it is a Reserve of Power and Authority to Parliament to bind us by such Laws as are made expresly to refer to
us," it is not only "a Limitation of the Power given to the
General Court" to Legislate, but it may whenever the Parliament shall think fit, render it of *no Effect*; for it puts it in the
Power of Parliament to bind us by as many Laws as they please,
and even to restrain us from making any Laws at all. If your
Excellency's Assertions in this and the next succeeding Part of
your Speech were well grounded, the Conclusion would be
undeniable, that the Charter even in this Clause, "does not
confer or reserve any Liberties" worth enjoying, "but what
would have been enjoyed without it;" saving that within any of
his Majesty's Dominions we are to be considered barely as *not
Aliens.* You are pleased to say, it cannot "be contended that by

the Liberties of free and natural Subjects" (which are expresly granted in the Charter to all Intents, Purposes, and Constructions whatever) "is to be understood an Exemption from Acts of Parliament because not represented there; seeing it is provided by the same Charter that such Acts shall be in Force." If, says an eminent Lawyer, "the King grants to the Town of D. the same Liberties which London has, this shall be intended the like Liberties." A Grant of the Liberties of free and natural Subjects is equivalent to a Grant of the same Liberties. And the King in the first Charter to this Colony expressly grants that it "shall be construed, reputed and adjudged in all Cases most favourably on the Behalf and for the Benefit and Behoof of the said Governor and Company and their Successors—any Matter, Cause or Thing whatsoever to the contrary notwithstanding." It is one of the Liberties of free and natural Subjects, born and abiding within the Realm, to be governed as your Excellency observes, "by Laws made by Persons in whose Elections they from Time to Time have a Voice." This is an essential Right. For nothing is more evident, than that any People who are subject to the unlimited Power of another, must be in a State of abject Slavery. It was easily and plainly foreseen that the Right of Representation in the English Parliament could not be exercised by the People of this Colony. It would be impracticable, if consistent with the English Constitution. And for this Reason, that this Colony might have and enjoy all the Liberties and Immunities of free and natural Subjects within the Realm, as stipulated in the Charter, it was necessary, and a Legislative was accordingly constituted within the Colony; one Branch of which consists of Representatives chosen by the People, to make all Laws, Statutes, Ordinances, &c. for the well ordering and governing the same, not repugnant to the Laws of England, or, as nearly as conveniently might be, agreeable to the fundamental Laws of the English Constitution. We are therefore still at a Loss to conceive where your Excellency finds it "*provided* in the same Charter, that such Acts," viz. Acts of Parliament made expressly to refer to us, "shall be in Force" in this Province. There is nothing to this Purpose expressed in the Charter, or in our Opinion even implied in it. And surely it would be very absurd, that a Charter, which is evidently formed upon a Supposition and

Intention, that a Colony is and should be considered as not within the Realm; and declared by the very Prince who granted it, to be not within the Jurisdiction of Parliament, should yet *provide*, that the Laws which the same Parliament should make expresly to refer to that Colony, should be in Force therein. Your Excellency is pleased to ask, "Does it follow that the Government by their (our Ancestors) Removal from one Part of the Dominions to another, loses its Authority over that Part to which they remove: And that they were freed from the Subjection they were under before?" We answer, if that Part of the King's Dominions to which they removed was not then a Part of the Realm, and was never annexed to it, the Parliament lost no Authority over it, having never had such Authority; and the Emigrants were consequently freed from the Subjection they were under before their Removal: The Power and Authority of Parliament being constitutionally confined within the Limits of the Realm and the Nation collectively, of which alone it is the Representing and Legislative Assembly. Your Excellency further asks, "Will it not rather be said, that by this their voluntary Removal, they have relinquished for a Time at least, one of the Rights of an English Subject, which they might if they pleased have continued to enjoy, and may again enjoy, whenever they return to the Place where it can be exercised?" To which we answer; They never did relinquish the Right to be governed by Laws made by Persons in whose Election they had a Voice. The King stipulated with them that they should have and enjoy all the Liberties of free and natural Subjects born within the Realm, to all Intents, Purposes and Constructions whatsoever; that is, that they should be as free as those who were to abide within the Realm: Consequently he stipulated with them that they should enjoy and exercise this most essential Right, which discriminates Freemen from Vassals, uninterruptedly in its full Sense and Meaning; and they did and ought still to exercise it, without the Necessity of returning, for the Sake of exercising it, to the Nation or State of England.

We cannot help observing, that your Excellency's Manner of Reasoning on this Point, seems to us to render the most valuable Clauses in our Charter unintelligible: As if Persons going from the Realm of England to inhabit in America, should hold and exercise there a certain Right of English Subjects; but in Order to exercise it in such Manner as to be of any Benefit to them, they must *not inhabit* there, but return to the Place where alone it can be exercised. By such Construction, the Words of the Charter can have no Sense or Meaning. We forbear remarking upon the Absurdity of a Grant to Persons born within the Realm, of the same Liberties which would have belonged to them if they had been born within the Realm.

Your Excellency is disposed to compare this Government to the Variety of Corporations formed within the Kingdom, with Power to make and execute By-Laws, &c. And because they remain subject to the Supreme Authority of Parliament, to infer that this Colony is also subject to the same Authority: This Reasoning appears to us not just. The Members of those Corporations are Resident within the Kingdom; and Residence subjects them to the Authority of Parliament, in which they are also represented: Whereas the People of this Colony are not Resident within the Realm. The Charter was granted with the express Purpose to induce them to reside without the Realm; consequently they are not represented in Parliament there. But we would ask your Excellency; Are any of the Corporations formed within the Kingdom, vested with the Power of erecting other subordinate Corporations? Of enacting and determining what Crimes shall be Capital? And constituting Courts of Common Law with all their Officers, for the hearing, trying and punishing capital Offenders with Death? These and many other Powers vested in this Government, plainly show that it is to be considered as a Corporation in no other Light, than as every State is a Corporation. Besides, Appeals from the Courts of Law here, are not brought before the House of Lords; which shows that the Peers of the Realm are not the Peers of America: But all such Appeals are brought before the King in Council, which is a further Evidence that we are not within the Realm.

We conceive enough has been said to convince your Excellency, that "when our Predecessors first took Possession of this Plantation or Colony by a Grant and Charter from the Crown of England, it *was not* and never had been the Sense of the Kingdom, that they were to remain subject to the Supreme Authority of Parliament." We will now with your Excellency's

Leave, enquire what *was* the Sense of our Ancestors of this very important Matter.

And as your Excellency has been pleased to tell us, you have not discovered that the Supreme Authority of Parliament has been called in Question even by private and particular Persons, until within seven or eight Years past; except about the Time of the Anarchy and Confusion in England, which preceeded the Restoration of King Charles the Second; we beg leave to remind your Excellency of some Parts of your own History of Massachusetts-Bay. Therein we are informed of the Sentiments of "Persons of Influence" after the Restoration, from which the Historian tells us, some Parts of their Conduct, that is of the General Assembly, "may be pretty well accounted for." By the History it appears to have been the Opinion of those Persons of Influence, "that the Subjects of any Prince or State had a natural Right to remove to any other State or to another Quarter of the World, unless the State was weakened or exposed by such Remove; and even in that Case, if they were deprived of the Right of all Mankind, Liberty of Conscience, it would justify a Separation, and *upon their Removal their Subjection determined and ceased.*" That "the Country to which they had removed, was claimed and possessed by independent Princes, whose Right to the Lordship and Sovereignty thereof had been acknowledged by the Kings of England," an Instance of which is quoted in the Margin; "That they themselves had actually purchased for valuable Consideration, not only the Soil, but the Dominion, the Lordship and Sovereignty of those Princes;" without which Purchase, "in the Sight of God and Men, they had no Right or Title to what they possessed. That they had received a Charter of Incorporation from the King, from whence arose a new Kind of Subjection, namely, "a voluntary, civil Subjection;" and by this Compact "they were *to be governed by Laws made by themselves.*" Thus it appears to have been the Sentiments of *private* Persons, though Persons by whose Sentiments the public Conduct was influenced, that their Removal was a justifiable Separation from the Mother State, upon which their Subjection to that State determined and ceased. The Supreme Authority of Parliament, if it had then ever been asserted, must surely have been called in Question, by Men who had advanced such Principles as these.

The first Act of Parliament made expresly to refer to the Colonies, was after the Restoration. In the Reign of King Charles the Second, several such Acts passed. And the same History informs us there was a Difficulty in conforming to them; and the Reason of this Difficulty is explained in a Letter of the General Assembly to their Agent, quoted in the following Words, "They apprehended them to be an Invasion of the Rights Liberties and Properties of the Subjects of his Majesty in the Colony, *they not being represented in Parliament*, and according to the usual Sayings of the Learned in the Law, the Laws of England were bounded within the four Seas, *and did not reach America*: However as his Majesty had signified his Pleasure that those Acts should be observed in the Massachusetts, they had made Provision by a Law of the Colony that they should be strictly attended." Which Provision by a Law of their own would have been superfluous, if they had admitted the Supreme Authority of Parliament. In short, by the same History it appears that those Acts of Parliament as such were disregarded; and the following Reason is given for it; "It seems to have been a *general* Opinion that Acts of Parliament had no other Force, than what they derived from Acts made by the General Court to establish and confirm them."

But still further to show the Sense of our Ancestors respecting this Matter, we beg leave to recite some Parts of a Narrative presented to the Lords of Privy Council by Edward Randolph, in the Year 1676, which we find in your Excellency's Collection of Papers lately published. Therein it is declared to be the Sense of the Colony, "that no Law is in Force or Esteem there, but such as are made by the General Court; and therefore it is accounted a Breach of their Privileges, and a Betraying of the Liberties of their Common-wealth, to urge the Observation of the Laws of England." And further, "That no Oath shall be urged or required to be taken by any Person, but such Oath as the General Court hath considered, allowed and required." And further, "there is no notice taken of the Act of Navigation, Plantation or any other Laws made in England for the Regulation of Trade." "That the Government would make the World believe they are a free State, and do act in all Matters accordingly." Again, "These Magistrates ever reserve to themselves a Power to alter, evade and disannul any Law or Command, not agreeing with their Humour or the absolute Authority of their Government, acknowledging no Superior." And further, "He (the Governor) freely declared to me that the Laws made by your Majesty and your Parliament, obligeth them in nothing, but what consists with the Interests of that Colony, that the Legislative Power and Authority is and abides in them *solely*." And in the same Mr. Randolph's Letter to the Bishop of London, July 14, 1682, he says, "This *Independency* in Government, claimed and daily practised." And your Excellency being *then* sensible that this was the Sense of our Ancestors, in a Marginal Note in the same Collection of Papers, observes, that "this," viz. the Provision made for observing the Acts of Trade, "is very extraordinary, for this Provision was an Act of the Colony declaring the Acts of Trade shall be in Force there." Although Mr. Randolph was very unfriendly to the Colony, yet as his Declarations are concurrent with those recited from your Excellency's History, we think they may be admitted for the Purpose for which they are now brought.

Thus we see, from your Excellency's History and Publications, the Sense our Ancestors had of the Jurisdiction of Parliament under the first Charter. Very different from that which your Excellency *in your Speech* apprehends it to have been.

It appears by Mr. Neal's History of New-England, that the Agents who had been employed by the Colony to transact its Affairs in England at the Time when the present Charter was granted, among other Reasons gave the following for their Acceptance of it, viz. "The General Court has with the King's Approbation as much Power in New-England, as the King and Parliament have in England; they have all English Privileges, and can be touched by *no Law*, and by no Tax but of their own making." This is the earliest Testimony that can be given of the Sense our Predecessors had of the Supreme Authority of Parliament under the present Charter. And it plainly shows, that they, who having been freely conversant with those who framed the Charter, must have well understood the Design and Meaning of it, supposed that the Terms in our Charter "full Power and Authority," intended and were considered as a *sole* and exclusive Power, and that there was no "Reserve in the Charter to the Authority of Parliament, to bind the Colony" by any Acts whatever.

Soon after the Arrival of the Charter, viz. in 1692, your Excellency's History informs us, "the first Act" of this Legislative was a Sort of Magna Charta, asserting and setting forth their general Privileges, and this Clause was among the rest, "No Aid, Tax, Tallage, Assessment, Custom, Loan, Benevolence or Imposition whatever, shall be laid, assess'd, impos'd or levied on any of their Majesty's Subjects, or their Estates, on any Pretence whatever, but by the Act and Consent of the Governor, Council and Representatives of the People assembled in General Court." And though this Act was disallowed, it serves to show the Sense which the General Assembly contemporary with the granting the Charter had of their sole and exclusive Right to Legislate for the Colony. The History says, "the other Parts of the Act were copied from Magna Charta;" by which we may conclude that the Assembly then construed the Words "not repugnant to the Laws," to mean, conformable to the fundamental Principles of the English Constitution. And it is observable that the Lords of Privy Council, so lately as in the Reign of Queen Anne, when several Laws enacted by the General Assembly, were laid before her Majesty for her Allowance, interpreted the Words in this Charter, "not repugnant to the Laws of England," by the Words "as nearly as conveniently may be agreeable to the Laws and Statutes of England." And her Majesty was pleased to disallow those Acts, not because they were repugnant to any Law or Statute of England, made expresly to refer to the Colony; but because divers Persons, by Virtue thereof, were punished without being tried by their Peers in the ordinary "Courts of Law," and "by the ordinary Rules and known Methods of Justice;" contrary to the express Terms of Magna Charta, which was a Statute in Force at the Time of granting the Charter, and declaratory of the Rights and Liberties of the Subjects within the Realm.

You are pleased to say, that "our Provincial or Local Laws have in numerous Instances had Relation to Acts of Parliament made to respect the Plantations and this Colony in particular." The Authority of the Legislature, says the same Author who is quoted by your Excellency, "does not extend so far as the Fundamentals of the Constitution." "They ought to consider the Fundamental Laws as sacred, if the Nation has not in very express Terms, given them the Power to change them. For the Constitution of the State ought to be fixed: And since that was first established by the Nation, which afterwards trusted certain Persons with the Legislative Power, the fundamental Laws are excepted from their Commission." Now the Fundamentals of the Constitution of this Province are stipulated in the Charter; the Reasoning therefore in this Case holds equally good. Much less then ought any Acts or Doings of the General Assembly, however numerous, to neither of which your Excellency has pointed us, which barely relate to Acts of Parliament made to respect the Plantations in general, or this Colony in particular, to be taken as an Acknowledgment of this People, or even of the Assembly, which inadvertently passed those Acts, that we are subject to the Supreme Authority of Parliament. And with still less Reason are the Decisions in the Executive Courts to determine this Point. If they have adopted that "as Part of the Rule of Law," which in Fact is not, it must be imputed to Inattention or Error in Judgment, and cannot justly be urged as an Alteration or Restriction of the Legislative Authority of the Province.

Before we leave this Part of your Excellency's Speech, we would observe, that the great Design of our Ancestors, in leaving the Kingdom of England, was to be freed from a Subjection to its spiritual Laws and Courts, and to worship God according to the Dictates of their Consciences. Your Excellency in your History observes, that their Design was "to obtain for themselves and their Posterity the Liberty of worshipping God in such Manner as appeared to them most agreeable to the sacred Scriptures." And the General Court themselves declared in 1651, that "seeing just Cause to fear the Persecution of the then Bishop, and High Commission for not conforming to the Ceremonies of those under their Power, they thought it their safest Course, to get to this Outside of the World, out of their View and *beyond their Reach.*" But if it had been their Sense, that they were still to be subject to the Supreme Authority of Parliament, they must have known that their Design might and probably would be frustrated; that the Parliament, especially considering the Temper of those Times, might make what ecclesiastical Laws they pleased, expressly to refer to them, and place them in the same Circumstances with Respect to religious Matters, to be relieved from which was the Design of their Removal. And we would add, that if your Excellency's Construction of the Clause in our present Charter is just, another Clause therein, which provides for Liberty of Conscience for all Christians except Papists, may be rendered void by an Act of Parliament made to refer to us, requiring a Conformity to the Rites and Mode of Worship in the Church of England, or any other.

Thus we have endeavoured to shew the Sense of the People of this Colony under both Charters; and if there have been in any late Instances a Submission to Acts of Parliament, it has been in our Opinion, rather from Inconsideration or a Reluctance at the Idea of contending with the Parent State, than from a Conviction or Acknowledgement of the Supreme Legislative Authority of Parliament.

Your Excellency tells us, "you know of no Line that can be drawn between the Supreme Authority of Parliament and the total Independence of the Colonies." If there be no such Line, the Consequence is, either that the Colonies are the Vassals of the Parliament, or, that they are totally Independent. As it cannot be supposed to have been the Intention of the Parties in the Compact, that we should be reduced to a State of Vassallage, the Conclusion is, that it was their Sense, that we were thus Independent. "It is Impossible, your Excellency says, that there should be two independent Legislatures in one and the same State." May we not then further conclude, that it was their Sense that the Colonies were by their Charters made distinct States from the Mother Country? Your Excellency adds, "For although there may be but one Head, the King, yet the two Legislative Bodies will make two Governments as distinct as the Kingdoms of England and Scotland before the Union." Very true, may it please your Excellency; and if they interfere not with each other, what hinders but that being united in one Head and common Sovereign, they may live happily in that Connection, and mutually support and protect each other? Notwithstanding all the Terrors which your Excellency has pictured to us as the Effects of a total Independence, there is more Reason to dread the Consequences of absolute uncontrouled Supreme Power, whether of a Nation or a Monarch, than those of a total Independence. It would be a Misfortune "to know by Experience, the Difference between the Liberties of an English Colonist and those of the Spanish, French and Dutch": And since the British Parliament has passed an Act which is executed even with Rigour, though not voluntarily submitted to, for raising a Revenue, and appropriating the same without the Consent of the People who pay it, and have claimed a Power making such Laws as they please to order and govern us, your Excellency will excuse us in asking, whether you do not think we already experience too much of such a Difference, and have not Reason to fear we shall soon be reduced to a worse Situation than that of the Colonies of France, Spain or Holland?

If your Excellency expects to have the Line of Distinction between the Supreme Authority of Parliament, and the total Independence of the Colonies drawn by us, we would say it would be an arduous Undertaking; and of very great Importance to all the other Colonies: And therefore, could we conceive of such a Line, we should be unwilling to propose it, without their Consent in Congress.

To conclude, These are great and profound Questions. It is the Grief of this House, that by the ill Policy of a late injudicious Administration, America has been driven into the Contemplation of them. And we cannot but express our Concern, that your Excellency by your Speech has reduced us to the unhappy Alternative, either of appearing by our Silence to acquiesce in your Excellency's Sentiments, or of thus freely discussing this Point.

After all that we have said, we would be far from being understood to have in the least abated that just Sense of Allegiance which we owe to the King of Great-Britain, our rightful Sovereign: And should the People of this Province be left to the free and full Exercise of all the Liberties and Immunities granted to them by Charter, there would be no Danger of an Independance on the Crown. Our Charters reserve great Power to the Crown in its Representative, fully sufficient to balance, analagous to the English Constitution, all the Liberties and Privileges granted to the People. All this your Excellency knows full well—And whoever considers the Power and Influence, in all their Branches, reserved by our Charter to the Crown, will be far from thinking that the Commons of this Province are too Independent.

———————

On Tuesday the 16th of February his Excellency was pleased to deliver the following Speech to both Houses in the Council Chamber, viz.

Gentlemen of the Council, and
Gentlemen of the House of Representatives,

THE Proceedings of such of the Inhabitants of the Town of Boston as assembled together and passed and published their Resolves or Votes as the Act of the Town at a legal Town-Meeting, denying in the most express Terms the Supremacy of Parliament, and inviting every other Town and District in the Province to adopt the same Principle and to establish Committees of Correspondence to consult upon proper Measures to maintain it, and the Proceedings of divers other Towns, in Consequence of this Invitation, appeared to me to be so unwarrantable and of such a dangerous Nature and Tendency, that I thought myself bound to call upon you in my Speech at Opening the Session, to join with me in discountenancing and bearing a proper Testimony against such Irregularities and Innovations.

I stated to you fairly and truly, as I conceived, the Constitution of the Kingdom and of the Province so far as relates to the Dependance of the latter upon the former; and I desired you, if you differed from me in Sentiments, to shew me with Candour my own Errors, and to give your Reasons in support of your Opinions, so far as you might differ from me. I hoped that you would have considered my Speech by your joint Committees, and have given me a joint Answer; but, as the House of Representatives have declined that Mode of Proceeding, and as your Principles in Government are very different, I am obliged to make separate and distinct replies.

I shall first apply myself to you,
Gentlemen of the Council,

The two first Parts of your Answer, which Respect the Disorders occasioned by the Stamp-Act and the general Nature of Supreme Authority, do not appear to me to have a Tendency to invalidate any Thing which I have said in my Speech; for, however the Stamp-Act may have been the immediate Occasion of any Disorders, the Authority of Parliament was notwithstanding denied in Order to justify or excuse them. And, for the Nature of the Supreme Authority of Parliament, I have never given you any Reason to suppose that I intended a more absolute Power in Parliament, or a greater Degree of active or passive Obedience in the People, than what is founded in the Nature of Government, let the Form of it be what it may. I shall, therefore, pass over those Parts of your Answer without any other Remark. I would also have saved you the Trouble of all those Authorities which you have brought to shew, that all Taxes upon English Subjects must be levied by Virtue of the Act not of the King alone but in Conjuction with the Lords and Commons, for I should very readily have allowed it; and I should as readily have allowed that all other Acts of Legislation must be passed by the same joint Authority, and not by the King alone.

Indeed, I am not willing to continue a Controversy with you upon any other Parts of your Answer. I am glad to find that Independence is what you have not in Contemplation; and that you will not presume to prescribe the exact Limits of the Authority of Parliament; only, as with due Deference to it, you are humbly of Opinion, that, as all human Authority in the Nature of it is and ought to be limited, it cannot constitutionally extend for the Reasons you have suggested, to the levying of Taxes in any Form on his Majesty's Subjects of this Province.

I will only observe, that your Attempts to draw a Line as the Limits of the Supreme Authority in Government, by distinguishing some natural Rights as more peculiarly exempt from such Authority than the rest, rather tend to evince the Impracticability of drawing such a Line; and that some Parts of your Answer seem to infer a Supremacy in the Province at the same Time that you acknowledge the Supremacy of Parliament, for otherwise the Rights of the Subjects cannot be the same in all essential Respects, as you suppose them to be, in all Parts of the Dominions, "under a like Form of Legislature."

From these, therefore, and other Considerations I cannot help flattering myself, that, upon more mature Deliberation and in Order to a more consistent Plan of Government, you will chuse rather to doubt of the Expediency of Parliament's Exercising its Authority in Cases that may happen, than to limit the Authority itself, especially as you agree with me in the proper Method of obtaining a Redress of Grievances by constitutional Representations, which cannot well consist with a Denial of the Authority to which the Representations are made; and, from the best Information I have been able to obtain, the Denial of the Authority of Parliament, expresly or by Implication, in those Petitions to which you refer was the Cause of their not being admitted, and not any Advice given by the Minister to the Agents of the Colonies.

I must enlarge and be much more particular in my Reply to you,

Gentlemen of the House of Representatives,

I shall take no Notice of that Part of your Answer which attributes the Disorders of the Province to an undue Exercise of the Power of Parliament, because you take for granted, what can by no Means be admitted, that Parliament had exercised its Power without just Authority. The Sum of your Answer so far as it is pertinent to my Speech, is this.

You alledge that the Colonies were an Acquisition of Foreign Territory not annexed to the Realm of England, and therefore at the *absolute* Disposal of the Crown; the King having, as you take it, a constitutional Right to dispose of and *alienate* any Part of his Territories not annexed to the Realm— that Queen *Elizabeth* accordingly conveyed the Property, *Dominion* and *Sovereignty* of *Virginia* to Sir *Walter Raleigh* to be held of the Crown *by Homage and a certain Render*, without reserving any Share in the Legislative and Executive Authority —that the subsequent Grants of America were similar in this Respect, that they were without any Reservation for securing the Subjection of the Colonists to the Parliament and future Laws of England,—that this was the Sense of the English Crown, the Nation and our Predecessors when they first took Possession of this Country—that if the Colonies were not then annexed to the Realm they cannot have been annexed since that Time—that if they are not now annexed to the *Realm* they are not Part of the *Kingdom*, and consequently not subject to the Legislative Authority of the Kingdom; for no Country, by the Common Law, was subject to the Laws or to the Parliament but the Realm of England.

Now if this your Foundation shall fail you in every Part of it, as I think it will, the Fabrick which you have raised upon it must certainly fall.

Let me then observe to you that, as English Subjects, and agreeable to the Doctrine of Feudal Tenure, all our Lands and Tenements are held mediately or immediately of the Crown, and although the Possession and Use or Profits be in the Subject, there still remains a Dominion in the Crown. When any new Countries are discovered by English Subjects, according to the general Law and Usage of Nations, they become Part of the State, and, according to the Feudal System, the Lordship or Dominion is in the Crown and a Right accrues of disposing of such Territories, under such Tenure or for such Services to be performed as the Crown shall judge proper, and whensoever any Part of such Territories, by Grant from the Crown, becomes the Possession or Property of private Persons, such Persons, thus holding under the Crown of England, remain or become Subjects of England to all Intents and Purposes, as fully as if any of the Royal Manors Forests or other Territory within the Realm had been granted to them upon the like Tenure. But that it is now, or was when the Plantations were first granted, the Prerogative of the Kings of England to alienate such Territories from the Crown, or to constitute a Number of new Governments altogether independent of the Sovereign Legislative Authority of the English Empire, I can by no Means concede to you. I have never seen any better Authority to support such an Opinion than an anonimous Pamphlet by which I fear you have too easily been mislead, for I shall presently shew you that the Declarations of King James the First, and of King Charles the First, admitting they are truly related by the Author of this Pamphlet, ought to have no Weight with you; nor does the Cession or Restoration, upon a Treaty of Peace, of Countries which have been lost or acquired in War militate with these Principles, nor may any particular Act of Power of a Prince in selling or delivering up any Part of His Dominions to a foreign Prince or State against the general Sense of the Nation be urged to invalidate them, and upon Examination it will appear that all the Grants which have been made of America are founded upon them and are made to conform to them, even those which you have adduced in Support of very different Principles.

You do not recollect that, prior to what you call the first Grant by Q. Elizabeth to Sir Walter Raleigh, a Grant had been made, by the same Princess, to Sir Humphrey Gilbert of all such Countries as he should discover which were to be *of the Allegiance of her, her Heirs and Successors* but, he dying in the Prosecution of his Voyage, a second Grant was made to Sir Walter Raleigh which, you say, conveyed the Dominion and Sovereignty without any Reserve of Legislative or Executive Authority *being held by Homage and a Render.* To hold by *Homage*, which implies Fealty, *and a Render* is Descriptive of Socage Tenure as fully as if it had been said to hold *as of our Manor of East Greenwich* the Words in your Charter. Now this alone was a Reserve of Dominion and Sovereignty in the Queen, her Heirs and Successors and, besides this, the Grant is made upon this express Condition, which you pass over, *that the People remain subject to the Crown of England*, the Head of that Legislative Authority which, by the English Constitution, is equally extensive with the Authority of the Crown throughout every Part of the Dominions. Now if we could suppose the Queen to have acquired separate from her Relations to her Subjects, or in her natural Capacity, which she could not do, a Title to a Country discovered by her Subjects and then to grant the same Country to English Subjects in her publick Capacity as Queen of England, still by this Grant she annexed it to the Crown. Thus by not distinguishing between the Crown of England and the Kings and Queens of England in their personal or natural Capacities, you have been led into a fundamental Error which must prove fatal to your System. It is not material whether Virginia reverted to the Crown by Sir Walter's Attainder or whether he never took any Benefit from his Grant, though the latter is most probable seeing he ceased from all Attempts to take Possession of the Country after a few Years Trial. There were, undoubtedly, divers Grants made by King James the First of the Continent of America in the Beginning of the 17th Century and similar to the Grant of Queen Elizabeth in this Respect, that they were dependant on the Crown. The Charter to the Council at Plimouth in Devon dated November 3d, 1620 more immediately respects us, and of that we have the most authentick Remains.

By this Charter, upon the Petition of Sir Ferdinando Gorges a Corporation was constituted to be and continue by Succession forever in the Town of Plimouth aforesaid, to which Corporation that Part of the American Continent which lies between the 40° and 48° Degrees of Latitude was granted *to be held of the King his Heirs and Successors as of the Manor of East Greenwich* with Powers to constitute subordinate Governments in America and to make Laws for such Governments, *not repugnant to the Laws and Statutes of England.* From this Corporation your Predecessors obtained a Grant of the Soil of the Colony of Massachusets-Bay, in 1627, and, in 1628, they obtained a Charter from King Charles the First making them a distinct Corporation, also within the Realm, and giving them full Powers within the Limits of their Patent, very like to those of the Council of Plimouth throughout their more extensive Territory.

We will now consider what must have been the Sense of the King of the Nation and of the Patentees at the Time of granting these Patents. From the Year 1602 the Banks and Sea Coasts of New-England had been frequented by English Subjects for catching and drying Cod-Fish. When an exclusive Right to the Fishery was claimed, by Virtue of the Patent of 1620, the House of Commons was alarmed and a Bill was brought in for allowing a free Fishery, and it was upon this Occasion that one of the Secretaries of State declared, perhaps as his own Opinion, that the Plantations were not annexed to the Crown and so were not within the Jurisdiction of Parliament. Sir Edwin Sandys, who was one of the Virginia Company and an eminent Lawyer, declared that he knew Virginia had been annexed and *was held of the Crown as of the Manor of East Greenwich* and he believed New-England was so also; and so it most certainly was. This Declaration, made by one of the King's Servants, you say shewed the Sense of the Crown and, being not secretly but openly declared in Parliament you would make it the Sense of the Nation also, notwithstanding your own Assertion that the Lords and Commons passed a Bill that shewed their Sense to be directly the contrary. But if there had been full Evidence of express Declarations made by King

James the First, and King Charles the First, they were Declarations contrary to their own Grants, which declare this Country to be held of the Crown and consequently it must have been annexed to it. And may not such Declarations be accounted for by other Actions of those Princes who when they were solliciting the Parliament to grant the Duties of Tonnage and Poundage with other Aids and were, in this Way, acknowledging the Rights of Parliament, at the same Time were requiring the Payment of those Duties with Ship Money, &c. by Virtue of their Prerogative?

But to remove all doubt of the Sense of the Nation and of the Patentees of this Patent or Charter in 1620 I need only refer you to the Account published by Sir Ferdinando Gorges himself of the Proceedings in Parliament upon this Occasion. As he was the most active Member of the Council of Plimouth and as he relates what came within his own Knowledge and Observation his Narrative, which has all the Appearance of Truth and Sincerity, must carry Conviction with it. He says that soon after the Patent was passed and whilst it lay in the Crown-Office he was summoned to appear in Parliament to answer what was to be objected against it, and the House being in a Committee and Sir Edward Coke that great Oracle of the Law, in the Chair, he was called to the Bar and was told by Sir Edward that the House understood that a Patent had been granted to the said Sir Ferdinando and divers other noble Persons for establishing a Colony in New-England, that this was deemed a Grievance of the Common-wealth *contrary to the Laws*, and to the Privileges of the Subject, that it was a Monopoly, &c. and he required the Delivery of the Patent into the House. Sir Ferdinando Gorges made no Doubt of the Authority of the House but submitted to their Disposal of the Patent as in their Wisdom they thought good "not knowing, under Favour, how any Action of that Kind could be a Grievance to the Publick seeing it was undertaken for the Advancement of Religion, *the Enlargement of the Bounds of our Nation*. &c. He was willing, however, to submit the whole to their honorable Censures." After divers Attendances he imagined he had satisfied the House that the planting a Colony was of much more Consequence than a simple disorderly Course of Fishing. He was, notwithstanding, disappointed and, when

the Publick Grievances of the Kingdom were presented by the
two Houses, that of the Patent for New-England was the first.
I don't know how the Parliament could have shewn more fully
the Sense they then had of their Authority over this new acquired Territory, nor can we expect better Evidence of the
Sense which the Patentees had of it, for I know of no historical
Fact of which we have less Reason to doubt.

And now Gentlemen I will shew you how it appears from
our Charter itself, which you say I have not yet been pleased to
point out to you except from that Clause which restrains us
from making Laws repugnant to the Laws of England, that it
was the Sense of our Predecessors at the Time when the Charter was granted that they were to remain subject to the Supreme Authority of Parliament.

Besides this Clause, which I shall have Occasion further to
remark upon before I finish, you will find that, by the Charter
a Grant was made of Exemption from all Taxes and Impositions upon any Goods imported *into New-England*, or exported from thence into England for the Space of twenty-one
Years, except the Custom of five per Cent upon such Goods as,
after the Expiration of seven Years, should be brought into
England. Nothing can be more plain than that the Charter, as
well as the Patent to the Council of Plimouth, constitutes a
Corporation in England with Powers to create a subordinate
Government or Governments within the Plantation, so that
there would always be Subjects of Taxes and Impositions both
in the Kingdom and in the Plantation. An Exemption for
twenty-one Years implies a Right of Imposition after the Expiration of the Term, and there is no Distinction between the
Kingdom and the Plantation. By what Authority, then, in the
Understanding of the Parties, were these Impositions to be
laid? If any, to support a System, should say by the King rather
than to acknowledge the Authority of Parliament, yet this
could not be the Sense of one of our principal Patentees Mr.
Samuel Vassall who at that Instant, 1628, the Date of the Charter, was suffering the Loss of his Goods rather than submit to
an Imposition laid by the King without the Authority of Parliament; and to prove that a few Years after it could not be the
Sense of the rest I need only to refer you to your own Records
for the Year 1642 where you will find an Order of the House of

Commons, conceived in such Terms as discover a plain Reference to this Part of the Charter, after fourteen Years of the Twenty-one were expired. By this Order the House of Commons declare that all Goods and Merchandize exported to New-England or imported from thence shall be free from all Taxes and Impositions both in the Kingdom *and in New-England* until the House shall take further Order therein to the contrary. The Sense which our Predecessors had of the Benefit which they took from this Order evidently appears from the Vote of the General Court, acknowledging their humble Thankfulness, and preserving a grateful Remembrance of the Honorable Respect from that high Court, and resolving that the Order sent unto them under the Hand of the Clerk of the Honorable House of Commons shall be entered among their Publick Records to remain there unto Posterity: And, in an Address to Parliament, Nine Years after, they acknowledge, among other undeserved Favours that of *taking off the Customs from them.*

I am at a Loss to know what your Ideas could be when you say that if the Plantations are not Part of the *Realm*, they are not Part of the *Kingdom*, seeing the two Words can properly convey but one Idea and they have one and the same Signification in the different Languages from whence they are derived. I do not charge you with any Design, but the equivocal Use of the Word Realm in several Parts of your Answer makes them perplexed and obscure. Sometimes, you must intend the whole Dominion which is subject to the Authority of Parliament, sometimes only strictly the Territorial Realm to which other Dominions are or may be annexed. If you mean that no Countries but the ancient territorial Realm can constitutionally be subject to the Supreme Authority of England, which you have very incautiously said is a Rule of the Common Law of England, this is a Doctrine which you will never be able to support. That the Common Law should be controuled and changed by Statutes every Day's Experience teaches, but that the Common Law prescribes Limits to the Extent of the Legislative Power, I believe has never been said upon any other Occasion. That Acts of Parliament for several Hundred Years past have respected Countries, which are not strictly within the Realm, you might easily have discovered by the Statute Books.

You will find Acts for regulating the Affairs of Ireland, though a seperate and distinct Kingdom. Wales and Calais, whilst they sent no Representatives to Parliament, were subject to the like Regulations. So are Guernsey, Jersey, Alderney, &c. which send no Members to this Day. These Countries are not more properly a Part of the ancient Realm, than the Plantations, nor do I know that they can more properly be said to be annexed to the Realm, unless the declaring that Acts of Parliament shall extend to Wales, though not particularly named shall make it so, which I conceive it does not in the Sense you intend.

Thus, I think, I have made it appear that the Plantations, though not strictly within the Realm, have from the Beginning been constitutionally subject to the Supreme Authority of the Realm and are so far annexed to it as to be, with the Realm and the other Dependencies upon it, one intire Dominion; and that the Plantation or Colony of Massachusetts-Bay in particular is holden as feudatory of the Imperial Crown of England: Deem it to be no Part of the Realm it is immaterial, for, to use the Words of a very great Authority in a Case in some Respects analogous, "being Feudatory the Conclusion necessary follows, that it is under the Government of the King's Laws and the King's Courts in Cases proper for them to interpose, though (like Counties Palatine) it has peculiar Laws and Customs, Jura Regalia, and complete Jurisdiction at Home."

Your Remark upon and Construction of the Words, *not Repugnant to the Laws of England*, are much the same with those of the Council; but can any Reason be assigned why the Laws of England as they stood just at that Period should be pitched upon as the Standard, more than at any other Period? If so, why was it not recured to when the second Charter was Granted, more than sixty Years after the first? It is not improbable that the original Intention might be a Repugnancy in general and, a Fortiori, such Laws as were made more immediately to Respect us, but the Statute of 7th and 8th, of King William and Queen Mary, soon after the second Charter, favours the latter Construction only, and the Province Agent, Mr. Dummer, in his much applauded Defence of the Charter, says that *then* a Law in the Plantations may be said to be repugnant to a Law made in Great Britain, when it flatly contradicts it so far as the Law made there mentions and relates to the Plantations. But, Gentlemen, there is another Clause both in the first and second Charter which, I think will serve to explain this or to render all Dispute upon the Construction of it unnecessary. —You are enabled to impose such Oaths only as are warrantable by, or not repugnant to the Laws and Statutes of the Realm. I believe you will not contend that these Clauses must mean such Oaths only as were warrantable at the respective Times when the Charters were granted. It has often been found necessary, since the Date of the Charters, to alter the Forms of the Oaths to the Government by Acts of Parliament, and such Alterations have always been conformed to in the Plantations.

Lest you should think that I admit the Authority of King Charles the Second in giving his Assent to an Act of the Assembly of Virginia, which you subjoin to the Authorities of James the First and Charles the First, to have any Weight, I must observe to you that I do not see any greater Inconsistency with Magna Charta in the King's giving his Assent to an Act of a Subordinate Legislature immediately or in Person than when he does it mediately by his Governor or Substitute but, if it could be admitted that such an Assent discovered the King's Judgment that Virginia was Independent, would you lay any Stress upon it when the same King was from Time to Time giving his Assent to Acts of Parliament which inferred the Dependence of all the Colonies, and had by one of those Acts declared the Plantations to be inhabited and peopled by his Majesty Subjects of England?

I gave you no Reason to Remark upon the Absurdity of a Grant to Persons born within the Realm of the same Liberties which would have belonged to them if they had been born within the Realm, but rather guarded against it by considering such Grant as declaratory only, and in the Nature of an Assurance that the Plantations would be considered as the Dominions of England. But is there no Absurdity in a Grant from the King of England of the Liberties and Immunities of Englishmen to Persons born in and who are to inhabit other Territories than the Dominions of England, and would such Grant, whether by Charter or other Letters Patent, be sufficient to make them inheritable, or to intitle them to the other Liberties and Immunities of Englishmen, in any Part of the English Dominions?

As I am willing to rest the Point between us upon the Plantations having been, from their first Discovery and Settlement under the Crown, a Part of the Dominions of England, I shall not take up any Time in remarking upon your Arguments to shew that since that Time, they cannot have been made a Part of those Dominions.

The remaining Parts of your Answer are principally intended to prove that, under both Charters, it hath been the Sense of the People that they were not subject to the Jurisdiction of Parliament, and, for this Purpose, you have made large Extracts from the History of the Colony. Whilst you are doing Honor to the Book, by laying any Stress upon its Authority, it would have been no more than Justice to the Author if you had cited some other Passages which would have tended to reconcile the Passage in my Speech to the History.—I have said that, except about the Time of the Anarchy which preceded the Restoration of King Charles the Second, I have not discovered that the Authority of Parliament had been called in Question even by particular Persons. It was, as I take it, from the Principles imbibed in those Times of Anarchy that the Persons of Influence, mentioned in the History, disputed the Authority of Parliament, but the Government would not venture to dispute it. On the contrary, in four or five Years after the Restoration, the Government declared to the King's Commissioners that the Act of Navigation had been for some Years observed here, that they knew not of it's being greatly violated and that such Laws as appeared to be against it were repealed. It is not strange that these Persons of Influence should prevail upon great Part of the People to fall in, for a Time, with their Opinions and to suppose Acts of the Colony necessary to give Force to Acts of Parliament; the Government, however, several Years before the Charter was vacated, more explicitly acknowledged the Authority of Parliament and voted that their Governor should take the Oath, required of him, faithfully to do and perform all Matters and Things enjoined him by the Acts of Trade. I have not recited in my Speech all these Particulars, nor had I them all in my Mind but, I think, I have said nothing inconsistent with them. My Principles in Government are still the same with what they appear to be in the Book you refer to, nor am I conscious that, by any Part of my Conduct, I have given Cause to suggest the contrary.

Inasmuch as you say that I have not particularly pointed out to you the Acts and Doings of the General Assembly which relate to Acts of Parliament, I will do it now, and demonstrate to you that such Acts have been acknowledged by the Assembly, or submitted to by the People.

From your Predecessors Removal to America until the Year 1640 there was no Session of Parliament, and the first short Session of a few Days only in 1640, and the whole of the next Session, until the withdraw of the King, being taken up in the Disputes between the King and the Parliament, there could be no Room for Plantation Affairs. Soon after the King's withdraw the House of Commons passed the memorable Order of 1642, and from that Time to the Restoration, this Plantation seems to have been distinguished from the rest, and the several Acts or Ordinances, which respected the other Plantations, were never enforced here, and, possibly, under Colour of the Exemption in 1642, it might not be intended they should be executed.

For 15 or 16 Years after the Restoration, there was no Officer of the Customs in the Colony, except the Governor annually elected by the People, and the Acts of Trade were but little regarded, nor did the Governor take the Oath required of Governors by the Act of the 12th of King Charles the Second, until the Time which I have mentioned. Upon the Revolution the Force of an Act of Parliament was evident in a Case of as great Importance as any which could happen to the Colony. King William and Queen Mary were proclaimed in the Colony, King and Queen of England, France and Ireland, *and the Dominions thereunto belonging*, in the Room of King James, and this not by Virtue of an Act of the Colony, for no such Act ever passed, but by Force of an Act of Parliament which altered the Succession to the Crown, and for which the People waited several Weeks with anxious Concern. By Force of another Act of Parliament, and that only, such Officers of the Colony as had taken the Oaths of Allegiance to King James deemed themselves at Liberty to take, and accordingly did take the

Oaths to King William and Queen Mary. And that I may mention other Acts of the like Nature together, it is by Force of an
Act of Parliament that the Illustrious House of Hanover succeeded to the Throne of Britain *and its Dominions*, and by
several other Acts, the Forms of the Oaths have from Time to
Time, been altered, and by a late Act that Form was established
which every one of us has complied with as the Charter in express Words requires and makes our Duty. Shall we now dispute whether Acts of Parliament have been submitted to when
we find them submitted to in Points which are of the very Essence of our Constitution? If you should disown that Authority
which has Power even to change the Succession to the Crown,
are you in no Danger of denying the Authority of our most
gracious Sovereign, which I am sure none of you can have in
your Thoughts?

I think I have before shewn you, Gentlemen, what must
have been the Sense of our Predecessors at the Time of the
first Charter, let us now, whilst we are upon the Acts and Doings of the Assembly, consider what it must have been at the
Time of the second Charter. Upon the first Advice of the Revolution in England, the Authority which assumed the Government instructed their Agents to petition *the Parliament* to
restore the first Charter, and a Bill for that Purpose passed the
House of Commons, but went no farther. Was not this owning
the Authority of Parliament? By an Act of Parliament, passed in
the first Year of King William and Queen Mary, a Form of
Oaths was established to be taken by those Princes and by all
succeeding Kings and Queens of England at their Coronation, the first of which is, that they will govern the People of
the Kingdom *and the Dominions thereunto belonging, according to the Statutes in Parliament agreed on, and the Laws and
Customs of the same.* When the Colony directed their Agents
to make their humble Application to King William to grant
the second Charter, they could have no other Pretence than as
they were Inhabitants of Part *of the Dominions of England*, and
they also knew the Oath the King had taken to govern them
according to the Statutes in Parliament; surely then, at the
Time of this Charter also, it was the Sense of our Predecessors,
as well as of the King and of the Nation that there was and
would remain a Supremacy in the Parliament. About the same

Time, they acknowledge, in an Address to the King, that they have no Power to make Laws *repugnant to the Laws of England*. And, immediately after the Assumption of the Powers of Government by Virtue of the new Charter, an Act passed to revive for a limitted Time all the Local Laws of the Colonies of Massachusetts-Bay and New-Plimouth, respectively, *not repugnant to the Laws of England*. And, at the same Session, an Act passed establishing Naval Officers in several Ports of the Province, for which this Reason is given, *that all undue Trading contrary to an Act of Parliament made in the 15th Year of King Charles the Second may be prevented in this their Majesty's Province*. The Act of this Province passed so long ago as the second Year of King George the first, for stating the Fees of the Custom-House Officers, must have relation to the Acts of Parliament by which they are constituted, and the Provision made in that Act of the Province for extending the Port of Boston to all the Roads as far as Cape-Cod, could be for no other Purpose than for the more effectual carrying the Acts of Trade into Execution. And, to come nearer to the present Time, when an Act of Parliament had passed in 1741, for putting an End to certain unwarrantable Schemes in this Province, did the Authority of Government, or those Persons more immediately affected by it, ever dispute the Validity of it? On the contrary, have not a Number of Acts been passed in the Province, that the Burdens to which such Persons were subjected might be equally apportioned, and have not all those Acts of the Province been very carefully framed to prevent their militating with the Act of Parliament? I will mention also an Act of Parliament made in the first Year of Queen Ann; altho' the Proceedings upon it more immediately respected the Council. By this Act no Office Civil or Military shall be void by the Death of the King, but shall continue six Months, unless suspended or made void by the next Successor. By Force of this Act, Governor Dudley continued in the Administration six Months from the Demise of Queen Ann, and immediately after, the Council assumed the Administration and continued it until a Proclamation arrived from King George, by Virtue of which Governor Dudley reassumed the Government. It would be tedious to enumerate the Addresses, Votes and Messages of both the Council and House of Representatives to the same

Purpose. I have said enough to shew that this Government has submitted to Parliament from a Conviction of it's constitutional Supremacy, and this not *from Inconsideration, nor meerly from Reluctance at the Idea of contending with the Parent State*.

If then I have made it appear, that both by the first and second Charters we hold our Lands and the Authority of Government not of the *King* but of the *Crown* of England, that being a Dominion of the Crown of England, we are consequently subject to the Supreme Authority of England, that this hath been the Sense of this Plantation, except in those few Years when the Principles of Anarchy which had prevailed in the Kingdom had not lost their Influence here; and if, upon a Review of your Principles, they shall appear to you to have been delusive and erroneous, as I think they must, or if you shall only be in Doubt of them, you certainly will not draw that Conclusion which otherwise you might do, and which I am glad you have hitherto avoided; especially when you consider the obvious and inevitable Distress and Misery of Independence upon our Mother Country, if such Independence could be allowed or maintained, and the Probability of much greater Distress, which we are not able to foresee.

You ask me if we have not Reason to fear we shall soon be reduced to a worse Situation than that of the Colonies of France, Spain or Holland. I may safely affirm that we have not; that we have no Reason to Fear any Evils from a Submission to the Authority of Parliament, equal to what we must feel from its Authority being disputed, from an uncertain Rule of Law and Government. For more than seventy Years together the Supremacy of Parliament was acknowledged without Complaints of Grievance. The Effect of every Measure cannot be foreseen by human Wisdom. What can be expected more from any Authority than when the Unfitness of a Measure is discovered, to make it void? When upon the united Representations and Complaints of the American Colonies any Acts have appeared to Parliament to be unsalutary, have there not been repeated Instances of the Repeal of such Acts? We cannot expect these Instances should be carried so far as to be equivalent to a Disavowal or Relinquishment of the Right itself. Why then shall we fear for ourselves and our Posterity, greater rigour of

Government for seventy Years to come than what we and our Predecessors have felt in the seventy Years past.

You must give me Leave, Gentlemen, in a few Words to vindicate myself from a Charge, in one Part of your Answer, of having, by my Speech, reduced you to the unhappy Alternative of appearing by your Silence to acquiesce in my Sentiments, or of freely discussing this Point of the Supremacy of Parliament. I saw, as I have before observed, the Capital Town of the Province, without being reduced to such an Alternative, voluntarily not only discussing but determining this Point, and inviting every other Town and District in the Province to do the like. I saw that many of the principal Towns had followed the Example, and that there was imminent Danger of a Compliance in most if not all the Rest, in Order to avoid being distinguished. Was not I reduced to the Alternative of rendering myself justly obnoxious to the Displeasure of my Sovereign by acquiescing in such Irregularities, or of calling upon you to join with me in suppressing them? Might I not rather have expected from you an Expression of your Concern that any Persons should project and prosecute a Plan of Measures which would lay me under a Necessity of bringing this Point before you? It was so far from being my Inclination, that nothing short of a Sense of Duty to the King, and the Obligations I am under to consult your true Interest could have compelled me to it.

Gentlemen of the Council, and
Gentlemen of the House of Representatives,

We all profess to be the loyal and dutiful Subjects of the King of Great-Britain. His Majesty considers the British Empire as one entire Dominion, subject to one Supreme Legislative Power, a due Submission to which is essential to the Maintenance of the Rights, Liberties and Privileges of the several Parts of this Dominion. We have abundant Evidence of his Majesty's tender and impartial Regard to the Rights of his Subjects; and I am authorized to say that "his Majesty will most graciously approve of every Constitutional Measure that may contribute to the Peace, the Happiness, and Prosperity of his Colony of Massachusetts-Bay, and which may have the

Effect to shew to the World that he has no Wish beyond that of reigning in the Hearts and Affections of his People."

To this Speech His Majesty's Council on the 25th of February *sent to his Excellency the following Answer, by* Harrison Gray, James Russell, James Pitts, Stephen Hall, *and* James Humphry, *Esq'rs*; viz.

May it please your Excellency,
As a small Part only of your Excellency's last Speech to both Houses is addressed to the Board, there are but a few Clauses on which we shall Remark.

With Regard to the Disorders that have arisen, your Excellency and the Board have assigned different Causes. The Cause you are pleased to assign, together with the Disorders themselves, we suppose to be Effects arising from the Stamp-Act, and certain other Acts of Parliament. If we were not mistaken in this, which you do not assert, it so far seems to invalidate what is said in your Speech on that Head.

We have taken Notice of this, only because it stands connected with another Matter, on which we would make a few further Observations. What we refer to is the general Nature of Supreme Authority. We have already offered Reasons, in which your Excellency seems to acquiesce, to shew that, though the Term *Supreme* sometimes carries with it the Idea of *unlimitted* Authority, it cannot, in that Sense, be applied to that which is human. What is usually denominated the Supreme Authority of a Nation must nevertheless be limitted in it's Acts to the Objects that are properly or constitutionally cognizable by it. To illustrate our Meaning, we beg Leave to quote a Passage from your Speech, at the Opening of this Session, where your Excellency says, "so much of the Spirit of Liberty breathes through all Parts of the English Constitution, that although from the Nature of Government there must be one Supreme Authority over the whole, yet this Constitution will admit of Subordinate Powers with Legislative and Executive Authority, greater or less, according to Local and other Circumstances."— This is very true, and implies, that the Legislative and Executive Authority granted to the Subordinate Powers should extend and operate as far as the Grant allows; and that, if it does not exceed the Limits prescribed to it, and no Forfeiture be incurred, the Supreme Power has no rightful Authority to take away or diminish it, or to substitute its own Acts in Cases wherein the Acts of the Subordinate Power can, according to its Constitution, operate. To suppose the contrary is to suppose, that it has no Property in the Privileges granted to it, for if it holds them at the Will of the Supreme Power, which it must do by the above Supposition, it can have no Property in them: upon which Principle, which involves the Contradiction, that what is granted is in Reality not granted, no Subordinate Power can exist. But as in Fact the two Powers are not incompatible, and do subsist together, each restraining its Acts to their Constitutional Objects, can we not from hence see how the Supreme Power may supervise, regulate, and make general Laws for the Kingdom, without interfering with the Privileges of the Subordinate Powers within it? And also see how it may extend its Care and Protection to its Colonies, without injuring their Constitutional Rights?—What has been here said concerning Supreme Authority has no Reference to the Manner in which it has been in Fact exercised, but is wholly confined to its general Nature; and if it conveys any just Idea of it, the Inferences that have been at any Time deduced from it, injurious to the Rights of the Colonists, are not well founded; and have probably arisen from a Misconception of the Nature of that Authority.

Your Excellency represents us as introducing a Number of Authorities merely to shew, that "all Taxes upon English Subjects must be levied by Virtue of the Act, not of the King alone, but in Conjunction with the Lords and Commons," and are pleased to add, that "you should very readily have allowed it; and you should as readily have allowed, that all other Acts of Legislation must be passed by the same joint Authority, and not by the King alone."—Your Excellency "would have saved us the Trouble of all those Authorities:" and on our Part we should have been as willing to have saved your Excellency the Trouble of dismembering our Argument, and from thence taking Occasion to represent it in a disadvantageous Light, or rather totally destroying it.

In Justice to ourselves it is necessary to Recapitulate that

Argument adduced to prove, that the Inhabitants of this Province are not constitutionally subject to Parliamentary Taxation. In order thereto we recurred to Magna Charta and other Authorities. And the Argument abridged stands thus—That from those Authorities it appears an Essential Part of the English Constitution, "that no Tallage, or Aid, or Tax, shall be laid or levied, without the Good-will and Assent of the Freemen of the Commonalty of the Realm." That from Common Law, and the Province Charter, the Inhabitants of this Province are clearly intitled to all the Rights of free and natural Subjects within the Realm: That among those Rights must be included the essential one just mentioned concerning Aids and Taxes; and therefore that no Aids or Taxes can be levied on us constitutionally without our own Consent signified by our Representatives. From whence the Conclusion is clear, that therefore the Inhabitants of this Province are not constitutionally subject to Parliamentary Taxation.

We did not bring those Authorities to shew that Tax Acts, or any other Acts of Parliament, in order to their Validity, must have the Concurrence of the King, Lords, and Commons; but to shew, that it has been, at least from the Time of Magna Charta, an essential Right of free Subjects within the Realm, to be free from all Taxes but such as were laid with their own Consent. And it was proper to shew this, as the Rights and Liberties, granted by the Province Charter, were to be equally extensive, to all Intents and Purposes, with those enjoyed by free and natural Subjects within the Realm. Therefore to shew our own Rights in Relation to Taxes, it was necessary to shew the Rights of Freemen within the Realm, in Relation to them: and for this Purpose those Authorities were brought, and not impertinently, as we humbly apprehend. Nor have we seen Reason to change our Sentiments with Respect to this Matter or any other contained in our Answer to your Excellency's Speech.

In the last Clause of your Speech, your Excellency informs the two Houses, "you are Authorized to say, that his Majesty will most graciously approve of every Constitutional Measure, that may contribute to the Peace, the Happiness and Prosperity of his Colony of Massachusetts-Bay."—We have the highest Sense of his Majesty's Goodness in his gracious Disposition to approve of such Measures, which, as it includes his Approbation of the Constitutional Rights of his Subjects of this Colony, manifests his Inclination to protect them in those Rights; and to remove the Incroachments that have been made upon them. Of this Act of Royal Goodness they are not wholly unworthy, as in Regard to Loyalty, Duty and Affection to his Majesty, they stand among the foremost of his faithful Subjects.

———————

And on Tuesday March 2*d, Mr.* Hancock, *Mr.* Gorham, *Major* Fuller, *Capt.* Greenleafe, *Capt.* Heath, *Mr.* Phillips, *Capt.* Nye, *Capt.* Brown *of* Watertown, *and Capt.* Gardner, *a Committee of the House of Representatives, waited on the Governor with their Answer as follows,* Viz.

May it please your Excellency,

IN your Speech at the Opening of the present Session, your Excellency express'd your Displeasure at some late Proceedings of the Town of Boston, and other principal Towns in the Province. And in another Speech to both Houses we have your repeated Exceptions at the same Proceedings as being "unwarrantable," and of a dangerous Nature and Tendency; "against which you thought yourself bound to call upon us to join with you in bearing a proper Testimony." This House have not discovered any Principles advanced by the Town of Boston, that are unwarrantable by the Constitution; nor does it appear to us that they have "invited every other Town and District in the Province to adopt their Principles." We are fully convinced that it is our Duty to bear our Testimony against "Innovations of a dangerous Nature and Tendency:" But is clearly our Opinion, that it is the indisputable Right of all or any of his Majesty's Subjects in this Province, regularly and orderly to meet together to state the Grievances they labor under; and to propose and unite in such constitutional Measures as they shall judge necessary or proper to obtain Redress. This Right has been frequently exercised by his Majesty's Subjects within the Realm; and we do not recollect an Instance, since the happy Revolution, when the two Houses of Parliament have been called upon to discountenance or bear their Testimony against it, in a Speech from the Throne.

Your Excellency is pleased to take Notice of some things which we "alledge" in our Answer to your first Speech; and the Observation you make, we must confess, is as natural and as undeniably true, as any one that could have been made, that "if our Foundation shall fail us *in every Part of it*, the Fabrick we have rais'd upon it, must certainly fall." You think, this Foundation will fail us; but we wish your Excellency had condesended to a Consideration of what we have "adduced in Support of our Principles." We might then perhaps have had some things offered for our Conviction, more than bare Affirmations; which, we must beg to be excused if we say, are far from being sufficient, though they came with your Excellency's Authority, for which however we have a due Regard.

Your Excellency says that "as English Subjects and agreeable to the Doctrine of the Feudal Tenure all our Lands are held mediately or immediately of the Crown." We trust your Excellency does not mean to introduce the Feudal System in it's Perfection; which to use the Words of one of our greatest Historians, was "a State of perpetual War, Anarchy and Confusion; calculated solely for Defence against the Assaults of any foreign Power, but in it's Provision for the interior Order and Tranquility of Society extremely defective." "A Constitution so contradictory to all the Principles that govern Mankind, could never be brought about but by foreign Conquest or native Usurpation:" And a very celebrated Writer calls it "that most iniquitous and absurd Form of Government by which human Nature was so shamefully degraded." This System of Iniquity by a strange Kind of Fatality, "though originally form'd for an Encampment and for Military Purposes only, spread over a great Part of Europe:" and to serve the Purposes of Oppression and Tyranny "was adopted by Princes and wrought into their Civil Constitutions;" and aided by the Canon Law, calculated by the Roman Pontiff, to exalt himself above all that is called God, it prevailed to the almost utter Extinction of Knowledge, Virtue, Religion and Liberty from that Part of the Earth. But from the Time of the Reformation, in Proportion as Knowledge, which then darted its Rays upon the benighted World, increas'd and spread among the People, they grew impatient under this heavy Yoke: And the most virtuous and sensible among them, to whose Stedfastness we in this distant Age and Climate are greatly indebted, were determined to get rid of it: And tho' they have in a great Measure subdued it's Power and Influence in England, they have never yet totally eradicated its Principles.

Upon these Principles the King claimed an absolute Right to and a perfect Estate in all the Lands within his Dominions; but how he came by this absolute Right and perfect Estate is a Mystery which we have never seen unravelled, nor is it our Business or Design at present to enquire. He granted Parts or Parcels of it to his Friends the Great Men, and they granted lesser Parcels to their Tenants: All therefore derived their Right and held their Lands, upon these Principles, mediately or immediately, of the King; which Mr. *Blackstone* however calls "in Reality a meer Fiction of our English Tenures."

By what Right in Nature and Reason the Christian Princes in Europe claimed the Lands of Heathen People, upon a Discovery made by any of their Subjects, is equally mysterious: Such however was the Doctrine universally prevailing when the Lands in America were discovered; but as the People of England upon those Principles held all the Lands they possessed by Grants from the King, and the King had never granted the Lands in America *to them*, it is certain they could have no Sort of Claim to them: Upon the Principles advanced, the Lordship and Dominion like that of the Lands in England, was in the King solely: and a Right from thence accrued to him of disposing such Territories under such Tenure and for such Services to be performed, as the King or Lord thought proper. But how the Grantees *became* Subjects of England, that is the Supreme Authority of the Parliament, your Excellency has not explained to us. We conceive that upon the Feudal Principles all Power is in the King; they afford us no Idea *of Parliament*. "The Lord was in early Times the Legislator and Judge over all his Feudatories," says Judge Blackstone. By the Struggles for Liberty in England from the Days of King John to the last happy Revolution, the Constitution has been gradually changing for the better; and upon the more rational Principles that all Men by Nature are in a State of Equality in Respect of Jurisdiction and Dominion, Power in England has been more equally divided. And thus also in America, though we hold our Lands agreeably to the Feudal Principles of the King; yet our Predecessors wisely took care to enter into Compact with the King that Power here should also be equally divided agreeable to the original fundamental Principles of the English Constitution, declared in Magna Charter, and other Laws and Statutes of England, made to confirm them.

Your Excellency says, "you can by no Means concede to us that it is now or was when the Plantations were first granted the Prerogative of the Kings of England to constitute a Number of new Governments altogether independent of the Sovereign Authority of the English Empire." By the Feudal Principles upon which you say "all the Grants which have been made of America are founded" "the Constitutions of the Emperor have the Force of Law." If our Government be considered as merely Feudatory, we are subject to the King's absolute Will, and there is no Room for the Authority of Parliament, as the Sovereign Authority of the British Empire. Upon these Principles, what could hinder the King's constituting a Number of independent Governments in America? That King Charles the First did actually set up a Government in this Colony, conceding to it Powers of making and executing Laws, without any Reservation to the English Parliament, of Authority to make future Laws binding therein, is a Fact which your Excellency has not disproved if you have denied it. Nor have you shewn that the Parliament or Nation objected to it, from whence we have inferred that it was an acknowledged Right. And we cannot conceive, why the King has not the same Right to alienate and dispose of Countries acquired by the Discovery of his Subjects, as he has to "restore upon a Treaty of Peace Countries which have been acquired in War," carried on at the Charge of the Nation; or to "sell and deliver up any Part of his Dominions to a foreign Prince or State, against the General Sense of the Nation" which is "an Act of Power" or Prerogative which your Excellency allows. You tell us that "when any New Countries are discovered by English Subjects, according to the general Law and Usage of Nations, *they become Part of the State*." The Law of Nations is or ought to be founded on the Law of Reason. It was the Saying of Sir Edwin Sandis, in the great Case of the Union of the Realm of Scotland with England, which is applicable to our present Purpose, that "there being no Precedent for this Case in the Law, the Law is deficient; and the Law being deficient, Recourse is to be had to Custom; and Custom being insufficient, we must recur to natural Reason," the greatest of all Authorities, which he adds "is the Law of Nations." The Opinions therefore, and Determinations of the greatest Sages and Judges of the Law in the Exchequer Chamber ought not to be considered as decisive or binding in our present Controversy with your Excellency, any further than they are consonant to *natural Reason.* If however we were to recur to such Opinions and Determinations we should find very great Authorities in our Favour, to show that the Statutes of England are not binding on those who are not represented in Parliament there. The Opinion of Lord Coke that Ireland was bound by Statutes of England wherein they *were named*, if compared with his other Writings, appears manifestly to be grounded upon a Supposition, that Ireland had by an Act of their own, in the Reign of King John, consented to be thus bound, and upon any other Supposition this Opinion would be against *Reason*; for *Consent only* gives human Laws their Force. We beg Leave, upon what your Excellency has observed of the Colony becoming a Part of the State, to subjoin the Opinions of several learned Civilians, as quoted by a very able Lawyer in this Country; "Colonies, says Puffendorf, are settled in different Methods. For either the Colony *continues a Part* of the Common Wealth it was set out from; or else is obliged to pay a dutiful Regard to the Mother Common Wealth, and to be in Readiness to defend and vindicate its Honor, and so is united by a Sort of unequal Confederacy; or lastly, is *erected into a separate Common Wealth* and *assumes the same Rights*, with the State it descended from." And King Tullius, as quoted by the same learned Author from Grotius, says "We look upon it to be neither Truth nor Justice that Mother Cities ought of Necessity and *by the Law of Nature* to *rule over the Colonies.*"

Your Excellency has misinterpreted what we have said, "that no Country by the Common Law, was subject to the Laws or the Parliament but the Realm of England," and are pleased to tell us that we have expressed ourselves "*Incautiously.*" We beg Leave to recite the Words of the Judges of England in the beforementioned Case to our Purpose. "If a King go out of

England with a Company of his Servants, Allegiance remaineth among his Subjects and Servants, altho' he be out of his Realm *whereto his Laws are confined.*" We did not mean to say, as your Excellency would suppose, that "the Common Law prescribes Limits to the Extent of the Legislative Power," though we shall always affirm it to be true of the Law of Reason and natural Equity. Your Excellency thinks you have made it appear, that the Colony of Massachusetts-Bay is "holden as feudatory of the Imperial Crown of England;" and therefore you say, "to use the Words of a very great Authority in a Case in *some Respects* analogous to it," being feudatory it necessarily follows, "that it is under the Government of the King's Laws." Your Excellency has not named this Authority; but we conceive his Meaning must be, that being Feudatory, it is under the Government of the King's Law, *absolutely*; for as we have before said the Feudal System admits of no Idea of the Authority of Parliament, and this would have been the Case of the Colony but for the Compact with the King in the Charter.

Your Excellency says, that "Persons thus holding *under the Crown* of England remain or *become* Subjects of England;" by which we suppose your Excellency to mean, subject to the Supreme Authority of Parliament "to all Intents and Purposes as fully as if any of the Royal Manors, &c. within the Realm had been Granted to them upon the like Tenure." We apprehend with Submission, your Excellency is Mistaken in supposing that our Allegiance is due to the Crown of England. Every Man swears Allegiance for himself to his own King in his Natural Person. "Every Subject is presumed by Law to be Sworn to the King, which is to his Natural Person," says Lord Coke. *Rep. on Calvins Case.* "The Allegiance is due to his Natural Body." And he says "in the Reign of Edward II. the Spencers, the Father and the Son, to cover the Treason hatched in their Hearts, invented this damnable and damned Opinion, that *Homage* and Oath of Allegiance was more by Reason of the King's Crown, that is of his politick Capacity, than by Reason of the Person of the King; upon which Opinion they infer'd execrable and detestable Consequents." The Judges of England, all but one, in the Case of the Union between Scotland and England, declared that "Allegiance followeth the natural Person not the politick;" and "to prove the Allegiance to be tied to the Body natural of the King, and not to the Body politick, the Lord Coke cited the Phrases of diverse Statutes, mentioning our *natural* liege Sovereign."—If then the Homage and Allegiance is not to the Body politick of the King, then it is not to him as the Head or any Part of that Legislative Authority, which your Excellency says "is equally extensive with the Authority of the Crown throughout every Part of the Dominion;" and your Excellency's Observations thereupon must fail. The same Judges mention the Allegiance of a Subject to the Kings of England who is out of the Reach and Extent of the Laws of England; which is perfectly reconcileable with the Principles of our Ancestors quoted before from your Excellency's History, but upon your Excellency's Principles appears to us to be an Absurdity. The Judges, speaking of a Subject, say, "although his Birth was out of the Bounds of the Kingdom of England, and *out of the Reach and Extent of the Laws of England*, yet if it were *within the Allegiance of the King of England*, &c. Normandy, Acquitain, Gascoign, and other Places within the Limits of France, and consequently out of the Realm or Bounds of the Kingdom of England, were in Subjection to the Kings of England. And the Judges say, "*Rex et Regnum* be not so Relatives, as a King can be King but of one Kingdom, which clearly holdeth not but that his Kingly Power extending to divers Nations and Kingdoms, all owe him equal Subjection and are equally born to the Benefit of his Protection, and altho' he is to govern them *by their distinct Laws*, yet any one of the People coming into the other is to have the Benefit of the Laws wheresoever he cometh." So they are not to be deemed Aliens, as your Excellency in your Speech supposes in any of the Dominions; all which accords with the Principles our Ancestors held. "And he is to bear the Burden of Taxes of the *Place where he cometh*, but living in one or for his Livelihood in one, *he is not to be taxed in the other*, because Laws ordain Taxes, Impositions and Charges as a Discipline of Subjection particularized to every particular Nation:" Nothing we think can be more clear to our Purpose than this Decision, of Judges, perhaps as learned as ever adorned the English Nation; or in Favor of America in her present Controversy with the Mother State.

Your Excellency says, that by our not distinguishing between the Crown of England and the Kings and Queens of England in their personal or natural Capacities, we have been led into a fundamental Error." Upon this very Distinction we have availed ourselves. We have said that our Ancestors considered the Land which they took Possession of in America as out of the Bounds of the Kingdom of England, and out of the Reach and Extent of the Laws of England; and that the King also even in the Act of granting the Charter, considered the Territory as *not within* the Realm; that the King had an absolute Right in himself to dispose of the Lands, and that this was not disputed by the Nation; nor could the Lands on any solid Grounds be claimed by the Nation, and therefore our Ancestors received the Lands by Grant from the King, and at the same Time compacted with him and promised him Homage and Allegiance, not in his publick or politick but natural Capacity only.—If it be difficult for us to show how the King acquired a Title to this Country in his natural Capacity, or separate from his Relation to his Subjects, which we confess, yet we conceive it will be equally difficult for your Excellency to show how the Body Politick and Nation of England acquired it. Our Ancestors supposed it was acquired by neither; and therefore they declared, as we have before quoted from your History, that saving their actual Purchase from the Natives, of the Soil, the Dominion, the Lordship, and Sovereignty, they had in the Sight of God and Man, no Right and Title to what they possessed. How much clearer then in natural Reason and Equity must our Title be, who hold Estates dearly purchased at the Expence of our own as well as our Ancestors Labour, and defended by them with Treasure and Blood.

Your Excellency has been pleased to confirm, rather than deny or confute a Piece of History which you say we took from an anonimous Pamphlet, and by which you "fear we have been too easily misled." It may be gathered from your own Declaration and other Authorities besides the anonimous Pamphlet, that the House of Commons took Exception, not at the King's having made an absolute Grant of the Territory, but at the Claim of an exclusive Right to the Fishery on the Banks and Sea Coast, by Virtue of the Patent. At this you say "the House of Commons was alarmed, and a Bill was brought in for allowing a free Fishery." And upon this Occasion your

Excellency allows, that "one of the Secretaries of State declared that the Plantations were not annexed to the Crown, and so were not within the Jurisdiction of Parliament." If we should concede to what your Excellency supposes might possibly or "perhaps" be the Case, that the Secretary made this Declaration "as his own Opinion," the Event showed that it was the Opinion of the King too; for it is not to be accounted for upon any other Principle, that he would have denied his Royal Assent to a Bill formed for no other Purpose, but to grant his Subjects in England the Privilege of Fishing on the Sea Coasts in America. The Account published by Sir Ferdinando Gorges himself, of the Proceedings of Parliament *on this Occasion*, your Excellency thinks will remove all Doubt of the Sense of the Nation and of the Patentees of this Patent or Charter in 1620. "This Narrative, you say, has all the Appearance of Truth and Sincerity," which we do not deny: And to us it carries this Conviction with it, that "what was objected" in Parliament was, the exclusive Claim of Fishing only. His imagining that he had satisfied the House after divers Attendances, that the Planting a Colony was of much more Consequence than a *simple disorderly Course of Fishing*, is sufficient for our Conviction. We know that the Nation was at that Time alarmed with Apprehensions of Monopolies; and if the Patent of New-England was presented by the two Houses as a Grievance, it did not show, as your Excellency supposes, "the Sense they then had of their Authority over this new-acquired Territory," but only their Sense of the Grievance of a Monopoly of the Sea.

We are happy to hear your Excellency say, that "our Remarks upon and Construction of the Words *not repugnant to the Laws of England*, are much the same with those of the Council." It serves to confirm us in our Opinion, in what we take to be the most important Matter of Difference between your Excellency and the two Houses. After saying, that the Statute of 7th and 8th of William and Mary favors the Construction of the Words as intending such Laws of England as are made more immediately to respect us, you tell us, that "the Province Agent Mr. Dummer in his much applauded Defence, says that *then* a Law of the Plantations may be said to be repugnant to a Law made in Great-Britain, when it flatly contradicts it so far as

the Law made there mentions and relates to the Plantations."
This is plain and obvious to common Sense, and therefore
cannot be denied. But if your Excellency will read a Page or
two further in that excellent Defence, you will see that he
mentions this as the Sense of the Phrase, as taken from an Act
of Parliament, rather than as the Sense he would chuse himself
to put upon it; and he expresly designs to shew, in Vindication
of the Charter, that in that Sense of the Words, there never was
a Law made in the Plantations repugnant to the Laws of Great-
Britain. He gives another Construction much more likely to
be the true Intent of the Words; namely, "that the Patentees
shall not presume under Colour of their particular Charters to
make any Laws *inconsistent with the Great Charter and other
Laws of England, by which the Lives, Liberties, and Properties of
Englishmen are secured.*" This is the Sense in which our Ancestors understood the Words; and therefore they were unwilling
to conform to the Acts of Trade, and disregarded them till
they made Provision to give them Force in the Colony by a
Law of their own; saying, that "the Laws of England did not
reach America: And those Acts were an Invasion of their
Rights, Liberties and Properties," because they were not "represented in Parliament." The Right of being governed only by
Laws which were made by Persons in whose Election they had
a Voice, they looked upon as the Foundation of English Liberties. By the Compact with the King in the Charter, they were
to be as free in America, as they would have been if they had
remained within the Realm; and therefore they freely asserted
that they "were to be governed by Laws made by themselves
and by Officers chosen by themselves." Mr. Dummer says, "It
seems reasonable enough to think that the Crown," and he
might have added our Ancestors, "intended by this Injunction
to provide for all its Subjects, that they might not be oppressed
by Arbitrary Power—but—being still Subjects, they should be
protected by the same mild Laws and enjoy the same happy
Government as if they continued within the Realm." And
considering the Words of the Charter in this Light, he looks
upon them as designed to be a Fence against Oppression and
despotic Power. But the Construction which your Excellency
puts upon the Words, reduces us to a State of Vassallage, and
exposes us to Oppression and despotic Power, whenever a

Parliament shall see fit to make Laws for that Purpose and put them in Execution.

We flatter ourselves that from the large Extracts we have made from your Excellency's History of the Colony, it appears evidently, that under both Charters it hath been the Sense of the People and of the Government that they were not under the Jurisdiction of Parliament. We pray you again to recur to those Quotations and our Observations upon them: And we wish to have your Excellency's judicious Remarks. When we adduced that History to prove that the Sentiments of *private* Persons of Influence, four or five Years after the Restoration, were very different from what your Excellency apprehended them to be when you delivered your Speech, you seem to concede to it by telling us "it was, as you take it, from the *Principles imbibed* in those Times of Anarchy (preceeding the Restoration) that they disputed the Authority of Parliament;" but you add, "the Government would not venture to dispute it." We find in the same History a Quotation from a Letter of Mr. *Stoughton*, dated 17 Years after the Restoration, mentioning "the Country's not taking Notice of the Acts of Navigation *to observe them.*" And it was, as we take it, after that Time, that the Government declared in a Letter to their Agents, that they had not submitted to them; and they ventured to "dispute" the Jurisdiction, asserting that they apprehended the Acts to be an Invasion of the Rights, Liberties and Properties of the Subjects of his Majesty in the Colony, *they not being represented in Parliament;* and that "the Laws of England *did not reach America.*" It very little avails in Proof that they conceded to the Supreme Authority of Parliament, their telling the Commissioners "that the Act of Navigation had for some Years before been observed here, that they knew not of its being greatly violated, and that such Laws as appeared to be against it were repealed." It may as truly be said now, that the Revenue Acts are observed by some of the People of this Province; but it cannot be said that the Government and People of this Province have conceded that the Parliament had Authority to make such Acts to be observed here. Neither does their Declaration to the Commissioners that such Laws as appeared to be against the Act of Navigation were repealed, prove their Concession of the Authority of Parliament, by any means so much as their making Provision for giving Force to an Act of Parliament within this Province, by a deliberate and solemn Act or Law of their own, proves the contrary.

You tell us, that "the Government four or five Years before the Charter was vacated more explicitly," that is than by a Conversation with the Commissioners, "acknowledged the Authority of Parliament, and voted that their Governor should take the Oath required of him faithfully to do and perform all Matters and Things enjoined him by the Acts of Trade." But does this, may it please your Excellency, show their explicit Acknowledgment of the Authority of Parliament? Does it not rather show directly the contrary: For, what need could there be for their Vote or Authority to require him to take the Oath already required of him by the Act of Parliament, unless both he and they judged that an Act of Parliament was not of Force sufficient to bind him to take such Oath? We do not deny, but on the contrary are fully persuaded that your Excellency's Principles in Government are still of the same with what they appear to be in the History; for you there say, that "the passing this Law plainly shows the wrong Sense they had of the Relation they stood in to England." But we are from hence convinced that your Excellency when you wrote the History was of our Mind in this Respect, that our Ancestors in passing the Law discovered their Opinion that they were without the Jurisdiction of Parliament: For it was upon this Principle alone that they shewed the wrong Sense they had in your Excellency's Opinion, of the Relation they stood in to England.

Your Excellency in your second Speech condescends to point out to us the Acts and Doings of the General Assembly which relates to Acts of Parliament, which you think "demonstrates that they have been acknowledged by the Assembly or submitted to by the People:" Neither of which in our Opinion shows that it was the Sense of the Nation, and our Predecessors when they first took Possession of this Plantation or Colony by a Grant and Charter from the Crown, that they were to remain subject to the supreme Authority of the English Parliament.

Your Excellency seems chiefly to rely upon our Ancestors, after the Revolution "proclaiming King William and Queen Mary in the Room of King James," and taking the Oaths to them, "the Alteration of the Form of Oaths from Time to Time," and finally "the Establishment of the Form which every one of us has complied with, as the Charter in express Terms requires and makes our Duty." We do not know that it has ever been a Point in Dispute whether the Kings of England were ipso facto Kings in and over this Colony or Province. The Compact was made between King Charles the First, his Heirs and Successors, and the Governor and Company, their Heirs and Successors. It is easy upon this Principle to account for the Acknowledgment of and Submission to King William and Queen Mary as Successors of Charles the First, in the Room of King James: Besides it is to be considered, that the People in the Colony as well as in England had suffered under the TYRANT James, by which he had alike forfeited his Right to reign over both. There had been a Revolution here as well as in England. The Eyes of the People here were upon William and Mary, and the News of their being proclaimed in England was as your Excellency's History tells us, "the most joyful News ever received in New-England." And if they were not proclaimed here "by virtue of an Act of the Colony," it was, as we think may be concluded from the Tenor of your History; with the general or universal Consent of the People as apparently as if "such Act had passed." It is *Consent alone*, that makes any human Laws binding; and as a learned Author observes, a purely *voluntary* Submission to an Act, because it is highly in our Favor and for our Benefit, is in all Equity and Justice to be deemed as not at all proceeding from the *Right* we include in the Legislators, that they thereby obtain an *Authority* over us, and that ever hereafter we must obey them of *Duty*. We would observe that one of the first Acts of the General Assembly of this Province since the present Charter, was an Act requiring the taking the Oaths mentioned in an Act of Parliament, to which you refer us: For what Purpose was this Act of the Assembly passed, if it was the Sense of the Legislators that the Act of Parliament was in Force in the Province. And at the same Time another Act was made for the Establishment of other Oaths necessary to be taken; both which Acts have the Royal Sanction, and are now in Force. Your Excellency says, that when the Colony applied to King William for a second Charter, they knew the Oath the King had taken, which was to govern them according to the Statutes in Parliament, and (which your Excellency here omits) *the Laws and Customs of the same.* By the Laws and Customs of Parliament, the People of England freely debate and consent to such Statutes as are made by themselves or their chosen Representatives. This is a Law or Custom which all Mankind may justly challenge as their *inherent* Right. According to this Law the King has an undoubted Right to govern us. Your Excellency upon Recollection surely will not infer from hence, that it was the Sense of our Predecessors that there was to remain a Supremacy in the English Parliament, or a full Power and Authority to make Laws binding upon us in all Cases whatever, in that Parliament where we cannot *debate* and *deliberate* upon the Necessity or Expediency of any Law, and consequently without our Consent, and as it may probably happen destructive of the first Law of Society, the Good of the Whole. You tell us that "after the Assumption of all the Powers of Government, by Virtue of the new Charter, an Act passed for the reviving for a limited Time all the local Laws of the Massachusetts-Bay and New-Plymouth respectively, not repugnant to the Laws of England. And at the same Session an Act passed establishing Naval Officers, that all undue Trading contrary to an Act of Parliament—may be prevented." Among the Acts that were then revived we may reasonably suppose was that whereby Provision was made to give Force to this Act of Parliament in the Province. The Establishment therefore of the Naval Officers was to aid the Execution of an Act of Parliament for the Observance of which within the Colony the Assembly had before made Provision after free Debates with their own Consent and by their own Act.

The Act of Parliament passed in 1741, for putting an End to several unwarrantable Schemes, mentioned by your Excellency, was designed for the general Good, and if the Validity of it was not disputed, it cannot be urged as a Concession of the supreme Authority, to make Laws binding on us *in all Cases whatever:* But if the Design of it was for the general Benefit of the Province, it was in one Respect at least greatly complained of by the Persons more immediately affected by it; and to remedy the Inconvenience, the Legislative of this Province pass'd an Act, directly militating with it. Which is the strongest evidence, that altho' they may have submitted *sub silentio* to some Acts of Parliament that they conceived might operate for their Benefit, they did not conceive themselves bound by any of its Acts which they judged would operate to the Injury even of Individuals.

Your Excellency has not thought proper to attempt to confute the Reasoning of a learned Writer on the Laws of Nature and Nations, quoted by us on this Occasion, to shew that the Authority of the Legislature does not extend so far as the Fundamentals of the Constitution. We are unhappy in not having your Remarks upon the Reasoning of that great Man; and until it is confuted, we shall remain of the Opinion, that the Fundamentals of the Constitution being excepted from the Commission of the Legislators, none of the Acts or Doings of the General Assembly, however deliberate and solemn, could avail to change them, if the People have not in very express Terms given them the Power to do it; and that much less ought their Acts and Doings however numerous, which barely refer to Acts of Parliament made expresly to relate to us, to be taken as an Acknowledgment that we are subject to the Supreme Authority of Parliament.

We shall sum up our own sentiments in the Words of that learned Writer Mr. Hooker, in his Ecclesiastical Policy, as quoted by Mr. Locke, "The lawful Power of making Laws to command whole political Societies of Men, belonging so properly to the same intire Societies, that for any Prince or Potentate of what Kind soever, to exercise the same of himself, and not from express Commission immediately and personally received from God, is no better *than mere Tyranny*. Laws therefore they are not which *publick Approbation* hath not made so," for "Laws human of what Kind soever are available by Consent." "Since Men naturally have no full and perfect Power to command whole politick Multitudes of Men, therefore, utterly without our Consent we could in such Sort be at no Man's Commandment living. And to be commanded we do not consent, when that Society whereof we be a Part, hath at any Time before consented." We think your Excellency has not proved, either that the Colony is a Part of the politick Society of England, or that it has ever consented that the Parliament of England or Great Britain should make Laws binding upon us in all Cases whatever, whether made expresly to refer to us or not.

We cannot help before we conclude, expressing our great Concern, that your Excellency has thus repeatedly, in a Manner insisted upon our free Sentiments on Matters of so delicate a Nature, and weighty Importance. The Question appears to us to be no other, than Whether we are the Subjects of absolute unlimitted Power, or of a free Government formed on the Principles of the English Constitution. If your Excellency's Doctrine be true the People of this Province hold their Lands of the Crown and People of England, and their Lives, Liberties and Properties are at their Disposal; and that even by Compact and their own Consent. They are subject to the King as the Head *alterius Populi* of another People, in whose Legislative they have no Voice or Interest. They are indeed said to have a Constitution and a Legislative of their own, but your Excellency has explained it into a mere Phantom; limitted, controuled, superceded and nullified at the Will of another. Is this the Constitution which so charmed our Ancestors, that as your Excellency has informed us, they kept a Day of solemn Thanksgiving to Almighty God when they received it? And were they Men of so little Discernment, such Children in Understanding, as to please themselves with the Imagination that they were blessed with the same Rights and Liberties which natural born Subjects in England enjoyed, when at the same Time they had fully consented to be ruled and ordered by a Legislative a Thousand Leagues distant from them, which cannot be supposed to be sufficiently acquainted with their Circumstances, if concerned for their Interest, and in which they cannot be in any Sense represented.

On Saturday the 6th *of* March, *his Excellency was pleas'd to put an End to the Session, after delivering the following* SPEECH *to both Houses,* viz.

Gentlemen of the Council, and
Gentlemen of the House of Representatives,
I THINK it incumbent on me to make some Observations, before I put an End to the Session, upon your last Messages to

me on the Subject of your Constitutional Dependance upon the Supreme Authority of the British Dominions. As the Council admit a partial Dependence, and suppose it to be consistent with the Principles and Nature of Government, I shall only endeavour very briefly to shew the contrary.

In your first Message, Gentlemen of the Council, you made some Strictures upon the Nature of the Supreme Authority in Government, both divine and human, the latter of which you determined could not be absolute and unlimitted. I thought the Distinction between divine and human Power not pertinent, and in Answer to you, I only remarked, that I had given you no Reason to suppose I intended a more absolute Power in Parliament than what is founded in the Nature of Government, and this, in your second Message, you construe an Acquiescence in your Reasons, which it certainly was not. You go on however to explain your Meaning by asserting, that "what is usually denominated the Supreme Authority of a Nation must be limited in its Acts to the Objects that are properly or constitutionally Cognizable by it."

Before you thus defined the Nature of Supreme Authority, I wish you had considered more fully what Objects there can be in a Government which are not cognizable by such Authority. You instance in a *subordinate* Power in Government which, whilst it keeps within its Limits, is not subject to the Controul of the *supreme* Power. Is there no Inconsistency in supposing a *subordinate* Power without a Power *superior* to it? Must it not so far as it is without Controul be, itself, Supreme?

It is essential to the Being of Government that a Power should always exist which no other Power within such Government can have Right to withstand or controul: Therefore, when the word *Power* relates to the Supreme Authority of Government it must be understood *absolute* and *unlimited*.

If we cannot agree in these Principles which no sensible Writer upon Government has before denied, and if you are still of Opinion that two Jurisdictions, each of them having a Share in the Supreme Power, are compatible in the same State, it can be to no Purpose to Reason or Argue upon the other Parts of your Message. Its enough to observe that this Disagreement in our Principles will have its Influence upon all the Deductions which are made from them.

I will also consider the last Message from you, Gentlemen of the House of Representatives, upon the same Subject, in as few words as the Importance of it will admit.

You say you have not discovered that the Principles advanced by the Town of Boston are unwarrantable by the Constitution. Whether they are or are not, will depend upon the Determination of the Point which you are now controverting. Your not having discover'd that the other Towns and Districts in the Province, were invited by the Town of Boston to adopt their Principles, must proceed from Inattention. Have not the Doings of that Town been sent through the Province, accompanied with a circular Letter, "desiring a free Communication of Sentiments," and, among other Expressions of the like Tendency, lamenting the Extinction of Ardor for civil and religious Liberty if it should be the general Voice of the Province, that the Rights as stated do not belong to them, and trusting that this cannot be the Case. If this is not inviting to adopt their Principles, I have mistaken their Sense and Meaning. The consequent Doings of so many other Towns shew that they understood them as I have done. I am sure I have no Disposition to represent unfavourably the Doings of any Town in the Province.

You assert "that it is the indisputable Right of all or any of His Majesty's Subjects in this Province *regularly and orderly* to meet together to state the Grievances they labour under," &c. I never denied it. Does it follow that it is *regular* and *orderly* for the Inhabitants of Towns, in their Corporate Capacity, to meet and determine upon Points which the Law gives them no Power to act upon? You have not asserted that it is, but you have not declared that it is not, as I thought a Regard to the Peace and Order of the Province made our Duty.

If the Fundamentals of our Government were not disputed, these Irregularities would appear to you in a very strong Light and you would join in discountenancing them.

To support your Principle that you hold your Lands and derive your Authority of Government from the *Kings* of England and not from the *Crown* of England you have very largely handled the Doctrine of Feudal Tenures. I observed to you in my last Speech that you had been misled by the Authority of an anonimous Pamphlet. I am now obliged to observe that you are again misled by having a general View of this

Doctrine brought before you, as it respects States or Governments under absolute Monarchs, and not as it is connected with or grafted upon the English Constitution. I shall not therefore spend Time in examining the Principles of your System, it being immaterial to the Point between us whether they are just or not. Instead thereof I will, in as brief and clear Terms as I can, lay this Doctrine before you as it relates to the Government of England.

Let me then observe to you, that from the Nature of Government a Supreme Legislative Power must always exist over all the Parts and all the Affairs of every Dominion—that in absolute Monarchies the Legislative and executive Powers are united in the Prince or Monarch—that in the English Constitution there is, and always has been, a Legislative Power distinct from the regal or executive Power—that the Feudal System, in your View of it and without correcting, could not be introduced into the English Government without changing the Constitution from a mixed to an absolute monarchical Government—that this System nevertheless has been introduced, the Constitution of a mixed Government still remaining, and consequently the System has been corrected or altered. What this Alteration has been will appear from Historical Facts. Before the Reign of William the First the Traces of Feudal Tenure are faint, the Evidence of a Legislative Power, an Assembly or Council of Wise Men, distinct from the Regal Power is strong and sufficient. After William had obtained the Crown, the other Nations of Europe being under this System, & particularly his Dominions in Normandy, and Wars being more frequent & Commerce small, and the Means of furnishing Money, the Sinews of War, difficult if not impracticable, meerly for the Defence of the Kingdom this Polity was so far established as that all the Landholders were made to contribute, by Military or other Services, to the Defence of the State, and for this Purpose, and by a Fiction only, the Lands were in Form acknowledged to have been originally in the King and held of him by his Subjects, and by this Form subjected to a supposed just Proportion of the Defence and Support of the Kingdom. This Establishment appears to have been made, not by an Act of Regal Power alone but by the Authority of the great Council of the Nation or Assembly of the Realm, and the Legislative

Authority still remained, according to its Nature, paramount and above all other Powers in the Dominion, and accordingly from Time to Time the Abuses of the Feudal Power either in the Sovereign or in such as held under him were corrected by the Supreme Legislative, and Magna Charta itself was framed and agreed upon, principally if not altogether for this Purpose. In succeeding Ages, as Commerce and Money increased and the Means of supporting War became more easy, these Military Services were gradually taken away, either, by Purchase or commuting for other Services or certain Rents, so that at the Period when America was first granted, the Remains were inconsiderable and the Lands of the Kingdom were held, generally, by what is called Socage Tenure or, in other Words, an Acknowledgment of Fidelity to the Sovereign, and a certain Rent which was in Name only, or of Value so inconsiderable as not to be demanded. The original Claim in the Sovereign, whether at first a Fiction or not, so far remained as that all Forfeitures, all Escheats, all new discovered Lands accrued to him, unless the Supreme Legislative should limit the Right to them, or otherwise dispose of them. This was the State of Feudal Tenure in England at the Time when the first Charter was granted, and the Difference between your System and mine will appear by this familiar Instance: Louis the 13. of France, I think the same Year the Massachusetts Patentees obtained the Grant of that Colony, by a Royal Edict granted to one Hundred Associates the Country of Canada, with Powers of Government and all the Privileges of natural born Subjects of France to all who should go and Inhabit or be Born there, with other very great Powers and Privileges. This, then, appears to be the different State of the People of the two Colonies. Louis, being an absolute Monarch, the Regal and Legislative Power were united in him. The Inhabitants of Canada therefore were subject to him and to every succeeding King of France as their Supreme Lord who, by Virtue of his uncontroulable Power, might at any Time revoke the Royal Edict at Pleasure, or dissolve any Charter whatsoever even though like the famous Edict of Nantes it had been declared irrevocable. Charles, having in him the regal Power only, could Grant no more than was in him, and the Legislative Power which was in the Parliament must still remain there, and consequently the Subjects of England continued when in the Colony still subject to the regal constitutional Power of Charles and the supreme Legislative Power of Parliament. And, I think, nothing is more certain than that the constitutional Restraint of the regal Power in Charles prevented the Charter from being revoked and annulled in less than Ten Years after the Date of it.

If this brief Account of Feudal Tenure, as it is Part of the English Constitution, be just, as I shall think it is until I have better Authority than any I have yet seen to the contrary, the Fabrick which you have raised will still fail of Support, for it wholly depends upon very different Principles, and upon what you hope I do not mean to introduce, viz. the Feudal System in its Perfection. If this Support fails, there is but little Occasion for me to remark upon the other Parts of your Message, and I shall pass them over, except such as may tend to make wrong Impressions upon any unwary Readers.

You cannot conceive "why the King has not the same Right to alienate and dispose of Countries acquired by the Discovery of his Subjects as he has to restore upon a Treaty of Peace Countries acquired in War carried on at the Charge of the Nation, or to sell and deliver up any Part of his Dominions against the general Sense of the Nation." I will venture to conjecture a Reason. By the English Constitution the sole Power of making War and Peace is in the King. It often happens that the restoring and ceding Acquisitions made in War is absolutely necessary to the Re-establishment of Peace, and if the King was restrained from such Restorations or Cessions an unsuccessful War might be perpetuated to the Destruction of the Kingdom. This Power therefore seems necessarily to result from this Prerogative of the Crown. And for selling any Part of the Dominions against the general Sense of the Nation I never supposed it to be a Part of the Prerogative, but have called it an Act of *Power*, by which I thought no candid Reader would understand any Thing but *meer Power*.

Your Attempt to shew that new discovered Countries do not become Part of the State, from the Authority of Puffendorff, &c. will fail, because the Instance given by him of a Colony erected into a separate Common Wealth plainly appears by the Context to be by the Leave or Consent of the

Parent State, and it does not appear that the other Cases were not so.

Your Remark upon the Authority I bring to shew that the Colony, being feudatory, is under the Government of the King's Laws, is very singular. You suppose it must mean the King's Laws *absolutely*, or as you explain it, not the Laws of Parliament. Do any of you remember ever to have seen the Expression, *the King's Laws*, meaning the King of England, used in any other Sense than *the Laws of the Realm?* You say I have not named the Authority. The Case I refer to is the King against Crowle, in the 2d. Vol Burrow's Reports, and for the Authority, which you will find mentioned there, I am not able to name a greater.

I would pass over in Silence your Attempt to shew that Allegiance is due to the natural Person and not to the Body Politick of the King, if I had not been well informed that the artificial Reasoning of Lord Chief Justice Coke upon the Doctrine of Allegiance, in the noted Case of Calvin, as you have recited it, had great Weight with some of the Members of the House. But have you recited this Case truly? After all the Refinements on this Subject does it appear that they can amount to any Thing more than that Allegiance is not due to the Politick Capacity *only?* And is it not expresly said that the natural Person of the King is ever accompanied with the Politick Capacity, and the Politick Capacity as it were appropriated to the Natural Capacity? Or have you any clear Idea of Allegiance to a King in his natural Capacity without any Relation to his political Capacity? From this Authority misunderstood you infer that I am mistaken in supposing your Allegiance to be due to the *Crown* of England. Without any Refinements, it is plain that it was one Condition, on the Performance whereof the first Charter depended, that Allegiance should be borne to King Charles his Heirs and *Successors*. Wherever therefore the Succession to the Crown shall go there Allegiance is to follow. The Condition in the second Charter is the same, and this is enough for my Purpose, which was to shew that in whatever Person the Regal Authority shall be, there your Allegiance is due. I wish you had omitted all you have said upon this Subject, for neither the Reasoning of Lord Coke, nor the Declarations of the Judges, in any Measure tend to the Purpose for which you produce them.

Your Assertion that Parliament, in regulating the Fishery, had nothing in View but to prevent a Monopoly of the Sea, and claimed no Authority over the Plantations or Lands in America, has only your own Authority to support it. It appears from the Debates in Parliament, that it was the Refusal of the Patentees to suffer Fish to be dried upon the Land within their Patent, by any Person who had not Licence from them, which was complained of as a Grievance, and the Bill was brought in to remove this Grievance: The King might very well refuse his Assent, not because Parliament had no Jurisdiction, but because he did not think fit to join with the Lords and Commons in an Act which invalidated or abridged those Privileges in a Patent of Lands which by his Royal Prerogative he had a Right to grant.

I will make no particular Remarks upon those Parts of your Message which relate to the Sense the People have had of their Constitution, as there can be no End to Disputes upon Facts which by small Deviations from the true State of them may be made to serve one Side or the other.

It is evident that the first Settlers of this Colony left England with a just Sense of their Dependance—that the Sense continued until the Principles of Anarchy in England spread in America, and it is conceded that these Principles were avowed by many of the Inhabitants here for near twenty Years after they were exploded in England. It is equally certain, that at the Time of the Revolution the People returned to a just Sense of the Supremacy of Parliament, and I think I may very safely say that the oldest Person in the Province has never heard the Supremacy called in Question until within a few Years past.

You again express your Concern that I should thus repeatedly insist upon your giving your free Sentiments on so delicate a Subject as the Authority of Parliament. In the Beginning of your Message you vindicate the Town of Boston & the other Towns in the Province, which have met together and determined upon the same Subject, and made their Proceedings Matter of Record and published them in News-Papers; and yet in the Close of it you assert that the Subject is too delicate and of too great Importance for you to consider. Certainly then it must have been extremely irregular in the Towns to take upon them separately to determine Points which they had no Authority to determine, and in this Way to influence if not determine the Acts and Doings of their Representatives in General Assembly, who cannot have the same Freedom of thinking and acting, after their Constituents have determined and resolved, as they had before.

Gentlemen of the Council
   and House of Representatives,

I am sensible that nice Distinctions of civil Rights and legal Constitutions are far above the Reach of the Bulk of Mankind to comprehend. There are, however, a few plain fundamental Principles of Government which carry within themselves such Evidence as cannot be resisted, and are no sooner proposed than assented to—Such as these—That in every Government there must be somewhere a supreme uncontroulable Power, an absolute Authority to decide and determine—That two such Powers cannot coexist, but necessarily will make two distinct States—That in a State of Society we give up Part of our natural Liberty in order to secure that legal Freedom which it is the great End of Government to maintain and preserve—That a Right in Individuals or Parts of a Government to judge of the Decisions of the Supreme Authority and to submit or not submit as they think proper, cannot consist with a State of Government and must work the Dissolution of it. Whilst these Principles had their due Influence we enjoyed all that Freedom and all those other Blessings which a State of Government will admit of. Our Connection with our Parent State secured these Blessings to us, and by Means of a nominal Dependence we possessed as great a Share of real Freedom as the Parent State itself upon which we are said to depend.

I have laid before you, Gentlemen, what appeared to me to be the true Constitution of the Province, and recommended an Adherence to it because I believed it would restore us to and continue us in that happy State in which we flourished so long a Course of Years.

Certainly it is of the utmost Importance to you that these Points should be settled, for I know of no Maxim in the Law of greater Truth than this. *Where the Constitution is contested and the Laws are vague and uncertain, there, will be the greatest Slavery.*

[Thomas Jefferson], A Summary View of the Rights of British America. Set Forth in Some Resolutions Intended for the Inspection of the Present Delegates of the People of Virginia. Now in Convention. Williamsburg, 1774.

In response to the Coercive Acts, fifty-five delegates from twelve colonies (all except Georgia) met at Philadelphia in September 1774 for the First Continental Congress. Unable to attend the convention that elected Virginia's delegates, Thomas Jefferson prepared instructions for them that he hoped would be embodied in an address to the king. They were never officially acted upon, though without his knowledge they were printed in Williamsburg as *A Summary View of the Rights of British America* and would exercise wide influence. Compared to other public expressions of American opinion in 1774, Jefferson's pamphlet was extremely radical. Convinced, like other Americans, that the British government was pursuing "a deliberate and systematical plan of reducing us to slavery," he came close to describing the colonies as independent states that had been settled by Britons in the same way England had been settled by the Saxons. The fantasy of a golden Anglo-Saxon age of pure liberty and equality that existed before the imposition of the Norman yoke in 1066 was central to the most alienated strain of eighteenth-century radical Whig thinking, and Jefferson was one of the few American writers who invoked this potent myth.

He went on to imply that the relationship between the colonies and Britain was fundamentally a commercial one, no different from those which Britain had with other states with whom it traded. As such, he declared, the British Parliament was "foreign to our constitutions, and unacknowledged by our laws," and consequently it "has no right to exercise authority over us." Instead of being under Parliament, each of the separate colonies was related only to the king, "who was thereby made the central link connecting the several parts of the empire."

This extraordinary notion has been called the "commonwealth" view of the empire because it anticipated the Statute of Westminster of 1931 that established the modern British Commonwealth. Each member of the Commonwealth has an independent sovereign legislature and is tied to the other members solely by its allegiance to the common monarch.

A
SUMMARY VIEW
OF THE
RIGHTS
OF
BRITISH AMERICA.
SET FORTH IN SOME
RESOLUTIONS
INTENDED FOR THE
INSPECTION
OF THE PRESENT
DELEGATES
OF THE
PEOPLE OF VIRGINIA.
NOW IN
CONVENTION.

By a NATIVE, and MEMBER of the
HOUSE of BURGESSES.

WILLIAMSBURG:
PRINTED BY CLEMENTINA RIND

EST PROPRIUM MUNUS MAGISTRATUS INTELLIGERE, SE GERERE PERSONAM CIVITATIS, DEBEREQUE; EJUS DIGNITATEM & DECUS SUSTINERE, SERVARE LEGES, JURA DISCRIBERE, EA FIDEI SUÆ COMMISSA MEMINISSE.

CICERO DE OF. L. 1, C. 34.

It is the indispensable duty of the supreme magistrate to consider himself as acting for the whole community, and obliged to support its dignity, and assign to the people, with justice, their various rights, as he would be faithful to the great trust reposed in him.

THE PREFACE OF THE EDITORS.

THE following piece was intended to convey to the late meeting of DELEGATES the sentiments of one of their body, whose personal attendance was prevented by an accidental illness. In it the sources of our present unhappy differences are traced with such faithful accuracy, and the opinions entertained by every free American expressed with such a manly firmness, that it must be pleasing to the present, and may be useful to future ages. It will evince to the world the moderation of our late convention, who have only touched with tenderness many of the claims insisted on in this pamphlet, though every heart acknowledged their justice. Without the knowledge of the author, we have ventured to communicate his sentiments to the public; who have certainly a right to know what the best and wisest of their members have thought on a subject in which they are so deeply interested.

A Summary View of the Rights of
British America, &c.

RESOLVED, that it be an instruction to the said deputies, when assembled in general congress with the deputies from the other states of British America, to propose to the said congress that an humble and dutiful address be presented to his majesty, begging leave to lay before him, as chief magistrate of the British empire, the united complaints of his majesty's subjects in America; complaints which are excited by many unwarrantable encroachments and usurpations, attempted to be made by the legislature of one part of the empire, upon those rights which God and the laws have given equally and independently to all. To represent to his majesty that these his states have often individually made humble application to his imperial throne to obtain, through its intervention, some redress of their injured rights, to none of which was ever even an answer condescended; humbly to hope that this their joint address, penned in the language of truth, and divested of those expressions of servility which would persuade his majesty that we are asking favours, and not rights, shall obtain from his majesty a more respectful acceptance. And this his majesty will think we have reason to expect when he reflects that he is no more than the chief officer of the people, appointed by the laws, and circumscribed with definite powers, to assist in working the great machine of government, erected for their use, and consequently subject to their superintendance. And in order that these our rights, as well as the invasions of them, may be laid more fully before his majesty, to take a view of them from the origin and first settlement of these countries.

To remind him that our ancestors, before their emigration to America, were the free inhabitants of the British dominions in Europe, and possessed a right which nature has given to all men, of departing from the country in which chance, not choice, has placed them, of going in quest of new habitations, and of there establishing new societies, under such laws and regulations as to them shall seem most likely to promote public happiness. That their Saxon ancestors had, under this universal law, in like manner left their native wilds and woods in the north of Europe, had possessed themselves of the island of Britain, then less charged with inhabitants, and had established there that system of laws which has so long been the glory and protection of that country. Nor was ever any claim of superiority or dependence asserted over them by that mother country from which they had migrated; and were such a claim made, it is believed that his majesty's subjects in Great Britain have too firm a feeling of the rights derived to them from their ancestors, to bow down the sovereignty of their state before such visionary pretensions. And it is thought that no circumstance has occurred to distinguish materially the British from the Saxon emigration. America was conquered, and her settlements made, and firmly established, at the expence of individuals, and not of the British public. Their own blood was spilt in acquiring lands for their settlement, their own fortunes expended in making that settlement effectual; for themselves they fought, for themselves they conquered, and for themselves alone they have right to hold. Not a shilling was ever issued from the public treasures of his majesty, or his ancestors, for their assistance, till of very late times, after the colonies had become established on a firm and permanent footing. That then, indeed, having become valuable to Great Britain for her commercial purposes, his parliament was pleased to lend them assistance against an enemy, who would fain have drawn to herself the benefits of their commerce, to the great aggrandizement of herself, and danger of Great Britain. Such assistance, and in such circumstances, they had often before given to Portugal, and other allied states, with whom they carry on a commercial intercourse; yet these states never supposed, that by calling in her aid, they thereby submitted themselves to her sovereignty. Had such terms been proposed, they would have rejected them with disdain, and trusted for better to the moderation of their enemies, or to a vigorous exertion of their own force. We do not, however, mean to under-rate those aids, which to us were doubtless valuable, on whatever principles granted; but we would shew that they cannot give a title to that authority which the British parliament would arrogate over us, and that they may amply be repaid by our giving to the inhabitants of Great Britain such exclusive privileges in trade as may be advantageous to them, and at the same time not too restrictive to ourselves. That settlements having been thus effected in the wilds of America, the emigrants thought proper to adopt that system of laws under which they had hitherto lived in the mother country, and to continue their union with her by submitting themselves to the same common sovereign, who was thereby made the central link connecting the several parts of the empire thus newly multiplied.

But that not long were they permitted, however far they thought themselves removed from the hand of oppression, to hold undisturbed the rights thus acquired, at the hazard of their lives, and loss of their fortunes. A family of princes was then on the British throne, whose treasonable crimes against their people brought on them afterwards the exertion of those sacred and sovereign rights of punishment reserved in the hands of the people for cases of extreme necessity, and judged by the constitution unsafe to be delegated to any other judicature. While every day brought forth some new and unjustifiable exertion of power over their subjects on that side the water, it was not to be expected that those here, much less able at that time to oppose the designs of despotism, should be exempted from injury.

Accordingly that country, which had been acquired by the lives, the labours, and the fortunes, of individual adventurers, was by these princes, at several times, parted out and distributed among the favourites and followers of their fortunes,* and, by an assumed right of the crown alone, were erected into distinct and independent governments; a measure which it is believed his majesty's prudence and understanding would prevent him from imitating at this day, as no exercise of such a

---

* 1632 Maryland was granted to lord Baltimore, 14. c. 2. Pennsylvania to Penn, and the province of Carolina was in the year 1663 granted by letters patent of majesty, king Charles II. in the 15th year of his reign, in propriety, unto the right honourable Edward earl of Clarendon, George duke of Albemarle, William earl of Craven, John lord Berkeley, Anthony lord Ashley, sir George Carteret, sir John Coleton, knight and baronet, and sir William Berkley, knight; by which letters patent the laws of England were to be in force in Carolina: But the lords proprietors had power, *with the consent of the inhabitants*, to make bye-laws for the better government of the said province; so that no money could be received, or law made, without the consent of the inhabitants, or their representatives.

power, of dividing and dismembering a country, has ever occurred in his majesty's realm of England, though now of very antient standing; nor could it be justified or acquiesced under there, or in any other part of his majesty's empire.

That the exercise of a free trade with all parts of the world, possessed by the American colonists, as of natural right, and which no law of their own had taken away or abridged, was next the object of unjust encroachment. Some of the colonies having thought proper to continue the administration of their government in the name and under the authority of his majesty king Charles the first, whom, notwithstanding his late deposition by the commonwealth of England, they continued in the sovereignty of their state; the parliament for the commonwealth took the same in high offence, and assumed upon themselves the power of prohibiting their trade with all other parts of the world, except the island of Great Britain. This arbitrary act, however, they soon recalled, and by solemn treaty, entered into on the 12th day of March, 1651, between the said commonwealth by their commissioners, and the colony of Virginia by their house of burgesses, it was expressly stipulated, by the 8th article of the said treaty, that they should have "free trade as the people of England do enjoy to all places and with all nations, according to the laws of that commonwealth." But that, upon the restoration of his majesty king Charles the second, their rights of free commerce fell once more a victim to arbitrary power; and by several acts* of his reign, as well as of some of his successors, the trade of the colonies was laid under such restrictions, as shew what hopes they might form from the justice of a British parliament, were its uncontrouled power admitted over these states. History has informed us that bodies of men, as well as individuals, are susceptible of the spirit of tyranny. A view of these acts of parliament for regulation, as it has been affectedly called, of the American trade, if all other evidence were removed out of the case, would undeniably evince the truth of this observation. Besides the duties they impose on our articles of export and import, they prohibit our going to any markets northward of Cape Finesterre, in the

* 12. c. 2. c. 18. 15. c. 2. c. 7. 25. c. 2. c. 7. 7. 8. W. M. c. 22. 11. W. 3. 4. Anne. 6. G. 2. c. 13.

kingdom of Spain, for the sale of commodities which Great Britain will not take from us, and for the purchase of others, with which she cannot supply us, and that for no other than the arbitrary purposes of purchasing for themselves, by a sacrifice of our rights and interests, certain privileges in their commerce with an allied state, who in confidence that their exclusive trade with America will be continued, while the principles and power of the British parliament be the same, have indulged themselves in every exorbitance which their avarice could dictate, or our necessities extort; have raised their commodities, called for in America, to the double and treble of what they sold for before such exclusive privileges were given them, and of what better commodities of the same kind would cost us elsewhere, and at the same time give us much less for what we carry thither than might be had at more convenient ports. That these acts prohibit us from carrying in quest of other purchasers the surplus of our tobaccoes remaining after the consumption of Great Britain is supplied; so that we must leave them with the British merchant for whatever he will please to allow us, to be by him reshipped to foreign markets, where he will reap the benefits of making sale of them for full value. That to heighten still the idea of parliamentary justice, and to shew with what moderation they are like to exercise power, where themselves are to feel no part of its weight, we take leave to mention to his majesty certain other acts of British parliament, by which they would prohibit us from manufacturing for our own use the articles we raise on our own lands with our own labour. By an act* passed in the 5th Year of the reign of his late majesty king George the second, an American subject is forbidden to make a hat for himself of the fur which he has taken perhaps on his own soil; an instance of despotism to which no parrallel can be produced in the most arbitrary ages of British history. By one other act,† passed in the 23d year of the same reign, the iron which we make we are forbidden to manufacture, and heavy as that article is, and necessary in every branch of husbandry, besides commission and insurance, we are to pay freight for it to

* 5. G. 2.
† 23. G. 2. c. 29.

Great Britain, and freight for it back again, for the purpose of supporting not men, but machines, in the island of Great Britain. In the same spirit of equal and impartial legislation is to be viewed the act of parliament,* passed in the 5th year of the same reign, by which American lands are made subject to the demands of British creditors, while their own lands were still continued unanswerable for their debts; from which one of these conclusions must necessarily follow, either that justice is not the same in America as in Britain, or else that the British parliament pay less regard to it here than there. But that we do not point out to his majesty the injustice of these acts, with intent to rest on that principle the cause of their nullity; but to shew that experience confirms the propriety of those political principles which exempt us from the jurisdiction of the British parliament. The true ground on which we declare these acts void is, that the British parliament has no right to exercise authority over us.

That these exercises of usurped power have not been confined to instances alone, in which themselves were interested, but they have also intermeddled with the regulation of the internal affairs of the colonies. The act of the 9th of Anne for establishing a post office in America seems to have had little connection with British convenience, except that of accommodating his majesty's ministers and favourites with the sale of a lucrative and easy office.

That thus have we hastened through the reigns which preceded his majesty's, during which the violations of our right were less alarming, because repeated at more distant intervals than that rapid and bold succession of injuries which is likely to distinguish the present from all other periods of American story. Scarcely have our minds been able to emerge from the astonishment into which one stroke of parliamentary thunder has involved us, before another more heavy, and more alarming, is fallen on us. Single acts of tyranny may be ascribed to the accidental opinion of a day; but a series of oppressions, begun at a distinguished period, and pursued unalterably through every change of ministers, too plainly prove a deliberate and systematical plan of reducing us to slavery.

* 5. G. 2. c. 7.

That the act* passed in the 4th year of his majesty's reign, intitled "An act for granting certain duties in the British colonies and plantations in America, &c."

One other act†, passed in the 5th year of his reign, intitled "An act for granting and applying certain stamp duties and other duties in the British colonies and plantations in America, &c."

One other act‡, passed in the 6th year of his reign, intituled "An act for the better securing the dependency of his majesty's dominions in America upon the crown and parliament of Great Britian;" and one other act§, passed in the 7th year of his reign, intituled "An act for granting duties on paper, tea, &c." form that connected chain of parliamentary usurpation, which has already been the subject of frequent applications to his majesty, and the houses of lords and commons of Great Britain; and no answers having yet been condescended to any of these, we shall not trouble his majesty with a repetition of the matters they contained.

But that one other act¶, passed in the same 7th year of the reign, having been a peculiar attempt, must ever require peculiar mention; it is intituled "An act for suspending the legislature of New York." One free and independent legislature hereby takes upon itself to suspend the powers of another, free and independent as itself; thus exhibiting a phœnomenon unknown in nature, the creator and creature of its own power. Not only the principles of common sense, but the common feelings of human nature, must be surrendered up before his majesty's subjects here can be persuaded to believe that they hold their political existence at the will of a British parliament. Shall these governments be dissolved, their property annihilated, and their people reduced to a state of nature, at the imperious breath of a body of men, whom they never saw, in whom they never confided, and over whom they have no

*4. G. 3. c. 15.
†5. G. 3. c. 12.
‡6. G. 3. c. 12.
§7. G. 3.
¶7. G. 3. c. 59.

powers of punishment or removal, let their crimes against the American public be ever so great? Can any one reason be assigned why 160,000 electors in the island of Great Britain should give law to four millions in the states of America, every individual of whom is equal to every individual of them, in virtue, in understanding, and in bodily strength? Were this to be admitted, instead of being a free people, as we have hitherto supposed, and mean to continue ourselves, we should suddenly be found the slaves, not of one, but of 160,000 tyrants, distinguished too from all others by this singular circumstance, that they are removed from the reach of fear, the only restraining motive which may hold the hand of a tyrant.

That by "an act* to discontinue in such manner and for such time as are therein mentioned the landing and discharging, lading or shipping, of goods, wares, and merchandize, at the town and within the harbour of Boston, in the province of Massachusetts Bay, in North America," which was passed at the last session of British parliament; a large and populous town, whose trade was their sole subsistence, was deprived of that trade, and involved in utter ruin. Let us for a while suppose the question of right suspended, in order to examine this act on principles of justice: An act of parliament had been passed imposing duties on teas, to be paid in America, against which act the Americans had protested as inauthoritative. The East India company, who till that time had never sent a pound of tea to America on their own account, step forth on that occasion the assertors of parliamentary right, and send hither many ship loads of that obnoxious commodity. The masters of their several vessels, however, on their arrival in America, wisely attended to admonition, and returned with their cargoes. In the province of New England alone the remonstrances of the people were disregarded, and a compliance, after being many days waited for, was flatly refused. Whether in this the master of the vessel was governed by his obstinacy, or his instructions, let those who know, say. There are extraordinary situations which require extraordinary interposition. An exasperated people, who feel that they possess power, are not easily restrained within limits strictly regular. A number of them

* 14. G. 3.

assembled in the town of Boston, threw the tea into the ocean, and dispersed without doing any other act of violence. If in this they did wrong, they were known and were amenable to the laws of the land, against which it could not be objected that they had ever, in any instance, been obstructed or diverted from their regular course in favour of popular offenders. They should therefore not have been distrusted on this occasion. But that ill fated colony had formerly been bold in their enmities against the house of Stuart, and were now devoted to ruin by that unseen hand which governs the momentous affairs of this great empire. On the partial representations of a few worthless ministerial dependents, whose constant office it has been to keep that government embroiled, and who, by their treacheries, hope to obtain the dignity of the British knighthood, without calling for a party accused, without asking a proof, without attempting a distinction between the guilty and the innocent, the whole of that antient and wealthy town is in a moment reduced from opulence to beggary. Men who had spent their lives in extending the British commerce, who had invested in that place the wealth their honest endeavours had merited, found themselves and their families thrown at once on the world for subsistence by its charities. Not the hundredth part of the inhabitants of that town had been concerned in the act complained of; many of them were in Great Britain and in other parts beyond sea; yet all were involved in one indiscriminate ruin, by a new executive power, unheard of till then, that of a British parliament. A property, of the value of many millions of money, was sacrificed to revenge, not repay, the loss of a few thousands. This is administering justice with a heavy hand indeed! and when is this tempest to be arrested in its course? Two wharfs are to be opened again when his majesty shall think proper. The residue which lined the extensive shores of the bay of Boston are forever interdicted the exercise of commerce. This little exception seems to have been thrown in for no other purpose than that of setting a precedent for investing his majesty with legislative powers. If the pulse of his people shall beat calmly under this experiment, another and another will be tried, till the measure of despotism be filled up. It would be an insult on common sense to pretend that this exception was made in order to restore its commerce to that great town. The trade which cannot be received at two wharfs alone must of necessity be transferred to some other place; to which it will soon be followed by that of the two wharfs. Considered in this light, it would be an insolent and cruel mockery at the annihilation of the town of Boston.

By the act* for the suppression of riots and tumults in the town of Boston, passed also in the last session of parliament, a murder committed there is, if the governor pleases, to be tried in the court of King's Bench, in the island of Great Britain, by a jury of Middlesex. The witnesses, too, on receipt of such a sum as the governor shall think it reasonable for them to expend, are to enter into recognizance to appear at the trial. This is, in other words, taxing them to the amount of their recognizance, and that amount may be whatever a governor pleases; for who does his majesty think can be prevailed on to cross the Atlantic for the sole purpose of bearing evidence to a fact? His expences are to be borne, indeed, as they shall be estimated by a governor; but who are to feed the wife and children whom he leaves behind, and who have had no other subsistence but his daily labour? Those epidemical disorders, too, so terrible in a foreign climate, is the cure of them to be estimated among the articles of expence, and their danger to be warded off by the almighty power of parliament? And the wretched criminal, if he happen to have offended on the American side, stripped of his privilege of trial by peers of his vicinage, removed from the place where alone full evidence could be obtained, without money, without counsel, without friends, without exculpatory proof, is tried before judges predetermined to condemn. The cowards who would suffer a countryman to be torn from the bowels of their society, in order to be thus offered a sacrifice to parliamentary tyranny, would merit that everlasting infamy now fixed on the authors of the act! A clause† for a similar purpose had been introduced into an act, passed in the 12th year of his majesty's reign, intitled "An act for the better securing and preserving his majesty's dockyards, magazines, ships, ammunition, and stores;" against which, as meriting the same censures, the several colonies have already protested.

* 14. G. 3.
† 12. G. 3. c. 24.

That these are the acts of power, assumed by a body of men, foreign to our constitutions, and unacknowledged by our laws, against which we do, on behalf of the inhabitants of British America, enter this our solemn and determined protest; and we do earnestly entreat his majesty, as yet the only mediatory power between the several states of the British empire, to recommend to his parliament of Great Britain the total revocation of these acts, which, however nugatory they be, may yet prove the cause of further discontents and jealousies among us.

That we next proceed to consider the conduct of his majesty, as holding the executive powers of the laws of these states, and mark out his deviations from the line of duty: By the constitution of Great Britain, as well as of the several American states, his majesty possesses the power of refusing to pass into a law any bill which has already passed the other two branches of legislature. His majesty, however, and his ancestors, conscious of the impropriety of opposing their single opinion to the united wisdom of two houses of parliament, while their proceedings were unbiassed by interested principles, for several ages past have modestly declined the exercise of this power in that part of his empire called Great Britain. But by change of circumstances, other principles than those of justice simply have obtained an influence on their determinations; the addition of new states to the British empire has produced an addition of new, and sometimes opposite interests. It is now, therefore, the great office of his majesty, to resume the exercise of his negative power, and to prevent the passage of laws by any one legislature of the empire, which might bear injuriously on the rights and interests of another. Yet this will not excuse the wanton exercise of this power which we have seen his majesty practise on the laws of the American legislatures. For the most trifling reasons, and sometimes for no conceivable reason at all, his majesty has rejected laws of the most salutary tendency. The abolition of domestic slavery is the great object of desire in those colonies, where it was unhappily introduced in their infant state. But previous to the enfranchisement of the slaves we have, it is necessary to exclude all further importations from Africa; yet our repeated attempts to effect this by prohibitions, and by imposing duties which might amount to a prohibition, have been hitherto defeated by his majesty's negative: Thus preferring the immediate advantages of a few African corsairs to the lasting interests of the American states, and to the rights of human nature, deeply wounded by this infamous practice. Nay, the single interposition of an interested individual against a law was scarcely ever known to fail of success, though in the opposite scale were placed the interests of a whole country. That this is so shameful an abuse of a power trusted with his majesty for other purposes, as if not reformed, would call for some legal restrictions.

With equal inattention to the necessities of his people here has his majesty permitted our laws to lie neglected in England for years, neither confirming them by his assent, nor annulling them by his negative; so that such of them as have no suspending clause we hold on the most precarious of all tenures, his majesty's will, and such of them as suspend themselves till his majesty's assent be obtained, we have feared, might be called into existence at some future and distant period, when time, and change of circumstances, shall have rendered them destructive to his people here. And to render this grievance still more oppressive, his majesty by his instructions has laid his governors under such restrictions that they can pass no law of any moment unless it have such suspending clause; so that, however immediate may be the call for legislative interposition, the law cannot be executed till it has twice crossed the atlantic, by which time the evil may have spent its whole force.

But in what terms, reconcileable to majesty, and at the same time to truth, shall we speak of a late instruction to his majesty's governor of the colony of Virginia, by which he is forbidden to assent to any law for the division of a county, unless the new county will consent to have no representative in assembly? That colony has as yet fixed no boundary to the westward. Their western counties, therefore, are of indefinite extent; some of them are actually seated many hundred miles from their eastern limits. Is it possible, then, that his majesty can have bestowed a single thought on the situation of those people, who, in order to obtain justice for injuries, however great or small, must, by the laws of that colony, attend their county court, at such a distance, with all their witnesses, monthly, till their litigation be determined? Or does his majesty seriously wish, and publish it to the world, that his subjects should give up the glorious right of representation, with all the benefits derived from that, and submit themselves the absolute slaves of his sovereign will? Or is it rather meant to confine the legislative body to their present numbers, that they may be the cheaper bargain whenever they shall become worth a purchase.

One of the articles of impeachment against Tresilian, and the other judges of Westminster Hall, in the reign of Richard the second, for which they suffered death, as traitors to their country, was, that they had advised the king that he might dissolve his parliament at any time; and succeeding kings have adopted the opinion of these unjust judges. Since the establishment, however, of the British constitution, at the glorious revolution, on its free and antient principles, neither his majesty, nor his ancestors, have exercised such a power of dissolution in the island of Great Britain; and when his majesty was petitioned, by the united voice of his people there, to dissolve the present parliament, who had become obnoxious to them, his ministers were heard to declare, in open parliament, that his majesty possessed no such power by the constitution. But how different their language and his practice here! To declare, as their duty required, the known rights of their country, to oppose the usurpations of every foreign judicature, to disregard the imperious mandates of a minister or governor, have been the avowed causes of dissolving houses of representatives in America. But if such powers be really vested in his majesty, can he suppose they are there placed to awe the members from such purposes as these? When the representative body have lost the confidence of their constituents, when they have notoriously made sale of their most valuable rights, when they have assumed to themselves powers which the people never put into their hands, then indeed their continuing in office becomes dangerous to the state, and calls for an exercise of the power of dissolution. Such being the causes for which the representative body should, and should not, be dissolved, will it not appear strange to an unbiassed observer, that that of Great Britain was not dissolved, while those of the colonies have repeatedly incurred that sentence?

But your majesty, or your governors, have carried this power beyond every limit known, or provided for, by the laws: After dissolving one house of representatives, they have refused to call another, so that, for a great length of time, the legislature provided by the laws has been out of existence. From the nature of things, every society must at all times possess within itself the sovereign powers of legislation. The feelings of human nature revolt against the supposition of a state so situated as that it may not in any emergency provide against dangers which perhaps threaten immediate ruin. While those bodies are in existence to whom the people have delegated the powers of legislation, they alone possess and may exercise those powers; but when they are dissolved by the lopping off one or more of their branches, the power reverts to the people, who may exercise it to unlimited extent, either assembling together in person, sending deputies, or in any other way they may think proper. We forbear to trace consequences further; the dangers are conspicuous with which this practice is replete.

That we shall at this time also take notice of an error in the nature of our land holdings, which crept in at a very early period of our settlement. The introduction of the feudal tenures into the kingdom of England, though antient, is well enough understood to set this matter in a proper light. In the earlier ages of the Saxon settlement feudal holdings were certainly altogether unknown; and very few, if any, had been introduced at the time of the Norman conquest. Our Saxon ancestors held their lands, as they did their personal property, in absolute dominion, disencumbered with any superior, answering nearly to the nature of those possessions which the feudalists term allodial. William, the Norman, first introduced that system generally. The lands which had belonged to those who fell in the battle of Hastings, and in the subsequent insurrections of his reign, formed a considerable proportion of the lands of the whole kingdom. These he granted out, subject to feudal duties, as did he also those of a great number of his new subjects, who, by persuasions or threats, were induced to surrender them for that purpose. But still much was left in the hands of his Saxon subjects; held of no superior, and not subject to feudal conditions. These, therefore, by express laws, enacted to render uniform the system of military defence, were made liable to the same military duties as if they had been feuds; and the Norman lawyers soon found means to saddle them also with all the other feudal burthens. But still they had not been surrendered to the king, they were not derived from his grant, and therefore they were not holden of him. A general principle, indeed, was introduced, that "all lands in England were held either mediately or immediately of the crown," but this was borrowed from those holdings, which were truly feudal, and only applied to others for the purposes of illustration. Feudal holdings were therefore but exceptions out of the Saxon laws of possession, under which all lands were held in absolute right. These, therefore, still form the basis, or groundwork, of the common law, to prevail wheresoever the exceptions have not taken place. America was not conquered by William the Norman, nor its lands surrendered to him, or any of his successors. Possessions there are undoubtedly of the allodial nature. Our ancestors, however, who migrated hither, were farmers, not lawyers. The fictitious principle that all lands belong originally to the king, they were early persuaded to believe real; and accordingly took grants of their own lands from the crown. And while the crown continued to grant for small sums, and on reasonable rents; there was no inducement to arrest the error, and lay it open to public view. But his majesty has lately taken on him to advance the terms of purchase, and of holding to the double of what they were; by which means the acquisition of lands being rendered difficult, the population of our country is likely to be checked. It is time, therefore, for us to lay this matter before his majesty, and to declare that he has no right to grant lands of himself. From the nature and purpose of civil institutions, all the lands within the limits which any particular society has circumscribed around itself are assumed by that society, and subject to their allotment only. This may be done by themselves, assembled collectively, or by their legislature, to whom they may have delegated sovereign authority; and if they are alloted in neither of these ways, each individual of the society may appropriate to himself such lands as he finds vacant, and occupancy will give him title.

That in order to enforce the arbitrary measures before complained of, his majesty has from time to time sent among us large bodies of armed forces, not made up of the people here, nor raised by the authority of our laws: Did his majesty possess such a right as this, it might swallow up all our other rights whenever he should think proper. But his majesty has no right to land a single armed man on our shores, and those whom he sends here are liable to our laws made for the suppression and punishment of riots, routs, and unlawful assemblies; or are hostile bodies, invading us in defiance of law. When in the course of the late war it became expedient that a body of Hanoverian troops should be brought over for the defence of Great Britain, his majesty's grandfather, our late sovereign, did not pretend to introduce them under any authority he possessed. Such a measure would have given just alarm to his subjects in Great Britain, whose liberties would not be safe if armed men of another country, and of another spirit, might be brought into the realm at any time without the consent of their legislature. He therefore applied to parliament, who passed an act for that purpose, limiting the number to be brought in and the time they were to continue. In like manner is his majesty restrained in every part of the empire. He possesses, indeed, the executive power of the laws in every state; but they are the laws of the particular state which he is to administer within that state, and not those of any one within the limits of another. Every state must judge for itself the number of armed men which they may safely trust among them, of whom they are to consist, and under what restrictions they shall be laid.

To render these proceedings still more criminal against our laws, instead of subjecting the military to the civil powers, his majesty has expressly made the civil subordinate to the military. But can his majesty thus put down all law under his feet? Can he erect a power superior to that which erected himself? He has done it indeed by force; but let him remember that force cannot give right.

That these are our grievances which we have thus laid before his majesty, with that freedom of language and sentiment which becomes a free people claiming their rights, as derived from the laws of nature, and not as the gift of their chief magistrate: Let those flatter who fear; it is not an American art. To give praise which is not due might be well from the venal, but would ill beseem those who are asserting the rights of human nature. They know, and will therefore say, that kings are the servants, not the proprietors of the people. Open your breast, sire, to liberal and expanded thought. Let not the name of George the third be a blot in the page of history. You are surrounded by British counsellors, but remember that they are parties. You have no ministers for American affairs, because you have none taken from among us, nor amenable to the laws on which they are to give you advice. It behoves you, therefore, to think and to act for yourself and your people. The great principles of right and wrong are legible to every reader; to pursue them requires not the aid of many counsellors. The whole art of government consists in the art of being honest. Only aim to do your duty, and mankind will give you credit where you fail. No longer persevere in sacrificing the rights of one part of the empire to the inordinate desires of another; but deal out to all equal and impartial right. Let no act be passed by any one legislature which may infringe on the rights and liberties of another. This is the important post in which fortune has placed you, holding the balance of a great, if a well poised empire. This, sire, is the advice of your great American council, on the observance of which may perhaps depend your felicity and future fame, and the preservation of that harmony which alone can continue both to Great Britain and America the reciprocal advantages of their connection. It is neither our wish, nor our interest, to separate from her. We are willing, on our part, to sacrifice every thing which reason can ask to the restoration of that tranquillity for which all must wish. On their part, let them be ready to establish union and a generous plan. Let them name their terms, but let them be just. Accept of every commercial preference it is in our power to give for such things as we can raise for their use, or they make for ours. But let them not think to exclude us from going to other markets to dispose of those commodities which they cannot use, or to supply those wants which they cannot supply. Still less let it be proposed that our properties within our own territories shall be taxed or regulated by any power on earth but our own. The God who gave us life gave us liberty at the same time; the hand of force may destroy, but cannot disjoin them. This, sire, is our last, our determined resolution; and that you will be pleased to interpose with that efficacy which your earnest endeavours may ensure to procure redress of these our great grievances, to quiet the minds of your subjects in British America, against any apprehensions of future encroachment, to establish fraternal love and harmony through the whole empire, and that these may continue to the latest ages of time, is the fervent prayer of all British America!

[James Wilson], Considerations on the Nature and the Extent of the Legislative Authority of the British Parliament. Philadelphia, 1774.

A Scottish-born graduate of the University of St. Andrews, James Wilson came to Pennsylvania in 1765 and read law with John Dickinson. He wrote the following pamphlet in 1768 but delayed publishing it until 1774—and for good reason. Because he denied the legislative authority of Parliament "*in every instance*," his pamphlet was as radical as Jefferson's. Wilson said that he had begun writing his pamphlet with an "expectation of being able to trace some constitutional Line between those cases, in which we ought, and those in which we ought not, to acknowledge the power of Parliament over us." But in the process he "became fully convinced, that such a Line does not exist; and that there can be no medium between *acknowledging* and *denying* that power in *all* cases." Wilson, in other words, posed the issue essentially as Hutchinson had. There was no middle ground: the colonists had to accept Parliament's authority in all cases whatsoever, or deny Parliament's authority in all cases whatsoever. This blunt alternative was dictated by the prevailing doctrine of sovereignty, which held that there had to be in every state one final, supream, irresistible, indivisible law-making authority.

By 1774 Wilson and other leading patriots had tired of trying to divide the indivisible and separate the inseparable and had come to accept the implications of this idea of sovereignty. But now this idea was to be applied to their separate provincial legislatures. Because two supreme law-making bodies could not exist in the same state, said John Adams, it had become clear to them "that our provincial legislatures are the only supream authorities in our colonies."

But this position was not, as Wilson recognized, a very satisfactory explanation of America's historical experience in the empire. The colonists had earlier acknowledged Parliament's right to regulate their trade, but could they continue to do so in light of Parliament's claim of sovereignty? Wilson suggested that the power of trade regulation might "be entrusted to the King, as a part of the Royal prerogative." Only a Philadelphia lawyer could have come up with such a shrewd but impossible solution. The best the Continental Congress could do was "cheerfully" but rather awkwardly consent to future parliamentary regulation of America's trade "from the necessity of the case, and a regard to the mutual interest of both countries."

CONSIDERATIONS

ON THE

NATURE

AND THE

EXTENT

OF THE

Legislative Authority

OF THE

BRITISH

PARLIAMENT.

PHILADELPHIA:

Printed and Sold, by WILLIAM and THOMAS BRADFORD,
at the *London Coffee-House.*

M.DCC.LXXIV.

ADVERTISEMENT.

THE following sheets were written during the late Non-Importation Agreement: But that Agreement being dissolved before they were ready for the Press, it was then judged unseasonable to publish them. Many will, perhaps, be surprised to see the Legislative Authority of the British Parliament over the Colonies denied *in every instance.* Those the writer informs, that, when he began this piece, he would probably have been surprised at such an opinion himself; for, that it was the *result,* and not the *occasion,* of his disquisitions. He entered upon them with a view and expectation of being able to trace some constitutional Line between those cases, in which we ought, and those in which we ought not, to acknowledge the power of Parliament over us. In the prosecution of his enquiries, he became fully convinced, that such a Line does not exist; and that there can be no medium between *acknowledging* and *denying* that power in *all* cases. Which of these two alternatives is most consistent with Law, with the principles of Liberty, and with the happiness of the Colonies, let the public determine. To them the writer submits his sentiments, with that respectful deference to their judgment, which, in all questions affecting them, every individual should pay.

AUGUST 17, 1774.

Considerations, &c.

No question can be more important to Great-Britain, and to the Colonies, than this—*Does the legislative authority of the British Parliament extend over them?*

On the resolution of this question, and on the measures which a resolution of it will direct, will depend, whether the Parent Country, like a happy Mother, shall behold her Children flourishing around her, and receive the most grateful returns for her protection and love; or whether, like a step-dame, rendered miserable by her own unkind conduct, she shall see their affections alienated, and herself deprived of those advantages, which a milder treatment would have ensured to her.

The British nation are generous: They love to enjoy freedom: They love to behold it: Slavery is their greatest abhorrence: Is it possible then, that they would wish themselves the authors of it? No. Oppression is not a plant of the British soil; and the late severe proceedings against the Colonies must have arisen from the detestable schemes of interested Ministers, who have misinformed and misled the people. A regard for that nation, from whom we have sprung, and from whom we boast to have derived the spirit, which prompts us to oppose their unfriendly measures, must lead us to put this construction on what we have lately seen and experienced. When therefore, they shall know and consider the justice of our claim—that we insist only upon being treated as Freemen, and as the Descendants of those British ancestors, whose memory we will not dishonour by our degeneracy, it is reasonable to hope, that they will approve of our conduct, and bestow their loudest applauses on our congenial ardour for Liberty.

But if these reasonable and joyful hopes should fatally be disappointed, it will afford us at least some satisfaction to know, that the principles on which we have founded our opposition to the late Acts of Parliament, are the principles of justice and freedom, and of the British constitution. If our righteous struggle shall be attended with misfortunes, we will reflect with exultation on the noble cause of them; and while suffering unmerited distress, think ourselves superior to the proudest slaves. On the contrary, if we shall be re-instated in the enjoyment of those rights, to which we are entitled by the supreme and controulable laws of nature, and the fundamental principles of the British constitution, we shall reap the glorious fruit of our labours; and we shall, at the same time, give to the world, and to posterity, an instructive example, that the cause of liberty ought not to be despaired of, and that a generous contention in that cause is not always unattended with success.

The foregoing Considerations have induced me to publish a few remarks on the important question, with which I introduced this Essay.

Those who allege that the Parliament of Great Britain have power to make Laws binding the American Colonies, reason in the following manner: "That there is and must be in every state a supreme, irresistible, absolute, uncontrouled authority, in which the *jura summi imperii*, or the rights of sovereignty reside:"* "That this supreme power, is, by the Constitution of Great-Britain, vested in the King, Lords, and Commons:"† "That, therefore, the Acts of the King, Lords, and Commons, or, in other words, Acts of Parliament, have, by the British Constitution, a binding Force on the American Colonies, they composing a part of the British Empire."

I admit that the principle, on which this argument is founded, is of great importance: Its importance, however, is derived from its tendency to promote the ultimate end of all government. But if the application of it would, in *any* instance, destroy, instead of promoting that end, it ought, in *that* instance to be rejected: For to admit it, would be to sacrifice the end to the means, which are valuable only so far as they advance it.

All men are, by nature, equal and free: No one has a right to any authority over another without his consent: All lawful government is founded on the consent of those, who are subject to it: Such consent was given with a view to ensure and to encrease the happiness of the governed above what they could enjoy in an independant and unconnected state of nature. The

* Blackstone, 48, 49.
† Ibid. 50, 51.

consequence is, that the happiness of the society is the FIRST law of every government.*

This rule is founded on the law of nature: It must control every political maxim: it must regulate the Legislature itself.[†] The people have a right to insist that this rule be served; and are entitled to demand a moral security that the Legislature will observe it. If they have not the first, they are slaves; if they have not the second, they are, every moment, exposed to slavery. For "civil liberty is nothing else but natural liberty, divested of that part which constituted the independance of individuals by the authority which it confers on sovereigns, attended with a right of insisting upon their making a good use of their authority, and with a moral security that this right will have its effect."[‡]

Let me now be permitted to ask—Will it ensure and encrease the happiness of the American Colonies, that the Parliament of Great-Britain should possess a supreme irresistible uncontroled authority over them?—Is such an authority consistent with their liberty? Have they any security that it will be employed only for their good? Such a security is absolutely necessary. Parliaments are not infallible: They are not always just. The members, of whom they are composed, are human; and, therefore, they may err: They are influenced by interest; and, therefore, they may deviate from their duty. The acts of the body must depend upon the opinions and dispositions of the members: The acts of the body may, then, be the result of error, and of vice. It is no breach of decency to suppose all this: The British Constitution supposes it: "It supposes that Parliaments may betray their trust, and provides, as far as human wisdom can provide, that they may not be able to do so long, without a sufficient control."[§] Without provisions for this purpose, the temple of British liberty, like a structure of ice, would

---

* The right of sovereignty is that of commanding finally—but in order to procure real felicity; for if this end is not obtained, sovereignty ceases to be a legitimate authority. BURL. 32.
[†] The law of nature is superior in obligation to any other. BLACKSTONE 41.
[‡] BURLAMAQUI.
[§] Dissert. on parties. Let. II. 12.

instantly dissolve before the fire of oppression and despotic sway.

It will be very material to consider the several securities, which the inhabitants of Great-Britain have, that their liberty will not be destroyed by the legislature, in whose hands it is entrusted. If it shall appear, that the same securities are not enjoyed by the Colonists; the undeniable consequence will be, that the Colonists are not under the same obligations to entrust their liberties into the hands of the same legislature: For the Colonists are entitled to *all* * the privileges of Britons. We have committed no crimes to forfeit them: We have too much spirit to resign them. We will leave our posterity as free as our ancestors left us.

To give to any thing that passeth in Parliament the force of a law, the consent of the King, of the Lords, and of the Commons† is absolutely necessary.‡ If, then, the inhabitants of Great Britain possess a sufficient restraint upon *any* of these branches of the legislature, their liberty is secure, provided they be not wanting to themselves. Let us take a view of the restraints, which they have upon the *House of Commons.*

They elect the members of that House. "Magistrates, says Montisquieu, are properly theirs, who have the nomination of them." The members of the House of Commons, therefore, elected by the people, are the magistrates of the people; and are bound, by the ties of gratitude for the honour and confidence conferred upon them, to consult the interest of their constituents.

The power of elections has ever been regarded as a point of the last consequence to all free governments.§ The independant exercise of that power is justly deemed the strongest

---

* As the law is the birthright of every subject, so wheresoever they go, they carry their laws with them. 2. WILLIAM's reports. 75.

† The Commons of England have a great and considerable right in the Government; and a share in the Legislature without whom no law pass. Lord RAYMOND's reports. 950.

‡ 4. Institute. 25.

§ The Athenians, justly jealous of this important privilege, punished, with death, every stranger who presumed to interfere in the Assemblies of the people.

bulwark of the British liberties.* As such, it has always been an object of great attention to the legislature; and is expressly stipulated with the Prince in the Bill of Rights. All those are excluded from voting, whose poverty is such, that they cannot live independant, and must therefore be subject to the undue influence of their superiors. Such are supposed to have no will of their own; and it is judged improper that they should vote in the representation of a free state. What can exhibit, in a more striking point of view the peculiar care which has been taken, in order to render the election of members of parliament entirely free? It was deemed an insult upon the independant Commons of England, that their uninfluenced suffrages should be adulterated by those, who were not at liberty to speak as they thought, though their interests and inclinations were the same. British liberty, it was thought, could not be effectually secured, unless those who made the laws were freely, and without influence, elected by those, for whom they were made. Upon this principle is reasonably founded the maxim in law—That every one, who is capable of exercising his will, is party, and presumed to consent to an Act of Parliament.

For the same reason that persons, who live dependant upon the will of others, are not admitted to vote in elections, those who are under age, and therefore incapable of judging; those who are convicted of perjury or subornation of perjury, and therefore unworthy of judging; and, those who obtain their freeholds by fraudulent conveyances, and would therefore vote to serve infamous purposes, are all likewise excluded from the enjoyment of this great privilege. Corruption at elections is guarded against by the strictest precautions, and most severe penalties. Every elector, before he polls, must, if demanded by a candidate or by two electors, take the oath against bribery, as prescribed by 2. Geo. 2. c. 24. Officers of the excise, of the customs, and of the post-offices—Officers concerned in the duties

---

* The English freedom will be at an end whenever the Court invades the free Election of Parliaments. RAPIN.

A right that a man has to give his vote at the election of a person to represent him in Parliament, there to concur to the making of laws, *which are to bind his Liberty and Property*, is a most transcendant thing and of an high nature. Lord RAYMOND's reports. 953.

upon leather, soap, paper, striped linens imported, hackney coaches, cards and dice, are restrained from interfering in elections under the penalty of £ 100 and of being incapable of ever exercising any office of trust under the King.

Thus is the freedom of elections secured from the *servility*, the *ignorance*, and the *corruption* of the electors; and from the interposition of officers depending immediately upon the Crown. But this is not all. Provisions, equally salutary, have been made concerning the qualifications of those, who shall be elected. All imaginable care has been taken, that the Commons of Great-Britain may be neither *awed*, nor *allured*, nor *deceived* into any nomination inconsistent with their liberties.

It has been adopted as a general maxim; that the Crown will take advantage of every opportunity of extending its prerogative in opposition to the privileges of the people; that it is the interest of those who have *pensions*, or *offices at will* from the Crown, to concur in all its measures; that mankind in general will prefer their private interest to the good of their country; and that, consequently, those who enjoy such pensions or offices are unfit to represent a free nation, and to have the care of their liberties committed to their hands.* All such officers or pensioners are declared incapable of being elected Members of the House of Commons.

But these are not the only checks which the Commons of Great Britain have upon the conduct of those, whom they elect to represent them in Parliament. The interest of the Representatives is the same with that of their constituents. Every measure, that is prejudicial to the nation, must be prejudicial to *them*, and their posterity. They cannot betray their electors, without, at the same time, injuring themselves. They must join in bearing the burthen of every oppressive act; and participate in the happy effects of every wise and good law. Influenced by these considerations, they will seriously and with attention examine every measure proposed to them; they will behold it in every light, and extend their views to its most distant consequences. If, after the most mature deliberation, they find it will be conducive to the welfare of their country, they will support

---

* There are a few exceptions in the case of officers at will.

it with ardour: If, on the contrary, it appears to be of a danger-ous and destructive nature, they will oppose it with firmness.

Every social and generous affection concurs with their inter-est in animating the representatives of the Commons of Great Britain to an honest and faithful discharge of their important trust. In each patriotic effort, the heart-felt satisfaction of hav-ing acted a worthy part vibrates in delightful unison with the applause of their countrymen, who never fail to express their warmest acknowledgements to the friends and benefactors of their country. How pleasing are those rewards! How much to be preferred to that paltry wealth, which is sometimes pro-cured by meanness and treachery! I say *sometimes*; for mean-ness and treachery do not always obtain even *that* pitiful reward. The most useful ministers to the crown, and therefore the most likely to be employed, especially in great emergencies, are those who are best beloved by the people; and those only are beloved by the people, who act steadily and uniformly in support of their liberties. Patriots, therefore, have frequently, and especially upon important occasions, the best chance of being advanced to offices of profit and power. An abject com-pliance with the will of a imperious Prince, and a ready dispo-sition to sacrifice every duty to his pleasure, are sometimes, I confess, the steps, by which only men can expect to rise to wealth and titles. Let us suppose, that in this manner, they are successful in attaining them. Is the despicable prize a sufficient recompence for submitting to the infamous means, by which it was procured; and for the torturing remorse, with which the possession of it must be accompanied? Will it compensate for the merited curses of the nation and of posterity?

These must be very strong checks upon the conduct of every man, who is not utterly lost to all sense of praise and blame. Few will expose themselves to the *just* abhorrence of those, among whom they live; and to the excruciating sensations, which such abhorrence must produce.

But lest all those motives, powerful as they are, should be insufficient to animate the representatives of the nation to a vigorous and upright discharge of their duty, and to restrain them from yielding to any temptation, that would incite them to betray their trust; their constituents have still a farther secu-rity for their liberties in the frequent election of Parliaments.

At the expiration of every Parliament, the people can make a distinction between those who have served them well, and those who have neglected or betrayed their interest: They can bestow, unasked, their suffrages upon the former in the new election; and can mark the latter with disgrace, by a mortifying refusal. The constitution is thus frequently renewed and drawn back, as it were, to its first principles; which is the most effectual method of perpetuating the liberties of a state. The people have numerous opportunities of displaying their just importance, and of exercising, in person, these natural rights. The representatives are reminded whose creatures they are; and to whom they are accountable for the use of that power, which is delegated unto them. The first maxims of jurisprudence are ever kept in view—THAT ALL POWER IS DERIVED FROM THE PEOPLE—THAT THEIR HAPPINESS IS THE END OF GOVERNMENT.

Frequent new Parliaments are a part of the British constitution: By them only the King can know the immediate sense of the nation. Every supply, which they grant, is justly to be considered as a testimony of the loyalty and affection, which the nation bear to their Sovereign; and by this means a mutual confidence is created between the King and his subjects. How pleasing must such an intercourse of benefits be! How must a father of his people rejoice in such dutiful returns for his paternal care! With what ardour must his people embrace every opportunity of giving such convincing proofs, that they are not insensible of his wise and indulgent rule!

Long Parliaments have always been prejudicial to the Prince, who summoned them, or to the people, who elected them. In that called by King Charles I, in the year 1640, the Commons proceeded at first, with vigour and a true patriotic spirit, to rescue the kingdom from the oppression, under which it then groaned—to retrieve the liberties of the people, and establish them on the surest foundations—and to remove or prevent the pernicious consequences, which had arisen, or which, they dreaded, might arise from the tyrannical exercise of prerogative. They abolished the courts of the star chamber and high commission: They reduced the forrests to their antient bounds: They repealed the oppressive statutes concerning knighthood: They declared the tax of ship-money to be illegal: They presented the petition of rights, and obtained a ratification of it from the crown. But when the King unadvisedly passed an Act to continue them till such time as they should please to dissolve themselves how soon—how fatally did their conduct change! In what misery did they involve their country! Those very men, who, while they had only a constitutional power, seemed to have no other aim but to secure and improve the liberty and felicity of their constituents; and to render their Sovereign the glorious ruler of a free and happy people—those very men, after they became independant of the King and of their electors, sacrificed both to that inordinate power, which had been given them. A regard for the public was now no longer the spring of their actions: Their only view was to aggrandize themselves, and to establish their grandeur on the ruins of their country. Their views unhappily were accomplished. They over-turned the constitution from its very foundation; and converted into rods of oppression those instruments of power, which had been put into their hands for the welfare of the state; but which those, who had formerly given them, could not now re-assume. What an instructive example is this! How alarming to those, who have no influence over their legislators—who have no security but that power, which was originally derived from the people, and was delegated for their preservation, may be abused for their destruction! Kings are not the only tyrants: The conduct of the long Parliament will justify me in adding, that Kings are not the severest tyrants.

At the Restoration, care was taken to reduce the House of Commons to a proper dependance on the King: but immediately after their election they lost all dependance upon their constituents, because they continued during the pleasure of the Crown. The effects soon dreadfully appeared in the long Parliament under Charles IId. They seemed disposed ingloriously to surrender those liberties, for which their ancestors had planned, and fought and bled: And it was owing to the wisdom and integrity of two virtuous Ministers of the Crown,* that the Commons of England were not reduced to a state of slavery and wretchedness by the treachery of their own representatives, whom they had indeed elected, but whom they could

* The Earls of Clarendon and Southampton.

not remove. Secure of their seats, while they gratified the Crown, the Members bartered the liberties of the nation for places and pensions; and threw into the scale of prerogative all that weight, which they derived from the people, in order to counter-balance it.

It was not till some years after the Revolution, that the people could rely on the faithfulness of their Representatives, or punish their perfidy. By the Statute 6. W. and M. c. 2. it was enacted, that Parliaments should not continue longer than *three* years. The insecure situation of the first Prince of the *Hanoverian* line, surrounded with rivals and with enemies, induced the Parliament, soon after his accession to the throne, to prolong this term to that of *seven* years. Attempts have since that time been frequently made to reduce the continuance of Parliaments to the former term: And such attempts have always been well received by the nation. Undoubtedly they deserve such reception: For long Parliaments will naturally forget their dependance on the people: When this dependance is forgotten, they will become corrupt: "Whenever they become corrupt, the Constitution of England will lose its liberty—it will perish."*

Such is the provision made by the Laws of Great Britain, that the Commons should be faithfully represented: Provision is also made, that faithful Representatives should not labour for their constituents in vain. The Constitution is formed in such a manner, that the House of Commons are *able* as well as *willing* to protect and defend the liberties entrusted to their care.

The Constitution of Great-Britain is that of a limited monarchy; and in all limited monarchies, the power of preserving the limitations must be placed somewhere. During the reigns of

---

* MONTESQ. b. 11. c. 6.

If the legislative body were perpetual; or might last for the life of the Prince who convened them, as formerly and were so to be supplied by occasionally filling the vacancies with new representatives; in these cases, if it were once corrupted, the evil would be past remedy: But when different bodies succeed each other, if the people see cause to disapprove of the present, they may rectify its faults in the next. A legislative Assembly also, which is sure to be separated again, will think themselves bound in interest as well as duty to make only such laws as are good. BLACKSTONE, 189.

the first Norman Princes, this power seems to have resided in the Clergy and in the Barons by turns. But it was lodged very improperly. The Clergy zealous only for the dignity and pre-eminence of the church, neglected and despised the people, whom, with the soil they tilled, they would willingly have considered as the patrimony of St. Peter. Attached to a foreign jurisdiction, and aspiring at an entire independance of the civil powers, they looked upon the prerogatives of the Crown as so many obstacles in the way of their favourite scheme of supreme ecclesiastical dominion; and therefore seised, with eagerness, every occasion of sacrificing the interests of their sovereign to those of the Pope. Enemies alike to their King and to their country, their sole and unvaried aim was to reduce both to the most abject state of submission and slavery. The means employed by them to accomplish their pernicious purposes were, sometimes, to work upon the superstition of the people, and direct it against the power of the Prince; and, at other times, to work upon the superstition of the Prince, and direct it against the liberties of the people.

The power of preserving the limitations of monarchy for the purposes of liberty was not more properly placed in the Barons. Domineering and turbulent, they oppressed their vassals, and treated them as slaves; they opposed their Prince, and were impatient of every legal restraint. Capricious and inconstant, they sometimes abetted the King in his projects of tyranny; and, at other times, excited the people to insurrections and tumults. For these reasons, the Constitution was ever fluctuating from one extreme to another; Now despotism—now anarchy prevailed.

But after the representatives of the Commons began to sit in a separate House, to be considered as a distinct branch of the legislature; and as such, to be invested with separate and independant powers and privileges; then the constitution assumed a very different appearance. Having no interest contrary to that of the people, from among whom they were chosen, and with whom, after the session, they were again to mix, they had no views inconsistent with the liberty of their constituents, and therefore could have no motives to betray it. Sensible that prerogative, or a discretionary power of acting where the laws are silent, is absolutely necessary, and that this prerogative is most properly entrusted to the executor of the laws, they did not oppose the exercise of it, while it was directed towards the accomplishment of its original end: But sensible likewise, that the good of the state was this original end, they resisted, with vigour, every arbitrary measure, repugnant to law, and unsupported by maxims of public freedom or utility.

The checks, which they possessed over prerogative, were calm and gentle—operating with a secret, but effectual force—unlike the impetuous resistance of factious Barons, or the boisterous fulminations of ambitious Prelates.

One of the most ancient maxims of the English law is, That no freeman can be taxed at pleasure.* But taxes on freemen were absolutely necessary to defray the extraordinary charges of government. The consent of the freemen was, therefore, of necessity to be obtained. Numerous as they were, they could not assemble to give their consent in their proper persons; and for this reason, it was directed by the constitution, that they should give it by their representatives chosen by and out of themselves. Hence the indisputable and peculiar privilege of the House of Commons to grant taxes.[†]

This is the source of that mild but powerful influence, which the commons of Great-Britain possess over the Crown. In this consists their security, that prerogative, intended for their benefit, will never be exerted for their ruin. By calmly and constitutionally refusing supplies, or by granting them only on certain conditions, they have corrected the extravagancies of some Princes, and have tempered the head-strong nature of others; they have checked the progress of arbitrary power, and have supported with honour to themselves, and with advantage to the nation, the character of grand inquisitors of the realm. The proudest Ministers of the proudest Monarchs have trembled at their censures; and have appeared at the bar of the House to give an account of their conduct, and ask pardon for their faults. Those Princes, who have favoured Liberty, and

---

* Bacon's Abridgment of the law, 568.

[†] *Note*, It is said in divers records, "per communitatem Angliæ probis concess." Because all grants of subsidies or aids by Parliament do begin in the House of Commons, and first granted by them: also because in effect the whole profit which the King reapeth, doth come from the Commons. Coke's Institutes, 29.

thrown themselves upon the affections of their people, have ever found that Liberty, which they favoured, and those affections which they cultivated, the firmest foundations of their throne, and the most solid support of their power. The purses of their people have been ever open to supply their exigencies: Their swords have been ever ready to vindicate their honour. On the contrary, those Princes, who, insensible to the glory and advantage of ruling a free people, have preferred to a willing obedience the abject submission of slaves, have ever experienced, that all endeavours to render themselves absolute were but so many steps to their own downfall.

Such is the admirable temperament of the British constitution! Such the glorious fabric of Britain's liberty—the pride of her citizens—the envy of her neighbours—planned by her legislators—erected by her patriots—maintained entire by numerous generations past! May it be maintained entire by numerous generations to come!

Can the Americans, who are descended from British ancestors, and inherit *all* their rights, be blamed—can they be blamed BY THEIR BRETHREN IN BRITAIN—for claiming still to enjoy those rights? But can they enjoy them, if they are bound by the Acts of a British Parliament? Upon what principle does the British Parliament found their power? Is it founded upon the prerogative of the King? His prerogative does not extend to make laws to bind any of his subjects. Does it reside in the House of Lords? The Peers are a collective, and not a representative body. If it resides any where, then, it must reside in the House of Commons.

Should any one object here, that it does not reside in the House of Commons *only*, because that House cannot make laws without the consent of the King and of the Lords; the answer is easy. Though the concurrence of all the branches of the Legislature is necessary to every law; yet the same laws bind different persons for different reasons, and on different principles. The King is bound, because he assented to them. The Lords are bound, because they voted for them. The Representatives of the Commons, for the same reason, bind themselves, and those whom they represent.

If the Americans are bound neither by the assent of the King, nor by the votes of the Lords to obey Acts of the British

Parliament, the *sole* reason, why they are bound, is, because the representatives of the Commons of Great-Britain have given their suffrages in favour of those Acts.* But are the Representatives of the Commons of Great Britain the Representatives of the Americans? Are they elected by the Americans? Are they such as the Americans, if they had the power of election, would probably elect? Do they know the interest of the Americans? Does their own interest prompt them to pursue the interest of the Americans? If they do not pursue it, have the Americans power to punish them? Can the Americans remove unfaithful members at every new election? Can members, whom the Americans do not elect; with whom the Americans are not connected in interest; whom the Americans cannot remove; over whom the Americans have no influence.—Can such Members be stiled, with any propriety, the magistrates of the Americans? Have those, who are bound by the laws of magistrates not their own, any security for the enjoyment of their absolute rights—those rights, "which every man is entitled to enjoy, whether in society or out of it?"† Is it probable that those rights will be maintained? Is it "the primary end of government to maintain them?"‡ Shall this primary end be *frustrated* by a political maxim intended to *promote* it?

But from what source does this mighty, this uncontrouled authority of the House of Commons flow? From the collective body of the Commons of Great-Britain. This authority must therefore originally reside in them: For whatever they convey to their representatives, must ultimately be in themselves.§ And have those, whom we have hitherto been accustomed to consider as our fellow subjects, an absolute and unlimited power over us? Have they a natural right to make laws, by which we may be deprived of our properties, of our liberties, of our lives? By what title do they claim to be our masters?

---

* This is allowed even by the advocates for parliamentary power; who account for its extension over the Colonies upon the very absurd principle of their being *virtually* represented in the House of Commons.
† Blackstone, 123.
‡ Blackstone, 124.
§ It is self-evident that the power, with relation to the part we bear in the legislation, is absolutely, is solely in the electors. We have no legislative authority but what we derive from them. Debates of the Commons, vol. 6. p. 75.

What act of ours has rendered us subject to those, to whom we were formerly equal? Is British Freedom denominated from the *soil*, or from the *People* of Britain? If from the latter, do they lose it by quitting the soil? Do those, who embark, free-men, in Great-Britain, disembark, slaves, in America? Are those, who fled from the oppression of regal and ministerial tyranny, now reduced to a state of vassalage to those, who, then, equally felt the same oppression? Whence proceeds this fatal change? Is this the return made us for leaving our friends and our country—for braving the danger of the deep—for planting a wilderness, inhabited only by savage men and savage beasts—for extending the dominions of the British Crown—for encreasing the trade of the British merchants—for aug-menting the rents of the British landlords—for heightening the wages of the British artificers? Britons should blush to make such a claim: Americans would blush to own it.

It is not, however, the ignominy only, but the danger also, with which we are threatened, that afflicts us. The many and careful provisions which are made by the British Constitution, that the electors of members of Parliament may be prevented from chusing Representatives, who would betray them; and that the Representatives may be prevented from betraying their constituents with impunity, sufficiently evince, that such precautions have been deemed absolutely necessary for secur-ing and maintaining the system of British liberty.

How would the Commons of Great-Britain startle at a pro-posal, to deprive them of their share in the Legislature, by rendering the House of Commons independent of them! With what indignation would they hear it! What resentment would they feel and discover against the authors of it! Yet the Com-mons of Great-Britain would suffer less inconvenience from the execution of such a proposal, than the Americans will suffer from the extension of the legislative authority of Parliament over them.

The Members of Parliament, their families, their friends, their posterity must be subject, as well as others, to the laws. Their interest, and that of their families, friends and posterity cannot be different from the interest of the rest of the nation. A regard to the former will, therefore, direct to such measures as must promote the latter. But is this the case with respect to

America? Are the Legislators of Great-Britain subject to the laws which are made for the Colonies? Is their interest the same with that of the Colonies? If we consider it in a large and comprehensive view, we shall discern it to be undoubtedly the same; but few will take the trouble to consider it in that view; and of those who do, few will be influenced by the consideration. Mankind are usually more affected with a near though inferior interest, than with one, that is superior, but placed at a greater distance. As the conduct is regulated by the passions, it is not to be wondered at, if they secure the former by measures, which will forfeit the latter. Nay the latter will frequently be regarded in the same manner as if it were prejudicial to them. It is with regret that I produce some late regulations of Parliament as proofs of what I have advanced. We have experienced what an easy matter it is for a Minister, with an ordinary share of art, to persuade the Parliament and the people, that taxes laid on the Colonies will ease the burdens of the Mother Country; which, if the matter is considered in a proper light, is, in fact, to persuade them, that the stream of national riches will be encreased by closing up the fountain, from which they flow.

As the Americans cannot avail themselves of that check, which interest puts upon the members of Parliament, and which would operate in favour of the Commons of Great-Britain, though they possessed no power over the Legislature; so the love of reputation, which is a powerful incitement to the Legislators to promote the welfare, and obtain the approbation, of those among whom they live, and whose praises or censures will reach and affect them, may have a contrary operation with regard to the Colonies. It may become popular and reputable at home to oppress us. A candidate may recommend himself at his election by recounting the many successful instances, in which he has sacrificed the interests of America to those of Great-Britain. A Member of the House of Commons may plume himself upon his ingenuity in inventing schemes to serve the Mother Country at the expence of the Colonies; and may boast of their impotent resentment against him on that account.

Let us pause here a little.—Does neither the love of gain, the love of praise nor the love of honour influence the members of the British Parliament in favour of the Americans? On what principles, then—on what motives of action can we depend for the security of our Liberties, of our Properties, of every thing dear to us in Life, of Life itself? Shall we depend on their veneration for the dictates of natural justice? A very little share of experience in the world; a very little degree of knowledge in the history of men will sufficiently convince us, that a regard for justice is by no means the ruling principle in human nature. He would discover himself to be a very sorry statesman, who would erect a system of jurisprudence upon that slender foundation. "He would make," as my Lord Bacon says, "imaginary laws for imaginary commonwealths; and his discourses, like the stars, would give little light, because they are so high."

But this is not the worst that can justly be said concerning the situation of the Colonies, if they are bound by the Acts of the British legislature. So far are those powerful springs of action, which we have mentioned, from interesting the members of that legislature in our favour, that, as has been already observed, we have the greatest reason to dread their operation against us. While the happy Commons of Great-Britain congratulate themselves upon the Liberty, which they enjoy, and upon the provisions—infallible, as far as they can be rendered so by human wisdom—which are made for perpetuating it to their latest posterity; the unhappy Americans have reason to bewail the dangerous situation, to which they are reduced; and to look forward, with dismal apprehension, to those future scenes of woe, which, in all probability, will open upon their descendants.

What has been already advanced, will suffice to shew, that it is repugnant to the essential maxims of jurisprudence, to the ultimate end of all governments, to the genius of the British constitution, and to the liberty and happiness of the Colonies, that they should be bound by the legislative authority of the Parliament of Great-Britain. Such a doctrine is not less repugnant to the voice of her laws. In order to evince this, I shall appeal to some authorities from the books of the law, which shew expressly, or by a necessary implication, that the Colonies are not bound by the Acts of the British Parliament; because they have no share in the British legislature.

The first case I shall mention was adjudged in the 2d year of

Richard IId. It was a solemn determination of all the Judges of England, met in the exchequer-chamber, to consider whether the people in Ireland were bound by an Act of Parliament made in England. They resolved, "That they were not, as to such things as were done in Ireland; but that what they did out of Ireland, must be conformable to the laws of England, because they were the subjects of England. Ireland, said they, has a Parliament, who make laws; and our statutes do not bind them; BECAUSE THEY DO NOT SEND KNIGHTS TO PARLIAMENT: But their persons are the subjects of the King, in the same manner as the inhabitants of *Calais, Gascoigne,* and *Guienne.*"*

This is the first case, which we find in the books upon this subject; and it deserves to be examined with the most minute attention.

1. It appears, that the matter under consideration was deemed, at that time, to be of the greatest importance: For ordinary causes are never adjourned into the Exchequer-Chamber; only such are adjourned there as are of uncommon weight, or of uncommon difficulty. "Into the Exchequer Chamber, says my Lord Coke, all cases of difficulty in the King's Bench, or Common Pleas, &c. are, and of antient time have been, adjourned, and there debated, argued, and resolved, by all the Judges of England and Barons of the Exchequer."† This Court proceeds with the greatest deliberation, and upon the most mature reflection. The case is first argued on both sides by learned Counsel; and then openly on several days, by all the Judges. Resolutions made with so much caution, and founded on so much legal knowledge, may be relied on as the surest evidences of what is law.

2. It is to be observed, that the extent of the legislative authority of Parliament is the very *point* of the adjudication. The decision was not incidental or indigested: It was not a sudden opinion, unsupported by reason and argument: It was an express and deliberate resolution of that very doubt, which they assembled to resolve.

---

*4. Modern Reports. 225. 7. Coke's Reports, 220. Calvin's case.
† Institutes, 110.

3. It is very observable, that the reason, which those reverend sages of the law gave, why the people in Ireland were not bound by an Act of Parliament made in England, was the same with that, on which the Americans have founded their opposition to the late Statutes made concerning them. The Irish did not send Members to Parliament; and, therefore, they were not bound by its Acts. From hence it undeniably appears, that parliamentary authority is derived SOLELY from representation —that those, who are bound by Acts of Parliament, are bound for this ONLY reason, because they are represented in it. If it were not the ONLY reason, parliamentary authority might subsist independent of it. But as parliamentary authority fails wherever this reason does not operate, parliamentary authority can be founded on no other principle. The law never ceases, but when the reason of it ceases also.

4. It deserves to be remarked, that no exception is made of *any* Statutes, which bind those, who are not represented by the makers of them. The resolution of the Judges extends to *every* Statute: They say, without limitation—"our Statutes do not bind them." And indeed the resolution ought to extend to every Statute; because the reason, on which it is founded, extends to every one. If a person is bound, ONLY because he is represented, it must certainly follow that wherever he is *not* represented he is *not* bound. No sound argument can be offered, why one Statute should be obligatory in such circumstances, and not another. If we cannot be deprived of our property by those, whom we do not commission for that purpose; can we, without any such commission, be deprived, by them, of our lives? Have those a right to imprison and gibbet us, who have not a right to tax us?

5. From this authority it follows, that it is by no means a rule, that the authority of Parliament extends to all the subjects of the Crown. The inhabitants of Ireland were the subjects of the King as of his crown of England; But it is expressly resolved, in the most solemn manner, that the inhabitants of Ireland are not bound by the Statutes of England. Allegiance to the King and obedience to the Parliament are founded on very different principles. The former is founded on protection: The latter, on representation. An inattention to this difference

has produced, I apprehend, much uncertainty and confusion in our ideas concerning the connexion, which ought to subsist between Great-Britain and the American Colonies.

6. The last observation, which I shall make on this case, is, that, if the inhabitants of Ireland are not bound by Acts of Parliament made in England; *a fortiori*, the inhabitants of the American Colonies are not bound by them. There are marks of the subordination of Ireland to Great-Britain, which cannot be traced in the Colonies. A writ of error lies from the King's Bench* in Ireland, to the King's Bench, and consequently to the House of Lords, in England; by which means the former kingdom is subject to the control of the Courts of Justice of the latter kingdom. But a writ of error does not lie in the King's Bench, nor before the House of Lords, in England, from the Colonies of America. The proceedings in their Courts of Justice can be reviewed and controled only on an appeal to the King in Council.†

The foregoing important decision, favourable to the liberty of all the dominions of the British crown, that are not represented in the British Parliament, has been corroborated by subsequent adjudications. I shall mention one that was given in the King's Bench in the fifth year of King William and Queen Mary between *Blankard* and *Galdy*.‡

The plaintiff was Provost-Marshal of Jamaica, and, by articles, granted a deputation of that office to the defendant, under an yearly rent. The defendant gave his bond for the performance of the agreement; and an action of debt was brought upon that bond. In bar of the action, the defendant pleaded the Statute of 5. Ed. 6. made against buying and selling of offices that concern the administration of justice, and averred that this office concerned the administration of justice in Jamaica, and that, by virtue of that Statute, both the bond and articles were void. To this plea the plaintiff replied, that Jamaica was an island inhabited formerly by the Spaniards, "that it was conquered by the subjects of the kingdom of England, commissioned by legal and sufficient authority for that

*4. Institute 256.

† BLACKSTONE 108. 231.

‡ SALKELD'S reports, 411. 4. Modern Reports, 215.

purpose; and that since that conquest its inhabitants were regulated and governed by their own proper Laws and Statutes, and not by Acts of Parliament or the Statutes of the kingdom of England." The defendant, in his rejoinder, admits that, before the conquest of Jamaica by the English, the inhabitants were governed by their own laws, but alleges that "since the conquest it was part of the kingdom of England, and governed by the Laws and Statutes of the kingdom of England, and not by Laws and Statutes peculiar to the island." To this rejoinder the plaintiff demurred, and the defendant joined in demurrer.

Here was a cause to be determined judicially upon this single question in law—*Were the Acts of Parliament or Statutes of England in force in Jamaica?* It was argued on the opposite sides by Lawyers of the greatest eminence, before Lord Chief Justice Holt (a name renowned in the law!) and his brethren the Justices of the King's Bench. They unanimously gave judgment for the plaintiff; and, by that judgment, expressly determined— *That the Acts of Parliament or Statutes of England were not in force in Jamaica.* This decision is explicit in favour of America; for whatever was resolved concerning Jamaica is equally applicable to every American Colony.

Some years after the adjudication of this case, another was determined in the King's Bench relating to Virginia; in which, Lord Chief Justice Holt held, that the laws of England did not extend to Virginia.*

I must not be so uncandid as to conceal, that in Calvin's case, where the abovementioned decision of the Judges in the Exchequer Chamber, concerning Ireland, is quoted, it is added, by way of explanation of that authority,—"which is to be understood, unless it (Ireland) be especially named." Nor will I conceal that the same exception† is taken notice of, and seems to be allowed, by the Judges in the other cases relating to America. To any objection that may, hence, be formed against my doctrine, I answer, in the words of the very accurate Mr. Justice Foster, that "general rules thrown out in argument,

---

* Salkeld's Reports, 666.
† This exception does not seem to be taken in the case of II Richard 2, which was the foundation of all the subsequent cases.

and carried farther than the true state of the case then in judgment requireth, have, I confess, no great weight with me."*

The question before the Judges in the cases I have reasoned from, was not how far the naming of persons in an Act of Parliament would affect them; though unless named, they would not be bound by it: The question was, whether the legislative authority of Parliament extended over the inhabitants of Ireland or Jamaica or Virginia. To the resolution of the latter question the resolution of the former was by no means necessary, and was, therefore, wholly impertinent to the point of the adjudication.

But farther; the reason assigned for the resolution of the latter question is solid and convincing: The American Colonies are not bound by the Acts of the British Parliament, because they are not represented in it. But what reason can be assigned why they should be bound by those Acts, in which they are specially named? Does naming them give those, who do them that honor, a right to rule over them? Is this the source of the supreme, the absolute, the irresistable, the uncontrouled authority of Parliament? These positions are too absurd to be alledged; and a thousand judicial determinations in their favour would never induce one man of sense to subscribe his assent to them.†

The obligatory force of the British statutes upon the Colonies, when named in them, must be accounted for, by the advocates of that power, upon some other principle. In my Lord

---

* Foster's Crown Law, 313.

†Where a decision is manifestly absurd and unjust, such a sentence is *not law*. Blackstone, 70.

The legality of the opinion; "That the people in Ireland were bound by the statutes of England, when particularly named by them," seems afterwards to have been doubted of by Lord Coke himself, in another place of his works. After having mentioned the resolution in the Exchequer Chamber in the time of Richard IId. and having taken notice that question is made of it in some of the books, and particularly in Calvin's case, he says, "That the question concerning the binding force of English statutes over Ireland is now by common experience and opinion without any scruple resolved; That the Acts of Parliament, made in England, since the Act of the 10th H. 7, (he makes no exceptions) do not bind them in Ireland; but all Acts made in England before 10 H. 7, BY THE SAID ACT MADE IN IRELAND, AN. 10, H. 7, C. 22, do bind them in Ireland." 12 Report, 111.

Coke's Reports, it is said, "That albeit Ireland be a distinct dominion, *yet, the title thereof being by conquest*, the same, by judgment of law, may be, by express words, bound by the Parliaments of England." In *this* instance, the obligatory authority of the Parliament is plainly referred to a *title by conquest*, as its foundation and original. In the instances relating to the Colonies this authority seems to be referred to the same source: For any one, who compares what is said of Ireland, and other conquered countries, in Calvin's case, with what is said of America, in the adjudications concerning it, will find that the Judges, in determining the latter, have grounded their opinions on the resolutions given in the former.* It is foreign to my purpose to enquire into the reasonableness of founding the authority of the British Parliament over Ireland upon the title of conquest though I believe it would be somewhat difficult to deduce it satisfactorily in this manner. It will be sufficient for me to shew, that it is unreasonable, and injurious to the Colonies to extend that title to them. How come the Colonists to be a conquered people? By whom was the conquest over them obtained? By the House of Commons? By the constituents of that House? If the idea of conquest must be taken into consideration when we examine into the title by which America is held, that idea, so far as it can operate, will operate in favour of the Colonists, and not against them. Permitted and commissioned by the Crown, they undertook, at their own expence, expeditions to this distant country, took

---

* It is plain that Blackstone understood the opinion of the Judges—that the Colonies are bound by Acts of the British Parliament, if named in them—to be founded on the principle of conquest. It will not be improper to insert his commentary upon the resolutions respecting America. "Besides these adjacent islands (Jersey, &c.) our more distant Plantations in America and elsewhere are also, in some respects, subject to the English laws. Plantations, or Colonies in distant countries, are either such where the lands are claimed in right of occupancy only, by finding them desart and uncultivated, and peopling them from the Mother-Country; or when already cultivated, they have been either gained by conquest, or ceded to us by treaties. Our American plantations are principally of this latter sort; being obtained in the last century, either *by right of conquest*, and driving out the natives (with what natural justice I shall not at present enquire) or by treaties.

Lord Chief Justice HOLT, in a case above-cited, calls Virginia a conquered country.

possession of it, planted it, and cultivated it. Secure under the protection of their King, they grew and multiplied, and diffused British freedom and British spirit, wherever they came. Happy in the enjoyment of liberty, and in reaping the fruits of their toils; but still more happy in the joyful prospect of transmitting their liberty and their fortunes to the latest posterity, they inculcated to their children the warmest sentiments of loyalty to their sovereign, under whose auspices they enjoyed so many blessings, and of affection and esteem for the inhabitants of the Mother Country, with whom they gloried in being intimately connected. Lessons of loyalty to Parliament indeed, they never gave: They never suspected that such unheard of loyalty would be required. They never suspected that their descendants would be considered and treated as a conquered people; and therefore they never taught them the submission and abject behaviour suited to that character.

I am sufficiently aware of an objection, that will be made to what I have said concerning the legislative authority of the British Parliament. It will be alleged, that I throw off all dependance on Great-Britain. This objection will be held forth, in its most specious colours, by those, who, from servility of soul, or from mercenary considerations, would meanly bow their necks to every exertion of arbitrary power: It may likewise alarm some, who entertain the most favourable opinion of the connexion between Great-Britain and her Colonies; but who are not sufficiently acquainted with the nature of that connexion, which is so dear to them. Those of the first class, I hope, are few; I am sure they are contemptible, and deserve to have very little regard paid to them: But for the sake of those of the second class, who may be more numerous, and whose laudable principles atone for their mistakes, I shall take some pains to obviate the objection, and to shew that a denial of the legislative authority of the British Parliament over America is by no means inconsistent with that connexion, which ought to subsist between the Mother Country and her Colonies, and which, at the first settlement of those Colonies, it was intended to maintain between them: But that, on the contrary, that connexion would be intirely destroyed by the extension of the power of Parliament over the American plantations.

Let us examine what is meant by a *Dependance* on Great-

Britain: For it is always of importance clearly to define the terms that we use. Blackstone, who, speaking of the Colonies, tells us, that "they are no part of the Mother Country, but distinct (though *dependant*) dominions,"* explains dependance in this manner. "Dependance is very little else, but an obligation to conform to the will or law of that superior person or state, upon which the inferior depends." "The original and true ground of this superiority in the case of Ireland, is what we usually call, though somewhat improperly, the right of conquest; a right allowed by the law of nations, if not by that of nature; but which, in reason and civil policy, can mean nothing more, than that, in order to put an end to hostilities, a compact is either expressly or tacitly made between the conqueror and the conquered, that if they will acknowlege the victor for their master, he will treat them for the future as subjects, and not as enemies."†

The original and true ground of the superiority of Great-Britain over the American Colonies is not shewn in any book of the law, unless, as I have already observed, it be derived from the right of conquest. But I have proved, and I hope satisfactorily, that this right is altogether inapplicable to the Colonists. The original of the superiority of Great-Britain over the Colonies is, then, unaccounted for; and when we consider the ingenuity and pains which have lately been employed at home on this subject, we may justly conclude, that the only reason why it *is* not accounted for, is, that it *cannot* be accounted for. The superiority of Great-Britain over the Colonies ought, therefore, to be rejected; and the dependence of the Colonies on her, if it is to be construed into "an obligation to conform to the will or law of the superior state," ought, in *this* sense, to be rejected also.

My sentiments concerning this matter are not so singular. They coincide with the declarations and remonstrances of the Colonies against the statutes imposing taxes on them. It was their unanimous opinion, that the Parliament have no *right* to exact obedience to those statutes; and, consequently, that the Colonies are under no *obligation* to obey them. The dependence of the

* Blackstone, 107.
† Ibid. 103.

Colonies on Great-Britain was denied in those instances; but a denial of it in those instances is, in effect, a denial of it in all other instances. For, if dependence is an obligation to conform to the will or law of the superior state; any exceptions to that obligation must destroy the dependence. If, therefore, by a dependence of the Colonies on Great-Britain, it is meant, that they are obliged to obey the laws of Great-Britain, reason, as well as the unanimous voice of the Americans, teaches us to disown it. Such a dependence was never thought of by those who left Britain, in order to settle in America; nor by their Sovereigns, who gave them commissions for that purpose. Such an *obligation* has no correspondent *right*: For the Commons of Great-Britain have no dominion over their equals and fellow subjects in America: They can confer no right to their delegates to bind those equals and fellow subjects by laws.

There is another, and a much more reasonable meaning, which may be intended by the dependence of the Colonies on Great-Britain. The phrase may be used to denote the obedience and loyalty, which the Colonists owe to the *Kings* of Great-Britain. If it should be alledged, that this cannot be the meaning of the expression, because it is applied to the *kingdom*, and not to the *King*, I give the same answer that my Lord Bacon gave to those, who said that allegiance related to the *kingdom* and not to the *King*; because in the statutes there are these words: "born within the allegiance of *England*," and again, "born without the allegiance of *England*." "There is no trope of speech more familiar, says he, than to use the *place* of addition for the *person*. So we say commonly, the line of York, or the line of Lancaster, for the lines of the Duke of York, or the Duke of Lancaster. So we say the possessions of Somerset or Warwick, intending the possessions of the Dukes of Somerset, or Earls of Warwick. And in the very same manner, the statute speaks, allegiance of England, for allegiance of the King of England."*

Dependence of the Mother Country seems to have been understood in this sense, both by the first planters of the Colonies, and also by the most eminent Lawyers, at that time, in England.

Those who launched into the unknown deep, in quest of

*4. Bacon's works, 192, 193. Case of the postnati of Scotland.

new countries and habitations, still considered themselves as subjects of the English Monarchs, and behaved suitably to that character; but it no where appears, that they still considered themselves as represented in an English Parliament, or that they thought the authority of the English Parliament extended over them. They took possession of the country in the *King's* name: They treated, or made war with the Indians by *his* authority: They held the lands under *his* grants, and paid *him* the rents reserved upon them: They established governments under the sanction of *his* prerogative, or by virtue of his charters. No application for those purposes was made to the Parliament: No ratification of the charters or letters patent was solicited from that Assembly, as is usual in England with regard to grants and franchises of much less importance.

My Lord Bacon's sentiments on this subject ought to have great weight with us. His immense genius, his universal learning, his deep insight into the laws and constitution of England are well known and much admired. Besides, he lived at that time when settling and improving the American Plantations began seriously to be attended to, and successfully to be carried into execution.* Plans for the government and regulation of the Colonies were then forming; and it is only from the first general idea of these plans that we can unfold, with precision and accuracy, all the more minute and intricate parts, of which they now consist. "The settlement of Colonies, says he, must proceed from the option of those, who will settle them, else it sounds like an exile: They must be raised by the *leave*, and not by the *command* of the *King*. At their setting out, they must have their commission, or letters patents from the *King*, that so they may acknowledge their DEPENDENCY UPON THE CROWN of England, and under his protection." In another place he says, "that they still must be *subjects* of the realm"[†] "In order to regulate all the inconveniencies, which will insensible grow upon them," he proposes, "that the King should erect a subordinate

* During the reign of Queen Elizabeth, America was chiefly valued on account of its mines. It was not till the reign of James I. that any vigorous attempts were made to clear and improve the soil.
† The Parliament have no subjects. My Lord Bacon gives in this expression, an instance of the trope of speech beforementioned. He says, the subjects of the '*realm*', when he means the subjects of the *king* of the realm.

council in England, whose care and charge shall be, to advise, and put in execution, all things which shall be found fit for the good of those new Plantations; who, upon all occasions, shall give an account of their proceedings to the *King* or to the *Council-Board*, and from THEM receive such directions, as may best agree with the government of that place."* It is evident, from these quotations, that my Lord Bacon had no conception, that the Parliament *would* or *ought* to interpose† either in the settlement or the government of the Colonies. The only relation, in which he says, the Colonists must still continue, is that of subjects: The only dependency, which they ought to acknowledge, is a dependency on the Crown.

This is a dependence, which they have acknowledged hitherto; which they acknowledge now; and which, if it is reasonable to judge of the future by the past and the present, they will continue to acknowledge hereafter. It is not a dependence, like that contended for on Parliament, slavish and unaccountable, or accounted for only by principles, that are false and inapplicable: It is a dependence founded upon the principles of reason, of liberty, and of law. Let us investigate its sources.

The Colonists ought to be dependent on the King, because they have hitherto enjoyed, and still continue to enjoy his protection. Allegiance is the faith and obedience, which every subject owes to his Prince. This obedience is founded on the protection derived from government: For protection and allegiance are the reciprocal bonds, which connect the Prince and his subjects.‡ Every subject, so soon as he is born, is under the royal protection, and is entitled to all the advantages arising from it. He therefore, owes obedience to that royal power, from which the protection, which he enjoys, is derived. But while he continues in infancy and non-age, he cannot perform the duties which his allegiance requires. The performance of

---

* 1. Bacon's works, 725, 726.
† It was chiefly during the confusions of the republic, when the King was in exile, and unable to assert his rights, that the House of Commons began to interfere in Colony matters.
‡ Between the Sovereign and subject there is duplex et reciprocum ligamen; quia sicut subditus Regi tenetur ad obedientiam; ita Rex subdito tenetur ad protectionem: Merito igitur ligeantia dicitur a ligando, quia continet in se duplex legamen. 7 Report. 5a. CALVIN's Case.

them must be respited till he arrive at the years of discretion and maturity. When he arrives at those years, he owes obedience, not only for the protection, which he now enjoys; but also for that, which, from his birth, he has enjoyed; and to which his tender age has hitherto prevented him from making a suitable return. Allegiance now becomes a duty founded upon principles of gratitude, as well as on principles of interest: It becomes a debt, which nothing but the loyalty of a whole life will discharge.* As neither climate, nor soil, nor time entitle a person to the benefits of a subject; so an alteration of climate or soil or of time cannot release him from the duties of one. An Englishman, who removes to foreign countries, however distant from England, owes the same allegiance to his King there which he owed to him at home; and will owe it twenty years hence as much as he owes it now. Wherever he is, he is still liable to the punishment annexed by law to crimes against his allegiance; and still entitled to the advantages promised by law to the duties of it: It is not *cancelled*; and it is not *forfeited*. "Hence all children born in any parts of the world, if they be of English parents continuing at that time as liege subjects to the King, and having done no act to forfeit the benefit of their allegiance, are ipsa facto naturalized: And if they have issue and their descendants intermarry among themselves, such descendants are naturalized to all generations."†

Thus we see, that the subjects of the King, though they reside in foreign countries, still owe the duties of allegiance, and are still entitled to the advantages of it. They transmit to their posterity the privilege of naturalization, and all the other privileges which are the consequences of it.‡

---

* The King is protector of all his subjects: In virtue of this high trust, he is more particularly to take care of those who are not able to take care of themselves, consequently of infants, who, by reason of their nonage, are under incapacities; from hence natural allegiance arises, as a debt of gratitude, which can never be cancelled, though the subject owing it goes out of the kingdom, or swears allegiance to another Prince. 2. WILLIAM's Reports, 123, 124.

† BACON's Argument in the case of postnati of Scotland.

‡ Natural born subjects have a great variety of rights, which they acquire by being born in the King's legiance, and can never forfeit by any distance of place or time, but only by their own misbehaviour; the explanation of which rights is the principal subject of the law. BLACKSTONE. 371.

Now we have explained the dependence of the Americans. They are the subjects of the King of Great-Britain. They owe him allegiance. They have a right to the benefits which arise from preserving that allegiance inviolate. They are liable to the punishments which await those who break it. This is a dependence, which they have always boasted of. The principles of loyalty are deeply rooted in their hearts; and there they will grow and bring forth fruit, while a drop of vital blood remains to nourish them. Their history is not stained with rebellions, and treasonable machinations: An inviolable attachment to their sovereign, and the warmest zeal for his glory shine in every page.

From this dependence, abstracted from every other source, arises a strict connection between the inhabitants of Great-Britain and those of America. They are fellow subjects; they are under allegiance to the same Prince; and this union of allegiance naturally produces an union of hearts. It is also productive of an union of measures through the whole British dominion. To the King is entrusted the direction and management of the great machine of government. He therefore is fittest to adjust the different wheels, and to regulate their motions in such a manner as to co-operate in the same general designs. He makes war: He concludes peace: He forms alliances: He regulates domestic trade by his prerogative; and directs foreign commerce by his treaties, with those nations, with whom it is carried on. He names the officers of government; so that he can check every jarring movement in the administration. He has a negative in the different legislatures throughout his dominions, so that he can prevent any repugnancy in their different laws.

The connection and harmony between Great-Britain and us, which it is her interest and ours mutually to cultivate; and on which her prosperity, as well as ours, so materially depends; will be better preserved by the operation of the legal prerogatives of the Crown, than by the exertion of an unlimited authority by Parliament.*

THE END.

* After considering, with all the attention of which I am capable, the foregoing opinion,—*That all the different Members of the British Empire are* DISTINCT

STATES, INDEPENDANT OF EACH OTHER, BUT CONNECTED TOGETHER UNDER THE SAME SOVEREIGN IN RIGHT OF THE SAME CROWN—I discover only one objection that can be offered against it. But this objection will, by many, be deemed a fatal one. "How, it will be urged, can the Trade of the British Empire be carried on, without some power, extending over the whole, to regulate it? The legislative authority of each part, according to your doctrine, is confined within the local bounds of that part: How, then, can so many interfering interests and claims, as must necessarily meet and contend in the commerce of the whole, be decided and adjusted?"

Permit me to answer these Questions by proposing some others in my turn. How has the Trade of Europe—How has the Trade of the whole Globe, been carried on? Have those widely-extended plans been formed by one superintending power? Have they been carried into execution by one superintending power? Have they been formed—have they been carried into execution, with less conformity to the rules of justice and equality, than if they had been under the direction of one superintending power?

It has been the opinion of some Politicians, of no inferior note, that all regulations of Trade are useless; that the greatest part of them are hurtful; and that the stream of Commerce never flows with so much beauty and advantage, as when it is not diverted from its natural channels. Whether this opinion is well founded or not, let others determine. Thus much may certainly be said, that Commerce is not so properly the object of Laws, as of Treaties and Compacts. In this manner, it has been always directed among the several nations of Europe.

But if the Commerce of the British Empire must be regulated by a general superintending power, capable of exerting its influence over every part of it, why may not this power be entrusted to the King, as a part of the Royal prerogative? By making Treaties, which it is his prerogative to make, he directs the Trade of Great-Britain with the other States of Europe: And his Treaties with those States have, when considered with regard to his subjects, all the binding force of Laws upon them.[†] Where is the absurdity in supposing him vested with the same right to regulate the Commerce of the distinct parts of his dominions with one another, which he has to regulate their Commerce with foreign States. If the history of the British Constitution, relating to this subject, be carefully traced, I apprehend we shall discover, that a prerogative in the Crown, to regulate Trade, is perfectly consistent with the principles of law. We find many authorities that the King cannot lay impositions on Traffic; and that he cannot restrain it ALTOGETHER, nor confine it to *Monopolists*: But none of the authorities, that I have had an opportunity of consulting, go any farther. Indeed many of them seem to imply a power in the Crown to regulate Trade; where that power is exerted for the great end of all prerogative—the public good.

If the power of regulating Trade be, as I am apt to believe it to be, vested, by the principles of the constitution, in the Crown, this good effect will flow from the doctrine: A perpetual distinction will be kept up between that power, and a power of laying impositions on Trade. The prerogative will extend to the former: It can, under no pretence, extend to the latter: As it is *given*, so it is *limited*, by the Law.

[†] *The King may make a treaty with a foreign State, which shall irrevocably bind the Nation.* BLACKSTONE. 252.

[William Henry Drayton], A Letter from Freeman of South-Carolina, to the Deputies of North-America, Assembled in the High Court of Congress at Philadelphia. Charleston, 1774.

William Henry Drayton was a planter from an established South Carolina family. Sent to England in 1750 for his education, first at the prestigious Westminster School and eventually at Balliol College, Oxford, Drayton returned to South Carolina in 1763 and was elected to the colony's assembly in 1765. His reputation for gambling (at which he was unlucky) and frequent absences from the assembly led in 1768 to his defeat at the hands of a schoolmaster. Initially he did not support the popular side in the imperial debate, refusing to speak out against the Townshend duties and strongly objecting to the coercive methods used by extralegal associations to enforce the nonimportation movement. He was especially contemptuous of the role played by Charleston artisans in supporting the boycott of British goods. It was inconceivable to him that educated gentlemen should have to consult "with men who never were in a way to study, or to advise upon any points, but rules on how to cut up a beast in the market to the best advantage, to cobble an old shoe in the neatest manner, or to build a necessary house. . . . Nature never intended that such men should be profound politicians or able statesmen."

In 1771 Drayton secured a Crown appointment to the colony's Council. Unsatisfied, he continued to seek other royal offices in the colony, and though he secured a judicial position, he was for the most part unsuccessful. After coming to realize that many royal officials and nearly all of his fellow council members were placemen from Britain with no roots in South Carolina society, he began rethinking his attitude towards royal authority. Provoked by the Coercive Acts—"the *Tragedy of five Acts*," he called them—Drayton joined the ranks of the popular Whig opposition.

In this pamphlet addressed to the First Continental Congress Drayton ranged over the whole of English history but focused especially on those rights that had been reaffirmed by the Glorious Revolution of 1688–89. Like many other Americans in the imperial debate, he was especially angry that judges in the colonies served at the pleasure of the Crown. This deviation from the standard practice in the mother country, where as a consequence of the parliamentary Act of Settlement of 1701 judges served during good behavior, was another indication that the colonists were to be denied their traditional rights as Englishmen. The issue was no longer the right of the mother country to tax America, "but, whether she has a constitutional right to exercise *Despotism* over America!" Drayton circulated his pamphlet widely, sending copies to the Continental Congress and to leading British ministers. He now gloried in being part of the American cause.

A LETTER

FROM

FREEMAN

OF

SOUTH-CAROLINA,

TO THE

DEPUTIES

OF

NORTH-AMERICA,

ASSEMBLED IN

THE HIGH COURT OF CONGRESS

AT

PHILADELPHIA.

SOUTH-CAROLINA:
CHARLES-TOWN, PRINTED BY PETER TIMOTHY.
M, DCC, LXXIV.

To the Deputies of North-America;
in General Congress.

GENTLEMEN!

WHEN the people of England, in the early part of the last century, were oppressed by illegal Taxes, violation of property, billeting Soldiers and martial law; there was reason to apprehend some insurrection, from the discontents which prevailed. They believed their liberties were on the point of being ravished from them, and Charles the First, found himself under an absolute necessity to summon a Parliament, to meet early in the Year 1628.—On the first day of their meeting, to deliberate upon a subject of no less importance than, to reinstate a good correspondence between the Crown and People;—and before the Commons had entered into any Debates; an anonymous letter to them, touching the inconveniences and grievances of the State, was communicated to the Members; and it was called a Speech without doors.

Upon Subjects of grievance similar with, yet infinitely more serious than, those of that period;—now, at a time threatening, not insurrection from discontents, but,—a civil war from despair; —and, by the same mode of address as was used to that House of Commons, I thus have the Honour, publicly to make known my sentiments to the Deputies of North-America: Deputies elected to meet in General Congress, to deliberate upon a subject, of at least as high import to the British Crown and People of America, as that Parliament had to discuss, relative to the Crown and People of England.—I here religiously wish, that the Claims of this Congress, may be as favourably admitted, as were the Claims of that Parliament;—and that the similitude between the two periods may then finally end. For we know, the subsequent years of Charles's administration, *encreased* the Public discontents to that degree; that at length, the People in their might arose, and took up Arms against the Sovereign!

Hitherto charactered by my Countrymen, as most zealous for the Prerogative in opposition to the Liberty of the Subject; I am conscious my principle of conduct has been misunderstood. As far as my small abilities enabled me, as an independent and honest middle branch of Legislature ought to act; so, in private and in public Stations have I endeavoured at one time, to oppose the Exuberances of Popular Liberty; and at another, the stretches of the Government Party, when I thought either advanced, beyond the Constitutional line of propriety.—In short, I wish to form a Political Character, by the Picture *Junius* gave of a virtuous Duke of Bedford.—"Willing to support the just measures of Government, but determined to observe the conduct of the Minister with suspicion, he would oppose the violence of faction with as much firmness, as the encroachments of prerogative."—And before *Junius* was known, I had established it as a first principle, not to proceed any farther with any party, than I thought they travelled in the *Constitutional Highway.*

Hitherto, I have opposed the local popular policy of this Colony. I thought the principles of action were unconstitutional; I am of the same opinion;—I may be wrong—my judgment is my guide.—But now! the *Tragedy of five Acts*, composed in the last Session of Parliament, in my opinion, violates all the rules of the Political drama, and incapacitates me from saying one word in favour of Administration.—Nay, the same Spirit of indignation which animated me to condemn popular measures in the year 1769, because, although avowedly in defence of Liberty, they absolutely violated the freedom of Society, by demanding Men, under pain of being stigmatized, and of sustaining detriment in property, to accede to Resolutions; which, however well-meant, could not, *from the apparent constraint they held out*, but be grating, very grating to a Freeman; so, the *same Spirit* of indignation, yet incapable of bending to measures violating Liberty, actuates me in like manner, *now to assert* my Freedom *against the malignant* nature of the late five Acts of Parliament.—As then, a certainty of sustaining a heavy loss of property, and of acquiring a heavy load of public odium, did not intimidate me from persevering in a conduct I thought right: so, now that the Liberty and Property of the American is at the pleasure of a Despotic power, an Idea of *a risque of life itself* in defence of my hereditary rights, cannot appal me, or make me shrink from my purpose, when perhaps those rights, can be maintained *only by a temporary suspension* of the rules of constitutional proceedings. Tenacious and jealous of my Liberty, I do not change *my* *ground*, because I in turn face *opposite* quarters making the attack. Thus, from *one and the same center of action and principle of conduct*, I opposed succeeding violations of my rights,—*then*, by a temporary Democracy—*now* by an established Monarchy. —If I did not act *thus consistently*, it might well be asked, why did I with so much spirit oppose my Countrymen *in the year* 1769, and remain silent *now*, that injuries of a much *more* alarming nature, are threatened *from another quarter?*—I consider myself thus fully obliged to anticipate, any uncandid and unworthy reflections, that might possibly be made of my being fickle and unsteady, or *influenced* by disgust;* as I have written against *popular* measures, and *now* write against those

---

* The full intention of Parliament respecting America became known here, by the arrival of the Acts at the same time when accounts were received that Administration had nominated an Assistant Judge, regularly bred to the Bar, in the room of Mr. Justice Murray deceased; and a change of conduct taking place in the author at this crisis, some imputed it to disgust rather than to principle. —The author was aware of such a construction, but he was incapable of being intimidated from a System he thought right. The following extract will shew, that the late appointment from home was expected, and therefore could have no influence upon his present conduct.

"On Tuesday last a Commission passed the Great Seal of this province, appointing the Honourable William-Henry Drayton, Esquire, to the office of Assistant-Judge, in the room of John Murray, Esquire, deceased. We hear that when His Honour the Lieutenant-Governor, and His Majesty's Council were in Deliberation to nominate a Gentleman of a proper rank and character to the office of Assistant-Judge, it was allowed that no such person at the bar would, for such a consideration, be induced to quit his practice, and that as no other person of rank and character would chuse to run the risk of being superseded by the appointment of a Barrister from England: so it would be highly indelicate to offer the post to any such. The case seemed difficult, yet of necessity a Judge must be appointed: After some time spent in agitating this subject, Mr. Drayton offered his service in that station UNTIL A BARRISTER SHOULD BE APPOINTED BY THE KING; which public spirited Behaviour was very readily and unanimously approved by the Lieutenant-Governor and Council."—*General Gazette*, No 801. Jan. 28. 1774.

When Mr. D. was pro tempore appointed Post Master General, in the year 1771, and made application at home to be confirmed, Lords Sandwich and Hillsborough did him the honour to acquaint him, that they personally applied on his behalf to Lord Le Despencer, one of the Post Masters General, who acquainted them, the office had been for some time previously engaged. —Mr. D. was not disgusted here, although he made application—in the present case he has never made the least solicitation, and engaged in the station exactly in the manner related in the Gazette.

of *Administration*. Each of the five late Acts of Parliament relating to America, encreased my alarms in a progressive degree;
they all run counter to my Ideas of the *constitutional power* of
Parliament.—Either they are utterly illegal, as the Acts of a whole
Session,* of the second Richard, and two Acts,† in particular, of
Henry the eighth, were deemed to be, and therefore done away
by subsequent Parliaments; or, I am utterly ignorant of the nature
of the English constitution or Parliament.—Let this alternative be
as it may; every Man has feelings, and must act by them.

The question now, is not whether Great-Britain has a right
to *Tax* America against her consent;—but, whether she has a
constitutional right to exercise *Despotism* over America!—What
can be more despotic in any government, than, in one Colony‡
to revoke Charter rights: to alter the law: to annihilate an essential branch of the Legislature in *favour of the People*, and in
its room to place an establishment existing but *at the Will of
the Sovereign!*—In another§ in effect to annihilate the antient
code of law, as well of the Vanquished as of the Conquerors,
subjecting the existence of the Common law, to the pleasure
of the Crown: to declare the people, *English People!* shall not
have representation; and to empower the Governor and Council to make laws for them.—What is this, but to enable the Crown,
by an *Instruction*, to give Law to the People! What is this, but *the
same power* that Henry the eighth had, by a *Proclamation*, to
give law to the People of England!—And what greater power
has the Sovereign at Constantinople, over a province in the
East, than the Sovereign at London now has over a province in
the West!—At a stroke to annihilate the right of representation,
and the common law from among English subjects, nay, *English
People!*—to empower Bashaws, in their little Divans to promulge
such laws to people of English blood, as, from time to time,
under the form of instructions, shall be penned by the English
Reis Effendi!—Such powers cannot legally exist in Britain.—
Than, that such powers should be exercised over us;—it will be

---

* Anno XI.
† 28 Henry 8. To enable Kings by their letters Patent to repeal laws during
their minority. 31 Henry. To give the Kings Proclamations the force of an Act
of Parliament.
‡ Massachusetts-Bay.
§ Quebeck.

better O! Americans! that we should not be.—The highest Despotism is now exercised over Quebeck; and remember! it is true to a proverb, *multis minatur, uni qui injuriam facit.*

But, affairs may yet be well, notwithstanding the gloomy face of our political atmosphere.—Our Ancestors of England, were often obliged to claim their rights, when they were in danger of losing them. Let Us follow so successful an example. On such a subject, let the Americans Address the Throne with all due respect to Majesty; and at the same time with attention to their own dignity as Freemen.—The stile of the Lord Keeper to Charles the First on a similar occasion, is a case in point.

"May it please your most Excellent Majesty." Your People of America by their Deputies assembled in General Congress, "taking into consideration that, *the good intelligence* between your Majesty and your People" of America, "*doth much depend upon your Majesty's answer* upon their" claim "of rights. With unanimous consent, do now become most humble Suitors unto your Majesty, that You will be pleased to give a clear and *satisfactory* answer"* to,

THE AMERICAN CLAIM OF RIGHTS.

That whereas, discontents, Jealousies, and alarms have unhappily pervaded, overspread and distressed the British Subjects, settled on the Continent of North-America, to the great endangering the Public Peace,

1. By Acts of the British Parliament, taxing those American Freeholders, *although* they have not any representation, *of their own election*, in Parliament.

2. By the constitution of Council established among them by the Royal Mandamus. Seeing they act as a second branch of the Legislature, entirely dependent upon the pleasure even of the Governor:—that Placemen dependent upon the Crown, being Strangers *ignorant* of the interests and laws of the Colonies, are sent from England to fill seats in Council, where they often form a majority;—as Legislators, determining the most weighty affairs of the Colony;—and as Chancellors, decreeing in Suits relating to the most valuable property of the Subject.

* 8 Parl. Hist. 202.

3. By there not being any constitutional Courts of Ordinary and of Chancery in America; and by Appeals being under the jurisdiction of the King and Privy Council, as the dernier resort.

4. By the Judges holding their seats at the will of the Crown: a tenure dangerous to the liberty and property of the Subject; and *therefore* justly abolished in England.

5. By Judges now adays granting to the Customs, to lie dormant in their possession, WRITS OF ASSISTANCE in the nature of *General Warrants*; by which, *without any crime charged and without any suspicion*, a petty officer *has power* to cause the doors and locks of any Man to be broke open, to enter his most private cabinet; and thence to take and carry away, whatever he shall in his pleasure deem uncustomed goods.

6. By the oppressive powers vested in the Courts of Admiralty.

7. By the British Parliament claiming and exercising a power to bind the Colonies *in all cases* whatsoever. To suspend the Legislature of New-York: to divest the Americans of the value of their lawful property at pleasure, and even without any form of trial: to annul and make void lawful contracts in trade: to oblige Judges to take bail in Cases of murder: to enable Persons charged with murder in Massachusetts Bay, *to fly* the Colony: to annihilate an ancient* branch of the Legislature *in favour of the People*, and in its room to constitute one entirely *dependent upon the pleasure of the Crown*: to deprive subjects of English blood of the right of representation in the Colony of Quebeck; and to enable the Governor and Council there to make laws for them; thereby in effect leaving it *in the power of the Crown, whether or not, or in what degree*, such Subjects *shall enjoy* the benefit of *Magna Charta* and *the Common Law*, under *a Crown*, which *is itself limited and controuled* by *Magna Charta* and *the Common law!*—And, for the purposes of repeating and continuing, all these grievances and heavy oppressions herein specified;—to establish the Romish Religion, in a very considerable part of the British Empire; and to *quarter* Soldiers in America, against the *consent* of the Freeholders.—All which are illegal, and directly contrary to the *Franchises* of America.

And therefore, the Americans represented by their Deputies

* About 200 Years.

aforesaid, taking into their most serious consideration, the best means to avert the calamities of Civil War: to restore public tranquillity: and to preserve *without dispute*, the supremacy of the Crown and British Dominion over America; "Do in the first place, as their Ancestors in like case have usually done, for the vindicating and asserting their ancient Rights and Liberties, declare;"*

1. That the Americans being descended from the same Ancestors with the people of England, and owing fealty to the same Crown, are therefore equally with them, entitled to the common law of England formed by their common Ancestors; and to all and singular the benefits, rights, liberties and claims specified in Magna Charta,† in the Petition of Rights,‡ in the Bill of Rights,§ and in the Act of Settlement.¶ They being no more, than principally *declaratory of the grounds* of the fundamental laws of England.** Therefore,

2. That the British Parliament ought not to have, and cannot of right possess any Power to Tax, or in any shape to bind American Freeholders of the British Crown; seeing it is against the Franchises of the land, because their consent is not signified in Parliament, by *a Representation of their own election*.††

3. That the constitution of the present Councils in America, by Mandamus, be utterly abolished; as being injurious to the Subject, and destructive of a free constitution of Government. —That of right, there ought to be an independent and permanent middle branch of Legislature, between the Crown and People; and, that as it ought of right to arise by the Royal Creation, so, the Members of it, ought of right, to be called out of American Families;—that the majority of the Council of State to the Governor, ought of right to consist of men connected with the colony, by birth or fortune; and that the Governor, or Council of State, cannot of right possess any Judicial Power whatsoever.

* Bill of Rights, W. & M.
† 9 Henry 3.
‡ 3 Car. 1.
§ 1 Will. & Mary.
¶ 12 & 13 Will. 3.
** 2 Inst. Proem.
†† 7 Parl. Hist. 371.—Year Books, 20 H. 6. 8.—2 R. 3. 12—25 Car. 2. c. 9.

4. That of right, there ought to be in each Colony, constitutional Courts of Ordinary and of Chancery; that for the ease of the subject, at such a vast distance as he is from England, appeals from the American Courts of Chancery, ought to be made to the Upper House of Assembly of each Colony respectively, and from thence to the House of Lords in Great-Britain; the only constitutional *dernier resort* for justice in the Empire.

5. That equally as the People of England are interested in the independence of their Judges; so, are we interested in the independence of our Judges; and upon principles of common and impartial Justice, claim that their commissions should run, *quam diu se bene gesserint.*

6. That no Writs of assistance ought to be issued to the Customs, but in the nature of Writs or Warrants to search for goods stolen; *General Writs or Warrants* being illegal.

7. That the powers of the American Courts of Admiralty, unnecessarily and oppressively trenching upon the property and liberty of the subject; therefore they ought to be modelled, more agreeable to the genuine principle of the Common Law.

8. That the King's Prerogative ought not, and cannot of right, be more extensive in America, than it is by law limited in England.

9. That the Americans, are of natural right entitled, to all and singular those inherent though latent powers of Society, necessary for the safety, preservation and defence of their just claims, rights and liberties herein specified; which no contract, no constitution, no time, *no climate* can destroy or diminish.*

"And they do claim, demand, and insist upon all and singular the premises, as their undoubted rights and Liberties; and that no Declarations, Judgments, Doings, or Proceedings, to the prejudice of the People in any of the said premises, ought in any wise to be drawn hereafter into consequence or example."†

To which demand of their rights, they are particularly encouraged, by a reliance on the Virtues of their Sovereign Lord George; convinced that this their demand, is the most peaceable means they have to obtain a full redress and remedy

* 1 Blackstone, 245.
† Bill of Rights, 1. W. & M.

therein; on which the good Intelligence, between His Most Sacred Majesty and His oppressed People of America, doth much depend.

Having therefore an entire confidence, that the Crown of Great-Britain will preserve them from the Violation of their Rights, which they have here asserted; and from all other attempts upon their Rights and Liberties; the said People of America by their Deputies aforesaid, do resolve;*

1. That they do of right owe, and will loyally maintain to the Crown of Great-Britain, like faith and allegiance as the people of England, from whose Ancestors they are descended.

2. That the Americans will grant general Aids to the British Crown, upon the same principles of requisition and grant, that aids are constitutionally required of and granted in the Parliament of Great-Britain.

3. That all General Aids from America to the Crown, and laws binding the whole Continent of North-America; shall from time to time, according to Parliamentary proceedings, be granted, enacted and received in a HIGH COURT OF ASSEMBLY of North-America; convened by the King's Writs to the two Houses of Assembly of each Colony respectively; to chuse an equal number of Persons in each House, as their and each of their Representatives in THE HIGH COURT of ASSEMBLY.

4. That the Act of the High Court of Assembly, having specified to the Colonies their respective proportions and quotas of an American general Aid; the said quotas shall be raised in the respective Colonies, by their respective Legislatures, and paid within a limited time to be expressed, and under certain penalties to be specified in the Act of General Aid.

5. That the High Court of Assembly, shall not however, be deemed or construed to possess any right or power, but, of a general nature; as, that all penalties and Acts of Legislation to be enacted in it, shall *in the same degree*, bind all and each of the Colonies.—Each Colony regulating her internal local Policy as heretofore, by her own internal legislature.

SUCH seem to be the Grievances and Claims of America; and the form of Legislature laid down in the Resolves, seems to be drawn

* Ibid.

up upon constitutional principles of English legislation—
Some such system of Government seems absolutely necessary.
—And, without a system of a general nature, the Colonies
acting independently of each other, they will scarce agree upon
their proportionable quotas of a general aid to the Crown.—
Each will plead her own inability, and magnify the wealth of
her Neighbour.—But, this policy could not be adopted with
the least success in a High Court of Assembly, where each
Member would be well acquainted with the real state and
ability of each Colony.—Indeed this would be an absolutely
necessary Study, lest by the ignorance or *laches* of any Member,
his Colony, and consequently his Estate, should bear a greater
proportion of the aid, than otherwise would be rated.—And if
the whole Continent should be thought too extensive under
one Legislature, that impropriety could be easily remedied, by
dividing the whole into two Districts as nearly equal as may be:
a division naturally pointed out, by every principle of true
policy.

Without doubt it may be said, nothing is easier than to draw
up a catalogue of Assertions, and to term one part grievances,
and the other part rights.—I admit the propriety of such an
observation; and therefore I will attempt to shew, that the
present state of American grievances, are too well founded in
fact; and her claims too just, to be speciously contradicted.

The subject of the American taxation, has been treated of in
so great a variety of manner, within these late years, that scarce
any thing new, is now left to be said on a point of so great
importance.—However, passing over the general arguments
which have been so lately formed, I will step back one hundred
years, and with a late Great Commoner, I will consider the
subject, illuminated by the Ideas of the Illustrious dead.—Ideas
so far of importance, that they are of the highest authority,
being no less than those of a High Court of Parliament.

The Preamble to the Act* allowing to the County of
Durham an actual representation in Parliament, gives the Ideas
of the Legislature, on the subjects of Taxation and actual representation, in the clearest terms.—"Whereas the Inhabitants
of the County Palatine of Durham, *have not hitherto had* the

* 25 Car. 2.

liberty and privilege of electing and sending any Knights and Burgesses to the High Court of Parliament, *although* the Inhabitants of the said County Palatine are liable to all payments, rates and subsidies granted by Parliament, equally with the inhabitants of other Counties, Cities and Boroughs in this Kingdom, and *are therefore* concerned *equally* with others the Inhabitants of this Kingdom, *to have Knights and Burgesses* in the said High Court of Parliament *of their own election.*" &c.— Hence it is clear, there cannot be a constitutional taxation, without an actual representation: or, why an actual representation now allowed to the County of Durham? This happened in the year 1672, and to all intents and purposes, must be considered as an *adjudged case* on the point.—Wherefore then has the case been over-ruled in our day, and America taxed without representation in Parliament?—I am answered, America is *virtually* represented?—But, was not Durham *as virtually* represented? Is there any other difference, than that the fiction of *virtual representation*, is much easier comprehended with respect to *Durham*, than *America?*—However, *that species of representation*, was *not thought* to be a *constitutional warrant to Tax* a small County, not equal to one half part of one of the smallest of our Colonies; but, now after a century, it is thought to be a species of representation, suitable to the meridian of America!

The original establishment of Councils in the Royal Governments on this Continent; consisted principally, and in a manner to all intents and purposes, of Men *of property established* in the Colony. Such a Council could not but be well acquainted with the interests of the country, and be no less ready and zealous to promote them at the hazard of their seats. Such men stood in no awe of a Minister, yet they rendered the most essential services to the Crown, as well as to the People.—But now, the System of appointment is reversed:—We see in Council more strangers from England, than Men of rank in the Colony!— Counsellors! because they are sent over to fill offices of 200*l.* or 300*l.* per annum, as their only subsistence in life! Thus, Strangers not to be supposed very solicitous about the prosperity of the Colony, in which they have *no interest but their commissions*, are, as Legislators, to determine upon the *res ardua* of the State; and ignorant of *our law*, and too often *unexpectedly* so of the English law, they are, as Chancellors, to decree in cases of the most important value to the Colonist.— Unfortunate Colonist! by the Minister abroad, thus are you delivered over a sacrifice at home, to the ignorance and necessities of a Stranger, by the Hand of power imposed upon you as a judge!

The unconstitutional formation of the Courts of Ordinary and of Chancery in America, and the Jurisdiction of the King and Privy Council over Appeals from this continent, I shall wave with intention to take up those subjects in a subsequent part of this letter; and as the dependence of the Judges upon the Crown for their daily subsistence, seems to have been the cause of *general Writs* of assistance having been issued, I shall class those subjects together; and likewise the opposite conduct of two sets of Judges *learned in the law*; the one, *Men of Property*—the other, Men without the *visible Shadow* of independence—hence the only apparent motive for a contrariety of conduct on the same question.—A few years ago, the Bench of Justice in this Colony, was filled with *Men of Property*, and if all of them were not learned in the law, there were some among them, who taught their Brethren to administer Justice *with public approbation*; and one* of them in particular had so well *digested* his reading, altho' he had never eat commons at the Temple, that he was without dispute *at least* equal *to* the law learning *of* the present Bench.—To this *independent and well informed* Bench of Judges, the Attorney General, *ex officio*, on the part of the Customs, from time to time during several years, made application to obtain Writs of Assistance,—of a more pernicious nature than General Warrants.—The demand even under the direction of an Act of Parliament; was constantly refused.—The Judges knew it trenched too severely and unnecessarily upon the safety of the subject, secured by Magna Charta, who the great Sir Edward Coke declared, "*is such a fellow, that he will have no Sovereign.*"[†] *Hence*, the Judges knew the Statute could not legally operate, and therefore, that it was absolutely void in law. At length one of them privately, and with such sound reasoning, delivered his Sentiments on

---

* Rawlins Lowndes, Esq.
[†] 8. Parl. Hist. 119.

the subject to the Attorney General, that he replied, he was not desirous to enter into *the merits* of the application, and therefore should forbear making any others upon the subject. —And thus were the Houses, the Castles of English Subjects preserved inviolate, when the Bench was filled by Men of *independence, as well as of knowledge*. But, no sooner was the Bench filled by Men who depended upon the smiles of the Crown for their daily bread, than the Attorney General, *ex officio*, returned to the attack, and carried the point even by *a coup d'essai*. There was no investigation of *the merits*, the General Writ, or rather, the *General Warrant* for breaking open doors at the pleasure of a petty officer, was granted as a matter of course, and without any hesitation.—The *contrast*, and the causes are striking, and need no comments.—Equally unnecessary is it for me to say any thing, to shew the oppression to which the Subject is exposed, in being dragged into the Admiralty Courts in America!

And such are the grievances, under which the Americans have long laboured. We expected nothing in addition, but to be drained of our Gold and Silver by taxes against our Consent, and to be over-run by troops of hungry placemen.—But, how short-sighted is Man!—The old grievances of America, were no more than the Harbingers of a more formidable band of oppressive measures!—A very few months ago we should have thought a man mad, who, under the spirit of prophecy, should have presented America with a view of only a part of the seventh paragraph of grievances!—But, not allowing myself now to be detained in my advance, by any reflections upon the Americans being divested of the value of their property: the annulling lawful contracts in trade: the obliging Judges to take bail in cases of murder: the enabling Persons charged with murder in Massachusetts-Bay, to *fly* the Colony:—I hold on my way to fly at objects of more importance,—of greater grievance!—The encrease of Royal Power by annihilation of Popular Rights, in Massachusetts-Bay—a Despotism over English People, by Act of Parliament established in Quebeck!

To consider these objects with propriety, it is necessary to take the subject up *ab origine*; and in that point of view, to examine the King's legal power in Massachusetts-Bay, and in Quebeck, when the Crown first acquired civil Dominion in those Countries. It may be said, that as Quebeck is a country obtained by Arms, and the Colony of Massachusetts-Bay was founded without violence; therefore there is a wide distinction between them, and the King may legally form laws, to bind the conquered and his natural subjects settled among them, although he cannot exercise such a power over the Colony founded without violence. But in truth, the English law considers the Colony of Massachusetts-Bay and the Province of Quebeck by one and the same principle, and the late conduct of Parliament has confirmed this doctrine, by giving to the King *an absolute Power in the one, and as great an encrease in the other* as he now chose to exercise. And, if in States exactly similar in the Eye of the law, the Crown can legally acquire and exercise over the one, *a despotic power* totally different from, and for ever *heterogeneous* to the *genus* of the natural and true *powers of the English Crown*; what fiction of argument shall prevent the same power being exercised over the other, and in short over all the Colonies in America, since the law considers them all but in one and the same light?

It is laid down that, "in *conquered or ceded* countries, that have already laws of their own, the King may indeed alter and change those laws; but 'till he does actually change them, the ancient laws of the Country remain, unless *such* as are against the law of God, as in the case of an Infidel country."* And that "our American Plantations are principally of this sort, being obtained either *by right of conquest* and driving out the Natives, *or by treaties*."†—What reading can be even desired more in point to shew, that Quebeck, Massachusetts-Bay, Virginia and Carolina are exactly in one and the same situation?—Which of the British Colonies in America is it, that the Crown has not "obtained either *by right of conquest* driving out the natives, *or by treaties*" with them: or *by conquest of or by treaties* with the French and Spaniards, who had first acquired the territory in *like manner* from the Natives?—Admitting that the Crown may alter the antient laws of the conquered, yet I cannot be of opinion, that *in those conquered or ceded* States, the Crown can legally acquire a power over *Subjects of English blood*, destruc-

---

* 7. Rep. 17 Calvin's case. Show. Parl. C. 51.
† 1 Blackstone 107.

tive of those rights which are peculiar to the blood: Rights evidenced by Magna Charta, and defended by the fundamental
laws of England!—Rights, evidence and laws which the Prerogative of the Crown cannot overthrow, nor the Parliament
change to the prejudice of the People interested in their preservation! The Parliament have no such power delegated to
them.—They cannot legally form any laws, *heterogeneous* to
the purposes of their own creation and existence.—As the Sap
peculiar to a Tree, must necessarily and invariably produce
similar effects in a Plant of the same Species, as far as the infancy of the latter will admit, being at the same time *incapable*
of producing in it, any appearance heterogeneous to the Parent
Tree: so the American Plant, being animated with the same
species of Sap with the English Tree, the Plant *however connected* with the Parent Tree, cannot naturally produce any
heterogeneous appearance. Thus even allowing the Constitutional power of Parliament, to pervade the English States in
America, it can naturally produce *those effects only*, of which the
Colonies are capable; and cannot legally produce in their Legislatures any appearance, heterogeneous to its own nature and
capability of action. Thus, it has not any legal or natural power
to make the British Crown absolute in Quebeck, because it
cannot make the Crown absolute in Great-Britain; neither can
Parliament vest in the Crown more power in the Legislature of
Massachusetts-Bay, than it is *capable* of exercising in the Em-
perial Legislature. The *genus* of the English Crown cannot
naturally admit of, nay, it would be absolutely destroyed by, a
heterogeneous ability from Parliament, to exercise in England,
either of the species of power that it now exercises at Quebeck
or Massachusetts-Bay. The People never delegated to Parliament, any Ability to aggrandize the Crown, with any such
powers, which are heterogeneous to the ability of the one to
vest, or to the nature of the other to admit. The prerogative of
Parliament, although, more exalted, yet is but of *the same
genus* with that of the Crown, which "hath a prerogative in all
things that are not *injurious* to the Subject, for in them all it
must be remembered, that the King's prerogative stretcheth
not to the doing of any *wrong*."*—When did the People of

* Finch II, 84. 85.

England delegate to Parliament, a power to *injure* the People of America, and do them *wrongs*, by in effect giving the Crown two voices in the legislature of Massachusetts-Bay; by incapacitating Subjects of English blood in Quebeck from enjoying the benefits of Representation there; and by enabling the Crown, through the Channel of the Governor and Council, to prescribe law to *those* Subjects, Illustrious Heirs of Magna Charta and the Common law!—Would not the People of England think themselves *injured and wronged*, if the Parliament should vest similar powers in the Crown to be exercised over them? Are the Americans less sensible of *injuries and wrongs?*—Are they less able to discern them?—I hope they will prove a genuine English descent, by a display of that great, generous and free Spirit, which has hitherto charactered their illustrious Ancestors.—In short, I cannot see that the Parliament, at any rate, can legally exercise over the Colonies, any powers which it cannot exercise over Great-Britain. The Parliament cannot there annihilate or constitute a Sovereign to Magna Charta—the Great Coke has said, "Magna Charta is such a fellow, that he will have no Sovereign." How then has the Parliament acquired a power, and how has it dared, to constitute the King so despotic in any part of the British Empire, as there to aggrandize him a Sovereign to this same Magna Charta!—The Roman Legislature having vested in Cæsar, unconstitutional authority in the Provinces, he was at length enabled, only by the means of this authority, to overthrow even the Roman Liberties and Constitution; and upon their ruins, to establish a Despotism throughout the whole Empire!

I cannot but now return to consider an object I held as of an inferior nature, when Despotism was in view. It is the privilege granted to persons charged with murder in the Colony of Massachusetts-Bay, to apply for the Governor's Mittimus to take their trials in any other Colony, or in Great-Britain! It is nothing less, than enabling the accused to stand trial in a Country, where by a thousand accidents or stratagems, the enormity of the crime *may not be known*. Upon which proceedings, an elegant writer furnishes me with a most just Idea. "No oppression is so heavy as that which is inflicted by the perversion and exorbitance of legal authority: as when plunder bears the name of impost,"* and murder being perpetrated by authority of law; the Villain escapes conviction, *flying the Country*, by the secure conveyance of *a mittimus* from the Magistrate!—This policy is new in the English Jurisprudence, for, it is not to be assimilated to the Act for trial of the Rebels of 1745 in London. They were carried to London for their *surer conviction*,—besides, they were taken in arms, in open Rebellion. And I dare venture to say, whoever drew the act in question, took the policy from antiquity, at the time of the first Roman Emperors. For, Tacitus somewhere says, that when the Legions being encamped, were oppressed by their Centurions, and in a clamorous manner demanded justice of the Generals: to save the accused from the vengeance of the injured, they at once ordered them to Prison, under pretence of future punishment; but in truth only to screen them from the popular fury, and to enable them to escape the doom due to their crimes.

When the first Charles billeted Soldiers upon his Subjects, the Commons of England presented[†] to the King, a Petition for redress of that grievance. In it they asserted, "that whereas by the fundamental laws of this Realm, every Freeman hath, and of right ought to have, a full and absolute property in his Goods and Estate; and that therefore the billeting and placing Soldiers in the House of any such Freeman *against his Will*, is directly contrary to the said Laws."[†]—An assertion which the Americans may use with equal propriety, against the quartering Soldiers among them, by authority of Parliament.

The arguments relative to Durham, have fully proved, that to be constitutionally *bound* by Parliament, *the people to be so bound*, must constitutionally give their *consent* in Parliament; *by representation* of their *own election, as* other Counties *have*. And, as this kind of consent is necessary to taxation, so, when the property of a Freeman is to be legally submitted to the quartering and billeting Soldiers, the above assertion of our honest Forefathers teaches us to say, the *consent* of the Freeman is indispensibly necessary. A consent that we know can be

* Rambler. No. 145.
† Anno 1628.
‡ 7 Parl. Hist. 447.

constitutionally given only in Parliament, by representation *of his own election*. A representation which the Americans have at no time ever had in the High Court of Parliament, and therefore they are not constitutionally bound to pay taxes, or to provide quarters for Soldiers, by authority of Parliament.

But, Soldiers are nevertheless to be quartered in the houses of American Freemen, even against their consent.—Similar causes generally produce similar effects; and what a train of mischiefs have had birth from such a measure in England! The above Petition to Charles presented to his view, a most fearful Arrangement.

"1. The Service of Almighty God is hereby greatly hindered, the People in many places not daring to repair to the Church, lest in the mean time the Soldiers should rifle their Houses.

2. The ancient and good Government of the Country is hereby neglected, and almost contemned.

3. Your Officers of Justice in performance of their duties, have been resisted and endangered.

4. The Rents and Revenues of your Gentry, greatly and generally diminished; Farmers to secure themselves from the Soldiers insolence, being, by the clamour and solicitation of their fearful and injured Wives and Children, enforced to give up their wonted Dwellings, and to retire themselves into places of more secure Habitation.

5. Husbandmen, that are as it were the Hands of the Country, corrupted by ill example of the Soldiers, and encouraged to idle life, give over work; and rather seek to live idly, at another man's charge, than by their own labour.

6. Tradesmen and Artificers almost discouraged; by being forced to leave their Trades, and to employ their time in preserving themselves and their families, from Violence and Cruelty.

7. Markets unfrequented, and our ways grown so dangerous, that the People dare not pass to and fro upon their usual occasions.

8. Frequent Robberies, Assaults, Batteries, Burglaries, Rapes, Rapines, Murders, barbarous Cruelties, and other most abominable Vices and Outrages are generally complained of, from all parts where these Companies have been and have their abode; few of which insolencies have been so much as questioned, and fewer, according to their demerit, punished."

Without doubt, it will be said, the excellent discipline at present established among the British soldiery, will effectually secure the Americans from such horrid Mischiefs.—But, I cannot be persuaded from an opinion, that when Soldiers have a good opportunity, they *will rifle in the absence of their Landlords*: —That drunk, they sometimes will be, and then, nay even when sober, they may be induced *to obstruct the Officers of Justice*, as in the case of General Gansel:—That Wives and Children cannot but be *under terrors and fears* of a Soldiery, quartered among them, to awe Society into Slavery:—That the lower rank of People *is apt to be corrupted* by the residence of a Soldiery, and thereby easily *encouraged to leave their trades*, and to "*live idly at another man's charge*": That ways *will be dangerous*, and *Robberies, Batteries, Burglaries, Rapes, and Seductions*, will be unavoidable, even under the discipline established among British Troops, quartered as Curbs upon the Americans. For to make the Americans *feel the Curb*, they will be *decently turbulent*, even by private allowance.

Thus it is as clear as the Sun at Noon, that the taxation of America: The Constitution of Councils by mandamus, and the manner of filling them: the want of Constitutional Courts of Ordinary and of Chancery, and Appeals being under the jurisdiction of the King in Council: the dependence of the Judges upon the Crown: the granting Writs of Assistance to the Customs: the oppressive powers vested in the Courts of Admiralty: the British Parliament exercising a Power to bind the Colonies in all cases whatsoever, from the violation of private Property, even up to the establishment of a Despotism in America; and the billeting Soldiers in America, are all unconstitutional, illegal, and oppressive.—Grievances!—crying aloud for redress, and heightened by a keenly affecting sensation, arising from the appearance of the British Arms by Land and Sea, now threateningly advanced, to continue and to enforce such oppressions, and to compel America to bow the Neck to Slavery!

Having thus seriously viewed and ascertained, a state of Grievances pregnant with horrible uproar and wild confusion: —We will now, no less minutely view the foundations, from which the Americans build their claim of Rights and Liberties.

In the same degree with the People of England, are the Americans of the lawful Posterity of those Freemen, who enjoyed the benefits of the Common Law of England, and who ascertained their ancient and unalienable Rights and Liberties, by Magna Charta, and by the Petition of Right; liberties recognized anew by the Bill of Rights, and by the Act of Settlement, And therefore are the Americans, equally with the people of England, entitled to those liberties which are emphatically termed the unalienable liberties of an Englishman.—And from such a title, does America derive her Freedom.—A title of infinitely more importance, than the Colony Charters from the Crown.

Therefore, like the people of Durham, the Americans being Freeholders of the British Crown, these cannot constitutionally be taxed by Parliament, without their consent signified by a representation there of their own election, *as* the people of Durham being other freeholders of the British crown *have* there.—And this precedent of Durham, at once flies at the novel doctrine, distinguishing between taxation and legislation.— We have already found, that to be constitutionally taxed, the people of Durham had *such a representation* in Parliament, of their own election *as* other Counties *have* there: that is, a *representation* endowed with such powers, being of such a nature, and *for such ends as* other Counties *have* in Parliament. In short, the acquiring a representation for the purpose of taxation, *ipso facto* works a representation at once *complete for every legislative purpose*: otherwise the representation allowed the County of Durham would not be such a one, *as* other Counties *have* in Parliament. Hence, we cannot see that there is any distinction, in the nature of a representation for the purpose of taxation or of legislation. And, I must confess, that it seems astonishing, at least to my very limited understanding, that any man should say, it is absolutely necessary, *to obtain the American's consent* implied by *actual representation* in Parliament, or, it is *not lawful to take one shilling* out of his pocket by taxation; and yet, *without his consent, it is lawful to divest* him of the value of *his whole property*, and eventually *take his life* by legislation! For my part, I cannot unravel the apparent absurdity of the position; I must leave that work to more comprehensive understandings, and I will continue to think, that there is much less ceremony necessary to take a shilling belonging to me, than my whole estate or my life. If a man has a legal right to take the two latter against my consent, I cannot see any reason, why he cannot as legally take the first without even asking my pleasure.—But, the favourers of this apparent absurdity, seem to have forgot a first principle in Government, which effectually destroys their position. They say, that altho' *consent* by representation, is absolutely necessary to the taxation of America, yet, British legislation may legally operate over America, without, and even *against her consent.* But the great Locke and Hooker,* are of a contrary opinion, and in the most explicit terms. As a first principle of lawful legislation, they lay down, that, the *consent of the society* over which the legislation is to be exercised, is absolutely, indispensably necessary; either to be expressed by *themselves,* or, *by authority from them*; otherwise the legislation "is no better than a mere tyranny." —America has at no time ever given any *such consent*; and therefore, any taxation or legislation, by the British Parliament over America against her consent, "is no better than a mere tyranny."†

The claim of a second, or middle branch of legislature in the Colonies: to be permanent and not subject to removal by the Crown, and to be called out of American families; is certainly unexceptionable. We do not yet desire Dignities, Lordships, and Dukedoms; but we have an equitable right to the benefit of the English constitution, formed by the courage and wisdom of our ancestors, for the equal benefit *of all* their posterity. —A second branch of legislature, permanent and not subject to removal by the *Crown or People*, is an essential part of that constitution; and therefore we equitably claim such an independent branch of legislature.—We likewise with the utmost propriety, claim that this branch shall be formed out of American families; as men so interested, will be more zealous for the interests of America, than strangers destitute of property and natural alliance in the Colonies. Thus, from the same principle it is likewise obvious, that the majority of the Council of state to the Governor, ought of right and of equity, to consist of

* Locke on Civil Gov. 205—Eccl. Pol. l. 1. Sect. 10.
† Hooker's Ecc. Pol. l. 1. Sect. 10.

men connected with the Colonies by fortune.—In what light would the people of England hold the King's Privy Council, if a majority of it consisted of upstarts *in the society*, destitute of the shadow of an estate, depending upon the pleasure of the Crown for their daily bread?—And from the same causes that the people of England found it necessary for the preservation of Justice,* to annihilate by an express statute,[†] *all judicial power whatever* in the King and Privy Council; so, for the same reason it is necessary, that judicial powers in the Governors and Councils ought likewise to be annihilated, for the good of the people of America; since no man will contend, that powers which by undue influence were dangerous in the hands of the King and his Council, will be of public advantage, and not in the least exposed to undue influence, in the Virtuous hands of needy Governors, and their hungry dependent Councils.— Nothing therefore is more to be avoided in a free constitution, than uniting the provinces of a Judge and Minister of State;[‡] *a fortiori* a Governor, who is the executive power; "which union might soon be an overballance for the legislative."[§]

Hence it is evident, that a Governor's exercising the functions of a Judge, threatens the very existence of the Freedom of a State; and I shall proceed to demonstrate, that such a dangerous junction of power, is directly contrary to the Common Law.

The Governor is the Executive power in the Colony. But although representing the Sovereignty of the King, and wielding his Executive authority: he cannot possess or exercise any of the Royal powers, prerogatives and attributes, than such as are delegated to him in the Royal Commission. It is laid down, that the King cannot *Personally* distribute Justice, having delegated his *whole Judicial power to the Judges* of his several Courts,[¶] which are the grand depository of the fundamental laws of the Kingdom.**—Hence it is clear, *the King cannot delegate to his Governor*, the Representative of his Sovereignty,

---

* 1 Blackstone, 269.
[†] 16 Car. 1. c. 10.
[‡] 1 Blackstone, 269.
[§] ibid.
[¶] 2 Inst. 186.
** 2 Hawk. P. C. 2.

any of the powers of the Ordinary or the Chancellor *to be exer-cised by him*, seeing he himself *cannot in his own Royal Person exercise any Judicial power whatsoever*. No, he has not even the power of a common Magistrate to arrest any man for treason or felony.*—Thus, the Governor like the King, *quoad hoc* cannot be any more than the reservoir from whence right and equity are conducted, "by the Judges of his several Courts," to every individual.†

Thus disconsonant to the safety of a free Government, and to the principles of law, appears the formation of the American Courts of Ordinary and of Chancery. And therefore, there cannot be any thing unreasonable, in our desiring Courts formed upon a basis, by experience found to be most adequate to the sure distribution of justice to the subject.—Neither is there any impropriety in desiring, that appeals may in the first instance, go to a constitutional middle branch of legislature in the Colonies.—For the expence of making appeals to England is so enormous, and the manner of conducting them to the best advantage by the presence of the parties, so impracticable to most of the Colonists; that being thus unable to make and plead to appeals in England, they have been, are and may be often obliged to submit to judgments and decrees in the Col-onies, deemed by the learned, illegally made by men, whom the *Royal Appointment* constitutes Judges, and *which is* but too often, the only *honourable mark* of their abilities in law. Here, I might by a number of instances, prove the propriety of this observation in an undeniable manner—but, I cannot condescend to hang up particular characters to the contempt of America—my letter is of too important a nature—I owe a propriety of conduct to my own character. I therefore resume the subject of appeals to the middle branch of legislature in the Colonies.—But, can the Americans reasonably require this mode of appeal, when the Irish are obliged to pass by their House of Lords, and to carry their appeals to the House of Peers in England?—Yes, their local situation entitles them to so equitable a distinction.—The Irish are, comparatively, at the door of the Supreme Tribunal in England; but the Americans

* 2 Inst. 186.
† 1 Blackstone, 265.

are at the distance of 3000 miles from that dernier resort. And, to attend appeals to the best advantage, the latter must unavoidably be exposed to a long absence at a vast distance from their domestic affairs, to great charges of voyage, and to great risque at Sea: Whereas, the Irish in a few hours sailing, and the absence of a few days, can superintend their appeals in London, as well as their domestic affairs in Dublin.—And is no mode of proceeding allowable, to give some adequate relief in a grievance arising from local situation?—Whence came the institution *of Circuits*, but from such an equity! And surely America! three millions of people! are no less equitably entitled to a proper relief in a similar grievance.—We do not claim a dernier resort among us, as the Irish House of Lords arrogated to themselves; therefore the *principle of law* * which made it necessary to deprive them of the power of hearing appeals, cannot be applied to America.—No! America means loyally to preserve sacred, the superiority of the Imperial State, if the parental justice of the Imperial Authority and Power, will permit her to act thus, according to the filial dictates of her constitutional Faith and Allegiance.

Having thus supported the equity of appeals to Tribunals in the Colonies, it is our next step, to support the propriety of appeals from thence to the House of Lords in England.

There is a position in law, that, whenever a question concerning property arises in America; as the dernier resort, the King in his Council exercises original jurisdiction therein, upon principles of feudal sovereignty.† And upon this doctrine it is, that our appeals have not yet reached the House of Lords.—To oppose this position, I shall make use of two others; the one, ancient, the other, very modern.—It is laid down as common law, by Sir Edward Coke, that the King cannot *personally* distribute justice, having delegated his *whole judicial power to the judges* of his several Courts.—Hence it must follow that the King in his person, cannot exercise an original judicial

---

* That a dernier resort cannot be lodged in a dependent state, because the law, appointed or permitted to such inferior dominion, might be insensibly changed within itself, without the assent of the Superior, to the disadvantage or diminution of the superiority. VAUGH. 402.

† 1 Blackstone, 231.

power upon the principles of feodal sovereignty, over the property of a country having the benefit of the common law. —The question therefore is, whether or not America is such a Country?

The nature of the operation of the Common Law, in establishments of natural English Subjects in America, as it is a point that has been more minutely enquired into within these eight or ten years, than ever it was at any time before; so without doubt, that point of law is better understood at this day, than at any time preceding.—Hence, notwithstanding it has been laid down, that the Common Law has no natural operation in the American Colonies obtained by conquest or treaties;* yet the more modern and better position now established as a settled point is, that English Subjects emigrating from England to Colonize America, carry with them inherently in their persons, a title, which is unalienable, and which no time or climate can invalidate, to enjoy the benefits of the common law in America; where, upon their arrival, it is *eo instanti* of force.— And such were the *Lares* our Forefathers religiously embarked with themselves, to protect them and their Posterity, in the Wilds of America! Thus undoubtedly possessed of the Birthrights of Englishmen, Rights evidenced by Magna Charta! shall we suffer them to be frittered away, or in any degree to be invalidated by a *fiction*, and artificial refinement of original judicial power, upon principles of feodal sovereignty?—Shall an *original Sovereignty, long annihilated in the English Crown* by common law, now be permitted to revive by a fiction, *to destroy original Rights*, expressly and often ascertained by the Forefathers of the Americans, and admitted as often by the Kings of England? —To expect this, is to think the Americans have no reasoning faculties.—But supposing the position to be true, that the common law not naturally operating in America, the Crown therefore possessed in appeals, an original jurisdiction, upon the principles of feodal Sovereignty. Yet of what importance can this be in support of the jurisdiction, since it must cease when the common law operates, which it has long since done in America; and besides the Crown in the most express terms has relinquished such a jurisdiction, if it could have had any

* 1 Blackstone, 107.

such, by the Charters granted to the American Colonies?—In these Charters, the Crown has covenanted with the Emigrants to America, that they, and *their descendants* there to be born, shall be in all things held, treated and *reputed as* the liege faithful people of us, our heirs and successors born within this our kingdom, to have and enjoy all Liberties, *Franchises and Privileges* of this our Kingdom of England, *as our Liege People* born within the same.*—Can words be more explicit?—Has not the Crown by this covenant, relinquished the Idea of feodal Sovereignty? Otherwise, how are the Americans to be deemed to have and enjoy all the Liberties and Franchises of England, *as and in like manner* with the liege People born there?—And as we know the Crown has no feodal Sovereignty over them, and cannot exercise any original jurisdiction over their Appeals; so neither can it legally arrogate a right to exercise an original jurisdiction over Appeals from America, whose inhabitants the Crown has, by Charters, declared shall be held, and reputed *to have and enjoy* all the Liberties and Franchises of England, in like manner *as the People* of England themselves. —At this period, the King's right to an Appellate Jurisdiction over disputes about American property, seems absolutely annihilated, to all intents and purposes to which arguments can operate.—However, I shall continue the subject, in order to settle it by a point of law.

It is laid down, that the powers which are vested in the Crown by the laws of England, are necessary for the support of Society; and do not intrench any farther on our natural liberties, than is expedient for the maintenance of our civil.† Nothing can be more equitable than such a principle of law. America joins issue upon it. She pleads that the *civil liberties* of Great-Britain and of America, cannot sustain any prejudice by American appeals being carried to the House of Lords, and produces that mode of proceeding from Ireland, as evidence of the propriety of the plea.—*Bracton* says, *Nihil aliud potest Rex, nisi id solum quod de jure potest*—How then, by any fiction, can the prerogative withhold appeals from being carried to the House of Lords, when such a measure *is not* "*expedient*

* Carolina Charter, 17 Car. 2.
† 1 Blackstone, 237.

for the maintenance of our civil liberties?"—Or how can the
Prerogative militate, to the partial violation of an express Statute* enacting, that the King and Privy Council shall not "by
English Bill, Petition, Articles, Libel *or any other arbitrary way*
whatsoever, examine or draw into question, determine or dispose of the lands, tenements, hereditaments, goods or chattels
of any of the subjects of this Kingdom?"—Were not our Forefathers Englishmen, and are not we, their descendants, subjects
of England? Yes, but the Statute does not respect Americans,
no mention is made of them.—Strange! that it must be construed so very strictly, as not to admit the common import of
the words, "*any* of the subjects," nay, the commonly equitable
construction of those words.—Can it be imagined that the
Justice, and equitable policy of that Parliament, meant to subject the Americans of that period, to the Judgment of a tribunal
they themselves no longer dared to trust?—Would not such a
sacrifice of the Americans, be the highest violation of Justice?
The Parliament thought so, and included the Americans under
the expression "ANY *of the Subjects* OF *this Kingdom*," in like
manner as Ireland is construed to be included under the general words "*within* ANY OF *the King's dominions*.[†] Thus, I
may safely lay it down, as a point of law not to be denied, that
the Statute of Charles, does *incapacitate* the King and Privy
Council from exercising, over *the property* of Americans, *Subjects* of the English Crown, *any judicial* power whatsoever,
except in appeals from the Court of Admiralty.[†] And farther,
that no Act of Assembly of a dependent Colony, an inferior
state, *can* vest in the English Crown, the Imperial state, any
power or jurisdiction to be exercised in the Imperial state, or
even to appertain to the Crown of England, which the law of
the Imperial dominion of England expressly says *cannot vest*
in, or appertain to the Crown to be exercised over "*any* of the
Subjects *of* the Kingdom."—I here rest the point relative to
the King's appellate jurisdiction over American property. I
shall however, continue the subject upon an entire *new ground*
of argument, not with any design, more firmly to establish our

* 16 Car. 1. c. 10.
† 1 Blackstone, 101.
‡ 6 Anne, C. 37.

claim of exemption from such a jurisdiction, but for the sole purpose of claiming objects, in their nature unlimited, and of the utmost importance to the Liberties of America.

It is laid down, that the fundamental rights of Englishmen, is that *residuum* of natural liberty, which is not required by the laws of Society to be sacrificed to public convenience.*—Hence, I may safely lay it down, that at any time when, the public convenience no longer requiring, the law of the Society remits a sacrifice of a particular Natural liberty; then that natural liberty reverts *eo instanti* to the residuum, for the benefit and advantage of the common and joint heirs of that residuum, to all intents and purposes, as if it had never at any time been separated from it, to be sacrificed to the public convenience. Thus, there cannot at any time be any encrease of liberty to the English Subject, but what his Ancestor coeval with the Constitution was absolutely possessed of, and then separated from the residuum, to be sacrificed as long as the public convenience should require it, with remainder-over to revert to the residuum vesting in his Heirs. The conclusion therefore must be, that whenever an Act of Parliament remits the Sacrifice of a natural liberty, and thereby *ipso facto* re-annexes it to the main Stock of the residuum, it becomes a part of that residuum as if it had never been separated from it; and the Americans being with the People of England, equal Heirs of this residuum, however encreased by the *remainders-over* resulting to it, must at once enter into possession of this natural liberty, now *again* become a component part of the residuum, without any necessity of their being mentioned in the Public Act, signifying that the public convenience no longer requires a Sacrifice, of that particular natural liberty, or exemption from the jurisdiction of the Crown. Upon these principles, the Americans may justly claim to participate, in *every restoration* of natural right, liberty, or exemption in any shape, from the Royal influence, power and jurisdiction, which the People of England shall at any time receive:—By the independence of the Judges, assuring to the Public a security against the influence of the Crown; as well as the being delivered from the Royal power, by their Properties being exempted from the Jurisdiction of the King and Privy

* I Blackstone, 129.

Council. A tribunal, which, as it has been, so, it may again be thought, inclined to pronounce that for law, which may be most agreeable to themselves.* And what just reason can there be, that the property of the Americans should be under the juris-diction of a tribunal, which the People of England themselves dare no longer trust? Why this odiously unjust distinction, be-tween people of the same blood and allegiance? But this is not the only harsh partiality of the English domination.—Why is it a principle of their law, that from all the dominions of the Crown, *except Great-Britain and Ireland*, an appellate jurisdic-tion in the last resort, is vested in the King and Privy Council, upon the principles of feudal sovereignty?[†] Upon what princi-ple of law is this exception grounded in favour of Ireland?—Let us examine into the nature of her dependence upon the Crown of Great-Britain, and let my purpose, to form a comparison between the liberties of Ireland and America, justify my con-tinuing the Subject of Appeals. The original and true ground of this dependence, is by conquest.[‡]—So far then, the nature of the acquisition of the *terra firma* of Ireland and America, is in law considered alike; and therefore as the King may alter the original laws of the acquired Indian and French territories in America, so he may in like manner alter at his will and pleasure, the laws of the acquired territory of Ireland, and by conse-quence, the Crown cannot but have an appellate jurisdiction in the last resort, over the Irish, Indians and French, *equally* conquered, and inhabiting countries equally acquired, by con-quest or by treaties and cession. As this must be granted, then, whence comes the exception in favour of Ireland?—I cannot see that it has arisen any otherwise, than by a Statute there, confirming, as Sir Edward Coke[§] apprehends, the letters patent of King John, ordaining, in right of the dominion by conquest, that Ireland should be governed by the laws of England; that is the common law, instead of the Brehon law of Ireland.[¶]— If thus, the common law of England obtaining in Ireland,

* 1 Blackstone, 269.
† 1 Blackstone, 269.
‡ 1 Blackstone, 231.
§ 2 Inst. 141.
¶ Vaugh 294.—2 Pryn. Rec. 85.—7 Rep. 23.

emancipated, as it certainly did, the *originally conquered Inhabitants* of the territory, from the King's appellate jurisdiction upon principles of feodal Sovereignty; *the English Colonies and Settlements in America* must, *a fortiori*, be equally emancipated by the same operation of the Common Law, first established in most of them, by Acts of their Assemblies, and now in all, by the late doctrine, that the law is the inherent natural right of every English Settlement in America. And if, notwithstanding, the common law operating in America, equally as in Ireland, the King still exercises over the former, an original appellate jurisdiction in the last resort, upon principles of feodal sovereignty, by what *law not applicable* to the former, is the latter emancipated from that *jurisdiction, originally applicable* to each?—A Statute* of George the first, annihilated the appellate Jurisdiction of their House of Lords—there was *no Statute directing*, that Appeals from Ireland should go to the House of Lords in England, and *therefore it is evident* they found their way there, and *by the conveyance and mere operation of the Common Law*. America, not having any appellate jurisdiction in the dernier resort within herself, was then, in that respect, in the same situation in which Ireland was reduced by the Act of George the first, and the common law being of force *equally in the two Colonies*, why should not Appeals from America as from Ireland, equally find their way to the House of Lords in England, *by the same conveyance and mere operation of the same common law?*—The Irish, Indians and French were originally Aliens, and it seems incomprehensible to me, that the English Colonists in America, can, by any fiction of law, so lose their natural rights of inheritance under the English Crown, as to be reduced, to the situation of Aliens *conquered*, and *therefore* bound to admit the law of the conquering Monarch. In short, the English Colonies in America, are taxed *against* their consent; their criminals have a power, by English law, *to fly* from their just vengeance; the value of their property *is taken from them*, and vested in the Crown; *Despotism* is established, in an English Province *containing* 150,000 *French Souls*, as a *Precedent* and *Terror* to the rest of the Continent—BECAUSE the English Colonists of America *quitted* their native Country, to

* 6 Geo. I. c. 5.

better their own fortunes, and *to* ENABLE *Great-Britain to form* the most lucrative Colonies a Parent State ever possessed—to establish the most powerful Empire the World ever saw—and to be at present in her turn the rising Power in Europe.

A most striking instance of *justice and gratitude* to Colonists, who, according to the present system of Europe, form the Basis of the British Grandeur!—Colonists! who being justly and tenderly treated, bid fair to render the British Empire, more powerful, more glorious, and more durable, than any we find recorded in historic page.—But Alas! instead of Parental tenderness, we experience a Step-Mother's severity—instead of justice, we receive marks of the most unfeeling ingratitude!—Why should not the English Colonists in America, enjoy the same national rights, which the English Colonists in Ireland possess? Are not their rights the same, equally derived from one and the same source?—It is with indignation the Americans, blood of the blood of the Imperial People, see themselves, by their own blood, refused the most valuable civil rights; which they have readily granted to the very Irish, an Alien race, conquered by their common Forefathers.—The Irish carry their appeals to the same dernier resort, and there, on equal terms, litigate their disputes with their conquerors. But the Americans, like a vanquished People, are obliged, in the dernier resort, to appeal to the King in Council; and as King John gave the Irish Law, in right of dominion by conquest, so the Americans, altho' of the blood of the conquerors, are under the hard necessity of receiving that for law, which their own natural Monarch shall be pleased to pronounce!—Sorely as Ireland is pressed, how preferable is her political Situation to that of America! Ireland a country conquered, and fattened by the slaughtering sword of England, and now, in *a considerable proportion, peopled* with English Colonists, gives Aids to the Crown, only at her own pleasure; for the Imperial People do not Tax her, because her Representatives "*are not summoned to the English Parliament:*"* and again, "Ireland hath a Parliament of its own, and our Statutes do not bind them, *because they do not send Knights to our Parliament.*"†

---

* Year Books. 20 Hen. VI. 8.
† 2 Ric. III. 12.

—Constitutional as this doctrine is, it will not avail the English Colonists, by whom I may say *America is peopled*. O Americans! *You* are taxed, although *your* "Knights are not summoned," and the English Statutes, are construed to bind *you*, although *you* "do not send Knights," to the British Parliament:—like a conquered People, you hold your property, but by the law of the Monarch, pronounced by the *advice of the Minister!*— Americans, now, no longer expect spontaneous justice, from the British Dominion, and it is with indignation, that even without any *political reason of State*, they see themselves postponed in favour, and in important religious and Civil rights, to the People of Ireland whom our Fathers conquered. Rights! worthy of being recovered, at the expence of slaughtered *hecatombs* of heroes.—The Americans are but upon a footing with the most trifling appendages of the British Crown, and formerly, appendages of Normandy, herself but a Dutchy in France!—Know yourselves, O Americans! You are but upon the same establishment, you enjoy but the same civil rights with the People of Guernsey, Jersey, Sark and Alderney. People like yourselves subject to the taxation, and Legislation of the British Parliament, and to the Royal award in disputes of property!

I here beg leave to make two observations, which I hope will be admitted with candour. That my frequent repetition of particular words, was ventured upon solely with a view to enforce, and put in the most striking light, arguments, which, without such repetitions, might not have appeared so pointed: And that every disagreeable word respecting the Irish Nation, was hazarded only with the same intention.

While Hannibal thundered at the Gates of Rome, such was the fortitude of the Romans, a people destined to be *Populum latè regem*, that in the Forum was sold and bought, even the very ground on which Hannibal was encamped. The Romans opposed him with a vigour, the more formidable, by being temperate. The event was suitable to the conduct. Let us imitate such an example. Let us not give up our rights, because a military government is formed, upon principles of the most baneful policy to the liberties of America, to extend along, almost, our whole Western frontier; an appearance infinitely more formidable, to the Sea Coast Colonies, than the late chain of Forts in that quarter, commanded under French commissions; a government accustomed to Despotism from its first existence; a people who have always hated, and, by their Spiritual Rulers, will ever be taught to hate us, as *Heretics*, and *Enemies of the Grand Monarque*, and, by their political rulers, to hate us as *Enemies to Despotism.*—Let us not despair, because armies are, as I may say, encamped upon our rights. No! we will still consider them, our property, as the Romans did their Soil, which Hannibal covered with his Numidians, and which he held planted with his hostile ensigns.

The Eyes and Attention of America, nay of Europe, are fixed upon the American Congress—O Deputies! I doubt not, but that you will act worthy of such an expectation.—Calmly deliberate upon, then respectfully and boldly declare the Grievances and Rights of America.—Be wisely cautious what you determine, but let your determinations be, as fixed as Fate. And, by a firm demand of our Liberties, shew a genuine descent from our Patriotic Forefathers at Runningmede; in consequence of whose conduct, our Gracious Sovereign now possesses the Imperial Crown of Great-Britain, his Subjects derive the continuance of their Liberties, and I, an American, have a title to write my name

FREEMAN.

South-Carolina, Charles-Town, August 10, 1774.

Some Fugitive Thoughts on a Letter Signed Freeman, Addressed to the Deputies, Assembled at the High Court of Congress in Philadelphia. Charleston, 1774.

Although South Carolina Whigs welcomed Drayton's *Freeman* pamphlet, supporters of the British government were appalled, believing the pamphlet to be "full of the most seditious sentiments" and "altogether tending to excite a spirit of disaffection and rebellion in the Minds of his Majesty's subjects." Lieutenant Governor William Bull, Drayton's uncle, was infuriated by the pamphlet and considered removing his nephew from the council; he eventually decided that such a removal would only make Drayton a martyr in the "eyes of the discontented," whom "he has been courting with unwearied diligence." Two judges from Ireland were insulted by Drayton's labeling them ignorant and corrupt placemen without roots in Carolina society, and they challenged him to a duel. Drayton agreed but proposed that they "settle the Affair like a Gentleman—by sword—a Gentleman's Weapon," insuring that the duel never came off. Eventually Drayton's patriotic harangues from the bench and in the press wore out the patience of Crown officials in both Charleston and London, and he was replaced as assistant judge by yet another political appointee from Britain. As Drayton was the last native Carolinian holding a major judgeship, all the province's top judicial positions were therefore occupied by appointees from Britain.

The identity of "Back Settler," the author of *Some Fugitive Thoughts*, is unknown, but he was obviously one of Drayton's growing number of enemies. He was an extreme enthusiast for parliamentary sovereignty, pointing out correctly that the Bill of Rights, the Petition of Rights, the Act of Settlement, even the Magna Charta, were "subject to the Controul of Parliament" and "confirm its imperial Authority." Even "the Crown and Dominions of the State" were under "the unmeasurable Power of Parliament." When the colonists came to America, "Back Settler" concluded, "they brought with them their Allegiance, an indelible Mark of their Subjection to a *British* Parliament." Here the author seems to be redefining the meaning of "allegiance." As a remnant of the personal lord-vassal relation of the feudal past, allegiance was traditionally understood to be owed to the king, not to Parliament, whose authority was based instead on its embodiment of all the social estates of the realm.

"Back Settler" may have misunderstood the meaning of allegiance, but he was clear about the ruinous implications of all the appeals by American Whigs, especially those in the south, to the same liberty that existed in England, where the 1772 *Somerset* court decision had apparently made slavery unconstitutional. "A general Manumission of Negroes," he warned, "is a Doctrine badly calculated for the Meridian of either *America* or the [West Indian] Islands."

SOME FUGITIVE

THOUGHTS

ON A LETTER

Signed FREEMAN,

ADDRESSED TO THE

DEPUTIES,

ASSEMBLED AT

The High Court of CONGRESS in

PHILADELPHIA.

By A BACK SETTLER.

SOUTH-CAROLINA.
Printed in the Year M DCC LXXIV.

To the Impartial Publick.

FULLY convinced of the Necessity which exists, that a strict Union between the Head and Members of the *British* Empire should take Place, no Person can harbour a sincerer Veneration for every Branch of it, or would more cordially rejoice in every Incident which had a Tendency to promote the Honour and Happiness of the Whole. Problematical as this Language may appear, in such as are disposed to offer modern publick Opinions, I can with Truth aver, that it is in Conformity to this Veneration, and that Conviction, I now attempt to expose the Imbecility of a Pamphlet signed *Freeman*, which lately made its Appearance, and point out a few of the many Absurdities with which it teems.

Men, who, to humour unprovoked Resentment on the one Hand, or to serve unjustifiable Purposes on the other, would invert the Order of Things, as well as the Grounds of established Policy, should be deemed Enemies to Society; but when this Principle of Corruption is extended, and Persons of distinguished Characters and upright Lives are singled out as Objects for Envy and Disappointment to wreck their Effects on, we may, without hesitating, proceed a Step further and venture to pronounce such, the Author of Calumnies, and destitute of every Species of honourable Feeling.

I must freely confess my present Difficulty. In this little Pamphlet, I could wish to give some exact Portrait of *Freeman*, but am at a Loss in the Choice of Colours. Whether I should consider him as patriotick or ministerial, heterodox, or orthodox, *simplex vel unus, compositus vel idem*, or both, or either, or neither, I cannot with Candour determine? But as it is not in the least my Intention to censure a Man who, in a personal Capacity, cannot much obstruct the publick Good, I will only confine myself to such Arguments as tend to illustrate the relative Connexion which subsists between *Great-Britain* and her Colonies.

I am well aware of the many Disadvantages which accompany an Attempt of this Nature. The best of Men are at Times liable to receive wrong Impressions, under the Influence of which many are apt to consider Objects only in that Point of

View which favours the natural Bias of the Mind. An Habit of thinking thus acquired is not readily erased; indeed with Time it collects a Strength in the Fancy frequently too solid for the most forcible Appearance of Reason or Argument to subdue. It is not to be then wondered that many Persons should be dazzled by those false Lights which are often displayed for sinister Purposes, though in other Respects possessed of a good Share of Understanding, as well as Integrity, Qualities which, in general, characterize *Americans*.

As I solemnly declare that I do not wear the Features of any Party, the impartial Publick may safely rely on the Candour of such Reasons as will be used in investigating the Nature of that Right of Dominion which *Great-Britain* claims over the Colonies of *North-America*. It is the immediate Inheritance of every Man born free, to give his Opinion on publick Affairs with Truth; as an Individual I claim that Right. My Opinion, however, shall be free, it must; for certainly it will be the Language of my Heart, unstudied, uncorrected.

The Sovereignty of a *British* Parliament over all the Dominions belonging to *Great-Britain* is so essential a Part of the Constitution, that the Right cannot be renounced without a Confusion of Ideas, or a treasonable Surrender. Notwithstanding that internal Evidence which arises in the Mind of a thinking Man to support the Truth of this Maxim, from a Survey of those Principles on which parliamentary Power is grounded, a Pamphlet, signed *Freeman*, was published a few Days since, replete with the most gross Strictures on the Conduct of his Majesty, his Ministers, his Parliament, with many others of his Majesty's Servants;—a Pamphlet, which, if accompanied with Grammar-Coherence, some Appearance of Decency, or shew of Reasoning, would evidently tend in its Consequences to subvert the Constitution, overturn a settled System of Subordination, and blot out that Ear-mark by which legal Dominion is distinguished.

The Arguments advanced by *Freeman* to sustain Positions in direct Contradiction to the inherent Rights of a State, are as incongruous as the Positions themselves are absurd. Since the first Establishment of Mankind into separate Societies, there was a supreme Power centered in some Part of the State or Society, for the Purpose of forming necessary Regulations for the Good of the Whole. It was justly presumed, that such Regulations, though essential for the Preservation of the Society, would not prove equally agreeable to each Individual, who might be left at Liberty to judge them a heavy Restraint on the Laws of Nature, there was a coercive Power, *ex necessitate*, established, which enjoined an implicit Obedience to such Laws as the Wisdom of the legislative Body judged proper to enact. The unequal Dictates of natural Law being thus wisely restrained, for the general Benefit of the Community, and reduced to a subordinate Limitation, no Arguments, on the supposed Impropriety of such Measures as were adopted by the acknowledged legislative Power could be admitted, being in their Nature opposed to those Principles on which the constitutional Power of the State or Society was founded.

On this Ground I will meet *Freeman*'s Opinion, and demonstrate its Incoherency: That Gentleman may, if he pleases, use the Dialect of metaphysical Jargon, I will confine myself to those plain Reasons which arise from a Contemplation of that constitutional Authority which is established in *Great-Britain*. His Opinion might possibly carry some Weight in *Foro Cœli*, but I strenuously deny that a Retrospect to the first Principles of our Constitution will render his Plea in Behalf of *American* Independence admissible at the Bar of an earthly Tribunal, guided by Wisdom or sound Policy. The Colonies were peopled and planted by *British* Subjects; at their Departure for *America*, they brought with them their Allegiance, an indelible Mark of their Subjection to a *British* Parliament; a Token of Obedience derived from their Ancestors, who were coeval with the Origin of the State, which no Change of Climate, no after-Act of theirs, could erase from their Persons. Thus circumstanced, the first Emigrants reached the western Continent, which had been previously declared to be subjected to the *English* State by the Discoverers thereof, agreeable to their Principles of Duty and Allegiance. The Proprietorship of those new Territories was granted by the executive Magistrate to the *Plymouth* Company, with Intent of promoting their Colonization; an Ability of forming such municipal Regulations for their Government, as were consistent with the relative Tie of Subjection they were under to the State, was also confirmed to the Company. They regularly exercised their Right of Power until their Priviledge ceased. Whatever local Regulations were made, were instituted in *England*. In like Manner the other Provinces of *America* were granted to different Persons, with Power of supreme Jurisdiction, though subservient to the Controul of Parliament: And no later than 1732, half a Dozen *English* Gentlemen regularly assembled at a Tavern in *London*, and there framed Laws for the Province of *Georgia*, for the Purpose of collecting a Revenue, *&c.* without the smallest Altercation held by the Inhabitants of that Province, concerning the Right of their Proprietors so to do. It must have required a wonderful Accession of Knowledge since the above Period, to discover; that a *British* Parliament, assembled in *Westminster-Hall*, cannot legally assume a Power which, when vested in Five or Six *British* Gentlemen, enjoying themselves over a Bottle at the *Crown-and-Anchor*, they held sacred, and with a placid Composure submitted to.

America is not a Part of the King's hereditary Estates; it constitutes a Share of the *British* Empire. The Dominion of the King in *America* arises from Parliament, which hath appointed him supreme Governor over all the Dominions of the State; and here I cannot sufficiently admire the Sophistry of Persons who affect Obedience to a Magistrate, and renounce at the same Time Subjection to that paramount Authority from which the Magistrate derives his Power. It is a very unlucky Circumstance, that Partizans for that Doctrine of Independence lately broached by *Freeman*, under a new political Phiz, cannot avoid the sad Alternative of either maintaining, that they are not Subjects to the King of *England*, or, if that be granted, of confessing their Depenence on a *British* Parliament, to the constituted chief Magistrate of which they humbly condescend to submit.

Parliament, foreseeing that the Crown might claim an exclusive Dominion over the Colonies, took an early Opportunity of asserting its Right. This Precaution in Parliament was very necessary. We find, that on a Complaint exhibited by the *New-England* Settlers to King *James* the First, against those who, under the Countenance of Parliament, carried on a Fishery on the Coasts, that many Outrages had been committed by Persons employed in that Business, on their Persons and Property, by cutting down Wood in their Enclosures, *&c.*

James was glad of this Pretext, thinking it would furnish him with a proper Excuse for usurping a sole and exclusive Right of Power. He therefore issued a Proclamation, not only for the Purpose of redressing Grievances complained of by the infant Settlers, but plainly importing the Idea of absolute Dominion, which in his regal Capacity he claimed. The *British* Senate now judged it high Time to interpose, and curb this gigantick Stride of Prerogative. The Affair being introduced into Parliament, *James* sent his Secretary with a Message desiring they may desist, as having no Authority over the Colonies;* but Parliament sensible of its Right, was not to be intimidated so far as to neglect a Matter of such Importance to the State, it resumed the Debates on that Subject, and expedited a Bill clearly thwarting the Assertions contained in the Royal Proclamation. Though this Bill miscarried in the Upper House, through the Machinations of the Duke of *Buckingham*, the Unanimity with which it passed the House of Commons, (there being only two dissenting Voices†) will remain a lasting Monument how conscious the Nation was of possessing a paramount Right over all the new Settlements and Territories acquired, conquered, or colonized, by its Subjects.

Parliament could not condescend to surrender into the Hands of the Crown a Right of so weighty a Concern. We accordingly find this Business taken up the Year following, in the House of Commons, and pursued with such Ardency,‡ that the King's Secretary gave up the Point. The supreme Jurisdiction of Parliament over the Colonies being thus established and acknowledged, by a Prince flushed with Ideas of divine Right, it cannot be doubted, that if its Competency was disputed, of exercising plenary Dominion over other Colonies, as well as *New-Plymouth*, it would have stept forth with the same Zeal, and incontrovertibly have determined its Right. Thus we see, that notwithstanding the Opinions Individuals now adays adopt, the Language of Parliament continues the same, with only this Difference, that the Struggle in the Reign of *James* the First was with the Crown, which attempted to oust it of its

* Commons Journal, 1622.
† The King's Secretary, and Mr. G—.
‡ Sir Edward Sackville's Speech, Com. Jour. 18th Feb. 1623.

supreme Jurisdiction, and that in the Reign of *George* the Third was with the Colonies, which contended for a Latitude of Independence inconsistent with every Idea of Subordination.

There is not the least Similitude between the two Periods of *Charles* the First and *George* the Third; nor would any Person draw the Portrait who had the smallest Particle of Respect for his Sovereign. Unhappy *Charles* became Heir to his Father's Follies as well as his Crown; taught from his Infancy to consider Parliaments as formal Expletives in the State, he judged them unnecessary when once they had ceased to echo the Will of the Sovereign, and determined to rule without them. In consequence of this fatal Resolution, arbitrary Exertions of the Prerogative grew into Use. Those were the Ills from which the Troubles of that Reign sprung. The House of Commons could no longer endure the continual Attacks which were made on its Privileges: It therefore, (not the People, as *Freeman* observes) arose in its Might, and established its undoubted Right. This was not a Contest between the Prince and a particular Body of his Subjects; it was strictly a Case in which the Sovereign was Plaintiff and Parliament Defendant: The Claim of the Crown was absolute and sole Dominion: Parliament demurred; and since no other Court of Judicature could determine this important Cause, the Appeal, from Necessity, lay to the God of Hosts. What a foul and ungenerous Misrepresentation! to combine the Events of two Princes Reigns, and assimilate them, where there is not the most distant Parity to justify the Observation; the one having usurped the Authority of Parliament, and substituted his will for Law; the other so tender of the Rights of his People, as not to proceed in the smallest Affairs without collecting the Sense of his Senate.

I will now consider the Weight of those Reasons which *Freeman* urges, to exempt *America* from Taxation by a *British* Parliament.

1. "That the *Americans* being descended from the same Ancestors with the People of *England*, and owing Fealty to the same Crown, are therefore equally with them entitled to the common Law of *England*, formed by their common Ancestors; and to all and singular the Benefits, Rights, Liberties and Claims, specified in *Magna Charta*, in the Petition of Rights, in the Bill of Rights, and in the Act of Settlement. They being no

more than principally declaratory of the Grounds of the fundamental Laws of *England*.

"Therefore, that the *British* Parliament ought not to have, and cannot of Right possess any Power to tax, or in any Shape to bind *American* Freeholders of the *British* Crown, seeing it is against the Franchises of the Land, because their Consent is not signified in Parliament, by a Representation of their own Election." The other principal Objection is, I think, the *adjudged Case in Point of* Durham.

Having already admitted the *Americans* (*though not descended from the same Ancestors with the People of* England, being a Compound of *English, Scots, Irish, French, Dutch,* &c. *New-York* in particular, was a *Dutch* Settlement until the Reign of *Charles* the Second, and was subject to the States of *Holland,* which gave Law and collected a Revenue therein) to be entitled to such Rights as *Englishmen* legally should enjoy, I cannot see a single Inference that arises from the Concession, to justify *Americans* in withdrawing an Obedience to such Laws as the Wisdom of the *English* State judges convenient to enact. It is the heavy Misfortune of *Freeman*, to quote Cases which, if properly considered, overthrow the Principles he would wish to establish. I must confess his Case is desperate; having impatiently solicited the Touch of Corruption for a long Series of Years, and meeting with only contemptuous Repulses, a lamentable Circumstance, which, when coupled with a total and merited Disregard of his Countrymen, and an entire Shipwreck of private Fortune, in the Reduction of which, alas! the Nicks of *Seven* and *Eleven* bore no inconsiderable Share. I say, to remedy those Calamities, Prudence must necessarily dictate some Measures proper to be pursued; and in this Pursuit, what Choice could be so happily adopted as that which bore the Aspect of Popularity, and offered an Occasion of revenging himself on an *unfeeling* Ministry, unfeeling, alas! to the earnest and repeated Solicitations of *Freeman*. I hope this will prove a sufficient Answer to such as may be led to inquire with *Hudibras,*

> Why he chose that cursed Sin,
> Hypocrisy to set up in,
> Because it is the general Calling,
> The only Saint's Bell that rings all in.

The first Reason assigned by the Author of the Letter to the general Congress, is so unguardedly couched that it may be retorted, I fear, with too much Success. *Exempli gratia*; the *Americans* are formed of different People, *Dutch, French, Swedes, Germans, Scots, Irish* and *English*.

Each Individual brought with him those unalienable Rights which were his Inheritance in the Country from whence he emigrated.

Therefore each of those Persons is entitled to all and singular the Rights, Privileges and Benefits, which they legally could enjoy in their several Countries from which they extracted their Origin.

To prevent, however, the Absurdity and Confusion which take birth from the Jumble of Matter contained in the first Position of *Freeman*'s Letter, I have taken Care to secure, by legal Demonstration, to the *Americans* the Rights of *Englishmen*, in a former Part of this short Treatise.

Magna Charta comes next in Order, which is "*such a Fellow that he will have no Sovereign.*" If he is "such a Fellow," he must be formidable indeed; but that he is "no such Fellow," will, I think, incontestibly appear.

The first and principal Care of the Barons who obtained that memorable Charter, was to secure the Roman Catholick Religion: Their second Precaution was to lop off the luxuriant Branches of *Norman* Hardships. That which was granted to the Barons at *Runnemede*, and which *Freeman* hath so highly extolled, I account of little Weight, and this for two Reasons; the first, as not sufficient for redressing the Oppressions which the People then groaned under; the second, because the Acquisition of the Charter did not carry a legal Complexion, being obtained from a Prince in Duress. But that Charter of Immunities, which was confirmed by King *Henry* the Third to his Barons, with Amendments in Favour of the Subject, which is properly stiled *Magna Charta*, may deserve the Eulogium of *Freeman*. I will now clearly demonstrate, that *Magna Charta* hath been, and still is, subject to the Controul of Parliament; first, in the Article of Religion, which is totally changed from that Form which the Barons contended for in Blood, and indeed established. Here mark. This Alteration in Religion was adopted by Parliament, which did not presume *Magna Charta* to be a "Fellow superior" to *its* enacting Power.

The second Instance of doing away the Substance of the great Charter is evident from every Day's Practice. Whereas the twenty-ninth Chapter of *Magna Charta* expresses, that no free Man shall be disseized of his Lands or Tenements, or banished, or imprisoned, unless by the Judgment of his Peers; we notwithstanding see a Writ issues in the first Instance from the Courts, which requires special Bail, or in Default thereof an Imprisonment of the Person ensues, before the Cause comes to a Trial, or a Judgment of his Peers can be obtained. Lest this Custom should be deemed an Abuse, and uncountenanced by Parliament, we have only to refer to those various Acts of Insolvency made for the Relief of the Unhappy. Although those humane Laws free many Objects from the Claws of merciless Creditors, is it not clearly apparent, that by a Side-Wind they support, a Custom expressed in Cap. 29th of *Magna Charta*, to be oppressive and unwarrantable? Indeed the Wisdom of that Body which enacted a Law in the Reign of *Edward* the Third, that *Magna Charta* should be deemed and considered as the common Law of *England*, was not very conspicuous; for if it was the common Law of the Realm, or *lex non scripta*, and stood unrepealed by any Statute, it imported such absolute Authority and Verity in itself, as not to require the Aid of Parliament to sustain it. But when an Act had been passed for that Purpose, so far from confirming the Substance of the Charter for common Law, that every immemorial Custom or municipal Usage contained therein must immediately lose its Habit of Action, and assume the Name of *lex scripta*, thro' the legal Operation of that Statute. Even this Law, tho' not penned with a superabundant Share of Wisdom, is an incontestible Proof that Parliament only considered the great Charter as the best Confirmation of the Subjects Rights that could then be obtained, and by no Means fastened on it an Idea of an exclusive paramount Controul over subsequent Parliaments, which in Truth have repealed, explained or rescinded, almost every Article in this celebrated Charter, notwithstanding the blind Assertion, "that he is such a Fellow, that he will have no Sovereign." I will now proceed and speak on the *Petition of Rights*, which is the next in Order of Succession.

The Nature of this Petition is so unconnected with the Purpose it was intended to second, that the Author of the Letter to the Delegates must certainly have imagined no Person properly informed of our History would have ever perused it. Supplemental Acts of State to supply the Defect of Laws, Tonnage and Poundage, and a Collection of other Duties upon Merchandises of all Kinds, *all which had been positively refused to be granted by Act of Parliament*, with many other Impositions on Trade, formed the Basis on which the Superstructure of this Petition was raised. This also was a Contest between the *King and his Parliament*, and not in any Degree analagous to the Case of the *Americans*. I could say more on this Head; but behold the *Bill of Rights*, which claims some little Attention.

What new and curious Alliances are hourly forming! *Freeman* is become a Supporter of the Bill of Rights. How? From Habit of Body or Conviction of Mind? From neither! Having exhausted his Stock of ministerial Expectation, and soured by Disappointment, he hath publickly avowed his Apostacy, and prophecied the Approach of the final Ruin of *American* Freedom, with nearly as much Zeal as *George Fox* did the Destruction of the *English* Monarchy in 1660. However, it is Time to use a serious Dialect. The Bill of Rights hath not the smallest Tendency to support the Opinion of *Freeman*. This Bulwark of Freedom was erected for another Purpose: It was a positive Declaration made by Parliament, of those Conditions by which a Tenure of the *British* Crown could be held. The supreme Authority of Parliament, not only over all the *British* Dominions, but also over the Crown, was rendered manifest at this memorable Period; and the Subjection of the Colonies to Parliament cannot be more strongly featured than in that Resolve of the Assembly of *Virginia*, which unanimously agreed, That if "the Parliament had constituted the Prince of *Orange* King, *we, who are subject to Parliament, must acknowledge him likewise*." The fifth Position now only remains to be considered, which is the *Act of Settlement*; an Act equally fatal to the Designs *Freeman* would wish to inculcate as any of the preceding.

Surely the Planet which presided over this Gentleman's Nativity must have been of a very inauspicious Nature, and given early Omens of the left-handed Singularity of Fortune which was to accompany him in his political Walk of Life. That a Man, *pro causis*, may be an Enemy to others is not very uncommon; but when a Person becomes the bitterest Enemy of the Cause he intended to establish, it is a convincing Proof that he hath attained the Summit of Folly. The smallest Attention to those Principles on which the Act of Settlement was founded, will render the Truth of this Assertion incontrovertibly clear.

The Heart of Man could not devise an Expedient, or produce a Case wherein the unbounded Power of Parliament could appear in that Plenitude of legal Lustre with which it did in the Act of Settlement. The Ordinance formed for the Trial of *Charles* the First, was neither constitutional or parliamentary: The Grant of the Crown to King *William*, on the Abdication, wanted something of Form, and can only be justified on Principles of Necessity, by such as would draw Conclusions from abstracted Principles of Government; tho', as *Blackstone* observes, the safest Way for the Subject is to consider that Transaction on the Footing of solid Authority: But in the Act of Settlement Parliament actually appeared in the Zenith of its legal Omnipotence. By this Act we see Parliament modelling the Crown, and limiting it to Persons not in a regular but a parliamentary Order of Succession. And farther; the Issue of King *William*, by any other Queen except *Mary*, excluded from the Inheritance of their Father's Crown, to make Way for the Accession of the Princess *Anne* and her Issue to the Throne; on Failure of which, the Crown was to revert to the Issue of King *William*, if *in esse*; or, in Default thereof, the lineal Descendants of King *James* the First were to inherit; under which last Clause King *George* the First was called to the Empire, Great Grandfather to our present most gracious Sovereign, whose Life may God long perpetuate.

The Case of *Durham* is by no Means applicable to the Colonies: It is a County situated in *England*, and paid Taxes equally with the represented Places of that Kingdom before it obtained the Privilege of Representation. This County was ordered to send two Knights to represent it, at the first

Parliament of *Edward* the Third: Its Inhabitants presented a
Petition to *Mortimer* signifying their Poverty, and could not
well disburse Money for the Knights Attendance, but that, as
heretofore, they would contribute their Proportion of all general Assessments. We accordingly find, specified in *Doomesday-
Book*, the different Levies collected in *Durroman*, or *Durham*, as
it is now called, when general Aids were required. The two
cities in *England* most famed for Manufactures are now unrepresented, *viz. Bermingham* and *Manchester*. A single Doubt is
not to be started, that had they desired a Representation it
would have been allowed them. Indeed the former had the
Offer of Privilege made it in 1766, by the Marquis of *Rockingham*, but it was declined: The Inhabitants of those Towns are
a wise and loyal People, satisfied with the Blessings arising
from the auspicious Reign of the most humane Prince that
ever graced a Throne. They look for nothing more on that
Head, but bestow their whole Attention on the Acquisition of
Riches and Greatness.

When the Affair of *Durham* was agitated in the Reign of
Charles the Second, the Reasons quickly appeared for intro-
ducing the Motion in Behalf of its Representation. This was a
ministerial Manœuvre, to give Sir *John Willoughby*, a warm
Espouser of the Doctrine of passive Obedience, a Seat in the
House of Commons. The popular Party, headed by Sir *John
Coventry*, distinguished themselves in Opposition, in the Lower
House: As did the Earl of *Shaftsbury* in the Upper. It was,
however, agreed to, and a Right of Representation confirmed
to *Durham*.

By what strange Fatality hath the Author of the Letter to the
Delegates been induced to furnish his Adversaries with such a
Number of unsurmountable Arguments against himself? The
most learned of Men may at Times inattentively stumble into
an Error; but such a Catalogue of Absurdities is somewhat
uncommon, and must oust of him of all Benefit of Clergy in
the argumentative World.

Indeed the first Position laid down by this Gentleman,
"That the *Americans* being descended from the same Ancestors with the People of *England*," would imply a dangerous
Tendency, to deprive one Moiety of *Americans* of those specified Rights which, as *English* Subjects, they have a just Right to

exercise: For by this Method of Reasoning it would follow, that no *Americans* but such as were descended from the same Ancestors with the People of *England*, could with Propriety become Candidates for the chartered Rights of *Englishmen*. The *Americans*, however, are entitled in general to every legal Right a Subject can demand. Not on the Principle of "being descended from the same Ancestors with the People of *England*;" but for this Reason, that on their Arrival in *America*, they settled in a Colony, the Territory of which, with the whole Country adjoining, was declared by *Cabot*, who was authorised by *Henry* VII. to make Discoveries, to be subject to the *English* State, and to constitute a Part of its Dominions.

It is a Truth to which all Men have assented; that the *Swedes* were the first People who colonized both Sides of the River *Delaware*. They called this Settlement *New-Sweden*. They fortified it in several Places, and erected a Fort in particular, which they named *Elsenburgh*, a Name it still preserves. The *Dutch* laid a Claim to this Country, pretending that an *Englishman*, which they had appointed for the Purpose, was the first Discoverer thereof in 1609. They formed a Colony at the Mouth of *Hudson*'s River, which they named *New-Amsterdam* (now *New-York*) and the Country adjoining was called *New-Netherland*. They extended those Settlements as far as Fort *Orange* (now Fort *Albany*) which is a Distance of forty Leagues up the River. They also established a Colony on the Banks of *Connecticut* River. The prodigious Increase of the *Dutch* in those Parts rendered them formidable to the *Swedes*, who apprehending lest their more powerful Neighbours should wrest their Possessions from them, agreed to throw themselves under the Protection of the States of *Holland*; and accordingly made a formal Surrender of that Country to the *Dutch* Governor. Parliament considered those *Dutch* Settlements as bold Usurpations on a *British* Territory; a Conclusion which flowed from the Principle of *Cabot*'s Discovery. Therefore, in the Reign of *Charles* the Second, the House of Commons voted a large Sum for fitting out a Fleet for the Reduction of *New-Netherland*; which was accordingly effected, and the whole Country reduced to the Obedience of the *English* State.

As the Proprietory of *Maryland* had been granted by the Crown to Lord *Baltimore*, a Roman Catholick, that Nobleman's

Son brought over a great Number of respectable Popish Families from *Ireland*: These were the actual and primary Settlers of that Province. Therefore, agreeable to *Freeman*'s Logick, we must Reason thus:

The Inhabitants of *Maryland* being descended from the same Ancestors with the Papists of *Ireland*, have a Right, and ought to enjoy all and singular the Privileges and Immunities which Papists enjoy in *Ireland*.

But the Papists in *Ireland* being declared by Law incapable of exercising any of those Rights or Immunities which Protestants in that Kingdom hold and enjoy.

Therefore the Inhabitants of *Maryland*, &c.

The manifest Absurdity of such Logick is evidently conspicuous. Were I not well satisfied that *Freeman*'s Appetite for ministerial Goods was truly sickened, I would have concluded his Performance a high finished Stroke in Politicks, to subject three-fourths of *Americans* to the State of Aliens or Papists, under the outward Cloak of Patriotism. I have only continued that invidious Distinction between *English* and *Irish* which characterizes the Writer of the Letter to the Deputies, with a View of exposing the Fallacy of that Principle the Distinction was created to sustain.

I believe now I may venture to affirm, that *Magna Charta*, the *Petition of Rights*, the *Bill of Rights*, and the *Act of Settlement*, serve but to shew the unmeasurable Power of Parliament over the Crown and Dominions of the State. So distant are they from generating an Incapacity in the *British* Senate, that they confirm its imperial Authority. I cannot sufficiently wonder that *Freeman* should overlook the two principal Laws now extant, which establish the Subject's Right, *viz.* the 12th *Charles* the Second, and the *Habeas Corpus* Act. The former removed every Oppression affecting Property, by reducing the Lands of the Kingdom to free, or soccage Tenure: The latter effectually secured the Person of the Subject from every Attack that Tyranny could devise. It is therefore well observed by a learned Judge, that *Magna Charta*, and *Charta de Foresta*, only pruned off some of the out-shooting Branches of *Norman* Tyranny: But those two Acts of *Charles* the Second's Reign plucked up every Root from which Oppression could by any Possibility take Birth. How those two only Monuments of

British Freedom should escape the Notice of the learned Author of the Letter to the Delegates is inconceiveable to me: But, when we see a String of Laws appealed to, Laws, which, on a proper Information of their Tendency, incontrovertibly damn the Assertions of the Appealer, can we possibly prevent that risible *Ton* which every Muscle of the Face will naturally assume?

Seeing, therefore, that the various Arguments deduced to limit the taxing Attribute of Parliament have not only failed, but fatally operated to demonstrate its perfect Ability, I will now consider the Principles of feodal Power, on which the Sovereignty of the *British* State is founded. "Shall an original Sovereignty, long annihilated in the *English* Crown by common Law, now be permitted to revive by a Fiction, to destroy original Rights, expressly, and often ascertained by the Forefathers of the *Americans*, and admitted as often by the Kings of *England*? To expect this, is to think the *Americans* have no reasoning Faculties." Thus far *Freeman*.

It is evident, that a very reasoning Faculty is here required, to form even a distant Idea of what this loose and ungrammatical Jumble of Words would import; yet, lest it should appear to be the Production of a Mind totally lost in the wide Expanse of Space, I will beg leave to explain its Tendency: Which is, that there does not exist a legislative Power on Earth warranted with sufficient Authority to deprive a Man of any one original or natural Right which in a State of Nature he is entitled to. Wonderful Reasoning!—has this Phænomenon been sent on Earth to recall the original Jurisdiction of Societies? By a talismanick Wave to remit into the Hands of the People, those Powers delegated by their Ancestors for the Purpose of correcting the savage Abuse of natural Law! Has this *speculum Justitiæ* perfectly forgot the first Principles of common Law, which Lord *Coke* hath laid down, that no absolute Property is vested in a Subject; that every Idea of *allodial* Right ceased on the Introduction of the feudal System—a System on which the King's Right to collect Quit-rent and Crown-rent is founded? and indeed, until the Appearance of this celebrated Letter to the Delegates, was never contested. It may not be improper to observe, that Ideas of *feodal Sovereignty were actually supported by the common Law*, "not annihilated," as *Freeman* asserts; and in all Cases where the Terrors of this lordly Dominion, are now suspended; with Thankfulness we must attribute it to the Wisdom of that Parliament which passed the *Soccage-Act*, in the 12th Year of *Charles* the Second's Reign. By this excellent Law the Lands of the Kingdom were ascertained to their Proprietors; and Tenants were freed from the vexatious and galling Oppression which took Rise from the slavish Tenures their feodal Tyrants subjected them to, and were only liable to those Assessments which Parliament at different Times would judge proper to lay on.

Principles of *feodal Sovereignty being incorporated with, and supported by common Law*; and the Hardships springing from such Principles being removed by *Statute Law*, does it not follow, that *Freeman*, not content with subjecting one Moiety of the *Americans* to the hard Condition of Aliens or Papists, would further deprive the Whole, of those Exemptions from feodal Dominion, which their *English* Brethren claim under Force of a Statute? Yet, lest I should be accused of Misrepresentation in a Matter of this Importance, I think it incumbent on me to quote the Gentleman's own Words.—"But supposing the Position to be true, that the common Law not naturally operating in *America*, the Crown therefore possessed in Appeals, an original Jurisdiction, upon the Principles of feodal Sovereignty; yet of what Importance can this be in Support of the Jurisdiction, since it must cease when the common Law operates, which it has long since in *America*." This surely is the most unlucky Argument *Freeman* hath hitherto used: In whatever extreme of Opposition it is placed in, it will be still found to establish feodal Tyranny in *America*. If the common Law did not naturally operate in this Country, in such a Case the *Americans* would be subject to the Right of feodal Sovereignty claimed by a superior State. If the common Law did naturally operate, we have also seen it would not have exempted *Americans* from an Obedience with its harsh Dictates. Two Reasons which can be urged will free this Assertion from every Colour of Doubt. The first, because the Idea of feodal Jurisdiction *was founded on, and supported by common Law*. The second, that the Authenticity it had received, and still continues to receive, in our Courts, in all Cases wherein it is not abolished by Statute, both was, and is, given upon the supposed Idea of being a *municipal Usage* of the Land. In this Light it operated to an extreme in *England* until the Reign of *Charles* the Second, when an Act passed which entirely discountenanced all its oppressive Severities. It is therefore evident, that the Writer of the Letter to the Delegates hath mistaken the Nature of the feodal System, or he could not have been guilty of such a criminal Want of both Accuracy and Attention to the *American* Interest in a Point of this high Moment.

The *Americans* cannot be Candidates for more Immunities than their Brethren in *England claim by Law*. Now, unless *Freeman* makes it appear that the Law made in the Reign of *Charles* the Second extends to all the Colonies of *North-America*, it must give an incurable Wound to the flattering Hopes I entertained, that the *Americans* were free Men, and entitled to every plenary Right of Exemption from feodal Hardship, a Subject residing in *England* actually enjoys.

It is not to be here understood, that the 12th of *Char*. II. had any farther Tendency than to remove the arbitrary Restraint under which the Subject's Property was held, from illegal Stretches of feodal Principles. The Idea was left untouched: It was only the frightful Edifice that was raised on this visionary Foundation, which tumbled beneath that invaluable Law. The Basis being of a magical Composition withstood the Shock, and indeed could not disappear without a Repeal of the whole Body of both Statute and Common Law; the great Outlines of which, in common with the Codes of every Nation in *Europe*, are founded on this visionary Principle. The Happiness of the Subject was not however compleated by this Law; it is true his Property was thereby secured; the Safety of his Person was not yet provided for: But the thirtieth Year of this King's Reign produced another Law called the *Habeas Corpus* Act, which, in Conjunction with the former, effectuated the Redemption of the Subject's Property and Person from every Device of Tyranny. These two Laws are the Palladium of *British* Freedom.

Were *Freeman*'s Principles adopted, and every genuine Right of Liberty which is established in *England* made attainable in *America*, it would complete the Ruin of many *American* Provinces, as well as the *West-India* Islands. A general Manumission of Negroes is a Doctrine badly calculated for the Meridian of either *America* or the Islands; yet it is one of those

original Rights, the Exercise of which all human Forms immediately enjoy, by setting a Foot on that happy Territory where
Slavery is forbidden to perch.

As the Compliance of the Judges with the Motion for issuing Writs of Assistance, hath been construed an Effect of their
Dependance on the Crown; and as the Author of the Letter to
the Delegates hath been induced on this Supposition to draw a
Comparison between "two Sets of Judges *learned in the Law*,
the one *Men of Property*—the other, Men without the *visible
Shadow* of Independence," it may not be improper to consider
at large those Reasons which determined the Judges to comply
with the Motion.

But, before I enter into these Considerations, it will be
necessary to take a Review of the superiour Courts of Judicature, established for the Benefit of the Community, and for the
Support of our glorious and excellent Constitution, together
with the indispensible Duty of Justices appointed by the Royal
Order to preside in each.

These Courts are divided in two Parts, *viz.* Law and Equity:
Judges in the former are sworn, in their Dispensation of Jus-
tice, to be guided by the Common and Statute Law of the
Realm. Any wilful Appeal to private Opinion, in their solemn
Determinations, where there is a Record which attests, or an
Act that declares, how the Law in the particular Case stands, is
a criminal Deviation from their Duty, and a flagrant Breach of
Oath, for which they are liable to be prosecuted, and most se-
verely punished.

However, lest a rigorous Determination of a Court of Law
should affect the Subject in Cases wherein he lay exposed to
the *Letter* of the Law; and, as it was *impossible* for him to obtain
Redress from *Judges sworn* to act *according to Law*; a Court of
Equity was established, and endued with Powers to mitigate
the Rigour of such Decisions as appeared not consistent with
equitable Principles of Justice.

This short Review of the Duty of Judges being ended, I am
now left at Liberty to consider the Propriety of the Conduct of
that "*Set*" of Judges which unanimously agreed that Writs of
Assistance should issue.

The Attorney-General moved the Court of Common-Pleas
in *February* Term 1773, for a Writ of this Nature. A Gentleman

who took Notes on that Day, hath done me the Favour of communicating to me the Substance of the Chief Justice's Argument; I will beg leave to insert it here.

"Tolls or Duties upon Merchandises, now called Customs, have been long payable to his Majesty's Predecessors, Kings and Queens of *England*; so long as to induce many to believe that they were the Inheritance of the King by immemorial Usage or common Law. But my Lord *Coke*, in his 2d *Institute*, Page 58, in his Exposition of *Magna Charta*, clearly demonstrates, that these Customs derived their Authority under the Sanction of an Act of Parliament, and were not allowable by common Law; but were first granted to the Crown, by the Statute of *West*. 1st, in the Reign of *Edw*. I. so that by this we see the King's Rights to Customs established by Authority of Parliament almost 500 Years since; and they now constitute a Part of the King's extraordinary Revenue. At first they were granted for only stated Terms of Years; and afterwards to the different Kings for Life, by different Acts of Parliament. I shall, however, go no farther back than the Reign of *Charles* II. when the Act of Tonnage and Poundage passed, among the first Laws made after the Restoration—in the 12th of *Char*. II. Cap. 4. By that Act a Subsidy of Tonnage and Poundage was given to his Majesty for Life, and the Rates of Merchandise were settled, as they were then agreed upon, by the Commons in Parliament, and signed by their Speaker.

"The same Duties were afterwards granted for Life to *Jac*. II. and *W*. III. And by three different Acts of Parliament made since, *viz*. 9th *Anne*, Cap. 6, the 1st *Geo*. I. Cap. 12, and the 3d *Geo*. I. Cap. 7, they are made perpetual; so that the King's Right thereto appears to be clear and indisputable, under the several Acts of Parliament mentioned.

"Immediately after the Act of Tonnage and Poundage had passed, it became necessary to secure to the King the Payment of the parliamentary Revenue granted him by that Act, and to prevent him of being defrauded thereof.

"And accordingly, by the 12th of the same King, Cap. 19, it was enacted, That where Goods liable to Customs, Subsidy, or other Duties, by the Act of Tonnage and Poundage, shall be conveyed away without Entry or Agreement for the Customs; that on Oath thereof before the Lord Treasurer, or any of the

Barons of the Exchequer, or the chief Magistrate of the Port or Place where the Offence was committed, or of the Place next adjoining thereto, it shall be lawful for the Lord Treasurer, &c. to issue Warrants to any Person, or Persons, enabling him or them, with Assistance of a Sheriff, Justice of Peace, or Constable, to enter *any* House by *Day*, where such Goods are *suspected* to be concealed; and in case of Resistance, to break open such Houses and seize, &c. and all Officers and Ministers of Justice are required to be aiding and assisting thereto.—No House to be entered except within a Month after the Offence is committed; and Damages may be recovered against a false Informer.

"The Remedy provided by this last mentioned Act was what was first suggested for securing the Payment of the King's Customs; but a very short Experience of it shewed that it was defective, and did not answer the intended Purpose; for after an Information received by the Officers of the Customs, the Time spent in taking the necessary Steps for obtaining the Warrant, generally gave the Offenders an Opportunity of privately conveying away the Goods. A further Act was therefore necessary; and we accordingly find, that in less than two Years after, an Act was passed, entitled, *An Act for preventing Frauds and regulating Abuses in his Majesty's Customs.* It is the 14th *Char.* II. Cap. 11. the Preamble of which sets forth, that, 'Forasmuch as it appears that several unlawful and indirect Means and Devices are daily put in Practice, to export and import Goods and Merchandises prohibited by the Laws and Statutes of this Kingdom, as also to defraud the King's most excellent Majesty of his Dues, Customs and Subsidies, as well by secret and deceitful Designs, as by open Force and Violence used against the King's Majesty's Officers employed in the Affairs of the Customs; for the better preventing of which Frauds and Violences in Time to come,' by the said Act, it is among other Things enacted, 'That it shall be lawful for any Person or Persons, authorized by Writ of Assistance under the Seal of the Court of Exchequer, to take a Constable, Headborough, or other publick Officer, being near the Place, and in the Day time to go and enter into any House, Shop, Cellar, Warehouse, Room or other Place; and in case of Resistance, to break open

Doors, Chests, Trunks, or other Package, there to seize, *&c.* any Kinds of Goods or Merchandise prohibited and uncustomed.'

"By this Act the Remedy became as complete as possible; the Formality of making Oath before the Lord Treasurer, a Baron of the Exchequer, or a chief Magistrate, on every Information of uncustomed or prohibited Goods, is dispensed with, and no Time lost, and as little Opportunity as possible given to secrete the Goods. Under this Act of Parliament, the Officers of the Customs in *England* are constantly armed with a Writ of Assistance, which is issued by the Clerk of the Exchequer as a Thing of Course, without any particular Application to the Court. Thus the Power of the Custom-House Officer is given him by Act of Parliament, and the Writ facilitates the Execution thereof: It is a Notification to the Constable of the Character and Station of the Officer; and is at the same Time a Security to the Subject, against others who might pretend to that Character, without a Right to assume it. By the former Act, the Officer acted under the Authority of any inferior Magistrate; his Power now emanates from a higher and more solemn Authority; a Writ under the Seal of the Court of Exchequer—a Disobedience to which is a Contempt of the Court.

"It remains now to be considered, how these Powers came to be extended to the Officers of his Majesty's Revenue in *America*.

"The first Act of Parliament I shall take Notice of for this Purpose is the 7 & 8 of *Will.* III. Cap. 22. entitled, *An Act for the more effectual preventing of Frauds, and regulating Abuses in the Plantation-Trade in* America. By this Act, it is among other Things provided, 'That the Officers for managing and collecting his Majesty's Revenue, and inspecting the Plantation-Trade in any of the Plantations in *America*, shall have the same Powers and Authority to visit and search Ships, *&c.* and to enter Houses or Warehouses, to search for, and seize, prohibited or uncustomed Goods; and, that the like Assistance shall be given to the said Officers, in the Execution of their Office, as by the 14th *Char.* II. is provided for the Officers in *England*.'

"By this Act, it is evident the Intention of the Legislature was to cloath the Custom-House Officers in *America* with the same Powers as those in *England*. But as the 14 *Char*. II. directs the Writs of Assistance to issue from the Court of Exchequer, and as such Courts are not generally established in *America*, for that Reason it became a Doubt whether any other Court could legally issue such Writs.

"This made a further Act of Parliament necessary. Accordingly, by the 7th *Geo*. III. Cap. 46, after reciting the 14th *Char*. II. the 7 & 8 *Will*. III. and then reciting, That no Authority being expressly given by the Act of King *William*, to any particular Court to grant such Writs of Assistance for the Officers in the Plantations, it is doubted, whether such Officers can legally enter Houses, and other Places on Land, to search for and seize Goods in the Manner directed by the said recited Acts. 'To obviate such Doubts for the future, and in order to carry the Intention of the said recited Acts into effectual Execution, it is enacted by the 7th *Geo*. III. That from and after the 20th of *November* 1767, such Writs of Assistance, to authorize and empower the Officers of his Majesty's Customs, to enter, and go into any House, Warehouse, Shop, Cellar, or other Place, in the *British* Colonies or Plantations in *America*, to search for, and seize, prohibited and uncustomed Goods, in the Manner directed by the said recited Acts, shall, and may be granted by the superior or supreme Court of Justice, having Jurisdiction within such Colony or Plantation respectively.'"

This last Act, therefore, places the Matter beyond all Doubt. It is a polar Star by which, agreeable to their Oath of Office, the Opinion of Law-Judges must be guided, and their Determination concluded. It leaves not the smallest Opening for a shuffling Disposition *to run with the Hare, and hunt with the Hound*. A positive Refusal of a Judge to comply with an Act of Parliament, is a violent Breach of the Trust reposed in him, and includes a Prosecution for high and mighty Crimes and Misdemeanours.

These were the Reasons which influenced the Chief Justice to comply with the Motion. An extensive Acquaintance with the various Laws relating to the Customs, from the earliest Period to the present Time, informed this Ornament of the Bench how the Law stood; and a *Conscience not ungrateful* to the Remembrance of a solemn Oath, constrained him to determine according to Law. The three Assistant-Judges, Messrs. *Savage, Coslett*, and *Murray*, concurred unanimously in this Decision, and gave weighty and substantial Reasons for coinciding with the Chief Justice's Opinion. Even Mr. Justice *Fewtrell* (whose Conduct is misrepresented by *Freeman* on this Occasion) entertained no Doubt of the *Legality* of issuing Writs of Assistance; and only hesitated in concurring with the other Judges from an Uncertainty which was the superior Court of Justice, the Court of Chancery or the Court of Common-Pleas; a Doubt which would have been entirely removed, by an Appeal to the Decision of all the Judges in *England*, on a Question proposed by the Lord Chancellor *Talbot, Anno* 1735, which was the supreme Court of Justice in the Kingdom. The House of Lords and the King's Bench were declared to be the two supreme Courts of Justice.*

Having taken a comprehensive View of the Arguments which constrained one "Set" of Judges, "Men without the *visible Shadow* of Independence" to grant those Writs, it will be only fair to consider what Motives could restrain another "Set" of Judges, *Men of Property*, from issuing such Writs. But, before I proceed further, it will not be amiss to observe, that *Freeman* might have been contented with holding up his own Conduct to publick Ridicule, without introducing the Names of other Gentlemen to share a Part of his Calamity. It is with Regret I answer this Passage in his Letter, as I am necessitated to analyze somewhat unfavourably thereon; yet, perhaps, my Method of censuring may do the Gentlemen at least as much Honour, as the ill-favoured Eulogiums bestowed on them by the Author of the Letter to the Delegates.

The first Motive, therefore, which naturally occurs, why Judges, *Men of Property*, in a mercantile Colony like this, should determine contrary to *written Law*, might arise from a partial Adherence to Self-Interest. The *best* of Men, as Times now run, are induced to take every Step of aggrandizing their Fortunes. The Spirit of accumulating Dollars, when added to that dissolving Satisfaction of Mind which a free born Subject of *America* tastes in seeing a stately Slave stand on every Perch of his extensive Plantation, is somewhat allayed by the bitter

* Vide Observations on Lord *Ferrers*'s Trial before the Lords.

Remembrance of paying Tribute to *Cæsar*. I may with Truth here add, that our Brethren in *England* would heartily concur with *Americans*, in the Doctrine of paying neither Taxes or Customs (with which it must be allowed they are heavily laden) were they not compelled by the positive Injunction of a superior Power, and with which, as inferiors, they are bound to comply.

The second Reason, why *they refused* to grant those Writs, is humourously related by *Freeman*; because the Opinion of the Bench was guided by *Rawlins Lowndes*, Esq; who, *Freeman* asserts, was not bred regularly to the Profession of the Law; and the other Judges went to School to Mr. *Lowndes*, who taught them to quaff such large Draughts of Law, as quickly enabled them to *administer Justice with publick Approbation*. This is, I think, the richest and most expressive Description of Quackery that ever caught my Attention. Indeed Empyrism is displayed with such *Pathos*, that I would have considered it in no other Light than of a *Burlesque* on the "Set" of learned Judges referred to, was I not sensible that the ingenious Author of the Letter to the Delegates, intended, *sub ficto nomine*, to be the Herald of his own Fame, and by the Side-Wind of his *Eulogium* on the great Abilities of Mr. *Lowndes*, "who had never eat Commons at the Temple," formed a Design to establish an Idea of his own *uncommon* Powers, by the sole Strength of which he hath been enabled to make such a rapid Progress in *Law-Story*, without the *vulgar* Aid of a *Temple*-Erudition.

I can now sincerely aver, that nothing but a warm Wish of promoting an Union between the Mother-Country and her Colonies, induced me to answer the mad Arguments of a Man, who, soured by Disappointment, would widen the Breach of Discontent: But, *Americans!* resume your Understanding, and discountenance every Design of Faction. Famed as you are for Justice, Humanity and Honour; it would ill become Men, justly celebrated for such godlike Virtues, to submit their Judgment as a Prey for Artifice to sport with; or to suffer their Attention to be diverted into any Channel but that which alone can render them a great and flourishing People.

Imperial *Rome*, which once gave Law to the World, fell by publick Discontents, as much as by Debauchery. Whilst the *Romans* continued a firm united People, they extended their

Conquests over the Earth; but when Faction reared its Head, and Persons thought it their Interest to embrace Extremes, ambitious Men were not wanting to keep these Breaches open: It was then the ancient *Roman* Virtue began to decline. Publick Offices, which were in the Gift of the People, were generally filled by their designing Leaders; indeed the most flagrant and turbulent Characters were commonly preferred. The guilty Custom drawing into an Establishment, soon rendered the Air of *Italy* too polluted for *Freedom* or *Order* to dwell in; they therefore winged their Way: By which Flight the *Romans* lost themselves and the Empire of the World together.

I will conclude this Pamphlet with an Advice to *Freeman*.

> *Frange, miser, calamos vigilataque prælia dele,*
> *Qui facis in parva sublimia carmina cella,*
> *Ut dignus venias hederis & imagine macra.*

Let Flames on thy unlucky Papers prey,
And Moths thro' written Pages eat their Way;
Thy Loves, thy Wars, thy Praises be forgot,
And all become one universal Blot.
The Rest is empty Praise, an Ivy Crown,
Or the lean Image of a mean Renown.

A BACK SETTLER.

Keowee, Sept. 25th, 1774.

[Jonathan Boucher?], A Letter from a Virginian, to the Members of the Congress to Be Held at Philadelphia, on the First of September, 1774. New York, 1774.

This pamphlet has been attributed to Jonathan Boucher, an English-born Anglican clergyman who served parishes in Maryland and Virginia and was tutor to George Washington's stepson before fleeing to England in 1775. But since he made no mention of it in his later *Reminiscences of an American Loyalist*, the attribution remains doubtful. It may show some similarities of style, but in tone and substance it seems more moderate than Boucher's other writings—perhaps because he wanted it to be more persuasive to the Congress. But it is certainly the work of someone firmly attached to the "great Nation" of Great Britain, someone who was alarmed by all the demagoguery and political quackery spreading throughout the colonies. Nothing was more dangerous, the author claimed, than "the false Refinements of speculative Men, who amuse themselves and the World, with visionary Ideas of Perfection, which never were, nor ever will be found, either in publick or in private Life."

In 1797, in exile in England, Boucher collected thirteen sermons he claimed to have delivered in the colonies between 1763 and 1775 and published them with a ninety-page introduction as *A View of the Causes and Consequences of the American Revolution*. He began by calling the American Revolution "one of the most remarkable events of modern times." As the French Revolution demonstrated, it had made the idea of "a great political revolution" an acceptable commonplace; indeed, a revolution was "now regarded as so very ordinary an event, that, however it may agitate the world whilst it is passing, when passed it merits being recorded merely as a common epoch." Ultimately, Boucher could not see, "in point of principle, . . . a shade of difference between the American revolution and the French rebellion." The French Revolution was in fact the "acknowledged and most distinguished offspring" of the American—which to a conservative like Boucher meant that chaos and terror reigned on both sides of the Atlantic.

A LETTER

From a VIRGINIAN,

TO THE

Members of the Congress

TO BE HELD

AT PHILADELPHIA,

ON

The first of SEPTEMBER, 1774.

PRINTED IN THE YEAR 1774.

A Letter, &c.

GENTLEMEN,

IN Times of publick Danger, every Man has a Right to offer his Advice; there are some Men who think it their Duty to do it, although on common Occasions they may be naturally too diffident of their own Opinions, or too indolent, to give themselves the Trouble to obtrude them on the World. If such Men happen to mistake their Talents, not from Vanity but from an Excess of Zeal, and meddle officiously with Matters above their Reach, they may be forgiven on the Score of their Intention: Even a modest Man is apt to over-rate his own Judgment where his Affections and Interests are deeply concerned.

My Zeal therefore in the common Cause must serve for my Excuse, if in the Course of this Letter I should give my Opinion more confidently than I ought to do, and seem to think myself, which is a very common Case, much wiser than I am.

You are soon to meet on the most serious Occasion that ever presented itself to this Country since its Existence.

The Harmony which subsisted, with little or no Interruption, between Great-Britain and her Colonies, from their very Infancy until of late, is in Danger of being destroyed for ever. The Habits of Kindness and Affection, on one Side, and of Respect and Obedience, on the other, (which prevailed during so long a Period, were in the highest Degree conducive to the Prosperity of this Country in particular, and are still necessary to its Security and Happiness) are changed into Murmurings, Discontents, and Reproaches; and will soon end, without some very extraordinary Interposition, in mutual and implacable Hatred. Complaints of Grievances, real or imaginary, are heard from one End of these Colonies to the other; the Minds of the People appear to be agitated as at some great Crisis; they wish, by a publick Consultation, to be assured of the general Opinion, by a Representation of every Province, to collect the calm, deliberate Determination of all the Provinces, to establish some publick Mark of mutual Confidence, that they may hold it up to the Parent Country, in all its Weight and Importance. For this Purpose, Gentlemen, you are delegated to the Congress. An absolute, perfect Representation of the People, never existed perhaps, but in Theory. You, it is true, have not been summoned, or convened, by any formal constitutional Authority, or invested with any legislative Powers: But you have been chosen as freely as the Circumstances of the Times would admit; with less Cabal and Intrigue than is usually employed for a Seat in many of our legal provincial Assemblies, and without even the Suspicion of Venality, which is but too frequently and too generally practised among us for that Purpose. Your Persons, Characters, and Principles, are familiarly known to your Constituents; you have been recommended by the most Honourable of all Interests, the general Opinion of your Knowledge, Abilities and Virtues. We look up to you as the Oracles of our Country; your Opinions will have the Effect of Laws, on the Minds of the People, and your Resolves may decide the Fate of America. All Orders of Men, who enjoy the Happiness of living under a free Government, may boldly assume the Character of Politicians; they inherit a Right to it as much as the proudest Peer inherits a Right to his Seat in Parliament, however ridiculous the Proportion may appear to the Conceit and Arrogance of Men who think themselves born to domineer over their fellow Creatures at Pleasure. High Birth and Fortune, when they are not abused, confer the solid and splendid Advantages of Education and Accomplishments, extensive Influence, and incitement to Glory; but they give no exclusive Title to Common Sense, Wisdom, or Integrity. The lowest Orders of Men in such a Country, have an unalienable Property in their Industry, their Liberty, and their Lives, and may be allowed to set some Value at least on the only Property they can boast of: These may be all endanger'd, or lost, by the Conduct of their Governors, they have therefore a Right, as Freemen, to examine their Conduct, to censure, to condemn it; without this Right the freest Government on Earth would soon degenerate into the rankest Tyranny. The great Out-lines, the fundamental Principles of our Constitution, are within the Reach of almost every Man's Capacity; they require little more than Leisure to study them, Memory to retain them, and Candour to form a true Judgment of them; unhappily for the Order and Peace of Society, this inestimable Privilege is but too often abused. Men in general are govern'd more by their Temper than their Judgment; they have little Leisure and still less Inclination, to inform themselves exactly of the necessary constitutional Powers of the supreme Magistrate, or of their own legal Rights; they have been often told that Liberty is a very great Blessing; they talk incessantly of it, they find something inchanting in the very Sound of the Word; ask them the Meaning of it, they think you design to affront them; push them to a Definition, they give you at once a Description of the State of Nature. Their Ideas of the Nature, Origin and Conditions of civil Society in general, are just as confus'd and inaccurate; they take their political as they do their religious Opinions (upon Trust) from the Nursery, the Company they fall into, or the Professions and Scenes in which they are accidentally engaged. They find the Movement of the Passions a more easy and agreeable Exercise than the Drudgery of sober and dispassionate Enquiry. Hand Bills, News Papers, party Pamphlets, are the shallow and turbid Sources from whence they derive their Notions of Government; these they pronounce as confidently and dogmatically, as if a political Problem was to be solved as clearly as a Mathematical one; and as if a bold Assertion amounted to a Demonstration.

Ambition and Lust of Power above the Laws, are such predominant Passions in the Breasts of most Men, even of Men who escape the Infection of other Vices, that Liberty, legal Liberty, would be in continual Danger of Encroachments, if it were not guarded by perpetual Jealousy. Crafty designing Knaves, turbulent Demagogues, Quacks in Politics, and Impostors in Patriotism, have in all free Governments, and in all Ages, avail'd themselves of this necessary Spirit of Jealousy; and by broaching Doctrines unknown to the Constitution, under the Name of constitutional Principles, by bold Assertions, partial Representations, false Colourings, wrested Constructions, and tragical Declamations, have frequently imposed on the Credulity of the well-meaning deluded Multitude. Thus the most honourable Cause that wise and good Men can engage in, the Cause of Liberty, has been often disgraced; Nations once as free and as happy as ourselves, have been frighten'd into Anarchy, plung'd into all the Horrors of a civil War, and ended their miserable Career in the most humiliating and abject Slavery, until the sacred Name of Liberty has become a Word of Scorn and Mockery in the Mouths of Tyrants, and their abandoned Minions and Emissaries.

Such are the Calamities which have frequently arisen from an ardent mistaken Zeal, and from the false Refinements of speculative Men, who amuse themselves and the World, with visionary Ideas of Perfection, which never were, nor ever will be found, either in publick or in private Life. You, Gentlemen, cannot even be suspected of being under the Influence of such Delusions; there are many among you who are eminently learned, not only in the Laws of the Land, but in the Laws of Nature and Nations, in the general Laws of Reason and Justice, who know their Authority and revere them, not as they have been sometimes explained on the narrow illiberal Principles of party Spirit, but as they have been understood, and acknowledg'd by the Wise of all Ages, and have served for the Basis of the most perfect Systems of Legislation. These are the only Rules by which all political Opinions ought to be tried and examin'd, by which an honest Man and a good Citizen, can form a true Judgment of the Duty he owes to his King and his Country.

It would have been happy for the World on many melancholy Occasions, that the revealed Will of God, which ought to be the sole Rule of every Man's Conduct, the only transcendent Authority from which there lies no Appeal, had never received but one general Interpretation with Regard to the reciprocal Duties of the Sovereign and the People; but even that sacred and eternal Standard of Right and Wrong, in private Life has been alternately perverted and profan'd in the political World, by the indiscreet Zeal and wild Passions of mad Enthusiasts, or slavish Bigots, has been equally abused, to serve the Purposes of a Charles or a Cromwell, of a Gregory, or a Venner, to throw a Veil over the Horrors of Anarchy, and Rebellion, or to sanctify the ridiculous and damnable Doctrines of Non-resistance, and Passive-Obedience, on a proper Application of the general Doctrines, and Principles, I have mention'd, to the peculiar and local Circumstances of this Country; your Proceedings, and Resolves, ought to depend, by a competent Knowledge of the Character of the Times, when the Colony Charters were granted; of the Kings, by whom they were granted; of the People, to whom they were granted; of the Purposes for which they were ask'd and obtained; of the Tenor and Spirit of the Charters themselves, how they were understood, and construed by our Ancestors; by a Knowledge in short of the History of our Country, we may discover the general Constitution of the Colonies, and be able to judge whether the present Discontents are founded on Truth or Ignorance.

By a due and candid Examination of this very interesting Subject, it may perhaps appear, that the Character of the Times, when most of the Charters were originally granted, bore very little Resemblance to the present Times; that the inestimable Privileges of a modern Englishman, might indeed be found in some Degree, in the Letter of the Law, but had never been enjoyed, were generally very imperfectly understood, and rarely claimed by our Ancestors; that even these legal constitutional Privileges were encumbered with a Thousand legal Customs, which they patiently submitted to, altho' they would exceed the Patience of a modern Frenchman; that they felt and discover'd infinitely more Zeal, for their religious, than for their civil Liberty, and would have been contented with half the Privileges their Posterity enjoy, for an Act of Toleration. It will appear, that the Kings, by whom the Charters were granted, were not despotick Kings, that they constitutionally possess'd the executive, not the supreme legislative Power, of which they only made a Part; that in all Questions of Magnitude, they were under the Control of the other Parts of the legislative Power. That our Ancestors, were Subjects of the Kings of England, not as the Inhabitants of Guyenne formerly were, or as those of the Electorate of Hanover are now, but Subjects of an English Parliamentary King; Englishmen in the fullest Sense of the Word, with the same Habits and Manners, speaking the same Language, govern'd by the same Maxims, Customs and Laws, with scarce any Distinction, but the Latitude and Longitude of their new Residence.

That if their Charters were granted without the Concurrence of Parliaments, it was not because a Parliament had no Right to interfere, but because they did not in those Days appear of Importance enough to be agitated in the great Council of the Nation.

That altho' by their Charters, our Ancestors were empowered to make By-Laws for their own local Convenience, they were nevertheless expressly and formally restrain'd from making Laws repugnant to the Laws of England; and were universally understood, both there, and here, to owe in Common with all Englishmen, an Obedience to the Laws, from which no King could release them, because no King could dispense with the Laws. That from this parliamentary Authority, they never wish'd until of late, to be emancipated, but would rather have fled to it for Protection, from the arbitrary Encroachments of a James, or a Charles, armed with the Usurpations, and Abuses, of privy Seals, Benevolences, Proclamations, Star Chambers and High Commission Courts, and from the Enormities of the two succeeding Reigns; that such were the Practices of the Times, when our early Charters bear their Dates, that if they were not granted by parliamentary Kings, they were granted by Tyrants, and we shall gain nothing by recurring to first Principles.

That no political Society can subsist, unless there be an absolute supreme Power lodg'd somewhere in the Society, has been universally held as an uncontrolable Maxim in Theory, by all Writers on Government, from Aristotle down to Sidney and Lock, and has been as universally adopted in Practice, from the Despotism of Morocco, to the Republic of St. Marino; as long as Government subsists, Subjects owe an implicit Obedience to the Laws of the supreme Power, from which there can be no Appeal but to Heaven. We for some Years past have been multiplying ineffectual Resolves, Petitions, and Remonstrances, and advancing Claims of Rights, &c. Our Petitions have at last been neglected, or rejected, or censured; the Principles on which we found our Claims, have been formally denied. To what, or to whom, shall we have Recourse? Shall we appeal to the King of Massachusetts Bay, to the King of Connecticut, to the King of Rhode Island, against the King of Great Britain, to rescind the Acts of the Parliament of Great Britain, to dispense with the Laws, to which as a necessary and efficient Part of that Body, he has so recently given his Assent? Ridiculous as these Questions may appear, I am afraid they are but too much of a Piece with Doctrines which have been lately broached, inculcated every where, and almost every where receiv'd. The Colonies are constitutionally independant of each other: They formally acknowledge themselves loyal, and dutiful Subjects of his Majesty GEORGE the Third. But severally claim an Exemption from the Authority of the British Parliament. A Doctrine so repugnant to the Ideas of all our Fellow-Subjects in Great Britain, can I trust, have no Place in your Assembly. The Business you have to transact, is too serious to be trifled with; the Confidence reposed in you, too sacred to be sacrificed to idle Sophistry and visionary Distinctions; the Fate of America, may depend on your Resolves; they should be founded on Principles that are plain, and intelligible, that are marked with the Authority of universal Opinions and Truths.

The supreme Power of the British Parliament over her Colonies, was ever till very lately, as universally acknowledg'd, by ourselves, as by our Fellow-Subjects in England. It usurps no Claim to infallibility in its Opinions, but gives the Subject a legal Right of petitioning, remonstrating, of proposing Plans of Reformation, and Redress. Nevertheless, tho' it pretends not to Infallibility, like all other Governments, it requires an implicit Obedience to its Laws, and has a Right to enforce it. A Tribe of Savages, unrestrained by Laws, human or divine, may live in some Harmony, and endure for Ages, because in the State of Nature, there are at the most but two or three Subjects, to contend about, and the Individuals are reciprocally over-awed by the natural Rights of private Revenge. But in civil Society, composed as it commonly is, of such an infinite Number of heterogeneous and discordant Principles and Interests, in Trade, in Politics, and Religion, where Subjects of Contention present themselves by Thousands every Hour; no Constitution can subsist a Moment, without a constant Resignation of private Judgment, to the Judgment of the Publick.

What Part then, Gentlemen, have you left you to act, but to propose, with the Modesty of Subjects, some practicable Plan of Accommodation, and to obey? Shall the Time of so respectable an Assembly be squandered, in advancing Claims of Right, that have been urged, and rejected a thousand Times; that have been heard, considered, solemnly debated, and decided by the only Power on Earth, who has a Right to decide them? Shall the Opinions and Desires of a small Part of the Community, prevail against the Opinions, and Desires of the Majority

of the Community? What new Species of Eloquence can be
invented to persuade? What new Logick to convince the Understandings of our Fellow-Subjects? Shall the British Senate
be governed by the pernicious Maxims of a Polish Diet, and
the Veto of a single Member, or of a few Members, however
distinguished by extraordinary Wisdom, and Virtue, obstruct
or suspend, or annul the Legislation of a great Nation?

Those wise and virtuous Citizens themselves hold such
Doctrines in Derision. While a Question is in Agitation, they
debate with Freedom, but they claim no blind Submission to
their Opinions, no Authority, but the Authority of their Arguments. They arrogate not to themselves, a Monopoly of all the
Wisdom, and all the Virtue in the Nation. When the Question
is decided, they submit their private speculative Opinions, to
the Opinion of the Majority, to the Law of the Land. They
revere the Law, and make it the Rule of their Conduct.

You therefore, Gentlemen, the Delegates of a very numerous,
and respectable People, will surely think it below the Dignity
of your Character, to assemble with the Passions and Language
of a common Town Meeting, to sit in Judgment, like some
foreign Imperial Power on the Decrees of a British Legislature;
to arraign the Conduct of Administration, in the lofty em-
phatick Tone of a Manifesto. Can such Proceedings answer
any Purpose, but the dangerous Purposes of exasperating and
provoking the Indignation and Vengeance of all Orders and
Degrees of Men in the parent Country? Of alienating the Affections of the People here, seducing them from their Allegiance, inflaming their Passions, and exciting them to popular
Tumults, and Insurrections? The Order and Tranquillity of
Government frequently depends more upon the Manners and
Morals of the People, than upon their Laws and Institutions.
For the Honour of our native Country, there are I believe, few
Instances on Record, of any People under a free Government,
who have passed thro' the same Length of Period, with so few
civil Commotions, tho' the Powers of Government have never
been vigilantly exerted, nor the Laws held in any extraordinary
Veneration. But the Manners and Morals of our Countrymen,
are undebauched and innocent, compared with those of the
Inhabitants of older Countries, where the Instruments of
Corruption, and the Incitements to Vices and Crimes are more

general. The Danger is nevertheless the same, or greater. There are no People on Earth more secure from the humiliating Effects of Poverty, more superiour to the Smiles, or Frowns of Power, more unawed by the Distinctions of Birth and Fortune, more confident, or tenacious of their own Opinions, or more on a level with all the World in their Conversation and Behaviour. The Passions of such Men, agitated by false Principles, and mistaken Zeal, are more dangerous to the Repose of the World, than the Frenzy of the most dissolute, and abandon'd Slaves. You will surely beware how you inflame the Minds of such honest deluded Citizens, or the Time may come, perhaps it is not very distant, that you will wish, when it will be too late, to calm the Storm you have raised, and will tremble every Moment, lest it burst on your own Heads.

Upon the Subject of a Non-Importation and Non-Exportation Agreement, I am at a Loss what to say, it has been so often and so warmly recommended, as a specific Remedy for all our Complaints, has received the Sanction of such General Authority, that I am afraid it will look like an affront to the Understandings of my Fellow Citizens, an Apostacy from my native Country to insinuate the least Doubt of its Efficacy. Yet let me most earnestly conjure you, by the common Love we bear to that Country, by the Gratitude we owe to the parent Country, by the important Trust reposed in you, as you value your present and future Peace, and the Interests and Happiness of your Posterity, Beware how you adopt that Measure, how you engage in that strange conflict of Sullenness and Obstinacy, till you have given it the most calm and serious Deliberation.

The efficacy of the Measure, admitting it to be a practicable one, depends, I presume, upon the Importance of our Commerce with Great-Britain; it is possible that People in general here, may have been much deceived, in this Matter, by partial and exaggerated Calculations, made under particular Circumstances, during particular Periods, to serve the Purposes of Party. It would be difficult, if not impossible to ascertain the exact Value of it. But if we may trust to the Authority of Men of Eminence, who have treated this Subject, as Politicians at large, unbiassed by partial, local, or temporary Views, Men who have traced it through the Books of Custom-Houses,

Merchants, Brokers, Manufacturers, &c. the best Sources of Information; if we can depend on the Opinions of the most intelligent Merchants of our own Country; if we can believe our own Eyes, every Man of common Observation, and Reflection, must be assured, that the amount of British Manufactures imported into this Country, is very inconsiderable, compared with the Opinions about it, that are so industriously circulated thro' all the Colonies, and so generally received. Let us examine by the same Rule, the amount of the Inland, and Coasting Trade, of Great-Britain, and her Foreign Trade, with all the Nations on Earth; it will appear infinitely greater, than our Countrymen in general (accustomed from the Vanity natural to all Mankind to consider the little Scenes, and Transactions immediately under their Eyes, as Objects of the greatest Magnitude) can form any adequate Idea of. The Resources of her Trade are infinite, the Combinations of it, too various and complicated, the Revolutions of it, too sudden and frequent, to be easily explained, or understood. But we may judge of it, by the Result, and Effect of the whole, whenever the astonishing Power of the Nation is called forth into Exertion. Can we seriously believe, that this Wealth, and Power, is derived almost entirely, from her North-American Colonies? Can we, (who by our own Confessions do not yet enjoy even all the Necessaries of Life) can we reasonably hope, to starve into Compliance, so great, and so powerful a Nation? Shall we punish ourselves, like froward Children, who refuse to eat, when they are Hungry, that they may vex their indulgent Mothers? Or like desperate Gamesters, stake at one throw, our small, but competent, and happy Fortunes, against the successive Stakes, the accummulated Wealth of Ages? We may teize the Mother Country, we cannot ruin her. Let us beware how we engage in such an unequal Contest, lest while we are giving her a slight Wound, we receive a Mortal one.

If notwithstanding, we are confident, that the Measure of a Non-Importation, and Non-Exportation Agreement, bids fair to be a successful one; it certainly behoves us as Men, and as Christians to be sure, that it is a just Measure. A Combination to Ruin, or to obstruct the Trade of a fellow Citizen, who happens to differ from us, in his religious, or political Opinions, adopted in Passion, prosecuted by the Intrigues of a

Cabal, by Innuendoes, Insinuations, Threatnings, and publicly signed, by large Numbers of leading Men, would I presume, be a manifest Violation, of the Laws of God and Man, and would on Conviction, be severely punished in every Court of Justice in the Universe. In what Colours then will appear, the Combinations of a large, and respectable Body of Subjects, against the supreme Power of the Community? Adopted from the same Motives, prosecuted by the same Arts, and publickly signed, in the Face of the whole World? Happily for us, by the generous, and noble Spirit, of the British Constitution, our own Constitution, the Crime of Treason, which in almost every other Country, is vague, and undefined, often in the Breast of a venal, and corrupt Judge, and made not to warn, but to ensnare the People, is exactly and circumstantially, ascertained and defined.

Shall we abuse the Generosity, and Beneficence of Laws, made for our Protection? Shall we skulk, behind the Letter of the Law, while we wage War, against the Spirit of it. Because our Ancestors had foreseen the Possibility, of the Subjects levying Arms, against the State in Passion, and Despair, but knew no Instance on Record, of their having meditated, in cold Blood, its Destruction, and had therefore made no regular Provision against an Enormity, which they presumed, could never happen.

It is, I believe, sufficiently notorious, that there are great Numbers, of our Countrymen, from one End of this Continent, to the other, who are averse from this Measure, some of them from Opinion, others from Interest, and many from down-right Necessity.

For the Sake of common Humanity, Gentlemen, disdain to co-operate, with Hand Bills, with News Papers, with the high menacing Resolves of common Town Meetings; do not conspire with them, to reduce, under the Pains, and Penalties of Disgrace, and Infamy, Thousands of your Fellow Citizens, to the cruel Alternative, of involving themselves, their Wives, and Children, in Indigence, and Wretchedness; or of being publicly branded, and pointed out by the frantic Multitude, as Apostates, and Traitors to their Country.

Let us, in the Name of common Sense and Decency, be consistent. Shall we Proteus like, perpetually change our Ground, assume every Moment, some new and strange Shape, to defend, to evade? Shall we establish Distinctions, between internal, and external Taxation one Year, and laugh at them the next? Shall we confound Duties, with Taxes, and Regulations of Trade with Revenue Laws? Shall we rave against the Preamble of the Law, while we are ready to admit the enacting Part of it? Shall we refuse to obey the Tea Act, not as an oppressive Act, but as a dangerous, a sole Precedent of Taxation, when every Post-Day shews us a Precedent, which our Fore-Fathers submitted to, and which we still submit to, without murmuring? Shall we move Heaven, and Earth, against a trifling Duty, on a Luxury, unknown to nine Tenths of the Globe, unknown to our Ancestors! Despised by half the Nations of Europe! Which no Authority, no Necessity compels us to use? There are Thousands of honest industrious Families, who have no Resources, but in the Consequences of Exportation, and Importation. Shall we levy a Tax, upon these innocent Citizens, a Tax unheard of, disproportionate, a Tax, never suggested by the most inhuman Tyrant? A Tax, to the Amount of their daily Bread? Reflect one Moment, on the Terms, in which the Resolves of every Town Meeting, on this Continent, speak of the Boston Port Bill? Altho' it is little more, than a temporary Suspension, of the Trade, of that City, until Restitution, which God, and Man calls aloud for, be made. And altho' the Ports, at a very small Distance from Boston, and every other Port on the Continent, is as free as ever, shall we multiply these Calamities, ten Thousand Fold? For such Calamities, must be the inevitable Consequences, of a Non-Importation, and Non-Exportation Agreement. You ought therefore to be confident, that it will prove effectual before you adopt it. Can any Man seriously believe this, who is tolerably acquainted with the History, and present State, of these Colonies? Who has visited our principal Cities and Towns, and has observ'd by what Means they have risen to their Wealth, and Importance; how they daily increase, and how their Inhabitants subsist? The horrid Punishments, inflicted by despotic Princes, are commonly of little avail, against a contraband Trade, where any trifling extraordinary Profit, is an irresistable Temptation. What can we expect from a loose Agreement, where the sole Subsistence of Thousands is at Stake? In all trading Nations, where there are Duties, or

Prohibitions, there are Smugglers, there ever were, and ever will be, until we find some Nation, where every Individual, is a Patriot, or a Saint.

Such an Agreement will have the Defect and Impotence, of Laws, framed on monkish Ideas of Purity, against the indelible Feelings and Passions of Humanity. Can you hope, by Promises, by extorted Promises, to restrain Men from carrying on a clandestine Trade with Great Britain? Who Trade every Day, with our inveterate Enemies, in Defiance of all Law, and who grow Rich by the Spoils of the fair Trader? Will it not rather happen, as it has happen'd already, that Province will smuggle against Province, Citizen, against Citizen, till we are weary, and ashamed of being the Dupes, of each other, and become the Laughing Stock of the whole World?

Let us no longer deceive ourselves, with the vain Hopes, of a speedy Repeal of the Tea Act, because we triumphed in the Repeal of the Stamp Act; the Acts themselves, are totally different in their Principles, and their Operation, the Occasion, by no means Similar. We have advanced from one extravagant Claim to another, made such sudden Turnings, and Windings, taken such wild, and rapid Flights, that the boldest of our Followers, can follow us no longer; our most zealous Advocates, are ashamed to plead a Cause, which all Men, but ourselves, condemn. Can we any longer doubt that our Friends, on the other Side of the Atlantic, as well as our Enemies, altho' they may differ in the Mode, of exercising the Authority of Parliament over us, are almost universally agreed in the Principle? Are we not convinced from a thousand Testimonies, that the Clamour against us, is universal, and loud? Is this, Gentlemen, a Season to frighten the Parent Country, into a Repeal? No Man of Spirit in private Life, even on the slightest Quarrel, will submit to be bullied, and expos'd to the Scorn and Derision, of the little Circle he lives in. Can we seriously hope, that a great Nation, a proud Nation, will be insulted, and degraded, with Impunity, by her Colonies, in the Face of every rival Kingdom in Europe? Let us then, Gentlemen, relinquish for ever, a Project fraught with Absurdity, and Ruin. Let your Constituents hope, that the Occasion of such an important Assembly, will not be wantonly squander'd, in opprobrious Reproaches, in bidding Defiance to the Mother Country, but in digesting and proposing some new Plan of Accommodation, worthy her Notice and Acceptance. Disputes are generally vain, and endless, where there are no Arbitrators to award, no Judges to decree, where Arguments, suspected to be drawn from Interest, and Passion, are addressed to Interest, and Passion, they produce no Conviction. We may ring eternal Changes, upon Taxation, and Representation, upon actual, virtual, and Non-representation. We may end as we began, and disagree eternally; but there is one Proposition, a self-evident Proposition, to which all the World give their Assent, and from which we cannot withold ours; that whatever Taxation, and Representation may be, Taxation, and Government, are insep-arable. On the Subject of Taxation, the Authority of Mr. Lock, is generally quoted by our Advocates, as paramount to all other Authority whatever. His Treatise on Government, as far as his Ideas are practicable, with the corrupt Materials of all Governments, is undoubtedly, a most beautiful Theory, the noblest Assertion of the unalienable Rights of Mankind. Let us respect it as the Opinions of a wise, and virtuous Philosopher, and Patriot, but let us likewise, as good Subjects, revere the Laws of the Land, the collected Wisdom of Ages, and make them the sole Rule of our political Conduct. Let not Mr. Lock be quoted partially, by those who have read him, to mislead Thousands who never read him. When he is brought as an Authority, that no Subject can be justly taxed without his own Consent; why don't they add his own Explanation of that Consent? "i. e. The Consent of the Majority, giving it either by themselves, or their Representatives chosen by them." Do we compose the Majority of the British Community? Are we, or are we not of that Community? If we are of that Community, but are not represented, are we not in the same Situation with the numerous Body of Copy-holders, with the Inhabitants of many wealthy and populous Towns; in short, with a very great Number of our fellow Subjects, who have no Votes in Elec-tions? Shall we affirm that these are all virtually represented, but deny that we are so; and at the same Time, be too proud to solicit a Representation? or under the trite and popular Pre-tences, of Venality and Corruption, laugh at it as impracticable? Shall we plunge at once into Anarchy, and reject all Accommo-dation with a Government, (by the Confession of the wisest

Men in Europe, the freest and the noblest Government, on the Records of History) because there are Imperfections in it, as there are in all Things, and in all Men? Are we Confederates, or Allies, or Subjects of Great-Britain? In what Code of Laws, are we to search for Taxation, under the Title, and Condition, of Requisition, as we understand the Word? In what Theory of Government, ancient or modern? Is it to be found any where on Earth, but in modern Harangues, modern Pamphlets? And in these, only as temporary Expedients. The Supply of Government, must be constant, certain, and proportioned to the Protection it affords; the Moment one is precarious the other is so too; the Moment it fails, civil Society expires. We boast much of our bountiful Compliance with the Requisitions made during the last War, and in many Instances with Reason; but let us remember and acknowledge, that there was even then, more than one rich Province, that refused to comply, altho' the War, was in the very Bowels, of the Country. Can Great-Britain then, depend upon her Requisitions, in some future War, a Thousand Leagues distant from North-America, in which, as we may have no immediate local Interest, we may look perhaps, with little Concern.

From the Infancy of our Colonies, to this very Hour, we have grown up and flourished under the Mildness, and Wisdom of her excellent Laws; our Trade, our Possessions, our Persons have been constantly defended against the whole World, by the Fame of her Power, or by the Exertion of it. We have been very lately, rescued by her, from Enemies, who threatned us with Slavery, and Destruction, at the Expence of much Blood, and Treasure, and established after a long War, (waged on our Accounts, at our most earnest Prayers) in a State of Security, of which there is scarce an Example in History. She is ever ready, to avenge the Cause, of the meanest Individual among us, with a Power respected by the whole World. Let us then, no longer disgrace ourselves, by illiberal, ungrateful Reproaches, by meanly ascribing, the most generous Conduct, to the most sordid Motives; we owe our Birth, our Progress, our Delivery to her; we still depend on her for Protection; we are surely able to bear some Part of the Expence of it; let us be willing to bear it. Employ then, Gentlemen, your united Zeal and Abilities, in substituting some adequate permanent and effectual Supply (by some Mode of actual Representation) in the Place of uncertain, ineffectual Requisitions, or in devising some Means of reconciling Taxation, the indispensible Obligation of every Subject, with your Ideas of the peculiar and inestimable Rights of an Englishman.

These are Objects, worthy a Congress, Measures, that will confer lasting Benefits on your Country, and immortal Honour on yourselves.

If on the contrary, like Independent States, you arrogate to yourselves, the sole Right of judging and deciding in your own Cause; if you persist in denying the supreme Power of Parliament, which no Parliament will ever renounce, like Independent States, we have no Appeal but to the God of Battles. Shall we dare lift up our Eyes to that God, the Source of Truth and Justice, and implore his Assistance in such a Cause? There are Causes, where, in Spight of the ridiculous Tenets of pious, deluded Enthusiasts, or of the wicked and monstrous Doctrines, of Slaves and Tyrants; the very Principles, the original Principles on which civil Society depends, require, where God and Nature call aloud for Resistance. Such Causes existed in the horrid Catalogue of Oppressions and Crimes, under a Philip the Second, a Katharine of Medicis, and in the List of Grievances, during one Period at least, of the Reign of the ill-educated, the ill-advised, the unhappy Charles; on such melancholly Occasions, Men of Sentiment, Spirit and Virtue, the only genuine Sons of Liberty, engage in the honourable Cause of Freedom, with God on their Side, and indignantly sacrifice every Advantage of Fortune, every Endearment of Life, and Life itself. Do such Causes exist now among us? Did they ever exist? Are they likely to exist?

Open if it be not too late, the Eyes of our infatuated Countrymen; teach them to compare their happy Situation, with the Wretchedness of Nine Tenths of the Globe; shew them the general Diffusion of the Necessaries, the Conveniencies and Pleasures of Life, among all Orders of People here; the certain Rewards of Industry, the innumerable Avenues to Wealth, the native, unsubdued Freedom of their Manners, and Conversation; the Spirit of Equality, so flattering to all generous Minds, and so essential, to the Enjoyment of private Society, the entire Security of their Fortunes, Liberty, and Lives, the Equity, and

Lenity, of their civil and criminal Justice, the Toleration of their religious Opinions, and Worship.

Teach them to compare these invaluable Privileges and Enjoyments, with the abject and miserable State of Men debased by artificial Manners, lost to all generous and manly Sentiment, alternately crouching and insulting, from the vain and humiliating Distinctions of Birth, Place and Precedence, trembling every Moment for their Liberty, their Property, their Consciences and their Lives; Millions toiling, not for themselves, but to pamper the Luxury, and not riot of a few worthless, domineering Individuals, and pining in Indigence, and Wretchedness: Save them from the Madness, of hazarding such inestimable Blessings, in the uncertain Events of a War, against all Odds, against Invasions from Canada, Incursions of Savages, Revolt of Slaves, multiplied Fleets and Armies, a War which must begin where Wars commonly end, in the Ruin of our Trade, in the Surrender of our Ports and Capitals, in the Misery of Thousands. Teach them in Mercy, to beware how they wantonly draw their Swords in Defence of political Problems, Distinctions, Refinements, about which the best and the wisest Men, the Friends, as well as the Enemies of America, differ in their Opinions, lest while we deny the Mother Country, every Mode, every Right of Taxation, we give her the Rights of Conquest.

FINIS.

[Samuel Seabury], The Congress Canvassed: or, An Examination into the Conduct of the Delegates, at Their Grand Convention, Held in Philadelphia, Sept. 1, 1774. Addressed, to the Merchants of New-York. New York, 1774.

On September 9, 1774, a convention in Suffolk County, Massachusetts, issued a radical declaration. Pronouncing the Intolerable Acts unconstitutional, the Suffolk Resolves urged a boycott of British imports, advised the people of the colony to form their own government until the acts were repealed, and implored them to raise the militia and arm themselves. The resolves were forwarded to the Continental Congress, where they were formally endorsed on September 17. The Congress followed this bold step by issuing on October 14 a Declaration and Resolves asserting that the colonists were "entitled to a free and exclusive power of legislation in their several provincial legislatures, where their right of representation can alone be preserved, in all cases of taxation and internal polity." The Congress also formed the Continental Association and charged local committees with the authority to enforce the nonimportation, nonexportation, and nonconsumption of British goods. Mob intimidation and tar-and-feathering were to prove very effective tools for this enforcement.

This came as no surprise to Samuel Seabury, a Connecticut-born graduate of Yale and rector of St. Peter's Church in Westchester, New York. In the several pamphlets that he wrote under the pseudonym of "A Westchester Farmer," Seabury devoted much space to predictions that all the extra-legal committees and congresses being created would turn out to be oppressive. Americans, he claimed, were tamely surrendering their liberty and property to "an illegal, tyrannical Congress," which was "a body utterly unknown in any legal sense . . . a *foreign* power" that was being made into "an instrument of *injustice* and *oppression*." Seabury was especially alarmed by the creation of the Continental Association. To him these local committees were based on the same principle as "the *popish Inquisition*."

Seabury often shrewdly deployed popular Whig rhetoric to make his case, emphasizing, for example, that the delegates to the Congress, who had been appointed by the various colonial assemblies, were exercising powers that they never received directly from the people, and thus could not "in any *true* sense be called the *representatives of a province*." He was not unusual in his use of popular rhetoric. Those loyal to the British cause were often more Whig than Tory, and consequently they were normally careful not to denigrate the sacred rights of the people. If they did, they were soon set straight. When John Adams's newspaper opponent in Massachusetts, Daniel Leonard, suggested that the people might become tyrannical, Adams dismissed the notion as illogical. Only kings were capable of tyranny; the people stood for liberty. "A democratical despotism," Adams declared, "was a contradiction in terms."

In a postscript Seabury took notice of a pamphlet entitled *A Full Vindication of the Measures of Congress*, written anonymously by nineteen-year-old Alexander Hamilton, which was severely critical of an earlier piece by Seabury. He and Hamilton would exchange another round of pamphlets during the winter of 1774-5.

THE

CONGRESS

CANVASSED:

OR,

An EXAMINATION

INTO

The Conduct of the Delegates,

AT THEIR

GRAND CONVENTION,

Held in PHILADELPHIA, Sept. 1, 1774.

ADDRESSED,

To the MERCHANTS of *New-York.*

By *A.W.* FARMER.
Author of Free Thoughts, *&c.*

Hæc, per Deos immortales, utrum esse vobis consilia siccorum, an vinolentorum somnia: Et utrum cogitata sapientum, an operata furiosorum, videntur? Cicer. contra Rullum.

Do you look upon these Proceedings as the Counsels of Sobriety, or the Dreams of Inebriation? Do they seem to you the Deliberations of Wisdom, or the Ravings of Phrenzy?

PRINTED IN THE YEAR M,DCC,LXXIV.

The Congress Canvassed:
or, an examination into the
Conduct of the Delegates, &c.

addressed
to the MERCHANTS of NEW-YORK.

Gentlemen,

I SHALL make no apology for addressing myself to you, the Merchants of the city of New-York, upon the present unhappy and distressed state of our country. My subject will necessarily lead me to make some remarks on your past and present conduct, in this unnatural contention between our parent country and us. I am duly sensible of what importance you are to the community, and of the weight and influence you must have in the conduct of all our public affairs: I know that the characters of many of you are truly respectable, and I shall endeavour to express what I have to say to you, consistently with that decency and good manners which are due, not only to you, but to all mankind.

But you must not expect any undue complaisance from *me*.—You must be content with plain English, from a plain countryman; I must have the privilege of calling a fig,—a Fig; an egg, an Egg. If, upon examination, your conduct shall, in any instances, appear to be weak, you must bear to be told of it:—if wrong, to be censured:—if selfish, to be exposed:—if ridiculous, to be laughed at:—Do not be offended if I omit to say, that if your conduct shall appear to be honourable, that it shall be commended. Honourable and virtuous actions want no commendation,—they speak for themselves: They affect not praise, but are rather disgusted with it,—instead of heightening, it tarnishes their lustre. If you have acted from honourable motives, from disinterested principles, from true patriotism, —if justice and prudence, and a love of your country have been the guides of your conduct, you need fear no attack, nor the strictest scrutiny of your actions.

Nor, upon the other hand, ought you to be displeased with the man, who shall point out your errors, supposing you have acted wrong. To err is common,—I wish it was uncommon to

241

persist in error. But such is the pride of the human heart, that when we have once taken a wrong step, we think it an impeachment of our wisdom and prudence to retreat. A kind of sullen, sulky obstinacy takes possession of us; and though, in the hour of calm reflection, our hearts should condemn us, we had rather run the risk of being condemned by the world too, than own the possibility of our having been mistaken. Preposterous pride! It defeats the end it aims at: It degrades instead of exalting our characters, and destroys that reputation which it seems so solicitous to establish. To become sensible of our errors, and to mend them,—to grow wiser by our own mistakes, —to learn prudence from our own misconduct,—to make every fall a means of rising higher in virtue,—are circumstances which raise the dignity of human nature the nearest to that perfection of conduct which has never erred.

Possibly, in many instances, I shall need your candour: In one particular I must bespeak it. I live at a distance from the city, and visit it but seldom. The opinion I have formed of your conduct, depends, a good deal, upon report, and the common newspapers.—I have, however, endeavoured to get the best information I could; and I have not the least inclination to put unfair constructions upon your actions; and should I, in any instance, misrepresent you, I will, upon good information, make all proper acknowledgments. Under these circumstances, and with this disposition, I think I have a right to expect, that you will read this Address without prejudice, and judge of it with impartiality, and such a regard to truth and right, as every reasonable man ought to make the basis of his opinion in all discussions, and the rule of his conduct in all his actions.

You, sometime ago, Gentlemen, joined with the other citizens of New-York, in sending Delegates to represent your city in the Congress at Philadelphia. Let me intreat you to reflect a little upon the motives on which you then acted.—Did you expect that the Congress would consult upon, and enter into some reasonable and probable scheme for accommodating our unhappy disputes with our mother country, and of securing and rendering permanent our own privileges and liberties? Did you expect that they would endeavour, upon the true principles of legislation, to mark out the bounds of parliamentary authority over the colonies; on the one side ascertaining and securing the liberties of the colonists, and on the other giving full weight and force to the supreme authority of the nation over all its dominions? which is the only mode of settling finally and permanently our disputes with Great-Britain.—Or did you expect that the Congress would throw all into confusion,— revile and trample on the authority of Parliament, and make our breach with the parent state a thousand times more irreparable than it was before?

To say that the Congress have not acted in this manner is to talk *childishly*, without either reason or good sense on your side. Look at the Suffolk Resolves, from Massachusetts, which they adopted, "*approved and recommended.*"—Look into their addresses to the people of Great-Britain, to the inhabitants of the colonies in general, and to those of Quebec in particular. They all tend, under cover of strong and lamentable cries about liberty, and the rights of Englishmen, to degrade and contravene the authority of the British parliament over the British dominions; on which authority the rights of Englishmen are, in a great measure, founded; and on the due support of which authority, the liberty and property of the inhabitants, even of this country, must ultimately depend. They all tend to raise jealousies, to excite animosities, to foment discords between us and our mother country. Not a word of peace and reconciliation,—not even a soothing expression:—No concessions are offered on our part,—nor even a possibility of their treating with us left. The parliament must give up their whole authority,—repeal all the acts, in a lump, which the Congress have found fault with, and trust, for the future, to our humour, to pay them just so much submission as we shall think convenient.

To me, it is a difficult task to account for the conduct of those gentlemen who were delegated from your city. Their characters, their stations, their abilities, their knowledge of the rights of mankind, and of the laws and constitution of their country, all concurred to raise my expectations, that they would have been of principal advantage in the congress, by moderating and keeping within bounds the fiery intemperate zeal, which it was too apparent, many of the Delegates carried with them to that assembly. Cruelly was I disappointed, when the account was confirmed, that the congress had *unanimously* adopted the *Suffolk Resolves*. Chagrined and vexed, I waited impatiently for their whole proceedings. Their proceedings, at length appeared,—and unhappily, the names of every Delegate from this province, one only excepted, who, I have been since informed, was absent, appeared at the bottom of their ill-concerted association.

I must leave it to these gentlemen to account for their own conduct: But, at the same time, must observe, that if what is whispered abroad be true, they are highly concerned to vindicate their conduct to the public. I do not choose to make myself accountable for transient whisperings, and vague reports. It is said, however, that some matters were *run* upon them.—I use the very phrase that was made use of to me,—that they unfortunately agreed, before they proceeded to business, that neither *dissent* nor *protest* should appear on their minutes,— that by this agreement their hands were tied, and they were obliged, in honour, to sign the association, and give their voice in confirmation of all the proceedings.—Let these Gentlemen, however, remember, that though they might unfortunately, and imprudently have *tied up their own hands*, yet that their *feet* were at liberty; and that when they found the Congress were taking an undue advantage of them, and were driving matters to such a dreadful extremity, they ought, in justice to themselves and the public, to have walked off, and have *left* the Congress.

The conduct of the New-England Delegates does not appear to me so hard to explain. It is well known that the province of Massachusetts-Bay, have carried their opposition to the British government, to the most daring heighth. They set the example to the other colonies, of destroying the property of their fellow subjects, the East-India Company, in open defiance of the laws of the empire, to which they owed subjection, of the laws of the province in which they lived, and of the general laws of humanity. —They have wrested the command of the militia from his Majesty's Governor,—they have proscribed the legal Treasurer of the province, and without any course of law, proclaimed him a "traitor to the state;"—they are forming and disciplining regiments, providing ammunition and trains of artillery, to oppose the King's troops;—they have shut up, and rendered useless the legal courts of justice;—they have, by mobs and riots obliged many officers of the crown to resign their employments;—and in a variety of other instances have behaved themselves in such a manner, as to deserve the epithet of *rebellion*. The extravagancy of their demands, and of their conduct, are such, that no persons can attempt to vindicate them without giving up all pretensions to common sense.

Nor does this behaviour of the people of the Massachusetts appear to be the effect of any sudden emergency, but of premeditated design:—The three-penny duty on tea, they complied with, and imported near two thousand chests, embarrassed with it. But finding uneasiness and complaints in this province, New Jersey, and Pennsylvania, on account of that duty; and their assembly, being engaged with their governor, in some political disputes, which awakened their republican principles; they seem to have thought it a proper time to try, how far the other colonies could, by art, and management, be induced to take part with them. They knew, that while all remained in peace and quietness, they could do nothing. If the other colonies received their motions coolly, they could recede; if warmly, they could advance the farther.

The unlucky step that was taken at home, of sending Tea, belonging to the East India company, to be sold here, increased our discontent, as it added the dread of a monopoly, to the hardship of which we already complained, of having three-pence sterling exacted upon every pound of Tea imported into the colonies. This was a time not to be neglected by the Massachusetts people. Unhappily, the first ship, with the companies Tea arrived in *their* harbour. Instead of suffering the Tea to be landed and stored, and of shewing their patriotism in not buying and using it, they took the fatal resolution of destroying it. Having executed their rash purpose, they waited awhile to see what effect it would have in the other colonies. Finding themselves abetted and applauded by the more furious and fiery zealots among those people in the neighbouring governments, who have dignified themselves, and dishonoured the phrase, by stiling themselves SONS OF LIBERTY, they became more turbulent and unruly; and spurned all the advice of the more moderate and more worthy part among themselves, of offering to make restitution for the damages they had done.

Perceiving that the Tea-ships had been obliged to return from Philadelphia and New-York, without being suffered to enter their ports, and that the contagion of their ill example had spread as far as the latter city, and had, in a lawless riotous manner, brought destruction on the Tea, imported by Captain *Chambers*, they advanced a step farther. They, at first hesitatingly, afterwards more openly, proposed a Congress of Delegates, to meet at Philadelphia, about the first of September. Many moderate people, who wished nothing so much as a hearty reconciliation, and firm union with Great-Britain, eagerly embraced and helped forward the design. The Sons *of Liberty*,—N. B. I use the phrase only through courtesy,—exulted and applauded the scheme in such extravagant terms, that it was enough to make one think, that they imagined, that God himself could save their liberties in no other way. All the wisdom of the continent was to be drawn together in a *focus* at Philadelphia, like the rays of light in a burning-glass. *There* a regular American constitution was to be settled, and our liberties and privileges fixed on a foundation so stable, that neither Lord North, nor Old Time himself, should ever make any impression on them.

Many people, however, expected no good from this proposed Congress. They foresaw that few, except the wrongheaded, blustering people among the sons of liberty, and the more sly favourers of an American Republic, would give themselves much trouble about the election of Delegates, unless it were the vain and pragmatical, of no political principles, who hoped to rise into some degree of consequence, from helping forward a project that had the popular cry in its favour. However ill-grounded these apprehensions were thought to be at that time, experience hath shewn that they were but too well founded.

Even in this province, many undue and unfair advantages were taken. I say nothing of the election in the city, for I know little about it. But when you had chosen your Delegates, the supervisors in the several counties were applied to by the committee of your city, if I understood the matter right, to call the people together, and to choose committees; which committees were to meet in one grand committee; and this grand committee of committees were to choose the Delegates for the county;

or to declare their approbation of the New-York Delegates: And if any county or district did not meet and choose their committee, it was to be taken for granted, that they acquiesced in the New-York choice.

Here, Gentlemen, an unfair advantage was taken. You had no right to dictate to the counties in what manner they should proceed. You had no right to suppose that those districts, or those people who did not assemble, were in your favour. The contrary ought to have been supposed; and you ought to have considered those people and districts who did not assemble, as not choosing to have any Delegates in Congress at all. The people of your city can easily assemble; they have but a short walk to the city-hall or coffee-house. But it is not easy to assemble the people of a country-district. Besides, it is well known by all those, who know any thing of human nature, that those people who are fond of innovations in government, and of rendering themselves conspicuous in their neighbourhood, would be most likely to attend on such an occasion. And so it accordingly happened; for it is notorious that in some districts only three or four met and *those themselves* to be a committee on this most important occasion. So that, taking the whole province together, I am confident, your Delegates had not the voice of an hundreth part of the people in their favour.

You may say that the people might have assembled; and if they did not, their silence was to be taken for their consent. Not so fast, gentlemen. That they might have assembled, I know; but had *your* committee, or *their* own superiors, any right to *call* them together? Were they under any obligations to obey such notifications, as a superior's advertisement, founded on the authority of a New-York committee? You know they were not, and because they did not choose to obey it, must their rights and privileges be given up, to be torn, and mangled, and trampled on by an enthusiastic congress? Whatever you, gentlemen, may think of the matter, or whatever my fellow-countrymen may think of it, *I* disdain such abject submission to your committee, or your delegates, or congress. *I* will not hold *my* rights and privileges on so precarious a tenure.

I do not recollect the precise mode in which the delegates were generally chosen in the other colonies. If it was in a manner similar to that in which their election was conducted in this province, the same objections may be made to it. But here I expect an outcry of exultation and triumph. "The Delegates from several of the governments," cry the deep-throated sons of liberty "were appointed by their ASSEMBLIES; by the true and legal representatives of the people; and therefore were the true and legal delegates of the people." I hear you, gentlemen; and while I hear you, I pity your ignorance, tho' I am astonished at your impudence. It would be much to your advantage if you would learn a little common sense, if you would furnish yourselves with some small degree of understanding, before you set up to manage the affairs of government, and to decide so very peremptorily upon the rights and liberties of your fellow-subjects. Learn to view things in their true light; to consider them according to their real natures, and to speak of them with propriety; and then you *will* be heard and attended to. But a misguided fancy, a heated imagination, will only hurry you into contempt. Noise and blustering may make you appear of some consequence in a tavern or ale-house: Loud cries of liberty may catch the ignorant, and beguile the unwary: *Tar and feathers* may silence the pusillanimous: But if you would rise into real dignity, and merit the esteem of your fellow subjects, in settling the present distracted state of our country, you must obtain a knowledge of the first principles at least, of civil government; from *them* you must deduce your reasonings; to *them* you must conform your conduct.

Consider now, and tell me, what right or power has any assembly on the continent to appoint delegates, to represent their province in such a congress as that which lately met at Philadelphia? The assemblies have but a delegated authority themselves. They are but the representatives of the people; they cannot therefore have even the shadow of right, to delegate that authority to three or four persons, even should these persons be of their own number, which were delegated by the people to their whole body conjunctively. Delegates, so appointed, are, at best, but delegates of delegates, but representatives of representatives. And whatever assembly hath acted in this manner, hath betrayed the rights and privileges of the people whom they represented. It has exercised a power which it never received from the people, but which it has usurped over them; and instead of commendations and applause, it deserves only censure and reproach. Besides,

The people are not bound by any act of their representatives, till it hath received the approbation of the other branches of the legislature. No delegates, therefore, can in any *true* sense be called the *representatives of a province*, unless they be appointed by the joint act of the whole legislature of the province. When, therefore, the delegates at Philadelphia, in the preamble to their Bill of rights, and in their letter to his Excellency General Gage, stiled their body "a full and free representation of—" "all the colonies from Nova-Scotia to Georgia," they were guilty of a piece of impudence which was never equalled since the world began, and never will be exceeded while it shall continue.

Nor is it clear to me, that the legislature of any province have a power of appointing delegates to such a congress as lately met at Philadelphia. I am certain no provincial legislature can give them *such* powers as were lately exercised at Philadelphia.

The legislative authority of any province cannot extend farther than the province extends. None of its acts are binding one inch beyond its limits. How then can it give authority to a few persons to meet other persons, from other provinces, to make rules and laws for the whole continent? In such a case, the Carolinas, Virginia, Maryland, and the four New-England colonies, might make laws to bind Philadelphia, New-Jersey and New-York: that is—they might make laws whose operation should extend farther than the authority by which they were enacted, extended. Before such a mode of legislation can take place, the constitution of our colonies must be subverted, & their present independency on each other must be annihilated. And after it was accomplished, we should be in a situation a thousand times worse, than our present dependance on Great-Britain, should all the difficulties we complain of be real, and all the grievances some people affect to fear, fall upon us.

But it is time to attend upon the congress, and consider their proceedings. However chosen, or however appointed, on September the fifth, 1774, the delegates met in a Grand Continental Congress at Philadelphia, and became the object of Grand Continental Attention. For a considerable time, they affected the utmost secrecy. Their doors were shut, their whole proceedings were involved in privacy and darkness. Nothing transpired, nothing was heard; but that Mr. ——, I forgot his name, was continually posting from Boston to Philadelphia, and from Philadelphia to Boston. We pleased ourselves with the thoughts that all our grievances would now be decently and fairly represented, all our unhappy disputes with our mother country adjusted and settled, and every possibility of future contention obviated, by the joint wisdom, prudence and moderation of all the colonies. Like the country people in the fable, we stood all attentive to the *throes* and *pangs* of the *labouring* mountain,—agape, with the expectation of some mighty matter to be produced at the birth. I would to God our expectations, like theirs, had ended in laughter and merriment;—But alass! the *labour* of the congress produced, not a silly mouse, to make us laugh, but a venomous brood of scorpions, to sting us to death.

During that mysterious period of silence, when they kept the whole continent in suspense, they seem to have been in the state of a man who is determined upon some hazardous enterprize, but not having courage enough to set about it cooly and deliberately, is obliged to wait till accident, or his own efforts have raised his passions to a proper degree of fury: Or, like the inhabitants of New-Zealand, before they attack their enemies, they found it necessary to animate themselves by singing their war song, exercising their lances, and brandishing their patoo-patoos, that they might work themselves up into such a state of frenzy, as should apparently lessen the danger of those desperate measures, which they were already determined to pursue.

The people of Boston seem attentively to have regulated their conduct in such a manner, as should have the greatest tendency to inflame the minds of the congress when it should meet. While the members of that assembly were drawing together at Philadelphia, a report was spread from Boston that the navy and army had attacked the town. Posts were dispatched with the most hasty speed, from town to town, till the dreadful tidings arrived at Philadelphia. In New-England, all was hurry and confusion, "the pulpit-drum ecclesiastic," spread the alarm through Connecticut. They flew to arms, and marched off to attack the troops of *that King* whose *faithful and loyal subjects* they have repeatedly declared themselves to be; those very troops, which were employed in the support of his government, and in the protection of his subjects.

This false alarm answered two purposes. It tried the temper of the other New-England colonies, and convinced the Boston people, that they were ready to join them in their most extravagant schemes,—to rush headlong with them down the precipice of rebellion. It served also to inflame the congress, and to prepare the way for another Boston manœuvre.

The county of Suffolk, in the province of Massachusetts Bay, had, on the sixth and ninth of September, entered into a set of resolves, by which the authority of the government of Great-Britain was denied, the courts of justice shut up, his Majesty's counsellors, who did not resign their places by a day set them, viz. September 20th, were declared to be "obstinate and incorrigible enemies to their country." The command of the militia taken from the King, and lodged in the people; with several other positions and declarations equally seditious and rebellious. It was a matter of great consequence to the success of their schemes, to get these resolves ratified, and confirmed by authority of the congress. Now was the lucky time, the critical minute. Their passions were up, their reason disturbed, their judgment distorted; with the most inconsiderate rashness they took the fatal resolution of adopting "*approving and recommending*" the conduct of the Suffolk people, contained in their resolves of the 6th of September; thereby making those rebellious resolves, as far as in them lay, the act and deed of all his *Majesty's faithful subjects, in all the colonies, from Nova Scotia to Georgia.*

It is not my design to consider minutely this adopted brat of the congress—the Suffolk resolves.—Every person who wishes a reconciliation with Great-Britain; who desires to continue under her dominion and protection; who hopes to enjoy the security of law and good government, and to transmit our present free and happy constitution untainted and uncorrupted to his posterity; must condemn and abhor them. Nor will I enter on a particular examination of the other productions of the congress. To point out and animadvert on every thing in their addresses, &c. which deserved censure, would require a volume; nor would my patience hold out through so dirty a road, though I should find scarce any thing to impede my progress; but positive assertions, without proof; declamations, without argument; and railing, without modesty.

My business is to detect and expose the false, arbitrary, and tyrannical PRINCIPLES upon which the Congress acted, and to point out their fatal tendency to the interests and liberties of the colonies.

It was the general opinion and expectation of those people I conversed with, that the congress would form some reasonable and probable scheme of accommodating our unhappy disputes with the mother country, and of securing our own rights and liberties; and that in order to make our union with Great-Britain durable and permanent, they would endeavour to mark out the limits of parliamentary authority over the colonies; ascertaining, on the one hand, the liberties of the colonies, and on the other, giving full weight to the supreme authority of the nation over all its dominions. Had they attempted this, they would have done something towards accomplishing the important business on which they assembled. Though they might have executed it in an imperfect manner, it might probably have served for something to build upon; it would have been discussed here and at home; its errors pointed out; its advantages explained; its inconveniences obviated; and future improvements might have made it of real utility: At least, they would, by this conduct, have shewn their attention to the interests of the colonies, and would, even on that account, have deserved their regard; but they did nothing like this, on the contrary, they spent near, or quite, two months, in approving and commending the mad proceedings of the people of Boston, and writing inflammatory addresses to the people of Great-Britain, Quebec, and the other provinces; and in exercising *an assumed power of legislation*.

Should any person choose to controvert this last position, I appeal to the *Association* published by them, under the signature of their own names. Every article of this instrument was intended by them to have a force of the law. They have indeed used the *soft, mild, insinuating* term of *recommending* their laws to our observance, instead of the authoritative phrase of "Be it enacted, &c." because, their authority was not yet firmly settled. But they have *solemnly bound themselves and their constituents* —by whom they affect to mean every inhabitant of the colonies, from Nova-Scotia to Georgia—(happy Nova-Scotia!

happy Georgians who are out of their jurisdiction—) *to adhere firmly to their Association*;—they have appointed their officers to carry it into execution,—they have ordained penalties upon those that shall presume to violate it. The appointments of those officers, the mode of their proceeding, the penalties to be inflicted, are contained in the eleventh article of the association.

Upon this article I beg leave to make some remarks.

"A committee" is ordered "to be chosen in every county, city, and town;" and to give the weight to those committees, and to make them appear as much as possible like LEGAL OFFICERS *duly elected*, they are ordered to be chosen only "*by those who are qualified to vote for Representatives in the legislature.*" A strong circumstance to prove that the Congress intended to give the force of a law to their Association.

Their "business shall be attentively to observe the conduct of all persons touching this Association; and when it shall be made appear to the satisfaction of a majority of any such committee, that any person within the limits of their appointment has violated this Association, that such majority do forthwith cause the truth of the case to be published in the Gazette, to the end, that all such foes to the rights of British America may be publicly known, and universally contemned as the enemies of American liberty, and henceforth we respectively will break off all dealings with him or her."

Here, gentlemen, is a court established upon the same principles with the *popish Inquisition*. No proofs, no evidences are called for. The committee may judge from *appearances* if they please—for when it shall be made appear to a majority of any committee that the Association is violated, they may proceed to punishment, and *appearances*, you know, are easily *made*; nor is the offender's *presence* necessary. He may be condemned unseen, unheard—without even a possibility of making a defence. No jury is to be impannelled.—No check is appointed upon this court;—no appeal from its determination: Nor is it left accountable to any power on earth; so that if a majority of the committee should chance not to have the fear of GOD before their eyes—the Lord have mercy upon us all!

Next, look at the punishment to be inflicted upon any person, when it shall *appear* to a majority of any committee that he hath violated this Association:—The committee are to cause the truth of the case to be published in the Gazette.—Consider the matter gentlemen, fairly and cooly, without prejudice or partiality. Should committees be chosen, according to the purport of this eleventh article of the Association, in every *county, city and town,* from Nova-Scotia to Georgia—do you think that a majority of *every* such committee would consist of men of such *exact* honour and probity, as that we might in *all* cases ex pect the *truth,* the *whole truth, and nothing but the truth,* in their publications? Do we run no risk by committing such unbounded power into their hands? May they not sometimes wantonly abuse it? Especially as they are accountable to no superior tribunal;— without any other check on their conduct, than their own honour. Will their passions, their prejudices and prepossessions never warp them from *realities,* to judge by *appearances* only? They must be very extraordinary persons indeed.

When the *Popish* inquisition hath passed sentence of condemnation on any person, they have done their duty—the poor wretch is then delivered over to the secular power to be punished. In humble imitation of this humane and laudable practice, when the *committorial* inquisition has condemned any person, and published his sentence in the Gazette; they have done their duty; and then the poor culprit is to be delivered over to the power of the mob, for execution. He is to be considered as a *foe to the rights of British America, and universally contemned as the enemy of American liberty, and thenceforth* the parties of the Association *respectively will break off all dealings with him or her.*—Poor, unhappy wretch, how I pity thee! Cast out from civil society! Nobody to have any dealings with thee! None to sell thee a loaf of bread, or a pot of tea-water, but such miserable out-laws as thyself! Perhaps thou hast drank a dish of *tea,* or a glass of *Madeira,* or hast used an English *pin,* or eaten Irish *potatoe,* imported out of due time;—and hast had the truth of thy unhappy case published, by the inquisition, in the Gazette: And is there no relief! Must thou expect no mitigation of thy punishment? None, my friend; thou hast committed the unpardonable sin against the Congress; and the utmost vengeance that they can inflict awaits thee!—Comfort thyself however in this—that thou art in no worse state than a few honest people, of whom I have read, in an old neglected book, who were not allowed to *buy* or *sell*, because they had not the *mark of the beast* in their *foreheads*.

I beg your pardon, Gentlemen, for treating so serious a subject with ridicule. Look back, I beseech you, upon the conduct of the Congress—consider what a state they have brought you into—view well the difficulties that surround you. Perhaps you may be tempted to make light of them, and without much reflection, to say, that *all will be well*. But remember;—your liberties and properties are now at the mercy of a body of men unchecked, uncontrouled by the civil power. You have chosen your committee;—you are no longer your own masters:—you have subjected your business, your dealings, your mode of living, the conduct and regulation of your families, to *their* prudence and discretion. The public laws of the province are superseded by the laws of the Congress. The government of your city is, in a great measure, taken out of the hands of the magistrates; they cannot do their duty for the want of that support which all good men ought to give them:—Violence is done to private property, by riotous assemblies, and the rioters go unpunished; nay more;—are applauded for those very crimes which the laws of the government have forbidden, under severe penalties.

You seem to think yourselves perfectly safe and secure, because your committee consists of virtuous and honest men, and *they will* not hurt you. I have no inclination to detract from the virtue, or to impeach the honesty of the gentlemen of the committee. I hope their future conduct will justify your good opinion of them. It is best however to see the end of their committee-ship, before you give them the sanction of your approbation.—But is it then come to *this?*—Your committee *will* not hurt you. Are you content to have your liberty and property dependent on the *Will* of the committee? *You* that spurned at the thought of holding your rights on the precarious tenure of the *will* of a British ministry, as you have been pleased to speak; or of a British Parliament, can *you* submit to hold them on as precarious a tenure, the *will* of a New-York committee, of a continental congress?

You cannot, I think, want conviction, that your liberty and property are made subject to the laws of the Congress, and the will of the committee. If you do, look at the tenth article of the

Association. Any goods or merchandize that may arrive on your account between the first day of December, and the first day of February next, though you should have ordered them before the Congress had a being, must be reshipped by your *own* direction; and this direction you *must* give, under the penalty of being *gazetted*;—or, they must be delivered up to the committee of the county or town wherein they shall be imported, to be stored at your *own risk*;—or, they must be sold under the direction of the committee; and after you are reimbursed your first cost and charges, the profit is to be applied to the relieving such poor inhabitants of the town of Boston as are immediate sufferers by the Boston Port-Bill.—Good God! That men who exclaim so violently for liberty and the rights of Englishmen, should ever voluntarily submit to such an abject state of slavery! That *you*, who refuse submission to the Parliament, should tamely give up your liberty and property to an illegal, tyrannical Congress: For shame, gentlemen, act more consistently. You have blustered, and bellowed, and swaggered, and bragged, that no British Parliament should dispose of a penny of your money without your leave, and now you suffer yourselves to be *bullied* by a *Congress*, and *cowed* by a COMMITTEE, and through fear of the *Gazette*, are obliged to hold open your pocket, and humbly intreat that the gentlemen of the committee would take out *all* the profits of a whole importation of goods, for the benefit of the *Boston poor*.

In God's name, are not the people of Boston able to relieve their *own* poor? Must they go begging from Dan to Beersheba; *levying* contributions, and *exacting* fines, from Nova-Scotia to Georgia, to support a few poor people whom their perverseness and ill conduct have thrown into distress? If they are *really* under such violent concern for their poor, why don't they *pay* for the tea which they destroyed, and thereby qualify themselves to have their port opened?—this would effectually answer the purpose; and is only an act of bare justice which they ought to have done long ago:—They have made a great parade about employing their poor, in paving their streets, and repairing their wharves and docks;—are they unable to *pay* them for their labour? Can't they *spare* some small portion of that wealth, which is now pouring in upon them from the army and navy, for so good a purpose? Or will not the labour of the poor support them now, as well as formerly? Must they command the wealth of the continent, to ornament their town, and render it more commodious? Do they expect a *literal* completion of the promise, that the *Saints shall inherit the earth?* In my conscience, I believe they do. Nor can I, on this occasion, help recollecting the observation of a queer fellow some time ago. Discoursing with him on this very subject, he said, that the conduct of the Boston people seemed to him to indicate an opinion "that God had made Boston for himself, and all the rest of the world for Boston."

For Heaven's sake, gentlemen, have you no *poor* of your *own* to relieve? Are you sure that your non-importation, non-exportation, non-consumption schemes, will not draw the resentment of the British parliament on *you*, as well as on *Boston?*

I pretend not to a right of dictating to you; you have my free consent to dispose of your money as you please. If the people of Boston are unable to relieve their poor, they have an undoubted right to beg for them. And whether they are able or not, you have a right to give as much, and as often as you please. But what right had the *Congress* to give what did not *belong* to them? to give your money,—the profits arising from the sale of your goods,—without your consent?—But I forget myself,—they first proclaimed themselves your representatives, and then of course they had an undoubted, legal, constitutional right to all your substance. For you know, gentlemen, that representation and taxation go together. God and nature hath joined them.—But how, on this principle, you will keep your money out of the harpy-claws of the congress, I cannot conceive. They have shewn you already what they can do: And power is apt to be encroaching: the next congress may go farther: they have taxed you but lightly now; only the profits arising from goods imported in two months. But the *same power* that *now* takes the *profits*, may *next* take the *goods too*. I know not how you will help yourselves, unless you have prudence enough to recur to the first principles of government: And then you will find that *Legislation* and *Taxation* go together; and that no government ever yet had a being where they were divided. It is true, in the British government, for the greater security of the subject, all money-bills must take their rise in the House of Commons; nor will the commons, suffer the Lords or the King to amend or alter a money-bill: Notwithstanding which, it has no more force than an old almanack, and will raise no more money, till it has passed the House of Lords, and received the Royal Assent: That is, till it has received the sanction of the *whole legislature*, and become one of the *Laws of the Kingdom*.

After all, there is something, to me, very mysterious in the conduct of the congress on this point; and if I should not express myself clearly on it, I must be forgiven; and if I am not, I don't care much about it.—The congress seem to me, to oblige a man to give the profits of his goods to the Boston poor, whether he *will* or *not*; and at the same time to oblige him to be *willing* to do so, even *against* his *will*.—They seem to oblige him to reship his goods, or deliver them up to be stored or sold, whether he be *willing* or *unwilling*; at the same time they oblige him to be so far *willing*, as to direct it to be done, even *against* his *will*. This is too much like that divinity which obliges a man, even against his *will*, to be *willing* to be damned, before it allows him a chance for escaping. I don't understand this having two *wills*, a *willing will*, and an *unwilling will*. I don't see how a man can act *freely* upon *compulsion*. The goods are to be reshipped *at the direction of the owner*. Suppose he should be unwilling. *Unwilling* or *not*, he *must* be *willing*,—or the dread of the GAZETTE shall make him so. So that should any importer be so unfortunate as to have the arrival of his goods delayed, by any accident, till the beginning of December, he will be in the state of a man, who being condemned to be hanged, by a law made after his pretended crime was committed, was yet so cruelly treated by his judge, as to be obliged to hang himself; or at least, obliged, freely and willingly to give directions to somebody else to perform the friendly office for him. This is too much like the story of poor Jack's hanging bout, in the history of John Bull; and smells most confoundedly strong of passive obedience and non-resistance. *You* may embrace the doctrine, gentlemen, and act upon it too, if you please; but really it is too much for *me*. I cannot swallow it; and if I could, I am sure my stomach would never digest it.

I hope, Gentlemen, that you want no more proof, that the regulations of the congress have, and were intended to have, the force of laws;—nor that your liberty and property are now at the mercy of your committee. Say that it is not so, and we will put the matter on THIS footing:—There is not one of you that will dare to act contrary to the laws of the congress:—not one of you will run the risk of opposing the committee in the execution of the office lately established by their High Mightinesses the Delegates.—I am very certain that you do not ALL approve of these non-importation, non-exportation, and non-consumption schemes. *Some* of you *must* have too much sense and understanding not to perceive their *fatal tendency*. But not one of you will have courage enough to avow your sentiments, and oppose them. The first of you, whose goods shall arrive after the first of December, will, with unwilling steps, march willingly to the committee, your new masters, and give *Directions* to have them disposed of, just as *they* shall please to order. So you will act, and I know the reason you will assign for it,—You'll say, your *honour* is engaged;—that you consented to send Delegates to the congress,—and that you promised to abide by, and observe all their determinations and laws.—This indeed was unfortunate: It was much the same conduct with his, who swore to *et cæteras*. But let us examine how far your honour is *really* engaged by such a promise.

Government was intended for the security of those who live under it;—to protect the weak against the strong;—the good against the bad;—to preserve order and decency among men, preventing every one from injuring his neighbour. Every person, then, owes obedience to the laws of the government under which he lives, and is obliged in honour and duty to support them. Because, if *one* has a right to disregard the laws of the society to which he belongs, *all* have the *same* right; and *then* government is at an end. Your honour was therefore previously engaged to the government under which you live, before you promised to abide by the determinations of the congress. You had no right to make a promise implicitly to obey all their regulations, before you knew what they were, and whether they would interfere with the public laws of the government, or not. And you are so far from being bound in honour to *obey* any determinations of the congress, which interfere with the laws of the government, that you are really bound in honour to *oppose* them. Now, a little consideration will render it evident, that there is no such thing as carrying the regulations of the congress into execution, without transgressing the known laws, and contravening the legal authority of the government:—without injuring and oppressing your neighbours, who have as good a right to the protection of the laws, as *you* have.

Let it also be considered, that as no man has a legal right to do what the laws forbid, so every man has a legal right to do what they permit.

Now, by enforcing an observance of the determinations of the congress, in this province, you abrogate, or suspend, several of its laws, some of them essential to the peace and order of the government: You contravene its authority: You take the government of the province out of the hands of the governor, council and assembly, and the government of the city, out of the hands of the legal magistrates, and place them in a CONGRESS, a body utterly unknown in any legal sense! You introduce a *foreign* power, and make *it* an instrument of *injustice* and *oppression*.

The laws of this government forbid all riots, all instances of violence to others, either in abusing their persons, or depriving them of their property:—They forbid us to disturb or hinder any person in the prosecution of his lawful business;—that is, in doing what the law permits to be done.

Now, what law has forbidden the exportation of sheep? No law of the province. The farmer is permitted to sell them, and the buyer to carry them off, if he pleases.—But you have introduced a law of the congress, making that unlawful and impracticable which the laws of the province permit. And in carrying this regulation of the congress into execution, on a late occasion, a public law, which forbids all riots, was notoriously trampled upon, and a flagrant and oppressive act of injustice done to several of his Majesties subjects.

Can it be supposed, that your honour obliges you to perpetrate, or abet such actions? If not, it does not oblige you to conform to the regulations of the congress, or carry them into execution.

There is no *honour* but what is founded in *Justice* and *Virtue*. Take these away, and what is *called* so is a mere *name*; it may be whim, it may be caprice, it may be pride, it may be selfish-ness: But HONOUR it can *not* be.

Suppose one of your fellow-citizens should have a parcel of goods arrive after the first day of December, and should refuse to deliver them up to the disposal of the committee: Are you in *honour* bound to compel him? In importing the goods he has transgressed no law of God, of nature, nor of the province. On the contrary, the laws of God, of nature, and of the province, forbid you to molest him in the prosecution of his business. But you are introducing a regulation of the congress superior to the laws of God, of nature; and of the province:—A regula-tion that supersedes and vacates them all. Remember, gentle-men, that honour and duty are always consistent. Honour can never oblige a man to do that which his duty forbids him to do. Your duty requires you to obey the laws of the government in which you live, and to support their authority: But *this* honour you talk of, requires you to disobey the laws of the government, and to disannul their authority. It is therefore *false* and not *true* honour which obliges you to adhere to the regulations of the congress, and to endeavour to carry them into execution; for it obliges you to act in direct opposition to your duty, to the laws of the government, to the rights and privileges of your fellow-citizens, and to the general good of the whole province; nay, of *all* the provinces, from Nova-Scotia to Georgia.

Some carry the matter still further; they plead the necessity of the times, and pronounce boldly, that when any people are struggling for liberty, the operation of the laws must, of course, cease, and the authority of government subside: And in sup-port of this position, they alledge the instance of that memora-ble revolution in England, which placed the great King William on the throne. However necessary that revolution may have been to secure the rights and liberties of the English nation, no man, I am persuaded, who really loves his country, would wish to see it again torn by such violent convulsions as it then endured. People who talk so very feelingly, and with so much pleasure about revolutions, and who are ever ready to justify the most violent, and the most needless opposition to govern-ment, by the example of the great revolution in England, seem to me to be too fond of revolutions to be good subjects of any government on earth. However, let us examine a little how far the necessary struggles for liberty will justify that violence, which puts an end to the operation of the laws, and introduces anarchy, riots, and brutal force, in their stead.

The operation of the laws certainly ought not to cease any farther than the necessary struggles for liberty require. A small struggle will not justify a total subversion of law and good government. A struggle for liberty, however necessary it may be, which can be carried on consistently with the laws, and in due subordination to government, will never justify the breach of any one law, nor opposition to government in any instance. —To speak directly to our own case.

Had you, gentlemen, suffered the Tea belonging to the East India Company, to have been landed and stored, you would have been under no obligations to have bought it, or to have used it. It might have lain till doomsday, and would never have hurt you or your posterity. Your dispute with the mother-country, about the three-penny duty, would have been conducted consistently with the laws of the government, and no injury would have been done to any mortal. But this peaceable conduct comported not with the intemperate, fiery zeal of the *Sons of Liberty*. The cry *then* was, that there was not *virtue* enough in the city to prevent the Tea from being bought and used.—A strange alteration has happened in a short time.— You have *now* virtue enough to prevent, not only *Tea* from being bought and *used*, but *all* commodities from Great-Britain and Ireland, &c. from being *imported*. If you go on, gentlemen, your improvements in *virtue* will soon put you upon an *exact equality* with the New-England people, whom a late celebrated writer of your city stiled, the *most virtuous people on earth*! Instead of this peaceable conduct, every violent measure has been pursued; all means that tended to promote a reconciliation with Great-Britain, and to maintain the peace and order of the government in which we live, have been neglected. And to complete the folly of your conduct, you now resolve to adhere to the determinations of the congress, thereby precluding all possibility of accommodation with the mother-country, except upon our own terms, which never can be complied with, consistently with the dignity of the nation: You thereby also introduce a new authority into the province, highly derogatory from, and subversive of the power of the legislature: You establish a court of Inquisition, to decide, in the most arbitrary, tyrannical and unheard-of manner, upon the liberties and properties of your fellow-subjects, over whom you have no just or legal power: You lay an embargo upon all the produce of the farmers, and will thereby be enabled to purchase it at your own price: You have monopolized, into your own hands many of the necessaries and comforts of life, and you prevent any more from being imported; by which means you will command the purses of the good people of the province, and may extort what sums you please from them in payment for your goods: And lastly, you promote and encourage riots, mobs and tumults, and make them the means of carrying into execution that abominable system of oppression which the congress have devised for the future government of the continent.

All the hardships which you complain of, all the evils which you say, you fear, from the weight of parliamentary power, endured for a *Century*, would not injure this province so much as this mode of conduct continued only for a *twelvemonth*.

Where, I beseech you, was the necessity for all this so glaring, so violent an infringement of the laws of society, and of the rights of your fellow subjects? In truth, there never was, nor is there now, any other necessity than what you yourselves have made. Had you permitted the Tea to have been stored, and only refrained from purchasing it, you might have waited for the meeting of the assembly, without any manner of danger to your rights and privileges: and then you might have had the grievances you complain of, considered by the true and legal representations of the people: If they were found to be just, they would have been represented, and a remedy sought, in a legal constitutional way; without the subversion of the laws, without the oppression of individuals, and without detriment to the province.

Instead of this reasonable and manly mode of proceeding, you have, by your rash and precipitate conduct, cast a very undeserved odium on your representatives, and involved the province in confusion and danger.—Have your representatives neglected your interests?—Have they given up your liberties? —Have they betrayed your rights?—Have they shewn any *disposition* to do these things?—If not, why are they neglected? Why are they treated as though they were not worthy to be trusted.

Let it also be considered, that the assembly are a body known and acknowledged by the laws of the empire. Their representations would be considered, their petitions or remonstrances attended to. The supreme authority of the nation could treat with them without descending from its dignity. But the congress are a body unknown to the government. In a *legal* sense, they are no *body at all*. You cannot then expect, that their petitions, should they have made any, will be attended to, or their remonstrances regarded.

Let those, who are fond of pleading the necessities of the times, in excuse of the subversion of the laws, consider,—that violent and illegal measures, even in the most necessary struggles for liberty, can never be justified, till all legal and moderate ones have failed.—Supposing therefore, that all the complaints we make against the British Parliament and Ministry are founded in truth; and that all the evils which we foresee and foretel are really coming on us. We have no right to procede to such violent means of redress as the congress have directed, and you are executing, till the legal and constitutional applications of our Assembly have failed.

Let me now request of you, gentlemen, to look back, and consider the whole of the matter, and then determine for yourselves, whether you are bound by the principles of honour, of duty, or of conscience, to adhere to, or carry into execution, the regulations of the Congress, to the subversion of the laws, the disturbance of the peace, the oppression of the inhabitants, and the destruction of the property of the province in which you live?

Besides, are you sure, that while you are supporting the authority of the congress, and exalting it over your own legislature, that you are not nourishing and bringing to maturity, a grand American Republic, which shall, after a while, rise to power and grandeur, upon the ruins of our present constitution? To me the danger appears more than possible. The out-lines of it seem already to be drawn. We have had a grand Continental Congress at Philadelphia. Another is to meet in May next. There has been a Provincial Congress held in

Boston government. And as all the colonies seem fond of imitating the Boston politics, it is very probable that the scheme
will spread and increase; and in a little time, the *Common-Wealth*
be completely formed.

You may think this a chimera, a creature of my own brain,
and may laugh at it. But when you consider circumstances
with a more minute attention, possibly some foundation for
my suspicions may appear. That a majority of the people of the
Massachusetts-Bay have it in meditation to throw off their
subjection to Great-Britain, as soon as a favourable season
presents, can scarce admit of a doubt. The independency of
that province on the British Parliament, has been declared in
express terms. As yet they acknowlege King George the Third
for their King and liege Lord;—how long they will abide by
this acknowlegment is very uncertain. They are daily encroaching on the prerogatives of his crown, and the legal rights of his
throne. They have wrested the militia from the command of
his Governor, and are disciplining it to fight against his own
troops, whom they have called *military executioners*, and enemies to their state. They have obliged his servants to resign
their employments. They have shut up his courts of justice,
dissolved his government, and are erecting one of their own
modeling in its room.

They boast of the number and valour of their men, and have
given plain intimations, in the Suffolk Resolves, that they will
not always act on the *defensive*. I could enumerate more circumstances in support of my suspicions, but these are sufficient.

Only now suppose it possible that they should succeed, and
become a state independent on Great-Britain. The probable
consequence would be, that the other New-England colonies
would join them, and together with them, form one Republic.
When once they had arrived at this height of power, How long
do you suppose they would remain in peace with *this* government? Certainly only till a fair opportunity offered to attack it
with advantage. The New-England people have ever cast a
wishful eye on the lands of this province. Connecticut, Massachusetts, New-Hampshire, have all in their turns encroached
upon them; and their encroachments have not only been very
troublesome, but also very difficult to remove. A state of continual war with New-England, would be the inevitable fate of

this province, till submission on our part, or conquest on their part, put a period to the dispute. The consequences of such an event to the *landed interest* of this colony, need no enumeration.

Whenever the fatal period shall arrive, in which the American colonies shall become independent on Great-Britain, a horrid scene of war and bloodshed will immediately commence. The interests, the commerce of the different provinces will interfere: disputes about boundaries and limits will arise. There will be no supreme power to interpose; but the sword and bayonet must decide the dispute. We, indeed, in *words*, disclaim every thought and wish of separating our interests from hers: But in *deed* and *fact*, all the colonies from Nova-Scotia to Georgia, have run headlong into such measures, as must, if they prove successful, finally break intirely our connection with her, or reduce her to the disagreeable necessity of establishing her dominion over us, in conquest.

To talk of subjection to the *King* of Great-Britain, while we disclaim submission to the Parliament of Great-Britain, is idle and ridiculous. It is a distinction made by the American Republicans to serve their own rebellious purposes,—a gilding with which they have enclosed the pill of sedition, to entice the unwary colonists to swallow it the more readily down.—The King of Great-Britain was placed on the throne by virtue of an act of Parliament: And he is King of America, by virtue of being King of Great-Britain. He is therefore King of America by act of Parliament. And if we disclaim that authority of Parliament which made him our King, we, in fact, reject him from being our King; for we disclaim that authority by which he is a King at all.

Let us not, Gentlemen, be led away from our duty and allegiance, by such fantastical distinctions. They are too nice and subtil for practice; and fit only for Utopian schemes of government. We have so long paid attention to sophistical declamations about liberty and property, the power of government, and the rights of the people, the force of laws and the benefit of the constitution, that we have very little of any of them left among us: And if we continue to support and imitate the mad schemes of our eastern neighbours, in the manner we have done, in a very short time, we shall have none at all.

We have hitherto proceeded from bad to worse. It is time to consider and correct our conduct. As yet it has done us no good: If persisted in too far, it will bring ruin upon us. It is our duty to make some proposals of accomodation with our parent country: And they ought to be reasonable ones—such as might be made with safety on our part, and accepted with dignity on hers. But if we expect to oblige *her* to propose a reconciliation,—to ask and intreat us to accept of such and such terms, to force *her* to concede every thing, while we will concede nothing:—If we are determined to proceed as we have done,—continually rising in our demands and increasing our opposition, I dread to think of the consequence. The authority of Great-Britain over the colonies must cease; or the force of arms must finally decide the dispute. Many Americans are hardy enough to suppose, that, in such a contest, we should come off victorious: But horrid indeed would be the consequence of our success! We should presently turn our arms on one another;—province against province,—and destruction and carnage would dessolate the land. Probably it would cost the blood of a great part of the inhabitants to determine, what kind of government we should have—whether a Monarchy or a Republic. Another effusion of blood would be necessary to fix a Monarch, or to establish the common wealth.

But it is much more probable, that the power of the British arms would prevail: And then, after the most dreadful scenes of violence and slaughter.—CONFISCATIONS and EXECUTIONS must close the HORRID TRAGEDY.

A. W. FARMER.

November 28, 1774.

FINIS.

POSTSCRIPT.

FARMER A. W. has seen a pamphlet, entitled, "A full Vindication of the Measures of the Congress, &c." He is neither frighted nor disconcerted by it; nor does he find any thing in it to make him change his sentiments, as expressed in the *Free Thoughts*: If the author of the Vindication has any teeth left, here is another *file* at his service. *A. W.* would be well pleased with an opportunity of vindicating both his publications at the same time, and he will wait ten days for this *Friend to America*'s Remarks upon the *Examination into the Conduct of the Delegates*, which he supposes will be full time enough for so very accomplished a writer to *ridicule* all the *wit* contained in it. *A. W.* begs the author of the Vindication to consult Johnson's Dictionary, and see whether the expression, "and his *wit* ridiculed," be *classical* or not. He is persuaded that had the *Vindicator* possessed the least spark of genuine *wit*, he would have felt both the impropriety of the expression, and the impracticability of the attempt.

Dec. 16, 1774.

[Thomas Bradbury Chandler], A Friendly Address to All Reasonable Americans, on the Subject of Our Political Confusions: In Which the Necessary Consequences of Violently Opposing the King's Troops, and of a General Non-Importation Are Fairly Stated. New York, 1774.

By the beginning of 1775 the British government was preparing for military action, and the colonists, especially in New England, were preparing to resist it. In September 1774 just a rumor that Governor-General Gage's troops had bombarded Boston led thousands of militiamen from southern and western New England to mobilize and march on the Massachusetts capital. Before they learned that it was a false alarm and turned back, as many as twenty thousand had been on the road to Boston.

This rising tenor of militarism led to an exchange—initiated by the *Friendly Address to All Reasonable Americans* and continued in Pamphlets 28, 30, and 31—dealing with the prospect of armed conflict. Thomas Bradbury Chandler was one of the most eloquent of those who wrote on behalf of the British cause in the latter stages of the imperial debate, and with his emphasis on respect for authority and the higher powers he may also have been one of the most Toryish. Chandler was rector of St. John's Anglican Church in Elizabethtown, New Jersey, and an important leader in the effort to bring a bishop to the North American colonies. Without a bishop all Anglican clergy trained in the colonies had to travel to England to be ordained. The prospect of an episcopal hierarchy brought to the colonies lay behind much of the revolutionary activism of Congregationalists and Presbyterians in New England and the Middle Colonies.

At the outset of his pamphlet Chandler raised the standard Loyalist charge—that the American reaction seemed out of all proportion to the oppression they alleged. Indeed, by the standards of tyrannies experienced throughout history, the Americans were not an especially oppressed people. "Of all people under heaven," wrote Chandler, "the King's subjects in America, have hitherto had the least ground for complaint." In fact the colonists admitted they were freer and less burdened with cumbersome feudal and hierarchal restraints than any part of humanity in the eighteenth century. Thus Americans often assumed a conservative posture in their writings, insisting that they were struggling to preserve their traditional rights, not to remodel society according to some radical vision. But to those loyal to the empire, the possibility of an American rebellion remained totally incomprehensible. Never in history, wrote the Massachusetts Loyalist Daniel Leonard, had there been so much resistance with so "little real cause."

A

FRIENDLY ADDRESS

TO

ALL reasonable AMERICANS,

ON

THE SUBJECT OF

OUR

POLITICAL CONFUSIONS:

IN WHICH

THE NECESSARY CONSEQUENCES

OF

Violently oppofing the KING'S TROOPS,

AND OF

A GENERAL NON-IMPORTATION

ARE

FAIRLY STATED.

Am I *therefore* become your Enemy, becaufe I tell you the Truth?

ST. PAUL.

NEW-YORK:
Printed in the Year M,DCC,LXXIV.

A Friendly Address, &c.

Friends, Countrymen, and Fellow-Subjects!

"OUR civil government (says an excellent English Writer) is happily placed between the two extremes of *despotic power* and *popular licentiousness*: it is wisely composed of such a due mixture of the several simple forms of government, those of one, of a few, and of many, as to retain as far as possible the advantages, and to exclude the inconveniencies, peculiar to each; and the parts are so nicely combined and adjusted, that the several powers co-operate and move on together in concert and agreement, mutually tempering, limiting, and restraining, yet at the same time aiding, supporting, and strengthening each other."

This frame of government, for the admirable wisdom of its structure, has always been the wonder of the world; and under its protection and mild influence, the subjects of Great Britain are the happiest people on earth. But of all the subjects of Great Britain, those who reside in the American Colonies have been, and, were they sensible of their own advantages, might still be, by far the happiest: surrounded with the blessings of peace, health, and never-failing plenty—enjoying the benefits of an equitable and free constitution—secured by the protection and patronage of the greatest maritime power in the world—and contributing, in but a small proportion, to the support of the necessary public expences.

Under these advantages, the colonies have hitherto flourished beyond example. They have become populous, both by natural increase, and the yearly influx of foreigners, the sure indications of a happy country; and they have become rich, by practicing, at their ease, the peaceful arts of agriculture and commerce. And were they to pursue the same path which has brought them thus far, there is no doubt but they would go on to flourish and prosper in the same proportion, till, in process of time, they would excite either the admiration or envy of the whole human race. The advice therefore of MOSES to a people highly favoured of Heaven, is justly applicable to them; and nothing can be wanting to their happiness, but hearts to follow it, "Only *take heed to thyself*, says he, and keep thy soul diligently,

273

lest thou forget the things which thine eyes have seen, and lest they depart from thine heart, all the days of thy life."

But a far different prospect, at this time, presents itself to view. The darkness of a rising tempest is beginning to overspread our land. The thunder roars at a distance, and appears to be swiftly approaching. It is high time therefore to awaken the thoughtless to a sense of their danger, and to think of providing for our common safety.

There is, there can be, but one way to prevent the ruin that threatens us. Our own misconduct has brought it forward; and our immediate reformation must stop its progress. He must be blind, that is not convinced of this; and he must be infatuated, that will pursue the road, which evidently terminates in darkness and destruction.

Whether the British Parliament has been right or wrong in its late proceedings, towards the Colonies; our behaviour has been such as every government must and will think intolerable. If the supreme power of any kingdom or state, through want of due information or attention, should adopt measures that are wrong or oppressive, the subjects may complain and remonstrate against them in a respectful manner; but they are bound, by the laws of Heaven and Earth, not to behave undutifully, much more not to behave insolently and rebelliously. The bands of society would be dissolved, the harmony of the world confounded, and the order of nature subverted, if reverence, respect, and obedience, might be refused to those whom the constitution has vested with the highest authority. The ill consequences of open disrespect to government are so great, that no misconduct of the administration can justify or excuse it. The guilt of it is so aggravated, that Christians are required, under the heaviest penalty to avoid it, and to be *subject to the higher powers*, of whatever character, *for conscience's sake*. No tyrant was ever more despotic and cruel, than *Nero*, and no Court ever more corrupted than his; and yet to the government of this cruel and despotic tyrant, and his corrupt ministry, peaceable submission was enjoined by an Apostle, who had a due regard for the rights and liberties of mankind. To disturb or threaten an established government, by popular insurrections and tumults, has always been considered and treated, in every age and nation of the world, as an unpardonable crime:

and were we the subjects of the *Grand Turk*, it is as certain that we ought not to encourage such practices, as that St. Paul and St. Peter, who condemned them, were inspired men.

But my design is not to consider, how far the conduct of the Colonies is, or is not, conformable to the rules and precepts of the Christian religion; but, how far it is to be condemned or justified by the maxims of sound policy and prudence. Our temporal interest and safety are considerations which all will regard, how much soever they may slight or despise the obligations of religion.

The voice of complaint, to call it no worse, is now heard through every corner of our land; and we are daily exhorted to prepare for the defence of our liberties, and all that is sacred, with united efforts.—But before we proceed, it concerns us to be well informed, both as to our real danger, and the steps proper to be taken.

Were the Americans actually in a state of oppression, it would shew their wisdom and prudence, to submit with patience to their present condition, rather than to provoke the power that oppresses them, without some fair prospect of obtaining relief. One degree of distress, in consequence of the weight of illegal power, is a grievance; ten degrees of distress are proportionably a greater evil; but bad as it is, he must be an idiot or a madman, who would not prefer them to twenty. But it appears to me that, of all people under heaven, the King's subjects in America, have hitherto had the least ground for complaint; and that the present confusion of the Colonies has been occasioned by misinformations and false alarms. If none of our *legal* rights have been invaded, no injury has been done us; if we have not been injured, we have no room for complaint; and we can never be justified in resenting that, which it would be unreasonable to complain of.

My *Friends, Countrymen, and Fellow Subjects!* suffer, for a few minutes, an American, one who has often gloried in the title, who loves his country as much, and has as great a regard for its honour, as any of you, to reason and expostulate with you, in plain language, on a subject now of the highest importance, both to you and him.

You are taught to exclaim loudly against "the arbitrary proceedings of the British Parliament." But consider; wherein have they been arbitrary, and in what do you suffer? Why, it seems, "a duty of three pence a pound, has been laid, by Parliament, upon their teas exported to America; and we cannot purchase the tea, without paying the duty." But if this may be called a burden, so may the weight of an atom on the shoulders of a giant: besides, this burden may be easily avoided; for we have no occasion to purchase the tea, and unless we purchase it, we are under no obligations to pay the duty.

You will say: "the Parliament had *no right* to lay the duty." But I suspect we are, most of us, but indifferent judges of the rights of Parliament; or however, the Parliament must act according to their own judgment, and not according to ours, if it be different from theirs. They assert, and believe, that they have the right in question; and we have never proved that they have not. Nay, we ourselves have always believed and allowed that they have it, till the present occasion. I might add, that we have always allowed that they had a right to regulate not only the trade, but all concerns of the Colonies; such a power they have always exercised, and we have submitted to their acts. Thus, for instance, we have paid a duty on wine and molasses, in obedience to Parliament, and without protestations or remonstrances; and, for the same reasons, we are as much obliged to pay the duty on tea. If we would act consistently, we should either refuse to pay the duty on wine and molasses, or consent to pay it on tea; for it is, in both cases, imposed from the same principle, and has the same effect.

Perhaps it will be replied, "These and all other duties ought to be rejected, because they are *precedents*, and intended to prepare the way for higher demands; and if Parliament has a right to take from us one penny, without our consent, it has a right to strip us of our whole property, and to make us absolute slaves."

This, I believe, is the first time that a sovereign power has been in want of *precedents*, to justify its making laws to govern any part of its dominions. It is a contradiction in the nature of things, and as absurd as that a part should be greater than the whole, to suppose that the supreme legislative power of any Kingdom does not extend to the utmost bounds of that kingdom. If these Colonies, which originally belonged to *England*, are not now to be regulated and governed by the authority of *Great Britain*, then the consequences are plain; they are not dependant upon *Great Britain*—they are not included within its territories—they are no part of its dominions—the inhabitants are not English, they can have no claim to the privileges of Englishmen; they are, with regard to *England*, foreigners and aliens; nay, worse, as they have never been legally discharged from the duty they owed it, they are rebels and apostates. On the above supposition, they are, at best; as much the dominions of *Denmark* or *Russia*, as of *Great Britain*; for there can be no difference in this case, unless one has an authority over them, which the others have not. But if *Great Britain* possesses a sovereignty over the Colonies, she certainly has a right, at least, to regulate our commerce; and especially to regulate the importation of such articles of mere luxury, as we can choose whether we will be concerned with, or not, with but little inconvenience to ourselves. Now the present duty on tea is exactly such a regulation.

You allow that this duty is a thing that is but trifling in itself; but then you conceit that you ought to oppose it, because it is a *precedent*, which hereafter may be used to your disadvantage. I am sorry to see that men can be so easily deluded by such sophistry. Can you imagine that Parliament will not do whatever they think right to be done by them, without waiting for *Precedents*? Yet precedents of their own for regulating the trade of the Colonies, are not wanting. Every reign, since the Settlement of the Colonies has produced them; in consequence of which you are daily paying duties that, in every view, are as liable to exception, as the duty on tea. From hence it is evident, that you yourselves have no inclination to be governed by precedents, whatever regard the Parliament may be supposed to have for them.

As to the argument that, "If Parliament has a right to take from us one penny, without our consent, it has a right to strip us of our whole property;" altho' so great a man as Mr. LOCKE was the father of it, it appears to me to be weak and sophistical. A right to do what is reasonable, implies not a right to do what is unreasonable. A father may have a right over his son, so far as to send him on an errand, or upon any reasonable service, without having such an absolute authority as can oblige him to throw himself down a precipice, or to hang himself. In like manner, cases may happen, in which it would be reasonable for

Parliament to take from us some small matter, though we were unwilling to part with it; but the case can hardly be supposed, in which it would be reasonable to take from us every thing, unless we should have forfeited it. Every society has a right to make a moderate use of its power over its own members, but not to abuse it. There can be no right to do what is unquestionably *wrong*.

But you will say, it is *wrong* to tax us at all, *without our consent*. But the duty on tea, which has occasioned all our confusions, is not such a tax; for unless you consent to the tax, you are not to pay the duty. You may refuse it, if you please, without incurring any penalty, or considerable inconvenience. As to such taxes as arise from the general regulation of American commerce, they must be imposed without our formal consent, if they are imposed at all. For if all the Colonies must be consulted, and all must agree, before such a regulation can take place; it is easy to foresee, that nothing of this kind can be established, as nothing can be proposed, in which all the Colonies, having each its peculiar views and interests, would be likely to agree. Therefore *Great Britain* must either impose such duties upon our imports and exports, as may be thought proper for the good of the whole community, without our consent, or she must not attempt to regulate our trade; and if she is not to superintend and regulate our trade, she had better relinquish at once her claim of authority over her colonies; after which they cannot expect to enjoy her protection.

But you further object, that "if we are to be bound by laws to which we have never consented, we have not the rights of Englishmen." In answer to this, let me remind you, first of all, that it never was, nor can it be, the right of Englishmen to be exempted from the authority of an English or British Parliament. It is not a *proper* consent to the laws enacted by the British Parliament, but the being *bound* by those laws, that distinguishes a British subject from a foreigner. So long as a man resides within any dominions, he is a subject of it, and is obliged to submit to its laws, as far as they concern him, whether he approves of them or not. There are many people in England, who are natives of the country, that do not consent to acts of Parliament that are passed, unless by a bare *fiction of the law*; which can make a *nominal* consent, but *not a real* one. This is always the case of the Minority, where there is a division, whose votes are over-ruled by the major part; for the law necessarily passes, not only without, but contrary to, their consent.

Besides, there are millions of people residing in *England*, who have no votes in elections, and are never consulted about the expediency of laws. I hope these are all Englishmen, although they give no other consent to acts of Parliament, to which they are bound to submit, than what is implied in their freely residing within the jurisdiction and protection of Parliament. In this sense, the Americans, by fixing themselves, and continuing to reside, within the British dominions, consent to be governed by the British laws. When the Colonists first settled on English American ground, they well knew that the authority of Parliament was not to be suspended or withdrawn, in their favour; and they knew too, that they had no power of sending representatives to Parliament of their own choosing. *On these terms* they willingly settled here; and they have always enjoyed every advantage which they originally expected to receive, and which was contracted for in their stipulation with the Crown, and they can have no just reason to complain on this account. Yet notwithstanding all this, they have been lately told by their agents, who had it from the best authority, that if they chose to send over persons to represent them in Parliament, they should be admitted to seats in the House. In my opinion, they have done wisely in not accepting of the offer; but after refusing it, they have surely no reason to complain, that they have no representatives in the Parliament that must govern them.

It has been frequently asserted, in justification of your claim, that, "as the charters granted by the Crown, have allowed a legislative authority to the several Colonies, the inhabitants are to be bound by no laws, but what are made by their respective provincial legislatures, to which they consent by representation." With regard to this doctrine, I beg leave only to ask a few questions. Can you be made to believe, that it was ever the intention of the Crown, to establish by charter a power of legislation, in any of the Colonies, that is sovereign, independent, and incontrolable by the supreme authority of the nation? Can you imagine, that in any instance, more than a *subordinate* right of jurisdiction was meant, for the internal regulation of the district mentioned in the charter; or conceive that such a grant can place you beyond the reach of parliamentary authority? Would not the arguments that perhaps have deceived you, prove as strongly, that the charter of the city of *Albany*, granting a power to make laws for its internal regulation, *provided they are not contrary to the laws of the Province*, places the inhabitants of that city beyond the reach of laws made by the assembly of *New-York*?

You, one and all, talk of your rights by charter: but are not some of the Colonies without charters? And do all the charters convey exactly the same privileges and rights? Do any of them say, that you shall not be bound by laws made in Great Britain? Nay, does not the charter of *Pennsylvania* say expressly, that *taxes* may be laid upon the inhabitants *by act of Parliament*? None therefore have a right to plead their charters, in the present controversy, with the mother country, who reside in the colonies that are without charters, or in Pennsylvania; and it is high time for those who reside in the other colonies, to furnish some kind of evidence, that their charters give *them* the right for which they contend. They have not yet done this; they have not attempted to do it; I suspect they never will attempt it; and I challenge them to do it if they can. You may have heard some of them *declaim* on this topic, and you may hear them again; but, if you expect the *proof* called for, you will be disappointed.

What has been offered is in order to shew, that, in reality, no proper *right* of the colonies is infringed by the late act of Parliament, that imposes a small duty on the teas exported to America. And here it is worthy of notice, and we ought to attend to it all along as we proceed, that the colonies of *Rhode-Island, Connecticut, New-York, New-Jersey, Pennsylvania, Maryland, Virginia*, the *Carolinas* and *Georgia*, are not affected by any other of the late acts of Parliament; and have no dispute of their own with the mother country, but what arises from the tea-act.

But let us now *suppose*, that we have been really injured by this act; and that our paying the duty would be dangerous to our constitutional liberties. On this supposition, which the

Americans in general seem to have adopted as the true state of the case, the great question is,— *What method the colonies ought in wisdom to pursue, in order to get rid of the duty?*

Different measures have been already taken, in the different colonies, to avoid the operation of the act. In *South-Carolina*, the obnoxious tea was landed; but the inhabitants formed a resolution, to which they have the virtue punctually to adhere, not to purchase it. Happy would it have been for the colonies, if this measure had been universally taken! In that case, we should still have enjoyed tranquility, uninterrupted by seditious alarms; and the black cloud, charged with storm and thunder, that now darkens our land, would not have collected.

In most of the other colonies, the tea was not suffered to enter their ports; but it was sent back unhurt. This indeed, in all its circumstances, must be considered as a kind of insult upon government; but yet it was such a species of misbehaviour, as, in all probability, the nation would have overlooked, and many of the friends of America would have thought worthy of commendation. But, as the evil genius of the colonies would have it, the tea that was sent to *Boston*, was neither stored, nor sent back, but outrageously destroyed by the hands of violence.

Whatever may be thought of confining, or sending back the tea, there are but few people so abandoned to all sentiments of fitness, propriety, and justice, as to think the destruction of it excuseable; and the government at home, as all governments would in the like case, thought it unsufferable.—It was soon determined, to inflict an exemplary punishment upon the town that was guilty of such shameful and flagrant injustice; and an act was passed, for shutting up the port of *Boston*, till proper satisfaction should be made for so provoking an outrage.

It is certain, that all the Americans are out of the reach of this act; that it was not intended to affect them; and therefore that they have nothing immediately to do with it, excepting the inhabitants of *Boston* themselves. Accordingly I should have passed it by, as foreign from *our* part of the dispute, had it not been voted by all our county and provincial COMMITTEES, to be *dangerous to the liberties of the British colonies*. For this reason I shall offer some observations on what appears to have been the policy of the act; which I shall address to those only, who are so reasonable and modest as to allow, that the tea ought not to have been destroyed.

If the conduct of the Bostonians, in destroying the tea, was criminal, it deserved punishment; and punishments should always be regulated by the nature and degree of the crimes for which they are inflicted, and the circumstances that attended the commission of them. Now the crime of the Bostonians was a compound of the grossest injury and insult. It was an act of the highest insolence towards government; such as mildness itself cannot overlook or forgive. The injustice of the deed was also most atrocious: as it was the destruction of property to a vast amount, when it was known that the nation was obliged in honour to protect it. At the same time it was very notorious, that the intention of the perpetrators was, by this example, to lead and excite others, when the expected opportunity should present, to the same wanton excess of riot and licentiousness. Under these circumstances, sound policy was thought to require, that both a severe and a speedy punishment should be inflicted—severe, that it might bear some proportion to the guilt; and speedy, that it might prevent the like mischief in other instances.

Many, I know, who admit that Boston ought to have been punished, yet exclaim loudly against the punishment decreed by Parliament, as being too severe in its manner: And if any other punishment had been inflicted, many of them, I dare say, would have exclaimed still. For when people are once disaffected towards an administration, whether with or without just reason, they will always find some pretence for blaming any measure that can be taken by it.

As to the *severity* of the punishment in question, it was no more than shutting up a port, till satisfaction should be made for a flagrant injury and insult, of which it had been guilty. While this restraint was laid, a free use of all the neighbouring ports was allowed; so that no people but the inhabitants of the town of *Boston* were intended to be punished by this act; and a sufficient time was indulged *them* to remove all their vessels out of their harbour, that they might be usefully employed during the restraint of their port. And as soon as compensation should be made for the injury done, and a proper acknowledgment of the offence committed, every appearance shews that government intended to be satisfied, and to remove the punishment. For provision was made, that, on such an event, the King might immediately suspend the operation of the act, without waiting for the meeting, or the formal proceedings of the Parliament, which might require time. Surely none, who have as high a sense of public guilt, as of private, can think this punishment too severe for the crime, considered under all its aggravations. For, no people are entitled to the use of any advantage, which they wantonly abuse to the injury of others.

An outcry is also made, that "the punishment of the *Bostonians* was hasty and precipitant, offering no alternative, and not suffering the party to be heard." It is freely confessed that, in common cases, none ought to be punished without a regular trial and conviction. But here the case was uncommon and extraordinary. The most essential rights of government were audaciously invaded—the crime was notorious and unquestionable—a regular trial must have been the work of time—and while this would be depending, it was imagined the evil would spread. Both the letter and spirit of the law had been openly insulted and defied, by the people in Boston; and, in such a case, the *forms* of the law, in bringing them back to a sense of their duty, when it was apprehended that the delay of punishment would be dangerous to the community, were thought to be dispensible. Such considerations indeed will not authorise a judge, or any court of justice, to proceed in this compendious manner; but when a case comes before the whole legislative body, they have always the power to dispense with the ordinary forms, and to do what is conceived to be most conducive to the public safety. For, to use the words of the justly celebrated Dr. BLACKSTONE, "The bare idea of a state, without a power, somewhere vested, to alter every part of its laws, is the height of political absurdity."

It is moreover objected, that "such a mode of punishment involves the innocent in the same calamity with the guilty." In answer to which, it is sufficient to observe, that this inconvenience must always attend all punishments inflicted on a people, whether by God or man, and necessarily arises from the condition of the world. There is no body of people so bad, but many innocent persons are intermixed with them. At the very worst, there is always a number of innocent children, who are connected with, and dependent upon, the proper delinquents. The consequence of which is, that no people, and commonly no individual, can possibly be punished, without hurting some innocent persons. The objection therefore, if it has any weight, will hold good against all public, and most private punishments, of what kind soever. In the town of *Boston* there are many innocent, worthy and respectable persons (many more than is commonly imagined) who are as free from the public guilt, and hold it in as much abomination, as any men within his Majesty's dominions. For their sake, more especially, those who have the greatest regard for the honour of government, wish that the punishment could have been avoided. But as this was politically impossible, they must bear their own share, with prudence and patience, as well as they can,—enjoying a consciousness of their own innocence,—maintaining their integrity, "in the midst of a crooked and perverse generation"—and looking forward to that time, which I hope is not distant, when they may expect to be distinguished with such favours as the public can give.

The *resolves* of the above-mentioned *committees* also express, that their brethren in *Boston*, meaning the offenders against government, are to be considered "as suffering in the common cause of American liberty." But I hope the *licentiousness* of their behaviour, is not avowed to be any part of the system of *American liberty*; and I should be extremely sorry to find, that the *common cause of the colonies* requires such defences as theirs. If a raving enthusiast, in order to promote the cause of American liberty, should take it in his head to assassinate his Prince, and afterwards should be punished for his treason; he might with equal propriety, be considered as suffering in the cause of American liberty. But, in that case, I believe no sober Americans would think themselves bound to abet the assassination; and for the same reasons, we are under no obligations to abet the destructive violence of the people in *Boston*, or to endeavour to skreen it from public justice. So far as they meant well, they ought to be commended; but so far as they did wrong, they ought to be condemned. And we both expose ourselves, and injure our cause, by appearing to countenance their lawless and unwarrantable proceedings.

The same *resolves* also condemn, *as oppressive and dangerous*, the other *act* for altering the administration of justice in the *Massachusetts-Bay*; and it has been used as an instrument, in the hands of our popular incendiaries, for farther enflaming the minds of the Americans against the King and his Ministers. But it deserves notice, that the alteration made by the act, is rather an imaginary than a real evil. For it introduces into that province a regulation, which is far from being inconsistent with the happiness of the people; as it only reduces them to a form of proceedings, under which the inhabitants of *New-York* and *New-Jersey* have been as happy as any people in *America*. Indeed it abridges them of some privileges that had been granted by charter. But no privileges are curtailed by the act, but such as had been abused and forfeited over and over, and such as probably would continue to be abused, to the great injury and disturbance of that province, as well as to the dishonour and reproach of the nation. It is the opinion of the best friends to the rights of mankind, that charters *may* be forfeited; and, it is a proof of the mildness, not of the rigour, of the administration, that the *Massachusetts* charter, after so many abuses and provocations, has not been totally vacated, rather than abridged.

Besides the two last-mentioned acts, there is a third, for settling *the government of Quebec*, which has been as successfully applied to the same noble purpose of enraging the Americans against the measures of government; and more lies and misrepresentations concerning this act have been circulated, than one would think malice and falsehood could invent. It is positively asserted, and generally believed, on the evidence of positive assertions, that by this act the Popish religion is *established*, throughout the vast extent of country now subject to the government of *Quebec*; and that the Protestant religion is there obliged to skulk in corners, not daring to lift up its head. Whereas, if we have recourse to the words of the act, we shall see, that the Popish religion is no more than *tolerated* within that dominion; which was one of the conditions on which the country surrendered itself to the crown of Great Britain; and that a proper foundation is laid for the establishment of the Protestant religion, which is meant to take place. Tithes, which are the property of the tolerated Romish church in all the parishes, are indeed ordered to be paid, as formerly, to the minister of the parish; but the very moment a man declares himself a Protestant, he is freed, by the act, from the obligation to pay tithes to the Popish incumbent. In that case, it is provided, that "his Majesty, his heirs or successors, may make such provision out of the—— accustomed dues and rights, for the encouragement of the *Protestant religion*, and for the maintenance of a *Protestant clergy* within the said province, *as he or they shall, from time to time, think necessary and expedient.*" It is true, the Papists in *Canada* might have had a toleration less generous than is granted them, without the Parliament's allowing to the clergy their tithes, or to the parishes their churches. But such a toleration, although it might have fulfilled the letter of the articles of the treaty, would not have answered their expectations, nor have left upon their minds favourable impressions of the British justice and honour. If we had taken from them their churches, or stripped the clergy of their tithes, which might have been done with equal propriety, it would probably have encreased the number of his Majesty's disaffected American subjects; which appears to be too great without them. And as to *trials by juries*, they are affirmed to be excluded by the act; but the assertion is groundless and false. Juries are no more excluded from *Canada*, than they are excluded from the other American colonies. They have never been established by act of Parliament in any of the colonies, excepting the late act for the regulation of the *Massachusetts-Bay*. They owe their being in *America* to acts of our provincial Assemblies, confirmed at home; and the provincial legislature of *Canada* may introduce them as soon as they please, and it is expected that they will, as soon as the inhabitants desire them, or the state of the country will admit of them.*

I have taken this notice of the three last acts relating to the colonies, in order to shew, that in themselves they are not of so alarming a nature as has been represented, and that they wear

---

* See this point cleared up, in a candid and satisfactory manner, in a pamphlet entitled, *The Justice and Policy of the Act of Parliament, for making more effectual Provision for the Government of Quebec,* which has been lately reprinted by Mr. GAINE. See also a defence of the general policy of this act, in *A Letter (said to be wrote by Lord Lyttelton) to the Earl of Chatham,* reprinted by Mr. RIVINGTON.

not that tremendous aspect which our wild imaginations have given them. Two of them were meant as punishments for crimes against the state, and to make examples of those who were considered as the greatest offenders, and from whose republican spirit a general mischief was apprehended. The design of the other act was to secure to a new colony the religious toleration it had a *right* to demand, and otherwise to ease the minds of a numerous body of people, whose behaviour towards government had been decent and unexceptionable since they owed it allegiance, and who were likely to prove his Majesty's *most loyal and faithful subjects* in his American dominions.

Notwithstanding all that has been suggested, and in spite of all that can be said, I am aware our political incendiaries will go on in their own way, and still contend, that these acts are tyrannical and arbitrary, and threaten the destruction of American liberty. But if we would recollect ourselves, and attend a moment to the conduct and characters of these men, we should be convinced that no representations of theirs are worthy of regard. For, in all their motions, they discover themselves to be under the undue influence of prejudice and passion. Thro' this dark and misty medium every object appears to them under a violent distortion; and as thus distorted, they must describe it to others. No wonder then, that they put the very worst constructions upon, and assign the very worst motives for, all the proceedings of the British Parliament.

However, let us now suppose the truth and reality of the facts as stated by them; yet the inferences they intend, will by no means follow. Supposing Popery were actually *established* in *Canada*, on the request of the inhabitants; would it follow, that it was designed also to establish it in the other colonies, where the inhabitants are averse to it? Can any man, in his senses, believe this to be the design of Parliament? Again: supposing the punishment inflicted on the Bostonians to be arbitrary and severe; yet those who are free from their guilt, and mean not to contract it, have no reason to fear the like punishment. "For rulers are not a terror to good works, but to the evil. Wilt thou then not be afraid of the power? Do that which is good, and thou shalt have praise of the same: for he is the minister of God to thee for good. But if thou do that which is evil, be afraid; for he beareth not the sword in vain; for he is the minister of God, a revenger to execute wrath upon him that doth evil." So far as we are innocent, we are safe; but if we undertake to justify or abet the crimes of others, we share in their guilt; and particularly, if we are fomenters of the sedition that rages in *Boston*, we must take the consequence.

But the Bostonians, you say, are *over-punished*. If that be the case, they are entitled to our pity, and to our influence in obtaining a mitigation of their punishment. But this can be no reason, for our putting ourselves in the same predicament with them, for making ourselves partners in their guilt, or for bringing upon ourselves a similar punishment. We must be fools to think of doing this; and if they desire us to do it, their modesty is like that of *the fox in the fable*, who, because he happened to have lost his own tail, requested of his brother foxes, that they would all suffer their tails to be cut off too. But the foxes had more wisdom than to comply; and so should we have. As the punishment of the Bostonians was designed to be local, and peculiar to them; we have no business to cause it to be general. Their case is not yet ours; and, God grant that it never may be!

The proper dispute subsisting between Great Britain and any of her colonies, excepting that of the *Massachusetts Bay*, is only *de Lana Caprina*, about an act imposing a duty of *three pence a pound* upon tea. This is the only ground *we* have for complaining of the administration; and yet this has occasioned, throughout our colonies, such an indecent and violent opposition to government as is truly astonishing. Can such behaviour on so slight a provocation, proceed from *dutiful and loyal subjects*? No; it is impossible. Whatever we may think, or say, of ourselves; if we had any true principles of *loyalty*, or any tolerable sense of the *duty* that is due to the supreme legislative power, under which the providence of God, and our consent, have placed us, no trifling considerations could prevail with us to behave towards it in so petulent and disrespectful a manner. But there is too much reason to believe, that our minds are unprincipled, and our hearts disposed for rebellion. Ever since the reduction of *Canada*, we have been bloated with a vain opinion of our own power and importance. Our ease has produced pride and wantonness. We have been intoxicated with such draughts of liberty, as our constitutions would not bear; and under this intoxication, we have conceited that all the privileges indulged us were the effects of fear. From thinking, we have proceeded to speaking, disrespectfully of our mother country; and our language now is—"It is contrary to reason and nature, that the petty island of *Britain* should govern, and give laws to, the extensive and mighty regions of *America*."

Yet whatever *time* may produce, at present the petty island of *Britain* is able to govern ten such *Americas* as this, if she will exert her power. But she wishes by lenity and forbearance and indulgence (I will venture to use these words, notwithstanding her demand of a duty of three pence a pound upon her tea, if we see fit to make use of it) I say, she wishes by lenity, forbearance and indulgence to secure our affections, and to render us sensible, that our greatest political happiness must arise from her smiles and fostering protection. We should be fully convinced of this, were it not for our ignorance, and want of consideration; and willing to confess it, were it not for our pride. But if we determine to deny her authority, or to question her *right* to command us; she will prove to the world, and bring us to confess, that though she is ancient, she is not superannuated or exhausted; and that she still possesses the spirit and vigour that have animated her best years.

Were she only to do nothing, but barely to leave the Colonies to themselves with their jarring principles, and interests, and projects; we should soon see province waging war against province, and our country would be involved in such misery and distress as are beyond all our present conceptions. Should it be known abroad that *Great-Britain* had withdrawn her protection, and would no longer interest herself in our preservation and safety; within the compass of one year our sea-ports would be ravaged, and our vessels plundered or seized as soon as they left our harbours. We should therefore soon feel the necessity of purchasing the protection of some maritime power, and on terms not of our proposing, but of theirs; and which could never be able to secure us against any hostile attempts of *Great-Britain*, should she see fit to make any; while she maintains that Empire of the sea which she now holds, and of which all the Maritime powers of the world are unable to dispossess her.

But replies the ignorant and deluded American: "Notwithstanding all that can be said of the naval strength of *Great-Britain*, it is asserted by our patriotic leaders, and we have reason to think, that these colonies, of themselves, are able to withstand all her force." The judgment of Heaven visibly appears in this dreadful infatuation. It was but a few years ago, that we believed, and found by experience, that the colonies were unable to withstand the militia of *Canada*, supported by a few regiments of regular troops from *France*. That this was the general opinion, most of us may remember; and it is evident from the messages that passed between Governor SHIRLEY and the House of Representatives of *Boston*, from the address of the assembly of *Virginia* to the King at the beginning of the late war, and from many other authentic documents of that period. The Colonies then humbly and ardently implored that *Great-Britain* would speedily step in to their rescue, and preserve them from a destruction that threatened to overwhelm them. Their prayers were soon heard; and what was the consequence we all know. The strong bulwarks and fortresses of *Canada* were stormed, and the country conquered by the discipline and invincible bravery of but a small part of the British troops.

There is no room to doubt but such an army as was employed in the reduction of *Canada* would be more than sufficient for the conquest of all the disaffected American Colonies, should such a resolution become necessary in order to reduce them to obedience. For they are open and accessible on every quarter, and have not a single fortress to cover them, nor one regiment of regular troops to defend them; and they are without military stores, without magazines, and without the skill that is necessary for supporting an army. Under such circumstances what would the boasted numbers of our inhabitants avail us against an attack from *Great-Britain*? If an army was sent in upon us, which a body of forty thousand of our militia was unable to withstand (for it is impossible that a greater number of undisciplined men could act to advantage) it would be able to carry desolation through the whole country; and all the men in the Colonies were they firmly united, would not be able to oppose it. But yet if the army here supposed, should be found unequal to the design of reducing the Colonies, *Great-Britain* could send of her own troops a second, of equal strength to the assistance of the first; to these she could add a third of *Hessians*, a fourth of *Hanoverians*, and so on till the work were compleated. She could easily take possession of all our sea-coasts where our wealth is principally seated, and force us to fly into the back parts of the country for immediate safety. There an army of *Canadians* might be ordered to meet us, and unnumbered tribes of *savages* might be let loose upon us at the same time, while our lands would lie uncultivated, our stores exhausted, our families unsheltered, and those that happened to escape the sword, glittering and flaming both in the front and rear of our settlements, would soon perish by sickness or famine.

All that is here mentioned *Great-Britain* is able to do; and all this I believe she *would* do, should she be obliged to enter into a war with the Colonies—provided the Americans had resolution and *firmness* enough (for so some would call it) to hold out to such extremity. But I am too well acquainted with their character to expect that they would prove thus *obstinate* in the day of trial. When they come to find that on their side there can be no prospect of victory, but that every day must deepen their distress and render their condition worse and worse; their natural understandings will return to them, and irresistibly plead the necessity of a submission as soon as possible. In that case happy would it be for them, if they could be considered only as conquered enemies; but alas! they must be viewed in the light of *vanquished rebels*, and treated accordingly. Their leaders must be given up into the executioner's hands; confiscations of their estates forfeited by rebellion, must follow, and all must be left at the mercy of their vanquishers. When one people is conquered by another in war, private property is restored to its former possessors; but when rebellions are crushed, the most to be expected is, that the lives of those that belong to the lower classes will be spared.

To this wretched and accursed state of rebellion, the principles that have been propagated, and several steps that have been taken in the American Colonies directly tend. Nay, a rebellion is *evidently commenced* in *New-England*, in the county of *Suffolk*, without room for retreating. The inhabitants of that large and populous county have openly bid defiance to the united authority of the King, Lords and Commons assembled in Parliament; they have most contemptuously rejected the regulations of their courts of justice &c. established by Parliament; and not only so, but they have set up in *direct opposition* to their authority, a government of their own. In the spirit of outrageous licentiousness, they have compelled by brutal violence, those respectable gentlemen that held Commissions under the Crown, to resign them in forms of their own inditing, and to relinquish their stations; and they have appointed others of the same factious and turbulent disposition with themselves to fill their places, till their long-projected *republic**

* I am persuaded that there are not many men in the other Colonies of any denomination, who have not a general prevailing principle of affection, esteem and veneration for our civil Constitution, however it may be darkened by the gross exhalations occasioned by the heat of the present disputes. But in *New-England* I conceive, the real sentiments of the people are of a *peculiar* complexion. Many of the first settlers imported with them an aversion to the *regal* part of our Constitution, and were thorough-paced *Republicans*. To every species of monarchy they were as inveterate enemies as any of their brethren, whom they left behind them in *England*; some of whom could not bear to read the word *King* in their *Bibles*, but wherever it occurred they substituted *Civil Magistrate* in its place. It is well known that even good old father BAXTER was a remarkable instance of this nature. In the time of CROMWELL's usurpation, he published his book of *Saints everlasting Rest*, in which he thought fit to use the phrase of *The* PARLIAMENT OF HEAVEN, instead of saying *The* KINGDOM OF HEAVEN.[†] Now those original settlers of *New-England* stiffly maintained, and zealously endeavored to propagate their own antimonarchical principles; and those principles have been handed down by an uninterrupted succession, from father to son, and from generation to generation, to the present day.

Although many of their descendants have acquired liberal sentiments, and have renounced the bigotry and prejudices of their well-meaning fore-fathers, whether relating to matters of religion or government; yet this is by no means the case with regard to the body of the people. They still retain an hereditary aversion to the frame of the English Constitution, and to the controll of monarchy; and this aversion has been from time to time, occasionally animated and inflamed by a set of *Pulpit-Incendiaries*, for which that part of the country has been ever famous. By these and other instruments they have been prepared whenever the word is given, to declare and exert themselves at all hazards for an *independent* government of their own modelling.

The confusions of the present time have been thought to afford a favorable opportunity, for putting their design in execution. The Colonies are discontented, and it has been imagined that they might all be persuaded to encourage the attempt. On this presumption, the decree has gone forth to *erect*

[†]GREY's *answer to* NEAL.

shall be settled, which is the glorious object. They have already if we may believe *credible information*, marked out the inland town of *Worcester* for the *seat of this Republic*; they are now collecting an artillery for its defence, and some of them have nominated the man who is to be their PROTECTOR.

Whether this be so or not, it appears from *authentic intelligence*, dated *Boston* September 27th, that they have done as bad.* For *the* SELECT MEN *and the* COMMITTEE *of* CORRESPONDENCE have proclaimed the King's troops to be public ENEMIES, and declared to Mr. SCOT that *he* DESERVED *immediate* DEATH, *for selling warlike stores* to them; *and the people* actually did assemble *to put* THIS *sentence in execution, but Mr.* SCOT *was so fortunate as to make his escape.* And besides this the King's *General* and *Governor* farther complains of their continual acts of hostility. "Orders, says he, are given to prevent all supplies for *English* troops: Straw purchased for their use is daily burnt, vessels with bricks sunk, carts with wood overturned, and thus even the King's property is destroyed in every manner in which it can be effected." And he justly observes that all this is "not the effect of rash tumult, but of evident system."

Now these rebellious Republicans, these hair-brained fanaticks, as mad and distracted as the ANABAPTISTS *of* MUNSTER, are the people whom the American Colonies wish to support! It seems to be a mark of *judicial infatuation* inflicted on us by the righteous judgment of Almighty God, that we of the other Colonies can *think* of espousing *such* a cause, and of *risquing* every thing that is dear, *against such inexpressible odds*—in support of a scheme which all of us, but a few Presbyterians and Independents, in our hours of reflexion, if we have any, must despise and abhor.

The hopes of all moderate and considerate persons among us, whose numbers I believe are not small, were long fixed upon the general *American Congress.* They imagined it to be

---

the Republic; the *Rubicon* has been passed, and there can be no thoughts of retreating. They have drawn the sword, with an aim to plunge it into the bowels of our ancient and venerable Constitution; and henceforward the scabbard must become useless. The cry now is: *We have no part in* DAVID, *neither have we inheritance in the son of* JESSE: *Every man to his tent*, O ISRAEL.

* See Mr. GAINE's *Mercury* of October 10.

the business and design of this grand COMMITTEE OF COM-MITTEES, to find out some way consistent with our claims for obtaining the restoration of our common tranquillity, and a happy reconciliation of Great-Britain to her Colonies. The *known* character of *some* Gentlemen appointed as Delegates, and the *supposed* character of *most* of the others, led us to expect from them all that we wanted; and to believe that the united wisdom of the Americans would shine in full splendor at the *Congress*, and that the prudence and policy of the Counsels there taken would be such, as would have done honour to an Assembly of the greatest sages of antiquity. But—the poor Americans are doomed to disappointment. The first discovery of the sentiments of the *Congress* was shocking. Every thing was kept secret for some weeks, and we flattered ourselves with hoping for the best. But when the news arrived at *Philadelphia*, that the people of SUFFOLK had OPENLY REVOLTED FROM THEIR ALLEGIANCE to the *King* and his *government*; in a sudden transport of joy, the veil of the *Congress* was drawn back, and a mystery revealed that filled the minds of many with surprize and astonishment; the mystery was, that the Gentlemen of the *Congress*, in whom we confided as the faithful guardians of the *safety*, as well as *rights* of America, were *disposed* to enter into a league offensive and defensive, with its *worst enemies* the New-England and other Presbyterian Republicans. This fact is notorious to the world; it can neither be denied nor palliated; for they hastily and eagerly published, (and it was the first thing that they *did* publish) their cordial approbation of the *Suffolk Resolves* for erecting an *Independent Government* in *New-England*; and recommended to the Americans the support of those measures *with united efforts*. From that time every moderate man among us has despaired of seeing any good produced by the *Congress*; and from that time every thing that was bad has been growing worse.

Ex illo fluere, ac retro sublapsa referri spes danaum.

Friends, Countrymen and Fellow-Subjects! let me entreat you to rouse up at last from your slumber, and to open your eyes to the danger that surrounds you—the danger of your being hurried into a state of rebellion before you are aware of it, and of suffering all that resentment which a mighty nation can discharge upon a defenceless people. Whether *Great-Britain* did right or not, in imposing the duty on tea, and whether we pay it or not, are matters of trifling consequence: But whether we shall bring down upon our own heads the full weight of her vengeance, and undergo all the horrors of a civil war, or not, are matters of dreadful importance to *us*. If you persist in the steps which many of you have taken; and especially if you go on to encourage the New-England fanaticks to attack the King's troops, whenever they can meet them; the time cannot be distant, in which both you and they will be legally proclaimed *Rebels and Traitors*—they as principals, and you as their abettors. You may still profess yourselves to be his *Majesty's most dutiful and loyal subjects*, as you did in your late RE-SOLVES, and as the leaders in the grand rebellion of 1641 did, in their messages to the King immediately after the battle of *Edge-Hill*, where they had fought against him in person; but this will not skreen you from vengeance. No: HAVOC will be the cry; and *the dogs of war* will be let loose to tear out your vitals. Then, if not before then, the *Dæmon* of discord will rise to distract you. Brother must fight against brother, and friend against the friend of his bosom. In short, the country that is now "fair as *Eden*," will become a field of blood, overspread with desolation and slaughter. I tremble, and my blood retires to my heart at the prospect of such amazing anguish and misery. The sun and the moon begin already to be darkened and the stars to withdraw their shining. O all-pitying Heaven! Preserve me! Preserve my friends! Preserve my country!

If we are now upon the brink of a horrid civil war, and there be no hopes of relief from the wisdom, prudence and good temper of the *Congress*, there can be but one way of safety left; which is, that we all endeavor to see with our own eyes, and make use of our own understandings, and resume the liberty of thinking, and speaking, and acting for ourselves. Let us then like men of sense, sit down calmly and count the cost, in the first place, before we undertake to finish the work proposed to us. Let us consider, before we proceed farther and get more deeply embarrassed, whether we are able to go through with our enterprize against *Great-Britain*, or not: And, I am persuaded, it will soon appear to be impossible.

What then remains to be done? Our blessed Savior, for our instruction, supposes a case, in which the inequality of strength was not comparable with ours, and tells us how common sense would determine. "What King, says he, going to make war against another King, sitteth not down first, and consulteth whether he be able with ten thousand to meet him that cometh against him with twenty thousand? Or else, while the other is a great way off, he sendeth an ambassage, and desireth conditions of peace."* Here one Independent state is supposed to be at war with another; but, upon conviction of the superior power of its antagonist, instead of rushing on to destruction, it proposes a treaty of accomodation, upon such conditions as the situation of affairs would admit of, and as *speedily* as possible. This divine parable instructs us, that when it appears that we are not able, without the utmost hazard, to go forward with any warlike design, the only way is to retreat from it as soon as we can, and secure to ourselves such advantages as may be still in our power. This would shew our wisdom and discretion, were our cause allowed to be ever so just, and had we no peculiar connexion with the power we were disposed to contend with. For it is an eternal maxim, which holds in all cases, that a less evil is to be chosen, when it frees us from a greater. But in our case, where the justice of our cause is at best but *doubtful*; and when the power to be opposed is that, which has cherished us in its bosom, and kindly protected us from our earliest infancy—which we have always heretofore acknowledged our obligations to obey—to which many of us have solemnly sworn allegiance—and which has seldom thwarted our inclinations at all, and never but in matters of comparatively trifling consequence:—In this case, I say, the necessity of such accomodating measures strikes us with still more irresistible evidence.

If those who have been most active among us, in raising seditious tumults, and in filling the country with distraction, will not be persuaded, by the foregoing considerations, to recede, it is hoped that others will; and it would be no small point gained, in favor of the Colonies, if those who are friends to order and government, and enemies to the riots and distur-

---

* *Luke* xiv. 31, 32.

bances of abusive *mobs*, would assume the courage openly to declare their sentiments. All those who are still loyal to their sovereign, should do the same. His Majesty's good subjects of the town of *Rye*,* to their lasting honour, have set the example. Not only their names, but their numbers, are very respectable; and, were the example to be followed, through all the towns and districts of our several Colonies, I doubt not but it would appear, to the confusion of some among us, that, in every province, there are more than *seven thousand men who have not bowed the knee*, and who will not bow it, to the *Baal* of independency. And I now congratulate all such on the pleasure of finding, from the information of Gentlemen of unquestionable veracity, that the *Resolves* from *Georgia* were far from expressing *the sense of the inhabitants* of that grateful and loyal Province; but that they were framed only by a company of hot-headed fellows, met together in a tavern.†

I will only observe farther on this subject, that all who have the courage now to declare themselves friends to Government, will undoubtedly think themselves bound in honour, interest and conscience, to resort to the King's *Standard*, when it comes to be erected in our different Colonies, should that melancholly event happen; and these, of themselves, will compose a body, which, in a good cause, will be formidable to its opposers. But many thousands of others, and indeed the greater part of those who shall not have rendered their cases desperate, when they see the danger thus nearly approaching, and the storm ready to burst, will be glad to fly for shelter too to the Royal standard, if human nature continues the same that it ever has been; and they will be zealous to *signalize* themselves in the King's service, in order to render unquestionable that loyalty which was formerly suspicious. It is morally certain that, in the day of trial, a large majority of the Americans will heartily unite with the King's troops, in reducing *America* to order. Our violent republicans will then find themselves deserted by thousands and thousands in whom they now confide; and inexpressibly dreadful must be their disappointment. "O!

* See Mr. RIVINGTON's *Gazetteer* of October 13.
† RIVINGTON's *Gazetteer*, ut sup.

that they were *wise*, that they *understood* this, that they would *consider* their LATTER END!"

I shall say no more on the supposed case of our waging WAR AGAINST THE KING, and entering into a STATE OF REBELLION; the thoughts of which, all sober men, and all conscientious men, and all who prefer the good of their country to the gratification of their own obstinate humors, must reject with horror.

But another scheme is proposed, at first view less shocking, which also appears to be recommended by the *Congress*, and which many at present are inclined to adopt; I mean, *a general non-importation agreement* throughout the Colonies. Against a proposal of this nature I have two objections to offer: Namely, that it will greatly distress a country which I love; and that it will not answer the purpose.

In order (N. B.) to get rid of a duty of *three pence a pound on tea*, it is proposed to stop all importation from *Great-Britain*, and even from the *West-India Islands*, till the act imposing it shall be repealed. But a remedy of this kind is ten thousand times worse than the disease. It is, for the wisdom of it, like cutting off an arm, in order to get rid of a small sore in one of the fingers.

On a late trial of non-importation from *Great-Britain* only, as soon as the stores of English goods began to be exhausted, every family among us experienced such inconveniences and difficulties, as produced a general murmur and complaint. For although the articles imported from *England* are not absolutely necessary to support *animal* life; yet it was found that the *civilized* life we had been used to, and which is necessary to the happiness of all but savages, depended, in no small degree, upon our importations from *Great-Britain*. And had the non-importation continued much longer, it would have excited insurrections in most parts of the country.

But a non-importation from the *West-Indies* would still more tenderly affect us. For to say nothing of *Rum*, or of *Molasses* for the use of our distilleries, without which more than a hundred thousand American dram-drinkers would soon be clamorous; the want of the single article *Sugar* would distress every family upon this Continent. For this, in the quantity that is necessary, we could find no sufficient substitute: the hardened juice of our *Maple*, where it could be had, would be but a sorry one; and as to *Honey*, we all know its use; and were our stock of it ever so large, it would prove but a bad sweetner of the bitter draught of a non-importation.

Here then it is proposed, that, to the non-importation which we have experienced and could hardly bear, another should be added, that would affect us still worse; and that a double weight should be fastened upon those shoulders, which were ready to give way under a single one. But this is not the worst of the case. It is generally believed, and intimations from *England* have confirmed the opinion, that if the Colonies should resolve to import nothing from *Great-Britain* and the *West-Indies*, they will not be suffered to import from any other quarter—not even the salt that is necessary to cure their winter's provisions, or to season their porridge: And besides this, that an absolute *non-exportation* will be ordered, and not a single vessel suffered to go out of our harbours. Such an order, we know, can effectually be executed, with the greatest ease. It is but commanding the several Custom-Houses to grant no clearances; and then every vessel that offered to sail, would be a lawful seizure. A few of the King's frigates would be sufficient to do the business, for all the Colonies on the Continent. Two or three of them stationed at the *Capes of Virginia*, would command every vessel belonging to the Ports, and to the fine navigable rivers, of *Virginia* and *Maryland*. As many stationed at the *Capes of Delaware*, would secure *Pennsylvania* and *West-Jersey*—and so of the rest.

Now a total stagnation of all foreign commerce, would at once place us in a glorious and blessed state. In the first place, all that live by this commerce would be thrown out of employ. Our *sailors* would be turned ashore; our ships would rot in our harbours; and our estates, which consist of wharfs or warehouses, would become as worthless, as those of the same nature are at present in the town of *Boston*. Our *ship-builders*, and their attendants, their *smiths, carmen &c.* with all that are employed in the business of cordage and rigging, must be immediately discharged. The numerous body of *pilots* and *boatmen* must be turned adrift. Nor would it fare much better with our *shop-keepers* and *merchants*, whose families are supported by the profits arising from their respective occupations. The expensive business of all our *iron-works* must stop; and the many thousands which they provide for, must, unprincipled as those wretches commonly are, be let loose upon the country, to get their living as they can.

Now all these classes of people, and many others which I have not enumerated, must have a support, and but few of them will be able to support themselves; and if their poverty is not relieved to their satisfaction, they will soon learn to carve for themselves. There are but few parishes and counties among us, which have not complained of the burthen of their own poor. But what will they say, when the burthen comes to be encreased an hundred-fold, as it necessarily must, when a general non-importation and non-exportation take place; and all their wonted resources fail them at the same time. The want of the money, of which we have been lately drained, in order to pamper the Boston fanaticks, will then be severely felt: Nor can we expect any return of assistance in our distress from that Province, as their sufferings will be much greater than ours.

In the Province of the *Massachusetts Bay*, there is a large number of populous sea-port towns, which have no other support than their fishery. The town of *Gloucester* has three hundred schooners employed in that service, with a proportionable number of hands. In the town of *Marblehead* there are supposed to be near four thousand men, and many of them with families, that know of no other means of subsistence than the cod-fishery. I might mention *Plymouth, Salem, Beverly* and a number of other towns, that are nearly in the same situation. Now, when all these fishermen are turned ashore, and their vessels become useless; they must, with their unprovided families, disperse themselves amongst the inhabitants, and while the country affords any thing to eat, they will not starve.

But to return to these Colonies. I have mentioned the distress that must immediately overwhelm many orders of people, on a general stagnation of commerce; but have said nothing of our Farmers, or those that live by the cultivation of their lands.—These may think themselves a kind of *privileged* persons, and imagine that such a revolution of affairs will affect them but little; yet a very short experience will open their eyes, and convince them of the contrary. It is their farms, as all other resources will fail, that must support all the abovementioned thousands of distressed people. Who must furnish them with food? None can do it, but, THE FARMERS. Who must supply them with cloathing? THE FARMERS. Who must shelter many of them in their houses? THE FARMERS. And can they expect pay for all this? Alas! those poor creatures will have nothing to make payment with. And if they are employed as labourers, they are all unacquainted with the business; and their labour will turn to but little account. Indeed, were the markets abroad open, the farmer might somewhat increase the quantity of his beef, his wheat and other produce, by their means, so that his bargain would be less intolerable. But the foreign consumption, on which he is now growing rich, will entirely cease; and there will be no demand for his beef, and his wheat and other produce. All that he raises must perish on his hands, except what he expends in his own family, and on the poor that will be pressing upon him.

When all people are thus distressed; when every mind is uneasy and discontented; it will be natural for them to fall to reproaching one another, with being the authors of this general calamity. This will be productive of eternal quarrels, and riots, and disturbances, and acts of violence, amongst ourselves; and then our misery will be compleat.

Yet after all, were it likely that these political agonies and convulsions would produce a repeal of the act in dispute, it would be *some* alleviation of our misfortunes to consider, that we should gain by them *Three pence a pound*, on all the tea we should have occasion to purchase. But my *second* objection against a general non-importation agreement is, that it will not answer the purpose.

After what has been said and done by the Colonies, a general non-importation agreement will be considered by *Great Britain* as an act of hostility, intended to *compel* her to relinquish her claim; and she will not submit to be conquered by *such* weapons, any more than by force of arms. It is not pretended that she is altogether invulnerable in this part. The blow would reach her, and be felt by her; but the wound would not be mortal. The strength and vigour of her constitution would bear much more, than we are able to inflict. But—the shaft, ungraciously aimed at the vitals of our Mother, on the rebound may prove fatal to ourselves.

A total stagnation of commerce would affect *Great Britain*, in much the same manner, that it would affect her colonies, or any other commercial people; that is, it would rob her of her subsistance. But a partial stagnation could not affect her in the same manner that we should be affected by a total stagnation. Now, the non-importation in question, while it would cause a total stagnation of our commerce, would produce no more than a partial stagnation of hers; and consequently would not place her in a situation so distressing, as it would place us. Her trade is not confined to her American Colonies. She has ships and factories in every quarter of the globe; and the treasures of the East and West are perpetually flowing in upon her. She receives no necessary or useful articles from these Colonies, but what she formerly received, and may at any time be supplied with, from foreign nations. Her manufactures that are consumed in the Colonies, she can shortly find ways to dispose of at other markets.

There is one branch of this hopeful project, that will contribute immediately and directly to the advantage of *Great Britain*, almost in the same proportion that it will distress ourselves. The Reader scarcely needs to be told, that what is here meant, is the stopping all intercourse and communication between the Colonies and the *West-Indies*. As soon as this takes place, the markets of Great Britain will be supplied, not only with the quantity of goods from the *West-Indies* which they have formerly received, but with the addition of all that is now consumed in the American Colonies. The British merchants will likewise have the advantage of supplying the Islands with many articles, which at present are not scored in any of their invoices.

The West-Indians themselves indeed may be somewhat injured and disconcerted at first, by the execution of this part of the plan; but far less, than seems to be generally expected and intended by us. The Island of *Jamaica* can supply her Planters with all kinds of provisions, but butter and flour; and with all the lumber that may be required, for a hundred years to come, excepting staves and heading for their *Rum Puncheons*. These she has often received from *Hamburgh*, from whence she might receive them again. But there will be no occasion for sending so far. *Canada* can supply her, and all the other islands, with these articles, as well as with flour, in any quantity that may be ordered; to say nothing of Georgia and the two Floridas, which abound in common lumber, at the service of the *Windward, Leeward,* and *Caribbee* Islands. So that after the first year, new channels may be opened, plans formed, and correspondences settled, in such a manner, that the *West-Indies* may be nearly as well supplied without our assistance, as they now are with it; and with some articles, perhaps better.

But supposing the contrary; yet what should we gain by this curious bargain? Why, the ill-will and resentment of all the West-Indians. For some years past, they have cultivated a peculiar friendship with the North-American Colonies, and proposed to themselves much happiness from a closer alliance.

They have sent hither their children, in large numbers, for their education: and many of them have brought over their families, and liberally spent the incomes of their estates among us. But when they find that, we can so ingeniously contrive schemes to distress them without benefiting ourselves; as they are generally not wanting in spirit, they will be apt to resent such ill usage, by withdrawing their sons and their families from among us, and perhaps by breaking off all further connexion with us in the way of commerce.

From what has been said, it will naturally be concluded, that by a general non-importation agreement we shall carry on a very unequal warfare with Great Britain; which will much sooner compel us to yield, than her to comply. The want of her North-American trade may hurt her, but it will not reduce her to extremity; and, if I may judge from my own feelings, nothing but the utmost extremity will induce her, where she believes she has right of her side, and where her honour is deeply at stake, to give up the point in dispute.

At the time of our former non-importation, the case was materially different. The *Stamp-act* was so contrary to all our ideas of American rights, and so much was offered against the policy of the act, both here and at home, that there was no difficulty in repealing it. Afterwards when we exclaimed against the duties imposed upon paper, glass, &c. and agreed not to import the several articles loaded with duties, our views were comparatively moderate, and we had a large body of friends in England to support us. And were the proposition now only not to import, or to consume, the tea that is charged with the duty; the case would be the same that it was then—we should have the same friends that we then had—and the duty would probably be removed, on the same principle that those duties then were. But our conduct now is so wild and distracted—our tumults and disorders are carried to so unreasonable and unwarrantable a length—nay, such a spirit of rebellion has broke forth among us, and such a determined enmity against the *supremacy* of *Great Britain* now predominates in the Colonies, that we have hardly a single friend remaining in *England*. Even the Manufacturers join with all other orders of people, in condemning our extravagance; and, which is still more, the Writers and Speakers against the King's ministry allow that it is inexcusable.

It appears, therefore, that nothing will be likely to procure a repeal of the *Tea-act*, or the removal of any other grievance of the like kind, but, the restoration of peace and order amongst ourselves—a candid acknowledgment of our political errors and offences—a formal allowance of the rightful supremacy in general, of *Great Britain*, over the American Colonies—a declaration of our aversion to a state of independency, with a *corresponding behaviour*—a respectful remonstrance on the subject of taxation—an assurance of our willingness to contribute, in some equitable proportion, towards defraying the public expences—and the proposal of a reasonable plan for a general American constitution. This, it is humbly conceived, was to have been the business of the *Congress*; and if they had acted upon these principles, and with such views, not only the present, but all future generations, would *call them blessed*.

Notwithstanding all unfavorable symptoms and appearances, I would not presume to form a final judgment of the *Congress*, till their whole plan of proceedings shall be known. It is possible, that all that has been wrong may be rectified in the end; and that moderate and wise measures, tending to restore the tranquility, the happiness, the honour and safety of the Colonies, may at last be concerted. Should this appear, in the general result of their councils, the members will be entitled to the grateful respect of every American, and the mistakes made in the former part of their proceedings ought never to be mentioned to their disadvantage. But, on the other hand, should it appear, that they mean to encourage acts of hostility against Great Britain, or to support the madmen of *New-England* in their scheme of an *Independent Republic*: in that case, I affirm, that the *Original Contract* between them and the *most respectable* part of their constituents will be *dissolved*—that we shall be at full liberty to consult our own safety, in the manner we shall think most conducive to that end—and that we shall owe them no greater respect and obedience, than they themselves pay to the British Parliament.

The foregoing considerations are addressed—not to those obstinate, hot-headed Zealots, who are at the bottom of all our confusions; for arguments would be as much wasted upon them, as upon men that are intoxicated with liquor—but to *all reasonable Americans*, to those who are still in the exercise of their understandings, and whose minds are open to conviction. People of this character, it is presumed, will see the necessity of giving up the present system of American politics, as essentially wrong and destructive; and of entering unanimously upon moderate and conciliating measures, as they regard the restoration of peace and tranquility in this, heretofore, happy country.

The great object in view, should be a general *American Constitution*, on a free and generous Plan, worthy of *Great Britain* to give, and of the colonies to receive. This is now become necessary to the mutual interest and honour, both of the Parent Kingdom and its American offspring. Such an establishment is only to be obtained by decent, candid and respectful application; and not by compulsion or threatening. To think of succeeding by force of arms, or by starving the nation into compliance, is a proof of shameful ignorance, pride and stupidity. All such projects must operate ten times more forceably against ourselves, than against *Great Britain*. They are, at best, but *Penny wise*, and *Pound foolish*; and therefore inconsistent with every maxim of sound wisdom and genuine Patriotism.

All violent opposition to lawful authority partakes of the nature of rebellion; and a rebellion of the Colonies, whether it should prove successful or unsuccessful, would necessarily terminate in ruin and destruction. We are now in the utmost danger of being hurried, before we are sensible of it, into this desperate and dreadful state,* when most of us think that we have grievances to complain of, in consequence of the exercise of unconstitutional power; and when many are practicing every wicked art to seduce us from our allegiance. It therefore highly concerns us to be upon our guard, at such a critical season as this. A small degree of reflection would convince us, that the grievances in question, supposing them to be real, are, at most, no more than a just ground for decent remonstrance, but not a sufficient reason for forcible resistance. These two things are widely and essentially different; and if we mistake one for the other, the consequence may be fatal.

It has been fully shewn, that a rebellion of the colonies can have no reasonable prospect of succeeding; and that it must prove the destruction of all that are concerned in it. But supposing that it were likely to succeed, it is of the utmost importance to consider, what we should gain by it; which would be, after the desolation of our country, and the sacrifice of thousands of lives, an exemption from the authority of the British Parliament, and subjection to the authority of an American republic. A blessed exchange this! especially if we take into the account

---

* Among the various denominations of Americans, most men would be startled and shocked at the proposal of entering into an open *rebellion*; but seditious principles, that directly lead to, and must finally bring on, a rebellion, have been gradually instilled into many of them, without alarming their apprehensions, under the cover of fair and specious pretences. Wrong principles are naturally productive of wrong conduct; and one wrong step prepares the way to another, and that to another, till at last there can be no retreating.

Nemo repente fit turpissimus, i. e. No one arrives at a gross and enormous pitch of wickedness at once, is an old and just observation; and it is particularly true with regard to *rebellion*. The grand English rebellion, in the last century, was a remarkable proof of it. In the first place, men gave way to unfavourable suspicions concerning the King and his Ministers, and thus lost the reverence that is due to the regal authority. They then began to take pleasure in blackening the King's character, and in giving an invidious turn to all his actions. From this they proceeded to *caballing* against him; and, at last, they took up arms, deluded with the pretence of liberty and property, and religious rights. And when they had once taken up arms against their Sovereign, they found it necessary to destroy him, for their own security. This soon brought on a general destruction of liberty and property, and the ruin of the nation, as well as of themselves. Such is the common progress, and the effect, of rebellions in general.

the character of our future masters. The principal conductors of the rebellion, would naturally have the principal authority in the republic; and these are men, whose tyrannical usurpation would be more oppressive, than the scorpion power of the most despotic Prince in Europe. There would be no peace in the colonies, till we all submitted to the republican zealots and bigots of New-England; whose tender mercies, when they had power in their hands, have been ever cruel, towards all that presumed to differ from them in matters either of religion or government.

As soon therefore, as people of this stamp come to be in possession of an established authority, which would be the case should the rebellion succeed, the dire effects of their persecuting, and intolerant spirit will be dismally felt by all that shall have courage to *dissent*; particularly, the members of the Church of England, the Friends or people called Quakers, the Baptists, those that belong to the German and Dutch Churches, and the moderate and candid part of the Presbyterians themselves. All these classes of people then, by promoting the present scheme for an independent government, are absurdly acting against their own interest and honour, and contributing to prepare yokes for their own necks.

O my infatuated Countrymen! My deluded Fellow-Subjects, and Fellow-Christians! Open your eyes, I entreat you; awake from your dreams, and regard your own safety!

As to you, who are members of the *Church of England*; it is amazing, that any of you should be so blind to your own interests, and such apostates from common sense, as to countenance and co-operate with a plan of proceedings, which, if it succeeds, will at once distress and disgrace you. You are endeavouring to provide arms for your enemies, and to put power into the hands of those who will use it against you. You are setting up a sort of people for your masters, whose principles you despise, and who were always fond of subduing by the iron rod of oppression, all those, whose principles or sentiments were different from their own. Their inveterate enmity to the Church of *England*, has polluted the annals of the *British* history. Their intolerance in *England*, towards the members of the Church, when the sovereign power was usurped by them, is recorded in characters of blood; and the same spirit was

dreadfully triumphant in *New-England*, from the first settlement of the country, till the mild disposition of Parliamentary
power interposed to restrain it. In 1629, they banished and transported even some of the original patentees of *New-England*, who
were men of abilities and of a respectable character, merely
because they discovered them to be Churchmen, declaring to
them as they sent them off, that NEW-ENGLAND *was* NO PLACE
FOR SUCH AS THEY.* Their descendants, who inherit their
principles, are the very persons that will govern you, if the
projected revolution should take place. As they have now
broke loose from the authority of Parliament, which for some
time past restrained them from mischief, they begin to appear
in their natural colours. They have already resumed the old
work of persecuting the Church of *England*, by every method
in their power. The members of it are daily misrepresented,
insulted, and abused by them; and they have lately driven several of its clergy from their parishes and families, which are left
in a state that is truly deplorable.

The pretence indeed is, that the members of the Church in
New-England are thus roughly treated, on account of their
political, and not of their *religious* principles. But, Good God!
is there to be no liberty of the press, no liberty of speaking, no
liberty even of thinking, on political subjects, where those republicans have the ascendant? This is despotism with a vengeance; and such as we must be all fools if we voluntarily
submit to. Nor will the case be at all better, with regard to religion. For it is a truth, which the history of all ages confirms,
that those who will distress men on account of their *political*
principles, will not scruple to persecute them for the sake of
their *religious* principles, when they have it in their power.

You then, who are members of the Church of *England*,
must renounce your principles relating both to religion and
government, or you can expect no quarter under the administration of such intemperate zealots. You must cease to be
Church-men, or become victims of their intolerance. Indeed it
must be confessed, and I am sorry to say, that many of you
appear already to have renounced one half of your principles;

---

* This appears from a valuable book written by a cotemporary author Mr.
MORTON, and entitled, *New-England's Memorial*.

or you could not proceed, as you do, in direct opposition to the established rules and doctrines of the Church. The principles of submission and obedience to lawful authority, are as inseparable from *a sound, genuine member* of the Church of *England*, as any religious principles whatever. This Church has always been famed and respected for its *loyalty*, and its regard to order and government. Its annals have been never stained with the history of plots and conspiracies, treasons and rebellions. Its members are instructed in their duty to government, by Three *Homilies* on *Obedience*, and six against *Rebellion*, which are so many standing lessons to secure their fidelity. They are also taught to pray in the Litany, that the Almighty would preserve them, "from all sedition, privy conspiracy and rebellion." And more than one solemn office is provided, for the annual commemoration of former deliverances from the power of those, whether *Papists* or *Protestants*, "who turn religion into rebellion, and faith into faction." But if you regard none of these things, you are untoward, undutiful, and degenerate sons of the Church; and she will be ashamed to own you for her children.

However, even those of you who are but half-principled in the doctrines of the Church, will be looked upon with an evil eye, under the intended republic; and they must give up the other moiety of their principles, before they can be secure against harm or molestation. The Church of England has always been the great obstacle in the way of those republican fanaticks; and when once they are established, no appearance of a Church-man will escape their resentment, or be tolerated among them.

Nor will it fare better with the *Friends*, or people called *Quakers*; however peaceable in their disposition, or however useful members of society. What they formerly suffered in *New-England* under the same sort of men that must and will govern this country, if it should be withdrawn from the jurisdiction of the British parliament, is too well known, and can never be forgotten. You, my respected friends, have experienced the genuine spirit and temper of their authority; and you can never wish to have your necks again encumbered with that *Presbyterian* yoke of bondage, which neither you nor your fathers were able to bear. On the other hand, you have the sense to see, and the gratitude to confess, that you have been happy under the relief and protection afforded you by the King and Parliament, in common with other good subjects. You will therefore *remember* (to use your own expressive language) "that, as under divine Providence, you are indebted to the King and his royal ancestors, for the continued favour of enjoying your religious liberties, you are under deep obligations (on *this* occasion) to manifest your loyalty and fidelity; and to discourage every attempt which may be made by any, to excite disaffection, or disrespect to him."

The *Baptists* have never had fair quarter allowed them by the demagogues of *New-England*; and they are perpetually complaining, from year to year, of the acts of oppression and violence with which they are harassed by them. Now if the people of *New-England* have been thus intolerant, towards those that differed from them only with regard to the case of baptism, while they possessed an authority that was subordinate to the British Parliament; what cruelty, towards all that dissent from them, may be expected, should they be armed with absolute and incontrolable power?

As to the *Germans* and *Dutch*, to whose industry and good behaviour the Colonies are greatly indebted; if they should become subject to the jurisdiction abovementioned, they will be considered as persons, not only of a different religion, but of different nations and languages, from whom they have such an aversion, that they have never admitted them to settle in *New-England*; and consequently all the Colonists who are of a *foreign* growth or extraction, must expect to meet with a double portion of rancour and severity from their new masters.

Nor can the moderate part of the *Presbyterians*, and *Congregationalists* themselves, have any prospect of continuing free from molestation under their government. Nothing can be more odious to bigots, than generosity and candour; or more intolerable in the opinion of the furious, than moderation and meekness. This assertion might be supported by the history of all ages and nations; but we need not go far for a confirmation of it. For among the Presbyterians and Independents in the Colonies, when the meek and the moderate, the candid and generous have been brought before the tribunals of the bigotted and furious, as has frequently happened; they have been treated with as much unrelenting rancour and roughness, as if they had been Mahometans and Heathens. So that there is no chance or probability, if the latter should come to the possession of despotic power, which is the aim of the revolution they propose; that their dispensations towards the former, would be less cruel than they commonly have been.

In a word: no order or denomination of men amongst us would enjoy liberty or safety, if subjected to the fiery genius of a New-England Republican Government; the little finger of which we should soon experience to be heavier than the loins of Parliament. *This* has sometimes chastised us with *whips*, when we deserved punishment; but *that* would torment us with *scorpions*, whether we deserved it or not.

POSTSCRIPT.

I Have said [see page 285.] that the Popish religion is not established in *Canada* by the late act, but *only tolerated*; and that this was one of the *conditions* on which the country surrendered to the crown of *Great Britain*. Since the greatest part of this *Address* was printed off, the papers published by the *Congress* have come to hand; in which they say, that "the Roman Catholic Religion, instead of being *tolerated*, as stipulated by the treaty of peace, is *established*," by the act.

In order that the reader may see with his own eyes, and judge for himself of this matter, I will present him with the following *Extracts*, from the *Treaty of Surrender*, the *Definitive Treaty* of Peace, and the ACT *for more effectual provision, &c.*

EXTRACT *from the* CAPITULATION *of* CANADA.

Art. XXVII. "The *free exercise* of the catholic, apostolic, and Roman religion, shall subsist *entire*; in such manner, that all the states and people of the towns and countries, places, and distant posts, shall continue to assemble in the churches, and to frequent the sacraments as heretofore, without being molested in any manner *directly or indirectly.*

"These people shall be obliged by the English government, to pay to the priests the *tithes*, and all the taxes they were used to pay, under the government of his most Christian Majesty."

GRANTED, *as to the free exercise of their religion. The*

obligation of paying the tithes to the priests, will depend on the King's pleasure.

Art. XXVIII. "The Chapter, Priests, Curates, and Missionaries, shall continue with an *intire liberty,* their exercise and function of their Cures in the parishes of the towns and countries."

GRANTED.

EXTRACT *from the* TREATY *of* PARIS.

Art. IV. So far as relates to the matter in question. "His Britannic Majesty on his side, agrees to grant the liberty of the catholic religion to the inhabitants of *Canada.* He will consequently give the most effectual orders, that his new Roman catholic subjects may profess the worship of their religion, according to the rites of the Romish church, as far as the laws of *Great Britain* permit."

EXTRACT *from the* CANADA-ACT.

"And for the more perfect security and ease of the minds of the inhabitants of the said province, it is hereby declared, that his Majesty's subjects professing the religion of the Church of *Rome,* of and in the province of *Quebec, may* have, hold and enjoy the free exercise of the religion of the Church of *Rome, subject to the King's supremacy,* declared and established by an act made in the first year of the reign of Queen *Elizabeth,* over all the dominions and countries which then did, or thereafter should belong, to the Imperial Crown of this realm; and that the clergy of the said Church *may* hold, receive and enjoy, their accustomed dues and rights, *with respect to such persons only,* as shall profess the said religion.

"*Provided nevertheless,* that it shall be lawful for his Majesty, his heirs and successors, to make such provision out of the rest of the said accustomed dues and rights, for the *encouragement* of the *Protestant Religion,* and for the *maintenance* and *support* of a *Protestant Clergy* within the said province, as he or they shall, from time to time, think necessary and expedient."

The next clause of the act provides an oath of allegiance, to be taken by the Canadian Papists, instead of the oath required by the 1st *Elizabeth.* The succeeding clause enacts, "that all his Majesty's Canadian subjects, within the province of *Quebec, the religious orders and communities only excepted,* may also hold and enjoy their property and possessions," &c. The last clause provides, that the King shall have the power of "*creating*, constituting, and appointing such courts of—ECCLESIASTICAL *Jurisdiction*, within and for the said province of *Quebec*, and appointing from time to time, the judges and officers thereof, as his Majesty, his heirs and successors, shall think necessary and proper for the circumstances of the said province."

Thus we see in what manner the toleration of the Popish religion was secured to the Canadians by treaty; and the act of Parliament allows them no more than, *the free exercise of their religion, without being molested*, in the public use of it, and that *entire liberty* in religious matters, for which they had stipulated.

Indeed the parochial Clergy, are permitted to enjoy those *tithes*, by which they had been always supported. This was proposed in the treaty; but it was neither granted, nor rejected, by the British General, who left it to depend upon the King's pleasure. After thirteen years experience of the dutiful, peaceable and good behaviour of his Canadian subjects, and at a time when his other American subjects were become turbulent, licentious, and refractory, the King, to whose goodness the matter had been referred, thought proper, with the approbation and consent of Parliament, to comply with the reasonable expectations and requests of the Canadians, in allowing the clergy to enjoy their wonted support, under certain restrictions and limitations. But this indulgence by no means converts the stipulated toleration into an establishment, as the Gentlemen of the Congress are pleased to assert.

Tithes in *Canada* are the *property* of the Romish church; and permitting a tolerated church to enjoy its own property, is far short of the idea of an establishment. If the city of New-York should be conquered by the Papists from *France*, or the Independents from *New-England*, (which I believe in my conscience would be much the worst event of the two) and at the time of its surrender, the corporation of *Trinity-Church* should contract for the *free exercise of their religion*, &c. the confirmation of this liberty, with a permission still to enjoy the estate that belongs to them, (upon which some people have long cast an envious and wishful eye) would not amount to what is commonly understood by a religious establishment. An established religion, is a religion which the civil authority engages, not only to protect, but to support; and a religion that is not provided for by the civil authority, but which is left to provide for itself, or to subsist on the provision it has already made, can be no more than a tolerated religion.

Now the Popish religion in *Canada* the Government is under no engagement to provide for; it is only allowed to enjoy such provision as it has made for itself, in a general way; and then this proposition is curtailed, whenever a Papist embraces the Protestant religion; and the various religious orders and communities are entirely dispossessed of their respective effect. But it evidently appears from the act, that it is the object of Government to make provision, as fast as the state of the country will admit of it, "for the *encouragement* of the *Protestant religion*, and for the *maintenance and support* of a *Protestant Clergy*."

From what has been offered, the inference is clear, that the Popish religion is only tolerated in *Canada*; and that it is meant to establish the Protestant religion in that colony. If, after all, men will confound the meaning of words, and make no distinction between *toleration* and *establishment*, they degrade themselves into the rank of quibblers and praters, and it is loss of time to dispute with them.

[Philip Livingston], The Other Side of the Question: or, A Defence of the Liberties of North-America. In Answer to a Late Friendly Address to All Reasonable Americans, on the Subject of Our Political Confusions. New York, 1774.

A member of the famous Livingston clan of New York, Philip Livingston had attended the Stamp Act Congress in 1765 and later became speaker of the New York assembly. In the complicated family politics of New York, Livingston was often the voice of moderation. Although he opposed the Stamp Act and the Coercive Acts he always paid, as he said in 1764, "the greatest deference to the wisdom and justice of the British parliament." Even as late as 1774 he still wanted somehow "to secure and establish the freedom of America" while at the same time recognizing "the sovereignty of that supreme legislature, which ought certainly to govern the whole empire." Although in 1774–75 he served actively in the Continental Congress as a delegate from New York, he was not present in July 1776, believing that independence was "the most vain, empty, shallow, and ridiculous project." Nevertheless, he reluctantly signed the Declaration of Independence the following month.

John Adams called his congressional colleague—who, he pointedly observed, had been "in Trade" and was now a man of means, living upon his income—"a great, rough, rappid Mortal," who blustered away out of fear that independence would result in "civil Wars among ourselves to determine which Colony should govern all the rest." According to Adams, Livingston, like many delegates from the Middle Colonies, seemed to dread the "Levelling Spirit" of New England and "the Goths and Vandalls" who had hanged Quakers there. For his part the Massachusetts delegate did not see much of value in New York. Passing through the city en route to attend the Congress in Philadelphia, Adams noted in his diary that he had "not seen one real Gentleman, one well bred Man." There was no agreeable conversation, no modesty, no real attention paid to one another. "They talk very loud, very fast, and alltogether. If they ask you a Question, before you can utter 3 Words of your Answer, they will break out upon you, again—and talk away."

THE

Other Side of the Queſtion:

OR,

A DEFENCE

OF THE

LIBERTIES of NORTH-AMERICA.

IN

ANSWER

TO A LATE

FRIENDLY ADDRESS

TO

All Reaſonable Americans,

ON

THE SUBJECT OF OUR

POLITICAL CONFUSIONS.

By A CITIZEN.

NEW-YORK:
Printed by JAMES RIVINGTON, fronting HANOVER-SQUARE.
M,DCC,LXXIV.

The Other Side of the Question:

or, A Defence of the Liberties of North-America, &c.

A Certain Friendly Address to all reasonable Americans, was just now put into my hands. Some people perhaps have read it, for I am told it was published six days ago; wherefore, after perusing, it seems proper to make a short answer to this performance: not because it is well written, or because there is the least danger any man will become a proselyte to the doctrines contained in it; but for the following reasons, which candor obliges me to mention.

First. I answer this pamphlet, for the very purpose which alone the pamphlet itself is likely to effect,—to encourage the paper manufactory.

Secondly. I answer it for the sake of the Printer, who must be sadly out of pocket, by publishing such woeful performances: And therefore he is hereby requested to print this in a large type, and the like, so as to make the most on't.

Thirdly. I write, because from the futility of the author's reasoning, no body else may think it worth the trouble. And if so, why then he would very naturally conclude that he had written an excellent unanswerable treatise, which conclusion might inflate the poor creature's vanity, in such manner as to tempt him into other imprudencies of the same kind. The public thanks therefore will be my due, for removing, or at least preventing a common nuisance.

Lastly. I am prompted to this undertaking out of regard to the fair-sex. For many weak women may be exceedingly frighted by that awful compound of threats, and texts, and homilies.

Now then, gentle reader, having told thee the origin. I shall next acquaint thee with the character of this new acquaintance, which my Master James hath introduced to thy hand.—I will not, as is too common with controversial people, whether politic, or polemic: I will not, I say, use any acrimonious expressions, against this unhappy author; for whose weaknesses and wanderings, I have the utmost pity and compassion. On the contrary, I shall treat him with the greatest gentleness and respect, owing in some measure to my very great reverence for the Clergy, one of which he is, as I have been informed. And truly the frequent quotations from scripture, together with the illiberal language contained in his pamphlet, will naturally lead folks to believe so. For it unfortunately happens, that the generality of these Gentlemen, from an ungain habit they acquire by abusing the poor Devil, are too apt to vilify and asperse their neighbours. Some exceptions there are, it must be acknowledged, which may be attributed to this; that a few individuals have kept better company, and seen more of the polite world, than the rest of their order. But alack and alas! I fear me our author is not one of these rare birds, for the household proverbs and tales with which his piece is interlarded, (if I may venture on something like his own language) make the odds at least a pound to a penny against him.

And now reader, if by chance thou art a Presbyterian, or Congregationalist, or other Dissenter from the Episcopalian Church, to which I myself belong; permit me to apologize for the rude and opprobrious terms made use of against you by our author. These things ought in common charity to be forgiven, inasmuch as they seem to have proceeded from ignorance and the want of better language.—And do not, I beseech you, conclude too hastily against his brethren, I have several friends and acquaintance among them, who are really Gentlemen. Wherefore it is my earnest desire, that if in the hurry of composition (for I have but three days to write this in the midst of other affairs) if I say any thing should fall from my pen, which can be construed a reflection on the Clergy, it is my desire that it should be instantly erased.—I honour them much for their piety, learning, and strictly loyal attachment to our Sovereign.

An old Mathematician (I think they call him Archimedes) had such confidence in his art and machines, as to declare he would move the earth itself, if he could get a place to stand on. But please your worships, while he was upon the thing which was to be moved, had he worked his heart out, 'twould not have budged an inch.—In imitation of this venerable screw-driver, may we not lay down the following logical maxim. A man may prove impossibilities if you will concede his postulata.—Thus, in order to demonstrate that black is white, or in other words, that black and white are the same thing, I ask only this admission; that there is no difference between them.

He who in conversation with half a dozen friends, should in a similar manner begin any argument whatever, by affirming the thing to be proved, would he not raise a laugh at his expence? Now, all America contends for rights, which we aver to have been invaded, violated, destroyed, and a certain writer attempts to prove this contest, treasonable and rebellious; what shall we think of a writer, who begins an address on this subject, not to half a dozen, or half a hundred, but to all *reasonable* Americans, with the following proposition? "Of all the subjects of Great-Britain, those who reside in the American colonies, are and might still be enjoying the benefits of an equitable and free constitution." As to his quotation from an "excellent writer," it may shew the Gentleman's reading, but can never help his argument; and therefore I shall pass it over in silence, to the examination of those excellencies, which he himself hath fabricated.

If by the term, subjects of Great-Britain, he means subjects to the King of Great-Britain, and subordinate to the Parliament of that Kingdom, it is an inaccuracy, which, considering what follows, may be easily forgiven. But if these words are intended to insinuate, that the people of America are subject to laws made by the Parliament of Great-Britain, in all cases whatever, then we shall find, that the first ground this great Archimedes intends to fix his reasoning machine on, is what follows. Americans are subject to the will of a Parliament which they have no vote in choosing, and being so subject, enjoy a free and equitable constitution. To which I have only two small exceptions: first, these are the very points to be proved, and secondly, they involve a flat contradiction. Now then, supposing these things admitted, after all, twist them and turn them as you please, still must you come back in a circle to the place from whence you set out; still luckless Philosopher you grovel on the earth.

Shortly after follows another false proposition. America contributes but a small proportion to support the public expences. This for argument sake, I will grant. I will grant what I suppose he meant; namely, that America contributes but little to *defray* the public expences which other folks support. I am not captious in my temper, nor do I mean to cavil about words, for then I should never have done.

Then comes a page about Moses, thunder, blindness, darkness and destruction. As these things are quite out of my way, I shall not meddle with them; but proceed to the next, the scope of which seems to be this, Whether parliament hath been right or wrong, we are bound by the laws of Heaven to obey its mandates. And in quality of good Christians, we must be subject to the Ministers, be they who they will, for conscience sake. Let who will be King, our author is Vicar of Bray. To elucidate all which doctrines, he observes, that if the greatest tyrant on earth (Nero for instance) should usurp and establish a domination over us, the harshest and most cruel, yet so heinous is the offence of disturbing an established government, that a due regard for the rights and liberties of mankind, would prompt us to a peaceable submission. To this submission we are enjoined, it seems, by the Christian religion; and to disturb or threaten such a government, is an unpardonable crime, and has been considered as such, in every age and nation of the world. All which is mighty reasonable. Wherefore it follows clearly, that those persons who, within these four or five centuries, contended for, and by degrees established our glorious constitution. "A frame of government, says our author, which has always been the wonder of the world, under the protection of which, the subjects of Great-Britain are the happiest people on earth." I say, those persons who have rendered these British subjects so happy, and transmitted to them all the rights and privileges they enjoy, those persons, according to the above doctrine, must be damned to all eternity for their pains.—This may be religion, I am sure it is not common sense. But be that matter as it will, I shall not hesitate to declare, in imitation of honest Sir Toby; I had rather trust God Almighty with my soul, than the British Parliament with my estate. Moreover, for the HONOUR of the Church of England, I do entreat all other Sectaries to believe, that very few of its members hold the same creed with this writer.

However, having introduced Nero, Saint Peter, Saint Paul, and the Grand Turk, in company together; he descends from his pulpit, leaves these dignified personages to shift for themselves, and opens the design of his pamphlet: which he tells us, is not religion, "but to consider how far the conduct of the colonies is to be condemned or justified by the maxims of sound policy and prudence." For it seems pretty well settled even in his idea, that notwithstanding that same Christian system he talks of "our temporal interest and safety, are considerations which all will regard;" in which opinion I do most heartily concur with him.

After this follows a little more declamation, which you may see if you have the pamphlet, if not, send for it to the Booksellers, and you will find a sort of syllogism to shew; that resentment is unjustifiable, and complaint unreasonable, if our legal rights have not been invaded.—Legal rights,—and why that term, legal rights? Do you mean, my Reverend Sir, that any right (that of taxing ourselves for instance), if it be not confirmed by some statute law, is not a legal right; and therefore an invasion of such right, will neither justify resentment, nor authorise complaint? I am afraid you do,—and yet I hope not; for this also is one point to be proved in support of your hypothesis. In the name of America I deny it. But if you mean to speak fairly, and if by *legal rights* you mean what you ought to make your own argument conclusive, namely, those rights which we are entitled to by the eternal laws of right reason; then the remainder of your task will be to shew, that our rights have not been invaded, and if that can be done, then to be sure our complaints are groundless.

Now then let us see what the Friendly Address says upon this subject. Why the first observation is, that the duty on tea is no tax; for unless we purchase it we don't pay the duty, therefore it is quite in our option, whether we will pay it or no. What can be more equitable?—I remember, about twelve years ago, there was a madman in the Philadelphia hospital, who imagined himself monarch of the country thereabouts; and among other wild projects, such as might be expected from a creature in that situation, he had one to tax the air. But may it please your Majesty, will such a tax be right? Air was always common and free, in the time of your Majesty's royal progenitors and predecessors. Will not your subjects think this an arbitrary law, like the poll tax? Arbitrary! cried the prince, enraged; and like the poll tax too! What rebels! Why, unless they breathe, they don't pay the duty, therefore it is quite in their option whether they will pay it or no. What can be more equitable. I pitied the poor man because he was mad.

But you say tea is a luxury. In some respects it may be so. And how, and where, shall we draw a line, between the luxuries and the conveniences of life? Or by what right can the one be taken away, which will not affect the other? Those who may rightfully deprive us of luxuries, by the same rule may as rightfully deprive us of conveniences too. And if in the plenitude of that power, which our author so apostolically hath conferred, they should deign to leave unto us the necessaries of life, pray by what standard shall we determine these necessaries?

> ———— ————Our basest beggars,
> Are in the poorest things superfluous.
> Allow not nature more than nature needs,
> Man's life is cheap as beast's.

But to return.—Our author next supposes, that he is arguing with some honest American, who should deny the right of Parliament to lay this duty on tea. To obviate this he quotes precedent. The American is then supposed to observe, that the precedent itself was wrong, wherefore no right could originate from it; but that together with other similar wrongs, it ought to be done away. So is the argument stated by himself. And he then, upon a supposition that this tea duty is quite distinct from a tax attempts to shew, that Parliament had a right to levy it, merely as a regulation of trade. Pray read the eighth and ninth pages

——— ———— ——— ———— ——— ———— ——— ———— ———

Have you read them?—Why now your honour, I will undertake to confute every thing contained there. I will undertake to shew, that the author's reasoning does not apply to his purpose or subject, any more than the words Denmark and Russia, which as you see are printed in large Italicks.—But what will it signify to take up so much of your attention; when it is very like you had better be thinking on some other affair. His consequence may be well supported on rational ground; though, to his misfortune, he could not discover it. The right of Great-Britain to *regulate* the trade of the colonies, shall be admitted. But that the duty on tea is a *regulation* of trade and not a tax; this is the very matter in controversy.

We are now arrived at the confutation of one of Mr. Locke's arguments; which, says our author, "appears to me weak and sophistical."—The argument as quoted by himself, stands thus: "If parliament has a right to take from us one penny without our consent, it has a right to strip us of our whole property." To confute which he observes, "A right to do what is reasonable, implies not a right to do what is unreasonable." And after a short similitude about father and son, he says, "Cases may happen, in which it would be reasonable for Parliament to take from us some small matter, though we were unwilling to part with it; but the case can hardly be supposed, in which it would be reasonable to take from us every thing, unless we should have forfeited it." And so concludes, "There can be no right to do wrong."—And this is the confutation.—I was some time puzzled to make any thing of it; but by comparing one part with another, we may at least guess that he means what follows: By the words, reasonable to take from us, &c. I presume he intends, a right to take from us. For, reasonable, in the proper sense of the word, will not answer his purpose at all; because if we invert the proposition, it will be as *reasonable* for the Legislature of this province to take from the people of England, a small matter without *their* consent. But that any such right could exist, the author of the Address would hardly allow. Throughout this admirable confutation therefore, let us substitute right for reasonable, and wrong for unreasonable, and then it will stand thus: *A right to do what is right, implies not a right to do what is wrong. To take from us one penny without our consent is right, but to strip us of our whole property is wrong. Therefore, Parliament may have a right to take from us one penny, without our consent, which is right; but this right does not necessarily imply, that Parliament has a right to strip us of our whole property, which is wrong. Therefore Mr. Locke's argument is confuted.* And in the same way I will undertake to confute Euclid's Elements, from one end to the other.—Examine this argument, this fine argument. It rests upon the assertion, that in some cases Parliament may have a right to take a small matter from us without our consent, which assertion is the very thing denied. And so the Gentleman's wits and faculties, after prancing and curveting through a whole section, bring him not one inch nearer the end of his journey, than he was when he first set out.

So here again he labours at a distinction between the duty on tea, and a tax. But as to any difference between them, that you know is quite another affair. No matter for the difference, provided there be a distinction. May it please your Reverence, whenever you are at a loss for matter to vamp up into the shape of another Address; I have a dozen or two such distinctions, which are very heartily at your Reverence's service, very heartily I do assure you.

Ah! what have we here? Another dissertation on the British right of regulating American trade? Yes. Here it is, hip and thigh, import and export, back stroke and fore stroke; blessings on us, I say. What a pity it is, that our author would not content himself with a simple assertion here, as he has done in those instances, which really required proof. Most unfortunately, in endeavouring to establish what we would readily grant; he lays his foundation on arguments, which would overthrow every principle of American liberty. I declare, reader, it is not my intention to cheat you, by re-printing quotations from the Address. But unless you have bought it, I do not know how otherwise to manage matters.

The same want of penetration, which led our author to imagine Mr. Locke's argument weak and sophistical, now bewilders him with a JackO'Lanthorn, in the shape of the word Englishmen. His drift is to shew, we may be bound by laws we do not consent to, and yet possess all the rights of *English*-men. For, says he, Englishmen can have no right to be exempted from the authority of an English Parliament. After this he blunders a little about majority and minority, hints at virtual representation, and says something of English American ground. To answer which at once, those who do not immediately perceive the fallacy, are desired to consider, that the persons who make laws for England, are to be bound by them when they have done. And that no existence whatever, except Almighty God, can have a natural right to make laws binding on others, which the law-maker is exempt from. True it is such power may be usurped, or through political necessity conceded. Usurped as the British power of taxing America, conceded as the power of regulating trade, which after such concession, becomes a right. Greater rights they cannot have; unless some mode can be invented, to incorporate us into the grand legislature of the empire, on constitutional principles. But let us examine his English argument. The word English above, is printed in Italicks, and separated from the word, men. In reading the sentence, leave out *English* and the argument is gone. Now I do aver, and will maintain, that to consent to laws binding upon us, is one of those rights which we enjoy as men, and not merely as English-men. In quality of rational and free agents, we enjoy it. A right granted by our Creator, when he formed us of the clod. That great charter by which he confirmed it, may be read in the human frame: A charter sealed with the breath of life. To this right every man is and must be entitled; it is annexed as an inseperable appendage to our existence, and altho' the English law hath secured it to the English subject, yet a Frenchman or Turk is as much entitled to it, by the law of nature. That this title hath not been ratified by political institutions, is *his* misfortune, and *I* am sorry for it.

So you see, reader, all this trouble might have been spared, if the poor creature had not most unluckily laid hold of that said word, English: which indeed from the face of his performance, he does not appear to understand. The last part of the argument we arc now upon, arises from a fact I am not inclined to dispute, though I do not believe it. He avers that we have been offered representatives in the Common's House, if we would send them over. Be this as it may, I agree with him that we have done wisely in not accepting the offer if ever it was made. Or in other words, to have accepted it, would have been folly. Now then hear him. "After refusing it, they have no reason to complain." That is to say, because we have *not* committed folly, we have no right to complain of injustice, Yet this is an Address to all *reasonable* Americans.

The next attempt of this masterly Address, is to impeach the validity of those compacts, which several colonies have made with the crown. These compacts can be considered in no other light, than as covenants by the King, in consideration of settling the desart; that he would protect the settlers and their dependants, in the enjoyment of their natural rights. If his Majesty chuses to withdraw this protection—be it so. The King can do no wrong. But I wish there had been a lineal warrantee from his ministers. Some of them are of noble descent, and I have so high an opinion of the honour of British

Peers, that I believe few of them would infringe such solemn agreements. However, suppose the King should withdraw this protection,—Are our rights therefore annihilated? No. Those rights were conferred by the King of Kings, and no earthly Potentate can take them away.

Not long since I saw a Letter from a Veteran, to the Officers of the Army at Boston: I pray the author to receive my thanks, for the great pleasure enjoyed in the reading of it. I think I could easily perceive in it, the traces of that manly, generous, brave, and free disposition; which mark the character of the Soldier and the Gentleman.

> If, to his share some little errors fall,
> View his kind heart, and you forgive them all.

I am almost afraid to return immediately to the Address, because comparisons are odious. Make none, gentle reader, I beseech thee; but observe our author here insinuates, that he hath shewn, "that in reality no proper *right* of the colonies is infringed by the late act of Parliament." Pray now, how hath he shewn it? Why by three assertions, neither of which is in the least proved, as I took occasion to observe before in treating of them respectively.—The first is, that the duty on tea is no tax. The second, that if a tax, it is a small one, and Parliament hath a right to take from us a small matter without our consent. And the third, that a man may be rightfully bound by laws which he does not, and cannot assent to.

These are the main pillars of this formidable argument; not one of which hath the least solidity: And therefore the provident author, fearful perhaps of their instability, before he ventures to charge us with sedition, privy conspiracy and rebellion, to anathematise us for false doctrine, heresy, and schism; or to reproach us for hardness of heart, and contempt of his word and command; reverts to his original considerations, about prudence and policy, on what he calls the supposition, and Americans the fact, that we have been really injured.

But these considerations, do not seem to be well considered; because he takes it for granted in the first instance, that the people of Boston were criminal in destroying the tea. And the word Boston, some how or other fascinating his imagination, he is hurried away with a torrent of invectives. The destruction of the tea, says he, "was a compound of the grossest injury and insult, an act of the highest insolence to government, such as mildness itself cannot overlook or forgive." The only fault of all this and some more of the same kind is, that it is rather misplaced; for it would answer tolerably well in a sermon against blasphemy.

Let me intreat the reader's attention to a simple tale: Those who are inclined to doubt it, will find unquestionable evidence in a pamphlet, called, A true State of the Proceedings in the Parliament of Great-Britain, and in the Province of the Massachusetts-Bay, &c.

In the year 1761, 1762, 1763, the duteous conduct of the Massachusetts, was exemplary and acknowledged.—In 1764, the stamp-act was threatened, and a duty imposed for raising a revenue in America. The House of Representatives resolved, that it is unconstitutional, to take their money without their consent. In 1765, the several Assemblies petitioned against the stamp-act; which they had no right to do, because—*it was a Money Bill*: consequently the petitions were disregarded, and the bill was passed. The Massachusetts then proposed a Congress of Delegates from the several Assemblies; and the Congress petitioned the King: but the Congress was an unconstitutional body; wherefore our gracious master (that year) was afflicted with a great deafness. In 1766, the Assembly petitioned against their Governor, one Francis Bernard, for assuming, with his Council, the powers of legislation. This accusation was very just, and therefore to make it was very impertinent. A Nonimportation in America, opened the ears of the Parliament in England; and in 1766, the Stamp Act was repealed. In 1767, another revenue act passed; whereupon the Assembly of that province presented a petition at the foot of the throne; and wrote to the other Assemblies to join in it, which was a piece of great presumption. In 1768, the Assembly was ordered to rescind the resolve, by which those letters had been written, on pain of dissolution; which peremptory mandate produced a petition, and also a letter to the secretary of state.—About the same time some seamen were pressed contrary to an act of parliament; the people of Boston petitioned their governor on this affair; but his Excellency had no business to interfere in the Admiral's department. A vessel also was seized in a manner which irritated the mob, and they were such scoundrels as to resent the insult; consequently they were guilty of treason and rebellion, for drubbing the worthy collector. An army was sent there immediately, but then there was an act of parliament against quartering them on the people, therefore the governor issued his commission, to dispense with the act, for a royal martyr had done so before him. The people then petitioned the governor to call an assembly; this was refused, for business could better be done without one. Disappointed in this, they appointed a convention, the members whereof irritated by what they called their wrongs, presented another humble petition to the King; wherefore in 1769, the troops, out of a just contempt for their pusilanimity, shot three brace by way of starting the covey. But it was impossible his Majesty's troops could have been the aggressors; therefore there must have been an insurrection of the people. This was clearly the case also from Judge Oliver's narration; yet near an hundred credible witnesses, had the impudence to swear, that his narration was false. Consequently to repair the breach in his character, it was necessary that he should be appointed Lieutenant Governor, which happened accordingly. In 1769, the Assembly presented another petition, against their governor Bernard. He prorogued the Assembly, went to England immediately, obtained an order for a hearing on the petition upon the 28th of February, and got the prorogation of the Assembly continued until the 14th of March. Notwithstanding all this, the Assembly never supported their charge with any proof; because the prorogations rendered it impossible; consequently the petition was groundless, vexatious and scandalous, as every body will easily see. In the year 1772, 1773, the Assembly took the liberty to petition again, which was at least forward and ill-bred, wherefore no notice was taken of what they alledged. In December 1773, the dutiable Tea arrived. I have during the course of this story, omitted many things which were thought very grievous by the people of the Massachusetts bay, for the sake of brevity, and because the recital of all their complaints might possibly inflame mens minds at this dangerous juncture; a thing I would wish to avoid, for I have great respect for the clergy.

In December 1773, the dutiable Tea arrived at Boston. It was evident that if this commodity was landed, there would be many purchasers among the governors creatures. Prudence therefore required, that it ought to be sent back. The governor would not permit this, and the necessity was then clear, either that the Tea must be destroyed, or the act submitted to. Wearied out with long oppression, and driven to desperation by repeated insults, a few daring men went disguised to the ship and destroyed the Tea.—Upon this tale I shall make no comment, it needs none. But to relieve the reader's attention, I will mention an incident of a more lively complexion:—Two young gentlemen found a cat sitting peaceably in one corner of the parlour: She was a gentle animal, and a good mouser. Young men love fun, so they shut the door and windows, and ferrited her about, till she and they were heartily tired: At length, in a violent leap from her persecutors, the cat fell in the midst of an elegant set of china: to lose a China cup and saucer, by means of a vile cat, was too much to be patiently borne, and poor puss was murdered for not scampering up the chimney.

Now after this digression, let us return to the pamphlet, and see what is said about the punishment of this crime, which mildness itself could neither overlook nor forgive. A very mild punishment says he, for it was only shutting up the port. Now shutting up the port, was, as we all know, only destroying the trade; and that is only a trifle, as we shall see by and by. "Surely, (cries our author) none who have as high a sense of public guilt as of private, can think this punishment too severe for the crime, considered under all its aggravations. For no people are entitled to the use of any advantage, which they wantonly abuse to the injury of others." These observations are calculated to shew the equity of the port bill; let us see then, whether our author hath fortunately stumbled upon sound reason in this instance, after failing so often.—The advantage which the Bostonians are deprived of, is their trade; and therefore their trade must be the thing which they wantonly abused. Now, by what figure of speech, the destruction of the Tea can be called a matter of trade, or what kind of trade it is, I am at a loss to conceive.—Do not say, that this is a verbal criticism. Such things I reserve for authors of greater perspicuity. The equity of every punishment depends on its relation to the crime. Now allowing, that the destroyers of the Tea, were guilty of a violent outrageous riot; I shall be glad to know, what kind of relation there is in the nature of things, between a riot committed by thirty or forty men, and the ruin of many honest tradesmen, by a total supension of that commerce on which they subsist. Yet this is a MILD and a JUST punishment. I have candidly exhibited the delinquencies of this people; were I to give them a name, nothing but that love of peace which sanctifies every means to obtain it, nothing but that should prevent me, from branding their conduct as a tameness under insults which provoke them.

The next attempt of our worthy pamphleteer is to shew, that "the punishment of the Bostonians, was not hasty and precipitate." He reasons thus: In common cases, a criminal ought to be heard; but this is an uncommon case; courts of justice ought not to condemn unheard, but the legislature may. Now let us scrutinize the intrinsic value of these suggestions. A fellow steals a sheep, or a horse, or ravishes your wife, or murders your father. Justice holds up on high her equal scales; she cries out aloud to the human heart, let him be heard in his defence; rather ninety-nine guilty escape, than one innocent perish: but should a man burn the tooth-pick of a court mistress, or prevent the prime minister from pissing in his pocket, or destroy some musty Tea, to save his estate; in such uncommon case, especially if ninety-nine innocent are to suffer, lest one guilty escape; in such uncommon case the maxim is, let them not be heard. Do you ask why? The answer is plain: If suffered to make a defence, they cannot be convicted.—So much for the case: Now for the tribunal.—If a man commits any of the crimes first mentioned against the known laws of the land, subject to a certain penalty, the maxim is, let him be heard. But as to the last sort, punishable by a new law, in a new mode, both framed after the fact committed, policy is of opinion, that they should not be heard, lest the varlets should except to her mode of proceedings against them. All which is addressed to the *reasonable* Americans.

But (says he in the next paragraph) to involve the innocent with the guilty, is an inconvenience which always *necessarily* attends punishments inflicted on a people, whether by God or man. And again, it was *politically* impossible to select the innocent of Boston from the guilty. We all remember the story of Sodom and Gomorrah. It is an excellent lesson to the Princes of the earth. The inhabitants of these cities, infamous by their vices to the last degree, became so obnoxious to the Supreme Being, that in anger, he resolved to destroy them. Yet had there been five men, only five men, who walked uprightly before God; had only five such men dwelt in Sodom and Gomorrah, no fire had descended from Heaven to consume them. But alas! Because among thirty thousand souls in Boston, thirty have offended; in vain shall the multitude plead innocence, as an exemption from ruin. Blush Humanity! This is thy political necessity, which must hereafter justify the laying that defenceless town in ashes, and drenching it in the blood of its inhabitants.

> —— ——Merciful Heaven!
> Thou rather with thy sharp, and sulph'rous bolt,
> Split'st the unwedgeable, and gnarled oak,
> Than the soft myrtle. Yea, but man, proud man!
> Drest in a little brief authority;
> Most ignorant of what he's most assur'd,
> His glassy essence: Like an angry ape,
> Plays such fantastick tricks before high Heaven,
> As makes the Angels weep.

Because thirty have offended, a whole colony is punished. And for what offence? An offence so small, so disproportionately punished, that the general voice of the continent hath declared, that they suffer in the cause of American liberty. Here our author begins to leave the paths of logic, and to enter the alleys of Billingsgate. Beneath his forming hand, American liberty starts forth a monster of licentiousness. And in his idea, to skreen our miserable fellow-creatures from that PUBLIC JUSTICE which hath been created for them; is giving shelter to the raving enthusiast, who hath murdered his prince.—Bold metaphors and florid language, are the magnificent trappings of reason and truth; and when falshood or folly is thus arrayed, it provokes at once our indignation and contempt.

But neither bold metaphors, nor yet bold language, serve some causes so well as bold assertions. I have heard of lawyers,

who by the assistance of that invincible front which is the pre-
scriptive privilege of their profession, frame evidence as they
go along, and speak fluently on facts which never existed. In
like manner and in humble imitation, to evince the propriety
of the act, for new modelling the government of Massachusets;
our author scruples not to affirm, that "no privileges are curtailed by the act, but such as had been abused and forfeited,
over and over, to the great injury and disturbance of that
province, as well as to the dishonour and reproach of the nation." The institutions of this act, as to their matter I do not
object to; for it hath long been my opinion, that the government of that colony was in its form and complection, too like
a Republic, for the true spirit of our constitution. But as to
the manner; even supposing these regulations to be a decree
substantially just, and made by a court having proper jurisdiction, still there is manifest impropriety.—It is, and while I
have existence, it shall be my sentiment; that no man, no body
of men, in any cause, before any tribunal, can be legally affected
by any determination, where an opportunity is not given, for
making a defence. Had this been done in the present instance,
perhaps his Majesty's Ministers would not have deemed them
so criminal, as they now do. But waving this idea, I am sure
the author of the Address at least, after the pointed assertions
he has made, ought in common justice to have shewn, how the
privileges he speaks of had been *abused and forfeited.* This,
however he thought it prudent to omit.—

That Administration is irritated with Boston, that it hath
cause to be irritated, I freely acknowledge: And *this* is the cause
of the anger they feel, and the revenge they have taken. The
people of that town, and the colony it belongs to, have been
forward and active, in stating and demanding, their rights and
liberties; they have addressed, petitioned, and remonstrated to
Ministers, Parliament, and King; they have sounded the alarm,
when the enemy attacked our privileges; and they have been
the grand obstacle to an American tyranny. If to do thus is a
forfeiture of privileges; if to do thus is an abuse of them, who
would hold such privileges on such tenure? Most readily do I
grant, that it was a dishonour and a reproach to the nation,
and its rulers too; that they so often made use of their right to
petition and to remonstrate. Great was the cause, or such

frequent complaints would not have been obtruded. For this was their guilt, this was their impertinence;—suffering they complained.

We come now to the Quebec Act. On this subject I shall not minutely follow our author, for the substance of what he says, being levelled at the following propositions of the Congress; that the government of Canada is rendered arbitrary, that the people are deprived of trial by jury, and that the Roman Catholick religion is established; if I shall be able to shew that these propositions are true, then what he hath said to the contrary, will be of no avail. And first, what can be more arbitrary than this? A Governor and Council appointed by, and dependent on the Crown, are the legislature of a whole region. They may sit at home, and frame edicts for the extremest parts of that vast province, without any one check from the people. They may tax the colony as they please, or hand it over to be fleeced by the British Commons. They may invent new crimes, and affix to them such new penalties, and make them cognizable before such new Courts, as they shall think meet at their sovereign will and pleasure, they may seize and imprison any member of the community; or else more certainly and entirely, to ruin and oppress him, they may cause some minion of power to institute an action for his whole substance, and try him and condemn him, by the arbitrary principles, and more arbitrary judges of the civil law. For, in the second place, it is clear to a demonstration, that trials by jury cannot be had there now; and it is equally clear that they never can exist hereafter, unless the Governor and Council chuse to risk and diminish their power, by introducing this free and generous branch of English jurisprudence. How probable is it that they will thus put a curb on their own wantonness, I leave any man in his senses to determine. But thirdly, it is not civil tyranny alone, which is planted in Quebec, to overshadow that immense country. From the same poisonous root, arises the most horrible religious tyranny, that my mind is capable of conceiving.— What establishment can any religion have in any country on earth, unless it be a legal provision for the support of its clergy? Look thro' Europe. See if Popery is in any other manner established in any one country, than by payment of tythes, and protection of Priests. Is not this an establishment? Is it not more? Is it not an encouragement? He who would go farther, must resort to fire and sword; the arguments of those barbarous ages and nations, whose annals disgust humanity. But the objection is, that when any man is converted, his Majesty may if he pleases, encourage the Protestant Clergy as he pleases, out of the tythes paid before to the Roman Priest. Allowing this argument to have weight, which indeed it has not; pray what likelihood is there that any man will be converted? Protestantism is the tender child of freedom and science: How then can it exist in the bold bosom of ignorant despotism? Without the patronage of one earthly friend. Without a single rag to cover its nakedness. In ancient days the Romish Church was a firm barrier against the incroachments of Royal prerogative. The Clergy dependent on the Pope as their universal head, defied the menaces of kingly power. Thus were popular privileges in those times frequently protected by popular superstition. Our Ministers by a refinement of modern policy, have adopted the Church of Rome as a twin-sister to the Church of England. Our subtle Ministers have placed the King of England in the same situation with the Roman pontiff. Every dignitary of the Church is dependent on him, besides which he hath full power to appoint such Ecclesiastical Courts, with such jurisdictions as he shall think meet. Thus, all the bigotry, all the superstition of a religion abounding in both, beyond any which the world hath beheld; all, all is in his Royal hand to be used at his Royal will and pleasure. To this full supremacy over their souls, are joined the fullest temporal powers, both legislative and judicial; so that like the ancient Patriarchs, he is King, Priest and Prophet. To finish the dreadful system, add all the executive powers of the State, and encircle the whole with a standing army, 'tis then compleat. These are facts? And whenever a wicked monarch in vengeance shall arise; then shall we behold him, the civil and religious tyrant, of a province which extends over half the Continent of America. Such is the tendency of the Canada Bill. View it, consider it, ponder upon it, in the coolest, most temperate disposition; behold its consequences, and the mild eye of reason will be clouded with a tear.

The next part of the Address is to shew, that the other Colonies need not trouble their heads about Boston or Quebec. As to what he says about Quebec, I believe with him, that there is no intention of introducing Popery into the other colonies. Our Ministers, or rather Masters, have more understanding than to entertain so wild an opinion. Nor would I perswade mankind to become Knights Errant, and wantonly undertake the quarrels, and fight the battles of other people. But I will leave it to any man, nay, I would almost appeal to the author of the address himself, to determine; whether a country has not great reason to fear the loss of its liberties, when surrounded by a multitude of slaves; especially when those slaves are inbued with principles inimical to it, and united together in one common interest, profession and faith, under one common head, and supported by all the weight of a large empire. Does not experience give additional force to every solicitous apprehension?

His ideas about Boston amount to this: that we should act like wise foxes, for fear of being docked: or, in plain English, view with unconcern the destruction of that capital, without daring to interpose for its preservation. I beg pardon for repeating a vulgar story: A Scotchman upon his arrival at an inn filled with travellers, crept into bed between an Englishman and an Irishman: towards the morning the Englishman was awaked by an inundation from his new bed-fellow, "zounds, says he, what are you about?" Hoot, hoot, mon, cried the politic Scot, "lye down quiet; I have done worse to him behind me."

But the author of the address tells us: the dispute with Great-Britain is *de lana caprina*. I learnt a little Latin at school, so with the help of my scholarship, and from what follows, I conjecture that this means goats wool:—That this to say, all the grievances America has laboured under for a dozen years past, amount to a meer trifle; which is so shockingly absurd, that it would be ridiculous to honour it with the ceremony of a confutation.

As to the thought of establishing a republic in America, breaking off our connexion with Great-Britain, and becoming independent: I consider it as the most vain, empty, shallow, and ridiculous project, that could possibly enter into the heart of man. I do not believe there are five hundred on the continent, who have the least pretensions to common sense, and who would not risque their dearest blood, to prevent such measures: This supposition, therefore, and what relates to it, I consider meerly as an introduction to his censures on the Congress. These censures seem to be the main business and intention of the pamphlet. If therefore in the avowed purpose of it (a consideration of the opposition in America on principles of prudence and policy) I shall be able to shew, that the author is much mistaken in condemning those measure which the Congress hath adopted; then all his declamation upon that subject, will be as the idle wind, which passeth away and is heard no more.

The first reflections he casts on this respectable body, are for adopting the Suffolk resolves. The asperity and bitterness which appears in this part of the pamphlet, are to be attributed to the great warmth of the reverend composer. Reproaches from an angry man are easily forgiven; and that meekness of disposition which attends the ministers of peace, will I hope moderate the unchristian transports of our authors zeal, as soon as his mistakes are discovered. By a member of the Congress, whose honor and veracity stand unimpeached, I am authorized to declare, that the Congress did not adopt the Suffolk resolves. That these resolves were never so much as read for debate; and that upon the common reading, the sense of that body was, that it was proper to recommend moderate and pacific conduct, supported by firmness and resolution. The language of the Congress, in consequence of this determination is as follows:

Resolved unanimously,

That we thoroughly approve the wisdom and fortitude, with which opposition has been hitherto conducted: and earnestly recommend a perseverance in the same firm and temperate conduct, as expressed in the resolution &c. Now then I appeal to the world, whether this is the cordial approbation of an independent government. Whether it is a transport of joy on the news of revolt. Whether it is a league with the worst enemies of America, surely it is not. The fair reputation of those Gentlemen who composed the Congress, render such imputations almost unpardonable. It is a duty therefore incumbent on the author of the Address, to make some public acknowledgement; many did indeed expect that some constitution would have been pointed out, to secure and establish the freedom of America, and the sovereignty of that supreme legislature, which ought certainly to govern the whole empire. This is a consummation devoutly to be wished for, but it is not the work of a moment. Besides, it might have been thought presumptuous in them to undertake what is properly the business of the British Parliament, and the respective legislatures of the Continent. Why then are those persons, who have generously devoted their services to the Public, why are they to be censured, for a sin of omission; which at any rate is pardonable on the score of human infirmity?

Much paper is consumed in the Address, to paint those horrors which await on civil war. To this I have no objection. For there is not a creature living, to whom such a prospect is more terrible than myself. And I dare say, a candid description of my own feelings on the subject, would convey as genuine marks of detestation for that horrible catastrophe, as the laboured periods of the author before us. But I see no reasons for such apprehensions. Neither do I think that man a friend to either country, who speaks of war between them except in the stile of contempt. To imagine that America can cope with Great Britain, is the excess of stupidity. And even if we were capable of the contest, were we certain of obtaining victory, I should pray that the hand in which I hold my pen, might wither e'er it drew the sword.—But let not the dread of power, draw off our attention from the pursuit of freedom. Let us in every instance follow that example which our author recommends. In imitation of the inhabitants of Rye; whenever either duty to the mother country, or enthusiasm in the cause of humanity, shall hurry us beyond the true line, of patriotism or obedience, let us take the earliest opportunity to retract our errors, and acknowledge our mistakes.—Resistance against oppression, is the undoubted privilege of mankind; but civil resistance alone, is justifiable in civil society.

I come now to what our author hath said of the non-importation agreement.—This he likens to the cutting off an arm, for a sore on one of the fingers. Similies are very agreeable and proper, where they tend to throw light on the subject.— Now, if a man hath a sore on his finger, he will naturally put a plaister to it. If the finger grows worse, and he grows timid, he sends for a surgeon. If the topical applications of the surgeon are inefficacious, and a gangrene ensues, the parts are scarified, and the bone cleansed. If this fails of success, and corruption spreads along the limb, and threatens the vitals, the only hope which remains is from amputation. True it is, the patient may loose much blood by the incision of his arteries, and death itself may be the consequence. But by undergoing it he has a chance for life, and otherwise his case is desperate. As an encouragement in such difficult emergencies, the scriptures tell us, if thy member offendeth thee, cut it off, and cast it away.

Now, reader, let me entreat your patience a little while longer. Pray observe. The liberties of this country have been infringed in an article of trade. Common sense informs us, that if one imposition is admitted, another will follow. Petitions and remonstrances, have been presented in vain. When we refused the dutiable commodity, it was almost forced upon our acceptance. No hope therefore remains from common efforts. And the question is reduced to this short alternative: Which is most advantageous, commerce or freedom? One or the other, we must forego. The one for a time, or the other forever. I will wave the common observation, which is level to the lowest capacity, that without freedom trade cannot flourish. But I must beg leave to examine, from reason and experience, Whether a cessation of trade will not procure us relief?

Nothing is more evident, than that the trade between Britain and the northern colonies, brings yearly very large sums of money to the latter. That the balance of all the other trade she enjoys, is on the whole against her. And that her annual expences amount to an enormous sum, great part whereof is paid into foreign countries, as interest for the national debt. Is it not then equally evident, that a suspension of her commerce with us, must greatly distress her? And to heighten this distress, what can be more effectual than to embarrass her trade with the islands? Every good heart would wish to avoid this, and it is not our smallest misfortune, that to make men reason, we must make them feel. Happy would it be if the authors of our misery, were the only sufferers. To effect this desirable purpose we had but one way, which was to injure the revenue, in such manner as to hold them up to the resentment of the nation;

and this has been done.—The wisest measures may fail, but these at least promise success.—Great-Britain may indeed very easily put an entire stop to all our commerce. But this (if we may believe the Address) is a mild punishment on Boston. And if so, why cannot we all undergo it? No, says he, inflicted on all of us, it would be very severe. It would so, but I trust not lasting. Will a stoppage of our trade, pay the debts we owe in England? Will shutting up our ports, breed sailors for the navy of Britain? Millions in Europe are fed by the American plough; while bread can be purchased on this continent will they starve? Will the Monarchs of France and Spain see their subjects perish, that Americans may be reduced to slavery? All these things may happen, and after all, this country is capable of supporting its inhabitants.

Great are the difficulties we labour under, and many are the obstacles we must surmount. For the road to freedom and virtue, is not strewed with flowers, but sprinkled with thorns. Perhaps our fortitude is not equal to the task, if so, we deserve the consequences. But remember, that the mother-country must suffer with her colonies: Remember, that a Non-Importation has once procured a redress of our grievances. Remember that Concord is the parent of success. Remember, that the worst which can possibly befal us, even at the last, is that very slavery which we must now resist or submit to. O AMERICANS! these considerations are submitted to you. Attend, and may the God of wisdom, who foreknoweth all human events, so direct you, as is most conformable to the mysterious intentions of his Divine Providence. For the good of his creatures, must be the will of him who is infinite goodness.

POSTCRIPT.

I thought it right to meet the author on his own ground, and therefore no notice is taken in the foregoing sheets, of that very *equitable* Bill, which makes offences in the colonies, triable in England. A Bill by which the most criminal partizan of government may be screened from punishment. A Bill by which any poor man in America, may be torn from all the tenderest connections of life; dragged in chains across the Atlantic Ocean, and left there friendless and forlorn, with the blessed alternative to starve or hang. This also is public justice —mild punishment—and political necessity.

FINIS.

Ebenezer Baldwin, "An Appendix, Stating the Heavy Grievances the Colonies Labour under from Several Late Acts of the British Parliament, and Shewing What We Have Just Reason to Expect the Consequences of These Measures Will Be." From Samuel Sherwood, A Sermon, Containing, Scriptural Instructions to Civil Rulers, and All Free-Born Subjects. New Haven, 1774.

Ebenezer Baldwin, a 1763 graduate of Yale College, was the minister of the Congregational Church in Danbury, Connecticut. In seeking "to enlighten the people of a country town, not under the best advantages for information from the news papers and other pieces . . . to a sense of the danger in which their liberties are now involved," he set forth in the following piece, attached as an appendix to a sermon by a fellow Connecticut minister, as clear and succinct a summary of the fears and anxieties of Americans in 1774 as could be found anywhere. Like Jefferson and many other Americans, Baldwin concluded from the events that had occurred since 1765 that the British ministry and Parliament had formed "a settled fix'd plan for *inslaving* the colonies."

This belief in conspiracies was common to the age. Lacking our modern repertory of impersonal forces, such as "industrialization" or "urbanization," to explain complicated combinations of events, this early modern culture tended to think that things did not just happen, but were brought about, step by step, by the will and intention of individuals. Although the increasing complexity of the world was exceeding people's capacity to explain it in personal terms, many Americans and Britons both still sought to hold particular individuals morally responsible for the course of events. The American colonists were not alone in seeing plots and conspiracies at work; George III and other British officials did as well. Events in Massachusetts in 1768, for example, convinced the House of Lords that "wicked and designing men" in the colonies were "evidently manifesting a design . . . to set up a new and unconstitutional authority independent of the crown of England."

Desperate to hold the empire together, Benjamin Franklin was one of the few who complained of "desclaimers on both sides the water" seeking "to sow the seeds of dissension, and blow up the flames of discord, where every prudent consideration calls for concord and harmony." He could not understand such people. "To suspect plots and deep designs where none exist, to regard as mortal enemies those who are really our nearest and best friends, and to be very abusive": what could these symptoms suggest, he pronounced in 1768, but a kind of "insanity of *head*."

A

SERMON,

C O N T A I N I N G,

Scriptural Inftructions to Civil Rulers, and all Free-born Subjects.

In which the Principles of found Policy and good Government are eftablifhed and vindicated ; and fome Doctrines advanced and zealoufly propagated by NEW-ENGLAND TORIES, are confidered and refuted.

Delivered on the public F A S T,

AUGUST 31, 1774.

With an Addrefs to the FREEMEN of the Colony.

By *Samuel Sherwood*, A. M.

Paftor of a Church of Chrift in FAIRFIELD.

Alfo, An A P P E N D I X,

Stating the heavy Grievances the Colonies labour under from feveral late Acts of the Britifh Parliament, and fhewing what we have juft Reafon to expect the Confequences of thefe Meafures will be.

By the Rev. EBENEZER BALDWIN, of Danbury.

And the chief Captain anfwered, With a great fum obtained I this freedom ; and Paul faid, but I was born free.
ACTS xxii, 28.
Sit Denique Infcriptum in fronte unius Cujufque Civis quid De Republica fentiat. CICERO.
Patria mihi mea vita multo eft Carior. CICERO.

New-Haven, Printed by *T.* and *S. GREEN.*

And in every province whithersoever the king's command-
ment, and his decree came, there was great mourning
among the Jews, and fasting and weeping, and wailing,
and many lay in sackcloth and ashes.

Esther.

Behold, we are servants this day, and for the land that thou
gavest unto our fathers to eat the fruits thereof, and the
good thereof, behold we are servants in it. And it yieldeth
much increase unto the kings whom thou hast set over us,
because of our sins: also they have dominion over our
bodies, and over our cattle, at their pleasure, and we are
in great distress.

Nehemiah.

PREFACE.

THE substance of the following Appendix was composed,
with a view to enlighten the people of a country town, not
under the best advantages for information from the news pa
pers and other pieces wrote upon the controversy, into the
true state of the present unhappy disputes between Great Britain and the colonies; for this reason it still appears in the form
of an address to the people. It has been thought the publication of it might answer valuable purposes, to rouse others in
the western part of this colony, who are much in the same situation with the people for whose information it was first composed, to a sense of the danger in which their liberties are now
involved. The Author is very willing to contribute his mite to
the common cause of liberty; and is very glad of an opportunity to subjoin the following Address as an appendix to a discourse so well adapted (as he imagines the foregoing is) to lead
people to a sense of the true nature of civil government, and of
the absurdity of many ridiculous whims; which some among us
have the impudence to attempt to maintain in direct opposition to those principles, which have seated the present Royal
Family on the British throne.

Should this appendix fall into the hands of any, that have

347

been more awake to a sense of our danger; than what hath been the case in the western parts of this colony; the author hopes they will readily overlook the mention of many things, which must be trite and common to them; as the particular mention of them was necessary to the design in view.

The silence of others on a subject of so much importance, and (as many think) so necessary to be wrote upon at the present time, must plead in excuse of the Clergy, if they write upon a subject by some deemed too political for their province: But let it be remembered that clergymen are freemen as well as others; have civil rights and privileges in common with their fellow subjects; are capable of feeling oppression as well as others: why then is there not an equal obligation on them, as on others, to stand forth in defence of their country, and endeavour to sound the alarm, when they see every thing that is dear and valuable in the utmost danger? Were a house on fire and the family securely sleeping while the flames were surrounding them; would it not be the height of folly, for those that were by, to stand disputing who was the properest person to give the alarm, and awake them from their dangerous repose? Much like this is it, to dispute who are the properest persons, the clergy or others, to point out to their fellow subjects the danger their country is in. The present crisis calls for the vigorous exertions of every rank and order of men.

The Author is not insensible that it is more fashionable to write *anonimously* upon such subjects as these, and would it equally answer the end proposed, he would very gladly lie concealed: But he thinks the public are liable to be greatly imposed upon on the one side and the other by anonymous publications; as in that case no-body is responsible for what is asserted. And as there are no sentiments in the following composition, which he is ashamed to own; or unwilling the world should believe are his—no facts asserted but what he verily believes to be true. He can't but think it may better subserve the purpose for which it is published, to have his name prefix'd; than to be published without a name.

Appendix.

NEVER was there a period so alarming to the English American colonies as the present is; never one that called for the careful attention, the prudent, yet vigorous exertion of every freeman in the colonies as the present doth! For when our lives, and our property are subject to the arbitrary disposal of others; what have we valuable we can call our own? The disposal of our property is now openly claimed by others; by a body, in which we have no representation; and upon which we have not the least check or controul: and charters, heretofore deemed *sacred* and inviolable; by which, we have been wont to suppose, was secured to us the quiet possession of our lives and properties, are now wantonly violated without even the form of a trial; and such modes of judicial proceedings introduced into a neighbouring province, as very much subject the lives of the people to the arbitrary disposal of their governor. And doubtless this is but a specimen of the plan adopted with regard to all the provinces; which will soon be introduced, if this first attempt succeed. We have to expect, if the measures adopted are carried into execution, we shall hold both our lives and our property in coming time upon the most precarious tenure. These measures you see are carrying into execution by the terror of military force both by sea and by land. And if our lives and our property are to be held by such a precarious tenure as the arbitrary will of those, who may be set over us, what is there in life or property worth the possessing? Will not the being in constant and perpetual fear of the deprivation of both, imbitter all the comforts of life? Could you take a view of the nations which are groaning under arbitrary and despotic government; you would never imagine what I say to be chimerical. We have not (blessed be God) as yet experienced the galling chains of slavery; tho' they have been shook over our heads. For this reason few perhaps among us, realize the horrors of that slavery, which arbitrary and despotic government lays men under.

Some possibly may think me extravagant in asserting there never was so alarming a period to the English American colonies, as the present is: But I cannot think any one needs any more, than to be thoroughly acquainted with the present state of public affairs, to be wholly of my opinion. We have, it is true, in times past, been alarmed with the horrors of war: the savages have committed shocking murders and made terrible devastations upon our exposed frontiers; but these were but temporary evils: while the present (if God prevent not) will extend their influence to all succeeding generations. And is the death of a number of individuals in war so great a calamity to the public, as a whole country's being enslaved, and the lives and the properties not only of the present, but of succeding generations subjected to the caprice of arbitrary rulers?

Under the administration of *Sir Edmund Andross*, near ninety years ago, very gloomy indeed was the prospect to our fathers: yet in many respects not so gloomy as at the present day. Charters, 'tis true, were *then* taken away; but they were taken away under colour of law; upon trial in courts of justice: But *now* they are taken away, without so much as a pretence of law; without so much as a trial, or hearing of the party concerned, by the almost omnipotent power claimed by the British parliament: And when only the courts of justice are corrupted, there is more hopes things may revert to a right channel; than when the corruption lies in the supreme legislative body. At *that time* the arbitrary measures pursued proceeded only from an arbitrary prince; *now*, from an arbitrary parliament. *Then* the nation was awake to the arbitrary measures pursuing: *now* they supinely slumber. *Then* Britain felt the weight of the iron hand of tyranny; while *now* they imagine their burdens relieved by the oppression of America. Which circumstances rendered the continuance of arbitrary government vastly less likely at that time, than at the present day. It is not therefore, without a cause, that the whole continent seems as it were struck with horror and amazement; that the attention of almost every American is roused to the present state of our public affairs. And tho' some may be transported with a wild and enthusiastic rage in the cause of liberty, and some others may be stupid and insensible of real danger; yet all the more sober thinking part feel impressed with a deep and solicitous concern for the event of these things. But in a place remote from public intelligence as this is, few comparatively can have opportunity to peruse the public papers, and other writings, which may open to us the present alarming situation of our country. Many, therefore, are perhaps little acquainted with what our danger is. They do not themselves as yet feel the weight of oppression. They hear the noise of danger echoed round the country, but know very little of what gives the alarm. For the information of such as have not been under advantages for proper intelligence, I will briefly as I can relate to you what hath been done by the British parliament with regard to America, which gives the present alarm.—What the grievances are we labour under from these acts of the British parliament—what we have just reason to fear the consequences of these measures will be—then just hint at a few things proper for us to do in the present alarming crisis.

Here I may premise, that the English American colonies, at least I may say the New-England colonies were settled without any cost to the crown. Private adventurers that they might enjoy the sweets of both civil and religious liberty, in a great measure denied them in their native land, ventured into this, then a howling wilderness; and at their own expence laid the foundation of these flourishing colonies. All they received from the king was charters securing to them the rights and privileges of Englishmen in this new-found world: here amid numerous wars with the barbarous savages in their infant state, they defended themselves without any expence to the crown. Afterwards when the nation was engaged in war, they complied with every requisition from the king. They exerted themselves beyond their abilities in two expensive expeditions against Canada, in the reigns of William & Anne, which proved unsuccessful. In the war before the last, at their own motion, and almost wholly at their own expence, they took the important fortress of Louisbourg, which gave peace to Europe. In the last war 'tis fresh in every one's memory how chearfully they complied with every requisition of men or money from the Crown: for several years near a quarter of the militia of New-England were in actual service. Yet, with what alacrity performed? Who ever heard a murmur or complaint of our expence of blood and treasure, tho' Britain reaped the profit of our conquests, as all the conquered lands were theirs? Britain was so sensible of the spirited exertions of the Colonies at that time;—sensible they had contributed more than their proportion, that they refunded to them a considerable part of their expence. Hitherto they had neither claimed, nor exerted any right to tax the Colonies: and every one, who remembers that time, knows how ardent our affections were to the mother country, we gloried in our relation to Britain—were ready to fight and bleed for her glory and honour.

As America was much the seat of the last war, the troops sent here from the mother country, opened a much freer communication between Great Britain and the Colonies, the state of the colonies was much more attended to in England, than it had been in times past. And as in a country like this, where property is so equally divided, every one will be disposed to rival his neighbour in gaudiness of dress, sumptuousness of furniture, &c. All our little earnings therefore went to Britain to purchase mainly the superfluities of life. Hence the common people here make a show, much above what they do in England. The luxury and superfluities in which even the lower ranks of people here indulge themselves, being reported in England by the officers and soldiers upon their return, excited in the people there a very exalted idea of the riches of this country, and the abilities of the inhabitants to bear taxes. The ministry soon conceived hopes that a large revenue might be raised from America.—A revenue that would be solely at their own disposal, whereby they might provide for great numbers of their dependants, and mightily enlarge their influence over the parliament, to secure a majority in their measures. Accordingly in a few years after the conclusion of the late war; the British parliament, for the first time, laid a tax upon America, by what was called the *stamp-act*: by which almost every written instrument of a public nature was subject to a high duty. Requisitions of men or money were no longer made as usual from the king to the colonies: but their money is now to be extorted from them by an act of the British parliament. 'Tis doubtless fresh in your memories, what an alarm this *new* claim of parliament gave to the colonies; what unanimous and vigorous opposition was made to the execution of the act: the stampt papers were either destroyed, or kept from being distributed throughout America: Trade with Great Britain was in a good degree suspended:—In short, a glorious struggle was made against this *first* exertion of a parliamentary claim of taxation over America. The issue of the struggle was happy.

The parliament the next session, repealed the act, tho' not upon the principles it could have been wished for, i. e. of its being *unconstitutional*; but upon the footing of its being *inexpedient* and ill-suited to the state of the colonies. The parliament still claimed a right of making statutes to bind the colonies in all cases whatsoever. They still claimed the right of taxing them at pleasure. Duties were accordingly laid upon sundry articles of merchandize payable upon their landing in America, as on *tea, glass, painters colours*, &c. part of which were afterwards taken off by parliament. There are also duties that have heretofore been laid on other articles of trade; but as they were supposed to be laid only to defray the expences of regulating trade; the colonies acquiesced in them without any complaint: but the duties on tea, &c. being for the express purpose of raising a revenue to his majesty, and being in consequence of the parliament's claim to make statutes to bind the colonies in all cases whatsoever, excited continual murmurs and complaints in the colonies: however as the tax was inconsiderable, it raised no considerable tumults. Soon after this *new admiralty courts* were erected throughout America. The powers of which courts were extended much beyond what they are in England, or what they had been in America. But as I have not by me, the act of parliament constituting those courts, I can only observe upon them in general as what Americans complain of. An expensive *Board of Commissioners* for managing the revenue were constituted with the most extravagant powers.—They have power to constitute as many under officers as they please; they are impowered to demand *general warrants* from the judges of courts in America: i. e. warrants to search any body, and any where for contraband goods; under pretence of which, they may search any man's most private apartments; not even his desk or drawers, or any thing would be secure. But as I am not possessed of the act constituting this board, I cannot be further particular upon it. The judges of the admiralty and the commissioners have both the most extravagant salaries; the former each *six hundred*, the latter *five hundred* pounds sterling per annum, paid out of the American revenue, besides the perquisites of their offices. And yet it has been reported of one at least of these judges of admiralty, that for two years or more he has had but one case to try.

These, with a swarm of petty custom-house officers appointed by the commissioners, exhaust almost the whole of the revenue. It is said, there was but 86*l.* the last year paid into the king's exchequer. So that all the money raised is spent to maintain a set of *idle drones* in ease and luxury, without doing any service to their king or country. The colonies from a reluctance to pay these, as they deemed them, unconstitutional duties, have, it is probable, purchased a considerable part of their teas from the Dutch; by which means the quantity imported from Great Britain hath been much less since the duty was laid than before; which caused an immense quantity of tea to lie upon the hands of the *East-India* company. With the approbation, if not by the proposal of the ministry, they resolved to send a large quantity of it to America upon their own risk. Several ships loaded with tea were accordingly sent to several different ports in America. This gave a general alarm thro' the Colonies. They tho't the mother country was now resolved to fasten the chains of slavery upon them; as they would not leave us at our own option whether we would import the Tea or not; but were resolved to force it upon us. A general resolution seems therefore to have been come into throughout the colonies, not to suffer the tea to be landed. Accordingly at Philadelphia, New-York and Portsmouth, and I am apt to think from some other parts of America also, they persuaded the masters of the ships to return to England, without unlading. At Boston, the governor would not suffer the tea ship to pass the castle without a clearance. A clearance could not be obtained without she entered and unladed. So that there was no other alternative, the people must either suffer the tea to be landed or destroy it; accordingly a number of persons went in disguise and emptied it all into the sea. At New-York also a quantity of the same tea was destroyed in like manner. When news was received in England, of the destroying of the tea in Boston; the ministry thinking that a proper opportunity now presented, for carrying the designs they had long since formed into execution, immediately hurried thro' the parliament, the act for blocking up the harbour of the town of Boston. This act forbids the shipping or landing any kind of merchandize whatsoever, (except fuel and victuals for the necessary sustenance of the inhabitants of the town) any where within Boston bay. Vessels, bound for Boston with provisions, must first be searched at Marblehead, must take an officer on board, and enter at Salem, before they may proceed to the town. By this act all the trade of the town of Boston is stopped, which was the whole support of the town; and 'tis calculated to distress them much in procuring provisions. Any attempt to lade or unlade merchandize is punished with a fine of treble their value; with a forfeiture of the vessels or carriages used in lading or unlading. The officers on the station are to be fined 500*l.* if they so much as connive at any breach of this act: and all forfeitures or penalties are to be recovered in the *courts of admiralty*, where the king is both party and judge. The repealing this act the parliament have put out of their own power, by lodging it with the king; who when he shall judge that peace is restored in the town of Boston, may appoint so many wharves or landing places as he pleases; and if any goods or merchandize be afterwards landed upon any wharves or landing places not appointed or licensed by him, the penalties of the act will notwithstanding take place; and even this, i. e. the licensing any wharves the king is restricted from doing, not only 'till it shall appear to his majesty that satisfaction is made to the East India company for the tea destroyed; but till the governor has certified that reasonable satisfaction hath been made for all the injuries done to the custom house officers in times past. This bill, so pregnant with mischief, was hurried with the greatest precipitancy thro' both houses of parliament; the design was for a while kept entirely secret, lest there should be petitions against the bill. They never proposed to the inhabitants of Boston whether they would make satisfaction for the injuries done or not. They never gave them any opportunity to speak a word in their own defence;—a privilege allowed to the meanest criminal in every court of justice. Altho' solicited in both houses, they would not so much as suffer their agent to speak in their behalf.

This Act hath been followed by two others respecting that province equally alarming, hurried thro' the parliament with the same precipitant haste as the other; without notifying the province to appear in their own defence, or allowing their agent to speak in their behalf. The one is intituled *An act for the better regulating the government of the province of Massachusetts-Bay.* Whereby in direct violation of the privileges granted by charter, the appointment of the council is taken out of the hands of the general assembly and vested with the king; the governor's power is greatly enlarged, so that he may appoint all the judges, justices, sheriffs and other inferior officers, and remove them at pleasure without any concurrence of council. The inhabitants are forbid to assemble in town meeting except by special license obtained from the governor; only in their annual meeting, and then to transact no other business than just the appointment of town-officers. Jurors, that were before returned by the impartial method of drawing them out of a box, are now to be summoned at the pleasure of the sheriff. And lest all this should not be sufficient to screen the soldiers or the officers either of the governor or of the custom-house, who should happen to commit murder upon the inhabitants, from deserved punishment: There is another act passed, intituled *An act for the impartial administration of justice*, &c. which impowers the governor upon the indictment of any of the soldiers, officers, &c. for any capital offence, when acting in execution of any of these laws, or under the direction of any magistrate, to remove the trial into any other province, or if he sees fit, into Great-Britain: obliging the prosecutor and witnesses to appear there or to drop the prosecution. This is the substance of the late acts respecting the Massachusetts; which are now rigorously carrying into execution: A large fleet blocking up their harbour, and six or seven regiments of soldiers quartered in the town of Boston, beside some others in the neighbourhood.

There is another act lately passed in the British parliament, for regulating the government of the province of Quebec, which greatly alarms the nation in general as well as America in particular. Thousands of English people have settled in that province under the faith of a royal proclamation, that the English laws should take place there, and a government like that of the other colonies as soon as the circumstances of the province would permit. But by this act all the *French* laws in being before the conquest are restored—*Popery* is established and provision is made for the legal support of the popish clergy by the collection of tythes.—Trials by jury are taken away, and the whole legislative power lodged in a council appointed by the king; what aspect this may have upon us shall be considered hereafter.

Thus I have related the principal facts with respect to America on which the present grievances and dangerous prospects of the Americans are founded. I proceed now to consider what those grievances are, which we have cause to complain of, from these acts of the British parliament.

The first thing we complain of as a grievance is, that by taxing the colonies for the purpose of raising a revenue, and claiming a right to make laws or statutes in all cases binding on the Colonies, the parliament claim what they have no right to, by the British constitution, and thereby deny us our *natural* rights as men, and our *constitutional* rights as Englishmen. This I will consider somewhat particularly, as 'tis at the foundation of our complaints: for if the parliament have rightfully such a power as this, the Americans only are to blame in the present disputes, that subsist between Great-Britain and the Colonies: In order to which we may with propriety advert a little to the foundation of civil government in general, and the principles of the British government in particular.

That, which induces any number of individuals to enter into compact for civil government, is the greater security of their lives and properties; which in a state of nature are exposed to every invader, and liable to be taken away with impunity by any one that is stronger than we. In a society formed for the purposes of government, there is the united power of the whole to suppress such injurious invaders. It is the duty of those who thus combine together for government to give up so much of their property into the hands of those who are intrusted with authority, as is necessary to carry on government: But then it would be very preposterous, when they entered into society to secure their property, to give it up to be wholly at the disposal of any one man or body of men: this would be to put their property in a worse state than the state of nature. 'Tis therefore to be presumed that every body of people entering into compact for civil government will keep the disposal of their property in their own hands, and make grants of it to their rulers as the exigencies of government shall require: otherwise they put it into the power of their rulers to exercise every kind of tyranny over them. And thus it is said with the greatest propriety, that every man hath a natural right to dispose of his *own* property. And every man hath a natural right to life, unless he hath been guilty of such conduct, that by the laws of nature he forfeits it; i. e. hath so conducted that it is evident others cannot be secure in the possession of their lives and properties without life is taken from him: Another benefit of society therefore is to have persons appointed, who can be trusted, to judge when this is the case; that we may not be liable to have our lives taken away at the capricious pleasure of every one, that may judge we have forfeited them; as is the case in a state of nature: But then as life is our most darling possession, no body of men acting rationally will intrust this power with any man or number of men, without using every precaution for the right exercise of it.

The English constitution most admirably provides for the security both of our lives and our properties. In that great *charter* of liberties, commonly called *Magna Charta*, which our ancestors obtained by the most painful struggles; 'tis a fundamental article that no man shall be taxed but by his own consent: But as every individual of the nation cannot meet to grant taxes; there becomes a necessity of their meeting by representation; and accordingly the British parliament represent all the people of Great-Britain; are chosen by them, and the *sole* right of granting money is vested in them: Neither the king nor house of lords have power to raise one penny of money upon the subject; And as the parliament when they grant money to the king, tax themselves in common with others, and as they are exposed to lose their places the next election, if they do not conduct according to the mind of their constituents; the people have the greatest security that can be, that they will grant no more money than what the purposes of government, the good of the community, and the honour of the nation require. So likewise are our lives most admirably guarded in that charter of privileges which our forefathers obtained: In which 'tis provided that no man shall be imprisoned but by the laws of the land—No man's life shall be taken away, (either by the king or judges appointed by him,) but by the voice of his country represented by twelve honest men of the neighbourhood where the crime is committed, called together in some impartial manner; who, 'tis to be presumed, can have no interest in acting otherwise than justly. These two. viz. the right of taxing themselves, and trials by jury, especially in capital cases, have ever been deemed by the people of England their fundamental privileges; the violation of which was the principal cause of that dreadful civil war in England about a century ago, which at last brought an arbitrary king to the block. A violation of these, with other attempts to subvert the constitution, dethroned king JAMES the second, and advanced WILLIAM and MARY to the throne. So jealous have Englishmen ever been of these important rights and privileges. Now the first of these the parliament go directly in the face of, when they lay taxes on the Americans; as we are not represented in the British parliament, and by reason of our distance can never have an equal representation there. When they lay taxes on us, they feel none of the burdens they impose; and we have no influence over them, as the people of England have, by dropping the members of parliament, if they conduct wrong, at the next election. They do in reallity take away our money from us by force, and make a present of it to the king. 'Tis not that we are against contributing to defray the expences of government, that causes us to complain of these taxes: But because our money is forced from us in an illegal manner, in direct violation of that fundamental privilege of Englishmen, *a right to tax themselves.* The colonies are represented in their respective general assemblies, and no where else; and whenever the King hath made requisitions to them of men and money, they have ever readily granted them: And would his majesty *ask* his good subjects in America, as he doth the people of Britain assembled in parliament, for money to defray the charges of government, I am bold to say they would readily grant it.

Altho' the privilege of trial by juries is not as yet taken away from the colonies in general; yet the advantage of it is much lessened in the province of the Massachusetts-Bay; as it is in the power of the sheriff to pack such a jury as he pleases; who being appointed *solely* by the governor, it may be presumed will ever be a *creature* of his; and also by the governor's having power to remove capital trials out of the province, or even to Britain, where a jury cannot be supposed so adequate judges, as one collected from the neighbourhood where the crime was committed. The admiralty courts, 'tis complained of, are in many cases an infringment upon this important privilege. In Canada trial by juries is wholly taken away; and who but justly fears that this is a sample by which the other colonies may e're long be modelled.

The late acts respecting the province of the Massachusetts-Bay are looked upon by Americans to be *grievous* in many respects; to that province immediately; to the other colonies as they afford a precedent of the treatment they may expect to receive, whenever they shall happen to fall under the resentment of the British court, and as it opens to view the plan adopted for the government of the colonies. To begin with that called the *port act*, or the act for blocking up the harbour of the town of Boston.

And first, if we look into the preamble of this act, we shall find the reasons assigned are, that *divers ill affected persons have fomented and raised dangerous commotions,* &c. *in which certain valuable cargoes of tea were destroyed.* Here you see 'tis supposed that the whole people are not guilty, but only *divers ill affected persons,* yet the whole town is punished, *men, women, and children.* Why did not the parliament enable his majesty to punish those *ill affected persons,* and not bring ruin on a whole country for the crime of a few individuals? 'Tis not probable that more than a hundredth part of the inhabitants of Boston were concerned in this affair, yet this is the only reason assigned for punishing the whole. Is it not the part of justice to sever between the guilty and the innocent and not to punish all in the lump? And have not other colonies been guilty of the like conduct? New-York destroyed a considerable quantity of the same tea. Philadelphia forcibly sent back a large cargo to the great detriment of the East-India company; yet Boston only is singled out to be the object of ministerial vengeance. It plainly appears they mean to take but *one* at a time, and thus by dividing the colonies to bring them one after another to submit to the yoke.

Again, if you look further into this monstrous production, you will find that all the immense estates lying in wharves, water lots, &c. clear round Boston bay are really *confiscated* to the king: for if ever satisfaction is made according to the requirements of the act, 'tis expressly left with the king, to license only such wharves and landing places as he pleases. Now wharves are worth nothing, if there may be no landing upon them: their water lots are worth very little, if they may not build wharves upon them; or may not use them when built. So that the property of these estates, all in a manner that is valuable in them, is wrested from the original owners and vested with the king: With equal right might the parliament vote to the king the landed estate of any person in this or any other province: And if because there hath been a riot or mischief done by some individuals, the parliament may vote to the king the estate of any person that happens to lie in the town or country where committed: In what a dreadful situation are we? Here is not only claimed, but actually exercised; not merely a right of taxation, but of granting our estates, just as the British parliament pleases. A precedent justly alarming to all the colonies!

If you look still further into this oppressive act, you will find it inforced by such penalties as never act was. If any goods are landed or shipped from any wharf or landing-place within Boston bay; not only the vessel and cargoes, with all the horses, carriages, cattle and every utensil concerned in carrying them are forfeit; but a fine treble the value of the goods at the highest price is laid upon any person that shall be so much as aiding or abetting. What shocking severity! And where are these fines to be recovered? Not in the common courts of justice where there might be a fair trial by jury: but in the courts of admiralty; where the king, who is to receive the fine, is both judge and jury, as well as party concerned. And the difficulties every vessel is laid under that goes in with provisions, seem as if designed, if not to starve them, at least to raise the price of provisions so high, as to force them to yield. And lest the officers on the coast should have some humane and compassionate feelings towards their distressed fellow subjects in Boston; a fine of 500*l.* sterling is laid on any one that shall so much as connive at the least breach of the act.

Again 'tis put out of the power of parliament to grant redress to Boston: 'tis lodged with the king when to remove the rigours of the act: yet he is restricted 'till full satisfaction is made for the tea destroyed by, or in behalf of the town of Boston; but who can it be expected will do it in their behalf?

and the town can do it in no other way than by a tax upon the inhabitants, thus involving the innocent with the guilty.* And not only so, but till the governor certifies satisfaction hath been made to the custom-house officers and others for all the

* The following quotation I find in the London Magazine for July 1774. p. 345. From a pamphlet entituled, *Observations on the act of parliament commonly called the Boston Port Bill*, &c. *By Josiah Quincy, junr. Esq; Counsellor at Law in Boston*. Which, as it contains a further difficulty to the inhabitants of Boston's complying with the requirements of the act than what had occurred to my mind, I take the liberty to add by way of note.

"It must again be noticed that no relief is to be had 'until full satisfaction hath been made *by* or *on* behalf of the inhabitants of said town of Boston.' Now to suppose that any in England or Europe would make satisfaction on behalf of said inhabitants was unnatural, if not absurd; but what is more to the point, it was certainly *unparliamentary*. The remaining alternative is that satisfaction must be made *by* Boston.

Every person knows that towns in this province cannot raise or appropriate any monies, but by the express provisions and direct authority of law: it is a matter of equal notoriety, that all town assessments of money are expressly confined by the 4. Wm. & Mar. c. 13. to the maintenance and support of the ministry schools, the poor, and defraying of other *necessary town charges*. A law which received the royal approbation almost a century ago.

Will any now say, that the monies appointed to be paid to the East India house come within the words of *necessary town charges*? When did the town contract the debt or how are they subject to the payment of it? Had the Parliament seen fit to enact, that monies requisite to satisfy the India merchants should be so *considered*, two questions (not of quick decision) might then have arisen: the one touching the validity and obligatory force of the statute; the other, whether it would then come within the intent and design of the province law. For past doubt, our provincial legislators had no such charge (as the one here supposed) in view, when they made the law of Wm. and Mary; and in this way therefore the matter could not be brought within its provision. Parliament must then make a new act to enable and impower Boston to pay the India company, before the town can comply with the terms of relief of their trade. In the mean while, what is to be the situation of Boston, and the inhabitants of the globe, with whom they have such extensive connections? But it is very apparent, that the parliament have not as yet enacted the payment of this satisfaction as a *town charge*. They have only placed it in the option of the town, to make that payment or submit to the consequences. That payment, we affirm, *they cannot make, without breach of the law of the land*. New and unheard of therefore is the state of this people. They must sustain the severest afflictions, they must stand the issue of distracting remedies or—violate one of the most known and practised laws of the land. Let us search the history of the world; let us inspect the records of a Spanish Inquisition; let us enter the recesses of an ottaman court; nay, let us traverse the regions of romance and fable—where shall we find a parrallel?

abuses they have received for several months before. Now how is it possible to know when they have complied with the requirements of the act? Let them be ever so much disposed to make satisfaction, no mortal can tell when it is done. They are left wholly at the mercy of their governor; who by office, if not by inclination (as one expresses it) is supposed to be a mere tool of arbitrary power. Never was there a completer instrument of tyranny, (if any are wicked enough to make such an use of it) than the Boston port act.

And over and above all this, this act which brings such an heavy calamity upon the town of Boston and the whole province, and establishes such a fatal precedent with respect to the parliament's power over the colonies, was passed without ever allowing the party therein concerned, an opportunity to make their defence, or even so much as their agents to speak in their behalf; and when (as has been often reported) full satisfaction was offered by the merchants in London for all damage the East-India company had suffered from the destroying of their tea.

"Here the sons of tyranny in America; the base advocates for parliamentary power; may see the blessed fruit of their doctrine: may see a specimen of what the other Colonies may expect from that exorbitant power they are at such pains to justify." Strange that any should dare to hold up their heads among a free people in defence of such oppressive claims, as are here exerted.

But let us attend to the other late acts respecting the province of the Massachusetts-Bay; both of which were hurried thro' the parliament with the utmost precipitancy, without ever allowing the province condemned an opportunity to speak in their own behalf. One of these in open defiance of the royal charter, in which the word of the king most solemnly given had guaranteed to them that form of government, they had enjoyed for near a century past, essentially changes their form of government,—vests the king with a power of appointing another branch of their legislature beside the governor.—Extends the power of the governor to the most exorbitant lengths, and almost nullifies that birth right of Englishmen, trials by jury. If charters, if the solemn promises of kings are to be thus trifled with, what security can we have in any thing?

Under the faith of charters solemnly given, our fathers planted this wilderness; built towns and cities—extended the commerce, the power, the glory of Britain. But now these sacred privileges thus solemnly confirmed are to be subject to the caprice of an insolent minister. And then the principle upon which the parliament avowedly proceeded, that whenever they judged it expedient & advantageous to the public, they had a right to set charters aside, greatly aggravates the evil. For upon this principle, if they judge it expedient, they may set aside all grants of land, all patents from the king (for none of these are more solemn or sacred than charters) and thus might cause all our lands to revert into the hands of the king. This principle nullifies all security of our property. In short, upon this principle the parliament may in the plenitude of their power, deprive us of every valuable enjoyment we possess.

The other act, which allows the governor to remove capital trials out of the province even to England, seems calculated with a most barefaced design to screen the soldiers and custom-house officers from punishment, when they should be guilty of any excesses. As tho' a merciless soldiery and those harpies and blood-suckers the officers of the customs would not be rigorous enough in executing these arbitrary laws, without a promise of impunity. For who would run the risk to cross the atlantic, more than 3000 miles to carry on a prosecution against them? Or if adventrous eno', how would it be possible to procure evidence? The language of it therefore is nearly this, let the soldiers commit what murders they please, they shall be liable to no punishment therefor.

Think now what a dreadful situation a people must be in, with an army of soldiers quartered among them; with another army of tax-gatherers encamped in all their trading places: both of which know they are sent for the express purpose of bearing down and humbling the people; and that to encourage them in their insolence, they have the greatest prospect of impunity, let them commit what crimes they please. These naturally insolent when under every restraint the civil authority can put them, what may it be expected they will be, when these restraints are taken away, and they as it were invited to be insolent and overbearing to the people? What hopes of redress can a people entertain, let them be injured ever so much? Let individuals in Boston be allowed as wicked as any are disposed to make them; yet surely the people have reason to complain of these acts, which inflict a punishment so far exceeding the crime; involve the innocent with the guilty, and are such complete engines of tyranny in the hands of any that shall be wicked enough to improve them as such.

Again the *Quebec government act* the colonies have just reason to complain of. First as it establishes the *popish* religion: by the articles of capitulation the inhabitants of Canada were indeed to have a toleration, but not an establishment. But *popery* is now established, tythes are collected by law for it's support; which shews such a disregard for the *protestant* religion as we never should expect in the reign of one of the house of *Hanover*, who were called to the British throne to be guardians of the protestant religion. And tho' there are thousands of English settled in that province, yet no provision is made for the support of a protestant clergy; there is only a reserve, that the king may make such provision, if he sees fit. Now when such favour is shewn to the bloody religion of Rome, it argues either a *favourable* disposition in the parliament towards that religion; or that it is done, in order to carry on some other *favorite* scheme. Again trials by juries are abolished by this act: which is injurious, at least to the English inhabitants, who under the faith of a royal proclamation, promising English privileges have settled there. As the government of Canada is now entirely after the model of the arbitrary government of France, 'tis to be feared this is designed as a precedent for what is to be done in the other colonies; or at least we may suppose, without much conjecture, that the French inhabitants of Canada are gratified with an establishment of *popery* and a restoration of their former laws; to engage them to be *true* to the ministry in any future struggles with the colonies: A military government is continued there; that they may always have a good body of troops at hand, to join the Canadians and Indians to pour down upon the back of us, if the ministry should find occasion to use them. And that this *French* arbitrary government may take in as much of America as possible, it's limits are extended southward to the Ohio, and westward to the Missisippi: so that it comprehends an extent of teritory almost as large as all the other provinces. When this vast extent of territory comes to be filled up with inhabitants, near half America will be under this arbitrary *French* government. So that upon the whole the Quebec act doubtless wears as threatning an aspect upon Americans as any act that hath been passed by the British parliament. Thus I have hinted to you some of the principal grievances which the Americans judge they labour under from the *late* acts of the British parliament.

Indulge me a little longer while I endeavour to point out what we have *just* reason to fear the consequences of these measures will be. If we view the whole of the conduct of the ministry and parliament, I do not see how any one can doubt but that there is a settled fix'd plan for *inslaving* the colonies, or bringing them under arbitrary government, and indeed the nation too. The present parliament have ever been (by all accounts) more devoted to the interest of the ministry, than perhaps ever a parliament were. Now notwithstanding the excellency of the British constitution, if the ministry can secure a majority in parliament, who will come into all their measures, will vote as they bid them; they may rule as absolutely as they do in *France* or *Spain*, yea as in *Turkey* or *India*: And this seems to be the present plan to secure a majority of parliament, and thus enslave the nation with their own consent. The more places or pensions the ministry have in their gift; the more easily can they *bribe* a majority of parliament, by bestowing those places on them or their friends. This makes them erect so many new and unnecessary offices in America, even so as to swallow up the whole of the revenue. The king is not at all the richer for these duties. But then by bestowing these places—places of considerable profit and no labour, upon the children or friends, or dependants of the members of parliament, the ministry can secure them in their interest. This doubtless is the great thing the ministry are driving at, to establish arbitrary government with the consent of parliament: And to keep the people of England still, the first exertions of this power are upon the colonies. If the parliament insist upon the right of taxing the colonies at pleasure, the least we can expect is, to be tax'd as heavily as we can possibly bear, and yet support our lives; for as the members of parliament feel no burdens themselves by what they lay upon us, and are under no danger of losing their places by taxing us, so long as they can persuade the people of England they are lightening their burdens thereby; they are under no motives of interest to abstain from loading us with taxes as heavy as we can possibly groan under. Doubtless they will be cautious enough, to introduce these heavy taxes gradually, lest they excite too great commotions in this country: But let the *right* be once fix'd and established; it will be very easy to keep adding tax to tax; till the loads grow so heavy and are so fast bound, that we can never shake them off. Nothing most certainly but a principle of justice will keep them from it; and what can we expect from this quarter, when in open defiance of the *English* constitution, they claim a right to tax us, and thus deprive us of our dearest privileges?

In the mean time we must expect our *charters* will fall a sacrifice to these arbitrary claims. Charter governments have long been disagreable to the powers in Britain. The *free* constitution of these colonies makes them such nurseries of freemen as cannot fail to alarm an arbitrary ministry. They only wait a favourable opportunity to abolish their charters, as they have done that of the Massachusetts-Bay. We know the principle the parliament have adopted and openly profess to act upon, that they have a right to alter or annihilate charters when they judge it convenient: And we may depend upon it, whenever they shall think it can be done without raising too great commotions in the colonies, they will judge it convenient. Some may imagine it was the destroying the tea induced the parliament to change the government of the Massachusetts-Bay. If it was, surely 'tis very extraordinary to punish a whole province and their posterity thro' all ages, for the conduct of a few individuals. How soon will a riot or some disorder of a few individuals, afford them a pretext for the like treatment of all the other charter governments. I believe, however, it may be made very evident, that the destroying the tea was not the reason for altering the government of the Massachusetts-Bay; but that it was a fix'd plan long before, and they only waited a colourable pretext for carrying it into execution. It has been reported by gentlemen of unquestionable veracity, that they had incontestible evidence that the two bills for altering the government of the Massachusetts-Bay were ordered by the council to be drawn up by the crown lawyers more than two years ago. Now if this be true (as it undoubtedly is) 'tis quite certain the ministry were only waiting for some colourable pretext for carrying their design into execution. The charter governments are by this precedent reduced not merely to the greatest uncertainty of the continuance of their charters; but may be quite certain, if the present plan is prosecuted, they will be taken away, and these colonies reduced, (if nothing worse) to the state of the royal governments; their governors, councils, judges, &c. will be appointed from England, with high and extravagant salaries.

There is great reason to fear the next step will be the vacating all grants and patents of land from the king; that all our landed property may revert to his majesty; to be regranted under such *quit rents and services* as those in power shall see fit to impose: Nor will *this fear* appear chimerical to any one that duly considers what hath been already done, and what the plan is, which the ministry are doubtless pursuing. 'Twould be weak policy indeed for an arbitrary ministry to push with all their horns at first. But certainly it doth not require very great sagacity to see that their measures are tending to this. When it was resolved to introduce arbitrary and despotic government into the colonies in the reign of king JAMES 2d. when Sir *Edmond Andross* was governor of New-England; the *first* step was to vacate the charters; the very *next* to revoke the grants of land that had been made:* which was done, in his short administration in a great number of instances; and people were obliged to take out *new* patents at a most exorbitant price. We see our charters are already struck at; a claim is advanced by the parliament to dissolve them at pleasure: And what is there more sacred in grants of land, than in charters; that the former may not be annulled with as much right as the latter. Our fathers when they planted this wilderness, placed equal

---

* The charter being vacated, the people were told that their titles to their estates were of no value. The expression in vogue was, that "the calf died in the cow's belly." "The fees for the patents varied according to circumstances both of persons and estates. In the complaint to king James, it is alleged that the fees of some amounted to 50l. Prudence was used. Men's titles were not questioned all at once. Had this been the case according to the computation then made, all the personal estates in the colony, would not have paid the charge of the new patents."

Gov. Hutchinson's Hist. Mas. vol. i. *p.* 359.

confidence in the royal word pledged in their charters; as in the patents by which they held their land: and deemed the privileges granted in the former of as much worth; as the property granted by the latter. The principle upon which the parliament proceeded in vacating the Massachusetts charter; will equally warrant them, whenever they shall see fit, to vacate all our grants of lands, i. e. when they shall judge it expedient, or for the good of the nation. If the parliament should once take it into their wise heads, that it is expedient, or for the general good, that all lands in America should revert to the crown, that they may be regranted all upon the same tenure,—upon large *quit-rents* to defray the charges of government; what will hinder their carrying it into execution? And indeed the Boston *port act* doth actually afford us a precedent of the exercise of this power: all their wharves and water-lots round the whole of Boston bay, are really *confiscated* to the king (as we have already shewn.) Now what is this but a vote of parliament to take away our landed property. And that power which hath been once exercised have we not all reason to fear will be exercised again.

And have we not just grounds to fear that all this will not be the completion of their oppressive plan, if the ministry find themselves successful in their first attempts? By the *Quebec-Act* we find the parliament claim a power to establish in *America*, the same arbitrary government that takes place in *France*.—To take away trials by juries:—to set aside general assemblies:—to vest the king with a power to appoint legislative councils &c. Now this act not only respects the *French* inhabitants (who having been long used to slavish subjection, and not knowing the benefit of any other form of government, are possibly well eno' pleased with it, especially as the pill is gilded over with a full establishment of that religion, of which they are such bigotted professors); but it respects thousands of *English*, who have settled there since the conquest, and all such as may settle any where within that vast extended province in future time. By the same right they could establish this form of government over the *English* in Canada; they may do it in the other provinces. In the province of the Massachusetts-Bay, the important privilege of being tried by a jury, is greatly *lessened* by setting aside the equitable and impartial method by which juries were wont to be panel'd. Viewing the things that have taken place, is it without foundation that I express my fears, that the British ministry will e'er long find our general assemblies troublesome things?—a hindrance to government and the like, and so set them aside, under a notion of their being *inexpedient*, and lodge the whole legislative power in a council appointed by the king. This is the very thing that took place in *Sir Edmond*'s time. The whole legislative power was lodged in him and his council. And since the previous steps are so like what took place then, why may we not expect the consequent ones will be so too? And very likely the ministry may find *juries* equally a bar to the government they mean to establish: and so may persuade the parliament, on the footing of expediency to abolish them likewise.

And when our civil rights and privileges shall have thus fallen a sacrifice to tyranny and oppression, our religious liberties cannot long survive: for where hath it ever been known that civil and ecclesiastical tyranny and despotism have not yet gone hand in hand together. The latter is so necessary to uphold and support the former, that arbitrary princes or ministers of state have ever found their interest in the encouragement of it. And should America be forced to yield in the present struggle for civil liberty, we have no reason to expect but ecclesiastical tyranny, in some shape or other, will like a mighty torrent overspread our land. Those princes on the British throne since the reformation, who have been most disposed to trample upon the rights of the people, and to rule in an arbitrary and despotic manner; have ever caressed the papists and shewn a favourable disposition towards the bloody religion of Rome, as that religion is the surest prop to tyranny and despotism. This is evident during the reigns of all the several kings of the house of *Stewart*. Papists shared in the royal favour and were sheltered under royal protection. Continual attempts were made to bring the church of England to a greater conformity to the despotic church of Rome; 'till James 2d. more adventurous than his predecessors boldly attempts to subvert the constitution both in state and in church;—to introduce both tyranny and popery: which so alarmed the nation that they dethroned the tyrant; and placed a confirmed protestant on the British throne. Some late transactions shew a very favourable disposition in the present ministry and parliament towards the religion of Rome; how far they may attempt to introduce *it* into the English nation both in Britain and the colonies, God only knows. But thus much we may safely guess, without much danger of erring, that to introduce episcopacy with all those formidable powers with which it was clothed (which indeed were no obscure resemblance of the church of Rome) before the acts of parliament restraining and regulating prelatic power and ecclesiastical courts, passed in consequence of the revolution, will be a darling object with the present ministry, if they see a prospect of being able to carry their designs into execution. For ecclesiastical government must be conformed to the civil, and nothing short of this would be in any measure suited to the genius of that civil policy they are evidently aiming to establish in the colonies. And tho' such an establishment might not introduce fire and faggots; yet depositions of the clergy, fines, imprisonment, disfranchisements, confiscations, &c. with various corporal penalties, you may depend upon it, will be its dire attendants.

All these things, I make no doubt, will take place one after another, as fast as the ministry can bring their measures to bear; unless something occur in God's providence to hinder them.

View now the situation of America: loaded with taxes from the British parliament, as heavy as she can possibly support under,—our lands charged with the most exorbitant quit rents,—these taxes collected by foreigners, steeled against any impressions from our groans or complaints, with all the rapaciousness of Roman publicans—our charters taken away—our assemblies annihilated,—governors and councils, appointed by royal authority without any concurrence of the people, enacting such laws as their sovereign pleasure shall dictate—judges appointed from the same source, without any check from juries carrying their arbitrary laws into execution.—the lives and property of Americans entirely at the disposal of officers more than three thousand miles removed from any power to controul them—armies of soldiers quartered among the inhabitants, who know the horrid purpose for which they are stationed, in the colonies,—to subjugate and bear down the inhabitants—who know what a chance they stand for impunity, tho' they commit the greatest excesses. These will be ready, not only to execute every arbitrary mandate of their despotic masters; but self-moved (if like others of their profession) to commit every outrage upon the defenceless inhabitants.—Robberies, rapes, murders, &c. will be but the wanton sport of such wretches without restraint let loose upon us.—These will be at hand by force and arms to quell every rising murmur, to crush every rising groan or complaint e'er it be uttered. And whenever the iron hand of oppression shall excite opposition or raise insurrections among the people: (which will ever be the case under arbitrary and despotic government, till long use has rendered their necks callous and insensible to the galling yoke) Blood-thirsty soldiers will be let loose upon them. Those who survive their murdering hands and have the misfortune to be taken captive by them, will soon be dragged, by the sentence of more merciless judges, to the place of execution.—Nothing shall then be heard of but executions, forfeitures of estates, families reduced to beggery, orphans crying for bread, and such like scenes of distress. The spirits of the people soon grow depress'd—Industry and public spirit die away—Learning, Virtue and Religion are soon extinguished.—No comfort or happiness to be enjoyed in social life, every one will be jealous and distrustful of his nearest friends and neighbours. To such a dreadful state as this, my countrymen, the present measures seem to be swiftly advancing. What free-born Englishman can view such a state of abject slavery as this, tho' at the greatest distance, without having his blood boil with indignation?

Some perhaps may be ready to think the issue of these measures cannot be so bad as has been described. No wonder men used to freedom cannot at once realize all the horrors of slavery. But this is no worse a state, than what now actually takes place in a great part of the world: and why will not the same government produce the same effects in America?

Others may think the British ministry cannot have so bad a scheme as this in view, that officers appointed by the crown cannot be so cruel and barbarous as hath been represented. Probably the ministry mayn't have it all in view at present: probably these officers would not at first be so cruel and barbarous, but there is no telling what men will soon become when entrusted with arbitrary power: such power will more surely intoxicate men than the strongest spirits: the best of men cannot be safely trusted with it. Many men amiable in private life have become monsters of cruelty when entrusted with arbitrary power: such were many of the Roman emperors. Should governors and councils appointed by the crown be entrusted with legislative power over the colonies, and be supported by armies of soldiers quartered among the people, I see not what (according to the ordinary course of things) would keep them from even greater excesses than I have mentioned.

Or should the colonies refuse to receive the chains prepared for them, and the present measures issue in a hostile rupture between Great Britain and the colonies, which God forbid, and which I wish the ministry may not have in view to promote, see what precautions they have early taken either to ruin us, or force us to subjection. To the Canadians who have been long inured to arbitrary government, and so are become fit tools for inslaving others, they have granted an establishment of their religion, the restoration of their former laws, &c. to attach them to their interest:—have continued Canada a military government that they may have store of forces at hand; that they may let loose these with all the force of Canada and all the northern tribes of Indians upon our exposed and helpless frontiers. What else can they have in view in trying so much to gratify the French inhabitants of that province?

Now if the British parliament and ministry continue resolved to prosecute the measures they have entered upon, it seems we must either submit to such a dreadful state of slavery as hath been shewn will be the probable issue of their measures, or must by force and arms stand up in defence of our liberties. The thoughts of either of which is enough to make our blood recoil with horror. Can any person survey the events that have taken place, and yet remain so stupid as not to be shocked at the dreadful prospect before us? Is there a wretch so unfeeling, as not to feel grieved and affected at the injured and violated liberties of America? Is there that tool of arbitrary power among the free-born sons of America, that will dare hold up his head in defence of such measures as these? If there be any such, I am sure I cannot find it in my heart to wish them worse, than to feel the iron rod of slavery, that is now strook over America, till they are brought to a sounder mind.*

Having thus given a brief account of the late acts of the British parliament respecting the colonies;—of the grievances the colonies labour under therefrom, and of what the probable consequences of these measures will be, I will very briefly touch upon the last thing proposed viz. what can be done by us in such an alarming crisis.—Some perhaps may think me already too bold in speaking thus freely of the acts of the most respectable legislature in the British empire. But the more I consider the shocking tendency of them, the more difficult I find it to restrain myself within the bounds of decency.—I am sure however there is nothing *treasonable* in feeling oppession when oppressed—nor in groaning under the anguish of it—as yet I have done little more than express this.—Surely it cannot be *treason* to feel our burdens and weep and mourn and pray on account of them. To pray to God for redress is certainly innocent, and happy it is we have heaven to go to, tho' our prayers should be denied on earth. God hath once and again in answer to prayer wrought eminent deliverance for the oppressed. Remember how he delivered the Jews from Haman's cursed devices. Oft hath he delivered his people of old;—oft the people of New-England;—this affords great encouragement to be fervent in our supplications to the throne of grace.

---

* Such wretches as can meanly crouch to justify the late measures respecting the colonies may, for aught I know, be justly tax'd by the British parliament, as having given their consent, & could they be separated from the rest, I should have no great objection to their wearing the chains, they are so assiduously seeking to bring upon themselves, at least for a while. This thought, with the mean servility with which some *few* in the colonies justify the late unconstitutional acts of parliament taxing the colonies, &c. brings to my mind a short story related in Rider's History of England, vol. 22, p. 76.

"When Waller (the poet) was young, he had the curiosity to go to court; and he stood in the circle, and saw (James the first) dine; where among other company there were two Bishops, Neile and Andrews. The king with an audible voice proposed this question, Whether he might not take his subjects money when he wanted it, without all this formality of parliament? Neile replied, 'God forbid you should not, for you are the breath of our nostrils.' Andrews declined giving an answer, as he was not, he said, conversant in parliamentary cases; but upon the king's pressing him, and saying he would admit of no apology, the Bishop replied with much humour, 'Why then I think your majesty may very lawfully take my brother Neile's money; for he offers it.'"

The king's heart is in the hand of the Lord, as the rivers of water: he turneth it whithersoever he will. But little will prayer avail us without unfeigned repentance and humiliation before God under the heavy frowns of his righteous providence. We have more reason to be afraid of the vice and wickedness that abounds among us, than of all the arms of Britain. These give us reason to fear lest we have not virtue enough to make use of the properest means of redress, and lest heaven should fight against us. Were a general reformation to take place I make no doubt heaven would find a way for our relief. The present alarming situation of things therefore loudly calls upon us to examine what sins in particular have provoked heaven thus to come out in judgment against us; and perhaps there cannot be a better rule of determining than to enquire what sins these calamities are properly retributive of, and by this rule will not the enslaving the poor *Africans* in the colonies stand forth in the front of the dreadful catalogue? Are not the colonies guilty of forcibly depriving them of their natural rights? Will not the arguments we use in defence of our own liberties against the claims of the British parliament, equally conclude in their favour? And is it not easy, to see there is something retributive in the present judgments of heaven? We keep our fellow men in slavery—heaven is suffering others to enslave us. Again I must mention worldliness, covetousness, selfishness, dishonesty, disobedience to constitutional authority, and many other vices as contained in the dismal train, and for which we need to repent and humble ourselves before God; but as this is a topic handled in the preceding sermon 'tis altogether needless for me to enlarge upon it.

But if ever we would hope for redress from the grievances we labour under; 'tis not only necessary that we repent, reform and pray; but that we unitedly prosecute the most firm and prudent measures for the attainment of it. A very little attention must convince every one of the necessity of our being united. If the colonies are divided or the people in the several colonies are very considerably divided, we are undone. Nothing but the united efforts of America can save us: and if united, they must have that weight, which gives me the most sanguine hopes of success. It should then be the concern of every one to labour as far as his influence extends, to promote this necessary union. The determinations of the congress of delegates from the several colonies may be deemed the general voice of America. A concurrence with these we should every one labour to promote. If in every particular we should not be entirely suited; yet the dreadful consequences of disunion should make us cautious how we let it be known. The Congress we hear have come into a conclusion that we *import* no British goods. This is a measure for redress, of which we may very safely and easily make trial. We can with a little self-denial do without the superfluities we receive from Britain. This will doubtless be distressing to the Mother Country and may convince them of the necessity of continuing to us our dear bought rights and privileges. No friend of his country can hesitate a moment in such a cause to deny himself the superfluities of Britain. And should the Congress agree also upon *non-exportation*; and extend both this and the other, not only to Great-Britain but to Ireland and the West-Indies; a general compliance with which, will most certainly, according to the ordinary course of things, ensure us redress, and of which necessity most certainly will be a sufficient justification: Should this I say be agreed upon by the Congress; none I hope will be so inimical to his country, as to attempt to break the general union by refusing to comply therewith. But should there be any such; it becomes every one, that hath any regard to the liberties of his country, to treat with deserved neglect and abhorrence the wretch, that thus meanly seeks his own emolument upon the ruins of his country's liberties:—To break off all trade and dealings with such selfish miscreants; and make them sensible, that without injuring their lives or property, their injured country can make them feel the weight of her vengeance, and rue the day they ever suffered a selfish spirit to banish all love to their country from their breasts. Here is a sphere in which every one can contribute something to save his sinking country from ruin. Suffer me then to intreat you (of the western parts of the colony of Connecticut) in some proper way to shew your hearty concurrence with other parts of the continent in the cause of American liberty; and your resolution to concur with, and endeavour to carry into execution the conclusions of the American Congress; and to open your hearts to commiserate, and contribute to the relief of the suffering poor of the town of Boston. What hath been said I trust makes it sufficiently appear, that they are suffering in the common cause of American liberty. Allowing the conduct of those individuals who destroyed the tea as criminal as any are disposed to make it, yet the punishment is beyond all bounds disproportionate to the crime:—the innocent are involved with the guilty:—the requirements of the act are such, that it can never be known whether complied with or not:—The act is as compleat an instrument of tyranny as ever was formed.— If the requirements of the act should be complied with; yet all their estates lying in wharves, water-lots, &c. will still lie at the king's mercy. So that the act cannot be complied with without giving up the struggle for liberty. The design in bearing thus hard upon one colony is evidently to divide the colonies; and thus to bring them one after another to submit to the arbitrary claims of parliament. All their means of sub- sistence depended on their trade, which by this act is wholly taken away. So that without assistance from the other colo- nies, they must inevitably yield, unless so very patriotic, as to be willing to starve to death. Our turn may soon come when we may want the like kind assistance from our brethren. Only apply the golden rule of "doing to others as we would that they should do unto us," and surely we cannot hesitate to contribute to their relief. We in this colony are situated nearer to them and on various accounts are more nearly connected with them than most of the other colonies. Our trade hath been principally with them;—our religion and manners are very similar to theirs:—We originated mainly from the same ancestors; most of our towns derived their first inhabitants from that province; the rest are descended from ancestors that left their native land for the same cause with the Massa- chusetts planters: So that it will be to our lasting shame, if more backward to contribute to their relief, than other colo- nies much more remote, and under no such special connec- tions as we are. Many towns in the eastern and northern parts of this colony have sent very generously to their relief, others are now making collections for this purpose. But I hear noth- ing of any collections for Boston either in Fairfield or

New-Haven counties.* I should be very sorry if we in the western parts of the colony should prove the most backward. Providence hath bless'd us with plentiful crops, and thereby hath amply furnished us with the means of contributing to their relief, if we have hearts to use them. I wish the importance of contributing to the relief of Boston might be duly attended to, and that some measures might be come into in all our towns for trying the generosity of people for this purpose. I am sure they that have a sense of the worth of liberty and the importance of making a firm yet decent and harmless opposition to these oppressive measures, which are calculated to rivit the chains of slavery both upon us and our posterity, cannot hesitate a moment to contribute something generous for the relief of that suffering people. May Americans be united in a just sense of the worth of their civil rights and privileges, and in every laudable and righteous method for obtaining redress; and God grant their struggles in so glorious a cause may be crowned with happy success.

FINIS.

---

* I have heard since writing the above, that a handsome collection is likely to be made in the town of Fairfield: and that subscriptions are opened for the like purpose in the town of Stratford.

[Charles Lee], Strictures on a Pamphlet, Entitled, a "Friendly Address to All Reasonable Americans, on the Subject of Our Political Confusions." Addressed to the People of America. The Second Edition. New London, 1775.

In February 1775 the British government offered a mixed message of both carrot and stick. Lord North made a Conciliatory Proposal in Parliament that was designed to pick off the colonies one by one by promising not to tax any colony that voluntarily contributed to the support of the empire. At the same time Parliament responded to the Continental Congress's Declaration and Resolves by proclaiming Massachusetts in a state of rebellion and calling upon the king "to take the most effectual measures to enforce due obedience to the laws and authority of the supreme legislature." Actually the ministry had already decided upon the use of force and in January had ordered Governor-General Gage "to restore the vigour of Government" in Massachusetts.

The time had come for military men to step to the fore. Charles Lee was born in England and schooled in Switzerland before securing a commission in the British army. After serving in North America during the Seven Years War, he saw action as a colonel in the Portuguese army fighting the Spaniards and later with the Polish army. Returning to England, he became a fervid republican, complaining about the "dolt," George III. In 1773 he came to America as an enthusiastic supporter of the patriot cause. Although he was warmly embraced by Americans because of his military background, he was a troubled, argumentative man who easily made enemies.

Originally published in several cities as a pamphlet in late 1774, and reprinted in the newspapers of at least four colonies, Lee's pamphlet was a hard-hitting refutation of Chandler's *Friendly Address*. This second edition of 1775 was published in New London with a preface written by Silas Deane, who in 1776 became one of the commissioners in Paris charged with negotiating a military and commercial alliance with France.

The optimism of Lee's professional assessment of the difficulties British armies would face in America helps account for the pamphlet's popularity. The British people were "lost in corruption and lethargy," he wrote, and their armies were "composed of the refuse of an exhausted nation, few of whom have seen action of any kind." It was very doubtful that such an army would "be able to conquer two hundred thousand active, vigorous yeomanry, fired with the noble ardor, we see prevalent through the continent." If they were persuaded by Lee's assertion "that all the essentials necessary to form infantry for real service may be acquired in a few months," Americans could feel confident that they had the military capacity to take on the greatest power in the world.

STRICTURES

ON A

PAMPHLET,

ENTITLED,

A

"FRIENDLY ADDRESS

TO

ALL Reasonable AMERICANS,

ON THE

Subject of our political Confusions."

ADDRESSED TO THE

PEOPLE OF *AMERICA*.

" Let's canvass Him in his broad Cardinal's Hat."

Shakespear.

The SECOND EDITION :

To which is prefixed

An ADVERTISEMENT,

Wrote by a Gentleman in *CONNECTICUT*.

PHILADELPHIA, Printed :
NEW-LONDON : Re-printed and sold by T. GREEN.

M.DCC.LXXV.

ADVERTISEMENT.

SINCE the proceedings of the Continental Congress have been published, a profligate, venal printer, and two prostituted and shameless high church clergymen, in and near the city of New-York, have been incessantly employed, by every means in their power, to prevent their taking effect—with little prospect of success; still they are indefatigable; and no doubt the unparallel'd unanimity which prevails throughout this continent, operates on their slavish and malicious tempers, as a sting to urge them on, to the last extremes of folly, madness and desparation. The first piece which made its appearance, was intitled, *A friendly Address to all reasonable Americans*: since which, a number under various titles, have been published, all running so exactly in one stile, as to leave not the least doubt of their being children of the same parents. *The friendly Address*, on which the following strictures were made, has probably been read but by few, in this colony; nor is it very necessary, as the author of these strictures has faithfully referr'd to all, that is very material in the address, except the railing and abuse, with which it abounds, and of which these gentlemen appear so very fond, that it was thought best to let them enjoy them undisturbed, as their proper sphere to move and be distinguished in. The views of the friendly addressor, evidently are, to intimidate the colonists from defending their rights, by exaggerating the force that may be brought against them,—their own weakness and inability to resist, in case of any extremity, and the dreadful consequences of opposition.

As many weak persons, into whose hands the address may fall, or to whom particular passages of it may be recited, may through want of a full acquaintance with the truth of these facts, be led into wrong conclusions, the following strictures, are thought by many, deserving a new impression, and with this view, are sent to the press.

The authors of the pieces published against the proceedings of the Congress, have, without exception, gone no farther in argument, (if really their writings can deserve the name), than to take for granted, in the first place, the capital matter in

383

controversy—"*the supreme and unlimited power of parliament, to make laws, binding on the colonies, in all cases whatever*," and then have fell to abusing the Congress, and their constituents, for attempts to oppose this power. Their standing printer, is well known to deserve the character given him here,—has been proscribed, as to his papers, or publications, by some of the first provinces on the continent, and by a great majority of individuals in all of them; but he is doubtless looking for fame on any terms, and justly concludes, that being active in destroying the liberties of a continent, may as fairly intitle him to it, as the burning a temple, or any other such gallant exploit. And that the author, now well known to be a clergyman, with his brother in office, are justly characterized, the address, with the rest of their productions abundantly evinces. Take one sentiment of this reverend abuser of the liberties of America, and their supporters, as a sample of the whole. In justifying the Quebec bill, and its authors, he asserts,—That Americans and their affairs, had much better, in his opinion, be under the direction and management of the Roman catholics of Canada, or elsewhere, than of the dissenters of New England. If then, the author of this advertisement, has been wrong, in calling him a *prostituted high church clergyman*, he has, and is willing, to ask his, and the public's pardon; but the times calling upon us to treat men and things as what they really are, if the world judge the character just, it certainly is not unseasonably applied.

Z.

Strictures, &c.

To the PEOPLE of AMERICA.

A PAMPHLET, entitled *A friendly Address to all reasonable Americans*, advertised and sold by Mr. James Rivington, of New-York, is, of so extraordinary a nature that it is difficult for any Man, who is interested in the welfare of the Community (whatever contempt he may have for the performance,) to remain silent.—I know not whether the author is a Layman or Ecclesiastick, but he bears strongly the characters of the latter. —He has the want of candour and truth, the apparent spirit of persecution, the unforgivingness, the deadly hatred to Dissenters, and the zeal for arbitrary power, which has distinguished Churchmen in all ages, and more particular the *high* part of the Church of England; I cannot help therefore considering him as one of this order.

The design of his Pamphlet is manifestly to dissolve the spirit of union, and check the noble ardor prevailing through the continent; but his zeal so far out-runs his abilities, that there is the greatest reason to think that his Reverence has laboured to little effect.—His discretion seems to be still less than his genius.—A man of common judgment would not so wantonly have attacked the general reigning principles and opinions of a People, whom he intends to seduce or intimidate out of their rights and privileges: For instance, I believe there are at least ninety-nine Americans in a hundred, who think that Charles the First was an execrable tyrant, that he met with no harder fate than he deserved, and that his two sons ought in justice to have made the same exit. To descant therefore on the criminality of the resistance made to that tyrant; to affect on every occasion giving the title of rebellion to the civil war which brought him to justice, is a degree of weakness which no man who is not blinded by the dæmon of jacobitism could possibly be guilty of.—But to preach up in this enlightened age (as he does in almost express terms) passive obedience, is a mark of lunacy, or at least it proves that the moment a head begins to itch for a mitre, it loses the faculty of reasoning, for if the principle of passive obedience is admitted, the gracious Prince, for whom his Reverence professes so great a devotion is a down right usurper, and the Parliament of which he speaks so respectfully Lords and Commons, are rebels and traitors.

The doctrines he aims to inculcate are as follow—*That the Parliament has a right to tax you without your consent; that the duty upon tea is no tax; that this duty is your only grievance; that the cause of Boston is their own concern; that it is not your cause; that the punishment of Boston is a just punishment; that it is lenient; that it is not equal to their crimes; that the Bostonians are rebels, traitors, and pampered fanatics; that the Congress are little better; that no misconduct of administration can justify or excuse open disrespect; that submission is to be paid to the higher powers, whatever character they be; that an Apostle enjoined submission to the tyrant Nero; that of all people under heaven the Kings American subjects have the least cause for complaint; that the present confusion of the Colonies has been occasioned by false alarms; that none of your legal rights have been invaded; no injury has been done you, and consequently that you can never be justified in resenting that of which you have no reason to complain; that you are no judges of the rights of Parliament; that the Parliament ought to act according to their own judgment, not according to yours, even in things which concern you principally or solely; that they assert they have the right in question; that you have never proved they have not; that you have always believed or allowed they have it until the present occasion; that the Quebec Bill is a just and constitutional Bill; that the Canadians are likely to prove the best and most loyal subjects in his Majesty's American dominions; that there is too much reason to believe that the minds of the Americans are unprincipled, and their hearts disposed for rebellion; that since the reduction of Canada they have been bloated with a vain opinion of their own power and importance; that the Island of Great-Britain is able to govern* (that is to dragoon) *ten Americas; that the moment it is known that America is no longer under the protection of Great-Britain, all the maritime powers of Europe would join to ravage your sea ports, plunder and seize your ships merely for the pleasure of ravaging;* * *that all the maritime powers of the world*

---

* This is perhaps the most preposterous idea that ever was hatched in a distempered brain. America (more particularly since the distractions in Poland have taken place) has been the great granary or *cella penaria* of Europe.—Is it

would not dispossess Great-Britain of the empire of the sea even when America is separated from her. Now I challenge the whole world to produce so many wicked sentiments, stupid principles, audaciously false assertions, and monstrous absurdities crowded together into so small a compass. All his positions are indeed so self evidently, absurd and false, that it would be an insult to American understandings, seriously to attempt refuting them. I shall only beg leave to take notice of the curious argument he uses to prove the duty on tea to be no tax, it is that, *unless we consent to the tax we are not to pay the duty. We may refuse purchasing it if we please.* The same logic would demonstrate that a duty on beer, candles, or soap would be no tax, as we are not absolutely obliged to drink beer; we may drink water, we may go to bed before it is dark, and we are not forced to wash our shirts. His assertion that Great-Britain, when divorced from her Colonies, will still hold the empire of the seas in spite of all the powers of the world, is still more ingenious. It amounts to this, that *without the possible means of procuring timber, iron, plank, masts, pitch, tar, or hemp, to furnish out a single frigate, they may build more ships then all the world put together;* that *when her nursery for seamen is destroyed, and all the commerce on which the existence of seamen depends, is annihilated, they will then be able to man more fleets than the whole universe put together.* But I am ashamed of trespassing on the public patience, in making strictures on such ridiculous articles, I shall therefore pass to some questions which have not been so much agitated, and on which, if I mistake not, his reverence lays the greatest stress; for as he modestly declares, that he has no opinion of your courage, it was natural for him

---

possible to conceive that the different maritime powers should unite to deprive themselves of the chief means of subsistance, merely for the fun's sake? Is it not more natural to suppose they would out bid each other for your friendship and commerce on which so much depends? When the Low Countries withdrew themselves from the dominion of Spain, did England, France, and the other Powers immediately set about ravaging their sea ports and seizing their ships? Did they not, on the contrary, exert themselves directly and indirectly to assist them? The case is similar, the event would be similar; and that Great-Britain would not be powerful enough at sea, when separated from her Colonies; to prevent this assistance, I shall refer my readers to Massie's Estimates, the authority of which has never been disputed, and which demonstrate, that more than half the naval power of Great-Britain stands on her American foundation.

to consider intimidation and terror, as the most powerful figures of rhetoric. *Regular armies from Great-Britain, Hessians,
Hanoverians, royal standards erected, skilful Generals, legions of
Canadians, and unnumbered tribes of savages; swords flaming
in the front and rear, pestilence, desolation and famine,* are all
marshalled in a most dreadful order by this church militant
author.—But let us somewhat minutely examine the picture, and
see whether, stript of its false colouring, it has any thing really
terrifying. His reverence begins with assuring us, that there is
no room to doubt, but that such an army as was employed in
the reduction of Canada (that is an army of seven thousand
men) would be more than sufficient for the conquest of all the
disaffected American Colonies, (which are in fact all the Colonies.) Should *such* a resolution become necessary in order to
reduce them to obedience. For my own part I think there is
very great reason to doubt, that seven thousand, even of the best
troops, are able to conquer two hundred thousand of the most
disorderly peasantry on earth, if they are animated in defence
of every thing they hold most dear and sacred; and there is still
greater reason to doubt, that seven thousand very indifferent
troops, composed of the refuse of an exhausted nation, few of
whom have seen action of any kind, should be able to conquer
two hundred thousand active, vigorous yeomanry, fired with
the noble ardor, we see prevalent through the continent, all
armed, all expert in the use of arms almost from their cradles.
The success of Quebec it is true, does infinite honour to the
English arms, the army was, I believe, only seven thousand, the
enemy were perhaps more than double, but sixteen thousand
men are not two hundred thousand. The fate of Canada, depended upon one decisive action, but it is impossible to calculate how many victories must be gained before these Colonies
could be subdued, whereas a single victory gained by the Colonies must decide the contest in their favour. In the affair of
Quebec there is another circumstance to be considered, it was
Wolfe, who commanded; a man of the most wonderful talents,
formed to level all difficulties; to render the most despicable
soldiery, almost instantaniously, an army of Heroes.—In short,
the genius of the man was so extraordinary, the event was so
extraordinary that no inferences can be drawn from it; but this
without presumption may be asserted that no General now

existing in the British service, would with double or treble his number have succeeded in the same circumstances. One thing more I must add in honour of that illustrious personage, that the same greatness of soul which qualified him to conquer the natural hereditary enemies of his country, would have made him reject with horror the Hangman's office, which others who are not endowed with conquering attributes, will with readiness accept.

It is notorious that Mr. Wolfe was not only the first of soldiers, but that he was a most liberal virtuous citizen, that he was passionately attached to the liberties of his country, and of mankind; and that he was particularly an enemy to large standing armies in time of peace. It is on the other hand remarkable, that all the advocates for standing armies; all those who are the fondest of the saddling and parade of war are the most active in avoiding real service.

This tremendous soothsayer, on the supposition that so great a miracle should happen in our favour, as that the trifling body of five hundred thousand men though firmly united (for every man in America, firmly united, would not amount to less,) should be able to withstand his seven thousand; goes on to rattle in our ears, armies of Hessians and Hanoverians. I wish to Heaven he had for once deviated into probability and truth. I wish ten thousand of them could possibly be transported to morrow. The purpose they would answer, is a purpose devoutly to be wished for; they would be an addition to this continent of just so many useful and excellent citizens, for I will venture to affirm, (affirming is infectious) that in less than four months not two of these ten thousand would remain with their Colours. But does not this Reverend Gentleman know, that in the year 1764 a convention was formed by most of the Princes of the empire, at the head of which convention were the Emperor himself and the King of Prussia, to prevent the alarming emigrations which threatened depopulation to Germany? Does he not know that no troops can march out of the empire without the consent of the empire? Does he not know that the Elector of Hanover and the Emperor are upon exceedingly ill terms? Does he not know that the Elector of Hanover and the King of Prussia are still upon worse? Is he sure that the Landgrave of Hess would sell his troops (for as not one man would return back to their country, he must consider them as forever sold?) Is he sure that as the finances of Great-Britain stand, the vast sum necessary for this purchase would be conveniently found? Is he sure that the State of Hanover would consent to such a draining of their country? I know not how it is; but his most excellent Majesty GEORGE the Third, who in England is justly esteemed the most gracious of Sovereigns, the wisest, greatest, and best of Kings, is not very popular in the Electorate of Hanover. These people seem to think it hard that Two Hundred and Twenty Thousand Pounds should annually be drawn from them, for the purposes (as they conceive it) of corrupting the Members of St. Stephen's Chapel, in order to support the power and authority of a sett of men, who from the beginning have been enemies to the succession of the Hanover line, and who shewed a particular animosity to their last and favourite Prince, George the Second; but these difficulties (great and unsurmountable as to a common mortal they appear) our divine Exorcist has in an instant conjured down, and by a single motion of his enchanted wand, has transported whole armies, in spite of their respective Princes, and without the consent of their respective States, from the interior parts of Germany across the Atlantic into the plains of New-England and Pennsylvania. But he does not confine himself to the introduction of his Germans. He proceeds next to erect the Royal Standard, to which he tells us that all who have the courage to declare themselves now friends to government, will undoubtedly resort, and these he says in a good cause, will be of themselves formidable to their opposers: Dreadfully formidable they must be indeed: There would resort to it, let me see, (for the respectable town of Rye have declared themselves a kind of neutrals, *rather than friends to government*,) there would resort to it, Mr. Justice Sewell, the honourable Mr. Paxton, Brigadier Ruggles, and about eight or ten more mandamus Councilmen, with perhaps twice their number of Expectants, and not less than twenty of the unrecanted Hutchinsonian Addressers.—These the four Provinces of New-England alone would send forth.—New-York would furnish six, seven or probably eight volunteers from a certain knot, who are in possession or expectation of contracts, and the fourth part of a dozen of high flying Church of

England Romanised Priests.—I represent to myself the formidable countenance they will make, when arranged under the Royal or ministerial Standard; but what will add to the terror of the appearance, will be their Reverend Pontifex himself, whom I conceive marching in the front, an inquisitorial frown upon his brow, his bands and canonicals floating to the air, bearing a cross in his hands, with the tremendous motto. *In hoc signo vinces*, flaming upon it in capital letters of blood, leading them on, and exciting them to victory. It is impossible that men, who are not under an infatuation by the judgment of heaven should flatter themselves, that forty thousand American Yeomanry (for we are assured by the same great authority that more than forty thousand cannot be brought to action) should stand the shock of this dreadful Phalanx.

But I should beg pardon for attempting to be ludicrous upon a subject which demands our utmost indignation.—I shall now therefore on the presumption that the People of England should be so lost to sense, virtue and spirit as to suffer their profligate Misrulers to persevere in their present measures, endeavour to state to you what is their force, and what is yours.—I shall endeavour to remove the false terrors which this writer would hold out, in order to intimidate you from the defence of your liberties and those of your posterity, that he and his similars may wallow in sinecures and benefices heaped up from the fruits of your labour and industry.

Great-Britain has, I believe, of infantry at home (comprehend Ireland, and exclusive of the guards) fifteen thousand men.— They find the greatest difficulty in keeping the regiments up to any thing near their establishment—what they are able to procure are of the worst sort. They are composed of the most debauched Weavers 'prentices, the scum of the Irish Roman Catholics, who desert upon every occasion, and a few, very few, Scotch, who are not strong enough to carry packs—This is no exageration; those who have been lately at Boston, represent the soldiers there (one or two regiments excepted) as very defective in size, and apparently in strength: But we shall be told they are still regulars, & regulars have an irresistable advantage.—There is, perhaps, more imposition in the term *regular troops*, than in any of the jargon which issues from the mouth of a Quack Doctor. I do not mean to insinuate, that a disorderly mob are equal to a trained disciplined body of men; but I mean, that all the essentials necessary to form infantry for real service may be acquired in a few months.* I mean, that it is very possible for men to be cloathed in red, to be expert in all the tricks of the parade, to call themselves regular troops, and yet, by attaching themselves principally or solely to the tinsel and shew of war, be totally unfit for real service.—This, I am told, is a good deal the case of the present British Infantry: If they can acquit themselves tolerably in the puerile reviews exhibited for the amusement of royal Masters and Misses in Hyde Park or Wimbledon Common, it is sufficient.

In the beginning of the late war, some of the most esteemed regular regiments were sent over to this country; they were well dressed; they were well powdered; they were perfect masters of their manual exercise; they fired together in platoons; but fatal experience taught us, that they knew not how to fight.—While your Militia were frequently crowned with success, these regulars were defeated or baffled for three years successively in every part of the continent—at length, indeed, (after repeated losses and disgraces) they became excellent troops, but not until they had absolutely forgotten every thing which, we are assured, must render regulars quite irresistable. The corpse sent from this country under General Monkton was, I believe, for its number, one of the best armies that was ever led to conquest, and yet, if I have been rightly informed, there was not a single regiment of them that could got through the manual exercise, or at best, they performed it most wretchedly —It is likewise said, that when after their glorious and rapid conquest of Martinico, they were joined by the spruce regiments

---

* There connot be a stronger illustration of the truth here advanced, than the Prussian army.—They are composed of about one third of the King's own subjects, two thirds foreigners.—The third, consisting of his own subjects, are, when the exercising season is over, (which lasts six or seven weeks) suffered to return to their families, and attend to the business of husbandry—half of the other two thirds, consisting of foreigners, are not only permitted, but encouraged to work at their trades in the garrison towns, and never touch a musket for the rest of the year, so that, in fact, only one third are, in the modern language, to be called regular Soldiers;—these generally make their escape the first opportunity: It may be said, therefore, that the King of Prussia has gained all his victories with a sort of Militia.

from Europe; such was their uncouth appearance, that they were scarce honored with the title of Soldiers by those Gentlemen. Upon the whole, it is most certain, that men may be smartly dressed, keep their arms bright, be called regulars, be expert in all the anticks of a review, and yet be very unfit for real action.—It is equally certain, that a Militia, by confining themselves to essentials, by a simplification of the necessary manœuvres, may become, in a very few months, a most formidable infantry.—The Yeomanry of America have, besides infinite advantages, over the peasantry of other countries; they are accustomed from their infancy to fire arms; they are expert in the use of them:—Whereas the lower and middle people of England are, by the tyranny of certain laws almost as ignorant in the use of a musket, as they are of the ancient Catepulta. The Americans are likewise, to a man, skilful in the management of the instruments necessary for all military works; such as spades, pickaxes, hatchets, &c.—Taking, therefore, all circumstances into consideration, there will be no rashness in affirming, that this continent may have formed for action, in three or four months, an hundred thousand infantry: For as to the assertion of one friendly adviser, *that no more than forty thousand could act to advantage*, I confess I do not understand it, nor does he, I believe, understand himself.—If he means that sixty thousand men cannot be ranged in a field capable of containing only forty thousand, we shall all agree with him; but how in the operations of a war upon a vast continent double this number should be a disadvantage, I can have no conception.

Let one simple general plan be adopted for the formation and subdivision of your battalions; let them be instructed only in so much of the manual exercise as to prevent confusion, and accidents in loading and firing; let them be taught to form, to retreat, to advance, to change their front, to rally by their colours; let them be taught to reduce themselves from a line of fire to a line of impression, that is, from two deep, to four, six, or eight.—This is all so easy and simple, that it may be acquired in three months. Let some plan of this sort be adopted, I say, and there is no doubt but that, in the time I have prescribed, you may have an army on foot of seventy, eighty, or an hundred thousand men, equal to all the services of war.

Should this be admitted, it will still be objected, that you have no able officers to conduct you. I do not know that you have; but is it certain that those sent to dragoon you have better? I have taken some pains to inform myself what methods these Gentlemen, said to be bred to arms, take to qualify themselves in a superior degree for the profession. What is their routine of instruction? Do they read much? I am assured that they do not; from books alone the theory of war can be acquired, and the English service in times of peace affords them no practical lessons; for mounting guard once or twice a week, or the preparation for the review of a single regiment can never be esteemed as such.*

Another circumstance, Americans, may be added for your comfort. It has been allowed by some of the most candid of the regulars themselves, that during the last war upon this continent, your countrymen the provincial Field-Officers were in general more understanding and capable than their own of the same rank. But the history of the civil war in the year 1641, furnishes us with the strongest instances that excellent officers may be soon formed from Country Gentlemen, Citizens, Lawyers, and Farmers. The Parliament's army (or as our priestly writer would call them, the rebellious Republicans) were

---

* It is much to be lamented, that the Gentlemen of the Army do not apply more of the many leisure hours they have upon their hands to reading.—The majority of them are of a generous disposition, which, did they cultivate, by conversing with the great historians and orators of antiquity, and the more liberal political writers of our own country, a standing army would be something less an object of jealousy to all virtuous citizens.—We might perhaps see them instead of being advocates and partizans of the present Ministry, a check upon their wickedness.—I am inclined to think that few or none of the officers have condescended to inform themselves of the merit of the present contest.—Let me conjure them for once to read coolly and candidly the whole process, afterwards to lay their hands upon their hearts, and answer, whether the People of America in general, and of Boston in particular, are "more sinned against or sinning?"

Now I am upon the subject of the Officers of the Army, I take the opportunity of mentioning, with the respect due to him, one Gentleman of high rank amongst them—the tenure of his conduct while in command, was so liberal, and his letters, quoted in the House of Commons, were so fair, candid and friendly to this Continent, that he is entitled to the thanks of America.—He is indeed of a country that owes not only its prosperity but its existance to the same principles which actuate America.

chiefly composed of this class of men. In the beginning of this war, they were treated with the same affected contempt, and almost in the same opprobrious terms as you, the people of America, are by your friendly and decent adviser.

Whoever would infer from the tenore of these papers, that the writer is desirous of precipitating, or could look with indifference upon the calamities of a civil war, does him great injustice. He considers them with all the horror natural to a feeling man and honest citizen. He execrates the memory of those men to whom they may justly be attributed, but he is persuaded that they never originated, (at least in states of any considerable extent) in the turbulent dispositions of the people, nor in the arts of demagogues, but in the oppression of their rulers, in the wantonness, folly, pride, or avarice of Kings, Ministers, or Governors. The Grislers of Switzerland, the Granvels of Holland, the Lauds and Straffords of England, were the undoubted authors of the tragedies acted in their respective countries: And if this continent should be stained with the blood of a single citizen, it can never be charged to the unreasonable pretensions of the people, but to the Barnards, Hutchinsons, and some other traitors of a similar stamp.

He is convinced, that being prepared for a civil war is the surest means of preventing it; that to keep the swords of your enemies in their scabbards, you must whet your own.—He is convinced, that remonstrances, petitions, prayers and supplications will make no impression on our callous Court and abandoned Parliament; England, Ireland, America, even Guernsey, Jersey and Minorca are witnesses of their inefficacy.—He is convinced, that fear alone can operate; there are symptoms that it already begins to operate;—the monster, Tyranny, already begins to pant, press her now with ardor, and she is down; already the Ministry have expressed in their letters an inclination to make some concessions;—to meet you half way: Which, I suppose, may be construed thus, that as they find they have it not in their power to establish, by force, the despotism which they aimed at, they shall be very well satisfied, if you will just cede so much of your rights and privileges, as will enable them by extending their pecuniary influence and sapping your virtue, to take away the rest at their leisure.

There now remains, people of America, one consideration

which (however it may be taken) I think it my duty to offer. History tells us that the free states of Greece, Thebes, Sparta, Athens, and Syracuse, were all in their turns subjugated by the force or art of tyrants. They almost all in their turns recovered their liberty and destroyed their tyrants. The first act upon the recovery of their liberty was to demolish those badges of slavery, citadels, strong holds, and military tenements; the Switzers did the same; the people of England (lost in corruption and lethargy as they are) could never be prevailed upon to suffer barracks amongst them; even the courtly Blackstone is startled at the idea. No separate camps, no barracks, no inland fortresses says he, should be allowed; in fact, wherever barracks are, freedom cannot be said to exist, or she exists so lamely as scarcely to deserve the name.

It is worth your consideration Americans, whether these badges should remain or no. I shall now conclude, brave citizens, with invoking the Almighty God from whom all virtues flow, to continue you in that spirit of unanimity and vigour which must insure your success, and immortalize you through all ages, as the champions and patrons of the human race.

[Henry Barry], The Strictures on the Friendly Address Examined, and a Refutation of Its Principles Attempted. Addressed to the People of America. Boston, 1775.

Henry Barry was a young lieutenant in the 52nd Regiment of Foot of the British army stationed in Boston, and he was understandably eager to refute the disparaging picture of His Majesty's forces that Charles Lee had drawn. Not only were the British soldiers "highly trained and qualified for service," he argued, but the army in Boston was composed of many veterans led by "Generals of approved knowledge and experience in war." By contrast, the American yeomanry, "the most happy and comfortable of any in the world," was "ill prepared to support the fatigues, dangers and wants of long campaigns." Once engaged in fighting, they would "soon miss those solaces which domestic tranquility afforded them, and would revert to their pristine avocations and delights."

Henry published his pamphlet in January 1775, three months before the clash of arms at Lexington and Concord on April 19. The British, believing they were dealing only with mobs led by a few seditious instigators, sought to arrest the rebel leaders, seize their arms, and reassert royal control in Massachusetts. The loss of nearly 280 casualties to militiamen firing from behind trees and stone walls on the march back to Boston was eye-opening for the British commanders. Two months later at Bunker Hill the losses were even more stunning: the British suffered a thousand casualties, over forty percent of their force. General John Burgoyne explained why the British officers sent wave after wave of red coats up the hill into deadly fire. "The respect and control and subordination of Government," he said, "in great measure depends upon the idea that trained troops are invincible against any numbers or any position of untrained rabble; and this idea was a little in suspense since the 19th of April."

The experience at Bunker Hill changed the British perspective. The government now realized it was involved in a war, not a police action.

THE

STRICTURES

ON THE

FRIENDLY ADDRESS

EXAMINED,

AND

A Refutation of its Principles attempted.

ADDRESSED

TO THE

PEOPLE OF AMERICA.

Ne quid falſi dicere audeat, ne quid veri non audeat.

Printed in the Year 1775.

ADVERTISEMENT.

IF some small inaccuracies should occur, and he hopes there are no essential ones, the indulgence and candour of the public will make allowances for the hasty production of a day, without the use of books to which its author could have reference.

The Strictures on the Friendly Address Examined, &c.

FRIENDS, and FELLOW-SUBJECTS,

THE poisons which have lately been too lavishly scattered among you, call aloud for an antidote; and by their operations they appear to be of so deadly a kind as to require the immediate counteraction of some powerfully efficient recipe; till such an one is produced, a less forcible prescription may, by stopping their progress, be found salutary.

Of late two pamphlets have appeared, the authors of which the contending parties of this country seem to consider as the invulnerable champions of their different principles and interests, and each has therefore naturally attracted the attention of its friends and opposers; but the zeal of the whigs, in dispersing abroad their boasted and favourite production, has far outstripped that of the tories, who perhaps, not considering an appeal to the head as so adapted to the purposes of party as one to the heart, have not inserted the Friendly Address in a News-Paper;—have not considerably reduced its price; or sent it abroad gratis, as a stimulus to their friends:* These being the honours which party has conferred on the strictures on that performance, it may not be unamusing or unprofitable to examine on what foundation this boasted bulwark of faction is erected. This writer, like a true disciple of the noble author of the Characteristics, tries every thing by the touchstone of ridicule; but does he know that it can place all subjects, even the sacred precepts and mysteries of our holy religion, in the same point of view; and like the jaundiced eye, seeing through a tainted medium, reduce all objects, however varied in colours, to its own loathsome hue? He commences with a notable discovery from unerring signs, of his antagonist's profession; but I much query if any one, from his subsequent observations, would be induced to consider him a soldier.

---

* It is observable in these impressions, designed for general use, it has been thought adviseable to omit one of the best turned and best deserved compliments to an officer of high rank, that, in the compass of a small reading, I as yet remember to have seen:—Such insiduous arts, and such want of candor are inexcuseable, and would disgrace the noblest of causes.

The friends of British government in America are, I trust, not so contemptible as the picture of this stricturer would ludicrously display them; many have already declared their attachment to its cause, and fifty times their numbers, at present overwhelmed by popular fury, would in the day of trial avow it: I wish not to see *royal standards erected or swords flaming in the front and in the rear*, but alas! the melancholy face of affairs on this continent too strongly indicates it; and then I am convinced the regular troops would not on experience be found so contemptible as he endeavours to represent them; or that colony forces could be so easily raised and disciplined as he asserts: A *simplification* of manœuvres that can be learnt in *three months*, will not bring you, Americans, to that steadiness, that you shall with regularity and composure, like the English troops at Fontenoy, evolute in the face of a victorious and superior army: For my part, I will go further than even this rapid instructor, and engage to teach school-boys, with wooden guns on their shoulders, *to form and reduce from a line of fire to a line of impression* in half an hour; but to train men for war requires labour, experience and time; and to reduce them to perfect submission to every superior, is with difficulty effected in legal establishments, never in popular and tumultuous associations; deprived of that coersive power which in the former produces obedience, their leaders in vain seek by attentions and courtesies that compliance with their commands which the others derive from established undisputed authority.

A yeomanry like the American, the most happy and comfortable of any in the world, are but ill prepared to support the fatigues, dangers and wants of long campaigns; they would soon miss those solaces which domestic tranquility afforded them, and would revert to their pristine avocations and delights; their acquaintance with the use of implements of husbandry would stand them in but little stead, for to what purpose should they employ them? It has long been acknowledged a principle in war, that irregulars are not calculated for defence, but attack; their vigour and intrepidity may bear down all obstacles to the latter, but too surely they will fail in that patience and perseverance which is indispensably requisite for the former. When the New-England provincials, under General Pepperrell, in the year forty-five, attacked Louisbourg, they laughed at the regular methods of approach proposed to them, and by a concurrence of fortunate circumstances, united to valour, carried that important fortress; this is a fact which many of them can vouch, and most if not all the rest of them have heard repeatedly from their fathers, when recounting the atchievements of their youthful days; and they must then have also told them, that the petulance of their brave countrymen was more than once on the point of giving up that glorious enterprise.—Consider therefore, I adjure you, by those ties and relations which endear life, and strow flowers along the rugged path of its pilgrimage; consider, before you engage in an attempt of so serious, so hazardous a nature, as the opposing a royal and long constituted army, what may reasonably be expected from forces so liable to defections as the unrestrained and hastily levied troops of these colonies must ever be: Your numbers are also held forth to you as powerful and unconquerable, and I do not deny that on so extended a continent as this many armies of forty-thousand each might, in the various operations of a war, to advantage be employed; but supposing it possible for this even to be the case, what must be its unavoidable consequences? All your peasantry being engaged in martial expeditions, the land would want its culture, and a dearth in a very few months must infallibly ensue, which would deprive your soldiers of even necessary sustenance,* for they must forego at the commencement every idea and wish for their accustomed luxuries: Are you yet to be told that there are diseases which are endemic to a camp, and that when famine with "baneful smile" stalks through its avenues she will add fresh poignancy and malignancy to its inseparable disorders? From most of these evils your opponents will be free; from long practice their constitutions are habituated to the fatigues of the most rigid discipline, they may feel distemper but they are better enabled to repel it than you, unused to hardships, can possibly be; nor will they be haunted by the smallest dread of want; your ports, blocked up by the navy of England, though denying you relief, will afford them plentiful supplies, and in

---

* To strengthen this observation, Germany last war afforded melancholy proofs to what distress a country is reduced, when occupied by contending armies.

case of defeat a most sure retreat till augmented by numerous and powerful reinforcements; for remember, that Great-Britain, during last war, did at one time carry conquest through every quarter of the globe, and that you assisted her only in this.

Hitherto, Americans, I have only pointed out to you the instability of your own force; it behoves you as you have examined how far you can rely with safety on it to change the scene, and see how it stands opposed to that of your antagonists, and here the prospect is different, taught to conquer by discipline, they firmly confide in what they know is irresistable; and not distracted by jarring principles and movements; with them every part of the machine acts in harmony and concord, and every spring and every wheel conspires to produce its necessary efficient force.

It matters not of what persons armies are composed, since the profession has a natural tendency to create in them new principles and ideas of fortitude, submission and reliance on the wisdom and experience of their superiors: Your informant has told you the British troops are made up of "*the most debauched weavers prentices, the scum of the Irish Roman Catholics who desert upon every occasion, and a few, very few Scotch who are not strong enough to carry packs.*" I have cultivated an acquaintance with the most sensible of the military gentlemen, and have found them men of candour and worth; from their information and my own observation, I will now in these particulars lay before you a true and impartial state of the British army:* If that part which England affords is only *the most debauched weavers prentices*, whence arises the great interest which the

---

* The writer of the Strictures in stating the number of the British infantry, has, either through negligence or purposely, committed an error, by not including the marines: Their establishment is, I think, upwards of four thousand. This corps, though existing under a different act of Parliament, may properly be denominated an addition to the marching regiments, as in the expeditions of last war it frequently co-operated with them, and by its vigour and intrepidity contributed to their memorable successes. This is only produced as an instance of what occurs in every page, unfair reasoning from misrepresented facts; for a trifling peace establishment is not to be computed the force of Britain,—it is founded on a plan, recommended by Marshal Saxe for the French army, of having many battalions with more officers to each than requisite for the number of private men, that in case of necessity, new levies might be ingrafted on them and by that means a considerable body of troops, fit for actual service, be almost instantaneously compleated.

friends of many of them have with the country gentlemen, and which is often powerfully employed in soliciting their discharges? And by what arts have so many apprentices, without detection, deserted their masters, and broke their indentures? But all recruiting officers, and I suspect the Stricturer can affirm it, know that it is the country and not the towns which completes their battalions, that they beat up only on market-days when peasants not mechanics resort to them; and you can all of you judge from the appearance of those recruits which have been brought hither, if they were the produce of villages or cities. *The scum of the Irish Roman Catholics*, he tells you, forms the proportion from that country, but unfortunately two strong circumstances militate against this assertion, for the legislature of Ireland, from fatal experience, jealous of the Roman Catholics, has, under the severest penalties, prohibited them the use of arms, and disqualified them from forming a part of the defence of their country: Yet I am told that some few notwithstanding, are smuggled into the service, but this can only be in those regiments lately on that establishment, and in them very inconsiderable; the other circumstance is, a law which from the fear of depopulation, proscribes the enlisting any man for other than the establishment within that kingdom: His annexment that they *desert upon every occasion*, is not better grounded upon fact;—here the mention of desertion makes me wish to advert to this great source of triumph in your popular leaders; they proclaim to the world how numerous have the instances of it been from the army quartered in Boston, and yet, I am well informed, it is no more than has always been from a similar body of troops, even to the natural enemies of their country; and I heartily wish they could as easily reconcile to their consciences the seducing men from their allegiance and duty to the worst of crimes, perjury and the greatest of earthly evils, unprepared, and almost certain death if retaken: Our author makes up the small residue with *a few, very few Scotch, who are not strong enough to carry packs*: I am told, had he been at the trouble to examine muster rolls he would have found them not so inconsiderable; that this is probable we may reasonably conclude from the number of emigrants who have quitted that country to come here, and what their condition is, those who have seen them will judge:

In fine, what is actually the present state of the whole British army, one who has not seen all of it cannot with precision determine, but if I might judge from those regiments which, in their tour of duty, have been sent here, I should pronounce it more than versed *in the tricks of the parade*, I should pronounce it highly trained and qualified for service; but it is objected that *few of them have seen action* and therefore they are much to be *doubted*: Who can have told this author so? For most surely he has been strangely misinformed; of the little army stationed in this capital there are two of the Quebec and one of the Minden battalions, in which many of the officers and soldiers who conquered on those glorious days still remain, and in most of the other regiments which compose it many of the veterans of last war are to be found; and for my own part when I view this small but finely appointed army, and consider that it is under the command of two Generals of approved knowledge and experience in war, I feel much confidence in the difficulties it would be able to surmount, and the victories over irregulars which, in human probability, it would assuredly obtain.

In order to induce in you a belief of his military principles and knowledge, he produces an instance in proof from the constitution of the King of Prussia's army, but even was it, which I have the greatest reason to doubt, literally as he has stated, it cannot then, I apprehend, be brought as a precedent in this case, for there is no similarity between the connected and absolute power of that monarch over all his dominions and the distinct and widely separated colonies of North-America: Between supporting the authority of the lawful Sovereign and rebelling against him.

He tells you also, that *no inferences can be drawn* from the conquest of Quebec by the army under General Wolfe, but believe me he is much mistaken for last war will afford abundant proofs to the contrary: Was it the *conquering attributes**

---

* "*Would have made him, Wolfe, reject with horror the* HANGMAN's OFFICE, *which others, who are not endowed with his conquering attributes, will with readiness accept.*" When men of genius and education, in defiance of facts, descend from the delicacy of language to the scurrility of the lower orders, human nature stands appalled, and sorrowing laments the misapplication of knowledge and talents;—but disappointed ambition and its consequent disaffection will,

of Wolfe that unsupported carried on the six British battalions to glory and decisive victory at Minden? Or was it his genius that stormed the Moro? Or was it that hero who defended Arcot against all the force which France could muster in the East? His own instance, *the corps which General Monkton led to conquest*, wars against the assertion; all these were wrought by that spirit and strict discipline which has ever actuated and supported the British infantry. I mean not to tear from the laurelled bust of Wolfe those honors which deservedly deck it;—I know he was a soldier, a general, and what is more, a man; and though *it is notorious that he was particularly an enemy to large standing armies in time of peace*, it is *notorious* also, that in *time of peace* he formed the twentieth regiment, a model from which others learnt to conquer and extend the dominions of their country; and yet *he was a most liberal, virtuous citizen*, and sedulously preserved and improved the palladium committed to him by the constitution "for the safety of the kingdom, the defence of the possessions of the crown of Great-Britain, and the preservation of the balance of power in Europe."*

After having with many arguments and more humour taught you to despise the armies of Britain, he proceeds and attempts with the same weapons to convince you of security from invasion by foreigners and tells you of a convention of the empire in the year 1764; but *does he not know* that the resolves of that body have ever been held in derision by its members from the time that the Landgrave of Hess and Prince Maurice of Saxony laughed at the decree of the Aulic Council, and the Emperor Charles the Fifth, more powerful that any of his successors, till his Majesty of Prussia and the Elector of Hanover, stood unmoved, and sustained the thunders of the imperial ban? In fact it is not more regarded than a papal bull when it opposes the inclinations of a Monarch.—You all of you know what in England, France and Spain was formerly the power of the Lord

---

with the benevolent, plead some mitigation, even though the shaft is aimed at a character, which was once deservedly the subject of *his* highest admiration and praise.

* Vid. Preamble to the act for punishing mutiny and desertion.

Paramount over his Feudatories, and such is precisely the
present state of the Germanic body; and therefore I do not see,
why the Landgrave of Hess, if it suits his convenience, may not
send over as many of his troops as required; and should they
ever be solicited, I dare aver, that an idea of their not returning
will never occur to him or his ministers to prevent their being
dispatched, nay that they would lack faith even though our
Stricturer, in the spirit of vaticination, has predicted it;* but
how the Elector of Hanover, backed by the power of Britain to
enforce his commands, should want credit to procure a few
thousands of his own subjects, is what I cannot comprehend:†
It is as mysterious to me that Great-Britain, when divorced
from her colonies, should be destitute of every requisite for
supporting her navy, though she possesses the northern and
southern extremities of this continent, and her trade to Russia
and the Baltic is open and free, and she can from thence supply
herself with all the materials for shipbuilding on at least as
reasonable conditions as she does now from America.

This lively writer has amused you with many historical allusions, but, alas! they are seldom in point; that by which he
marks out the facility of forming *excellent officers* is a most
striking instance of this, for to what pitch must military knowledge have arrived in the times of the civil war, when two large
armies were for three days marching within ten miles of each
other, and both remained ignorant of their enemies situation?
—In this case it was chance or numbers that must decide, for
each was unacquainted with discipline; and if there were faction and agitators in the parliament army, the noble historian
of those troubles, and he would have wished to conceal it, tells
us that the royal forces were not less infested by dissension,
party and private opinion; if therefore the inference which in

---

* *This is perhaps the most preposterous idea that ever was hatched in a distempered
brain*; but I beg pardon, perhaps this author is intrusted with the purport of
the Observator on the Boston Port Bill's embassy, and can tell that he is sent
to divulge to the Landgrave of Hess this amazing secret.
† Britain has another resource, which has perhaps not occurred to the Friendly
Addresser or his critic: She is in the strictest alliance with Russia, whose
troops, come from ravaging the extensive provinces of Turkey, would overrun
this continent with the same facility they passed the Danube, still carrying
conquest in their front, and swept before them unnumbered fortresses.

the strictures is drawn from this uncommon and tempestuous period, is just, let every man of candour, reading and understanding determine.

The last *consideration*, Americans, *which he thinks it is his duty to offer you*, is, whether or no you shall demolish his Majesty's forts and barracks: I consider not by whom they were erected, or for what purpose, but, beyond doubt, the property of all such public buildings and of all public military stores is, for the security of the realm, vested in the crown; and to attempt to seize, retain, or destroy them, is by the law declared to be high-treason: His proposition therefore is, whether you shall at once plunge yourselves into open rebellion and thereby incur its penalties, or not: To what a precipice would this author lead you? When I look down my senses forsake me, and at the prospect my blood rushes tumultuously to, and retreats from its citadel, the heart. Yes, unhappy and infatuated citizens, with anguish I am forced to acknowledge, that such violences as he recommends, have in part been committed. O righteous God! do thou avert the justice of the empire, and, by inspiring its governing powers with thy milder attribute of mercy, snatch this deluded people from the imminent calamities, dangers, ruin, and destruction which await them!

FINIS.

[Joseph Galloway], A Candid Examination of the Mutual Claims of Great-Britain, and the Colonies: with a Plan of Accommodation, on Constitutional Principles. New York, 1775.

Joseph Galloway was a leading member of the Pennsylvania Assembly, a close confidant of Benjamin Franklin, and a Pennsylvania delegate to the First Continental Congress, where he proposed an inventive Plan of Union, which he included in the following pamphlet. The plan called for the creation of a president-general appointed by the king along with a grand council composed of representatives from each colony to be chosen every three years. Laws passed by either this grand council or by the British Parliament were to be subject to mutual review and approval.

It was a bold and ingenious scheme, and if it had been offered ten years earlier it might well have staved off a rebellion. John Jay and James Duane of New York and Edward Rutledge of South Carolina spoke for it, with Rutledge finding "it almost a perfect Plan." But on September 28, 1774, six colonial delegations voted to table it, with five opposed. Charles Thomson, the secretary of the Congress, inadvertently or not, failed to enter the plan in the Congress's journal. Three weeks later, on October 22, the Congress declined to take up the plan, with Thomson once again not bothering to enter in the journal this vote of rejection.

By October 1774, even if Galloway's plan had been adopted, it was unlikely that Congress could have reversed the transfer of authority that was taking place in the localities. Royal governors watched helplessly as their authority slipped away into the hands of committees of safety and provincial conventions. The Congress simply recognized these new local centers of power and gave them its blessing and the authority to enforce the economic sanctions against Britain.

A major critique of Galloway's pamphlet appeared in the *Pennsylvania Journal* of March 8, 1775, attributed to Thomson and John Dickinson, Galloway's opponents in the Pennsylvania Assembly. The critics turned Galloway's assertion that there must be in every state one final supreme legislative power against him, suggesting that the Assembly and Parliament could not both be the supreme legislative power in the colony; "for it would be 'irregular and monstrous' to suppose us subject to two Legislatures." As for the Plan of Union, it was dismissed as "confused, impracticable, and dangerous." The colonists were so suspicious of all distant power that even a grand council composed of their fellow Americans would not be trusted, an anticipation of the anti-federalist thinking that would emerge in the following decade. We should not leave "the liberties of a Country to the virtues of any men, however great or conspicuous," they warned. "We know too well the fallibility of human nature."

A

CANDID EXAMINATION

OF THE

MUTUAL CLAIMS

OF

GREAT-BRITAIN,

AND THE

COLONIES:

WITH

A PLAN

OF

ACCOMODATION,

ON

CONSTITUTIONAL PRINCIPLES.

NEW-YORK:
Printed by James Rivington, M,DCC,LXXV.

My dear Countrymen,

WHEN we see the country we live in, where agriculture, elegant and beneficial improvements, philosophy, and all the liberal arts and sciences have been nourished and ripened to a degree of perfection, astonishing to mankind; where wisdom and sound policy have even sustained their due authority, kept the licentious in awe, and rendered them subservient to their own, and the public welfare; and where freedom, peace and order, have always triumphed over those enemies to human happiness, oppression and licentiousness; now governed by the barbarian rule of frantic folly, and lawless ambition: When we see freedom of speech suppressed, the liberty and secrecy of the press destroyed, the voice of truth silenced: A lawless power established throughout the colonies, forming laws for the government of their conduct, depriving men of their natural rights, and inflicting penalties more severe than death itself, upon a disobedience to their edicts, to which the constitutional magistracy, in some places by force, and in others willingly, submit:—The property of the subject arbitrarily, and without law, taken from him, in pursuance of those edicts:—When, under their influence, America is arming in the east and west, against the parent state:—I say, when we see the colonies, needlessly, and while the path to their safety and happiness is plain, and open before them; thus pushing on with precipitation and madness, in the high road of sedition and rebellion, which must ultimately terminate in their misery and ruin: It is the duty of every man of the least abilities, to try to reclaim them from their folly, and save them from destruction, before it be too late.—With this design I am resolved to review the most important controversy, that ever was agitated between a state and its members; in hope, that my countrymen, too long seduced from their true interest, by false tho' specious arguments, will, at length, listen to reason and truth, and pursue those measures only, which lead to their safety and happiness.

In a controversy of so great moment, it is of the first importance to ascertain the standard by which it ought to be decided. This being unsettled, the merits can never be determined, nor any just decision formed. Hence it is, that we have seen all the

American writers on the subject, adopting untenable principles, and thence rearing the most wild and chimerical super-
structures. Some of them have fixed on, as a source from
whence to draw American Right, "the laws of God and nature,"
the common rights of mankind, "and American charters."
Others finding that the claims of the colonies could not be
supported upon those pillars, have racked their inventions to
find out distinctions, which never existed, nor can exist, in reason or common sense: A distinction between a right in parliament to legislate for the colonies, and a right to tax them
—between internal and external taxation—and between taxes
laid for the regulation of trade, and for the purpose of revenue.
And after all of them have been fully considered, even the authors themselves, finding that they have conveyed no satisfactory idea to the intelligent mind, either of the extent of
parliamentary authority, or of the rights of America, have exploded them, and taken new ground, which will be found
equally indefensible. I shall not attempt to account for a conduct which must appear so strange, when it is considered, that
the subject itself naturally, and familiarly, led to the only just
and proper means of deciding it. It is a dispute between the
supreme authority of the state, and a number of its members,
respecting its supremacy, and their constitutional rights. What
other source to draw them from, or standard to decide them
by, can reason point out, but the principles of government in
general, and of that constitution in particular, where both are
to be found, defined and established? Whoever searches for
them elsewhere, will search for them in vain, and ever confound the subject, perplex himself, and bewilder the reader.

In order then to ascertain the constitutional extent of parliamentary authority; to determine whether the colonies are
members of the British state; and if they are, to mark out their
just rights, and to propose a remedy to reconcile them, upon
principles of government and liberty; it is necessary, first, to
delineate those principles, which are essential in the constitution of all societies, and particularly in that of the British
government.

There is no position more firmly established, in the conduct
of mankind, Than that there must be in every state a supreme
legislative authority, universal in its extent, over every member.

This truth, the principles upon which all governments from the earliest ages have been established, uniformly demonstrate. This truth, the authority of all authors of credit will ever support.—This truth, the nature and reason of civil societies will for ever evince. Tully gives us this definition of government, "Multitudo juris consensu et utilitatis communione sociata. A multitude of people united together by a communion of interests, and *common laws* to which *they all submit with one accord*." Mr. Locke tells us, that "the first *fundamental positive law* of all common-wealths is, the establishing *the legislative power*. This legislative is not only the *supreme power of the common-wealth*; but is sacred and unalterable in the hands where the community have placed it." And in another place, he says, "there can be but one *supreme power*, which is the *legislative*, to which *all the rest* are, and must be, *subordinate*." The judicious Burlamaqui, in treating of the essential constitution of states, and of the manner in which they are formed, declares that in forming a society, "it is necessary to *unite forever* the *wills of all the members* in such a manner, that from that time forward they should never desire *but one and the same thing*, in whatever relates to the end and purpose of society. It is afterwards necessary, to establish a *supreme power*, supported by the strength of the whole body. That it is from this *union of wills and strength*, that the *body politic, or state, results*; and *without it we could never conceive a civil society*. That the state is considered as a body, or moral person, of which the *Sovereign* is the chief head, and the *subjects are the members*." And afterwards, in another part he says, "The state is a body, or society, animated by *one soul*, which directs *all its motions*, and makes *all its members* act after a *constant and uniform manner*, with a view to one and the *same end*, namely the *public utility*." And in another chapter, speaking of the characters of sovereignty, its modifications and extent, he avers, "that in every government there should be such a *supreme power*, is a point absolutely *necessary*; the very nature of the thing requires it; otherwise *it is impossible for it to subsist*. That this power is that *from which all others flow*, it being a supreme and independent power; that is, a power that judges finally of whatever is *susceptible of human direction*, and relates to the welfare and advantage of society." And *Acherley*, in his treatise on the Britannic constitution, proves with great strength of argument, "That the *supreme power* in every government and nation, is the *legislative power of making and altering those laws* of it, by which *every man is to be bound*, and to which he is to *yield obedience.*"

The evidence of all other authors of credit, even of those the most attached to republican forms of government, might be adduced, to demonstrate the same truths; but this must be unnecessary, when we refer to the forms of all civilized societies, whether monarchical, aristocratical, democratical, or mixed; and there find a sovereign legislature established, to which it is the duty of *every member uniformly to yield obedience*. A due attention to this universal principle, which seems too firmly settled to be shaken by any sophistical distinctions, would have saved the American writers from all their numerous absurdities. It would have shewn them, that the legislative authority in every government must of necessity be *equally supreme over all its members.*—That to divide this supremacy, by allowing it to exist in some cases, and not in all,—over a part of the members, and not the whole,—is to weaken and confound the operations of the system, and to subvert the very end and purpose for which it was formed; in as much as the vigour and strength of every machine, whether mechanical or political, must depend upon the consistency of its parts, and their corresponding obedience to the supreme *acting power*: And it would have shewn that there can be no alternative; either the colonies must be considered as complete members of the state, or so many distinct communities, in a state of nature, as independant of it, as Hanover, France, or Spain.

That there is such a supreme power established in the British society, which has from the time of its origin, exercised this universal authority over all its members, will not be denied. But where it is lodged; what are its modifications; and what are the powers subordinate to it, is a necessary enquiry. It will lead us to those principles which must decide many important questions in this great controversy; and in particular point out the absurdity, in the colonists, when they acknowledge allegiance to the King, and deny obedience to the laws of parliament.

The government of Great-Britain is of a particular kind. There is none now in the world like it. It is of a mixed form, composed partly of the principles of a monarchy, aristocracy, and democracy; and yet cannot with propriety be described, by the name of either of them. Its supreme legislative head is *lodged* in the King, Lords and Commons. To their authority every other power of the state is subordinate, and every member must yield full and perfect obedience. These three branches constituting but one supreme politic head, their power is equal and concurrent; their joint assent being necessary to the validity of every act of legislation. So that even in this department of the state, which is the highest and first in order, the King is not supreme; being only one of three equal in power. It cannot therefore be to the King, as legislator, that the colonists owe obedience and allegiance; because he has no such complete, independent capacity; he is not, by the constitution, a legislator, but only a part of one; and to submit to the power of a *part*, and not to the *whole*, is too great an absurdity for men of sense to adopt.

But as the legislature does not always exist, it could avail little, without some power to superintend the execution of its regulations. The appointment of a representative of the whole state, to see that its laws are duly carried into execution, was absolutely necessary. The King is that representative; and as such is vested with the executive power of the British government. But this power is a subordinate one, and perpetually liable to the alterations and controul of the supreme legislative authority; whose will, enacted into laws, is the sole guide and rule of its actions. Mr. Locke tells us, that the King "is to be considered as the image, phantom, or *representative of the common wealth, and by the will of the society declared in its laws*, and thus *has no will, no power*, but *that of the law*."

To him, in this representative capacity, and as supreme executor of the laws, made by *a joint power of him and others*, the oaths of allegiance are taken; and by him, that obedience in the subjects to the laws, which intitle them to protection in their persons and properties, is received. Is it then to him, as representative of the state, and executor of its laws, that the Americans profess their allegiance? This cannot be; because it would be owning an obedience to the laws of the state which he represents, and is bound to execute, and of which they uniformly deny the force and obligation. Hence these professions are not made to him either in his legislative, or executive capacities;

but yet it seems they are made to the King. And into this distinction, which is no where to be found, either in the constitution of the government, in reason or common sense, the ignorant and thoughtless have been deluded ever since the passing of the stamp-act, and they have rested satisfied with it without the least examination; for we find it in all the resolves and petitions of the American assemblies, town meetings, provincial committees, and even in the proceedings of the continental congress. And such have been the unhappy effects, that we have seen the officers of justice in America, who have taken the oaths to the British government, resolutely opposing the execution of those very laws, which they have sworn to obey and execute; and thus unwittingly sliding into the most palpable perjuries. I do not mean to offend the inventors of this refined distinction, when I ask them—Is this acknowledgment made to the King, in his politic capacity, as King of Great-Britain, or of America? If to him in the first, it includes a promise of obedience to the British laws, as I shall more fully prove hereafter. If in the second, as King of America, when did he assume that title, and by whom was it conferred? When was he crowned? On the contrary has he not invariably denied the existence of any such capacity in him, by an uniform conduct, in exerting his authority, to execute the British statutes in America?

In his representative capacity, the King also holds the great seal, or the seal of the state, and has right to affix it to all acts of the legislature, and such as he is impowered to do by his prerogative, and *no other*. He has also certain prerogatives, which are defined and known. By one of them he has right, under the great seal, to form any circle of territory, within the realm, and the subjects on it, into inferior bodies politic, and to vest them with the power to make municipal laws, for the regulation of its internal police, so far as it relates to the welfare of that circle only: But by no means to discharge them from their obedience to the supreme legislative authority. Because this would be to weaken, dismember, and in the end destroy the state, contrary to the intent for which the prerogative was vested in him, namely, the public good and safety.

Having thus established the necessity of a supreme legislative authority in every government, and shewn that it is an essential principle in the English state, and explained such other parts of the constitution as are necessary to my purpose; let us next enquire whether the colonies of right are members of that state, or so many independent communities, in a state of nature, with respect to it. For seeing a legislative authority competent, in all cases whatsoever, over every member, is necessary in every government; the colonies must stand in one or other of these predicaments.

The lands upon which the colonies are established must be considered, as they truly are, either discovered, or conquered territories. In either case the right of property is in the state, under the license or authority of which they were discovered or conquered. This property being vested in the state, no subject can lawfully enter upon, and appropriate any part of it to his own use, without a commission or grant from the immediate representative for that purpose. Hence we find in the histories of all civilized states, from the earliest ages to this day, the heads, or representatives of all governments, distributing such lands, by special grants, among their people, who in every instance which history affords, still retain the duties of subjects: And there is no position better established by the practice and usage of all societies, than that where a subject removes from one part of the territory of a government, to another part of the same, his political rights and duties remain as before; but where the subject of one state removes to the territory of another, and settles there, his political rights and duties are changed from those of the state from whence he removed, to those of the state under which he settles, and from which he receives protection. No person acquainted with politic law, or the practice of societies, in these respects, will assert the contrary. What then are the circumstances of America? Under what authority was it discovered? What was the intent of the discovery? By whom, and under what authority, has it been settled? A decision of these questions will lead us to a very important truth, viz. That the colonies are of Right members of the British government.

America was discovered in the latter end of the 15th century, by Sebastian Cabot, authorised for that special purpose, under the great seal of the state, affixed to his commission, by *Henry* 7. Representative of the British government. The *signature* of the great seal fully proves that the King did not in the granting this commission, consider himself as acting in his private, but in his politic capacity. In the first he had no right to affix it, in the second he had. The design in view was to encrease the territories, extend the commerce, and add to the wealth and power of the state. And therefore the discovery was made to the use of the state, and the territories became immediately subjcct to its supreme authority. No man in his sober senses will, I imagine, affirm that *Henry* 7. had in view the discovery of a country, into which his successors might give license to the members of the state to emigrate, with intent to become independent of its authority. Such a design is too absurd to be supposed ever to have been admitted into any system of policy; much less that of a Prince so justly famed for his wisdom.

Every colony in America, as well those under charters, as others, has been settled under the licence and authority of the great seal, affixed by the representative of the body politic of the British state. The property of the territory of America being in the state, and its members removing under its authority from one part of it to another, equally subject to its supreme jurisdiction; they of consequence, brought over with them all their political rights and *duties*, and amongst the rest, that of perfect obedience to its laws;—nor could they be lost or changed by an alteration of their local circumstances. Indeed nothing can be more explicitly confessed than this truth, in all the American declarations of their rights. I shall cite only those of the congresses which met at New-York in 1765, and at Philadelphia in 1774. By the first we are told, "that his *Majesty's* subjects in these colonies *are entitled to* all the *inherent rights and liberties* of his *natural* born subjects within the kingdom of Great-Britain." And in the second, "That our ancestors, who first settled these colonies, were, at the time of their emigration from the mother-country, *entitled to all the rights, liberties* and immunities of free and natural born subjects within the realm of England." And "that by such emigration they by no means forfeited, surrendered, or lost any of those rights;" Thus evidently deducing their title to their right, from the relation they bore, as members of the mother state. Conscious that they could not deduce them from any other source but the English government, as they no where else exist, they claim them under its title and authority. But can the wisest among them inform us, by what law, or upon what principle, they claim rights under the British government, and yet deny the obligation of those duties which subjects of that government owe to it? The rights and duties of the members of all societies are reciprocal. The one is the continuing consideration for the other. Either of them being destroyed, without the consent of the subjects to which both of them adhere, the other ceases. Therefore, should a state arbitrarily deprive its members of their just rights, and refuse to restore them, after it has been repeatedly, and respectfully required so to do, then their duties and obedience to the state cease, but not before: It being the design of every society, when formed, that its existence should be permanent, not of a temporary duration.

Here we may perceive some of those many inconsistencies and absurdities in which the advocates of America have weakly involved her cause. We see them calling the subjects in America, "subjects of his *Majesty*," in his political capacity, and as representative of the British state, bound in duty to execute its laws, in *every part* of its dominions; and in the same breath denying obedience to those laws. We see them claiming "all the inherent rights and liberties of natural born subjects" of the state, and denying the force of those duties, which are so inseparably united with those "rights and liberties." We hear them declare that they have not "forfeited, surrendered, or lost" the rights "they enjoyed at the time of their emigration;" and yet they will not comply with the duties upon the performance of which those rights depend. Thus it seems the American subjects have neither "forfeited, surrendered, nor lost," but still retain the rights they derive from the government of Great-Britain; but the government has either forfeited, surrendered, or lost its rights over Them. Indeed they have not told us how, or by what means, this forfeiture, surrender, or loss of rights in the British state, has happened: This, I believe, was a task impossible; and therefore carefully avoided. But what shall we think of the sagacity and foresight of these able politicians, when we find that the right claimed by parliament, and which they deny, may be established with equal reason and solidity, upon the same principles and deductions, on which they have rested the claims of America? May not the advocates for the parliamentary authority assert, "That at the time of the emigration of our ancestors," the legislative power had a constitutional authority over them, and every other member of the state; that by such emigration, which was an act of their own, as well as of the state, it neither "forfeited, surrendered, nor lost" that authority? And would not such a declaration be in reason, truth, and on the principles of the English constitution, as well founded, as that upon which the defenders of American rights have endeavoured to establish them?

But it may be said that America is settled by others, besides British subjects. Are They also members of the state, and subject to its authority? They most certainly are. They have by their own act become subjects, and owe obedience to its laws, as fully as any other members, as I have before shewn. But to confirm what I have already advanced upon this head, I shall add the opinion of Mr. *Locke*, because it has been often heretofore relied on by the American advocates, as worthy of credit. His words are,—"Whoever by *inheritance, purchase, permission, or otherwise*, enjoys *any part of the land* annexed to, and under the government of a common wealth, must take it with the condition it is under, that is of *submitting* to the government of the common wealth, under whose jurisdiction it is, as *far as any subject of it*." If the preceding principles and arguments be well founded, as they appear to be, from the usage, practice and policy of all societies; it follows, that whatever British subject, or foreigner, has, either under the sanction of the American charters, or otherwise, become an occupant of the English territories in the colonies, he is truly a member of the British state, and subject to the laws of its supreme authority.

I have thus far drawn my arguments chiefly from the policy of government in general, and of the English constitution in particular; and, I hope, with sufficient evidence, to prove the justness and truth of them: But as I mean fully to investigate, with the strictest candour, the rights of both the parties, and place them in their true light; it is of importance to consider whether their conduct, for upwards of a century, affords evidence of a denial, or confirmation of the principles I have maintained. And here we shall find, that the prerogatives of this supreme representative of the state, ever since the first settlement of the colonies, have been uniformly exercised, and submitted to, in all the colonies. All their political Executive powers have been derived from, and all their governments established by, it. It is in this representative capacity that the King has granted all the charters, appointed the governors, custom-house officers, &c. and granted authority to the governors to commissionate the inferior officers of justice, as well judicial as ministerial. From this source only all his legal powers, in respect to the colonies, can be drawn; there being no other capacity vested in him, from whence he could derive them. So that every officer in America, appointed by him, or under his authority, is truly the inferior and subordinate delegate of the King, Lords and Commons; receiving his authority from the supreme executive representative of the British state; all their powers being originally derived from, and limited by, its constitution and laws.

Upon the same principle, the supreme legislature has, upon many occasions, and at a variety of times, held forth and exercised its authority over the colonies; and they have yielded obedience to all the British statutes, in which they have been named; as well those imposing taxes on them, as those for regulating their internal police. The learned judges in England, and the judges and other officers concerned in the administration of justice in America, in conformity to this idea, of their being the inferior delegates of the British state, and of its authority over the colonies, have ever made those laws of parliament, where by words they have been extended to them, the test of their decisions, in all American disputes, without doubt or hesitation, until the year 1765, when our unhappy controversy commenced.

All the officers of government, every member of assembly, every foreigner before his naturalization, had always taken the oaths of allegiance, under the directions of the statutes, that have been made for that purpose. The words of the oath are the same with that administred to the subject in Britain, on the like occasions; and consequently must be of the same import, and carry with them the same obligations in every respect. Both in Britain and America the oaths are taken to the King, not in his private, but politic capacity; they are taken to him as representative of the whole state, whose duty it is to superintend the administration of justice, and to see that a faithful obedience is paid to the laws. These oaths are no more than renewals of the original covenant, upon which all governments

are formed: For in the constitution of all societies two covenants are essential; one on the part of the state, that it will ever
consult and promote the public good and safety; and the other
on the part of the subject, that he will bear fidelity and true
allegiance to the *sovereign, or supreme authority.* "This last
covenant," says the judicious Burlamaqui, "includes a submission of the *strength* and *will* of each *individual* to the *will* and
head of the society, as far as the public good requires; and thus
it is that a *regular state*, and *perfect government* is formed."
And the words of Mr. Locke are equally apposite, "The oaths
of allegiance are taken to the King, it is not to him as supreme
legislator, but as *supreme executor of the law*, made by a joint
power of *him and others; allegiance* being nothing but *obedience according to law*, which, when he *violates*, he has no right
to *obedience*, nor can *claim it* otherwise than in his *public person*, vested with the *power of the law.*" And in another place he
says, "That all obedience which by the most solemn ties any
one can be obliged to pay, *ultimately terminates in the supreme
power of the legislature*, and is directed by those laws which it
enacts." This being the nature of the oath of allegiance, and of
the obligations it enforces, no man of any understanding will
call for further proof, That all the officers of government in
America, who have taken these oaths, and those who have
submitted to their administration, while they were executing
the British statutes, considered themselves as subjects of the
state, owing obedience to its legislative authority.

In every government, protection and allegiance, or obedience, are reciprocal duties. They are so inseparably united that
one cannot exist without the other. Protection from the state
demands, and entitles it to receive, obedience and submission
to its laws from the subject: And obedience to the will of the
state, communicated in its laws, entitles the subject to its protection. A just sense of this truth has governed the conduct of
the state towards the colonies, and that of the colonies towards
the state, ever since their settlement. The colonists have not
only settled upon the lands of the state, under its licence and
authority, granted by its representative; but they have been
fostered, nourished and sheltered under its wings, and protected by its wealth and power. And as they have ever yielded
obedience to its laws, they have, whenever in danger, called for

its protection; and in the last war were saved from all the misery and slavery, which popish superstition and tyranny could inflict, when their inability to save themselves was universally known and acknowledged.

Seeing then that the colonies have, ever since their existence, considered themselves, and acted as perfect members of the British state, obedient to its laws, untill the year 1765: There must, one would imagine, be something lately discovered, which has convinced them of their mistake, and that they have a right to cast off their allegiance to the British government. We can look for this in no place so properly, as in the late declaration of American rights. Here we find it drawn from "the immutable laws of nature, the principles of the English constitution, and their several charters, or compacts." Should we fail in discovering it here, we may safely determine it is not any where to be found. We shall not find it in "the laws of nature;" the principles upon which those laws are founded, are reason and immutable justice, which require a rigid performance of every lawful contract;—to suppose therefore, that a right can thence be derived to violate the most solemn and sacred of all covenants; those upon which the existence of societies, and the welfare of millions depend; is, in the highest degree, absurd. And, I believe, we shall be equally unsuccessful in searching for it in the principles of the English constitution; because that constitution is formed to bind all the members of the state together, and to compel an obedience to its laws.—We must therefore find it in the American charters or compacts, or no where. And after we have looked there, we can discover no exemption, or discharge from the authority of parliament in any of them, save one, and there it is only partial; while other parts of the same charter declare the contrary, and expressly retain the submission of the subject to the British laws. But suppose there had been such an exemption in all of them, as clear as words could express it, it is a question which demands a solution, whether the King had a right, by the constitution, to grant it.

The original intent of the prerogative, under which the inhabitants of particular districts of territory have been incorporated into bodies politic, was to enable the representative of the state, to form inferior communities, with municipal rights and privileges. This was necessary to enable the executive power to carry into execution the operations of government with regularity and order. And in some instances it has been beneficial in promoting the trade, arts, and particular pursuits in business of such districts.—This prerogative is very antient, and well defined by usage and prescription. London held peculiar privileges long before the conquest. William the conqueror granted to that city two charters soon after. A great number of inferior societies have been since incorporated, by succeeding Kings, upon these principles; all of them under the great seal, and by the same authority under which the American charters were granted. Having so many precedents before us, we cannot be at a loss to ascertain the extent of this prerogative. The exercise of it for so many centuries will give satisfaction to every candid enquirer. Making this the test of decision, we shall find that no King has ever presumed to grant more than merely municipal powers and privileges, always leaving the subjects and the territory incorporated, under the supreme legislative authority. There being no *traces* of a farther extent of this prerogative, in the conduct of all the British Kings; the conclusion is, that no such power does, or ever did exist. Besides, this prerogative, like all others, is vested in the King, in trust, to promote, not to injure, the public good. And therefore, to assert that he may, under it, discharge these incorporated societies from their obedience to the supreme power, is to contend that, by virtue of the power which he holds in trust to strengthen, he may weaken,—and instead of maintaining and defending, he may destroy, the common wealth; which involves the most palpable contradiction.

Sufficient has been said to convince us, that the Kings of England can have no authority to discharge inferior bodies politic, from parliamentary authority. But as upon a satisfactory decision of the question, the claim of independency must stand or fall, I shall farther corroborate what I have said, with the most respectable authorities. The learned Pufendorf tells us, "With regard to all *lawful bodies*, it is to be observed, that whatever right they possess, or whatever power they hold over their members, is all under *the determination of the supreme authority*, which it ought on *no account to oppose, or over ballance*. For otherways, if there could be a body of men, not *subject to the regulation of the civil government*, there would be *a state within a state.*—If we look on these bodies, or systems, in a state already settled, we are then to consider what was the *intent of the supreme Governor*, in founding, or confirming, such a company. For if he hath given, or ascertained to them, in express words, *an absolute and independent right*, with regard to *some particular affairs* which concern the *publick administration*; then he hath *plainly* ABDICATED *part of his authority*, and by admitting *two heads* in the constitution, hath rendered it *irregular and monstrous.*" Mr. Locke says, "That the legislative authority *must needs be supreme*; and *all other powers*, in any members, or parts of society, *derived from, and subordinate* to it." And speaking of the King's exceeding his public trust, he affirms, "That when he quits his *representative capacity*, his *public will*, and acts by his own *private will, he degrades* himself, and is but *a single, private person, without power, without will, that has any right to obedience.*" And the same author would not scruple to declare, upon the principles he establishes in the latter part of his treatise: That a King who should have granted, in the American charters, a licence to the subjects of the state to emigrate, with a discharge from their obedience to the legislative authority, and should open such a door to a desertion of the principal territory, and dissolution of its government, would thereby forfeit his crown; and to prevent the mischief of such grant, the people might resume their original authority, if the mischief could not otherwise be prevented.

I have said before, whenever a state refuses to give protection to its subjects, and maintain their rights, there duty ceases. It may with equal truth be affirmed, that whenever subjects shall refuse to perform those duties, and yield that obedience which they are bound to perform and yield by the constitution, or original compact of society, they forfeit not only their right to the protection of the state, but every other right or claim under it; and the government may either punish them agreeably to its laws, or cease its protection over them, and annul the rights and privileges they derive from it. There is no truth more evident than that where a mutual covenant subsists, including a consideration perpetually to be performed on both sides, upon which the validity of the covenant rests, if either party refuse the performance on his part, the other is discharged

of course, and the party refusing loses his right and claim to
the performance of the other. If this assertion be just, and that
it is we shall find, whether we apply to the laws of nature, or
civil societies,—into what a dangerous predicament are the
Americans thrown by a denial of obedience to the authority of
parliament, which is one of the most essential duties! That
they have not, as the congress affirms, forfeited, surrendered,
or lost their rights, by their emigration, is true.—But that this
wise body of men have used their best endeavours, and pursued the most effectual measures to forfeit them, is equally
true. Let us suppose that the late congress had been a regular
and legal representative of all America, vested with authority,
by the consent of the colonists, to deny and withdraw their
obedience to the laws of the British state, as they have endeavoured to do; would not Great-Britain be justifiable in declaring, by an act of state, that all the rights and privileges which
the colonists derive under her, are forfeited? Shall the Americans have a right to withdraw from the state the performance
of their duties, and the state be bound to continue *them* in the
enjoyment of all their rights? Every principle of government
and common sense denies it.

Thus, in whatever light we view the subject; whether we
reason from the principles and policy upon which all governments are established, or those of the English constitution in
particular;—the right of property in the territory,—the authority under which the colonists have been settled,—the persons by whom settled,—their rights under the several charters
and compacts,—their conduct ever since their settlement,
down to the year 1765,—or from the conduct of the state down
to this day; we find that they are members of the British state,
and owe obedience to its legislative authority.

That America has been wandering in a wrong path, bewildered among the erroneous principles upon which her advocates have attempted in vain to support her rights, is apparent
from all her conduct; she began by denying the authority of
parliament, to lay internal taxes:—But finding that ground not
tenable, she next denied its power to lay either internal or external taxes: And at length has declared, that it can neither lay
internal nor external taxes, nor regulate the internal police of
the colonies. And yet such has been the implicit confidence,—

such the infatuation of the unthinking and deluded people, that they have believed at the time, that all those principles were so many solid pillars—and supports of their rights, and *truths as sacred as those in holy writ.*

It would not be unreasonable to think, that the arguments before offered, to expose the present unhappy measures of the colonies, would be sufficient for that purpose. But however that may be, as I am convinced they lead to the ruin of my country, I think it my duty to take a more particular view of them. The claims made by the last congress, and upon which, it seems, all America now rests, are, "That the colonies are entitled to *a free and exclusive right, or power of legislation* in their several provincial legislatures, where their right of representation can alone be preserved, *in all cases of taxation and internal polity, subject only to the negative of their Sovereign, in such manner as has been heretofore used and accustomed.*" No words can convey a more perfect claim of independency, on the British legislature, than those I have just transcribed. Because there is no act within the power of any legislature to pass, binding on any member of the state, but what must, in either the regulation or execution of it affect the internal police. States may make laws for the government of their subjects, while in foreign countries, or upon the sea; but as those laws can only be executed within the society, there being no jurisdiction, no officer of justice without, its internal police must be affected by them, according to the nature of the penalties, and the mode of recovering, or inflicting them, and in the most sacred things, life, liberty and property; these being the objects upon which penalties are laid. If this be true, and the colonies have a "free and exclusive legislation, in all cases of internal polity," the legislature of Great-Britain can have no more authority over them, than the parliament of Paris; and the colonies are as independent of the one as the other. But it seems under this claim of right, though the legislature of Great-Britain, which is supreme in power, having no superior, as I have shewn, shall have no right to make laws for us, nor even to repeal an act of assembly, of the colonies, however inconsistent with the laws of England, or destructive to the rights and interests of the nation; yet the legislation of the colonies is to be subject to the *repeal of the King.* Does not this ill-founded claim

involve the cause of America in an inextricable absurdity? Is not
this acknowledging a power in an inferior, and denying it in
the superior, from whom that inferior draws all its authority,
and by whom all its prerogatives, rights, and powers are governed, and controuled? The King, by the constitution, has no
capacity in which he does not represent the supreme legislature, or head of the state, as I have proved before. Nor can he
assume any other inconsistent with its rights. The power of
repeal, being a compleat legislative act, he can draw it from no
other fountain, but from his representation of the *whole legislative body*. Because as legislator, he holds only a third part of
the right, and upon no ground of reason, or propriety, can an
entire superior power be derived, from any part of the same
power.

   Here we have a full view of the plan of the delegates of
North-America, which, when examined, appears to be that of
absolute independence on the mother state. But conscious
that a scheme, which has so great a tendency to a forfeiture of
her rights, and so destructive to her safety and happiness,
could not meet with the approbation and support of the colonists in general, unless in some measure disguised; they have
endeavoured to throw a veil over it, by graciously concedeing
to the mother-state, a whimsical authority, useless and impracticable, in its nature. This is a stale device, common to
wrong-headed politicians, who have not reason and truth to
support their pretensions. But the veil is too thin. The herbage
is not sufficiently thick to conceal the covered snake, from the
eye of the candid and sensible enquirer. But let us hear them.
"But from the necessity of the case, and a regard to the mutual
interest of both countries," not from any *constitutional right*,
for this they have denied in the preceeding part of the resolve,
in all cases whatsoever, "we consent;" but to what do they
consent? "to the operations of," not to the right of making,
"such acts of the British Parliament as are," not such as shall be
hereafter, for they are, no doubt, to receive the sanction of this
wise and learned body, before they are valid, "bona fide restrained, to the regulation of our external commerce, for the
purpose of *securing* the commercial advantages of the *whole*, (i. e.
of our commerce) to the *mother country*, and the commercial
benefits of its *respective members*." Here is more art and finesse,

than an honest mind would wish to find in the conduct of any men, much less in those of character. It is easy to perceive from the import of these words, that should the British parliament be obliged to accept of their *concessions*, they concede nothing. They have taken especial care, that what they have consented to in one breath, should be blasted by the next. For there is no law of trade, that I know of, nor can such a law be formed, as shall *secure the* commercial advantages *of all the external American commerce* to the mother country, which is a part of the realm distinct from the colonies, and yet "secure to the colonies," as members, their commercial benefit. It would not have been any great deviation from the public duty of these gentlemen, had they dealt less in mysteries, and explained what laws they were, which answered those excellent purposes. Surely they could not mean those statutes, which enumerate American commodities, and compel us to land them in Britain, before they can be exported to foreign markets; nor those which oblige us to purchase their manufactures, and forbid us to get them from other countries.—These are so far from "securing," that they greatly diminish the commercial benefits of the colonies; and I know of no other that "secure" the advantages of our commerce "to the mother country."—But suppose there are such laws, who are to point them out in the volumes of the statutes? Who is to say whether a law answers this description? Is the legislature of Great-Britain to do this? No. Who then?— Why, the assemblies.—But the assemblies are disunited, and may differ as they have done, even in matters which concerned their essential safety, and there is no constitutional union, declaring the voices of a majority, binding on all.—Why then, since it can be no otherways, the point must be determined by an illegal, motley congress; some few of them to be appointed by the assemblies, if they can be so lost to their own, and the true interest of their constituents, as ever to appoint another; and the rest by a twentieth part of the people, the most ignorant and violent to be found among them. A blessed American constitution!

But should there be any such laws as the congress have described, it seems, they are to be still further limited, and to "exclude every idea of internal and external taxation, for raising a revenue in America." All the laws of trade, from whence the least aid arises to the crown for the protection of its dominions, are invalid, for want of this "consent," and to be abolished: But those which amount to an absolute prohibition, are agreed to. The statute imposing a small duty on foreign sugars and molasses, on their importation, and thereby enabling the colonists to establish new manufactures, and open new sources of foreign trade, shall not be obeyed; but had the parliament instead thereof passed an act totally prohibiting this part of our foreign commerce, under forfeiture of vessel and cargo, it would have met with the approbation and consent of these great and wise men, at least as to its "operations." Is it not strange, that when they were about to bring forth this ruinous principle, they could not perceive, that every greater power includes every inferior, relative power; and that the power to prohibit a particular trade includes, *from necessity*, that of permitting it, *on condition of paying an advantageous duty*?

To conclude my remarks upon this famous American bill of rights, this pillar of American liberties: It seems implicitly agreed, that with the "consent of America," both internal and external taxes may be laid by Parliament;—But they have not informed us in what constitutional, or legal mode, this consent is to be obtained, or given. They must have known, if they knew any thing, that there was none; and yet so far were they from meaning to propose any, that they ordered, in direct violation of their own rules, the only constitutional plan which was offered for that purpose, to be *rescinded* from their minutes, after it had been debated, and refered to further consideration; lest the good people of America should see and approve of it, depriving the member who proposed it, of that security, against misrepresentation, which he was in justice entitled to, and contrary to their duty to the colonies.—Such are the proceedings of the men, intrusted with the sacred rights and liberties of America! Such the disappointment of their constituents.—They thought that all wisdom, justice and policy were concentred in that learned body. And therefore they expected that some permanent system of union, between Great-Britain and the colonies, upon principles of government and liberty, would have been proposed to the mother state, and a path opened to a lasting and happy reconciliation. But alas! How mistaken! Nothing has been the production of their

two months labour, but the ill-shapen, diminutive brat, INDE-
PENDENCY. And conscious of its inability to defend itself, they
have exerted every nerve, to prevail on the people to adopt the
spurious infant of a day, and take up arms in its defence; to
rush into the blackest rebellion, and all the horrors of an unnatural civil war. To effect this wicked and horrid design, they,
in all their *sham* majesty of illegal power, resolve that if "the
late acts of parliament shall be attempted to be carried into
execution *by force*, that in such case, *All America* ought to
support the inhabitants of the Massachusets Bay, *in their opposition.*" Who is to superintend the execution of the laws,
against which this opposition is advised? This is the duty of his
Majesty, as representative of the state, who is authorised to do
it, by first calling on the aid of the civil power, and if that is not
sufficient, the military. The essential principles of government
justify it. Search for yourselves, my dear countrymen, look into
all the treatises on the crown law, and they will tell you, that
this opposition is clear, palpable treason and rebellion, which
will incur the forfeiture of your estates, and your lives. But this
is not all the mischief they have done, or attempted to do—as
if nothing would satisfy them, but your inevitable ruin.—They
have surrounded you with misery on all sides—have used their
utmost endeavours, to raise the hostile resentment of one of
the most powerful states upon earth against you, when nothing but her affection, lenity and mercy towards you, can prevent her from reducing you, in a short time, to the deplorable
condition of a conquered people. But if she should be so blind
to your and her own interest, as to give you independency,
which is the great aim of their conduct, they have prepared the
rods and scourges of their own tyranny to subdue your spirits,
and triumph over your invaluable rights and liberties. Under
this tyranny, edicts have been made and published; and so sacred are they to be held, that none is to presume to *meddle*
with, or determine any dispute arising on them, but the creatures of this illegal power. The severest of all penalties are ordained for a disobedience to them. Taxes have been imposed
on your property, and that property arbitrarily taken from you;
the liberty of the press, and even the liberty of speech is destroyed. The unthinking, ignorant multitude, in the east and
west, are arming against the mother state, and the authority of

government, is silenced by the din of war.—What think you, O my countrymen, what think you will be your condition, when you shall see the designs of these men carried a little farther into execution?—Companies of armed, but undisciplined men, headed by men unprincipled, travelling over your estates, entering your houses—your castles—and sacred repositories of safety for all you hold dear and valuable—seizing your property, and carrying havock and devastation wherever they head—ravishing your wives and daughters, and afterwards plunging the dagger into their tender bosoms, while you are obliged to stand the speechless, the helpless spectators. Tell me, oh! tell me—whether your hearts are so obdurate as to be prepared for such shocking scenes of confusion and death. And yet, believe me, this is a real and not an exaggerated picture of that distress, into which the schemes of those men, who have assumed the characters of your guardians, and dare to stile themselves his *Majesty's most loyal subjects*, will inevitably plunge you, unless you oppose them with all the fortitude which reason and virtue can inspire.

I have thus thought it my duty, in a case of such infinite importance to my country, to give the full weight to the arguments in favour of the right of parliament, and against those rash and violent measures which are hastening the ruin of America. I do not know, that I have exaggerated any. I mean, with the most benevolent attachment to her true interest, to lay the truth, the whole truth, and nothing but the truth, before my country, that she may impartially consider it, and give it that weight which reason and her own preservation shall dictate;—but hitherto I have only performed a part of my engagement. The rights of America remain to be considered and established. A task which the undertaker must perform with ineffable pleasure, as he is pleading a cause founded on the immutable principles of reason and justice—the cause of his country, and the latest posterity. He is endeavouring to restore an union between two great countries, whose interest and welfare are inseparable; and to recover those rights upon the enjoyment whereof the happiness of millions depends.

That America has rights, and most important rights, which she does not at present enjoy, I know; and that they are as firmly established, as those of the parliament, may be easily proved; but what those rights are—whence derived—how the exercise of them has been lost—and what is the only possible and safe mode of recovering them, are questions, a candid solution of which will throw full light upon this unhappy controversy.

After what has been said respecting the rights of parliament, and the duties of the British state, it cannot be difficult to determine from whence the rights of America are derived. They can be traced to no other fountain, but that wherein they were originally established. This was in the constitution of the British state. Protection from all manner of unjust violence, is the great object which men have in view, when they surrender up their natural rights, and enter into society. I have said before, that the right to this protection, and the duties of allegiance were reciprocal. By protection I do not mean protection from foreign powers only; but also against the private injustice of individuals, the arbitrary and lawless power of the state, and of every subordinate authority. Such being the right, unless the government be so formed, as to afford the subject a security in the enjoyment of it, the right itself would be of little estimation. The tenure would be precarious, and its existence of a short duration. In proportion to the stability of this security, all governments are more or less free, and the subject happy under them. Much therefore depends on the particular form, or constitution of the society. In a monarchy, where the supreme power is lodged in a single person, without any check or controul, the tenure is precarious; because it depends on the discretion and integrity of the Monarch. But in a free government of the mixt form, where the people have a right to a share, and compose a part of the supreme authority, its foundation will be solid, and its continuance permanent; because the people themselves, who are interested in its preservation, partake of the power which is necessary to defend it.

There is no society in the world where this right of protection is settled with so much wisdom and policy, as in the English constitution. The experience of ages affords numerous instances of its being invaded and impaired, but in a short time restored by its own energetic power. It is this part of the English government upon which authors dwell with rapture; as it constitutes its whole excellence, and forms its freedom.

Power naturally arising from property, it is evident from a view of the British constitution, in all its different stages, that the English government derives its power from the landed interest; that being the most permanent and unchangeable in its nature, of all kinds of property, and therefore most worthy of protection. And although we cannot trace this truth up to its origin, the necessary antient records being buried in the ruins of the monasteries, either before or after the conquest, yet the fact is sufficiently evident from very ancient histories and documents, as well as from the plan of government, used in England from time immemorial. All historians agree that the present form of government was settled in Britain, by our ancestors, the Anglo-saxons; and so far as we have any knowledge of their government, in their own country, we know that the *proprietors of the land*, gave their personal attendance in *the legislative council*, and *shared the power of making their laws*. After their conquest of Britain, *all those to whom the land* was apportioned, held a right to assist in the Saxon parliaments. And by the feudal law *every landholder*, met in the feudal courts, and gave his assent, or dissent, to the laws there proposed.

Such continued to be the form of the British government, until the dissolution of the heptarchy, and union of the seven kingdoms, when, we should not have thought it strange, had this principle been destroyed, or greatly impaired, in the convulsions which effected so great a revolution. But, on the contrary, although the numbers of people, and their remoteness from the place of convention, were greatly encreased by the union which rendered a personal exercise of the legislative power impracticable; yet in order to preserve in the government, this important principle, upon which all their rights and freedom depended, they adopted the policy of vesting the landed interest in each tything and borough, with a right to send representatives to their Wittena-Gemot, or Parliament.

Nor could the rage of conquest, and all the power of arms, abolish this first principle of English liberty and safety. William the first, at the time he conquered Britain, found it consistent with his interest and security, to preserve it inviolate: And when he thought it necessary to lessen the exorbitant power of the Saxon Earls, which endangered his safety, by dismembering the baronies from the counties, the Barons were vested with a right to represent their baronies, in the great national council. This was all the change which that great man ventured to make in the constitution; a change which made no essential difference, as to its freedom. For as every spot of land was before the conquest within some tything, so under this alteration every part of it was included, in some barony or borough, and all of them were represented in the legislative power, by the Barons, or Burgesses.

Upon this solid foundation continued the freedom of the English government, during the reigns of William Rufus, and Henry the first. In the civil war between Stephen and Maud and Henry the second, each party finding the power and influence of the Barons over their vassals too great, divided the conquered baronies into smaller *tenancies in chief*, and rewarded their friends with them. By this measure, and the like policy, which was afterwards pursued by King John, tenants in capite, or the lesser Barons, were so multiplied, that a very unequal representation of the landed interest arose. They held an equal share in the legislature, with the greater Barons; and being more numerous, and their interest in many respects different, they over-ruled, and often deprived the greater nobility of their rights. This grievance grew intolerable; and therefore, when King John found himself obliged to do justice to the nation, and restore the antient principle of the constitution, two several clauses were inserted in Magna Charta: By the first "the Archbishops, Abbots, Earls and *great Barons* of the realm," were to be "summoned *singly*" by the King's writs; and by the second, "all others who held in chief," viz. the lesser Barons, or tenants in capite, were to be "summoned in general." By this clause the lesser barons were separated from the greater, and lost their hereditary right of representing their lands *singly*, or in person; but being summoned to parliament "in general," they held the right of electing some of their body to represent them in the house of commons; and of participating the supreme legislative authority, by their delegates, who were thence forward stiled Knights of the shire.

Thus this right to protection from the state, stood secured in every alteration of the constitution, by preserving to the landholders a share in the authority of the supreme head, who were to regulate that protection, and every other matter susceptible of human direction, until the reign of Henry VI. when our ancestors, conceiving that it could not be rendered too secure, nor founded on a base too broad, they obtained, by act of parliament, a right in every freeholder of forty shillings per annum, to vote for knights of the shire.

In confirmation of this right, I shall only add that King John, in the great charter I have before mentioned, granted for the restoration of the rights of the subject, engages "not to impose any taxes without summoning the archbishops, the bishops, the abbots, the earls, the greater barons, and the *tenants in capite*." And by the 17th of Edward III. another charter, granted on the like occasion, it is expressly declared, that "*whatever concerns the estate of the realm, and the people*, shall be treated of in parliament by the King, with the consent of the prelates, earls, barons, and commonalty of the realm."

It would be endless to trace this truth through all the pages of the history of the English government. I have offered proofs sufficient to demonstrate that the Lords and Commons, who hold so large a share of the legislative authority, derive their *right from, and represent the lands* within the realm. I shall therefore only add, before I leave this point, That this power of legislation in the people, derived from the share they held in the lands, was originally, and yet is, of the essence of the English government; and ever was, and still continues to be, the only check upon the encroachments of power, the great security against oppression, and the main support of the freedom and liberty of the English subjects. And its excellence consists in affording, to every part of the realm, an opportunity of representing, by their delegates, at all times, their true circumstances, their wants, their necessities, and their danger, to the supreme authority of the nation, without a knowledge of which it is impossible to form just or adequate laws; and when represented, to consult, advise and decide upon such provisions, as are proposed for their relief, or safety; giving their negative to such as are mischievous or improper, and their assent to those which remove the mischief, or afford a remedy. Here we have a perfect idea of civil liberty, and free government, such as is enjoyed by the subject in Great-Britain.

But what are the circumstances of the American British subjects? Is there a *part or spot of the lands in America*, or are the owners or proprietors thereof *in right of such lands,* represented in the British parliament; or do they in any other manner partake of the supreme power of the state? In this situation of the colonies, is not the British government as absolute and despotic over them, as any Monarch whatever, who singly holds the legislative authority? Are not the persons, lives and estates of the subjects in America at the disposal of an absolute power, without the least security for the enjoyment of their rights? Most certain it is, that this is a situation which people accustomed to liberty cannot sit easy under.

From the preceeding remarks it partly appears in what manner the American subjects have lost the enjoyment of this inestimable right, though not the right itself, viz. by their emigration to a part of the territory of the state, for which the constitution had not provided a representation. America not being known or thought of when the constitution was formed, no such provision was then made. But the right to a share in the supreme authority was confined to the territory at that time, intended to be governed by it. And at the time our ancestors left the mother country, it seems none was established. How this happened is not material to my subject—they came over, perhaps, without thinking of the importance of the right;—or their poverty, which rendered the obtaining of it in any form impracticable, prevented their claim of it. However, it is certain that it was passed over in silence, as well by the state, as the people who emigrated; but has been neither forfeited, surrendered, nor lost. And therefore it ought to be restored to them, in such manner as their circumstances will admit of, whenever it shall be decently and respectfully asked for. Justice to the Americans, and sound policy, in respect to both countries, manifestly require it.

The emigrants enjoyed in Britain the perfect rights of English subjects. They left their native country with the consent of the state, to encrease her commerce, to add to her wealth, and extend her dominions. All this they have effected with infinite labour and expence, and through innumerable difficulties and dangers. In the infant-state of their societies, they were incapable of exercising this right of participating the legislative authority in any mode. The power of parliament was justifiable from necessity at that time over them; they stood in as much need of its protection, as children in an infant-state require the aid and protection of a parent, to save them from a foreign enemy, as well as from those injuries which might arise from their own indiscretions. But now they are arrived at a degree of opulence, and circumstances so respectable, as not only to be capable of enjoying this right, but from necessity, and for the security of both countries to require it.

The subjects of a free state, in every part of its dominions ought, in good policy, to enjoy the same fundamental rights and privileges. Every distinction between them must be offensive and odious, and cannot fail to create uneasiness and jealousies, which will ever weaken the government, and frequently terminate in insurrections; which, in every society, ought to be particularly guarded against. If the British state therefore means to retain the colonies in a due obedience on her government, it will be wisdom in her to restore to her American subjects, the enjoyment of the right of assenting to, and dissenting from, such bills as shall be proposed to regulate their conduct. Laws thus made will ever be obeyed; because by their assent, they become their own acts.—It will place them in the same condition with their brethren in Britain, and remove all cause of complaint; or, if they should conceive any regulations inconvenient, or unjust, they will petition, not rebel. Without this it is easy to perceive that the union and harmony, which is peculiarly essential to a free society, whose members are resident in regions so very remote from each other, cannot long subsist.

The genius, temper, and circumstances of the Americans should be also duly attended to. No people in the world have higher notions of liberty. It would be impossible ever to eradicate them: should an attempt so unjust be ever made: Their late spirit and conduct fully prove this assertion, and will serve as a clue to that policy by which they ought to be governed. The distance of America from Britain, her vast extent of territory, her numerous ports and conveniencies of commerce, her various productions, her increasing numbers, and consequently her growing strength and power, when duly considered—all point out the policy of uniting the two countries together, upon principles of English liberty. Should this be omitted, the colonies will infallibly throw off their connexion with the mother country.—Their distance will encourage the attempt, their discontent will give them spirit, and their numbers wealth and power, at some future day, will enable them to effect it.

If it be the interest of the mother country, to be united with the colonies, it is still more Their interest that the union should take place. Their future safety and happiness depend on it. A little attention to their circumstances will prove it. Each colony, in the present constitution, is capable, by its own internal legislature, to regulate its own internal police, within its particular circle of territory. But here it is confined; thus far, and no farther, can its authority extend,—one cannot travel into the bounds of the other, and there make, or execute, its regulations. They are, therefore, in respect to each other, so many perfect and independent societies; destitute of any political connection, or supreme authority, to compel them to act in concert for the common safety. They are different in their forms of government,—productions of soil, and views of commerce.—They have different religions, tempers, and private interests.—They, of course, entertain high prejudices against, and jealousies of, each other; all which must from the nature and reason of things always conspire to create such a diversity of interests, inclinations, judgements, and conduct, that it will ever be impossible for them to unite in any general measure whatever, either to avoid any general mischief, or to promote any general good. A retrospect to the conduct of the colonies, during the last war, will shew that this assertion is founded in fatal experience. It was owing to this disunited state of the colonies, and their conducting their policy upon these principles, that a small number of French subjects in Canada, acting on the reverse, were enabled to concert their plans with such superior wisdom, and to exert such a superior degree of strength, as to endanger the safety of all North America, which contained upwards of two millions of people, and obliged them to implore the assistance of the British government. In the application to the mother country for protection, this is fully acknowledged. "It now evidently appears," say the council and assembly of the Massachusets Bay, "That the French are advanced in the execution of a *plan, projected more than fifty years since*, for extending their possessions from the mouth of the Mississippi on the south, to Hudson's Bay on the north, for securing the vast body of Indians in that inland country, and for subjecting *this whole continent to the crown of France.*"* And from what cause did it happen that the English colonies, possessed of an hundred fold more wealth, and twenty times the number of people, could not oppose, with success, the force and schemes of a few? The same gentlemen tell us, "The French have but *one interest*, and keep but *one point* in view: The *English governments have different interests, are disunited: some of them have their frontiers covered by their neighbours; and not being immediately affected seem unconcerned.*" The commissioners from the several colonies at Albany, assign the same cause. "The colonies," they inform the crown, being "in a divided, disunited state, there has never been *any joint exertion of their force*, or *councils*, to repel or defeat the measures of the French;" and "particular colonies are *unable and unwilling* to maintain the cause of the whole." "That it seems *absolutely necessary*, that speedy and effectual measures be taken *to secure the colonies from the slavery they are threatened with.*" The prediction contained in these declarations turned out strictly true. As it was most just that the colonies should contribute towards their own protection, while the mother country was lavishing millions in their defence; requisitions were annually made of them. But what was the conduct of the colonies in this scene, so very interesting to them? It is enough for me here to assert, what was known to all at the time, and what there still remains abundant documents to prove—That altho' some of the colonies, which were in immediate danger, complied chearfully and in time; yet others, from various causes, complied too late to be of real service; and some gave nothing towards the general defence, even at times when the enemy was within their borders, and a considerable part of the colony was evacuated. What must have been the direful consequences of those omissions of duty in the colonies towards each other, had not the mother-country exerted her military abilities to save them? The danger, and all the horrors of French slavery, and popish superstition, which then threw us, at times, into the greatest despondency, are past, and we have forgot them! But let us not deceive ourselves; the

* Message from the Council and House of Representatives of the Massachusets Bay, in 1754.

same causes will ever produce the same effects.—The ambition of France is still alive and active, her power indeed is asleep, but only to wake at some future day. America is daily growing a more alluring object of her ambition. Her fleets, and those of her natural ally, the King of Spain, are encreasing. The practice of conquering and dividing territories and kingdoms, is become fashionable in Europe. Under this prospect of things, what can America expect, while she denies the authority of the mother-state; and by that denial incurs a forfeiture of her protection, and refuses to be united with her upon such principles as will entitle her to it. She must in all probability soon become the slave of arbitrary power, —of Popish bigotry and superstition.

But the miseries of a foreign yoke are not all the mischiefs which may attend her scheme of independency. Disputes will ever arise among the colonies. The seeds of controversy, respecting their several interests and boundaries, are already sown, and in full vegetation. Ambition and avarice are ever ready to exert their influence, whenever opportunity offers. America has many men of abilities and intrigue, who will at all times be ready to rise on the misfortunes and calamities of others. Disputes between Pennsylvania and Maryland began, and would have ended in a civil war, had not the authority of the state interposed. Similar disputes have subsisted between New-York and Connecticut; New-York and New-Jersey, and still subsist between New-York and New-Hampshire, Connecticut and Pennsylvania, and Pennsylvania and Virginia; all arising from the uncertainty of their boundaries, and right to the soil. In 1606 King James granted two charters, one to the Plymouth company, and the other to Sir Thomas Gates, and others; *including all the colonies.* The resumption of the first of these charters has been publickly avowed and attempted; and we have great reason to believe, that of the other is in contemplation. These, with many other causes, will afford plentiful sources of dispute between the several colonies; which can only be decided by the sword, there being no other power to appeal to. The northern colonies, inured to military discipline and hardships, will, in all probability, be the first to enter the list of military controversy; and, like the northern Saxons and Danes, carry devastation and havock over the southern; who, weak for want of discipline, and having a dangerous enemy within their own bowels, must, after suffering all the horrors of a civil war, yield to the superior force, and submit to the will of the conquerors.

We have now before us, all that we are to gain by this frantic attempt, to separate the colonies from Great-Britain. Should America fail in her military opposition, which she must infallibly do, they immediately become a conquered people, subject to such laws as the conquerors shall think proper to impose: —All our rights and privileges forfeited,—our loyalty justly distrusted—our ports secured by men of war,—our capital cities burthened with British troops,—and our wealth exhausted for their support. On the contrary, should we by any miraculous event succeed in this mad design, we must soon either become a prey to a foreign power; our laws, our manners and customs, our rights both civil and religious, and our inestimable religion itself, will be changed for the arbitrary customs, the slavery and bloody superstition of Rome: Or should we by any unforeseen accident, escape this deplorable situation, another awaits us, almost as shocking and distressing. Ambition and avarice will soon furnish the fewel, and blow up the flame of civil discord among ourselves. Some of these calamities must inevitably be the blessed consequences of this unnatural scheme.

It will now be asked, what then is to be done? Must we submit to parliamentary regulations, when we are not represented in that body? My answer is—That I am a friend to true liberty. I esteem it above all other temporal blessings, and *because* I esteem it, I disapprove of the independent measures of the congress; which, instead of tending to secure, or obtain it, lead to the destruction of *all liberty*, and the *most dangerous tyranny*. I do not differ from them in opinion, that America has grievances to complain of; but I differ from them in the mode of *obtaining redress*. I ever was convinced that Great-Britain was not so despicable in her power as to be hectored out of her rights by her subjects; or that she was so ignorant of the condition of the colonies, as to believe our pretensions to independency could be maintained. I foresaw what has now come to pass, that we must either submit to parliamentary authority,—or to be a conquered people,—or seek for redress in an *union* with the mother state. And my duty as a subject, my own interest, and the safety and happiness of my country, ever prevailed on me to prefer the last. Had this measure been adopted in the year 1766, in all probability, the rights of America would have been restored, and the most perfect harmony would have this day subsisted between the two countries: But unfortunately for America, such ground was at that time taken, as rendered it inconsistent with the honour and dignity of parliament to meet us.

Great pains have been taken by the American demagogues, to delude the unhappy people, whom they have doomed to be the dupes of their ambition, into a belief that no justice was to be obtained of his Majesty, and his houses of parliament; and that they had refused to hear our most reasonable petitions. Hence we have seen the best of Sovereigns treated with the grossest abuse and insult, the affections of his people alienated, and many of his faithful subjects, desponding of relief, taking up arms against his authority. It is high time that this fatal delusion should be exposed, and the good people of America disabused. It is true, that his Majesty and the two houses of parliament have treated petitions from the colonies with neglect; but what were those petitions? Did they rest on a denial of the essential rights of Parliament, or did they ask for the rights of the subject in America? A retrospect of all the petitions, ever presented to the throne on this subject, will shew that they conveyed to the royal ear, nothing but the language of independence. They disowned the power of the supreme legislature, to which, as subjects, they owe obedience, and denied a capacity in the colonies to be represented—and upon this ground they insisted on a repeal of the laws. Here they ended.—*No prayer, nor the least intimation of a desire to be united with Britain upon a just restoration of their rights!* Such were the petitions of the colonies, which were treated with neglect by the supreme power of the nation. And the reasonable and sensible man will now, on reflection, determine, whether it becomes us to resent a conduct of this kind, in our superiors, or rather to look back with astonishment at our folly, in permitting ourselves to be led by designing men, into such acts of disrespect and insult. Let us bring the case home to ourselves. The relation between the sovereign authority and its members, bears a true resemblance to that between parent and child. Their rights and duties are similar. Should a child take umbrage at the conduct of a parent, tell him that he was not his father, nor would he consider himself, or act, as his child *on any terms*; ought the parent to listen to such undutiful language, or could he be justly censured for treating it with neglect, or even with contempt?

In order to prevail on the congress to desert their scheme of independence, and to pursue those measures for restoring the rights of America, which carried with them a prospect of success; a member of the congress, as I mentioned before, proposed a plan of union between the two countries, which would have restored to the colonists the full enjoyment of their rights. I have often conversed with him on the subject, and well understand his principles, and what passed on the occasion. He waited with patience to see whether any rational scheme of union would be adopted by the congress,—determined to unite with them in any measure which might tend to a reconciliation between the two countries; but he waited in vain: And when he found them bewildered, perpetually changing their ground, taking up principles one day, and shifting them the next, he thought it his duty, however little the prospect of success, to speak his sentiments with firmness, and to endeavour to show them the true line of their duty. After proving the necessity of a supreme authority over every member of the state, tracing the rights of the colonies to their origin, and fixing them on the most solid principles; and thence shewing the necessity of an union with the mother state, for the recovery of them; he introduced the plan with the resolve which precedes it. But before he delivered it to be read, he declared, that he was sensible it was not perfect; that knowing the fundamental principles of every system must be first settled, he had, to avoid perplexity, contented himself with only laying down the great out-lines of the union; and should they be approved of, that he had several propositions of lesser consequence to make, in order to render the system more complete. The plan read, and warmly seconded by several gentlemen of the first abilities, after a long debate, was so far approved as to be thought worthy of further consideration, and referred under a rule for that purpose, by a majority of the colonies. Under this promising aspect of things, and an expectation that the rule would have been regarded, or at least that something rational would take place to reconcile our unhappy differences, the member proposing it was weakly led to sign the non-importation agreement, although he had uniformly opposed it; but in this he was disappointed.—The measures of *independence and sedition*, were soon after preferred to those of *harmony and liberty*; and no arguments, however reasonable and just, could prevail on a majority of the colonies to desert them. The resolve, plan, and rule referring them to further consideration, so inconsistent with the measures now resolved on, were expunged from the minutes; with what view let America determine: And while the enemies to the gentleman who proposed them, are abusing him for offering and publishing to the world the most infamous falshood, in representing it as ministerial, and sent over to him by Lord N——h; they have copies of it in their pockets, industriously concealing it from the world. With what view can this be, but that their malevolent aspersions may take the greater effect? In justice therefore to the character of this gentleman, and that America may see and judge for itself, they are here offered to its consideration.

RESOLVED,

That the Congress will apply to his Majesty for a redress of grievances under which his faithful subjects in America labour; and assure him, that the Colonies hold in abhorrence the idea of being considered independent communities on the British government, and most ardently desire the establishment of a Political Union, not only among themselves, but with the Mother State, upon those principles of safety and freedom which are essential in the constitution of all free governments, and particularly that of the British Legislature; and as the Colonies from their local circumstances, cannot be represented in the Parliament of Great-Britain, they will humbly propose to his Majesty and his two Houses of Parliament, the following plan, under which the strength of the whole Empire may be drawn together on any emergency, the interest of both countries advanced, and the rights and liberties of America secured.

A PLAN OF A PROPOSED UNION BETWEEN GREAT-BRITAIN AND THE COLONIES.

THAT a British and American legislature, for regulating the administration of the general affairs of America, be proposed and established in America, including all the said colonies; within, and under which government, each colony shall retain its present constitution, and powers of regulating and governing its own internal police, in all cases whatever.

That the said government be administered by a President General, to be appointed by the King and a grand Council, to be chosen by the Representatives of the people of the several colonies, in their respective Assemblies, once in every three years.

That the several Assemblies shall choose members for the grand Council in the following proportions, viz.

New-Hampshire,	Delaware Counties,
Massachusetts-Bay,	Maryland,
Rhode-Island,	Virginia,
Connecticut,	North-Carolina,
New-York,	South-Carolina,
New-Jersey,	and
Pennsylvania,	Georgia.

Who shall meet at the city of　　　　for the first time, being called by the President-General, as soon as conveniently may be after his appointment.

That there shall be a new election of members for the Grand Council every three years; and on the death, removal or resignation of any member, his place shall be supplied by a new choice, at the next sitting of Assembly of the Colony he represented.

That the Grand Council shall meet once in every year, if they shall think it necessary, and oftner, if occasions shall require, at such time and place as they shall adjourn to, at the last preceding meeting, or as they shall be called to meet at, by the President-General, on any emergency.

That the grand Council shall have power to choose their Speaker, and shall hold and exercise all the like rights, liberties and privileges, as are held and exercised by and in the House of Commons of Great-Britain.

That the President-General shall hold his Office during the pleasure of the King, and his assent shall be requisite to all acts of the Grand Council, and it shall be his office and duty to cause them to be carried into execution.

That the President-General, by and with the advice and consent of the Grand-Council, hold and exercise all the legislative rights, powers, and authorities, necessary for regulating and administring all the general police and affairs of the colonies, in which Great-Britain and the colonies, or any of them, the colonies in general, or more than one colony, are in any manner concerned, as well civil and criminal as commercial.

That the said President-General and Grand Council, be an inferior and distinct branch of the British legislature, united and incorporated with it, for the aforesaid general purposes; and that any of the said general regulations may originate and be formed and digested, either in the Parliament of Great-Britain, or in the said Grand Council, and being prepared, transmitted to the other for their approbation or dissent; and that the assent of both shall be requisite to the validity of all such general acts or statutes.

That in time of war, all bills for granting aids to the crown, prepared by the Grand Council, and approved by the President General, shall be valid and passed into a law, without the assent of the British Parliament.

I shall not affirm that this plan is formed upon the most perfect principles of policy and government; but as it is an universally prevailing opinion, that the colonies cannot be represented in parliament: I know of none other which comes so near to them; and it is most evident, upon a due consideration of it, that the rights of America would have been fully restored, and her freedom effectually secured by it. For under it, no law can be binding on America, to which the people, by their representatives, have not previously given their consent: This is the essence of liberty, and what more would her people desire?

The author of this plan seems to have formed it on a comprehensive view, of the regulations necessary to the interest and safety of the colonies. These he has divided into two classes: the first contain all such as the colony legislatures have a right to make, under the several constitutions, and to which they are adequate; these to remain under their decisions; it being declared in the plan, that "each colony shall retain its present constitution and powers of regulating and governing its own internal police in all cases whatever." The others, which are to be the objects of the deliberations and decisions of the grand council, relate to the general interests and security of the colonies, and are absolutely necessary for those purposes; such laws for granting aids to the crown, and levying taxes in just and reasonable proportions in the colonies—for regulating a general paper currency, and the value of foreign coins, which ought in all good policy, to be established on funds equally solid, and ascertained at the same value: Laws for regulating and quartering troops, which may be necessary for their general protection; for settling disputes between the colonies, respecting their boundaries—with a variety of other matters that must naturally arise from the jarring interests of the colonies, which will continually encrease with the encrease of their wealth and commerce. And as to those, it must be owned, that the colony legislatures are not adequate; but that they must be made either by the parliament, or by some new establishment for those purposes. The authority of the first was objected to; and as to the second, or any other system of union, it being incompatible with the scheme of independence, it was not thought worthy of attention.

Objections were indeed made to this plan, which it may not be improper here to mention. It was said, "that the delegates did not come with authority to consent to a political union between the two countries." To which many arguments were opposed, to show that they had such authority or none; and concluded with desiring, that if that was, in the opinion of the members, the case, yet that the congress ought in justice to their country to digest and form one, and recommend it to their respective assemblies; by whom it would be presented with more constitutional propriety than by any other body of men. It was further said, "that the members of the grand council would be corrupted, and betray the interest of the colonies." To this it was answered—That if American virtue was not firm enough to maintain American liberty, it could be supported by no wisdom or policy whatever; but suppose the people to be in so corrupt a state;—yet as the election of the members was to be triennial, they might change them every 3 years, and the sums of money, necessary to bribe the new members, would be too great to be supplied: That the most sensible writers on the side of liberty agreed, if the parliament of England was triennial, it would destroy the system of corruption. Besides, to avoid all risque of the contrary, they might, by altering one word in the plan, make the election duennial, or annual, which must certainly remove the objection. A third objection was, That it deprived the colony legislatures of a part of their rights: To which it was replied, that a colony legislature is capable of passing laws to regulate its internal police; but not adequate to any general regulation, not even in the necessary one of taxation. That there is no proposition more just, than that every colony, as a member of the state, ought to be obliged to contribute towards the defence of the whole, in proportion to the property and wealth which each colony possesses. That this is a primary consideration in every society; and that no one colony had a constitutional power to obtain the amount and value of the property of the others, by which to ascertain its proportion. Nor was there any authority whatever, save the British Parliament, to compel refractory colonies to do their reasonable duty, in this or any other general measure: and that this plan was so far from diminishing the rights of any colony legislature, that it extended them; by giving to each a new jurisdiction, to decide upon regulations which relate to the general police of all the colonies.

Such was the plan laid before the congress, the objections against, and the arguments in favour of it. They are here laid before the public, to enable them to judge for themselves, whether, as a representation in parliament, is generally supposed to be impracticable, any thing more consistent with their safety could have been adopted.

Had this unhappy controversy been of the first impression in the English government, I should not be surprised to find the advocates of America so much at a loss for principles upon which to ask for, and obtain her rights. I confess I know not whether to attribute their strange conduct to a total ignorance of the merits, or to a design from the beginning to throw off all political connections with the British government. However this may be, precedents are not wanting upon which to reason, and to form a remedy. The principality of Wales, the Bishop-rick of Durham, and the Palatinate of Chester, laboured under the like grievances; being bound by the laws of parliament for many years, without holding a share in the supreme authority. Great discontent arose from the slavish distinction between the subjects of the same state. The oppressed thought it their duty, as members of the state, to petition the parliament for a share in their authority. And such was the equity and justice of their claims, that they became thereupon vested with this important privilege. When Henry III. conquered Calais, and settled it with English merchants, with intent to extend his dominions, and encrease the commerce of the nation; it was held so incompatible with English liberty, that the authority of parliament should extend to members who did not partake of it, that they were incorporated with the English government, and shared in its legislature.

What then is to be done? Is it too late to recover from our madness, and to pursue the dictates of reason and duty? By no means. But it is high time we had changed our measures, and retreated from the dangers with which we are threatened. Let us, like men who love order and government, boldly oppose the illegal edicts of the congress, before it is too late,—pull down the licentious tyranny they have established, and dissolve their inferior committees,—their instruments to trample on the sacred laws of your country, and your invaluable rights. This done, and peace and order restored within your several provinces; apply to your assemblies, who are your constitutional guardians, and can alone procure a redress of your grievances. Entreat them in a respectful and dutiful manner, to petition his Majesty and his two houses of parliament—and in their petitions to assure them, "That you are sensible of the necessity of a supreme legislature over every member of the state; that you acknowledge yourselves subjects of the British government; that you have, through innumerable difficulties and perils, settled and improved a wilderness, extended the territories, and greatly encreased the wealth and power of the nation: That by such settlement you have lost the enjoyment of, though not the right to, some of the first and most excellent of the privileges of Englishmen: That the "English government is founded on freedom: That this freedom depends on its particular constitution, in which it is and ever was essential, that the landed interest, or the freeholders of every part of its territory, should participate in the supreme legislative authority, having a right to regulate their conduct, and a power over their lives, liberties and properties. That this privilege alone distinguishes British subjects from the slaves of the most despotic governments: That no *part of the lands in America*, nor the *proportion thereof in right of such lands*, enjoy their antient right of participating in the authority of parliament. And yet that laws have been made, by that authority, for levying taxes upon your property, for restraining and prohibiting your trade and commerce, for suppressing your manufactures, for regulating your internal police, and depriving you of many other rights, to which you are entitled as English subjects. That by such regulations you have been aggrieved and oppressed, and great discontent has arisen in the breasts of his Majesty's faithful American subjects, to the destruction of that harmony which ought to subsist between members of the same community, and great prejudice of the common wealth. That it is not for want of inclination, but capacity, arising from the disunited state of the colonies, that you have not discharged, with justice among yourselves, those duties which appertain to members of the state: And therefore pray, That you may not only be restored to this capacity, but to all the rights of Englishmen, upon such principles of liberty and policy, as shall best suit your local circumstances."

A petition of this kind, so reasonable and just, and so well founded and established on the principles of their own government, attended with such a plan of union as may be wisely digested by your several assemblies, there is no room to doubt, will be graciously received, and duly attended to by his Majesty and his two houses of parliament, and finally terminate in a full redress of your grievances, and a permanent system of union and harmony, upon principles of liberty and safety. But let me entreat you, not to trust these petitions to your agents alone; but follow the wise examples of the Grecian and Roman colonists, —send over with them one or more delegates, to remove the present prejudices, to create friends, and to solicit your cause. The expence will be trifling, their utility may be great,—the importance of your rights is infinite.

Thus I have, my dear countrymen, with the utmost candour and freedom, and the most benevolent regard for your true interest and happiness, laid before you the constitutional extent of parliamentary jurisdiction, and *deduced* your rights from the most solid foundation, and explained your duties. I have pointed out the mode which I am convinced, you ought to pursue for a restoration of those rights. I have showed you the folly of the scheme now in agitation for that purpose. My most sincere wish is, that you may avail yourselves of the information, and retreat from the danger and distress which threatens you, before it is too late. Permit me, before I conclude, to ask you a few serious questions. Do you mean to forfeit, by your rash and imprudent conduct, your right to the protection of the British state, and cut yourselves and your posterity off for ever from all the privileges of Englishmen? To relinquish your trade up the Mediterranean, in the British seas, and all the British ports? and suffer the produce of your soil, and the effects of your labour and industry to perish on your hands, for want of a market to dispose of them? Do you mean to desert all your present blessings, & retreat from superior force into a wilderness inhabited by wild beasts and savages, destitute of the necessaries of life, and incapable of obtaining them? Or do you mean to submit to the deplorable condition of a conquered people, subject to the oppression and tyranny of a military government, with British fleets directing that pittance of trade, which the conqueror may allow you to enjoy; and with British forces in all your capital cities, commanding your allegiance to the British state?

Do you wish to exchange the mild and equal rule of English customs and manners, and your inestimable religion, for the tyranny of a foreign yoke, and the bloody superstitions of popery? Or do you design to give up your present enjoyment of all the blessings of life, for the horrors and distress of a civil war, and the fatal consequences which must infallibly attend yourselves, and your latest posterity? Are you *still* resolved to surrender up your reason to the miserable sophistry and jargon of designing men, and to hazard all these direful misfortunes, rather than be united with your brethren and fellow subjects in Britain? If such be your dreadful resolutions, I, who have all that I hold dear and valuable among you, must content myself with sharing along with you the calamitous consequences of your frenzy, and the miserable fate of an American; with this only consolation, that I have honestly discharged my duty in warning you of your dangers, and endeavoured to pilot you into the haven of security and happiness.

FINIS.

[Samuel Johnson], Taxation No Tyranny; an Answer to the Resolutions and Address of the American Congress. London, 1775.

One of the most celebrated literary figures in eighteenth-century England, Samuel Johnson was naturally cantankerous, and early in his career was often opposed to government; but in the 1770s he wrote several pamphlets in support of ministerial policies. This one, commissioned by Lord North's ministry and published in March 1775, was the longest and most elaborate of Johnson's political tracts and it went through four editions in the first month. According to his celebrated biographer, James Boswell, Johnson came naturally to the assignment, having "long before indulged most unfavourable sentiments of our fellow-subjects in America. For, as early as 1769, I was told by Dr. John Campbell, that he had said of them, 'Sir, they are a race of convicts, and ought to be thankful for any thing we allow them short of hanging.'"

Relentless, colorful, and sarcastic, *Taxation No Tyranny* does not appear to be designed to change Americans' minds; indeed, at times it seemed to assume that the colonists were already "no longer subjects" of Britain. Instead, Johnson used his pamphlet to present the British case to the world to judge which side was right. And he took a very hard line. Too bad if the people of Boston were "condemned unheard." Since the "crime" of destroying tea was "manifest and notorious," there was "no need of a trial" to prove their guilt. In fact, Johnson took a harder line than the ministry wanted, since it was still hoping for some sort of settlement. Much to Johnson's annoyance, the government removed several incendiary passages before publication, including one in which Johnson wrote that if he were in charge, "the first thing he would do, would be to quarter the army on the citys, and if any refused free quarters, he would pull down the person's house, if it was joined to other houses, but would burn it if it stood alone." This deletion did nothing to undermine Johnson's core message, however: the Americans "leave us no choice but of yielding or conquering, or resigning our dominion, or maintaining it by force."

In September 1775 John Wesley, the founder of Methodism, published *A Calm Address to Our American Colonies*, the first eighteen pages of which were borrowed without attribution directly from Johnson's pamphlet—plagiarism being more acceptable in the eighteenth century than it is today.

Taxation no Tyranny;

AN

ANSWER

TO THE

RESOLUTIONS AND ADDRESS

OF THE

AMERICAN CONGRESS.

LONDON,

PRINTED FOR T. CADELL, IN THE STRAND.

MDCCLXXV.

Taxation No Tyranny.

IN all the parts of human knowledge, whether terminating in science merely speculative, or operating upon life private or civil, are admitted some fundamental principles, or common axioms, which being generally received are little doubted, and being little doubted have been rarely proved.

Of these gratuitous and acknowledged truths it is often the fate to become less evident by endeavours to explain them, however necessary such endeavours may be made by the misapprehensions of absurdity, or the sophistries of interest. It is difficult to prove the principles of science, because notions cannot always be found more intelligible than those which are questioned. It is difficult to prove the principles of practice, because they have for the most part not been discovered by investigation, but obtruded by experience, and the demonstrator will find, after an operose deduction, that he has been trying to make that seen which can be only felt.

Of this kind is the position, that *the supreme power of every community has the right of requiring from all its subjects such contributions as are necessary to the public safety or public prosperity*, which was considered by all mankind as comprising the primary and essential condition of all political society, till it became disputed by those zealots of anarchy, who have denied to the parliament of Britain the right of taxing the American colonies.

In favour of this exemption of the Americans from the authority of their lawful sovereign, and the dominion of their mother-country, very loud clamours have been raised, and many wild assertions advanced, which by such as borrow their opinions from the reigning fashion have been admitted as arguments; and what is strange, though their tendency is to lessen English honour, and English power, have been heard by English-men with a wish to find them true. Passion has in its first violence controlled interest, as the eddy for a while runs against the stream.

To be prejudiced is always to be weak; yet there are prejudices so near to laudable, that they have been often praised, and are always pardoned. To love their country has been considered as virtue in men, whose love could not be otherwise than blind, because their preference was made without a comparison; but it never has been my fortune to find, either in ancient or modern writers, any honourable mention of those, who have with equal blindness hated their country.

These antipatriotic prejudices are the abortions of Folly impregnated by Faction, which being produced against the standing order of Nature, have not strength sufficient for long life. They are born only to scream and perish, and leave those to contempt or detestation, whose kindness was employed to nurse them into mischief.

To perplex the opinion of the Publick many artifices have been used, which, as usually happens when falsehood is to be maintained by fraud, lose their force by counteracting one another.

The nation is sometimes to be mollified by a tender tale of men, who fled from tyranny to rocks and desarts, and is persuaded to lose all claims of justice, and all sense of dignity, in compassion for a harmless people, who having worked hard for bread in a wild country, and obtained by the slow progression of manual industry the accommodations of life, are now invaded by unprecedented oppression, and plundered of their properties by the harpies of taxation.

We are told how their industry is obstructed by unnatural restraints, and their trade confined by rigorous prohibitions; how they are forbidden to enjoy the products of their own soil, to manufacture the materials which Nature spreads before them, or to carry their own goods to the nearest market: and surely the generosity of English virtue will never heap new weight upon those that are already overladen, will never delight in that dominion, which cannot be exercised but by cruelty and outrage.

But while we are melting in silent sorrow, and in the transports of delicious pity, dropping both the sword and balance from our hands, another friend of the Americans thinks it better to awaken another passion, and tries to alarm our interest, or excite our veneration, by accounts of their greatness and their opulence, of the fertility of their land, and the splendour of their towns. We then begin to consider the question with more evenness of mind, are ready to conclude that those restrictions are not very oppressive which have been found consistent with this speedy growth of prosperity, and begin to think it reasonable that they, who thus flourish under the protection of our government, should contribute something towards its expence.

But we are then told that the Americans, however wealthy, cannot be taxed; that they are the descendants of men who left all for liberty, and that they have constantly preserved the principles and stubbornness of their progenitors; that they are too obstinate for persuasion, and too powerful for constraint; that they will laugh at argument, and defeat violence; that the continent of North America contains three millions, not of men merely, but of Whigs, of Whigs fierce for liberty, and disdainful of dominion; that they multiply with the fecundity of their own rattle-snakes, so that every quarter of a century doubles their numbers.

Men accustomed to think themselves masters do not love to be threatened. This talk is, I hope, commonly thrown away, or raises passions different from those which it intended to excite. Instead of terrifying the English hearer to tame acquiescence, it disposes him to hasten the experiment of bending obstinacy, before it is become yet more obdurate, and convinces him that it is necessary to attack a nation thus prolific while we may yet hope to prevail. When he is told through what extent of territory we must travel to subdue them, he recollects how far, a few years ago, we travelled in their defence. When it is urged that they will shoot up like the Hydra, he naturally considers how the Hydra was destroyed.

Nothing dejects a trader like the interruption of his profits. A commercial people, however magnanimous, shrinks at the thought of declining traffick, and an unfavourable balance. The effect of this terrour has been tried. We have been stunned with the importance of our American commerce, and heard of merchants with warehouses that are never to be emptied, and of manufacturers starving for want of work.

That our commerce with America is profitable, however less than ostentatious or deceitful estimates have made it, and that it is our interest to preserve it, has never been denied; but surely it will most effectually be preserved, by being kept always in our own power. Concessions may promote it for a moment, but superiority only can ensure its continuance. There will always be a part, and always a very large part of every community that have no care but for themselves, and whose care for themselves reaches little farther than impatience of immediate pain, and eagerness for the nearest good. The blind are said to feel with peculiar nicety. They who look but little into futurity, have perhaps the quickest sensation of the present. A merchant's desire is not of glory, but of gain; not of publick wealth, but of private emolument; he is therefore rarely to be consulted about war and peace, or any designs of wide extent and distant consequence.

Yet this, like other general characters, will sometimes fail. The traders of *Birmingham* have rescued themselves from all imputation of narrow selfishness by a manly recommendation to Parliament of the rights and dignity of their native country.

To these men I do not intend to ascribe an absurd and enthusiastick contempt of interest, but to give them the rational and just praise of distinguishing real from seeming good, of being able to see through the cloud of interposing difficulties, to the lasting and solid happiness of victory and settlement.

Lest all these topicks of persuasion should fail, the great actor of patriotism has tried another, in which terrour and pity are happily combined, not without a proper superaddition of that admiration which later ages have brought into the drama. The heroes of Boston, he tells us, if the Stamp Act had not been repealed, would have left their town, their port, and their trade, have resigned the splendour of opulence, and quitted the delights of neighbourhood, to disperse themselves over the country, where they would till the ground, and fish in the rivers, and range the mountains, AND BE FREE.

These surely are brave words. If the mere sound of freedom can operate thus powerfully, let no man hereafter doubt the story of the Pied Piper. *The removal of the people of Boston into the country* seems even to the Congress not only *difficult in its execution*, but *important in its consequences.* The difficulty of execution is best known to the Bostonians themselves; the consequence, alas! will only be, that they will leave good houses to wiser men.

Yet before they quit the comforts of a warm home for the sounding something which they think better, he cannot be thought their enemy who advises them to consider well whether they shall find it. By turning fishermen or hunters, woodmen or shepherds, they may become wild, but it is not so easy to conceive them free; for who can be more a slave than he that is driven by force from the comforts of life, is compelled to leave his house to a casual comer, and whatever he does, or wherever he wanders, finds every moment some new testimony of his own subjection? If the choice of evil is freedom, the felon in the gallies has his option of labour or of stripes. The Bostonian may quit his house to starve in the fields; his dog may refuse to set, and smart under the lash, and they may then congratulate each other upon the smiles of liberty, *profuse with bliss, and pregnant with delight.*

To treat such designs as serious, would be to think too contemptuously of Bostonian understandings. The artifice indeed is not new: the blusterer who threatened in vain to destroy his opponent, has sometimes obtained his end, by making it believed that he would hang himself.

But terrours and pity are not the only means by which the taxation of the Americans is opposed. There are those who profess to use them only as auxiliaries to reason and justice, who tell us that to tax the colonies is usurpation and oppression, an invasion of natural and legal rights, and a violation of those principles which support the constitution of English government.

This question is of great importance. That the Americans are able to bear taxation is indubitable; that their refusal may be over-ruled is highly probable: but power is no sufficient evidence of truth. Let us examine our own claim, and the objections of the recusants, with caution proportioned to the event of the decision, which must convict one part of robbery, or the other of rebellion.

A tax is a payment exacted by authority from part of the community for the benefit of the whole. From whom, and in what proportion such payment shall be required, and to what uses it shall be applied, those only are to judge to whom government is intrusted. In the British dominion taxes are apportioned, levied, and appropriated by the states assembled in parliament.

Of every empire all the subordinate communities are liable to taxation, because they all share the benefits of government, and therefore ought all to furnish their proportion of the expence.

This the Americans have never openly denied. That it is their duty to pay the cost of their own safety they seem to admit; nor do they refuse their contribution to the exigencies, whatever they may be, of the British empire; but they make this participation of the public burden a duty of very uncertain extent, and imperfect obligation, a duty temporary, occasional and elective, of which they reserve to themselves the right of settling the degree, the time, and the duration, of judging when it may be required, and when it has been performed.

They allow to the supreme power nothing more than the liberty of notifying to them its demands or its necessities. Of this notification they profess to think for themselves, how far it shall influence their counsels, and of the necessities alleged, how far they shall endeavour to relieve them. They assume the exclusive power of settling not only the mode, but the quantity of this payment. They are ready to co-operate with all the other dominions of the King; but they will co-operate by no means which they do not like, and at no greater charge than they are willing to bear.

This claim, wild as it may seem, this claim, which supposes dominion without authority, and subjects without subordination, has found among the libertines of policy many clamorous and hardy vindicators. The laws of Nature, the rights of humanity, the faith of charters, the danger of liberty, the encroachments of usurpation, have been thundered in our ears, sometimes by interested faction, and sometimes by honest stupidity.

It is said by Fontenelle, that if twenty philosophers shall resolutely deny that the presence of the sun makes the day, he will not despair but whole nations may adopt the opinion. So many political dogmatists have denied to the Mother Country the power of taxing the Colonies, and have enforced their denial with so much violence of outcry, that their sect is already very numerous, and the publick voice suspends its decision.

In moral and political questions the contest between interest and justice has been often tedious and often fierce, but perhaps it never happened before that justice found much opposition with interest on her side.

For the satisfaction of this inquiry, it is necessary to consider how a Colony is constituted, what are the terms of migration as dictated by Nature, or settled by compact, and what social or political rights the man loses, or acquires, that leaves his country to establish himself in a distant plantation.

Of two modes of migration the history of mankind informs us, and so far as I can yet discover, of two only.

In countries where life was yet unadjusted, and policy unformed, it sometimes happened that by the dissensions of heads of families, by the ambition of daring adventurers, by some accidental pressure of distress, or by the mere discontent of idleness, one part of the community broke off from the rest, and numbers, greater or smaller, forsook their habitations, put themselves under the command of some favourite of fortune, and with or without the consent of their countrymen or governours, went out to see what better regions they could occupy, and in what place, by conquest or by treaty, they could gain a habitation.

Sons of enterprise like these, who committed to their own swords their hopes and their lives, when they left their country, became another nation, with designs, and prospects, and interests, of their own. They looked back no more to their former home; they expected no help from those whom they had left behind: if they conquered, they conquered for themselves; if they were destroyed, they were not by any other power either lamented or revenged.

Of this kind seem to have been all the migrations of the old world, whether historical or fabulous, and of this kind were the eruptions of those nations which from the North invaded the Roman empire, and filled Europe with new sovereignties.

But when, by the gradual admission of wiser laws and gentler manners, society became more compacted and better regulated, it was found that the power of every people consisted in union, produced by one common interest, and operating in joint efforts and consistent counsels.

From this time Independence perceptibly wasted away. No part of the nation was permitted to act for itself. All now had the same enemies and the same friends; the Government protected individuals, and individuals were required to refer their designs to the prosperity of the Government.

By this principle it is, that states are formed and consolidated. Every man is taught to consider his own happiness as combined with the publick prosperity, and to think himself great and powerful, in proportion to the greatness and power of his Governors.

Had the Western continent been discovered between the fourth and tenth century, when all the Northern world was in motion; and had navigation been at that time sufficiently advanced to make so long a passage easily practicable, there is little reason for doubting but the intumescence of nations would have found its vent, like all other expansive violence, where there was least resistance; and that Huns and Vandals, instead of fighting their way to the South of Europe, would have gone by thousands and by myriads under their several chiefs to take possession of regions smiling with pleasure and waving with fertility, from which the naked inhabitants were unable to repel them.

Every expedition would in those days of laxity have produced a distinct and independent state. The Scandinavian heroes might have divided the country among them, and have spread the feudal subdivision of regality from Hudson's Bay to the Pacifick Ocean.

But Columbus came five or six hundred years too late for the candidates of sovereignty. When he formed his project of discovery, the fluctuations of military turbulence had subsided, and Europe began to regain a settled form, by established government and regular subordination. No man could any longer erect himself into a chieftain, and lead out his fellow-subjects by his own authority to plunder or to war. He that committed any act of hostility by land or sea, without the commission of some acknowledged sovereign, was considered by all mankind as a robber or a pirate, names which were now of little credit, and of which therefore no man was ambitious.

Columbus in a remoter time would have found his way to some discontented Lord, or some younger brother of a petty Sovereign, who would have taken fire at his proposal, and have quickly kindled with equal heat a troop of followers; they would have built ships, or have seized them, and have wandered with him at all adventures as far as they could keep hope in their company. But the age being now past of vagrant excursion and fortuitous hostility, he was under the necessity of travelling from court to court, scorned and repulsed as a wild projector, an idle promiser of kingdoms in the clouds: nor has any part of the world yet had reason to rejoice that he found at last reception and employment.

In the same year, in a year hitherto disastrous to mankind, by the Portuguese was discovered the passage of the Indies, and by the Spaniards the coast of America. The nations of Europe were fired with boundless expectation, and the discoverers pursuing their enterprise, made conquests in both hemispheres of wide extent. But the adventurers were contented with plunder; though they took gold and silver to themselves, they seized islands and kingdoms in the name of their Sovereigns. When a new region was gained, a governour was appointed by that power which had given the commission to the conqueror; nor have I met with any European but Stukeley of London, that formed a design of exalting himself in the newly found countries to independent dominion.

To secure a conquest, it was always necessary to plant a colony, and territories thus occupied and settled were rightly considered as mere extensions or processes of empire; as ramifications through which the circulation of one publick interest communicated with the original source of dominion, and which were kept flourishing and spreading by the radical vigour of the Mother-country.

The Colonies of England differ no otherwise from those of other nations, than as the English constitution differs from theirs. All Government is ultimately and essentially absolute, but subordinate societies may have more immunities, or individuals greater liberty, as the operations of Government are differently conducted. An Englishman in the common course of life and action feels no restraint. An English Colony has very liberal powers of regulating its own manners and adjusting its own affairs. But an English individual may by the supreme authority be deprived of liberty, and a Colony divested of its powers, for reasons of which that authority is the only judge.

In sovereignty there are no gradations. There may be limited royalty, there may be limited consulship; but there can be no limited government. There must in every society be some power or other from which there is no appeal, which admits no restrictions, which pervades the whole mass of the community, regulates and adjusts all subordination, enacts laws or repeals them, erects or annuls judicatures, extends or contracts privileges, exempt itself from question or control, and bounded only by physical necessity.

By this power, wherever it subsists, all legislation and jurisdiction is animated and maintained. From this all legal rights are emanations, which, whether equitably or not, may be legally recalled. It is not infallible, for it may do wrong; but it is irresistible, for it can be resisted only by rebellion, by an act which makes it questionable what shall be thenceforward the supreme power.

An English Colony is a number of persons, to whom the King grants a Charter permitting them to settle in some distant country, and enabling them to constitute a Corporation, enjoying such powers as the Charter grants, to be administered in such forms as the Charter prescribes. As a Corporation they make laws for themselves, but as a Corporation subsisting by a grant from higher authority, to the controll of that authority they continue subject.

As men are placed at a greater distance from the Supreme Council of the kingdom, they must be entrusted with ampler liberty of regulating their conduct by their own wisdom. As they are more secluded from easy recourse to national judicature, they must be more extensively commissioned to pass judgment on each other.

For this reason our more important and opulent Colonies see the appearance and feel the effect of a regular Legislature, which in some places has acted so long with unquestioned authority, that it has been forgotten whence that authority was originally derived.

To their Charters the Colonies owe, like other corporations, their political existence. The solemnities of legislation, the administration of justice, the security of property, are all bestowed upon them by the royal grant. Without their Charter there would be no power among them, by which any law could be made, or duties enjoined, any debt recovered, or criminal punished.

A Charter is a grant of certain powers or privileges given to a part of the community for the advantage of the whole, and is therefore liable by its nature to change or to revocation. Every act of Government aims at publick good. A Charter, which experience has shewn to be detrimental to the nation, is to be repealed; because general prosperity must always be preferred to particular interest. If a Charter be used to evil purposes, it is forfeited, as the weapon is taken away which is injuriously employed.

The Charter therefore by which provincial governments are constituted, may be always legally, and where it is either inconvenient in its nature, or misapplied in its use, may be equitably repealed, and by such repeal the whole fabrick of subordination is immediately destroyed, the constitution sunk at once into a chaos: the society is dissolved into a tumult of individuals, without authority to command, or obligation to obey; without any punishment of wrongs but by personal resentment, or any protection of right but by the hand of the possessor.

A Colony is to the Mother-country as a member to the body, deriving its action and its strength from the general principle of vitality; receiving from the body, and communicating to it, all the benefits and evils of health and disease; liable in dangerous maladies to sharp applications, of which the body however must partake the pain; and exposed, if incurably tainted, to amputation, by which the body likewise will be mutilated.

The Mother-country always considers the Colonies thus connected, as parts of itself; the prosperity or unhappiness of either is the prosperity or unhappiness of both; not perhaps of both in the same degree, for the body may subsist, though less commodiously, without a limb, but the limb must perish if it be parted from the body.

Our Colonies therefore, however distant, have been hitherto treated as constituent parts of the British Empire. The inhabitants incorporated by English Charters, are intitled to all the rights of Englishmen. They are governed by English laws, entitled to English dignities, regulated by English counsels, and protected by English arms; and it seems to follow by consequence not easily avoided, that they are subject to English government, and chargeable by English taxation.

To him that considers the nature, the original, the progress, and the constitution of the Colonies, who remembers that the first discoverers had commissions from the crown, that the first settlers owe to a charter their civil forms and regular magistracy, and that all personal immunities and personal securities, by which the condition of the subject has been from time to time improved, have been extended to the Colonists, it will not be doubted but the Parliament of England has a right to bind them by statutes, and *to bind them in all cases whatsoever*, and has therefore a legal and constitutional power of laying upon them any tax or impost, whether external or internal, upon the product of land, or the manufactures of industry, in the exigencies of war, or in the time of profound peace, for the defence of America, *for the purpose of raising a revenue*, or for any other end beneficial to the Empire.

There are some, and those not inconsiderable for number, nor contemptible for knowledge, who except the power of taxation from the general dominion of Parliament, and hold that whatever degrees of obedience may be exacted, or whatever authority may be exercised in other acts of Government, there is still reverence to be paid to money, and that legislation passes its limits when it violates the purse.

Of this exception, which by a head not fully impregnated with politicks is not easily comprehended, it is alleged as an unanswerable reason, that the Colonies send no representatives to the House of Commons.

It is, say the American advocates, the natural distinction of a freeman, and the legal privilege of an Englishman, that he is able to call his possessions his own, that he can sit secure in the enjoyment of inheritance or acquisition, that his house is fortified by the law, and that nothing can be taken from him but by his own consent. This consent is given for every man by his representative in parliament. The Americans unrepresented cannot consent to English taxations, as a corporation, and they will not consent as individuals.

Of this argument, it has been observed by more than one, that its force extends equally to all other laws, that a freeman is not to be exposed to punishment, or be called to any onerous service but by his own consent. The congress has extracted a position from the fanciful *Montesquieu*, that *in a free state every man being a free agent ought to be concerned in his own government*. Whatever is true of taxation is true of every other law, that he who is bound by it, without his consent, is not free, for he is not concerned in his own government.

He that denies the English Parliament the right of taxation, denies it likewise the right of making any other laws civil or criminal, yet this power over the Colonies was never yet disputed by themselves. They have always admitted statutes for the punishment of offences, and for the redress or prevention of inconveniencies; and the reception of any law draws after it by a chain which cannot be broken, the unwelcome necessity of submitting to taxation.

That a free man is governed by himself, or by laws to which he has consented, is a position of mighty sound; but every man that utters it, with whatever confidence, and every man that hears it, with whatever acquiescence, if consent be supposed to imply the power of refusal, feels it to be false. We virtually and implicitly allow the institutions of any Government of which we enjoy the benefit, and solicit the protection. In wide extended dominions, though power has been diffused with the most even hand, yet a very small part of the people are either primarily or secondarily consulted in Legislation. The business of the Publick must be done by delegation. The choice of delegates is made by a select number, and those who are not electors stand idle and helpless spectators of the commonweal, *wholly unconcerned with the government of themselves.*

Of Electors the hap is but little better. They are often far from unanimity in their choice, and where the numbers approach to equality, almost half must be governed not only without, but against their choice.

How any man can have consented to institutions established in distant ages, it will be difficult to explain. In the most favourite residence of liberty, the consent of individuals is merely passive, a tacit admission in every community of the terms which that community grants and requires. As all are born the subjects of some state or other, we may be said to have been all born consenting to some system of Government. Other consent than this, the condition of civil life does not allow. It is the unmeaning clamour of the pedants of policy, the delirious dream of republican fanaticism.

But hear, ye sons and daughters of liberty, the sounds which the winds are wafting from the Western Continent. The Americans are telling one another, what, if we may judge from their noisy triumph, they have but lately discovered, and what yet is a very important truth. *That they are entitled to Life, Liberty, and Property, and that they have never ceded to any sovereign power whatever a right to dispose of either without their consent.*

While this resolution stands alone, the Americans are free from singularity of opinion; their wit has not yet betrayed them to heresy. While they speak as the naked sons of Nature, they claim but what is claimed by other men, and have witheld nothing but what all withhold. They are here upon firm ground, behind entrenchments which never can be forced.

Humanity is very uniform. The Americans have this resemblance to Europeans, that they do not always know when they are well. They soon quit the fortress that could neither have been mined by sophistry, nor battered by declamation. Their next resolution declares, that *their ancestors, who first settled the Colonies, were, at the time of their emigration from the Mother-country, entitled to all the rights, liberties, and immunities of free and natural-born subjects within the realm of England.*

This likewise is true; but when this is granted, their boast of original rights is at an end; they are no longer in a State of Nature. These lords of themselves, these kings of *Me*, these demigods of independence, sink down to Colonists, governed by a Charter. If their ancestors were subjects, they acknowledged a Sovereign; if they had a right to English privileges, they were accountable to English laws, and what must grieve the Lover of Liberty to discover, had ceded to the King and Parliament, whether the right or not, at least the power, of disposing, *without their consent, of their lives, liberties, and properties.* It therefore is required of them to prove, that the Parliament ever ceded to them a dispensation from that obedience, which they owe as natural-born subjects, or any degree of independence or immunity not enjoyed by other Englishmen.

They say, That by such emigration they by no means forfeited, surrendered, or lost any of those rights; but that *they were, and their descendents now are, entitled to the exercise and enjoyment of all such of them as their local and other circumstances enable them to exercise and enjoy.*

That they who form a settlement by a lawful Charter, having committed no crime, forfeit no privileges, will be readily confessed; but what they do not forfeit by any judicial sentence, they may lose by natural effects. As man can be but in one place at once, he cannot have the advantages of multiplied residence. He that will enjoy the brightness of sunshine, must quit the coolness of the shade. He who goes voluntarily to America, cannot complain of losing what he leaves in Europe. He perhaps had a right to vote for a knight or burgess: by crossing the Atlantick he has not nullified his right; for he has made its exertion no longer possible. By his own choice he has left a country where he had a vote and little property, for another, where he has great property, but no vote. But as this preference was deliberate and unconstrained, he is still *concerned in the government of himself*; he has reduced himself from a voter to one of the innumerable multitude that have no vote. He has truly *ceded his right*, but he still is governed by his own consent; because he has consented to throw his atom of interest into the general mass of the community. Of the consequences of his own act he has no cause to complain; he has chosen, or intended to chuse, the greater good; he is represented, as himself desired, in the general representation.

But the privileges of an American scorn the limits of place; they are part of himself, and cannot be lost by departure from his country; they float in the air, or glide under the ocean.

Doris amara suam non intermisceat undam.

A Planter, wherever he settles, is not only a freeman, but a legislator, *ubi imperator, ibi Roma. As the English Colonists are not represented in the British Parliament, they are entitled to a free and exclusive power of legislation in their several legislatures, in all cases of Taxation and internal polity, subject only to the negative of the Sovereign, in such manner as has been heretofore used and accustomed. We cheerfully consent to the operation of such acts of the British Parliament as are* bona fide *restrained to the regulation of our external commerce—excluding every idea of Taxation, internal or external, for raising a revenue on the subjects of America without their consent.*

Their reason for this claim is, *that the foundation of English*

Liberty, and of all Government, is a right in the People to partic-
ipate in their Legislative Council.

They inherit, they say, *from their ancestors, the right which*
their ancestors professed, of enjoying all the privileges of English-
men. That they inherit the right of their ancestors is allowed;
but they can inherit no more. Their ancestors left a country
where the representatives of the people were elected by men
particularly qualified, and where those who wanted qualifications, or who did not use them, were bound by the decisions
of men whom they had not deputed.

The colonists are the descendants of men, who either had
no votes in elections, or who voluntarily resigned them for
something, in their opinion, of more estimation: they have
therefore exactly what their ancestors left them, not a vote in
making laws, or in constituting legislators, but the happiness
of being protected by law, and the duty of obeying it.

What their ancestors did not carry with them, neither they
nor their descendants have since acquired. They have not, by
abandoning their part in one legislature, obtained the power
of constituting another, exclusive and independent, any more
than the multitudes, who are now debarred from voting, have
a right to erect a separate Parliament for themselves.

Men are wrong for want of sense, but they are wrong by
halves for want of spirit. Since the Americans have discovered
that they can make a Parliament, whence comes it that they do
not think themselves equally empowered to make a King? If
they are subjects, whose government is constituted by a charter, they can form no body of independent legislature. If their
rights are inherent and underived, they may by their own suffrages encircle with a diadem the brows of Mr. Cushing.

It is farther declared by the Congress of Philadelphia, *that*
his majesty's Colonies are entitled to all the privileges and immu-
nities granted and confirmed to them by Royal Charters, or se-
cured to them by their several codes of provincial laws.

The first clause of this resolution is easily understood, and
will be readily admitted. To all the privileges which a Charter
can convey, they are by a Royal Charter evidently entitled. The
second clause is of greater difficulty; for how can a provincial
law secure privileges or immunities to a province? Provincial
laws may grant to certain individuals of the province the

enjoyment of gainful, or an immunity from onerous offices; they may operate upon the people to whom they relate; but no province can confer provincial privileges on itself. They may have a right to all which the King has given them; but it is a conceit of the other hemisphere, that men have a right to all which they have given to themselves.

A corporation is considered in law as an individual, and can no more extend its own immunities, than a man can by his own choice assume dignities or titles.

The Legislature of a Colony, let not the comparison be too much disdained, is only the vestry of a larger parish, which may lay a cess on the inhabitants, and enforce the payment; but can extend no influence beyond its own district, must modify its particular regulations by the general law, and whatever may be its internal expences, is still liable to Taxes laid by superior authority.

The Charters given to different provinces are different, and no general right can be extracted from them. The Charter of Pensylvania, where this Congress of anarchy has been impudently held contains a clause admitting in express terms Taxation by the Parliament. If in the other Charters no such reserve is made, it must have been omitted as not necessary, because it is implied in the nature of subordinate government. They who are subject to laws, are liable to Taxes. If any such immunity had been granted, it is still revocable by the Legislature, and ought to be revoked as contrary to the publick good, which is in every Charter ultimately intended.

Suppose it true that any such exemption is contained in the Charter of Maryland, it can be pleaded only by the Marylanders. It is of no use for any other province, and with regard even to them, must have been considered as one of the grants in which the King has been deceived, and annulled as mischievous to the Publick, by sacrificing to one little settlement the general interest of the Empire; as infringing the system of dominion, and violating the compact of Government. But Dr. Tucker has shewn that even this Charter promises no exemption from Parliamentary Taxes.

In the controversy agitated about the beginning of this century, whether the English laws could bind Ireland, Davenant, who defended against Molyneux the claims of England, considered it as necessary to prove nothing more, than that the present Irish might be deemed a Colony.

The necessary connexion of representatives with Taxes, seems to have sunk deep into many of those minds, that admit sounds without their meaning.

Our nation is represented in Parliament by an assembly as numerous as can well consist with order and dispatch, chosen by persons so differently qualified in different places, that the mode of choice seems to be, for the most part, formed by chance, and settled by custom. Of individuals far the greater part have no vote, and of the voters few have any personal knowledge of him to whom they entrust their liberty and fortune.

Yet this representation has the whole effect expected or desired; that of spreading so wide the care of general interest, and the participation of publick counsels, that the interest or corruption of particular men can seldom operate with much injury to the Publick.

For this reason many populous and opulent towns neither enjoy nor desire particular representatives: they are included in the general scheme of publick administration, and cannot suffer but with the rest of the Empire.

It is urged that the Americans have not the same security, and that a British Legislature may wanton with their property; yet if it be true, that their wealth is our wealth, and that their ruin will be our ruin, the Parliament has the same interest in attending to them, as to any other part of the nation. The reason why we place any confidence in our representatives is, that they must share in the good or evil which their counsels shall produce. Their share is indeed commonly consequential and remote; but it is not often possible that any immediate advantage can be extended to such numbers as may prevail against it. We are therefore as secure against intentional depravations of Government as human wisdom can make us, and upon this security the Americans may venture to repose.

It is said by the *Old Member* who has written an *Appeal* against the Tax, that *the produce of American labour is spent in British manufactures, the balance of trade is greatly against them; whatever you take directly in Taxes, is in effect taken from your own commerce. If the minister seizes the money with which*

the American should pay his debts and come to market, the mer-
chant cannot expect him as a customer, nor can the debts already
contracted be paid.—Suppose we obtain from America a million
instead of one hundred thousand pounds, it would be supplying
one personal exigence by the future ruin of our commerce.

All this is true; but the *old Member* seems not to perceive,
that if his brethren of the Legislature know this as well as
himself, the Americans are in no danger of oppression, since by
men commonly provident they must be so taxed, as that we
may not lose one way what we gain another.

The same *old Member* has discovered, that the judges formerly thought it illegal to tax Ireland, and declares that no
cases can be more alike than those of Ireland and America; yet
the judges whom he quotes have mentioned a difference. Ireland, they say, *hath a Parliament of its own.* When any Colony
has an independent Parliament, acknowledged by the Parliament of Britain, the cases will differ less. Yet by the 6 Geo. I.
chap. 5. the Acts of the British Parliament bind Ireland.

It is urged that when Wales, Durham, and Chester were divested of their particular privileges or ancient government, and
reduced to the state of English counties, they had representatives assigned them.

To those from whom something had been taken, something
in return might properly be given. To the Americans their
Charters are left as they were, except that of which their sedition has deprived them. If they were to be represented in Parliament, something would be granted, though nothing is
withdrawn.

The inhabitants of Chester, Durham, and Wales, were invited to exchange their peculiar institutions for the power of
voting, which they wanted before. The Americans have voluntarily resigned the power of voting to live in distant and separate governments, and what they have voluntarily quitted, they
have no right to claim.

It must always be remembered that they are represented by
the same virtual representation as the greater part of Englishmen; and that if by change of place they have less share in the
Legislature than is proportioned to their opulence, they by their
removal gained that opulence, and had originally and have now
their choice of a vote at home, or riches at a distance.

We are told, what appears to the *old Member* and to others a
position that must drive us into inextricable absurdity, that we
have either no right, or the sole right of taxing the Colonies.
The meaning is, that if we can tax them, they cannot tax themselves; and that if they can tax themselves, we cannot tax
them. We answer with very little hesitation, that for the general
use of the Empire we have the sole right of taxing them. If
they have contributed any thing in their own assemblies, what
they contributed was not paid, but given; it was not a tax or
tribute, but a present. Yet they have the natural and legal
power of levying money on themselves for provincial purposes,
of providing for their own expence, at their own discretion.
Let not this be thought new or strange; it is the state of every
parish in the kingdom.

The friends of the Americans are of different opinions. Some
think that being unrepresented they ought to tax themselves,
and others that they ought to have representatives in the British Parliament.

If they are to tax themselves, what power is to remain in the
supreme Legislature? That they must settle their own mode of
levying their money is supposed. May the British Parliament
tell them how much they shall contribute? If the sum may be
prescribed, they will return few thanks for the power of raising
it; if they are at liberty to grant or to deny, they are no longer
subjects.

If they are to be represented, what number of these western
orators are to be admitted. This I suppose the parliament must
settle; yet if men have a natural and unalienable right to be represented, who shall determine the number of their delegates?
Let us however suppose them to send twenty-three, half as many
as the kingdom of Scotland, what will this representation avail
them? To pay taxes will be still a grievance. The love of money
will not be lessened, nor the power of getting it increased.

Whither will this necessity of representation drive us? Is
every petty settlement to be out of the reach of government,
till it has sent a senator to Parliament; or may two or a greater
number be forced to unite in a single deputation? What at last
is the difference, between him that is taxed by compulsion
without representation, and him that is represented by compulsion in order to be taxed?

For many reigns the House of Commons was in a state of fluctuation: new burgesses were added from time to time, without any reason now to be discovered; but the number has been fixed for more than a century and a half, and the king's power of increasing it has been questioned. It will hardly be thought fit to new model the constitution in favour of the planters, who, as they grow rich, may buy estates in England, and without any innovation, effectually represent their native colonies.

The friends of the Americans indeed ask for them what they do not ask for themselves. This inestimable right of representation they have never solicited. They mean not to exchange solid money for such airy honour. They say, and say willingly, that they cannot conveniently be represented; because their inference is, that they cannot be taxed. They are too remote to share the general government, and therefore claim the privilege of governing themselves.

Of the principles contained in the resolutions of the Congress, however wild, indefinite, and obscure, such has been the influence upon American understanding, that from New-England to South-Carolina there is formed a general combination of all the Provinces against their Mother-country. The madness of independence has spread from Colony to Colony, till order is lost and government despised, and all is filled with misrule, uproar, violence, and confusion. To be quiet is disaffection, to be loyal is treason.

The Congress of Philadelphia, an assembly convened by its own authority, and as a seditious conventicle punishable by law, has promulgated a declaration, in compliance with which the communication between Britain and the greatest part of North America is now suspended. They ceased to admit the importation of English goods in December 1774, and determine to permit the exportation of their own no longer than to November 1775.

This might seem enough, but they have done more. They have declared, that they shall treat all as enemies who do not concur with them in disaffection and perverseness, and that they will trade with none that shall trade with Britain.

They threaten to stigmatize in their Gazette those who shall consume the products or merchandise of their Mother-country, and are now searching suspected houses for prohibited goods.

These hostile declarations they profess themselves ready to maintain by force. They have armed the militia of their provinces and seized the publick stores of ammunition. They are therefore no longer subjects, since they refuse the laws of their Sovereign, and in defence of that refusal are making open preparations for war.

Being now in their own opinion free states, they are not only raising armies, but forming alliances, not only hastening to rebel themselves, but seducing their neighbours to rebellion. They have published an address to the inhabitants of Quebec, in which discontent and resistance are openly incited, and with very respectful mention of *the sagacity of Frenchmen*, invite them to send deputies to the Congress of Philadelphia, to that seat of Virtue and Veracity, whence the people of England are told, that to establish popery, *a religion fraught with sanguinary and impious tenets*, even in Quebec, a country of which the inhabitants are papists, is so contrary to the constitution, that it cannot be lawfully done by the legislature itself, where it is made one of the articles of their association, to deprive the conquered French of their religious establishment; and whence the French of Quebec are, at the same time, flattered into sedition, by professions of expecting *from the liberality of sentiment, distinguishing* their *nation*, that *difference of religion will not prejudice them against a hearty amity*, because *the transcendent nature of freedom elevates all who unite in the cause above such low-minded infirmities*.

Quebec, however, is at a great distance. They have aimed a stroke from which they may hope for greater and more speedy mischief. They have tried to infect the people of England with the contagion of disloyalty. Their credit is happily not such as gives them influence proportionate to their malice. When they talk of their pretended immunities *guarrantied by the plighted faith of Government, and the most solemn compacts with English Sovereigns*, we think ourselves at liberty to inquire when the faith was plighted and the compact made; and when we can only find that King James and King Charles the First promised the settlers in Massachuset's Bay, now famous by the appellation of Bostonians, exemption from taxes for seven years, we infer with Mr. Mauduit, that by this *solemn compact*, they were, after the expiration of the stipulated term, liable to taxation.

When they apply to our compassion, by telling us, that they are to be carried from their own country to be tried for certain offences, we are not so ready to pity them, as to advise them not to offend. While they are innocent they are safe.

When they tell of laws made expressly for their punishment, we answer, that tumults and sedition were always punishable, and that the new law prescribes only the mode of execution.

When it is said that the whole town of Boston is distressed for a misdemeanor of a few, we wonder at their shamelessness; for we know that the town of Boston, and all the associated provinces, are now in rebellion to defend or justify the criminals.

If frauds in the imposts of Boston are tried by commission without a jury, they are tried here in the same mode; and why should the Bostonians expect from us more tenderness for them than for ourselves?

If they are condemned unheard, it is because there is no need of a trial. The crime is manifest and notorious. All trial is the investigation of something doubtful. An Italian philosopher observes, that no man desires to hear what he has already seen.

If their assemblies have been suddenly dissolved, what was the reason? Their deliberations were indecent, and their intentions seditious. The power of dissolution is granted and reserved for such times of turbulence. Their best friends have been lately soliciting the King to dissolve his Parliament, to do what they so loudly complain of suffering.

That the same vengeance involves the innocent and guilty is an evil to be lamented, but human caution cannot prevent it, nor human power always redress it. To bring misery on those who have not deserved it, is part of the aggregated guilt of rebellion.

That governours have been sometimes given them only that a great man might get ease from importunity, and that they have had judges not always of the deepest learning, or the purest integrity, we have no great reason to doubt, because such misfortunes happen to ourselves. Whoever is governed will sometimes be governed ill, even when he is most concerned in his own government.

That improper officers or magistrates are sent, is the crime or folly of those that sent them. When incapacity is discovered, it ought to be removed; if corruption is detected, it ought to be punished. No government could subsist for a day, if single errors could justify defection.

One of their complaints is not such as can claim much commiseration from the softest bosom. They tell us, that we have changed our conduct, and that a tax is now laid by Parliament on those which were never taxed by Parliament before. To this we think it may be easily answered, that the longer they have been spared, the better they can pay.

It is certainly not much their interest to represent innovation as criminal or invidious; for they have introduced into the history of mankind a new mode of disaffection, and have given, I believe, the first example of a proscription published by a Colony against the Mother-country.

To what is urged of new powers granted to the Courts of Admiralty, or the extension of authority conferred on the judges, it may be answered in a few words, that they have themselves made such regulations necessary; that they are established for the prevention of greater evils; at the same time, it must be observed, that these powers have not been extended since the rebellion in America.

One mode of persuasion their ingenuity has suggested, which it may perhaps be less easy to resist. That we may not look with indifference on the American contest, or imagine that the struggle is for a claim, which, however decided, is of small importance and remote consequence, the Philadelphian Congress has taken care to inform us, that they are resisting the demands of Parliament, as well for our sakes as their own.

Their keenness of perspicacity has enabled them to pursue consequences to a greater distance; to see through clouds impervious to the dimness of European sight; and to find, I know not how, that when they are taxed, we shall be enslaved.

That slavery is a miserable state we have been often told, and doubtless many a Briton will tremble to find it so near as in America; but how it will be brought hither, the Congress must inform us. The question might distress a common understanding; but the statesmen of the other hemisphere can easily resolve it. Our ministers, they say, are our enemies, and *if they should carry the point of taxation, may with the same army enslave us. It may be said, we will not pay them; but remember*, say the western sages, *the taxes from America, and we may add the men, and particularly the Roman Catholics of this vast continent will then be in the power of your enemies. Nor have you any reason to expect, that after making slaves of us, many of us will refuse to assist in reducing you to the same abject state.*

These are dreadful menaces; but suspecting that they have not much the sound of probability, the Congress proceeds: *Do not treat this as chimerical. Know that in less than half a century the quit-rents reserved to the crown from the numberless grants of this vast continent will pour large streams of wealth into the royal coffers. If to this be added the power of taxing America at pleasure, the crown will possess more treasure than may be necessary to purchase* the remains *of liberty in your island.*

All this is very dreadful; but amidst the terror that shakes my frame, I cannot forbear to wish that some sluice were opened for these streams of treasure. I should gladly see America return half of what England has expended in her defence; and of the stream that will *flow so largely in less than half a century*, I hope a small rill at least may be found to quench the thirst of the present generation, which seems to think itself in more danger of wanting money than of losing liberty.

It is difficult to judge with what intention such airy bursts of malevolence are vented: if such writers hope to deceive, let us rather repel them with scorn, than refute them by disputation.

In this last terrifick paragraph are two positions that, if our fears do not overpower our reflection, may enable us to support life a little longer. We are told by these croakers of calamity, not only that our present ministers design to enslave us, but that the same malignity of purpose is to descend through all their successors, and that the wealth to be poured into England by the Pactolus of America will, whenever it comes, be employed to purchase the remains of liberty.

Of those who now conduct the national affairs we may, without much arrogance, presume to know more than themselves, and of those who shall succeed them, whether minister or king, not to know less.

The other position is, that the *Crown*, if this laudable opposition should not be successful, *will have the power of taxing America at pleasure.* Surely they think rather too meanly of our apprehensions, when they suppose us not to know what they well know themselves, that they are taxed, like all other British subjects, by Parliament; and that the Crown has not by the new imposts, whether right or wrong, obtained any additional power over their possessions.

It were a curious, but an idle speculation to inquire, what effect these dictators of sedition expect from the dispersion of their letter among us. If they believe their own complaints of hardship, and really dread the danger which they describe, they will naturally hope to communicate their own perceptions to their fellow-subjects. But probably in America, as in other places, the chiefs are incendiaries, that hope to rob in the tumults of a conflagration, and toss brands among a rabble passively combustible. Those who wrote the Address, though they have shown no great extent or profundity of mind, are yet probably wiser than to believe it: but they have been taught by some master of mischief, how to put in motion the engine of political electricity; to attract by the sounds of Liberty and Property, to repel by those of Popery and Slavery; and to give the great stroke by the name of Boston.

When subordinate communities oppose the decrees of the general legislature with defiance thus audacious, and malignity thus acrimonious, nothing remains but to conquer or to yield; to allow their claim of independence, or to reduce them by force to submission and allegiance.

It might be hoped, that no Englishman could be found, whom the menaces of our own Colonists, just rescued from the French, would not move to indignation, like that of the Scythians, who, returning from war, found themselves excluded from their own houses by their slaves.

That corporations constituted by favour, and existing by sufferance, should dare to prohibit commerce with their native country, and threaten individuals by infamy, and societies with at least suspension of amity, for daring to be more obedient to government than themselves, is a degree of insolence, which not only deserves to be punished, but of which the punishment is loudly demanded by the order of life, and the peace of nations.

Yet there have risen up, in the face of the publick, men who, by whatever corruptions or whatever infatuation, have undertaken to defend the Americans, endeavour to shelter them from resentment, and propose reconciliation without submission.

As political diseases are naturally contagious, let it be supposed for a moment that Cornwal, seized with the Philadelphian frenzy, may resolve to separate itself from the general system of the English constitution, and judge of its own rights in its own parliament. A Congress might then meet at Truro, and address the other counties in a style not unlike the language of the American patriots.

"Friends and Fellow-subjects,

"We the delegates of the several towns and parishes of Cornwal, assembled to deliberate upon our own state and that of our constituents, having, after serious debate and calm consideration, settled the scheme of our future conduct, hold it necessary to declare in this publick manner, the resolutions which we think ourselves entitled to form by the immutable laws of Nature, and the unalienable rights of reasonable Beings, and into which we have been at last compelled by grievances and oppressions, long endured by us in patient silence, not because we did not feel, or could not remove them, but because we were unwilling to give disturbance to a settled government, and hoped that others would in time find like ourselves their true interest and their original powers, and all co-operate to universal happiness.

"But since having long indulged the pleasing expectation, we find general discontent, not likely to increase, or not likely to end in general defection, we resolve to erect alone the standard of liberty.

"*Know then*, that you are no longer to consider Cornwall as an English county, visited by English judges, receiving law from an English Parliament, or included in any general taxation of the kingdom; but as a state distinct, and independent, governed by its own institutions, administered by its own magistrates, and exempt from any tax or tribute but such as we shall impose upon ourselves.

"We are the acknowledged descendants of the earliest inhabitants of Britain, of men, who, before the time of history, took possession of the island desolate and waste, and therefore open to the first occupants. Of this descent, our language is a sufficient proof, which, not quite a century ago, was different from yours.

"Such are the Cornishmen; but who are you? who but the unauthorised and lawless children of intruders, invaders, and oppressors? who but the transmitters of wrong, the inheritors of robbery? In claiming independence we claim but little. We might require you to depart from a land which you possess by usurpation, and to restore all that you have taken from us.

"Independence is the gift of Nature, bestowed impartially on all her sons; no man is born the master of another. Every Cornishman is a freeman, for we have never resigned the rights of humanity; and he only can be thought free, who is not governed but by his own consent.

"You may urge that the present system of government has descended through many ages, and that we have a larger part in the representation of the kingdom, than any other county.

"All this is true, but it is neither cogent nor persuasive. We look to the original of things. Our union with the English counties was either compelled by force, or settled by compact.

"That which was made by violence, may by violence be broken. If we were treated as a conquered people, our rights might be obscured, but could never be extinguished. The sword can give nothing but power, which a sharper sword can take away.

"If our union was by compact, whom could the compact bind but those that concurred in the stipulations? We gave our ancestors no commission to settle the terms of future existence. They might be cowards that were frighted, or blockheads that were cheated; but whatever they were, they could contract only for themselves. What they could establish, we can annul.

"Against our present form of government it shall stand in the place of all argument, that we do not like it. While we are governed as we do not like, where is our liberty? We do not like taxes, we will therefore not be taxed; we do not like your laws, and will not obey them.

"The taxes laid by our representatives are laid, you tell us, by our own consent: but we will no longer consent to be represented. Our number of legislators was originally a burthen imposed upon us by English tyranny, and ought then to have been refused: if it be now considered as a disproportionate advantage, there can be no reason for complaining that we resign it.

"We shall therefore form a Senate of our own, under a President whom the King shall nominate, but whose authority we will limit, by adjusting his salary to his merit. We will not withhold our share of contribution to the necessary expence of lawful government, but we will decide for ourselves what share we shall pay, what expence is necessary, and what government is lawful.

"Till the authority of our council is acknowledged, and we are proclaimed independent and unaccountable, we will, after the tenth day of September, keep our Tin in our own hands: you can be supplied from no other place, and must therefore comply at last, or be poisoned with the copper of your own kitchens.

"If any Cornishman shall refuse his name to this just and laudable association, he shall be tumbled from St. Michael's Mount, or buried alive in a tin-mine; and if any emissary shall be found seducing Cornishmen to their former state, he shall be smeared with tar, and rolled in feathers, and chased with dogs out of our dominions.

From the Cornish Congress at Truro."

Of this memorial what could be said but that it was written in jest, or written by a madman? Yet I know not whether the warmest admirers of Pennsylvanian eloquence can find any argument in the Addresses of the Congress, that is not with greater strength urged by the Cornishman.

The argument of the irregular troops of controversy, stripped of its colours, and turned out naked to the view, is no more than this. Liberty is the birthright of man, and where obedience is compelled, there is no Liberty. The answer is equally simple. Government is necessary to man, and where obedience is not compelled, there is no government.

If the subject refuses to obey, it is the duty of authority to use compulsion. Society cannot subsist but by some power; first of making laws, and then of enforcing them.

To one of the threats hissed out by the Congress, I have put nothing similar into the Cornish proclamation; because it is too foolish for buffoonery, and too wild for madness. If we do not withhold our King and his Parliament from taxing them, they will cross the Atlantick and enslave us.

How they will come they have not told us: perhaps they will take wing, and light upon our coasts. When the cranes thus begin to flutter, it is time for pygmies to keep their eyes about them. The Great Orator observes, that they will be very fit, after they have been taxed, to impose chains upon us. If they are so fit as their friend describes them, and so willing as they describe themselves, let us increase our army, and double our militia.

It has been of late a very general practice to talk of slavery among those who are setting at defiance every power that keeps the world in order. If the learned author of the *Reflections on Learning* has rightly observed, that no man ever could give law to language, it will be vain to prohibit the use of the word *slavery*; but I could wish it more discreetly uttered; it is driven at one time too hard into our ears by the loud hurricane of Pennsylvanian eloquence, and at another glides too cold into our hearts by the soft conveyance of a female patriot bewailing the miseries of her *friends and fellow-citizens.*

Such has been the progress of sedition, that those who a few years ago disputed only our right of laying taxes, now question the validity of every act of legislation. They consider themselves as emancipated from obedience, and as being no longer the subjects of the British Crown. They leave us no choice but of yielding or conquering, of resigning our dominion, or maintaining it by force.

From force many endeavours have been used, either to dissuade, or to deter us. Sometimes the merit of the Americans is exalted, and sometimes their sufferings are aggravated. We are told of their contributions to the last war, a war incited by their outcries, and continued for their protection, a war by which none but themselves were gainers. All that they can boast is, that they did something for themselves, and did not wholly stand inactive, while the sons of Britain were fighting in their cause.

If we cannot admire, we are called to pity them; to pity those that shew no regard to their mother country; have obeyed no law which they could violate; have imparted no good which they could withold; have entered into associations of fraud to rob their creditors; and into combinations to distress all who depended on their commerce. We are reproached with the cruelty of shutting one port, where every port is shut against us. We are censured as tyrannical for hindering those from fishing, who have condemned our merchants to bankruptcy and our manufacturers to hunger.

Others persuade us to give them more liberty, to take off restraints, and relax authority; and tell us what happy consequences will arise from forbearance: How their affections will be conciliated, and into what diffusions of beneficence their gratitude will luxuriate. They will love their friends, they will reverence their protectors. They will throw themselves into our arms, and lay their property at our feet. They will buy from no other what we can sell them; they will sell to no other what we wish to buy.

That any obligations should overpower their attention to profit, we have known them long enough not to expect. It is not to be expected from a more liberal people. With what kindness they repay benefits, they are now shewing us, who, as soon as we have delivered them from France, are defying and proscribing us.

But if we will permit them to tax themselves, they will give us more than we require. If we proclaim them independent, they will during pleasure pay us a subsidy. The contest is not now for money, but for power. The question is not how much we shall collect, but by what authority the collection shall be made.

Those who find that the Americans cannot be shewn in any form that may raise love or pity, dress them in habiliments of terrour, and try to make us think them formidable. The Bostonians can call into the field ninety thousand men. While we conquer all before us, new enemies will rise up behind, and our work will be always to begin. If we take possession of the towns, the Colonists will retire into the inland regions, and the gain of victory will be only empty houses and a wide extent of waste and desolation. If we subdue them for the present, they will universally revolt in the next war, and resign us without pity to subjection and destruction.

To all this it may be answered, that between losing America and resigning it, there is no great difference; that it is not very reasonable to jump into the sea, because the ship is leaky. All those evils may befal us, but we need not hasten them.

The Dean of Gloucester has proposed, and seems to propose it seriously, that we should at once release our claims, declare them masters of themselves, and whistle them down the wind. His opinion is, that our gain from them will be the same, and our expence less. What they can have most cheaply from Britain, they will still buy, what they can sell to us at the highest price they will still sell.

It is, however, a little hard, that having so lately fought and conquered for their safety, we should govern them no longer. By letting them loose before the war, how many millions might have been saved. One ridiculous proposal is best answered by another. Let us restore to the French what we have taken from them. We shall see our Colonists at our feet, when they have an enemy so near them. Let us give the Indians arms, and teach them discipline, and encourage them now and then to plunder a Plantation. Security and leisure are the parents of sedition.

While these different opinions are agitated, it seems to be determined by the Legislature, that force shall be tried. Men of the pen have seldom any great skill in conquering kingdoms, but they have strong inclination to give advice. I cannot forbear to wish, that this commotion may end without bloodshed, and that the rebels may be subdued by terrour rather than by violence; and therefore recommend such a force as may take away, not only the power, but the hope of resistance, and by conquering without a battle, save many from the sword.

If their obstinacy continues without actual hostilities, it may perhaps be mollified by turning out the soldiers to free quarters, forbidding any personal cruelty or hurt. It has been proposed, that the slaves should be set free, an act which surely the lovers of liberty cannot but commend. If they are furnished with fire arms for defence, and utensils for husbandry, and settled in some simple form of government within the country, they may be more grateful and honest than their masters.

Far be it from any Englishman to thirst for the blood of his fellow-subjects. Those who most deserve our resentment are unhappily at less distance. The Americans, when the Stamp Act was first proposed, undoubtedly disliked it, as every nation dislikes an impost; but they had no thought of resisting it, till they were encouraged and incited by European intelligence from men whom they thought their friends, but who were friends only to themselves.

On the original contrivers of mischief let an insulted nation pour out its vengeance. With whatever design they have inflamed this pernicious contest, they are themselves equally detestable. If they wish success to the Colonies, they are traitors to this country; if they wish their defeat, they are traitors at once to America and England. To them and them only must be imputed the interruption of commerce, and the miseries of war, the sorrow of those that shall be ruined, and the blood of those that shall fall.

Since the Americans have made it necessary to subdue them, may they be subdued with the least injury possible to their persons and their possessions. When they are reduced to obedience, may that obedience be secured by stricter laws and stronger obligations.

Nothing can be more noxious to society than that erroneous clemency, which, when a rebellion is suppressed, exacts no forfeiture and establishes no securities, but leaves the rebels in their former state. Who would not try the experiment which promises advantage without expence? If rebels once obtain a victory, their wishes are accomplished; if they are defeated, they suffer little, perhaps less than their conquerors; however often they play the game, the chance is always in their favour. In the mean time, they are growing rich by victualing the troops that we have sent against them, and perhaps gain more by the residence of the army than they lose by the obstruction of their port.

Their charters being now, I suppose, legally forfeited, may be modelled as shall appear most commodious to the Mother-country. Thus the privileges, which are found by experience liable to misuse, will be taken away, and those who now bellow as patriots, bluster as soldiers, and domineer as legislators, will sink into sober merchants and silent planters, peaceably diligent, and securely rich.

But there is one writer, and perhaps many who do not write, to whom the contraction of these pernicious privileges appears very dangerous, and who startle at the thoughts of *England free and America in chains*. Children fly from their own shadow, and rhetoricians are frighted by their own voices.

Chains is undoubtedly a dreadful word; but perhaps the masters of civil wisdom may discover some gradations between chains and anarchy. Chains need not be put upon those who will be restrained without them. This contest may end in the softer phrase of English Superiority and American Obedience.

We are told, that the subjection of Americans may tend to the diminution of our own liberties: an event, which none but very perspicacious politicians are able to foresee. If slavery be thus fatally contagious, how is it that we hear the loudest yelps for liberty among the drivers of negroes?

But let us interrupt a while this dream of conquest, settlement, and supremacy. Let us remember that being to contend, according to one orator, with three millions of Whigs, and according to another, with ninety thousand patriots of Massachusets Bay, we may possibly be checked in our career of reduction. We may be reduced to peace upon equal terms, or driven from the western continent, and forbidden to violate a second time the happy borders of the land of liberty. The time is now perhaps at hand, which Sir Thomas Brown predicted between jest and earnest,

> *When America shall no more send out her treasure,*
> *But spend it at home in American pleasure.*

If we are allowed upon our defeat to stipulate conditions, I hope the treaty of Boston will permit us to import into the confederated Cantons such products as they do not raise, and such manufactures as they do not make, and cannot buy cheaper from other nations, paying like others the appointed customs; that if an English ship salutes a fort with four guns, it shall be answered at least with two; and that if an Englishman be inclined to hold a plantation, he shall only take an oath of allegiance to the reigning powers, and be suffered, while he lives inoffensively, to retain his own opinion of English rights, unmolested in his conscience by an oath of abjuration.

FINIS.

An Answer to a Pamphlet, Entitled Taxation No Tyranny. Addressed to the Author, and to Persons in Power. London, 1775.

"I think I have not been attacked enough for it," Boswell recalled Johnson observing of *Taxation No Tyranny* shortly after it was published. "Attack is the re-action; I never think I have hit hard, unless it rebounds." Of the several responses that did emerge, this one was among the more moderate. At least its author refrained from accusing Johnson, as another pamphleteer did, of being a Tory and Jacobite on every other page. (Though certainly a Tory, Johnson was no Jacobite, at least not at this time; indeed he was personally indebted to the House of Hanover for a royal pension granted in recognition of his literary merit.) Johnson had no patience for these critics who he felt were not only defending the American position but inciting the colonists to resist. Such "contrivers of mischief," he wrote, were as "detestable," as the rebels. "If they wish success to the Colonies, they are traitors to this country."

Near the end of this pamphlet the author cited Johnson's suggestion that the Americans' African slaves might be set free ("an act," said Johnson, "which surely the lovers of liberty cannot but commend"). In his tepid response, Johnson's anonymous critic could only charge that "you would establish a Saturnalia of cruelty, and expose these devoted men to the brutality of their own slaves, enflamed and irritated to retaliate traditionary wrongs, and to wreak a barbarous vengeance on the degraded masters."

He does not cite the most famous sentence in Johnson's pamphlet: the devastating query, "How is it that we hear the loudest yelps for liberty among the drivers of negroes?" It was indeed extraordinary, as Johnson noted, how often the colonists invoked "slavery" as the condition diametrically opposed to the "liberty" they were contending for. Some colonists, at least initially, could not see any connection between their yelps for liberty and their enslaving of Africans. John Dickinson, for example, having defined taxation without representation as "a state of the most abject slavery," went on to question whether it was even "possible to form an idea of slavery more *compleat*, more *miserable*, more *disgraceful*, than that of a people, where *justice is administered, government exercised*, and a *standing army maintained*, AT THE EXPENSE OF THE PEOPLE, and yet WITHOUT THE

497

LEAST DEPENDENCE UPON THEM." Many other Americans, however, did see the excruciating contradiction between their struggle for liberty and the holding of African slaves and were embarrassed by it. James Otis knew that "the Colonists are by the law of nature free born, as indeed all men are, white or black." Was it "right," he asked in his pamphlet of 1764, "to enslave a man because he is black?" In the end, in ways many of its participants surely did not intend, the Americans' debate over their rights and their freedom in the 1760s and 70s contributed decisively to the emergence of the antislavery movement in the last decades of the eighteenth century.

AN ANSWER TO A PAMPHLET,

ENTITLED

Taxation no Tyranny.

ADDRESSED TO THE

AUTHOR,

AND TO

PERSONS IN POWER.

LONDON:

Printed for J. Almon, opposite Burlington House, Piccadilly.

M DCC LXXV.

An Answer, &c.

THE importance of the subject, the crisis of time in which I write, and the notoriety of your stile and character, make it unnecessary for me to use a preface.

The very title of your pamphlet is delusion. No man has ever said that taxation is, in *itself*, tyranny; nor will you say, that it may not *become* so, by abuse, or by want of authority in the imposers of it. Had your title said, "that the British parliament is the *proper* and *constitutional* body for taxing the Colonies," you would not have mistated the question. But that would not have tended to ensnare an inattentive reader, by a disingenuous and a false implication.

You set out with this position. "That the supreme power of every community has the right of *requiring* from *all* its subjects such *contributions* as are *necessary* to the *public safety*, or *public prosperity*."

You pretend that this position is as old as Government, but it is evidently of modern structure. This appears from the word *requiring*. Your maxim, is, not that the supreme power has the right of *taxing*, but of *requiring contributions* from all its subjects; and is evidently framed for the present dispute, and for the identical idea of *requisition* from the Colonies. Now this, whether right or wrong, is certainly not an old, nor even now an established idea on either side of the Atlantic.

Further, if by the supreme power having a right to *require contributions*, you mean that it has a right to *tax*, you express yourself inaccurately; and if from that position you conclude, that the British parliament has a right to tax America, you but just assume what you ought to prove. For the very point in debate, is, whether the British parliament, though it be the supreme power of the whole empire as to many points, is so as to all; and particularly as to taxation. Now this being a question relating to the British government, it is evident, that it is not to be determined by a general maxim of government in abstract. It must be decided by the *fundamental principles* of the *British* constitution; by the *established practice* of it; and by the dictates of sound sense, of natural justice and of public convenience, applied to the ground of that constitution.

By your general terms the reader naturally supposes it only to be asserted, that the legislature of every community has the power you speak of. Now this, in abstract, sounds well. When we speak of *the* legislature of a community, we suppose only *one* legislature; and where there is but one, it must of *necessity* have the right you speak of; otherwise no taxes at all could be raiscd in that community. But then the proof arises from this necessity, which makes it absurd that it should be otherwise. Where therefore there is not the same necessity, the same absurdity will not arise; nor the same proof, by consequence, follow. Now the present dispute is, not with respect to this island alone, which certainly has but one legislature; but with respect to the British empire at large, in which there are *many* legislatures; or many assemblies *claiming* to be so. Here is the fallacy of your position. From the state of the British empire, composed of extensive and dispersed dominions, and from the nature of its government, a multiplicity of legislatures, or of assemblies claiming to be so, have arisen in one empire. It is in some degree a new case in legislation, and must be governed therefore more by its own circumstances, and by the genius of our peculiar constitution, than by abstract notions of government at large. Every colony, in fact, has two legislatures; one interior and provincial, viz. the colony assembly: the other exterior and imperial, viz. the British parliament. It would have been utterly absurd, that a provincial legislature should ever have subsisted, if it were not *practically* or *constitutionally necessary* for *certain* matters. It would be equally absurd, if the imperial legislature were to interpose in such matters; for if it should, one of two things must follow; either that the imperial legislature must in such matters yield to the provincial wherever they differed; or that it must prevail over it in points, from its own *practical*, or *constitutional unfitness* for which, the provincial legislature was formed; either of which would be perfectly absurd. Neither will the unity of the empire be in danger from the provincial legislature being thus exclusive as to points. It is perfectly sufficient, if the British legislature be supreme, as to all those things which are essential to Great Britain's being substantially the head of the empire; a line not very difficult to be drawn if it were the present subject. Neither is there any absurdity in there being two assemblies, each of them sufficient, or, if you will, supreme, as to objects perfectly distinct; for this plain reason, that, the objects being perfectly distinct, they cannot clash. The Colonist therefore, allowing that the supreme power or legislature, where there is but one, must have the right you speak of; will say, that with respect to him there are two, and that the provincial legislature is the supreme power as to *taxation* for his Colony. And so the controversy, notwithstanding your position, will remain just where it began.

But not to have done with your maxim. It says, that the supreme power has a right to require such contributions as are *necessary* to the *public safety* and *public prosperity*. If these words have any meaning but to deceive, they must mean, that this right of the supreme power has limits, viz. that it is only a right to impose or require such contributions as are *necessary* to the *safety* and *prosperity* of the *public*. Suppose the supreme power to exceed those limits. It then exceeds its right; it acts without authority; and in all just *reasoning* becomes as impotent as an unauthorized individual. As such it may be resisted, and as such resistance to it cannot be rebellion. In your fundamental position therefore you establish a limit to the supreme power, and by consequence a justification for resistance, if that limit is transgressed. And yet in every other place you assert, that Government is the *sole* judge; that if the people can withhold obedience in any case they are no longer subjects; that they are rebels; that they must be compelled; that Government is necessary to man, and that where *obedience* is not *compelled*, Government is at an end. You say, in a word, that the supreme power has limits, and that it has not limits; that Government has a duty, which it may transgress with impunity; and that the people have rights, which they cannot maintain without the guilt of rebellion. And all these contradictions you build upon the sorry and verbal sophism, that the legislature of every country is the *supreme* power, and being *supreme*, cannot be *controlled*. But the truth is, that it is no more than the *chief* power in *ordinary* course; but with an *eventual* controll. For in *extreme* cases, there is a controll in the hands of the whole people, with whom *alone* the supreme power *unlimited* of any community can reside; and with whom it *always* does reside, though in common course they delegate a portion of authority sufficient for legislation to others; but so, as that they are not

to subvert the constitution under which they act; nor to convert Government to the misery and ruin of the people, for
whose happiness and prosperity it was formed. This *final right*
of the people is *felt* and *exercised* in the most arbitrary Governments, though it is not only not professed in those countries,
but the doctrine of passive obedience maintained and perhaps
generally believed. So strong is nature, and so weak is sophistry
in extreme cases however, that more Turkish emperors have
been slain by their subjects, than kings in all the free monarchies
that have ever existed. But resistance in our constitution is not a
tacit reserve; it is an express doctrine of our Government in its
best times. It is then absurd to say, that the governing powers
are unlimited here, for a right of resistance implies a limit. If
there could be no *transgression* there could be no right to resist;
and a power that has *no limits*, cannot transgress.

Having thus done nothing, you proceed to a premature triumph over the arguments and principles of your adversaries
through forty pages, when you come to this proposition, "that
the legislature of a Colony is only the vestry of a larger parish."
This you assert, but you do not condescend to prove, or to
apply it. Let us try for a moment whether there is the smallest
analogy. The legislatures of the Colonies, for so you call them,
have parish vestries under them in America, similar to ours;
which bear the same relation to the provincial legislatures,
which British vestries bear to the British parliament. Now I do
not find that our vestries have other vestries subordinate to
them in like manner. Neither do I suppose, that the provincial
legislatures would have had such had they been considered as
similar to British vestries. The provincial legislatures are convened and dissolved by the immediate act of the crown in the
same manner as our parliament. Are the meetings of vestries so
summoned, or so discharged? Writs issue in America from the
crown to the sheriffs of the several counties to have a new
representative elected for every general assembly in each province. Is this a ceremony belonging to vestries? Their session
opens and closes like ours with a speech from the throne upon
the public business, and there is the same intercourse between
them and the executive as between the king and the British
parliament. Can this be said of vestries? They make laws of
all kinds, civil and criminal, which jurors, sheriffs, the king's

judges, all officers of judicature, and the whole province, are obliged to acknowlege as public law; and these laws require and receive the royal assent in like manner with British acts of parliament. Does this belong to vestry regulations? They vote men and money for public service and for military expeditions, witness the late war. Can this be alledged of vestries? Or would Mr. Grenville formerly, or the British parliament at this day, think of sending to any British vestry; or tell them, that if they would tax themselves for the public service, parliament would not tax them? I should be ashamed to dwell longer on such a dream.

Your next proposition is, that the Americans have no reason to complain, for that they are represented in the British parliament. And how do you prove this? In fact, though not in words, the proof you offer is this. That there are *many* in Great Britain, who, not being electors, are *not* represented; that *none* of the Americans are electors; and that, notwithstanding, they *are* represented. To soften this absurdity you borrow an idea which this controversy has created. It is, that there are *two kinds* of representatives, one actual, and the other virtual; that those who have votes are actually represented; and that those who have not votes are virtually represented. And therefore as it must be made out, that the Americans are represented in some manner or other, and as it is absurd to say that they are actually represented, it is thus deduced that they are represented virtually, and that they are very unreasonable, if they are not perfectly content. But I desire that the law-book may be produced, in which a *virtual* representative is once mentioned as a character known to our law or constitution. There is no such notice, I am bold to affirm, from the first year book down to the commentary of Blackstone. If therefore this idea is allowed at all, it must be allowed, not as a maxim of British law, but of general reason. As such it will apply equally to all governments as well as to that of Britain. Now if it be true, that every man is virtually represented in the legislature of his country, though he has no share in chusing it, then it is true that the Americans may be virtually represented in the British parliament. But it is equally true, that the same may be said of every nation under the sun, with respect to its legislature. The grand Signior for instance, has the legislature of the Turkish empire in his own person; he is the virtual representative of his people therefore; and his subjects consequently have the blessing of representation equally with the Americans; and thus all the governments of the world are happily brought to a level.

To comfort the Americans, it is your constant practice to tell them, that though they must have less freedom and constitutional privilege than their brethren at home, yet that the people of Great Britain have little of either. Thus you exaggerate the number of non-electors in Britain, and seem to impeach the constitution, as having been negligent of the people. In this whole business, I think you mistake the drift of the constitution, as I shall endeavour to shew. But first to touch it upon your own ground. Women and minors are a great majority of every people; yet in no constitution have they ever been electors. So far the British constitution has nothing particular to account for; and, as for the rest, let history answer. In our fœdal origin, the property of the state, that fell to commoners, was for the most part pretty equally divided into military freeholds, to which every privilege was at that time annexed, and particularly that of constituting county members. Moneyed property was little known, or attended to at first. As it grew, however, members for cities, towns and boroughs were, from time to time, *added*; that personal property might be represented in some measure, though not so accurately as freehold. The elective principle therefore was general and perfect, as property originally stood. If the course of time has altered this state, so as that the constitutional principle has become narrow in its operation, what follows? That some change should be made, in order that the constitutional principle should be restored to its full operation. That is, that the constitution should be revived at home, not destroyed at the other side of the Atlantic. Whereas your argument is, that because it is bad here, it should be rendered worse there; and because its image is somewhat impaired in Great Britain, that there should not be a shadow of it left in America.

Again—You tell the Americans that they are no great losers by not having a vote for their British representatives, for that those who have votes seldom know, or have seen the person whom they chuse. This is the fault of the individuals however, and the faults of British individuals are scarcely to be punished in the persons of Americans, by a deprivation of their privileges. Neither does this happen, except where the constitution has deviated from its original; and when therefore it ought rather to be restored to its purity, than its error propagated; I mean in the declining, or decayed boroughs. But if it is an absurd state of things, that the representative should not be known by his constituents, is it not absurd that America should be represented in Great Britain?

The principle of the constitution in this point was so strong, that by the common law, no man could be either an elector or a representative for any place, without *residing* on the spot. And upon the soundest reason. Men, at that unrefined period, *resided* on their *property*. There was therefore not only more personal knowledge and intercourse, but a greater community of the most solid interests, and of property above all, between men residing in the same county or town; than between persons (though of the same kingdom) who resided at a considerable distance from each other. Both representatives and electors were, like jurors, from the *vicinage*. This was the great and sound principle of our forefathers. They knew that government was an art, practical, not theoretic. It was not an abstract subtlety that contented them, but a solid and binding principle of social connexion. What that was precisely with respect to what is commonly called representation may deserve perhaps to be a little explained.

Words that are long in common use acquire so many senses, that they lose exactness. This perhaps is the case of the word representation. A representative, however, we understand to be a delegate; a person not self-authorized; but constituted by something else. I will call him member, as less equivocal. Now what is it which constitutes the member? I say the property of the county or borough; not the persons. Hence many persons in a county or borough have not votes; which ought not to be, if the persons in the county or borough were to constitute the member. But it is the property of the county or borough that is to do so; and therefore, property, *legally notified*, never fails to have a vote, that is, to make an elector; for electors are the medium through which property is to operate. This will be still more illustrated hereafter. Freehold property constitutes county representatives. Personal property constitutes all others.

To explain this. Personal property was considered by the old law, as *fugitive* and *unreal*, compared with freehold property; and the quantum of it possessed by any man is difficult to ascertain. Hence the law has not fixed the quantum, nor does it require the same precise proof of its existence as it does in freehold; but has contented itself with selecting certain marks, and which are such presumptions of personal property to a degree in the possessor, that the law allows them for a proof of it. Thus for instance, burgage tenure, birth, service, residence, paying certain rates, boiling a pot, &c. All these prove or presume some degree of personal property, and of connexion with the soil where they are found, and are admitted as proofs of it. This species of property, thus notified, constitutes members for boroughs, towns, and cities. Thus property is the universal constituent of the house of Commons. Honorary freemen, &c. I have not mentioned, being a modern device, unconnected with the constitution.

To pursue this idea. In ancient time the Commons had not very large properties. The large properties were in the barons; that is, in truth, the large properties made them barons. A man became a baron the moment he obtained a barony. Barons were not created by the crown at that time. It was an operation of property merely, not an act of the executive. Thus property constituted the baronage, and every man knows that the baronage is only another name for the peerage of England. A man who had a certain proportion of property of his own, was of course a peer. A number of small properties, belonging to other men, combined and centered in one man, by virtue of election, made him a commoner. One sat in right of his own property. The other sat in right of the property of others. But both sat equally by property. This accounts for some things that seem at first view irregular. For instance, the barons, in old time, sitting by their property, taxed themselves; that is, taxed their own property. But now, sitting by the act of the crown merely, without reference to property, the Commons, who continue to sit by property, have claimed the whole of taxation, and the Lords have ceded it to them. This shews to demonstration, that the body which is constituted by the property of any country, is the only body constitutionally qualified to tax that country; and consequently, that the provincial legislatures are the only assemblies constitutionally qualified to tax the provinces, and not the British House of Commons, which American property has no share in constituting. This shews, that by the fundamentals of the British government, property was the vital principle. It was that which constituted *both houses* of parliament. And for wise reasons. That the interest of the members might as much as possible coincide with their duty; that the former might act as a centinel upon the latter, and that the very thing which gave men a vote in the legislature, should superintend and sway the exercise of that vote. And surely in so ordaining, they shewed a more intimate knowledge of human nature, and more salutary views, than those men who now argue, that members will do their duty as well, who have no such motives of interest to prompt them to it, whatever they may have to the contrary; and that that assembly is, in all points, even to taxation itself, the fittest legislature for America, which has not an inch of American property in the whole structure and formation of it.

Having thus cleared to demonstration, I think, the fundamental principle of our government as to this subject, let me advert a little to the practice of the constitution, as it would have been on your principle, and as it actually has been.

Had the Norman conqueror returned to Normandy, and made that the seat of empire, the Norman states would have been the imperial legislature. Would he have been entitled, I ask, to tax his English subjects in his states of Normandy? You will not affirm it. Yet might he not say, "My Norman states made laws for all my subjects, when I had no subjects beyond Normandy; and why may they not continue to do so still, tho' my condition is altered in that respect? My Norman law has made no distinction concerning my subjects beyond sea; (for the prince might forget, that till he had subjects beyond sea, no mention of them could be expected.) I am too moderate to make these subjects beyond sea, dependant on myself. They shall be dependant on my Norman states; and there will be this comfort in it besides, that I can do what I please with my Norman states, whereas the popular assemblies beyond sea might be less manageable." This speech, no doubt, would be highly relished; the Norman states would be flattered; a great majority would vote for the doctrine; the minority would be

called an English faction and decried; and all would be harmony and satisfaction in Normandy. But how would it have
gone in England? I will answer this question for you. He must
have conquered it again, and again, and again. If he were once
worsted, he would have been undone, and every pause of
bloodshed would have been a renewal of war.

England, however, as I hope it always will, continued to be
the seat of empire to him and to his descendants. Did any of
them attempt to tax their dominions beyond sea in the legislature of England? Never. The Scotch have asserted, that they
conquered England; the English have asserted, that they conquered Scotland. Did either nation, though *contiguous*, ever
think of taxing the other in its domestic legislature? No such
thing was ever thought of. Henry the Fifth conquered France.
Did he or his son ever attempt to tax France in the English
parliament? Or if they had resided in France, would the states
of France have been the constitutional legislature for taxing
the English subject? You will not say it. Was Wales, though
conquered and contiguous, ever taxed by the English parliament till it sent representatives thither? Never. When the
crowns of England and Scotland were united in the person of
James the First, who made England the seat of empire, did the
parliament of England ever think of taxing Scotland? Or in
queen Anne's reign, when the Scotch were averse to a union,
were they ever told, that the English parliament could do the
business, if they were refractory; for that Scotland was represented in the parliament of England, though all the property
on the other side of the Tweed did not constitute one vote
towards constituting one member of that assembly? No man
ever dreamed of such a thing. Did Henry the Second, or any
of his successors, ever attempt to tax Ireland in the English
parliament, though conquered, and not very distant? No, you
confess. But the judges, you say, have mentioned a distinction
to account for this exemption, viz. that Ireland had a parliament of her own. But why was a parliament given to her? Because no man thought at that time, that the English parliament
was a constitutional or adequate legislature in ordinary, for
dominions beyond sea. Nor can I believe, that the judges
grounded their decision merely on the trisyllable, "parliament;" or that they had any other idea, than that Ireland

having a legislature, by whatever name, competent to taxation, it was not fitting that she should be taxed by the English parliament, in the constituting of which the property of Ireland had no share. Now this holds equally as to the provincial assemblies, and to the legislatures or states of every kingdom or province which I have before-mentioned; and therefore it is clear, that this universal practice was founded on a universal principle, that the parliament of England ought not to tax any part of the dominion, the property of which had not its due share in constituting that assembly. But there is an instance more precisely in point, and that is, the practice of parliament with respect to these very Colonies. From their origin till the commencement of this dispute, the parliament of England never attempted to tax them. It is confessed to have been a new idea, and as such principally it has been gloried in by Mr. Greenville and his friends. Will nothing convince men? I know, however, there are persons who will be ready to contradict this, and to mention, that the post-office is a tax. To this I answer, first, that it does not bear the letter and form peculiar to a tax law; and was not intended on the one side, nor received on the other as such; and therefore can be no precedent. At least, if it were intended so by you, the intention was masqued. There was concealment in the transaction, enough to destroy it in a court of equity. And if you set the example of litigiousness, and of little over-reachings to your dependencies, you will make them afraid of you in every part of your dealing; which will encrease your difficulties without end, and will begin with universal contention, as it will terminate in universal chicane. Next I answer, that the post-office was an *undertaking* first carried on by individuals at their private hazard; since adopted by the state, which stands in the place only of those individuals as to the dependencies; and that it is now as an *establishment*, maintained at the sole expence of Great Britain. She therefore has a right to say to any man, that if he makes use of that convenience he shall pay for it. It is a matter of compact, not of legislation, either in letter or in spirit. The Americans can send their letters by other conveyances. They have done so. And if they generally do otherwise, it is because they prefer the public vehicle to any other, not because they are confined to it. That is, they pay postage for the carriage of their letters, as they would pay a stage coach for the carriage of their persons. I deny, therefore, that there is a single instance in which the British parliament has taxed the Colonies. And you cannot deny that the British parliament has acknowledged, that the provincial assemblies *can* tax the provinces, and that, in *fact*, they have exercised that right in a manner the most meritorious towards this country. You cannot therefore contest their power of granting money, nor their inclination to grant reasonably; but you fear, that they will not grant unreasonably. You want therefore to deprive them of a negative, and to extort what you please by threatening, that you will tax them here, if they do not implicitly tax themselves in America. Not content with a reasonable resource in an application to their choice, you want to establish a boundless resource in their fears. Like our arbitrary princes, you are straining the prerogative of this country, that under the terror of it you may obtain what you do not chuse from an unconstitutional pride, or what, from its unreasonableness, you are afraid to ask. Your apprehensions that the Colonies might by Provincial Grants render the Crown independant, unless Parliament had a right to interpose, is only a pretence? Why have you ever let them make grants then? And is not your complaint that they have granted too little, not too much? But if that be your real fear, you can remedy it without a civil war. Pass an Act of Parliament, declaring that it shall not be lawful for the Crown to give the royal assent to any provincial grant without the approbation of Parliament. America will not refuse you a negative on her grants, but she will not relinquish a negative on your demands. I repeat, that the English Parliament has never taxed the Colonies. And if I could not, I should say, what all the world must acknowledge, that neither they, nor any body of people on earth, could defend their freedom for half a century, if a desultory and a questionable instance could overthrow it. It is not one problematical precedent that can be of any weight against a people. It must be by the general current of rational, unequivocal, and unoccasional practice, that the constitution of any country is to be tried.

And may not the Colonists well say, that it would be wonderful indeed if our Parliament had been designed to be an universal legislature to the ends of the earth, and as to all points? That our forefathers must have been not only wise men, which they were, but prophets, which they were not, if they could have foreseen our American acquisitions? And that no conclusion can be more certain, than that our Parliament, in fact, was not originally intended to tax them, because when it was formed there was no such thing in being. May they not say, that the only *equity* advanced in favour of the British claim, is, that the *Americans* are exactly in the same case with the *non-electors* of Britain? And may they not maintain that nothing can be more dissimilar? For that first the British non-elector has a strong influence upon the *elector*, by habits of personal intercourse and connexion; but that the American has none. Next, that the British non-elector may at any time acquire a vote by money or industry; but that the American never can. And lastly, that the British representative cannot tax the *non*-elector of Britain without taxing his constituents equally and himself: whereas every tax that he lays on America, is, in the first instance, a gain and exoneration to his constituents and himself, in the same manner exactly in which it is a burden to America. May they not say, that men may be much more safely trusted in imposing taxes which they are to *pay*, than in imposing taxes which they are to *receive?* That the former is fairly a legislative act of *taxation*; but that the latter is an arbitrary imposition of *tribute?* May they not ask, Whether the people of Great-Britain would think themselves as safe in being taxed by *virtual* representatives in *America*, as in being taxed by their *actual* representatives in *Great-Britain?* And whether they would not esteem such levies to be a *fine*, rather than a *tax*; and an *enaction*, rather than an *impost?* May they not say with some reason, that they wish you would know your own minds, and what would content you, and that you would decide for once, Whether the possession of the Colonies, upon the old terms, would be an advantage to you, or not? For that if it would not, you are doubtless at liberty to relinquish it; and that if it would, you have no right to be paid for it? Have they not some reason to say that you are paid for it already according to your original requisition? That the profits of their commerce, not taxes, were your object in colonizing; and that, possessing that, you have no right to a further payment by way of taxation? And that if they shall be able, and shall consent to contribute taxes, also that you should receive them rather as an over-payment, and as so much clear gain, than as a strict debt, or as a grounded demand? May they not say that it is rather hard that you should charge them with being a burden and a grievance to you if they chuse your protection; and accuse them of being rebels if they are content to be without it? May they not observe, perhaps, that you call your connexion with them by different names, according to the ends which you have to carry? That if you want taxes from them you call it protection; and that if they want rights and immunities from you, that you call it mastery and dominion? So that they may be beggared by taxes in return for being protected; and executed as rebels if they prefer independance? May they not say, when you complain of your taxes, that you could not pay those taxes if it were not for your commerce; and that a great and beneficial part of your commerce, is your *monopoly* of American traffic? If therefore your *monopoly* of American traffic supplies a good part of those taxes, is it just to say, that America does not contribute; or that she is not entitled to protection from any part of them? May she not also assert, that she is not the authoress of that debt with which you charge her? That the wars of King William and Queen Anne began it; that venal and unmanly counsels continued it; and that in the last war it was the Germanic, and not the American Continent, from which it received its final accumulation? That all these measures were the product of English Counsels, which were approved by the British Parliament, but over which the Colonies had no influence? That if the last war began about American boundaries, it was only because America is a British territory, and that it would equally have begun in whatever part of the dominion the encroachment had been made? And if you will have America to be particularly concerned in the commencement of that war, may she not be bold to say, that it was the conquests in America which your Colonists helped to make, and the cessions in America which they did not help to make, that accomplished the peace? Has she not reason to bid you look forward, and to tell you, that bending under that national debt, the Continent of Europe is not a scene on which you can act; and that it is by the American Continent only that the balance of Europe can be any longer in your hands? That by your great superiority of numbers there, you command both the Americas, command Spain and Portugal, influence France and other powers of Europe, and that therefore instead of checking their encrease by a jealous and hostile policy, you ought to encourage it by every just and generous institution: that instead of exasperating them by system, you should bind them to you by every demonstration of liberal attachment; and that you should leave them to conduct themselves to prosperity, without the alarming interposition of imperial authority, except where it is *bona fide* essential to preserve Great-Britain at the head of an united empire? And as taxing the Colonies in the British Parliament, or making them tax themselves by compulsory requisition from hence, is inconsistent with all the rights of British property; and as it is evident from your own past experience, that such a power is not necessary to the union of your empire, but probably inconsistent with it; have they not reason to hope that you will renounce the idea with a manly decision, and not hold over their heads, *in terrorem*, a claim, which even arbitrary countries do not exercise over their colonies, the establishments of which are maintained at the expence of the parent state, without raising in them any conception that their colonies are therefore useless, or that their empire is in danger of being dissolved?

Surely no man can doubt but that system of Colony Government is best by which you will derive the greatest benefit from your Colonies, with the least disquietude and discomfort to them and to yourselves. You will not let them go at large into manufactures or commerce. What follows? That they never can be opulent states, and not being so, that they never can be productive of any considerable revenue. Do not endeavour to unite incompatibilities. You have made your choice, and you have made a wise one. You have chosen the greater object in preference to the less. You have chosen copious returns of trade, rather than scanty resources of tribute. It would be absurd now to shake and to reverse your system for the purpose of going back to what you were right in originally relinquishing. And right too not only because it is in itself of more value, but because you can get much in this way without disgusting your Colonists; whereas you could get but little in the other with their total alienation. And that, for this plain reason;—that men can better bear to be deprived of many means of acquisition, than to lose all security in what they already possess. For men can be happy without wealth, but they cannot be happy with nothing. It was right also, because if your title to taxation was ever so clear, it is equally clear that you ought not to use it—witness the Stamp-act; a law particularly calculated to execute itself, digested by an acknowledged Financier, and prepared for by him as a great experiment, with much circumspection, and through a long period of time: And yet take the whole system, and you find a thousand errors in it, and inaptitudes to the place for which it was designed. What then would it be reasonable to expect from such a power in the hands of ordinary financiers, and in the common course of business, in which expedition, and round numbers, as it were, are preferred to accuracy or justice? What but eternal blunders, eternal miscarriages, and eternal feuds? What would be the consequence? You would hazard all your American commerce, and all your American empire for the shadow of revenue. Without a large army you could levy nothing. With a large army the expence would over-balance the receipts. If that army did not reside, all would be confusion the moment it departed; if it did reside, how could its ranks be kept full? Or how could it be prevented from becoming American? And if all these difficulties were removed, how could such a system be reconciled to the principle of your empire, which is free and commercial; and which cannot be either of these without being both? Rome, however, it may be said, governed her Provinces by armies. Be it so. But her empire was military, not commercial. War was to her, in some measure, what peace is to us. It fanned the principle of her government. Armies too were to Rome what Navies are to Great-Britain. Yet what was the consequence of this measure there? All manner of injustice and rapine spread through the Provinces under the sanction of the Roman banner. Some of the dependencies were ruined more quietly. Others revolted. Larger armies were called for. The ruin of some provinces, and the mighty armies sustained in others, exhausted the empire. The *distant legions* became tumultuary. One province was employed against it's neighbour. As one army was quieted, another mutinied. The Empire was tossed from hand to hand; and the Roman Government, once so famous, became a theatre of military ravage; full of contending Emperors, and conflicting Legions. The same tumults would close the scene with us; and the Empire would be dismembered by the very arms that were intended to unite it. For nothing that is unnatural can last. There would be this difference, however, that this measure might have seemed at first to be congenial, and even auxiliary to the principle of the Roman State; but in our Government it would be madness from the beginning. What follows? That if for ten thousand reasons you cannot govern by the sword, you have but one thing left, and that is, to govern by justice; and if this proposition revolts you, it is clear that you are not in a temper to govern.

That this system will dismember the empire, is one of those solemn absurdities which some men affect to believe, for the purpose of imposing upon others. Has your hitherto leaving them to tax, and in general to regulate themselves, overturned your empire? No.—It has made it.—Has Ireland having had a parliament for every purpose of legislation for six hundred years made her independent, or undutiful? You acknowledge the contrary. Indeed how is it possible any thing of this sort should happen? The British Parliament declares who shall be King for the whole empire; and without the assent of that King, no law can pass in any of the dependencies. Will that King dare to give, or will his Ministers dare advise him to give the royal assent to any law that will dismember the empire? Is it credible to suppose that he would forfeit the Crown of the whole Empire, to gratify or to conspire with a part of it, which he must lose together with that Crown? It is nonsense to suppose it. No law therefore can pass in any dependency, over which you have not a negative in *effect*, though not in *form*. Is this nothing? The power of peace and war, and the sword of the Empire, resides with Great-Britain. Your friends and enemies are of course the friends and enemies of the whole dominion. Is this nothing? You raise men for your fleets and armies throughout the whole. Is this nothing? The worst that can happen is that you may sometimes fail in getting money from them also. This too you will get in a reasonable degree, and with reasonable attention to them. Neither is all that they can ever contribute, over and above the maintainance of their local establishments, worth a civil war. For as to any significant remittances of revenue from America to Great-Britain, it is too absurd to talk about. Add to all I have said above, what is indeed revenue, and infinitely more than revenue: That Britain, as the head of a naval and commercial Empire, must be supreme in trade and commerce, naval and maritime regulation. Is this nothing? Or rather is it not every thing? Will you get nothing from your Colonies by such a system? I will be bold to say that you will get more than any nation under the sun ever obtained from Colonies before. What follows from all this? That you are going at this very moment, at the expence of every species of injustice and cruelty, to contend with your countrymen for nothing, at the hazard of every thing. If this is common sense go on with it.

You say it is strange that in this dispute Englishmen have become opponents to English honour and interest;—That perhaps it never happened before that justice found much opposition with interest on her side; and that the principles of the Congress, however *wild*, have united *all* the provinces against the mother country, from New England to South Carolina. Are not these circumstances, I ask, much stronger presumptions against you, than in your behalf? For is it possible to conceive, that a cause, in which no religious enthusiasm enters, which has nothing to appeal to but reason and justice, and against which the semblance of a national interest and honour is leagued—is it to be conceived that such a cause, if founded in fraud or falsehood, could have stood *ten year's* agitation without detection? Or that if it were not built on the most solid truth, and upon the most commanding justice, that so many provinces, with so many principles of discord to keep them asunder, would have united against a parent country so powerful, and to which the moment before they were so cordially united? And that such a combination in America, should not produce union in Great-Britain, even if before there had been nothing but enmity; instead of leaving this matter as it has done, to be the leading, and almost the only subject of controversy amongst us? And what can be more honourable to the character of this great and just nation, than that no sophism of perverted talents like yours; no pretexts even of national interest, or honour; nor all these, aided by the voice of Parliament itself, could warp the integrity of the public mind: or blind it to those rights in their countrymen, which the people of this kingdom, by such an unshaken adherence to them, have shewn they will not suffer to be torn from themselves?

You say that the Colonies of Britain differ from those of other nations, no otherwise than as the English constitution differs from theirs. The American agrees with you, and says that is in freedom. But that, not a modern device dressed up in deceitful words, but the solid freedom of the British constitution; which cannot exist without a *resident* legislature for domestic regulation in general, and for taxation particularly furnished with members *constituted* by the *property* of that country which they are to *tax*. He who goes *voluntarily* to America, you say, cannot complain of losing what he leaves in Europe; for that as a man can be but in one place at once, he cannot have the advantage of multiplied residence. But first, our Colonists were *not* mere voluntary emigrants. They went by the *invitation* of the State. A futile claim to an uncultivated territory was all you had. That you would have lost if you had not sent them to keep possession of it. They went therefore in the service of their country, and a hard service too. A barren, or over-wooded soil was what you gave them. You owe your title to that soil, at this moment, to their occupancy; they owe the fruits of it to their labour; and they pay the monopoly of its trade to your superior and parental relation. Men who stand in this situation are not lightly to be construed out of their privileges. They allow, by this change of place, that they lose their vote for a representative in Britain; and they claim in lieu of it, though by no means an equivalent, a vote for a representative in America. They say it is an inseparable quality of property by the British Government, to constitute the members of the legislature that are to tax that property; that as their property lies in America, it must constitute the members that are to tax America; but that it has no share in constituting the British House of Commons, and that therefore they are not to be taxed by that assembly.

You say that the Americans do not wish to send representatives to the British parliament, and I believe it. They see the difficulty, or rather impossibility of executing such an idea, and how unfairly, if it were possible, it is likely to be executed. They conclude, therefore, that they must be represented and taxed in America. But you conclude the reverse, that they ought to be taxed in England; and say, that there is little difference, if any, between a man's being *taxed* by *compulsion without representation*, and being *represented* by *compulsion* in *order* to be *taxed*. This seems, how consistently I know not, to state this as the alternative to which the American is reduced. And the American confesses that your doctrine at the best, does not mend that condition. For he says that if you *force* him to *receive* at the point of the *sword* a *fiction* of his being *virtually represented* here, that he will then be exactly in the state you describe, viz. that of being *represented* by *compulsion* in *order* to be *taxed*. And he admits that violence in the first instance, by taking his money by force without any law, would be less an insult to his understanding; and perhaps a less dangerous because a more alarming violation of his property.

And though every part of your publication breathes nothing but the spirit of tyranny, yet there is one passage so audacious that it deserves to be distinguished. In your 24th page you have these words, "an *English Individual* may by the supreme authority be deprived of liberty, and a *Colony* divested of its *powers*, for reasons of which that authority is the *sole* judge." If one Individual, or one Colony, can be thus deprived, so may all the Colonies together; so may every man in the community. For I defy any man to shew where any limitation exists, if any such power be admitted. By this doctrine, the Parliament, for reasons of which it is the *sole* judge; that is without assigning any reason at all, may make every man in the British Empire a slave in one day. That is to say, a body of men, taken from amongst ourselves, in number not above a thousand, collected in one spot of the Empire, under the most sacred trust for the service of the whole, are entitled to do that which no power on earth has a right to do, viz. to make slaves, at one blow, and without saying wherefore, of fourteen millions of fellow subjects, and of their posterity, to latest time, and throughout every quarter of the world. Is such language to be endured? Or can he be a friend to human nature who uses it?

With equal humanity in your 60th page, you say "if the Bostonians are condemned *unheard*, it is because there is no *need* of a *trial*. All trial is the investigation of something *doubtful.*" Your ideas of legislation we had before, and your *judicial* ideas are as intolerable. To say that a crime's being notorious, or asserted to be notorious, will justify condemnation unheard, is too insolent an imposition. Where is the Caligula who would not say that the guilt of the man, or of the province that he wanted to destroy, was notorious. If the assertion of the tyrant will convert cruelty into justice, no tyrant will ever be cruel. But the law of England is so different from your sentiment, that it presumes every man to be innocent, till his guilt is tried and established. That is, instead of condemning unheard, so long as any man is unheard, it acquits him.

Neither do you stop at barren tenets of tyranny; but endeavour to propagate them into act; and to stamp their image upon the measures of Government. You call aloud to the Crown, to new model; that is, to innovate charters. Yet what is your doctrine with respect to charters? It is that if these emigrants had gone without ceremony to seek their fortunes in any district which was unoccupied, or which by arms, address, or labour, they had acquired, they would have been independent states. But that by accepting these charters, the Colonists put themselves under the protection of the state, and by necessary implication under its jurisdiction and authority. Thus you confess that if it were not for these charters, they might have been independent; and yet in other places you say that it is to these charters they owe that they are freemen. At one time you state these charters as an invaluable favour conferred upon them, and at another, as an inextricable chain by which they are bound. You state it as a compact; and justly with respect to the Emigrants; for they gave up every thing here for what they obtained in America. What follows? That you cannot take that away from them without restoring, at least, what they gave up for it. Now what is that? All that they, and their descendants might have acquired by remaining in Great-Britain ever since, all which they have lost; and which is probably much more than they have gained. Now this I believe you would find it hard to calculate, and as hard perhaps to pay.—To return.—Who were the parties to this compact; The Colonists and the Crown; not the Parliament. Now if in such a transaction, the Parliament is not included, it is final against the Parliament. If on the other hand it is included, and that the Crown is to be considered as acting for the Parliament, I say that its act must be binding on both sides, or on neither. That is to say, that Parliament must be bound on one side, or the Colonist is not bound on the other. And this with good reason; first, because it is the nature of compact to be mutual, or null. And next, because if the terms were disagreeable to Parliament, Parliament had an opportunity of immediately undeceiving the Colonists, and declaring their dissent; which if they did not they are bound. Now did they make any such declaration? Nothing like it. I say then that the faith of Legislature is as much pledged by this subsequent and implied assent, as by an antecedent participation.

I have proved, that taxation by an Assembly, not constituted by the property which it taxes, is an idea repugnant to our constitution. Such a power, therefore, to exist at all, must be reserved in the most express terms. Now it is confessed that taxation is reserved only in one charter, that of Pennsylvania. By every other therefore it is excluded I say; and that, not only by constitutional inference, but by the cooperation of Parliament itself in the assent which it has given to these charters, as above explained. And to this natural construction of the charters as they stand expressed, I add the contemporary and continual construction which they have received from the conduct of Parliament, which best knew its own intentions, and which did not tax them: insomuch that the non-user may be better argued to be a tacit renunciation of taxation as to Pennsylvania, where the power was reserved; than as leaving a doubt but that there is no such right where it was not reserved. And shall any man say that such rights, purchased originally by what was relinquished here, purchased since by labour and service in America, and ratified by time, the arbiter of Governments— Shall any man say that such rights are to be blown away by the breath of the first idle disputant? Or that they are alterable or revocable every hour of the day; with this absurdity added to injustice, that they are alterable and revocable only on one side: that is to the injury of the Colonist for ever, and at no period of time to his benefit? And this without considering, that by your own doctrine these charters, instead of being annulled as the ground of their independance, ought to be held sacred and immutable as the source of your authority?

But not content with innovating charters, you advise that the Americans universally should be subjugated by stricter laws and stronger obligations. You exhort that national *vengeance* may be poured on the contrivers of mischief, and that no *mistakes* of *clemency* should prevent abundant forfeitures. Lest this should not be sufficiently harsh and humiliating, you suggest, that their slaves may be taken from them, though, by your laws, their property, and settled, with arms for their defence, in some simple, that is, arbitrary form of government. Thus you would establish a Saturnalia of cruelty, and expose these devoted men to the brutality of their own slaves, enflamed and irritated to retaliate traditionary wrongs, and to wreak a barbarous vengeance on their degraded masters. Lest even the common soldier should have too much tenderness for them, you are careful to represent them under every odious and disparaging image. You say, that we ought to resent our situation as the Scythians did of old when they found themselves excluded by their own *slaves*. You slander the very bounties of nature in them; and, as far as you can, degrade them below the rank of humanity.

Is this the language of a sober enquirer? As a philosopher, as a moralist, as a man, you ought to have cried out to the contending nations, "Infatuated as you are, whither do you rush? Though you may have some cause for difference with each other, you have much more still for concord." But you have scattered firebrands between them. You have endeavoured to ripen tumult to anarchy, and dissatisfaction to rebellion; and to transform punishment into waste and extirpation.

The tumour of your stile, the insolence of your manners, your rawness in the great principles of the subject which you treat, and your universal inaccuracy, or unfairness in arguing, are inferior considerations and faults that may be forgiven. But let it be remembered at all events, that with respect to this point you confess, that if the Americans are right, it is robbery in us, not rebellion in them. Now I ask any man, whether on this state it is so clear that America is wrong, and that it is not robbery in us, as that we should lightly run the risque of becoming murderers also; and murderers of our fellow-subjects into the bargain? Every lover of truth and liberty, every honest and conscientious man will feel this question. The soldier will feel it; the sailor will feel it; the free subject will feel it: the King and his Ministers will feel it.

FINIS.

Edmund Burke, The Speech of Edmund Burke, Esquire, on Moving His Resolutions for Conciliation with the Colonies, March 22d, 1775. New York, 1775.

Though American patriots had a more favorable view of Edmund Burke than he probably deserved, they did have a number of reasons to think highly of him. He was the parliamentary spokesman for those Whigs led by Lord Rockingham who during their brief ministry in 1766 had repealed the Stamp Act. In his *Thoughts on the Cause of the Present Discontents* (1770) Burke had voiced fears of a Tory cabal that had taken over the monarchy and was corrupting Parliament—confirming a conspiracy theory that Americans had long nourished. And in several speeches in the House of Commons he had expressed admiration for America and sympathy for its cause, most memorably in this remarkable two-and-a-half-hour speech on conciliation delivered in the House of Commons on March 22, 1775. The speech was quickly published, and passed through numerous editions in a matter of weeks. The text that follows is from the first American edition, published just six months after the speech was delivered.

But the sympathy that Burke and the Rockingham Whigs had for the American position was deceptive. It was true that they feared a monarchical conspiracy engineered by Lord Bute and other Tory "friends" of the king. But they never questioned the supreme authority of Parliament or its right to legislate for the colonies. They were the most devout of Whigs, deeply mistrustful of monarchy and instinctively attached to Parliament. Indeed, the Americans would have done well to recall that though they may have repealed the Stamp Act, it was the Rockingham Whigs who also passed the Declaratory Act, which asserted Parliament's complete supremacy over America. Burke's position on the American crisis was always to avoid "metaphysical distinctions" and "abstract ideas of right" (leave these "to the schools," he said in 1774, "for there only they may be discussed with safety"); instead, he said, exercise prudence and accommodation, keep trade flowing, let the cultural ties of affection flourish, and return to those earlier decades before 1763 when everyone prospered.

So suspicious of monarchy and so devoted to Parliament were the Rockingham Whigs that they could not tolerate the belated British concession expressed in the Carlisle Commission of 1778—which was essentially the position Americans had suggested in 1774, that is, thirteen legislatively independent colonies tied only to the king. Better to grant America complete independence, they concluded, than to keep an empire in which only the king ruled.

THE
SPEECH
OF

Edmund Burke, Esquire,

ON MOVING HIS

RESOLUTIONS

FOR

CONCILIATION

WITH THE

COLONIES,

MARCH 22d, 1775.

NEW-YORK:

PRINTED BY JAMES RIVINGTON. 1775.

The following are the nine Resolutions contained in Mr. Burke's Conciliatory Plan, *which he offered for the consideration of the House of Commons.*

1. "THAT the colonies and plantations in North-America, consisting of fourteen separate governments, and containing two millions of free inhabitants, have not had the liberty and privilege of electing and sending knights, citizens and burgesses to represent them in parliament;" which passed in the negative, ayes 78, noes 270.

2. "That the said colonies, &c. have been liable to, and bounden by several subsidies, payments, rates, and taxes, given and granted by parliament, though the said colonies and plantations have not their knights, &c. in said Parliament of their own election, to represent the condition of their country; by lack whereof they have been often grieved by subsidies, given and granted and assented to in the said court, in manner prejudicial to the commonwealth, quietness, rest, and peace of the subjects inhabiting within the same." Amendment proposed to leave out from the word *country* to the end of the resolution. Question put, that the words proposed to be left out, stand part of the question; it passed in the negative without a division. Then the main question so amended being put, it passed likewise in the negative.

3. "That each of said colonies, &c. hath within itself a body chosen in part, or in the whole, by the freemen, freeholders, or other inhabitants thereof, commonly called the General Assembly, or General Court, with powers legally to raise, levy and assess, according to the usage of such colonies, duties and taxes, towards defraying all public services." It passed in the negative.

4. "That the said General Assemblies, General Courts, or other bodies legally qualified as aforesaid, have at sundry times freely granted several large subsidies and public aids, for his Majesty's service, according to their abilities, when required thereto by letter from one of his Majesty's principal Secretaries of State; and that their right to grant the same, and the cheerfulness and sufficiency in the said grants, have been at sundry times acknowledged by Parliament." passed in the negative.

5. "That it hath been found by experience, that the manner of granting the said supplies and aids by those General Assemblies, hath been more agreeable to the inhabitants of the said colonies, and more beneficial and conducive to the public service, than the mode of giving and granting aids and subsidies in Parliament, to be raised and paid in said colonies." Passed in the negative.

6 and 7. "That the several acts passed in the 7th and 14th years of his present Majesty's reign relating to America, be repealed, and to explain an act of the 35th of Henry VIII. for the trial of treason, &c." Passed in the negative.

8. "That from the time when the General Assembly, &c. of any colony or plantation in North-America, shall have appointed, by act of Assembly duly confirmed, a settled salary to the offices of Chief Justices and Judges of the superior court, it may be proper that the said Chief Justices, &c. of the superior courts of such colony, shall hold his or their office and offices during their good behaviour; and shall not be removed therefrom, but when the said removal shall be adjudged by his Majesty, in Council, upon a hearing, on complaint from the General Assembly; or on a complaint from the Governor, or the Council, or the House of Representatives severally, of the colony in which said Chief Justice, &c. have exercised the said office." It passed in the negative.

9. "That it is proper to regulate the courts of Admiralty, or Vice Admiralty, authorised by the 15th chapter of 4th of George III. in such a manner as to make the same more commodious to those who sue or are sued in said courts." It passed in the negative.

Speech of Edmund Burke, Esq.

I HOPE, Sir, that, notwithstanding the austerity of the Chair, your good-nature will incline you to some degree of indulgence towards human frailty. You will not think it unnatural, that those who have an object depending, which strongly engages their hopes and fears, should be somewhat inclined to superstition. As I came into the House full of Anxiety about the event of my motion, I found to my infinite surprize, that the grand Penal Bill, by which we had passed sentence on the trade and sustenance of America, is to be returned us from the other House.* I do confess, I could not help looking on this event as a fortunate omen. I look upon it as a sort of providential favour; by which we are put once more in possession of our deliberative capacity, upon a business so very questionable in its nature, so very uncertain in its issue. By the return of this bill, which seemed to have taken its flight for ever, we are at this very instant nearly as free to choose a plan for our American government, as we were on the first day of the session. If Sir, we incline to the side of conciliation, we are not at all embarrassed (unless we please to make ourselves so) by any incongruous mixture of coercion and restraint. We are therefore called upon, as it were by a superior warning voice, again to attend to America; to attend to the whole of it together, and to review the subject with an unusual degree of care and calmness.

Surely it is an awful subject; or there is none so on this side of the grave. When I first had the honour of a seat in this House, the affairs of that continent pressed themselves upon us, as the most important and most delicate object of parliamentary attention. My little share in this great deliberation oppressed me. I found myself a partaker in a very high trust; and having no sort of reason to rely on the strength of my

---

* The act to restrain the trade and commerce of the province of Massachusetts-Bay and New-Hampshire, and colonies of Connecticut and Rhode-Island, and Providence Plantation in North-America, to Great-Britain, Ireland, and the British islands in the West-Indies; and to prohibit such provinces and colonies from carrying on any fishery on the Banks of Newfoundland, and other places therein mentioned, under certain conditions and limitations.

natural abilities for the proper execution of that trust, I was obliged to take more than common pains to instruct myself in every thing which relates to our colonies. I was not less under the necessity of forming some fixed ideas, concerning the general policy of the British Empire. Something of this sort seemed to be indispensible; in order, amidst so vast a fluctuation of passions and opinions, to concenter my thoughts; to ballast my conduct; to preserve me from being blown about by every wind of fashionable doctrine. I really did not think it safe, or manly, to have fresh principles to seek upon every fresh mail which should arrive from America.

At that period, I had the fortune to find myself in perfect concurrence with a large Majority in this House. Bowing under that high authority, and penetrated with the sharpness and strength of that early impression, I have continued ever since, without the least deviation, in my original sentiments. Whether this be owing to an obstinate perseverance in error, or to a religious adherence to what appears to me truth and reason, it is in your equity to judge.

Parliament, Sir, having an enlarged view of objects, made, during this interval, more frequent changes in their sentiments and their conduct, than could be justified in a particular person upon the contracted scale of private information. But though I do not hazard any thing approaching to a censure on the motives of former Parliaments to all those alterations, one fact is undoubted, that under them the state of America has been kept in continual agitation. Every thing administered as remedy to the public complaint, if it did not produce, was at least followed by, an heightening of the distemper; until, by a variety of experiments, that important country has been brought into her present situation; a situation, which I will not miscall, which I dare not name; which I scarcely know how to comprehend in the terms of any description.

In this posture, Sir, things stood at the beginning of the session. About that time a worthy member* of great parliamentary experience, who, in the year 1766, filled the chair of the American committee with much ability, took me aside; and lamented the present aspect of our politics, told me, things

* Mr. Rose Fuller.

were come to such a pass, that our former methods of proceeding in the House would be no longer tolerated. That the
public tribunal (never too indulgent to a long and unsuccessful
opposition) would now scrutinize our conduct with unusual
severity. That the very vicissitudes and shiftings of ministerial
measures, instead of convicting their authors of inconstancy
and want of system, would be taken as an occasion of charging
us with a predetermined discontent, which nothing could satisfy; whilst we accused every measure of vigour as cruel, and
every proposal of lenity as weak and irresolute. The public, he
said, would not have patience to see us play the game out with
our adversaries; we must produce our hand. It would be expected, that those who for many years had been active in such
affairs, should shew that they had formed some clear and decided idea of the principles of colony government; and were capable of drawing out something like a platform of the ground,
which might be laid for future and permanent tranquility.

I felt the truth of what my hon. friend represented; but I felt
my situation too. His application might have been made with
far greater propriety to many other gentlemen. No man was
indeed ever better disposed, or worse qualified, for such an
undertaking than myself. Though I gave so far into his opinion
that I immediately threw my thoughts into a sort of parliamentary form, I was by no means equally ready to produce
them. It generally argues some degree of natural importance
of mind, or some want of knowledge of the world, to hazard
plans of government, except from a seat of authority. Propositions are made, not only ineffectually, but somewhat disreputa-
bly, when the minds of men are not properly disposed for their
reception; and for my part I am not ambitious of ridicule; nor
absolutely a candidate for disgrace.

Besides, Sir, to speak the plain truth, I have in general no
very exalted opinion of the virtue of paper government; nor of
any politics, in which the plan is to be wholly separated from
the execution. But when I saw that anger and violence prevailed every day more and more, and that things were hastening towards an incurable alienation of our colonies, I confess
my caution gave way, I felt this as one of those few moments in
which decorum yields to an higher duty. Public calamity is a
mighty leveller, and there are occasions when any, even the

slightest chance of doing good must be laid hold on, even by the most inconsiderable person.

To restore order and repose to an empire so great and so distracted as ours, is merely in the attempt an undertaking that would ennoble the flights of the highest genius, and obtain pardon for the efforts of the meanest understanding. Struggling a good while with these thoughts, by degrees I felt myself more firm. I derived at length some confidence from what in other circumstances usually produces timidity. I grew less anxious even from the idea of my own insignificance, For, judging of what you are, by what you ought to be; I persuaded myself that you would not reject a reasonable proposition, because it had nothing but its reason to recommend it. On the other hand being totally destitute of all shadow of influence, natural or advantitious, I was very sure, that if my proposition were futile or dangerous, if it were weakly conceived, or improperly timed, there was nothing exterior to it, of power to awe, dazzle, or delude you. You will see it just as it is, and you will treat it just as it deserves.

The proposition is peace. Not peace through the medium of war. Not peace to be hunted through the labyrinth of intricate and endless negociations. Not peace to arise out of universal discord, fomented from principle in all parts of the empire. Not peace to depend on the juridical determination of perplexing questions; or the precise marking the shadowy boundaries of a complex government. It is simple peace sought in its natural course, and its ordinary haunts. It is peace sought in the spirit of peace, and laid in principles purely pacific. I propose by removing the ground of the difference, and by restoring the *former unsuspecting confidence of the colonies in the mother country*, to give permanent satisfaction to your people; and (far from a scheme of ruling by discord) to reconcile them to each other in the same act, and by the bond of the very same interest, which reconciles them to British government.

My idea is nothing more. Refined policy ever has been the parent of confusion, and ever will be so long as the world endures. Plain good intention, which is as easily discovered at the first view, as fraud is surely detected at last, is, let me say, of no mean force in the government of mankind. Genuine simplicity of heart is an healing and cementing principle. My plan, therefore, being formed upon the most simple grounds imaginable, may disappoint some people when they hear it. It has nothing to recommend it to the pruriency of curious ears. There is nothing at all new and captivating in it. It has nothing of the splendor of the project, which has lately laid upon your table, by the noble Lord in the blue riband.* It does not propose to fill your lobby with squabbling colony agents who will require the interposition of your mace, at every instant, to keep the peace amongst them. It does not institute a magnificent auction of finance, where captivated provinces come to general ransom by bidding against each other, until you knock down the hammer, and determine a proportion of payments, beyond all the powers of algebra to equalize and settle.

The plan which I shall presume to suggest, derives, however one great advantage from the proposition and registry of that noble Lord's project. The idea of conciliation is admissible. First, the House, in accepting the resolution moved by the noble Lord, has admitted, notwithstanding the menacing front of our address, notwithstanding our heavy bill of pains and penalties, that we do not think ourselves precluded from all ideas of free grace and bounty.

The House has gone farther, it has declared conciliation admissible, previous to any submission on the part of America. It has even shot a good deal beyond that mark, and has admitted that the complaints of our former mode of exerting the

---

* "That when the Governor, Council, or Assembly, or General Court, of any of his Majesty's provinces or colonies in America, shall *propose* to make provision, *according to the condition, circumstances,* and *situation* of such province or colony, for contributing their *proportion* to the *common defence* (such *proportion* to be raised under the authority of the General Court, or General Assembly of such province or colony and disposable by Parliament) and shall engage to make provision also for the support of the civil government, and the administration of justice, in such province or colony, it will be proper, *if such proposal shall be approved by his Majesty, and the two Houses of Parliament,* and for so long as such provision shall be made accordingly, to forbear, *in respect to such province or colony,* to levy any duty, tax, or assessment, or to impose any farther duty, tax, or assessment, except such duties as it may be expedient to continue to levy or impose for the regulation of commerce; the net produce of the duties last mentioned to be carried to the account of such province or colony respectively." Resolution moved by Lord North in the committee, and agreed to by the House, 27 Feb. 1775.

right of taxation were not wholly unfounded. That right thus exerted is allowed to have had something reprehensible in it; something unwise, or something grievous; since, in the midst of our heat and resentment, we of ourselves have proposed a capital alteration; and, in order to get rid of what seemed so very exceptionable, have instituted a mode that is altogether new; one that is, indeed wholly alien from all the ancient methods and forms of Parliament.

The principle of this proceeding is large enough for my purpose. The means proposed by the noble Lord for carrying his ideas into execution, I think, indeed, are very indifferently suited to the end; and this I shall endeavour to shew you before I sit down. But, for the present, I take my ground on the admitted principle. I mean to give peace. Peace implies reconciliation; and, where there has been a material dispute, reconciliation does in a manner always imply concession on the one part or on the other. In this state of things I make no difficulty in affirming that the proposal ought to originate from us. Great and acknowledged force is not impaired, either in effect or in opinion, by an unwillingness to exert itself. The superior power may offer peace with honour and with safety. Such an offer from such a power will be attributed to magnanimity. But the concessions of the weak are the concessions of fear. When such a one is disarmed, he is wholly at the mercy of his superior, and he loses for ever that time and those chances which, as they happen to all men, are the strength and resources of all inferior power.

The capital leading questions, on which you must this day decide, are these two. First, whether you ought to concede; and, secondly, what your concession ought to be. On the first of these questions we have gained (as I have just taken the liberty of observing to you) some ground. But I am sensible that a good deal more is still to be done. Indeed, Sir, to enable us to determine both on the one and the other of these great questions with a firm and precise judgment: I think it may be necessary to consider distinctly the true nature and the peculiar circumstances of the object which we have before us. Because after all our struggle, whether we will or not, we must govern America according to that nature, and to those circumstances, and not according to our own imaginations; not according to abstract ideas of right; by no means according to mere general theories of government, the resort to which appears to me, in our present situation, no better than arrant trifling. I shall therefore endeavour, with your leave, to lay before you some of the most material of these circumstances in as full and as clear a manner as I am able to state them.

The first thing we have to consider with regard to the nature of the object, is the number of people in the colonies. I have taken for some years a good deal of pains on that point. I can by no calculation justify myself in placing the number below two millions of inhabitants of our own European blood and colour, besides at least five hundred thousand others, who form no inconsiderable part of the strength and opulence of the whole. This, Sir, is, I believe about the true number. There is no occasion to exaggerate where plain truth is of so much weight and importance. But whether I put the present numbers too high, or too low, is a matter of little moment. Such is the strength with which population shoots in that part of the world, that state the numbers as high as we will, whilst the dispute continues, the exaggeration ends. Whilst we are discussing any given magnitude, they are grown to it. Whilst we spend our time in deliberating the mode of governing two millions, we shall find we have millions more to manage. Your children do not grow faster from infancy to manhood, than they spread from families to communities, and from villages to nations.

I put this consideration upon the present and the growing numbers in the front of our deliberations; because, Sir, this consideration will make it evident to a blunter discernment than yours, that no partial, narrow, contracted, pinched, occasional system, will be at all suitable to such an object. It will shew you that it is not to be considered as one of those *minima*, which are out of the eye and consideration of the law; not a paltry excrescence of the state; not a mean dependent, who may be neglected with little damage, and provoked with little danger. It will prove that some degree of care and caution is required in the handling such an object; it will shew that you ought not, in reason, to trifle with so large a mass of the interests and feelings of the human race. You could at no time do so without guilt, and be assured you will not be able to do it long with impunity.

But the population of this country, the great and growing population, though a very important consideration, will lose much of its weight if not combined with other circumstances. The commerce of your colonies is out of all proportion beyond the numbers of the people. This ground of their commerce indeed has been trode some days ago, and with great ability, by a distinguished person at your bar.* This gentleman after thirty-five years—it is so long since he appeared at the same place to plead for the commerce of Great-Britain, has come again before you to plead the same cause, without any other effect of time than that to the fire of imagination and extent of erudition, which even then marked him as one of the first literary characters of his age, he has added a consummate knowledge in the commercial interest of his country, formed by a long course of enlightened and discriminating experience.

Sir, I should be inexcusable in coming after such a person with any detail, if a great part of the members who now fill the House, had not the misfortune to be absent when he appeared at your bar. Besides, Sir, I propose to take the matter at periods of time somewhat different from his. There is, if I mistake not, a point of view from whence, if you will look at this subject, it is impossible that it should not make an impression upon you.

I have in my hand two accounts, one a comparative state of the export trade of England to its colonies, as it stood in the year 1704, and as it stood in the year 1772. The other a state of the export trade of this country to its colonies alone, as it stood in 1772, compared with the whole trade of England to all parts of the world (the colonies included) in the year 1704. They are from good vouchers; the latter period from the accounts on your table, the earlier from an original manuscript of Davenant, who first established the Inspector-General's office, which has been ever since his time so abundant a source of parliamentary information.

The export trade to the colonies consists of three great branches. The African, which terminating almost wholly in the colonies, must be put to the account of their commerce, the West Indian and North-American. All these are so interwoven that the attempt to separate them would tear to pieces the

* Mr. Glover.

contexture of the whole; and, if not entirely destroy, would very much depreciate the value of all the parts. I therefore consider these three denominations, to be, what in effect they are, one trade.

The trade to the colonies, taken on the export side, at the beginning of this century, that is, in the year 1704, stood thus:

Exports to North-America and the
    West-Indies, ... £.483,265
To Africa, ...   86,665
                                           569,930

In the Year 1772, which I take as a middle year between the highest and the lowest of those laid on your table, the accounts were as follow:

To North-America and the West Indies, ... £.4,791,734
To Africa, ... 866,398
To which, if you add the export trade to
    and from Scotland, which had in 1704 no   364,000
    existence, ...
                                    £.6,022,132

From five hundred and odd thousands, it has grown to six millions; it has encreased no less than twelvefold. This is the state of the colony trade, as compared with itself at these two periods, within this century. But this is not all. Examine my second account. See how the export trade to the colonies alone, in 1772, stood in the other point of view, that is, as compared to the whole trade of England, in 1704.

The whole export trade of England, including
    that to the colonies, in 1704, ... 6,509,000
Export to the colonies alone, in 1772, ... 6,024,000
                      Difference,   £.485,000

The trade with America alone is now within less than 500,000l. of being equal to what this great commercial nation, England, carried on at the beginning of this century with the whole world! If I had taken the largest year of those on your table, it would rather have exceeded. But it will be said, is not this American trade an unnatural protuberance, that has drawn the juices from the rest of the body? The reverse. It is the very food that has nourished every other part into its present magnitude. Our general trade has been greatly augmented; and augmented more or less in almost every part to which it ever extended; but with this material difference, that of the six millions which, in the beginning of the century, constituted the whole mass of our export commerce, the colony trade was but one twelfth part; it is now (as a part of seventeen millions) considerably more than a third of the whole. This is the relative proportion of the importance of the colonies at these two periods; and all reason concerning our mode of treating them must have this proportion as its basis, or it is a reasoning weak, rotten, and sophistical.

Mr. Speaker, I cannot prevail upon myself to hurry over this great consideration. It is good for us to be here. We stand where we have an immense view of what is, and what is past. Clouds indeed, and darkness rest upon the future. Let us, however, before we descend from this noble eminence reflect, that this growth of our national prosperity has happened within the short period of the life of man. It has happened within sixty-eight years. There are those alive, whose memory might touch the two extremities! For instance, my Lord Bathurst might remember all the stages of the progress. He was, in 1704, of an age at least to be made to comprehend such things, he was then old enough, *acta parentum jam legere, et quæ sit poterit cognoscere virtus*—Suppose, Sir, that the angel of this auspicious youth, foreseeing the many virtues, which made him one of the most amiable, as he is one of the most fortunate men of his age, had opened to him in a vision, that when, in the fourth generation, the third Prince of the House of Brunswick had sat twelve years on the throne of that nation, which (by the happy issue of moderate and healing councils) was to be made Great-Britain, he should see his son Lord Chancellor of England, turn back the current of hereditary dignity to its fountain, and raise him to an higher rank of peerage, whilst he enriched the family with a new one; if amidst these bright and happy scenes of domestic honour and prosperity, that angel should have drawn up the curtain, and unfolded the rising glories of his country, and whilst he was gazing with admiration on the then commercial grandeur of

England, the genius should point out to him a little speck, scarce visible in the mass of the national interest, a small seminal principle, rather than a formed body, and should tell him,—"Young man, there is America; which at this time serves for little more than to amuse you with stories of savage men, and uncouth manners; yet shall, before you taste of death, shew itself equal to the whole of that commerce which now attracts the envy of the world. Whatever England has been growing to by a progressive increase of improvement, brought in by variety of people, by succession of civilizing conquests and civilizing settlements in a series of seventeen hundred years, you shall see as much added to her by America in the course of a single life!" If this state of his country had been foretold to him, would it not require all the sanguine credulity of youth, and all the fervid glow of enthusiasm, to make him believe it? Fortunate man, he has lived to see it! Fortunate indeed if he lives to see nothing that shall vary the prospect, and cloud the setting of his day!

Excuse me, Sir, if turning from such thoughts I resume this comparative view once more. You have seen it on a large scale; look at it on a small one. I will point out to your attention a particular instance of it in the single province of Pennsylvania. In the year 1704 that province called for 11,459l. in value of your commodities, native and foreign. This was the whole. What did it demand in 1772? Why, nearly fifty times as much, for in that year the export to Pennsylvania was 507,909l. nearly equal to the export to all the colonies together in the first period.

I choose, Sir, to enter into these minute and particular details; because generalities, which in all other cases are apt to heighten and raise the subject, have here a tendency to sink it. When we speak of the commerce with our colonies, fiction lags after truth; invention is unfruitful; and imagination cold and barren.

So far, Sir, as to the importance of the object in the view of its commerce, as concerned in the exports from England. If I were to detail the imports, I could shew how many enjoyments they procure which deceive the burthen of life; how many materials which invigorate the springs of national industry, and extend and animate every part of our foreign and domestic commerce. This would be a curious subject indeed; but I must prescribe bounds to myself in a matter so vast and various.

I pass therefore to the colonies in another point of view, their agriculture. This they have prosecuted with such a spirit, that, besides feeding plentifully their own growing multitude, their annual export of grain, comprehending rice, has some years ago exceeded a million in value. Of their last harvest, I am persuaded they will export much more. At the beginning of the century some of these colonies imported corn from the mother country. For some time past the old world has been fed from the new. The scarcity which you have felt would have been a desolating famine, if this child of your old age, with a true filial piety, with a Roman charity, had not put the full breast of its youthful exuberance to the mouth of its exhausted parent.

As to the wealth which the colonies have drawn from the sea by their fisheries, you had all that matter fully opened at your bar; you surely thought these acquisitions of value, for they seemed even to excite your envy; and yet the spirit, by which that enterprizing employment has been exercised, ought rather, in my opinion, to have raised your esteem and admiration. And pray, Sir, what in the world is equal to it? Pass by the other parts, and look at the manner in which the people of New-England have of late carried on the whale fishery. Whilst we follow them among the tumbling mountains of ice, and behold them penetrating into the deepest frozen recesses of Hudson's-Bay and Davis's Straights, whilst we are looking for them beneath the arctic circle, we hear that they have pierced into the opposite region of polar cold; that they are at the antipodes, and engaged under the frozen serpent of the South. Falkland Island, which seemed too remote and romantic an object for the grasp of national ambition, is but a stage and resting place in the progress of their victorious industry. Nor is the equinoctial heat more discouraging to them than the accumulated winter of both the poles. We know that whilst some of them draw the line and strike the harpoon on the coast of Africa, others run the longitude, and pursue their gigantic game along the coast of Brazil.

No sea but what is vexed with their fisheries; no climate that is not witness to their toils. Neither the perseverance of Holland, nor the activity of France, nor the dextrous and firm sagacity of English enterprize, ever carried this most perilous mode of hardy industry to the extent to which it has been pushed by this recent people; a people who are still, as it were, but in the gristle, and not yet hardened into the bone of manhood. When I contemplate these things; when I know that the colonies in general owe little or nothing to any care of ours, and that they are not squeezed into this happy form by the constraints of watchful and suspicious government, but that through a wise and salutary neglect, a generous nature has been suffered to take her own way to perfection; when I reflect upon these efforts, when I see how profitable they have been to us, I feel all the pride of power sink, and all presumption in the wisdom of human contrivances melt and die away within me. My rigour relents. I pardon something to the spirit of liberty.

I am sensible, Sir, that all which I have asserted in my detail, is admitted in the gross; but that a quite different conclusion is drawn from it. America, gentlemen say, is a noble object. It is an object well worth fighting for. Certainly it is, if fighting a people be the best way of gaining them. Gentlemen, in this respect, will be laid to their choice of means by their complexions and their habits. Those who understand the military art, will of course have some predilection for it. Those who wield the thunder of the state, may have more confidence in the efficacy of arms. But I confess, possibly for want of this knowledge, my opinion is much more in favour of prudent management than of force; considering force not as an odious, but a feeble instrument for preserving a people, so numerous, so active, so growing, so spirited as this, in a profitable and subordinate connection with us.

First, Sir, permit me to observe, that the use of force alone is but temporary, it may subdue for a moment; but it does not remove the necessity of subduing again, and a nation is not governed, which is perpetually to be conquered.

My next objection is its uncertainty; terror is not always the effect of force; and an armament is not a victory. If you do not succeed, you are without resource; for, conciliation failing, force remains; but force failing, no farther hope of reconciliation is left. Power and authority are sometimes bought by kindness; but they can never be begged as alms by an impoverished and defeated violence.

A farther objection to force is, that you impair the object by your very endeavour to preserve it. The thing you fought for, is not the thing which you recover; but depreciated, sunk, wasted, and consumed in the contest. Nothing less will content me than whole America. I do not choose to consume its strength along with your own, because in all parts it is the British strength that I consume. I do not choose to be caught by a foreign enemy at the end of this exhausting conflict; and still less in the midst of it. I may escape, but I can make no insurance against such an event. Let me add, that I do not choose wholly to break the American spirit, because it is the spirit that has made the country.

Lastly, we have no sort of experience in favour of force as an instrument in the rule of our colonies. Their growth and their utility has been owing to methods altogether different. Our ancient indulgence has been said to be pursued to a fault. It may be so. But we know, if feeling is evidence, that our fault was more tolerable than our attempt to mend it, and our sin far more salutary than our penitence.

These, Sir, are my reasons for not entertaining that high opinion of untried force, by which many gentlemen, for whose sentiments in other particulars I have great respect, seem to be so greatly captivated. But there is still behind a third consideration concerning this object, which serves to determine my opinion on the sort of policy which ought to be pursued in the management of America, even more than its population and its commerce, I mean its temper and character.

In this character of the Americans, a love of freedom is the predominating feature, which marks and distinguishes the whole; and as an ardent is always a jealous affection, your colonies become suspicious, restive, and untractable, whenever they see the least attempt to wrest from them by force, or shuffle from them by chicane, what they think the only advantage worth living for. This fierce spirit of liberty is stronger in the English colonies probably than in any other people of the earth, and this from a great variety of powerful causes; which, to understand the true temper of their minds, and the direction which this spirit takes, it will not be amiss to lay open somewhat more largely.

First, the people of the colonies are descendants of Englishmen. England, Sir, is a nation which still I hope respects, and formerly adored her freedom. The colonists emigrated from you, when this part of your character was most predominant; and they took this bias and direction the moment they parted from your hands. They are therefore not only devoted to liberty, but to liberty according to English ideas, and on English principles. Abstract liberty, like other mere abstractions, is not to be found.—Liberty inheres in some sensible object; and every nation has formed to itself some favourite point which by way of eminence becomes the criterion of their happiness. It happened, you know, Sir, that the great contests for freedom in this country were from the earliest times chiefly upon the question of taxing. Most of the contests in the ancient commonwealths turned primarily on the right of election of Magistrates; or on the balance among the several orders of the state. The question of money was not with them so immediate. But in England it was otherwise. On this point of taxes, the ablest pens, and the most eloquent tongues have been exercised; the greatest spirits have acted and suffered. In order to give the fullest satisfaction concerning the importance of this point, it was not only necessary for those who in argument defended the excellence of the English constitution, to insist on this privilege of granting money as a dry point of fact, and to prove that the right had been acknowledged in ancient parchments and blind usages, to reside in a certain body called an House of Commons. They went much farther; they attempted to prove, and they succeeded, that in theory it ought to be so from the particular nature of a House of Commons as an immediate representative of the people; whether the old records had delivered this oracle or not. They took infinite pains to inculcate as a fundamental principle, that in all monarchies the people must in effect themselves mediately or immediately possess the power of granting their own money, or no shadow of liberty could subsist. The colonies draw from you, as with their life-blood, these ideas and principles. Their love of liberty, as with you, fixed and attached on this specific point of taxing. Liberty might be safe, or might be endangered in twenty other particulars, without their being much pleased or alarmed. Here they felt its pulse; and as they found that beat, they thought themselves sick or sound. I do not say whether they were right or wrong in applying your general arguments to their own case. It is not easy indeed to make a monopoly of theorems and corollaries. The fact is, that they did thus apply those general arguments; and your mode of governing them, whether through lenity or indolence, through wisdom or mistake, confirmed them in the imagination that they, as well as you, had an interest in the common principles.

They were farther confirmed in this pleasing error by the form of their provincial legislative assemblies. Their governments are popular in an high degree, some are merely popular; in all, the popular representative is the most weighty; and this share of the people in their ordinary government never fails to inspire them with lofty sentiments, and with a strong aversion from whatever tends to deprive them of their chief importance.

If any thing were wanting to this necessary operation of the form of government, religion would have given it a complete effect. Religion, always a principle of energy, in this new people, is no way worn out or impaired; and their mode of professing it is also one main cause of this free spirit. The people are protestants; and of that kind which is the most averse to all implicit submission of mind and opinion. This is a persuasion not only favourable to liberty, but built upon it. I do not think, Sir, that the reason of this averseness in the dissenting churches, from all that looks like absolute government, is so much to be sought in their religious tenets, as in their history. Every one knows, that the Roman Catholic religion is at least coeval with most of the governments where it prevails; that it has generally gone hand in hand with them; and received great favour and every kind of support from authority. The church of England too was formed from her cradle under the nursing care of regular government. But the dissenting interests have sprung up in direct opposition to all the ordinary powers of the world; and could justify that opposition only on a strong claim to natural liberty. Their very existence depended on the powerful and unremitted assertion of that claim. All protestantism, even the most cold and passive, is a sort of dissent. But the religion most prevalent in our northern colonies; where the church of England, notwithstanding its legal rights, is in reality no more than a sort of private sect; not composing most probably the tenth of the people. The colonists left England when this spirit was high; and in the emigrants was the highest of all, and even that strain of foreigners, which has been constantly flowing into these colonies, has, for the greatest part, been composed of dissenters from the establishments of their several countries; and have brought with them a temper and character far from alien to that of the people with whom they mixed.

Sir, I can perceive by their manner, that some gentlemen object to the latitude of this description; because in the southern colonies the church of England forms a large body, and has a regular establishment. It is certainly true. There is, however, a circumstance attending these colonies, which, in my opinion, fully counterbalances this difference, and makes the spirit of liberty still more high and haughty than in those to the northward. It is that in Virginia and the Carolinas, they have a vast multitude of slaves. Where this is the case in any part of the world, those who are free are by far the most proud and jealous of their freedom.—Freedom is to them not only an enjoyment, but a kind of rank and privilege. Not seeing there that freedom as in countries where it is a common blessing, and as broad and general as the air, may be united with much abject toil, with great misery, with all the exterior of servitude, liberty looks amongst them like something that is more noble and liberal. I do not mean, Sir, to commend the superior morality of this sentiment, which has at least as much pride as virtue in it, but I cannot alter the nature of man. The fact is so; and these people of the southern colonies are much more strongly, and with an higher and more stubborn spirit, attached to liberty than those of the northward. Such were all the ancient commonwealths; such were our Gothic ancestors; such in our days were the Poles; and such will be all masters of slaves, who are not slaves themselves. In such a people the haughtiness of domination combines with the spirit of freedom, fortifies it, and renders it invincible.

Permit me, Sir, to add another circumstance in our colonies, which contributes no mean part towards the growth and effect of this untractable spirit. I mean their education. In no country, perhaps, in the world, is the law so general a study. The profession itself is numerous and powerful, and in most provinces it takes the lead. The greater number of the deputies sent to the Congress were lawyers. But all who read, and most do read, endeavour to obtain some smattering in that science. I have been told, by an eminent bookseller, that in no branch of his business, after tracts of popular devotion, were so many books as those on the law exported to the plantations. The colonists have now fallen into the way of printing them for their own use. I hear that they have sold nearly as many of Blackstone's Commentaries in America as in England. General Gage makes out this disposition very particularly in a letter on your table. He states, that all the people in his government are lawyers, or smatterers in law; and that in Boston they have been enabled, by successful chicane, wholly to evade many parts of one of your capital penal constitutions. The smartness of debate will say that this knowledge ought to teach them more clearly the rights of legislature, their obligations to obedience, and the penalties of rebellion. All this is mighty well. But my honourable and learned friend* on the floor, who condescends to mark what I say for animadversion, will disdain that ground. He has heard, as well as I, that when great honours and great emoluments do not win over this knowledge to the service of the state, it is a formidable adversary to government. If the spirit be not tamed and broken by these happy methods, it is stubborn and litigious. *Abeunt studia in mores.* This study renders men acute, inquisitive, dextrous, prompt in attack, ready in defence, and full of resources. In other countries, the people, more simple, and of a less martial cast, judge of an ill principle in government only by an actual grievance; here they anticipate the evil, and judge of the pressure of the grievance by the badness of the principle. They augur misgovernment at a distance, and snuff the approach of tyranny in every tainted breeze.

The last cause of this disobedient spirit in the colonies is hardly less powerful than the rest, as it is not merely moral, but laid deep in the natural constitution of things. Three thousand miles of ocean lie between you and them. No contrivance can prevent the effects of this distance in weakening government. Seas roll, and months pass, between the order and the execution; and the want of a speedy explanation of a single point, is enough to defeat a whole system. You have, indeed, winged ministers of vengeance, who carry your bolts in their pounces

* The Attorney General.

to the remotest verge of the sea. But there a power steps in that limits the arrogance of raging passions and furious elements, and says, "So far shalt thou go, and no farther." Who are you, that should fret and rage, and bite the chains of nature? Nothing worse happens to you than does to all nations, who have extensive empire; and it happens in all the forms into which empire can be thrown. In large bodies, the circulation of power must be less vigorous at the extremities. Nature has said it. The Turk cannot govern Egypt, and Arabia, and Circassia, as he governs Thrace; nor has he the same dominion in Crimea and Algiers, which he has at Brussa and Smyrna. Despotism itself is obliged to truck and huckster. The Sultan gets such obedience as he can. He governs with a loose rein, that he may govern at all; and the whole of the force and vigour of his authority in his centre, is derived from a prudent relaxation in all his borders. Spain, in her provinces, is perhaps not so well obeyed as you are in yours. She complies too; she submits; she watches times. This is the immutable condition; the eternal law of extensive and detached empire.

Then, Sir, from these six capital sources of descent; of form of government; of religion in the northern provinces; of manners in the southern; of education; of the remoteness of situation from the first mover of government, from all these causes a fierce spirit of liberty has grown up. It has grown with the growth of the people in your colonies, and encreased with the encrease of their wealth; a spirit that unhappily meeting with an exercise of power in England, which, however lawful, is not reconcilable to any ideas of liberty, much less with theirs, has kindled this flame, that is ready to consume us.

I do not mean to commend either the spirit in this excess, or the moral causes that produced it. Perhaps a more smooth and accommodating spirit of freedom in them would be more acceptable to us. Perhaps ideas of liberty might be more reconcilable with an arbitrary and boundless authority. Perhaps we might wish the colonists to be persuaded that their liberty is more secure when held in trust for them by us (as their guardians during a perpetual minority) than with any part of it in their own hands. But the question is not whether their spirit deserves praise or blame. What, in the name of God, shall we do with it! You have before you, the object, such as it is, with all its glories, with all its imperfections on its head. You see the magnitude, the importance, the temper, the habits, the disorders.

By all these considerations we are strongly urged to determine something concerning it. We are called upon to fix some rule and line for our future conduct, which may give a little stability to our politics, and prevent the return of such unhappy deliberations as the present. Every such return will bring the matter before us in a still more untractable form. For what astonishing and incredible things have we not seen already? What monsters have not been generated from this unnatural contention? Whilst every principle of authority and resistance has been pushed, upon both sides, as far as it would go, there is nothing so solid and certain, either in reasoning or in practice, that has not been shaken. Until very lately, all authority in America seemed to be nothing but an emanation from yours. Even the popular part of the colony constitution derived all its activity, and its first vital movement, from the pleasure of the Crown. We thought, Sir, that the utmost which the discontented colonists could do, was to disturb authority; we never dreamt they could of themselves supply it; knowing in general what an operose business it is to establish a government absolutely new. But having, for our purposes, in this contention, resolved that none but an obedient assembly should sit, the humours of the people there, finding all passage through the legal channel stopped, with great violence broke out another way.

Some provinces have tried their experiment, as we have tried ours; and theirs has succeeded. They have formed a government sufficient for its purposes, without the bustle of a revolution, or the troublesome formality of an election. Evident necessity, and tacit consent, have done the business in an instant. So well have they done it, that Lord Dunmore (the account is among the fragments on your table) tells you, that the new institution is infinitely better obeyed than the ancient government ever was in its most fortunate periods. Obedience is what makes government, and not the names by which it is called, not the name of Governor, as formerly, or committee, as at present. This new government has originated directly from the people; and was not transmitted through any of the ordinary artificial media of a positive constitution. It was not a manufacture ready formed, and transmitted to them in that condition from England.

The evil arising from hence, is this; that the colonists having once found the possibility of enjoying the advantages of order, in the midst of a struggle for liberty, such struggles will not henceforward seem so terrible to the settled and sober part of mankind, as they had appeared before the trial.

Pursuing the same plan of punishing, by the denial of the exercise of government to still greater lengths, we wholly abrogated the ancient government of Massachusetts. We were confident that the first feeling, if not the very prospect of anarchy, would instantly enforce a complete submission. The experiment was tried. A new, strange, unexpected face of things appeared. Anarchy is found tolerable. A vast province has now subsisted, and subsisted in a considerable degree of health and vigour for near twelve months, without Governor, without public council, without judges, without executive magistrates. How long it will continue in this state, or what may arise out of this unheard of situation, how can the wisest of us conjecture? Our late experience has taught us, that many of those fundamental principles, formerly believed infallible, are either not of the importance they were imagined to be, or that we have not at all adverted to some other far more important, and far more powerful principles, which entirely over-rule those we had considered as omnipotent. I am much against any farther experiments which tend to put to the proof any more of these allowed opinions, which contribute so much to the public tranquility.

In effect, we suffer as much at home, by this loosening of all ties, and this concussion of all established opinions, as we do abroad. For, in order to prove that the Americans have no right to their liberties, we are every day endeavouring to subvert the maxims, which preserve the whole spirit of our own. To prove that the Americans ought not to be free, we are obliged to depreciate the value of freedom itself; and we never seem to gain a paltry advantage over them in debate, without attacking some of those principles, or deriding some of those feelings, for which our ancestors have shed their blood.

But, Sir, in wishing to put an end to pernicious experiments,

I do not mean to preclude the fullest enquiry. Far from it. Far from deciding on a sudden or partial view, I would patiently go round and round the subject, and survey it minutely, in every possible aspect. Sir, if I were capable of engaging you to an equal attention, I would state that, as far as I am capable of discerning, there are but three ways of proceeding relative to this stubborn spirit, which prevails in your colonies, and disturbs your government.

These are—to change that spirit, as inconvenient, by removing the causes. To prosecute it as criminal. Or to comply with it as necessary. I would not be guilty of an imperfect enumeration; I can think of but these three. Another has indeed been stated; that of giving up the colonies; but it met so slight a reception, that I do not think myself obliged to dwell a great while upon it. It is nothing but a little sally of anger, like the frowardness of peevish children, who, when they cannot get all they would have, are resolved to take nothing.

The first of these plans, to change the spirit as inconvenient, by removing the causes, I think is the most like a systematic proceeding. It is radical in its principle; but it is attended with great difficulties, some of them little short, as I conceive, of impossibilities. This will appear by examining into the plans which have been proposed.

As the growing population in the colonies is evidently one cause of their resistance, it was last session mentioned in both Houses, by men of weight, and received not without applause, that in order to check this evil, it would be proper for the crown to make no farther grants of land. But to this scheme, there are two objections. The first, that there is already so much unsettled land in private hands, as to afford room for an immense future population, although the crown not only with-held its grants, but annihilated its soil. If this be the case, then the only effect of this avarice of desolation, this hoarding of a royal wilderness, would be to raise the value of the possessions in the hands of the great private monopolists, without any adequate check to the growing and alarming mischief of population.

But if you stopped your grants, what would be the consequence? The people would occupy without grants. They have already so occupied in many places. You cannot station garrisons in every part of these desarts. If you drive the people from one place, they will carry on their annual tillage, and move with their flocks and herds to another. Many of the people of the back settlements are already little attached to particular situations. Already they have topped the Apalachian mountains, from thence they behold before them an immense plain, one vast, rich, level meadow; a square of five hundred miles. Over this they would wander, without a possibility of restraint; they would change their manners with the habit of their life; would soon forget a government by which they were disowned; would become hordes of English Tartars, and pouring down upon your unfortified frontiers a fierce and irresistible cavalry, become masters of your governors, and your counsellors, your collectors and comptrollors, and all the slaves that adhered to them.

Such would, and in no long time must, be the effect of attempting to forbid, as a crime, and to suppress as an evil, the command and blessing of Providence, "increase and multiply." Such would be the happy result of an endeavour, to keep as a lair of wild beasts, that earth, which God, by an express charter, has given to the children of man. Far different, and surely much wiser, has been our policy hitherto. Hitherto we have invited our people by every kind of bounty, to fixed establishments. We have invited the husbandman to look to authority for his title. We have taught him piously to believe in the mysterious virtue of wax and parchment. We have thrown each tract of land, as it was peopled, into districts, that the ruling power should never be wholly out of sight. We have settled all we could, and we have carefully attended every settlement with government.

Adhering, Sir, as I do to this policy, as well as for the reasons I have just given, I think this new project of hedging in population to be neither prudent nor practicable.

To impoverish the colonies in general, and in particular to arrest the natural course of their marine enterprizes, would be a more easy task, I freely confess it. We have shewn a disposition to a system of this kind; a disposition even to continue the restraint after the offence; looking on ourselves as rivals to our colonies, and persuaded that of course we must gain all that they shall lose. Much mischief we may certainly do. The power inadequate to all other things is often more than sufficient for this. I do not look on the direct and immediate power of the colonies to resist our violence as very formidable. In this, however, I may be mistaken. But when I consider, that we have colonies for no purpose but to be serviceable to us, it seems to my poor understanding a little preposterous, to make them unserviceable, in order to keep them obedient. It is, in truth, nothing more than the old, and as I thought, exploded problem of tyranny, which proposes to beggar its subjects into submission. But remember, when you have completed your system of impoverishment, nature still proceeds in her ordinary course; that discontent will increase with misery; and that there are critical moments in the fortune of all states, when they who are too weak to contribute to your prosperity, may be strong enough to complete your ruin. *Spoliatis arma supersunt.*

The temper and character which prevail in our colonies, are, I am afraid, unalterable by any human art. We cannot, I fear, falsify the pedigree of this fierce people, and persuade them that they are not sprung from a nation, in whose veins the blood of freedom circulates. The language in which they would hear you tell them this tale, would detect the imposition; your speech would betray you. An Englishman is the unfittest person on earth to argue another Englishman into slavery.

I think it is nearly as little in our power to change their republican religion, as their free descent; or to substitute the Roman Catholic as a penalty; or the Church of England as an improvement. The mode of inquisition and dragooning is going out of fashion in the old world, and I should not confide much to their efficacy in the new. The education of the Americans is also on the same unalterable bottom with their religion. You cannot persuade them to burn their books of curious science; to banish their lawyers from their courts of law; or to quench the lights of their Assemblies, by refusing to choose those persons who are best read in their privileges. It would be no less impracticable to think of wholly annihilating the popular Assemblies, in which these lawyers sit. The army, by which we must govern in their place, would be far more chargeable to us; not quite so effectual; and perhaps, in the end, full as difficult to be kept in obedience.

With regard to the high aristocratic spirit of Virginia and the southern colonies, it has been proposed, I know, to reduce it by declaring a general enfranchisement of their slaves. This project has had its advocates and panegyrists; yet I never could argue myself into any opinion of it.—Slaves are often much attached to their masters. A general wild offer of liberty would not always be accepted. History furnishes few instances of it. It is sometimes as hard to persuade slaves to be free, as it is to compel freemen to be slaves; and in this auspicious scheme, we should have both these pleasing tasks on our hands at once. But when we talk of enfranchisement, do we not perceive that the American master may enfranchise too, and arm servile hands in defence of freedom? A measure to which other people have had recourse more than once, and not without success, in a desperate situation of their affairs.

Slaves as these unfortunate black people are, and dull as all men are from slavery, must they not a little suspect the offer of freedom from that very nation which has sold them to their present masters? From that nation, one of whose causes of quarrel with those masters, is their refusal to deal any more in that inhuman traffic? An offer of freedom from England would come rather oddly, shipped to them in an African vessel, which is refused an entry into the ports of Virginia or Carolina, with a cargo of three hundred Angola Negroes. It would be curious to see the Guinea Captain attempting at the same instant to publish his proclamation of liberty, and to advertise his sale of slaves.

But let us suppose all these moral difficulties got over. The ocean remains. You cannot pump this dry; and as long as it continues in its present bed, so long all the causes which weaken authority by distance will continue. "Ye Gods, annihilate but space and time, and make two lovers happy!"—was a pious and passionate prayer, but just as reasonable as many of the serious wishes of very grave and solemn politicians.

If then, Sir, it seems almost desperate to think of any alterative course, for changing the moral causes (and not quite easy to remove the natural) which produce prejudices irreconcilable to the late exercise of our authority; but that the spirit infallibly will continue, and continuing, will produce such effects, as now embarrass us; the second mode under consideration is to prosecute that spirit in its overt acts as *criminal*.

At this proposition I must pause a moment. The thing seems a great deal too big for my ideas of jurisprudence. It should seem to my way of conceiving such matters, that there is a very wide difference in reason and policy, between the mode of proceeding on the irregular conduct of scattered individuals, or even of bands of men, who disturb order within the state, and the civil dissensions which may, from time to time, on great questions, agitate the several communities which compose a great empire. It looks to me to be narrow and pedantic, to apply the ordinary ideas of criminal justice to this great public contest. I do not know the method of drawing up an indictment against a whole people. I cannot insult and ridicule the feelings of millions of my fellow-creatures, as Sir Edward Coke insulted one excellent individual (Sir Walter Rawleigh) at the bar. I am not ripe to pass sentence on the gravest public bodies, entrusted with magistracies of great authority and dignity, and charged with the safety of their fellow-citizens, upon the very same title that I am. I really think, that for wise men this is not judicious; for sober men, not decent; for minds tinctured with humanity, not mild and merciful.

Perhaps, Sir, I am mistaken in my idea of an empire, as distinguished from a single state or kingdom. But my idea of it is this; that an empire is the aggregate of many states under one common head; whether this head be a monarch or a presiding republic. It does, in such constitutions, frequently happen (and nothing but the dismal, cold, dead uniformity of servitude can prevent its happening) that the subordinate parts have many local privileges and immunities. Between these privileges, and the supreme common authority, the line may be extremely nice. Of course disputes, often too, very bitter disputes, and much ill-blood will arise. But though every privilege is an exemption (in the case) from the ordinary exercise of the supreme authority, it is no denial of it. The claim of a privilege seems rather, *ex vi termini*, to imply a superior power. For to talk of the privileges of a state, or of a person, who has no superior, is hardly any better than speaking nonsense. Now in such unfortunate quarrels, among the component parts of a great political union of communities, I can scarcely conceive any thing more completely imprudent, than for the head of the empire to insist, that if any privilege is pleaded against his will, or his acts, that his whole authority is denied, instantly to proclaim rebellion, to beat to arms, and to put the offending provinces under the ban. Will not this, Sir, very soon teach the provinces to make no distinctions on their part? Will it not teach them that the government, against which a claim of liberty is tantamont to high treason, is a government to which submission is equivalent to slavery? It may not always be quite convenient to impress dependent communities with such an idea.

We are, indeed, in all disputes with the colonies, by the necessity of things, the judge. It is true, Sir. But I confess that the character of judge in my own cause, is a thing that frightens me. Instead of filling me with pride, I am exceedingly humbled by it. I cannot proceed with a stern, assured, judicial confidence, until I find myself in something more like a judicial character. I must have these hesitations as long as I am compelled to recollect, that, in my little reading upon such contests as these, the sense of mankind has, at least, as often decided against the superior as the subordinate power. Sir, let me add too, that the opinion of my having some abstract right in my favour, would not put me much at my ease in passing sentence, unless I could be sure that there were no rights which in their exercise under certain circumstances, were not the most odious of all wrongs, and the most vexatious of all injustice. Sir, these considerations have great weight with me, when I find things so circumstanced, that I see the same party, at once a civil litigant against me in a point of right; and a culprit before me, while I sit as a criminal judge, on acts of his whose moral quality is to be decided upon the merits of that very litigation. Men are every now and then put, by the complexity of human affairs, into strange situations; but justice is the same let the judge be in what situation he will.

There is, Sir, also a circumstance which convinces me that this mode of criminal proceeding is not (at least in the present stage of our contest) altogether expedient; which is nothing less than the conduct of those very persons who have seemed to adopt that mode, by lately declaring a rebellion in Massachusetts-Bay, as they had formerly addressed to have traitors brought hither under an act of Henry VIII. for trial. For though rebellion is declared, it is not proceeded against as such; nor have any steps been taken towards the apprehension or conviction of any individual offender, either on our late or our former address: but modes of public coercion have been adopted, and such as have much more resemblance to a sort of qualified hostility towards an independent power than the punishment of rebellious subjects. All this seems rather inconsistent, but it shews how difficult it is to apply these juridical ideas to our present case.

In this situation let us seriously and coolly ponder. What is it we have got by all our menaces, which have been many and ferocious? What advantage have we derived from the penal laws we have passed, and which, for the time, have been severe and numerous? What advances have we made towards our object by the sending of a force which, by land and sea, is no contemptible strength? Has the disorder abated? Nothing less.—When I see things in this situation, after such confident hopes, bold promises, and active exertions, I cannot, for my life, avoid a suspicion that the plan itself is not correctly right.

If then the removal of the causes of this spirit of American liberty be, for the greater part, or rather entirely, impracticable; if the ideas of criminal process be inapplicable, or, if applicable, are in the highest degree inexpedient, what way yet remains? No way is open but the third and last; to comply with the Americans spirit as necessary, or if you please, to submit to it as a necessary evil.

If we adopt this mode, if we mean to conciliate and concede, let us see of what nature the concession ought to be: To ascertain the nature of our concession, we must look at their complaint. The colonies complain that they have not the characteristic mark and seal of British freedom. They complain, that they are taxed in a Parliament, in which they are not represented. If you mean to satisfy them at all, you must satisfy them with regard to this complaint. If you mean to please any people, you must give them the boon which they ask; not what you may think better for them, but of a kind totally different. Such an act may be a wise regulation, but it is no concession; whereas our present theme is the mode of giving satisfaction.

Sir, I think you must perceive, that I am resolved this day to have nothing at all to do with the question of the right of taxation. Some gentlemen startle—but it is true. I put it totally out of the question. It is less than nothing, in my consideration. I do not indeed wonder, nor will you, Sir, that gentlemen of profound learning are fond of displaying it on this profound subject. But my consideration is narrow, confined, and wholly limited to the policy of the question. I do not examine, whether the giving away a man's money be a power excepted and reserved out of the general trust of government, and how far all mankind, in all forms of polity, are entitled to an exercise of that right by the charter of nature. Or whether, on the contrary, a right of taxation is necessarily involved in the general principle of legislation, and inseparable from the ordinary supreme power? These are deep questions, where great names militate against each other; where reason is perplexed, and an appeal to authorities only thickens the confusion. For high and reverend authorities lift up their heads on both sides, and there is no sure footing in the middle. This point is the *great Serbonian bog, betwixt Damiata and Mount Casius old, where armies whole have sunk.* I do not intend to be overwhelmed in that bog, though in such respectable company. The question with me is, not whether you have a right to render your people miserable; but whether it is not your interest to make them happy? It is not, what a lawyer tells me I may do, but what humanity, reason, and justice, tells me I ought to do. Is a politic act the worse for being a generous one? Is no concession proper, but that which is made from your want of right to keep what you grant? Or does it lessen the grace or dignity of relaxing in the exercise of an odious claim, because you have your evidence-room full of titles, and your magazines stuffed with arms to enforce them? What signify all those titles, and all those arms? Of what avail are they, when the reason of the thing tells me, that the assertion of my title is the loss of my suit; and that I could do nothing but wound myself by the use of my own weapons?

Such is stedfastly my opinion of the absolute necessity of keeping up the concord of this empire by a unity of spirit, though in a diversity of operations; that, if I were sure the colonists had, at their leaving this country, sealed a regular compact of servitude; that they had solemnly abjured all the rights of citizens; that they had made a vow to renounce all ideas of liberty, for them and their posterity, to all generations;

yet I should hold myself obliged to conform to the temper I found universally prevalent in my own day, and to govern two millions of men, impatient of servitude, on the principles of freedom. I am not determining a point of law; I am restoring tranquility, and the general character and situation of a people must determine what sort of government is fitted for them. That point nothing else can or ought to determine.

My idea, therefore, without considering whether we yield as matter of right, or grant as matter of favour, is *to admit the people of our colonies into an interest in the constitution*; and, by recording that admission in the Journals of Parliament, to give them as strong an assurance as the nature of the thing will admit, that we mean for ever to adhere to that solemn declaration of systematic indulgence.

Some years ago the repeal of a revenue act, upon its understood principle, might have served to shew, that we intended an unconditional abatement of the exercise of a taxing power. Such a measure was then sufficient to remove all suspicion; and to give perfect content. But unfortunate events, since that time, may make something further necessary; and not more necessary for the satisfaction of the colonies, than for the dignity and consistency of our own future proceedings.

I have taken a very incorrect measure of the disposition of the House, if this proposal in itself would be received with dislike. I think, Sir, we have few American financiers. But our misfortune is, we are too acute; we are too exquisite in our conjectures of the future, for men oppressed with such great and present evils. The more moderate among the opposers of parliamentary concession freely confess, that they hope no good from taxation; but they apprehend the colonists have farther views; and if this point were conceded, they would instantly attack the trade laws. These gentlemen are convinced that this was the intention from the beginning; and the quarrel of the Americans with taxation was no more than a cloak and cover to this design. Such has been the language even of a gentleman* of real moderation, and of a natural temper well adjusted to fair and equal government. I am, however, Sir, not a little surprised at this kind of discourse, whenever I hear it;

* Mr. Rice.

and I am the more surprised on account of the arguments which I constantly find in company with it, and which are often urged from the same mouths, and on the same day.

For instance, when we alledge that it is against reason to tax a people under so many restraints in trade as the Americans, the Noble Lord in the blue ribbon* shall tell you that the restraints on trade are futile and useless; of no advantage to us, and of no burthen to those on whom they are imposed; that the trade to America is not secured by the acts of navigation, but by the natural and irresistable advantage of commercial preference.

Such is the merit of the trade laws in this posture of the debate. But when strong internal circumstances are urged against the taxes; when the scheme is dissected; when experience and the nature of things are brought to prove, and do prove the utter impossibility of obtaining an effective revenue from the colonies; when these things are pressed, or rather press themselves so as to drive the advocates of colony taxes to a clear admission of the futility of the scheme; then, Sir, the sleeping trade laws revive from their trance; and this useless taxation is to be kept sacred, not for its own sake, but as a counterguard and security of the laws of trade.

Then, Sir, you keep up revenue laws which are mischievous, in order to preserve trade laws that are useless. Such is the wisdom of our plan in both its members. They are separately given up as of no value; and yet one is always to be defended for the sake of the other. But I cannot agree with the noble Lord, nor with the pamphlet from whence he seems to have borrowed these ideas, concerning the inutility of the trade laws. For without idolizing them I am sure they are still in many ways, of great use to us; and in former times, they have been of the greatest. They do confine, and they do greatly narrow, the market for the Americans. But my perfect conviction of this, does not help me in the least to discern how the revenue laws form any security whatsoever to the commercial regulations; or that these commercial regulations are the true ground of the quarrel; or, that the giving way in any one instance of authority, is to lose all that may remain unconceded.

One fact is clear and indisputable. The public and avowed

* Lord North.

origin of this quarrel, was on taxation. This quarrel has indeed brought on new disputes on new questions; but certainly the least bitter, and the fewest of all, on the trade laws. To judge which of the two be the real radical cause of quarrel, we have to see whether the commercial dispute did, in order of time, precede the dispute on taxation? There is not a shadow of evidence for it. Next, to enable us to judge whether at this moment a dislike to the trade laws be the real cause of quarrel, it is absolutely necessary to put the taxes out of the question by a repeal. See how the Americans act in this position, and then you will be able to discern directly what is the true object of the controversy, or whether any controversy at all will remain? Unless you consent to remove this cause of difference, it is impossible, with decency, to assert, that the dispute is not upon what it is avowed to be. And I would, Sir, recommend to your serious consideration, whether it be prudent to form a rule for punishing people, not on their own acts, but on your conjectures? Surely it is preposterous at the very best. It is not justifying your anger, by their misconduct; but it is converting your ill-will into their delinquency.

But the colonies will go further. Alas! alas! when will this speculating against fact and reason end? What will quiet these panic fears which we entertain of the hostile effect of a conciliatory conduct? Is it true that no case can exist, in which it is proper for the Sovereign to accede to the desires of his discontented subjects? Is there any thing peculiar in this case, to make a rule for itself? Is all authority of course lost, when it is not pushed to the extreme? Is it a certain maxim, that the fewer causes of dissatisfaction that are left by government, the more the subject will be inclined to resist and rebel?

All these objections being in fact no more than suspicions, conjectures, divinations; formed in defiance of fact and experience; they did not, Sir, discourage me from entertaining the idea of a conciliatory concession, founded on the principles which I have just stated.

In forming a plan for this purpose, I endeavoured to put myself in that frame of mind which was the most natural, and the most reasonable; and which was certainly the most probable means of securing me from all error. I set out with a perfect distrust of my own abilities; a total renunciation of every speculation of my own; and with a profound reverence for the wisdom of our ancestors, who have left us the inheritance of so happy a constitution, and so flourishing an empire, and what is a thousand times more valuable, the treasury of the maxims and principles which formed the one, and obtained the other.

During the reigns of the Kings of Spain of the Austrian family, whenever they were at a loss in the Spanish councils, it was common for their statesmen to say, that they ought to consult the genius of Philip the second. The genius of Philip the second might mislead them; and the issue of their affairs shewed, that they had not chosen the most perfect standard. But, Sir, I am sure that I shall not be misled, when in a case of constitutional difficulty, I consult the genius of the English constitution. Consulting at that oracle (it was with all due humility and piety) I found four capital examples in a similar case before me; those of Ireland, Wales, Chester, and Durham.

Ireland, before the English conquest, though never governed by a despotic power, had no parliament. How far the English Parliament itself was at that time modelled according to the present form, is disputed among antiquarians. But we have all the reason in the world to be assured that a form of Parliament, such as England then enjoyed, she instantly communicated to Ireland; and we are equally sure that almost every successive improvement in constitutional liberty, as fast as it was made here, was transmitted thither. The feudal baronage, and the feudal knighthood, the roots of our primitive constitution, were early transplanted into that soil; and grew and flourished there. Magna Charta, if it did not give us originally the House of Commons, gave us at least an House of Commons of weight and consequence. But your ancestors did not churlishly sit down alone to the feast of Magna Charta. Ireland was made immediately a partaker. This benefit of English laws and liberties I confess, as not at first extended to all Ireland. Mark the consequence. English authority and English liberty, had exactly the same boundaries. Your standard could never be advanced an inch before your privileges. Sir John Davis shews beyond a doubt, that a refusal of a general communication of these rights, was the true cause why Ireland was five hundred years in subduing; and after the vain projects of a military government, attempted in the reign of Queen

Elizabeth, it was soon discovered that nothing could make that country English, in civility and allegiance, but your laws and your forms of legislature. It was not English arms, but the English constitution that conquered Ireland.

From that time, Ireland has ever had a general Parliament, as she had before a partial parliament.

You changed the people; you altered the religion; but you never touched the form of the vital substance of free government in that kingdom. You deposed Kings; you restored them; you altered the succession to theirs, as well as to your own crown; but you never altered their constitution; the principle of which was respected by usurpation; restored with the restoration of Monarchy, and established, I trust for ever, by the glorious revolution. This has made Ireland the great and flourishing kingdom that it is; and from a disgrace and a burden intolerable to this nation, has rendered her a principle part of our strength and ornament. This country cannot be said to have ever formally taxed her. The irregular things done in the confusion of mighty troubles, and on the hinge of great revolutions, even if all were done that is said to have been done, form no example. If they have any effect in argument, they make an exemption to prove the rule.

None of your own liberties could stand a moment, if the casual deviations from them, at such times, were suffered to be used as proofs of their nullity. By the lucrative amount of such casual breaches in the constitution, judge what the stated and fixed rule of supply has been in that kingdom. Your Irish pensioners would starve, if they had no other fund to live on than taxes granted by English authority.

Turn your eyes to those popular grants, from whence all your great supplies are come; and learn to respect that only source of public wealth in the British empire.

My next example is Wales. This country was said to be reduced by Henry the third. It was said more truly to be so by Edward the first. But tho' then conquered, it was not looked upon as any part of the realm of England. Its old constitution, whatever that might have been, was destroyed; and no good one was substituted in its place. The care of that tract was put into the hands of Lords Marchers, a form of government of a very singular kind; a strange heterogeneous monster, something between hostility and government; perhaps it has a sort of resemblance, according to the modes of those times, to that of Commander in Chief at present, to whom all civil power is granted as secondary. The manners of the Welsh nation followed the genius of the government; the people were ferocious, restive, savage, and uncultivated; sometimes composed, never pacified. Wales within itself, was in perpetual disorder; and it kept the frontier of England in perpetual alarm. Benefits from it to the state, there were none. Wales was only known to England, by incursion and invasion.

Sir, during that state of things, Parliament was not idle. They attempted to subdue the fierce spirit of the Welsh by all sorts of rigorous laws. They prohibited by statute, the sending all sorts of arms into Wales, as you prohibit by proclamation (with something more of doubt on the legality) the sending arms to America. They disarmed the Welsh by statute, as you attempted (but still with more question on the legality) to disarm New-England by an instruction.

They made an act to drag offenders from Wales into England for trial, as you have done (but with more hardship) with regard to America. By another act, where one of the parties was an Englishman, they ordained that his trial should be always by English. They made acts to restrain trade as you do; and they prevented the Welsh from the use of fairs and markets, as you do the Americans from fisheries and foreign ports. In short, when the statute book was not quite so much swelled as it is now, you find no less than fifteen acts of penal regulation on the subject of Wales.

Here we rub our hands, a fine body of precedents for the authority of Parliament and the use of it! I admit it fully; and pray add likewise to these precedents, that all the while, Wales rid this kingdom like an *incubus*; that it was an unprofitable and oppressive burthen; and that an Englishman travelling in that country, could not go six yards from the high road without being murdered.

The march of the human mind is slow. Sir, it was not until after two hundred years, discovered, that by an eternal law, providence had declared vexation to violence; and poverty to rapine. Your ancestors did however at length open their eyes to the ill-husbandry of injustice. They found that the tyranny of a free people could of all tyrannies the least be endured; and that laws made against a whole nation were not the most effectual methods for securing its obedience. Accordingly in the 27th year of Henry VIII. the course was entirely altered. With a preamble stating the entire and perfect rights of the crown of England, it gave to the Welsh all the rights and privileges of English subjects. A political order was established; the military power gave way to the civil; the marches were turned into counties. But that a nation should have a right to English liberties, and yet no share at all in the fundamental security of these liberties, the grant of their own property, seemed a thing so incongruous, that eight years after, that is, in the 35th year of that reign, a complete and not ill proportioned representation by counties and boroughs was bestowed upon Wales, by act of Parliament; from that moment, as by a charm, the tumults subsided; obedience was restored; peace, order, and civilization, followed in the train of liberty. When the day star of the English constitution had arisen in their hearts, all was harmony within and without.

> *Simul alba nautis*
> *Stella refulsit,*
> *Defluit saxis agitatus humor:*
> *Concidunt venti, fugiuntque nubes:*
> *Et minax (quod sic voluere) ponto*
> *Unda recumbit.*

The very same year the county palatine of Chester received the same relief from its oppressions, and the same remedy to its disorders. Before this time Chester was little less distempered than Wales. The inhabitants without rights themselves, were the fittest to destroy the rights of others; and from thence Richard II. drew the standing army of Archers, with which, for a time, he oppressed England. The people of Chester applied to Parliament in a petition penned as I shall read to you:

> *To the King our Sovereign Lord, in most humbly wise shewn unto your Excellent Majesty, the inhabitants of your Grace's county palatine of Chester; That whereas the said county palatine of Chester is and hath been always hitherto exempt, excluded and*

separated out and from your high court of Parliament, to have any knights and burgesses within the said court; by reason whereof the said inhabitants have hitherto sustained manifold disheri-sions, losses and damages, as well in their lands, goods, and bodies, as in the good, civil, and politick governance and maintenance of the commonwealth of their said country: (2) And for as much as the said inhabitants have always hitherto been bound by the acts and statutes made and ordained by your said highness, and your most noble progenitors, by authority of the said court, as far forth as other counties, cities, and boroughs have been, that have had their knights and burgesses within your said court of Parlia-ment, and yet have had neither knight ne burgess there for the said county palatine; the said inhabitants, for lack thereof, have been oftentimes touched and grieved with acts and statutes made within the said court, as well derogatory unto the most ancient jurisdictions, liberties and privileges of your said county pala-tine, as prejudicial unto the commonwealth, quietness, rest, and peace of your Grace's most bounden subjects inhabiting within the same.

What did Parliament with this audacious address?—reject it as a libel? treat it as an affront to government? spurn it as a derogation from the rights of legislature? Did they toss it over the table? Did they burn it by the hands of the common hangman?—They took the petition of grievance, all rugged as it was, without softening or temperament, unpurged of the original bitterness and indignation of complaint; they made it the very preamble to their act of redress; and consecrated its principle to all ages in the sanctuary of legislation.

Here is my third example. It was attended with the success of the two former. Chester, civilized as well as Wales, has demonstrated that freedom and not servitude is the cure of anarchy; as religion, and not atheism, is the true remedy for superstition. Sir, this pattern of Chester was followed in the reign of Charles II. with regard to the county palatine of Durham, which is my fourth example. This county had long lain out of the pale of free legislation. So scrupulously was the example of Chester followed, that the stile of the preamble is nearly the same with that of the Chester act; and without af-fecting the abstract extent of the authority of Parliament, it recognizes the equity of not suffering any considerable district in which the British subjects may act as a body, to be taxed without their own voice in the grant.

Now, if the doctrines of policy contained in these preambles, and the force of these examples in the acts of Parliament, avail any thing, what can be said against applying them with regard to America? Are not the people of America as much Englishmen as the Welsh? The preamble of the act of Henry VIII. says, the Welsh speak a language no way resembling that of his Majesty's English subjects. Are the Americans not as numerous? If we may trust the learned and accurate Judge Barrington's account of North Wales, and take that as a standard to measure the rest, there is no comparison. The people cannot amount to above 200,000; not a tenth part of the number in the colonies. Is America in rebellion? Wales was hardly free from it. Have you attempted to govern America by penal statutes? You made fifteen for Wales. But your legislative authority is perfect with regard to America; was it less perfect in Wales, Chester, and Durham? But America is virtually represented. What! does the electric force of virtual representation more easily pass over the Atlantic, than pervade Wales, which lies in your neighbourhood; or than Chester and Durham surrounded by abundance of representation that is actual and palpable? But, Sir, your ancestors thought this sort of virtual representation, however ample, to be totally insufficient for the freedom of the inhabitants of territories that are so near, and comparatively so inconsiderable. How then can I think it sufficient for those which are infinitely greater, and infinitely more remote?

You will now, Sir, perhaps imagine, that I am on the point of proposing to you a scheme for a representation of the colonies in Parliament. Perhaps I might be inclined to entertain some such thought; but a great flood stops me in my course. *Opposuit natura.*—I cannot remove the eternal barriers of the creation. The thing in that mode, I do not know to be possible. As I meddle with no theory, I do not absolutely assert the impracticability of such a representation. But I do not see my way to it; and those who have been more confident, have not been more successful. However, the arm of public benevolence is not shortened; and there are often several means to the same end. What nature has disjoined in one way, wisdom may unite in another. When we cannot give the benefit as we would wish, let us not refuse it altogether. If we cannot give the principal, let us find a substitute. But how? Where? What substitute?

Fortunately I am not obliged for the ways and means of this substitute to tax my own unproductive invention. I am not even obliged to go to the rich treasury of the fertile framers of imaginary commonwealths; not to the Republic of Plato, not to the Utopia of More; not to the Oceana of Harrington. It is before me—It is at my feet, and the rude swain treads daily on it with his clouted shoon. I only wish you to recognize, for the theory, the ancient constitutional policy of this kingdom with regard to representation, as that policy has been declared in acts of Parliament; and, as to the practice, to return to that mode which an uniform experience has marked out to you, as best; and in which you walked with security, advantage, and honour, until the year 1763.

My resolutions therefore mean to establish the equity and justice of a taxation of America, by grant, and not by imposition. To mark the legal competency of the colony Assemblies for the support of their government in peace, and for public aids in time of war. To acknowledge that this legal competency has had a dutiful and beneficial exercise; and that experience has shewn the benefit of their grants, and the futility of parliamentary taxation as a method of supply.

These solid truths compose six fundamental propositions. There are three more resolutions corollary to these. If you admit the first set, you can hardly reject the others. But if you admit the first, I shall be far from solicitous whether you accept or refuse the last. I think these six massive pillars will be of strength sufficient to support the temple of British concord. I have no more doubt than I entertain of my existence, that, if you admitted these, you would command an immediate peace; and with but tolerable future management, a lasting obedience in America. I am not arrogant in this confident assurance. The propositions are all mere matters of fact; and if they are such facts as draw irresistible conclusions even in the stating, this is the power of truth, and not any management of mine.

Sir, I shall open the whole plan to you together, with such observations on the motions as may tend to illustrate them where they may want explanation. The first is a resolution—*That the*

colonies and plantations of Great-Britain in North-America, con-
sisting of fourteen separate governments, and containing two
millions and upwards of free inhabitants, have not had the liberty
and privilege of electing and sending any knights and burgesses,
or others to represent them in the high court of Parliament.—This
is a plain matter of fact, necessary to be laid down, and (excepting the description) it is laid down in the language of the constitution; it is taken nearly verbatim from acts of Parliament.

The second is like unto the first—*That the said colonies and*
plantations have been liable to, and bounden by, several subsidies,
payments, rates, and taxes, given and granted by Parliament,
though the said colonies and plantations have not their knights
and burgesses, in the said high court of Parliament, of their own
election, to represent the condition of their country; by lack
whereof they have been oftentimes touched and grieved by subsi-
dies given, granted, and assented to, in the said court, in a
manner prejudicial to the commonwealth, quietness, rest, and
peace, of the subjects inhabiting within the same.

Is this description too hot, or too cold, too strong, or too
weak? Does it arrogate too much to the supreme legislature?
Does it lean too much to the claims of the people? If it runs
into any of these errors, the fault is not mine. It is the language
of your own ancient acts of Parliament. *Non meus hic sermo,*
sed quæ præcepit Ofellus rusticus, abnormis sapiens. It is the
genuine produce of the ancient rustic, manly, home-bred sense
of this country—I did not dare to rub off a particle of the venerable rust that rather adorns and preserves, than destroys the
metal. It would be a profanation to touch with a tool the stones
which construct the sacred altar of peace. I would not violate
with modern polish the ingenuous and noble roughness of these
truly constitutional materials. Above all things, I was resolved
not to be guilty of tampering the odious vice of restless and
unstable minds. I put my foot in the tracts of our forefathers;
where I can neither wander nor stumble. Determining to fix
articles of peace, I was resolved not to be wise beyond what was
written; I was resolved to use nothing else than the form of
sound words; to let others abound in their own sense; and carefully to abstain from all expressions of my own. What the law
has said, I say. In all things else I am silent. I have no organ but
for her words. This, if it be not ingenious, I am sure is safe.

There are indeed words expressive of grievance in this second resolution, which those who are resolved always to be in the right, will deny to contain matter of fact, as applied to the present case; although Parliament thought them true, with regard to the counties of Chester and Durham. They will deny that the Americans were ever "touched and grieved" with the taxes. If they consider nothing in taxes but their weight as pecuniary impositions, there might be some pretence for this denial. But men may be sorely touched and deeply grieved in their privileges, as well as in their purses. Men may lose little in property by the act which takes away all their freedom. When a man is robbed of a trifle on the highway, it is not the two-pence lost that constitutes the capital outrage. This is not confined to privileges. Even ancient indulgences withdrawn, without offence on the part of those who enjoyed such favours, operate as grievances. But were the Americans then not touched and grieved by the taxes, in some measure, merely as taxes? If so, why were they almost all, either wholly repealed or exceedingly reduced? Were they not touched and grieved, even by the regulating duties of the sixth of George II? Else why were the duties first reduced to one third in 1764, and afterwards to a third of that third in the year 1766? Were they not touched and grieved by the stamp-act? I shall say they were, until that tax is revived. Were they not touched and grieved by the duties of 1767, which were likewise repealed, and which Lord Hillsborough tells you (for the ministry) were laid contrary to the true principle of commerce? Is not the assurance given by that noble person to the colonies of a resolution to lay no more taxes on them, an admission that taxes would touch and grieve them? Is not the resolution of the noble Lord in the blue ribband, now standing on your journals, the strongest of all proofs that parliamentary subsidies really touched and grieved them? Else, why all these changes, modifications, repeals, assurances, and resolutions?

The next proposition is—*That from the distance of the said colonies, and from other circumstances, no method hath hitherto been devised for procuring a representation in Parliament for the said colonies.*" This is an assertion of a fact. I go no further on the paper; though in my private judgment, an useful representation is impossible; I am sure it is not desired by them; nor ought it perhaps by us; but I abstain from opinions.

The fourth resolution is—*That each of the said colonies hath within itself a body, chosen in part, or in the whole, by the freemen, freeholders, or other free inhabitants thereof, commonly called the General Assembly, or General Court, with powers legally to raise, levy, and assess, according to the several usage of such colonies, duties and taxes towards defraying all sorts of public services.*

This competence in the colony Assemblies is certain. It is proved by the whole tenor of their acts of supply in all the Assemblies, in which the constant style of granting is, "an aid to his Majesty;" and acts granting to the crown have regularly for near a century passed the public offices without dispute. Those who have been pleased paradoxically to deny this right, holding that none but the British Parliament can grant to the crown, are wished to look to what is done, not only in the colonies, but in Ireland, in one uniform unbroken tenor every session. Sir, I am surprized, that this doctrine should come from some of the law servants of the crown. I say, that if the crown could be responsible, his Majesty—but certainly the ministers, and even these law officers themselves, through whose hands the acts pass, biennially in Ireland, or annually in the colonies, are in an habitual course of committing impeachable offences. What habitual offenders have been all Presidents of the Council, all Secretaries of State, all First Lords of Trade, all Attorneys and all Solicitors General! However, they are safe; as no one impeaches them; and there is no ground of charge against them, except in their own unfounded theories.

The fifth resolution is also a resolution of fact—*That the said General Assemblies, General Courts, or other bodies legally qualified as aforesaid, have at sundry times freely granted several large subsidies and public aids for his Majesty's service, according to their abilities, when required thereto by letter from one of his Majesty's Principal Secretaries of State; and that their right to grant the same, and their cheerfulness and sufficiency in the said grants, have been at sundry times acknowledged by Parliament.* To say nothing of their great expences in the Indian wars; and not to take their exertion in foreign ones, so high as the supplies in the year 1695; not to go back to their public contributions in the year 1710; I shall begin to travel only where the journals give me light; resolving to deal in nothing but fact, authenticated by parliamentary record; and to build myself wholly on that solid basis.

On the 4th of April 1748,* a committee of this house came to the following resolution:

RESOLVED,

That it is the opinion of this Committee, that it is just and reasonable that the several provinces and colonies of Massachusetts-Bay, New-Hampshire, Connecticut, and Rhode-Island, be reimbursed the expences they have been at in taking and securing to the crown of Great-Britain, the island of Cape Breton and its dependencies.

These expences were immense for such colonies. They were above £.200,000 sterling; money first raised and advanced on their public credit.

On the 28th of January 1756,† a message from the King came to us, to this effect—*His Majesty, being sensible of the zeal and vigour with which his faithful subjects of certain colonies in North-America have exerted themselves in defence of his Majesty's just rights and possessions, recommends it to this house to take the same into their consideration, and to enable his Majesty to give them such assistance as may be a proper reward and encouragement.*

On the 3d of February 1756,‡ the House came to a suitable resolution, expressed in words nearly the same as those of the message: but with the further addition, that the money then voted was as an encouragement to the colonies to exert themselves with vigour. It will not be necessary to go through all the testimonies which your own records have given to the truth of my resolutions. I will only refer you to the places in the journals:

Vol. XXVII.—16th and 19th May, 1757.
Vol. XXVIII.—June 1st, 1758—April 26th and 30th, 1759—
March 26th and 31st, and April 28th,
1760—Jan. 9th and 20th, 1761.
Vol. XXIX.—Jan. 22d and 26th, 1762—March 14th, 17th,
1763.

* Journals of the House, Vol. XXV.
† Journals of the House, Vol. XXVII.
‡ Ibid.

Sir, here is the repeated acknowledgment of Parliament, that the colonies not only gave, but gave to satiety. This nation hath formerly acknowledged two things; first, that the colonies had gone beyond their abilities, Parliament having thought it necessary to reimburse them; secondly, that they had acted legally and laudably in their grants of money, and their maintenance of troops, since the compensation is expressly given as a reward and encouragement. Reward is not bestowed for acts that are unlawful; and encouragement is not held out to things that deserve reprehension. My resolution therefore does nothing more than collect into one proposition, what is scattered through your journals. I give you nothing but your own; and you cannot refuse in the gross, what you have so often acknowledged in detail. The admission of this, which will be so honourable to them and you, will, indeed, be mortal to all the miserable stories, by which the passions of the misguided people have been engaged in an unhappy system.

The people heard, indeed, from the beginning of these disputes, one thing continually dinned in their ears, that reason and justice demanded, that the Americans, who paid no taxes, should be compelled to contribute. How did that fact of their paying nothing, stand, when the taxing system began? When Mr. Grenville began to form his system of American revenue, he stated in this house, that the colonies were then in debt two millions six hundred thousand pounds sterling money; and was of opinion they would discharge that debt in four years. On this state, those untaxed people were actually subject to the payment of taxes to the amount of six hundred and fifty thousand a year. In fact, however, Mr. Grenville was mistaken. The funds given for sinking the debt did not prove quite so ample as both the colonies and he expected. The calculation was too sanguine; the reduction was not compleated till some years after, and at different times in different colonies. However, the taxes after the war, continued too great to bear any addition, with prudence or propriety; and when the burthens imposed in consequence of former requisitions were discharged, our tone became too high to resort again to requisition. No colony, since that time, ever has had any requisition whatsoever made to it.

We see the sense of the crown, and the sense of Parliament,

on the productive nature of a revenue by grant. Now search the same journals for the produce of the revenue by imposition.—Where is it?—let us know the volume and the page?—What is the gross, what is the nett produce?—To what service is it applied?—How have you appropriated its surplus?—What, can none of the many skilful index-makers, that we are now employing, find any trace of it?—Well, let them and that rest together. But are the journals, which say nothing of the revenue, as silent on the discontent?—Oh no! a child may find it. It is the melancholy burthen and blot of every page.

I think then I am, from those Journals, justified in the sixth and last resolution, which is—*That it hath been found by experience, that the manner of granting the said supplies and aids, by the said General Assemblies, hath been more agreeable to the said colonies, and more beneficial, and conducive to the public service than the mode of giving and granting aids in Parliament, to be raised and paid in the said colonies.*—This makes the whole of the fundamental part of the plan. The conclusion is irresistible. You cannot say, that you were driven by any necessity, to an exercise of the utmost rights of legislature. You cannot assert, that you took on yourselves the task of imposing colony taxes, from the want of another legal body, that is competent to the purpose of supplying the exigencies of the state without wounding the prejudices of the people. Neither is it true that the body so qualified, and having that competence, had neglected that duty.

The question now, on all this accumulated matter, is,—Whether you will chuse to abide by a profitable experience, or a mischievous theory; whether you will chuse to build on imagination or fact; whether you prefer enjoyment or hope; satisfaction in your subjects, or discontent.

If these propositions are accepted, every thing which has been made to enforce a contrary system, must, I take it for granted, fall along with it, On that ground I have drawn the following resolution, which, when it comes to be moved, will naturally be divided in a proper manner: *That it may be proper to repeal an act, made in the seventh year of the reign of his present Majesty, intituled, An Act for granting certain duties in the British colonies and plantations in America; for allowing a drawback of the duties of customs upon the exportation from this kingdom, of coffee and cocoa nuts of the produce of the said colonies or plantations; for discontinuing the drawbacks payable on China earthen-ware exported to America; and for more effectually preventing the clandestine running of goods in the said colonies and plantations.—And that it may be proper to repeal an act, made in the fourteenth year of the reign of his present Majesty, intituled, An Act to discontinue in such manner, and for such time, as are therein mentioned, the landing and discharging, lading or shipping, of goods, wares, and merchandize at the town, and within the harbour of Boston, in the province of Massachusetts-Bay, in North-America—And that it may be proper to repeal an act, made in the fourteenth year of the reign of his present Majesty, intituled, An Act for the impartial administration of justice, in the cases of persons questioned for any acts done by them, in the execution of the law, or for the suppression of riots and tumults, in the province of Massachusetts-Bay in New-England.—And that it may be proper to repeal an act, made in the fourteenth year of the reign of his present Majesty, intituled, An Act for the better regulating the government of the province of the Massachusetts-Bay in New-England.—And also that it may be proper to explain and amend an act, made in the thirty-fifth year of the reign of King Henry VIII. intituled, An Act for the trial of treasons committed out of the King's dominions.*

I wish, Sir, to repeal the Boston Port-bill, because (independently of the dangerous precedent of suspending the rights of the subject during the King's pleasure) it was passed, as I apprehend, with less regularity, and on more partial principles than it ought. The corporation of Boston was not heard before it was condemned. Other towns, full as guilty as she was, have not had their ports blocked up. Even the restraining bill of the present session does not go to the length of the Boston Port-act. The same ideas of prudence, which induced you not to extend equal punishment to equal guilt, even when you were punishing, induce me, who mean not to chastise, but to reconcile, to be satisfied with the punishment already partially inflicted.

Ideas of prudence, and accommodation to circumstances, prevent you from taking away the charters of Connecticut, and Rhode-Island, as you have taken away that of Massachusetts colony, though the Crown has far less power in the two former provinces than it enjoyed in the latter; and though the abuses have been full as great and as flagrant in the exempted as in the punished. The same reasons of prudence and accommodation have weight with me in restoring the charter of Massachusetts-Bay. Besides, Sir, the act which changes the charter of Massachusetts is in many particulars so exceptionable, that, if I did not wish absolutely to repeal, I would by all means desire to alter it; as several of its provisions tend to the subversion of all public and private justice. Such, among others is the power in the Governor to change the Sheriff at his pleasure; and to make a new returning officer for every special cause. It is shameful to behold such a regulation standing among English laws.

The act for bringing persons accused of committing murder, under the orders of government, to England for trial, is but temporary. That act has calculated the probable duration of our quarrel with the colonies; and is accommodated to that supposed duration. I would hasten the happy moment of reconciliation; and therefore must, on my principle, get rid of that most justly obnoxious act.

The act of Henry VIII. for the trial of treasons, I do not mean to take away, but to confine it to its proper bounds and original intention; to make it expressly for trial of treasons (and the greatest treasons may be committed) in places where the jurisdiction of the crown does not extend.

Having guarded the privileges of local legislature, I would next secure to the colonies a fair and unbiassed judicature; for which purpose, Sir, I propose the following resolution: *That, from the time when the General Assembly or General Court of any colony or plantation in North-America, shall have appointed by act of Assembly, duly confirmed, a settled salary to the offices of the Chief Justice and other Judges of the Superior Court, it may be proper that the said Chief Justice, and other Judges of the Superior Courts of such colony, shall hold his and their offices during their good behaviour; and shall not be removed therefrom, but when the said removal shall be adjudged by his Majesty in Council, upon a hearing on complaint from the General Assembly, or on a complaint from the Governor or Council, or the House of Representatives severally, of the colony in which the said Chief Justice and other Judges have exercised the said offices.*

The next resolution relates to the Courts of Admiralty. It is this: *That it may be proper to regulate the Courts of Admiralty, or Vice Admiralty, authorized by the 15th chapter of the 4th of George the Third, in such a manner as to make the same more commodious to those who sue, or are sued in the said Courts, and to provide for the more decent maintenance of the Judges in the same.*

These courts I do not wish to take away; they are in themselves proper establishments. This court is one of the capital securities of the act of navigation. The extent of its jurisdiction indeed has been encreased; but this is altogether as proper, and is, indeed, on many accounts, more eligible, where new powers were wanted, than a court absolutely new. But courts incommodiously situated, in effect, deny justice; and a court partaking in the fruits of its own condemnation, is a robber. The congress complain, and complain justly, of this grievance.*

These are the three consequential propositions. I have thought of two or three more; but they come rather too near detail, and to the province of executive government, which I wish Parliament always to superintend, never to assume. If the first six are granted, congruity will carry the latter three. If not, the things that remain unrepealed, will be, I hope, rather unseemly incumbrances on the building, than very materially detrimental to its strength and stability.

Here, Sir, I should close; but that I plainly perceive some objections remain, which I ought, if possible, to remove.

The first will be, that in resorting to the doctrine of our ancestors, as contained in the preamble to the Chester act, I prove too much; that the grievance from a want of representation, stated in the preamble goes to the whole of legislation, as well as to taxation. And that the colonies grounding themselves upon that doctrine, will apply it to all parts of legislative authority.

To this objection, with all possible deference and humility, and wishing as little as any man living to impair the smallest particle of our supreme authority, I answer, that the words are

---

* The Solicitor-General informed Mr. Burke, when the resolutions were separately moved, that the grievance of the Judges partaking of the profits of the seizure, had been redressed by office; accordingly the resolution was amended.

the words of Parliament, and not mine; and that all false and inconclusive inferences, drawn from them, are not mine; for I heartily disclaim any such inference. I have chosen the words of an act of Parliament, which Mr. Grenville, surely a tolerably zealous and very judicious advocate for the sovereignty of Parliament, formerly moved to have read at your table, in confirmation of his tenets. It is true that Lord Chatham considered these preambles as declaring strongly in favour of his opinions. He was a no less powerful advocate for the privileges of the Americans. Ought I not from hence to presume, that these preambles are as favourable as possible to both, when properly understood; favourable both to the rights of Parliament, and to the privilege of the dependencies of this Crown? But Sir, the object of grievance, in my resolution, I have not taken from the Chester, but from the Durham act, which confines the hardship of want of representation to the case of subsidies; and which therefore falls in exactly with the case of the colonies. But whether the unrepresented counties were, *de jure*, or *de facto*, bound, the preambles do not accurately distinguish; nor indeed was it necessary; for, whether *de jure*, or *de facto*, the legislature thought the exercise of the power of taking, as of right, or as of fact without right, equally a grievance, and equally oppressive.

I do not know, that the colonies have, in any general way, or in any cool hour, gone much beyond the demand of immunity in relation to taxes. It is not fair to judge of the temper or dispositions of any man, or any set of men, when they are composed and at rest, from their conduct, or their expressions, in a state of disturbance and irritation. It is besides a very great mistake to imagine, that mankind follow up practically, any speculative principle either of government or of freedom, as far as it will go in argument and logical illation. We Englishmen stop very short of the principles upon which we support any given part of our constitution; or even the whole of it together. I could easily, if I had not already tired you, give you very striking and convincing instances of it. This is nothing but what is natural and proper. All government, indeed every human benefit and enjoyment, every virtue, and every prudent act, is founded on compromise and barter. We balance inconveniencies; we give and take; we remit some rights, that we may enjoy others; and, we chuse rather to be happy citizens, than subtle disputants. As we must give away some natural liberty, to enjoy civil advantages; so we must sacrifice some civil liberties for the advantages to be derived from the communion and fellowship of a great empire. But in all fair dealings the thing bought, must bear some proportion to the purchase paid. None will barter away the immediate jewel of his soul. Though a great house is apt to make slaves haughty, yet it is purchasing a part of the artificial importance of a great empire too dear, to pay for it all essential rights, and all the intrinsic dignity of human nature. None of us who would not risque his life, rather than fall under a government purely arbitrary. But, although there are some amongst us who think our constitution wants many improvements, to make it a complete system of liberty, perhaps none who are of that opinion, would think it right to aim at such improvement, by disturbing his country, and risquing every thing that is dear to him. In every arduous enterprize, we consider what we are to lose, as well as what we are to gain; and the more and better stake of liberty every people possess, the less they will hazard in a vain attempt to make it more. These are the cords of man. Man acts from adequate motives relative to his interest; and not on metaphysical speculations.—Aristotle, the great master of reasoning, cautions us, and with great weight and propriety, against this species of delusive geometrical accuracy in moral arguments, as the most fallacious of all sophistry.

The Americans will have no interest contrary to the grandeur and glory of England, when they are not oppressed by the weight of it; and they will rather be inclined to respect the acts of a superintending legislature; when they see them the acts of that power, which is itself the security, not the rival, of their secondary importance. In this assurance, my mind most perfectly acquiesces; and I confess, I feel not the least alarm, from the discontents which are to arise, from putting people at their ease; nor do I apprehend the destruction of this empire, from giving, by an act of free grace and indulgence, to two millions of my fellow-citizens, some share of those rights, upon which I have always been taught to value myself.

It is said indeed, that this power of granting vested in American assemblies, would dissolve the unity of the empire; which was preserved entire, although Wales, and Chester, and Durham, were added to it. Truly, Mr. Speaker, I do not know what this unity means; nor has it ever been heard of, that I know, in the constitutional policy of this country. The very idea of subordination of parts, excludes this notion of simple and undivided unity. England is the head; but she is not the head and the members too. Ireland has ever had from the beginning a separate, but not an independent, legislature; which, far from being distracting, promoted the union of the whole. Every thing was sweetly and harmoniously disposed through both islands for the conservation of English dominion, and the communication of English liberties. I do not see that the same principles might not be carried into twenty islands, and with the same good effect. This is my model with regard to America, as far as the internal circumstances of the two countries are the same. I know no other unity of this empire, than I can draw from its example during those periods, when it seemed to my poor understanding more united than it is now, or then it is likely to be by the present methods.

But since I speak of these methods, I recollect, Mr. Speaker, almost too late, that I promised, before I finished, to say something of the proposition of the noble Lord on the floor,[*] which has been so lately received, and stands on your journals. I must be deeply concerned, whenever it is my misfortune to continue a difference with the majority of this House. But as the reasons for that difference are my apology for thus troubling you, suffer me to state them in a very few words. I shall compress them into as small a body as I possibly can, having already debated that matter at large, when the question was before the Committee.

First, then, I cannot admit that proposition of a ransom by auction; because it is a mere project. It is a thing new; unheard of; supported by no experience; justified by no analogy; without example of our ancestors, or root in the constitution. It is neither regular parliamentary taxation, nor colony grant. *Experimentum in corpore vili*, is a good rule, which will ever make me averse to any trial of experiments on what is certainly the most valuable of all subjects; the peace of this empire.

Secondly, it is an experiment which must be fatal in the end

* Lord North.

to our constitution. For what is it but a scheme for taxing the colonies in the anti-chamber of the noble Lord and his successors? To settle the quotas and proportions in this House, is clearly impossible. You, Sir, may flatter yourself, you shall sit as state auctioneer with your hammer in your hand, and knock down to each colony as it bids. But to settle (on the plan laid down by the noble Lord) the true proportional payment for four or five and twenty governments, according to the absolute and the relative wealth of each, and according to the British proportion of wealth and burthen, is a wild and chimerical notion. This new taxation must therefore come in by the back-door of the constitution. Each quota must be brought to this House ready formed; you can neither add nor alter. You must register it. You can do nothing further. For on what grounds can you deliberate either before or after the proposition? You cannot hear the council for all these provinces, quarrelling each on its own quantity of payment, and its portion to others. If you should attempt it, the committee of provincial ways and means, or by whatever other name it will delight to be called, must swallow up all the time of Parliament.

Thirdly, it does not give satisfaction to the complaint of the colonies. They complain that they are taxed without their consent; you answer, that you will fix the sum at which they shall be taxed. That is, you give them the very grievance for the remedy. You tell them indeed, that you will leave the mode to themselves. I really beg pardon: it gives me pain to mention it; but you must be sensible that you will not perform this part of the compact. For, suppose the colonies were to lay the duties which furnished their contingent, upon the importation of your manufactures; you know you would never suffer such a tax to be laid. You know too, that you would not suffer many other modes of taxation. So that, when you come to explain yourself, it will be found, that you will neither leave to themselves the quantum nor the mode; nor indeed any thing. The whole is delusion from one end to the other.

Fourthly, this method of ransom by auction, unless it be *universally* accepted, will plunge you into great and inextricable difficulties. In what year of our Lord are the proportions of payments to be settled? To say nothing of the impossibility that colony agents should have general powers of taxing the colonies at their discretion; consider, I implore you, that the communication by special messages, and orders between these agents and their constituents on each variation of the case, when the parties come to contend together, and to dispute on the relative proportions, will be a matter of delay, perplexity, and confusion, that never can have an end.

If all the colonies do not appear at the outcry, what is the condition of those Assemblies, who offer by themselves or their agents, to tax themselves up to your ideas of their proportion? The refractory colonies, who refuse all composition, will remain taxed only to your old impositions; which, however grievous in principle, are trifling as to production. The obedient colonies in this scheme are heavily taxed; the refractory remain unburdened. What will you do? Will you lay new and heavier taxes by Parliament on the disobedient? Pray consider in what way you can do it. You are perfectly convinced that in the way of taxing, you can do nothing but at the ports. Now suppose it is Virginia that refuses to appear at your auction, while Maryland and North-Carolina bid handsomely for their ransom, and are taxed to your quota. How will you put these colonies on a par? Will you tax the tobacco of Virginia? If you do, you give its death-wound to your English revenue at home, and to one of the very greatest articles of your own foreign trade. If you tax the import of that rebellious colony, what do you tax but your own manufactures, or the goods of some other obedient, and already well-taxed colony? Who has said one word on this labyrinth of detail, which bewilders you more and more as you enter into it? Who has presented, who can present you, with a clue to lead you out of it? I think, Sir, it is impossible, that you should not recollect that the colony bounds are so implicated in one another, (you know it by your other experiments in the bill for prohibiting the New-England fishery) that you can lay no possible restraints on almost any of them which may not be presently eluded, if you do not confound the innocent with the guilty, and burden those whom upon every principle you ought to exonerate. He must be grosly ignorant of America, who thinks that, without falling into this confusion of all rules of equity and policy, you can restrain any single colony, especially Virginia and Maryland, the central, and most important of them all.

Let it also be considered, that, either in the present confusion, you settle a permanent contingent, which will and must be trifling; and then you have no effectual revenue; or you change the quota at every exigency; and then on every new repartition you will have a new quarrel.

Reflect, besides, that when you have fixed a quota for every colony, you have not provided for prompt and punctual payment. Suppose one, two, five, ten years arrears. You cannot issue a treasury extent against the failing colony. You must make new Boston port bills, new restraining laws, new acts for dragging men to England for trial. You must send out new fleets, new armies. All is to begin again. From this day forward the empire is never to know an hour's tranquility. An intestine fire will be kept alive in the bowels of the colonies, which one time or other will consume this whole empire. I allow indeed that the empire of Germany raises her revenue and her troops by quotas and contingents; but the revenue of the empire, and the army of the empire, is the worst revenue, and the worst army in the world.

Instead of a standing revenue, you will therefore have a perpetual quarrel. Indeed the noble Lord, who proposed this project of a ransom by auction, seemed himself to be of that opinion. His project was rather designed for breaking the union of the colonies, than for establishing a revenue. He confessed, he apprehended, that his proposal would not be to their taste. I say, this scheme of disunion seems to be at the bottom of the project; for I will not suspect that the noble Lord meant nothing but merely to delude the nation by an airy phantom which he never intended to realize. But whatever his views may be; as I propose the peace and union of the colonies as the very foundation of my plan, it cannot accord with one whose foundation is perpetual discord.

Compare the two. This I offer to give you is plain and simple. The other full of perplexed and intricate mazes. This is mild; that harsh. This is found by experience effectual for its purposes; the other is a new project. This is universal; the other calculated for certain colonies only. This is immediate in its conciliatory operation; the other remote, contingent, full of hazard. Mine is what becomes the dignity of a ruling people; gratuitous, unconditional, and not held out as matter of bargain and sale. I have done my duty in proposing it to you. I have indeed tired you by a long discourse; but this is the misfortune of those to whose influence nothing will be conceded, and who must win every inch of their ground by argument. You have heard me with goodness. May you decide with wisdom! For my part I feel my mind greatly disburthened, by what I have done to-day. I have been the less fearful of trying your patience, because on this subject I mean to spare it altogether in future. I have this comfort, that in every stage of the American affairs I have steadily opposed the measures that have produced the confusion, and may bring on the destruction of this empire. I now go so far as to risque a proposal of my own. If I cannot give peace to my country, I give it to my conscience.

But what (says the financier) is peace to us without money? Your plan gives us no revenue. No! But it does.—For it secures to the subject the power of *refusal*; the first of all revenues. Experience is a cheat, and fact a liar, if this power in the subject of proportioning his grant, or of not granting at all, has not been found the richest mine of revenue ever discovered by the skill or by the fortune of man. It does not indeed vote you £. 152,750:11:2¾ths, nor any other paltry limited sum.—But it gives the strong box itself, the fund, the bank, from whence only revenues can arise amongst a people sensible of freedom: *Posita luditur arca*. Cannot you in England; cannot you at this time of day; cannot you, an House of Commons, trust to the principle which has raised so mighty a revenue, and accumulated a debt of near 140 millions in this country? Is this principle to be true in England, and false every where else? Is it not true in Ireland? Has it not hitherto been true in the colonies? Why should you presume that, in any country, a body duly constituted for any function, will neglect to perform its duty, and abdicate its trust? Such a presumption would go against all government in all modes. But, in truth, this dread of penury of supply, from a free Assembly, has no foundation in nature. For first observe, that, besides the desire which all men have naturally of supporting the honour of their own government; that sense of dignity, and that security to property, which ever attends freedom, has a tendency to increase the stock of the free community. Most may be taken where most is accumulated.

And what is the soil or climate where experience has not uniformly proved, that the voluntary flow of heaped-up plenty, bursting from the weight of its own rich luxuriance, has ever run with a more copious stream of revenue, than could be squeezed from the dry husks of oppressed indigence, by the straining of all the politic machinery in the world.

Next we know, that parties must ever exist in a free country. We know too, that the emulations of such parties, their contradictions, their reciprocal necessities, their hopes and their fears, must send them all in their turns to him that holds the balance of the state. The parties are the gamesters; but government keeps the table, and is sure to be the winner in the end. When this game is played, I really think it is more to be feared, that the people will be exhausted, than that government will not be supplied. Whereas, whatever is got by acts of absolute power ill obeyed, because odious, or by contracts ill kept, because constrained; will be narrow, feeble, uncertain and precarious. "Ease would retract vows made in pain, as violent and void."

I, for one, protest against compounding our demands; I declare against compounding, for a poor limited sum, the immense, ever-growing, eternal debt, which is due to generous government from protected freedom. And so may I speed in the great object I propose to you, as I think it would not only be an act of injustice, but would be the worst œconomy in the world, to compel the colonies to a sum certain, either in the way of ransom, or in the way of compulsory compact.

But to clear up my ideas on this subject,—a revenue from America transmitted hither; do not delude yourselves, you never can receive it. No, not a shilling. We have experience, that from remote countries it is not to be expected. If, when you attempted to extract revenue from Bengal, you were obliged to return in loan what you had taken in imposition; what can you expect from North-America? For certainly if ever there was a country qualified to produce wealth, it is India; or an institution fit for the transmission, it is the East-India Company. America has none of these aptitudes. If America gives you taxable objects, on which you lay your duties here, and gives you, at the same time, a surplus by a foreign sale of her commodities to pay the duties on these objects which you tax at home, she has performed her part of the British revenue.

But with regard to her own internal establishments; she may, I doubt not she will, contribute in moderation. I say in moderation; for she ought not to be permitted to exhaust herself. She ought to be reserved to a war; the weight of which, with the enemies that we are most likely to have, must be considerable in her quarter of the globe. There she may serve you, and serve you essentially.

For that service, for all service, whether of revenue, trade or empire, my trust is in her interest in the British constitution. My hold of the colonies is in the close affection which grows from common names, from kindred blood, from similar privileges, and equal protection. These are ties, which, though light as air, are as strong as links of iron. Let the colonies always keep the idea of their civil rights associated with your government; they will cling and grapple to you; and no force under heaven will be of power to tear them from their allegiance. But let it be once understood that your government may be one thing and their privileges another; that these two things may exist without any mutual relation; the cement is gone; the cohesion is loosened; and every thing hastens to decay and dissolution. As long as you have the wisdom to keep the sovereign authority of this country as the sanctuary of liberty, the sacred temple consecrated to our common faith, wherever the chosen race and sons of England worship freedom, they will turn their faces towards you. The more they multiply, the more friends you will have; the more ardently they love liberty, the more perfect will be their obedience. Slavery they can have any where. It is a weed that grows in every soil. They may have it from Spain, they may have it from Prussia. But until you become lost to all feeling of your true interest and your natural dignity, freedom they have from none but you. This is the commodity of price, of which you have the monopoly. This is the true act of navigation, which binds to you the commerce of the colonies, and through them secures to you the wealth of the world. Deny them this participation of freedom, and you break that sole bond, which originally made, and must still preserve, the unity of the empire. Do not entertain so weak an imagination, as that your registers, and your bonds, your affidavits, and your sufferances, your cockets, and your clearances, are what form the great securities of your commerce. Do not dream that your letters of office, and your instructions, and your suspending clauses, are the things that hold together the great contexture of this mysterious whole. These things do not make your government. Dead instruments, passive tools as they are, it is the spirit of English communion that gives all their life and efficacy to them. It is the spirit of the English constitution, which infused through the mighty mass, pervades, feeds, unites, invigorates, vivifies every part of the Empire, even down to the minutest member.

Is it not the same virtue which does every thing for us here in England? Do you imagine then, that it is the land tax act which raises your revenue? that it is the annual vote in the committee of supply, which gives you your army? or that it is the mutiny bill which inspires it with bravery and discipline? No! surely no! It is the love of the people; it is their attachment to their government, from the sense of the deep stake they have in such a glorious institution, which gives you your army and your navy, and infuses into both that liberal obedience, without which your army would be a base rabble, and your navy nothing but rotten timber.

All this, I know well enough, will sound wild and chimerical to the profane herd of those vulgar and mechanical politicians, who have no place among us; a sort of people who think that nothing exists but what is gross and material, and who therefore, far from being qualified to be directors of the great movement of empire, are not fit to turn a wheel in the machine. But to men truly initiated and rightly taught, these ruling and master principles, which, in the opinion of such men as I have mentioned, have no substantial existence, are in truth every thing, and all in all. Magnanimity in politics is not seldom the truest wisdom; and a great empire and little minds go ill together. If we are conscious of our situation, and glow with zeal to fill our place as becomes our station and ourselves, we ought to auspicate all our public proceedings on America, with the old warning of the church, *Sursum corda!* We ought to elevate our minds to the greatness of that trust to which the order of Providence has called us. By adverting to the dignity of this high calling, our ancestors have turned a savage wilderness into a glorious empire; and have made the most extensive, and the only honourable conquests; not by destroying, but by promoting the wealth, the number, the happiness, of the human race. Let us get an American revenue as we have got an American empire. English privileges have made it all that it is; English privileges alone will make it all it can be. In full confidence of this unalterable truth, I now *(quod felix faustumque sit)* lay the first stone of the temple of peace; and I move you,

That the colonies and plantations of Great-Britain, in North-America, consisting of fourteen separate governments, and containing two millions and upwards of free inhabitants, have not had the liberty and privilege of electing and sending any knights and burgesses, or others, to represent them in the high court of Parliament.

Upon this resolution, the previous question was put, and carried; for the previous question 270, against it 78.

FINIS.

[Moses Mather], America's Appeal to the Impartial World. Hartford, 1775.

A descendant of the famous Puritan family, Moses Mather served for sixty-four years as minister of the Congregational Church in Middlesex (now Darien), Connecticut. He was a devout and fearless patriot, speaking out even in the face of a large number of Loyalists in his town. Because Middlesex was close to New York City, he would be twice taken captive by Loyalist raiding parties during the Revolutionary War.

First and foremost a theologian, over the course of his long career Mather gradually cast off traditional Calvinist doctrine in favor of an emphasis on reason and the ability of human beings to help bring about their own salvation. His political activism was indicative of the degree to which the clergy, especially the Congregationalists of New England, were involved in the mobilization of the American people into resistance and eventually revolution. Massachusetts Loyalist Peter Oliver was not exaggerating by much when he blamed the "black regiment" of the clergy for the breakup of the empire. Many of the clergy saw in the imperial crisis signs of the Second Coming of Christ and the Day of Judgment. The fusion of these kinds of millennial expectations with the more secular progressive thinking of the Enlightenment helped create the belief that America was on the verge of some momentous reformation. The city upon the hill, it was hoped, would soon assume a new republican character, becoming what Samuel Adams called "the *Christian* Sparta."

In this pamphlet, Mather focused purely on politics. Indeed, few colonial writers offered a more impressive analysis of what was happening between what he called the "two countries." Not only did he brilliantly examine the issues already raised in the imperial debate, but he opened new avenues of political and constitutional thinking. He explored the possibility of expatriation from one's country, emphasized the importance of education in inculcating virtue, and drew a distinction between ordinary legislation and the fundamental law of a constitution, a distinction that eventually came to separate American from English constitutionalism. He spelled out more precisely than most what it meant to have thirteen independent colonial legislatures each of which had a separate relationship to the king. And he turned the doctrine of sovereignty against the British by arguing that to admit the power of Parliament over the sovereign legislatures of each of the colonies "would be constituting an *imperium in imperio*, one supreme power within another, the height of political absurdity." The Reverend Mather was more than ready for independence.

A M E R I C A's
A P P E A L

T O

The Impartial W O R L D.

Wherein the RIGHTS of the *AMERICANS,* as MEN, BRITISH SUBJECTS, and as COLONISTS; the *Equity* of the *Demand*, and of the *Manner* in which it is made upon them by *Great-Britain*, are ſtated and conſidered.　　　And,

The *Oppoſition* made by the Colonies to Acts of Parliament, their reſorting to ARMS in their *neceſſary* DEFENCE, againſt the Military Armaments, employed to enforce them, VINDICATED.

Wo ! to thee that ſpoileſt when thou waſt not ſpoiled ; and dealeſt treacherouſly, and they dealt not treacherouſly with thee, &c.
　　　　　　　　　　　　　　　　　　Iſaiah xxxiii.

My bowels, my bowels ! I am pained at my heart, my heart maketh a noiſe in me ; I cannot hold my peace becauſe thou haſt heard, Oh my ſoul ! the ſound of the trumpet and the alarm of war.
　　　　　　　　　　　　　　　　　　Jer. iv.

And they anſwered the King, the man that conſumed us and deviſed againſt us, that we ſhould be deſtroyed from remaining in any of the coaſts of Iſrael, let, &c.　　　　　2 Sam. xxi.

===

H A R T F O R D :

Printed by EBENEZER WATSON, 1775

America's Appeal to the Impartial World.

A^T a time when we are called upon to surrender our liberties, our religion, and country; or defend them at the point of the sword, against those, that were our friends, our brethren, and allies, (whose swords, and ours, till lately were never drawn but for mutual defence; and in joint battalions, cemented in love, affinity, and valour, have wrought wonders, vanquished armies, and triumphed over the power of mighty potentates) nothing will inspire our councils with unanimity, our resolves with firmness, and render the exertions, the noble struggles of a brave, free and injured people, bold, rapid and irresistable, like a right understanding of the necessity and rectitude of the defence, we are compelled to make, in this unnatural contention.

To write upon a subject, that hath been so often and ably handled—a subject so important in its nature, so extensive in its consequences, in which the fate of America, the rights and liberties of millions, nay more, of mankind, are involved; and to trace those rights to their native original source, develope the fountain from whence derived; define their nature and immutability, and shew wherefore the arbitrary institutions of civil government (originally ordained to connect the strength of each, for the security of all) cannot destroy or alter them, requires a fund of abilities far beyond mine; yet, to attempt it, may serve to awaken and stimulate some masterly pen, to execute a task so arduous, and beneficial to the world. And should these imperfect considerations, on a subject so important, call forth the prolific fire of some great intuitive genius, to lighten upon the subject, on which I have only glimmered, and like a skilful physician, comprehending the disease and the remedy, point out the one, and prescribe the other, or some mighty deliverer, while others lop here and there a scattered branch, with unerring aim, to give a blow at the root, my end would be answered, my pains compensated, and my country rescued from the darkness that invelops, and from the misery and slavery that impend it. With these views, the following pages are humbly dedicated to the candour and patronage, of the impartial world; to whom, (under God) we make our appeal, with fervent desires, that He, who hath the hearts of King's in his hands suspends the fate of empires on his nod, and whom, even angry, conflicting elements instantly obey, would hush the civil tumults, still and dispel the thundering tempest, that darkens and disquiets our hemisphere.

I shall consider the subject under the following divisions.

I. The natural rights of the Americans, considered as men.

II. The rights of Americans antecedent to any charters, or colony constitutions under the crown.

III. Their rights subsequent to such charters, or colony constitutions.

IV. The equity of the demand made on the colonies, and of the manner in which it is made.

Free agency, or a rational existence, with its powers and faculties, and freedom of enjoying and exercising them, is the gift of God to man. The right of the donor, and the authenticity of the donation, are both incontestable; hence man hath an absolute property in, and right of dominion over himself, his powers and faculties; with self-love to stimulate, and reason to guide him, in the free use and exercise of them, independent of, and uncontrolable by any but him, who created and gave them. And whatever is acquired by the use, and application of a man's faculties, is equally the property of that man, as the faculties by which the acquisitions are made; and that which is absolutely the property of a man, he cannot be divested of, but by his own voluntary act, or consent, either expressed, or implied. Expressed, by actual gift, sale, or exchange, by himself, or his lawful substitute:—implied, as where a man enters into, and takes the benefits of a government, he implicitly consents to be subject to it's laws; so, when he transgresses the laws, there is an implied consent to submit to it's penalties.—And from this principle, all the civil exousiai,* or rightful authorities, that are ordained of God, and exist in the world, are derived as from their native source. From whence are authorities, dominions and powers? from God, the sovereign ruler, as the fountain, *through the voice and consent of the people.* For what purpose are they erected? *for the good of the people.* Wherefore the sovereign ruler, condescends to cloath, with authority, the

---

* Exousia, in the original, which is translated power, signifies a rightful authority or moral power, and stands opposed to dunamis, a natural power or might.

man who by the general voice, is exalted, from among the people, to bear rule; and to pronounce him his minister for their good. Hence, it is evident, that man hath the clearest right, by the most indefeasible title, to personal security, liberty, and private property. And whatever is a man's own, he hath, most clearly, a right to enjoy and defend; to repel force by force; to recover what is injuriously pillaged or plundered from him, and to make reasonable reprisals for the unjust vexation.* And, upon this principle, an offensive war may sometimes be justifiable, viz. when it is necessary for preservation and defence.

II. I am now to consider the rights of the Americans, antecedent to any charters or colony constitutions under the crown.

When our ancestors left the kingdom of England, they were subjects of that kingdom, and entitled to equal privileges with the rest of its subjects; when they came into America, where no civil constitutions were existing, they joined themselves to none: the lands which they entered and possessed, they acquired by purchase, or by conquest of the natives: they came over of themselves, viz. were not colonies sent out, to make settlements by government; not to mention the intolerable oppressions, by which they were driven out, crossed the Atlantick, and availed themselves of possessions, at their own risque and expence, and by their own sword and prowess. Now, in America, they were still subjects of the kingdom of England, or they were not; if the former, then they were entitled to enjoy, in America, the same or equal privileges, with those enjoyed by the subjects residing in England—if the latter, then that kingdom had no right of jurisdiction over them, and they were in a state of nature, at liberty to erect such a constitution of civil government as they should chuse. Upon the supposition that they were still subjects of that kingdom, let us consider what rights and privileges they were entitled to enjoy:

*I have not noticed the authority of parents over children, it not being to the argument, but remark, that the Creator, foreseeing the necessity of civil government, arising from the depravity of human nature, hath wisely formed our infancy, and childhood, feeble and dependent on the protection, and government of parents, thereby preparing us, in childhood, for dependence on, and subjection to civil government, in manhood.

1st. In regard to legislation.

2d. TAXATION.   And,

3d. THE mode of trial.

By nature, every man (under God) is his own legislator, judge, and avenger, and absolute lord of his property. In civil government, rightly constituted, every one retains a share in the legislative, taxative, judicial, and the vindictive powers, by having a voice in the supreme legislature, which enacts the laws, and imposes the taxes, and by having a right, in all cases wherein he is injured, to resort to, and demand redress, in a course of law, from the tribunal of the public, and the sword of state. And the English nation, early impressed, with these first great principles of natures dictates, erected a system of civil government, correspondent thereto; invested the parliament, which consisted of all the estates, that composed the nation, in epitome, with the supreme sovereignty of the kingdom; and in which, each estate made a part, and had a share, either personally or by actual representation, to advise, resolve, consent, or dissent, and in which, the concurrence of all three, viz. the King, Lords and Commons, was necessary, to every act of legislation. Thus the English government was constituted upon the foundation of reason; and the natural rights of the subjects, instead of being given up, or impaired, were confirmed, improved and strengthened, although the mode of exercising them was altered: Wherefore it is a maxim in the English laws, that to an act of parliament, every man, in judgment of law is party. The English constitution, like other imitations of nature, was a system of consummate wisdom, and policy, the balance of power, being so judiciously placed, as to connect the force, and to preserve the rights of all; each estate, armed with a power of self defence, against the encroachments of the other two, by being enabled to put a negative upon any or all of their resolves, neither the King, Lords or Commons, could be deprived of their rights or properties but by their own consent in parliament, and no laws could be made, or taxes imposed, but such as were necessary, and in the judgment of the three estates in parliament, for the common good, and interest of the realm. Most justly then did a celebrated French writer, treating of the English, and the excellence of their constitution, say, that England could never lose its freedom, until parliament lost its virtue. The English, animated with the spirit of freedom, to their immortal honor, anciently claimed these privileges, as their unalienable rights, and anxious to preserve and transmit them unimpaired to posterity; caused them to be reduced to writing, and in the most solemn manner to be recognized, ratified and confirmed, first by King John, then by his son Henry the IIId. in the 3d and 37th years of his reign, at Westminster-Hall, where Magna Charta was read in the presence of the Nobility and Bishops, with lighted candles in their hands; the King, all the while laying his hand on his breast, at last, solemnly swearing faithfully and inviolably to observe all things therein contained, as he was a man, a christian, a soldier and a King; then the Bishops extinguished the candles and threw them on the ground, and every one said, thus let him be extinguished and stink in hell, who violates this charter: Upon which there was universal festivity and joy, ringing of bells, &c. and again by Edward the 1st. in the 25th year of his reign, by the statute called *Confirmatio Cartarum*. Afterwards by a multitude of corroborating acts, reckoned in all, by Lord Cook, to be thirty-two, from Edw. 1st. to Hen. 4th. and since, in a great variety of instances, by the bills of right and acts of settlement; whereby Magna Charta, that great charter of liberties, hath been established as the standard of right throughout the realm, and all judgments contrary thereto declared void, it was ordered to be read twice a year in all the cathedral churches, and sentence of excommunication to be denounced against all, who by word or deed, acted contrary to, or infringed it.

2d. WITH REGARD TO TAXATION.

As the rights of private property are sacred, and no one can be divested thereof without his free consent: The English constitution, in this also religiously follows the dictates of reason: No subject of England can be constrained to pay any aids or taxes, even for the defence of the realm, or the support of government, but such as are imposed by his own consent, or that of his representative in parliament. By the stat. 25 Edw. 1st. c. 5 and 6, it is provided, that the King shall not take any aids or taxes, but by the common assent of the realm: And what that common assent is, is more fully explained, by the 34th of Edw. 1st. stat. 4, c. 1, which enacts, that no talliage or aid shall be taken, without assent of Archbishops, Bishops, Earls, Barons, Knights, Burgesses, and other freemen of the land; and by the 14th Edw. 3. stat. 2. it is provided, that the Prelates, Earls, Barons, Commons, and Citizens, Burgesses and Merchants, shall not be charged to make any aid, if it be not by the common assent of the great men, and Commons in Parliament: And as this fundamental principle had been shamefully violated by succeeding Princes, it was made an article in the petition of right, third of King Cha. I. that no man shall be compelled to yield any gift, loan, or benevolence, tax, or any such charge, without common consent, by act of Parliament; and again by the 1st of William and Mary, stat. 2, it is declared, that levying money for, or to the use of the crown, by pretence of prerogative, without grant of parliament, or for longer time, or in other manner, then the same is or shall be granted, is illegal; and that the subjects do claim, demand, and insist upon all and singular the premises, as their antient undoubted rights and liberties. Lastly, these rights and liberties were asserted and confirmed, in the act of settlement which limited the crown, to the illustrious house of his present Majesty, in the beginning of this century. Talliage from the French taille to cut, signifies a part cut or carved out of the whole estate, and in a law sense includes all subsidies, taxes, impositions, and duties whatsoever, none of which might be taken without common consent in parliament. Hence, it is the antient and unalienable right of the House of Commons, to originate all money bills, they being the free donations of the people, and not the exactions of the Prince; upon the principle that civil government is constituted for the good of the people, and not the people for government: And there is no difference in the reason and nature of the thing, between the King's levying money in England without consent of parliament, and the parliament's levying money in America without the consent of the Americans.

3d. IN REGARD TO THE MODE OF TRIAL.

As it is not the laws merely, that are made, considered in themselves, but the construction and sense put upon them, by the judges and triers, that falls upon the subject and affects him in his person and property; it was necessary that the constitution should guard the rights of the subject, in the executive as well as the legislative part of government: And no mode of trial would so effectually do this, be so unexceptionable, by reason of their equality, and the impartial manner in which they are taken and impanelled; so advantageous, on account of their knowledge of the parties, the credibility of the witnesses, and what weight ought to be given to their testimony, as that by our peers, a jury of the vicinity: For very good and wholsome laws may be perniciously executed. Wherefore it is expresly provided and ordained, in the Great Charter, chap. 29, "That no freeman shall be taken or disseised of his freehold, or liberties, or free customs, or be outlawed, or exiled, or any otherwise destroyed; and we will not pass sentence upon him, nor condemn him, but by lawful judgment of his peers; or by the laws of the land." By this no freeman might be molested in his person, liberty or estate, but according to the laws of the land, by lawful warrant, granted by lawful authority, expressing the cause for which, the time when, and place where he is to answer or be imprisoned, with the terms of his enlargement; nor have sentence passed upon him in any case, but by lawful judgment of his peers; who, in the instance of giving their verdict, do unanimously declare and announce the law, with respect to themselves, in like circumstances. It is, says Dr. Blackstone, the most transcendant privilege which "any subject can enjoy or wish for, that he cannot be affected in his property, his liberty or person, but by the unanimous consent of twelve of his neighbours and equals: And when a celebrated French writer concludes, that because Rome, Sparta, and Carthage, lost their liberties, therefore England must in time lose theirs, he should have recollected, that Rome, Sparta, and Carthage were strangers to trial by jury; and that it is a duty which every man owes to his country, his friends, his posterity and himself, to maintain, to the utmost of his power, this valuable constitution in all its parts, to restore it to its antient dignity, if at all impaired, or deviated from its first institution, &c. and above all, to guard with the most jealous circumspection, against the introduction of new and arbitrary methods of trial, which, under a variety of plausible pretences, may in time, imperceptably undermine this best preservative of English liberties." English subjects, therefore, could be bound by no laws, be liable to no taxes, but what were made and imposed by their own consent; not have any sentence passed upon them but by the judgment of their equals. Glorious constitution! worthy to be engraved in capitals of gold, on pillars of marble; to be perpetuated through all time, a barrier, to circumscribe and bound the restless ambition of aspiring monarchs, and the palladium of civil liberty; especially, when in addition to these, we consider the Habeas Corpus act, passed in 31 Car. II. that second Magna Charta and stable bulwark of the subjects liberties, which provides a remedy for the immediate relief of such as are unjustly imprisoned, under colour of law. And enacts, that no subject of this our realm, who is an inhabitant of England, Wales, or Berwick, shall be sent a prisoner to Scotland, Ireland, Jersey, Guernsey, or places beyond the seas, and all such imprisonments are declared illegal, the party causing them disabled to bear any office, incurs the penalty of a premunire, becomes incapable of the King's pardon, and also is to answer damages to the party aggrieved. "Of great importance, says the above cited author, to the public, is the preservation of personal liberty, for if once it was left in the power of any, the highest magistrate, to imprison arbitrarily, whomsoever he or his officers thought proper (as in France is daily practised by the crown) there would soon be an end to all other rights and immunities." How consistent with these principles, the present mode of administring government is, the impartial world may judge, by the late revenue and other acts of parliament, relative to America, directing its inhabitants to be imprisoned, and transported beyond sea for trial; erecting courts of admiralty, and other arbitrary tribunals, to decide in matters most interesting, without the intervention of a jury.

These privileges, important and inestimable as they are, every subject of the realm of England hath right to possess and enjoy. And the Americans, antecedent to their charters, &c. if they were still subjects of that realm, had right to have and enjoy in America. Now, if it was impossible for the Americans, in their situation, to enjoy the rights and privileges of the English government, it follows, that they were not amenable to its power, nor taxable for its support; *nam qui sentit onus, sentire debet commodum*, he that bears the burden ought to enjoy the blessing, and *vice versa*. Can any thing be more absurd, than that a man should be tied to a government, bound to yield subjection, and contribute support, wherever he is, on the face of the earth, without having any part or voice in its administration, or power to enjoy its immunities. And that it was impossible for the Americans to enjoy the privileges of the English government, is evident, there being no provision in the constitution for summoning members to parliament from the American world; and if there was, the local distance, the risk and uncertainty of crossing the atlantic, the disparity between the two countries, in respect of situation, numbers, age, abilities and other circumstances, would render any representation of America in the parliament of England, utterly impracticable and vain. So that our ancestors, in America, were unable to exercise and enjoy that capital right of all English subjects, viz. the having a voice in the supreme legislature, without which, as the *causa sine qua non*, the parliament of England could not bind them in any respect. Hence the right of subjectship, on the part of the Americans, and of jurisdiction over them by parliament, became dormant, ineffectual rights, incapable of being exercised; for the whole ground of the parliament's right to bind the Americans, consisted in their being subjects; and for that very reason, if they were subjects, the parliament could have no right to bind them, or exercise jurisdiction over them, without their consent.

I will now enquire, whether the Americans, antecedent to their charters, &c. are to be considered as being subjects of the kingdom of England, or not.

From what hath been already said, it is evident, that they either were not subjects of that kingdom, or as though they were not: But this will be further illustrated, by considering, in what subjectship consists: Compleat subjectship* consists in being under allegiance to the King, inhabiting territories within the kingdom, in having, or at least in being capable of having a voice in the supreme legislature, and enjoying, or in being able to enjoy the benefits and immunities of the government.

Allegiance, from *ligo*, to bind, is the bond that connects the subjects with their sovereign, and their sovereign with them: Hence the King is called their liege Lord, and they his liege subjects; because he is bound to protect and they to obey. And there are three kinds of allegiance, natural, acquired, and local,

* By this is meant one that is a subject of the kingdom as well as of the King.

every one born within the realm, is by birth, inheritable to the laws, intitled to the immunities of the government, and to the protection of the King; wherefore his allegiance, like St. Pauls, is natural: Every alien friend that comes into the realm, who by the King's letters patent is made a denizen, or by act of parliament is naturalized, hath an acquired allegiance; every alien friend that comes into the realm to reside for a time, oweth a local temporary allegiance, during his residence there. And the obligation to obedience in all these cases, arises from the reason and fitness of things, and is comprehensively expressed in this short law maxim, *protectio trahit subjectionem, & subjectio protectionem*, protection mutually entitles to subjection, and subjection to protection. Hence it follows (as mankind by joining to society do not mean, nor doth allegiance intend to confine them perpetually to dwell in one country) that when a person, under a natural, acquired, or local allegiance removes out of the realm to some distant climate, goes out of the protection of the King, and loses all benefit of the laws and government of the kingdom; his allegiance, which is mutual or not at all, ceaseth, for *cessante causa cesset effectus*, the cause or reason ceasing, which in this case is protection and the benefits of government, the effect, viz. the obligation of obedience also ceaseth. There is also what is called a legal allegiance, *ex provisione legis*, that is by positive institution, as the oath of allegiance taken by the subjects, wherein they swear to bear all true and faithful allegiance to the King; which is a counter part to the King's coronation oath, whereby he swears to protect his subjects in all their just rights, to abjure popery, and maintain the protestant religion, to govern the kingdom and administer justice according to the laws of the realm. Both which are only confirmations of the mutual obligations resulting from the relation, that subsists between them as King and subjects, and do attend upon and follow it, in its extent and duration. I am not insensible that it is a doctrine of antiquity, patronized by many, that natural allegiance is universal and perpetual; cannot be lost or forfeited, but by the commission of crimes, &c. but notwithstanding, I beg leave to suggest a few considerations on this point. The place of a man's birth, in respect to himself, is a matter of accident and necessity, and not of choice; and is a man so bound by accident and necessity, as to the place of his birth, that when he arrives to the age of discretion, he cannot remove into another kingdom and country, and become the subject of another prince? Doth not the obligation of subjection and obedience to parents, cease with our childhood and state of dependance, although that of respect and reverence ever remains? Should the King of Great-Britain voluntarily resign his crown, or abdicate the government, remove and reside in Italy, or enter into religion, whereby he would be civilly dead, would he, notwithstanding, be King, *de jure & de facto*, and would the subjects be under obligation of allegiance to him, as their liege Lord? incapable of placing another on the throne, without incurring the crime of treason, or being involved in the dilemma of owing subjection to two rightful sovereigns, at one time? If so, then he that is once King, can never be divested of royal authority, the principles of the revolution are false; and no new subjects can ever be acquired, for all are born under allegiance to some prince or state; where, upon these principles, they must ever remain, fixed as fate; and acquired allegiance, by act of parliament in England, is all a farce.

But be this as it may, yet should a number of the subjects of Great-Britain, under a natural allegiance to the King, by his licence remove voluntarily, or by accident be carried to some distant, uncivilized, or uninhabited country, where they should find it convenient and beneficial to settle; would they be incapable of erecting civil government, and making laws, for the well ordering of their affairs, independent of the King and kingdom? If so, they would be of all men most miserable, and their boasted subjectship would be their greatest calamity, because they have the rights of British subjects, they are rendered incapable of enjoying the rights of men. Upon this contracted principle, no new countries could be peopled, or new empires founded; but all things must remain as they were. And is the world and its empires so fixed and concluded by an unalterable fate? Are men, who were created in the image of their maker, to contemplate the heavens and soar above the stars, whose first great law was to increase, multiply and replenish the earth, and by experiencing the boundless profusion of divine goodness, learn to be profusely bounteous and good, to be so restrained? Is this becoming the dignity of their rational nature, and suited to the selfish* social passions, implanted in the human soul? Whose motives are our own good and the good of mankind: To attempt to eradicate or alter these, by the arbitrary restraints of civil government, is to impeach the wisdom of the Creator, for not suiting man's passions and faculties, to his station here, and offering violence to human nature. Let civil government then be suited to man's nature and passions, (I mean not the depraved, ungodly desires and cravings of tyranny, which grasps for universal despotic sway; or of licentiousness, that is ever impatient of all legal restraints, how ever reasonable and righteous) for if it is not, there will be a perpetual conflict between the regulations and restraints of government, and the reasonable desires and passions of the subjects.

It may be said, that the reason why natural allegiance is perpetual, is not merely on account of our being born, &c. but the protection and support of the government, afforded us where born; this is an obligation of debt. Much, most undoubtedly, we owe to our parents and to the government that supported and protected our infantile state: But is it true, that because we were once dependant, we must ever be so? Because we were once obliged, we can never be disengaged from the obligation? If it is, then all mankind are insolvents, servants of servants, the curse of Canaan is the portion of all: And every alien born is utterly incapable of ever becoming a subject of the kingdom of Great-Britain.

But to return, allegiance is due to the King in his natural and political capacity; and doth not necessarily superinduce an obligation of obedience to the power of parliament; for a person may be a subject of the King of England and not of the realm; be under allegiance to the King, yet owe no obedience to parliament; as was the case of Scotland, upon the accession of King James the 1st. to the throne of England, before the act of union; and as the case is at present with Hanover; and as was the case of Normandy, when William the Conqueror wore the crown of England.

The rights of a subject may be suspended for a time, with respect to the enjoyment and exercise of them, by some

---

* By selfish here is meant virtuous passions that prompt us to seek our own preservation &c. as self-love, &c.

temporary impediment, which when removed they revive: But when the obstacle that suspends and impedes the exercise and enjoyment of them, is universal, permanent and perpetual, it is an extinguishment of those rights. Thus much I thought necessary to observe, before I gave a relation of the cause and manner of our ancestors first coming and settling in America.

North-America was first discovered by Sebastian Cabot, in the reign of Henry the 7th, A. D. 1498, and was at that time inhabited by the Indian natives, who lived principally by hunting: In A. D. 1606 King James, by letters patent, erected two companies called the Virginia Companies, with power to make settlements in America. Though none were made in New-England by virtue of that authority. About the close of the sixteenth century, several attempts were made for settling Virginia, before any proved successful: The three first companies that came all perished, by hunger, diseases or Indian cruelty: The fourth was reduced to almost the same situation, when Lord Delaware came to their relief. Thus Virginia, being the first province that was settled in America, to her honour be it remembered, hath likewise been foremost in maintaining and vindicating the rights of the Americans.

In A. D. 1620, England, torn with religious dissentions, the friends of the reformation, persecuted with unrelenting cruelty, by the intolerant spirit that influenced government, were forced to renounce their religion and liberties, or assert them with their lives. The protestants, to the number of one hundred and fifty, who before had fled to Holland for safety, having made a purchase under the Plymouth Company, and obtained the royal licence, quitted their native country, preferring the enjoyment of their religion and liberty, in a howling desert, to the pomp and pleasures of luxury and sin in England; crossed the Atlantic and arrived at Plymouth in America in A. D. 1620, and by their own valour, industry, risk and expence (under the smiles of Heaven) acquired plantations, subdued savage enemies, built cities, turned the wilderness into fruitful fields, and rendered it vocal with the praises of their Saviour, and from small beginnings, in process of time, became great in number, and in extent of territory; Great numbers, not long after, from religious considerations, emigrating from England, came and settled the other colonies in America; for, says an

English historian, "it seems that all the provinces of North-America were planted from motives of religion." Thus was gradually unfolded the rudiments of a future empire, before in embryo.

Upon what principles then, could England have jurisdiction over the persons and properties of those brave and free adventurers who settled the colonies? Because England was most powerful? This would be founding right in might, an argument too absurd to need refutation, applied to any but the supreme Being; who, though almighty, yet can do no wrong. Or because they were once subjects of that kingdom? This, if it proves any thing, proves too much, as hath been shown. Or was it because the country was discovered by the King of England? Whatever rights accrue by first discovering a vacant country, accrue to the Prince, under whom it is made; and they are *jura coronæ*, rights of the crown, belonging to the King and not to the kingdom. But America, had long before been discovered and inhabited by numerous tribes of Indians, the original proprietors of the country; subjects capable of property, and who made a part of the human species, when the Almighty gave the earth to the children of men; and why black squalid hair, a tawny complexion, a particular manner of living, and ignorance of divine revelation, should be absolute disqualifications, to have and hold property, any more than a black skin, curled head, flat nose and bandy legs, should be the infallible criterion of slavery, I cant devise.

III. *Let us consider the Rights of the AMERICANS subsequent to their Charters and Colony Constitutions.*

As there are certain rights of men, which are unalienable even by themselves; and others which they do not mean to alienate, when they enter into civil society. And as power is naturally restless, aspiring and insatiable; it therefore becomes necessary in all civil communities (either at their first formation or by degrees) that certain great first principles be settled and established, determining and bounding the power and prerogative of the ruler, ascertaining and securing the rights and liberties of the subjects, as the foundation stamina of the government; which in all civil states is called the constitution, on the certainty and permanency of which, the rights of both the ruler and the subjects depend; nor may they be altered or changed by ruler or people, but by the whole collective body, or a major part at least, nor may they be touched by the legislator; for the moment that alters essentially the constitution, it annihilates its own existence, its constitutional authority. Not only so, but on supposition the legislator might alter it; such a stretch of power would be dangerous beyond conception; for could the British parliament alter the original principles of the constitution, the people might be deprived of their liberties and properties, and the parliament become absolute and perpetual; and for redress in such case, should it ever happen, they must resort to their native rights, and be justified in making insurrection. For when the constitution is violated, they have no other remedy; but for all other wrongs and abuses that may possibly happen, the constitution remaining inviolate, the people have a remedy thereby.

The Americans antecedent to their colony constitutions, must be considered either as the subjects of the kingdom of England, or as subjects of the King and not of the kingdom, or as subjects of neither; and their territory as belonging either to that kingdom, the King, or to neither. In which of these lights they should be considered, I leave the impartial world to judge. If the first, then the grants and patents from the crown conveyed nothing, *nam ex nihilo nihil gignitur*, for what the King had not he could not grant, and the colonies, besides their rights as English subjects, have acquired an indefeasable title, by prescription, to the lands they have possessed, to the privileges, immunities and exemptions they have enjoyed, and to all the powers of government, rights of jurisdiction, regalities, &c. which they have had and exercised, beyond which, the memory of man runneth not to the contrary. If the second, then by the royal grants, patents, &c. all the powers of government, rights of jurisdiction, liberties and privileges, with the property of the lands in fee, are passed from the crown, and vested in the colonies, absolutely and indefeasably, according to the tenor of their several grants and constitutions. If the last, then all these rights of jurisdiction, of property and liberty, were underived and self-originated. If, therefore, they were to be considered as English subjects, by the constitution of that kingdom, they had right to enjoy all these privileges; if not as English subjects, then they were theirs without being beholden therefor. In either view, therefore, they were entitled to have and enjoy all the rights, liberties and privileges, which, by their several constitutions, were granted and confirmed to them, antecedent thereto. And their constitutions are the original compacts, containing the first great principles, or stamina of their governments; combining the members, connecting and subordinating them to the King as their supreme head and liege Lord; also prescribing the forms of their several governments, determining and bounding the power of the crown over them, within proper limits, and ascertaining and securing their rights, jurisdictions and liberties; and are not to be compared to the charters of corporations in England (although they are to be deemed sacred) which are royal favours granted to particular corporations, beyond what are enjoyed by the subjects in common; if they should be forfeited and taken away the members will still retain the great essential rights of British subjects, and these original compacts were made and entered into by the King, not only for himself, but expressly for his heirs and successors on the one part, and the colonies, their successors and assigns on the other; whereby the connection was formed, not only between the parties then in being, but between the crown and the colonies, through all successions of each; and those compacts are permanent and perpetual, as unalterable as Magna Charta, or the primary principles of the English constitution: nor can they be vacated or changed by the king, any more than by the colonies, nor be forfeited by one more than the other; for they are mutually obligatory on both, and are the ligaments and bonds that connect the colonies with the king of Great-Britain, and the king with them: cut, therefore, and dissolve them, and the colonies will become immediately disunited from the crown, and the crown from them. Should the original parties to these constitutions awake in their tombs, and come forth (on a controversy that would awake the dead, could the dead be waked) and with united voice testify, that this was their original, true intent and meaning, would it not be awfully striking and convincing? But we have greater evidence; we have their original declaration, made in that day, deliberately reduced to writing, and solemnly ratified and confirmed, which is as follows: "We do, for us, our heirs and successors, grant to, &c. and their successors, by these presents, that these our letters patent, shall be firm, good, and effectual in the law, to all intents, constructions and purposes whatever, according to our true intent and meaning herein before declared, as shall be construed, reputed and adjudged most favourable on the behalf, and for the best benefit and behoof of the grantees, &c. notwithstanding any omissions therein, or any statute, act, ordinance, provision, proclamation or restriction heretofore made, had, enacted, ordained or provided, or any other matter, cause or thing whatsoever, to the contrary thereof, in any wise notwithstanding."

And the reasons for erecting these constitutions, are recited in the preamble of some of them, as follows, viz. "Whereas by the several navigations, discoveries, and successful plantations of divers of our loving subjects of this our realm of England, several lands, islands, places, colonies and plantations have been obtained and settled, &c. and thereby the trade and commerce there, greatly increased, &c. and that the same, or the greatest part thereof, was purchased and obtained, for great and valuable considerations, and some other parts thereof gained by conquest, with much difficulty, and at the only endeavours, expence and charge of them and their associates, and those under whom they claim, subdued and improved, and thereby become a considerable addition of our dominions and interest there. Now, KNOW YE, That in consideration thereof, and in regard the said colony is remote from other the English plantations in the place aforesaid, and to the end the affairs and business which shall from time to time happen, or arise concerning the same, may be duly ordered and managed; we have therefore thought fit, &c."

Through this portal, majesty itself, like the meridian sun, lightens upon the subject, and makes plain and clear a matter, which the wits and disputers of a venal age, would envelope in midnight obscurity. In consideration that these discoveries, settlements, &c. were obtained for great and valuable considerations, &c. and at their, viz. the colonist's only endeavours and expence of blood and treasure, and in regard that they are remote, so that they cannot otherwise enjoy the benefits of civil government, &c. therefore, it is most reasonable and necessary, that they should have a government of their own. These constitutions are in some respects various in different colonies; all have their assemblies, or parliaments, consisting of the governor, council, and the representatives of the people; invested with the supreme power of legislation and taxation; though in some, their laws are subject to be negativ'd by the royal dissent, within a limited time: in some, the governor and council are chosen by the people, in others, the council; and in some, both governor and council are appointed by the crown. All have their courts of judicature, to take cognizance of all causes, arising within their territorial limits, and the power of judging in the last resort, though this right hath been infringed in sundry instances, by appeals to the king and council. But how a judgment in England can be executed in America, according to the course of law, is to me a paradox.

Further, it is ordained and declared, "That all and every of the subjects of us, our heirs, &c. which shall go to inhabit in said colony, and every of their children that shall happen to be born there, or on the sea in going to or returning from thence, shall have and enjoy all liberties and immunities of free and natural subjects, within any the dominions of us, our heirs or successors, to all intents, constructions and purposes whatever, as if they and every of them were born within the realm of England." This doth not bring the Americans within the realm of England; but it proves them to be out of it: For were it not so, the granting to them and to their children privileges equal to natural subjects, born within the realm, would have been idle and unnecessary, being no more than they would have been entitled to without it, after setling the foundation principles, and enumerating a variety of capital articles in the constitution of their governments; to avoid prolixity and all mistake and omissions in a recital of their rights and priviledges; they are in short, summed up and declared to be similar and as ample in every respect, as those of the natural born subjects of the realm, to which the colonists are referred, to learn the full extent of their own; which demonstrates the similarity and likeness that subsists between the civil constitutions of the two countries; although several and distinct; and the lands are granted to be holden, not in capite, or by knight service, but in free and common soccage, as of the manor of East-Greenwich; paying therefor a certain proportion of the gold and silver ore, that should from time to time be found, &c. in lieu of all services, duties and demands whatsoever. Thus, whether the Americans, antecedent to their constitutions, were subjects of the kingdom of England or not, they have now the clearest right to enjoy the liberties and privileges of English subjects: and to hold their lands discharged of all duties and demands of every kind, except as above. And nothing is plainer, than that the colonists cannot enjoy such privileges, unless they have parliaments and assemblies of their own; invested with the supreme power of legislation and taxation, in which they may be represented, and for this I have a very great and antient authority, viz. the case of the Virginians, determined by one of the Kings of England, near a century and a half ago, which, to use the words of the English historian, is as follows: "The government of this province was not at first adapted to the principles of the English constitution, and to the enjoyment of that liberty, to which a subject of Great-Britain thinks himself entitled, in every part of the globe. It was governed by a Governor and Council appointed by the King of Great-Britain. As the inhabitants increased, the inconveniency of this form became more grievous; and a new branch was added to their constitution, by which the people, who had formerly no consideration, were allowed to elect their representatives from each county, with privileges resembling those of the representatives of the Commons of England; thus two houses, the upper and lower house of assembly were formed; the upper house appointed by the crown are stiled honourable, and answer in some measure to the house of peers in the British constitution. The lower house is the guardian of the people's liberties. And thus, with a Governor representing the King, and an upper and lower house of assembly, this government bears a striking resemblance to our own." Now, if the parliament hath right to bind the colonists in any instance of legislation and taxation, it hath in all: Wherein, then, will consist the similarity of the colony constitutions to that of Great-Britain? Wherein the power of their assemblies to guard the rights of the people? In fine, where is the boasted English liberties of the subjects? All laid in the dust, and the colonies subjected to be governed and taxed by the parliament, who are, and their constituents both, interested in augmenting their taxes and burdens.

Realm signifies kingdom; and kingdom signifies the country or countries, that are subject to one sovereign prince. And should a school boy be asked, whether America, which is three thousand miles distant, was within the kingdom of Great-Britain, both being subject to one prince, he must answer that it was not; but that it was within the kingdom of the King of Great-Britain and America. Nor are the following questions more difficult, viz. whether the House of Commons, who have only a representative authority, have right to bind those whom they do not represent? Or whether, in virtue of their being the representatives of the people in Great-Britain, they are the representatives of the people in America? viz. whether the Britons and the Americans are identically the same persons, or whether the Britons are, have, or ought to have, every thing, and the Americans nothing? If the colonies, when they were first constituted, were not subject to the jurisdiction of parliament, they are not become so, by any thing since: and that they were not is evident, not only from the declaration of the King in the constitutions, but by the royal conduct towards them from time to time, treating them as though they were not.

Upon the remonstrance of the Virginians against the imposition of duties on their trade, King Charles the second issued a declaration under his privy seal, dated 19th of April, A. D. 1676, "affirming, that taxes ought not to be laid upon the proprietors and inhabitants of the colony, but by the common consent of the General Assembly." And when a revenue was wanted for the support of civil government in Virginia, in A. D. 1679, an act was framed and sent over to be passed by their Assembly, in these words, "Enacted by the King's most excellent Majesty, by and with the consent of the General Assembly of the colony of Virginia, that a duty of, &c." which was accordingly passed into a law.

And it was declared by James the first and Charles first, when a bill was proposed in the House of Commons, and repeatedly and strenuously urged, to give liberty to the subjects of England to fish on the coast of America; "that it was unnecessary, that the colonies were without the realm and jurisdiction of parliament, and that the Privy Council would take orders in matters relating to them." And liberty of fishing in America, is reserved in some of the charters that were afterwards made; which shews that without such reservation, they would not have had right to fish on the coast of the colonies. And upon complaint of piracies, &c. committed off the coast of Connecticut, King Charles the second, in A. D. 1683-4, instead of causing an act of Parliament to be made to restrain and punish them, writes this letter to the General Assembly in Connecticut, which letter, is not extant in the hands of the Secretary. "Charles Rex, trusty and well-beloved, we greet you well: Whereas we are informed of great disorders and depredations daily committed, to the prejudice of our allies; contrary to treaties between us and a good correspondence that ought to be maintained between christian princes and states; and we having already given strict order in our Island of Jamaica, against such illegal proceedings, by passing a law for restraining and punishing privateers and pirates, &c. our will and pleasure is, that you take care that such a law (a copy whereof is herewith sent you) be passed within our colony, under your government, which you are to certify unto us by the first opportunity, so we bid you heartily farewell. Given at our Court at New-Market, the 8th day of March, A. D. 1683-4, in the 36th year of our reign. By his Majesty's command. L. Jenkins." And accordingly the bill was passed into a law by the General Assembly of Connecticut. Can it be supposed, that this bill would have been sent to Connecticut to be passed into a law, if the Parliament had had jurisdiction thereof? Further, Great-Britain sending their culprits into banishment in America, demonstrates, that America is out of the jurisdiction of that kingdom, for banishment consists in putting a subject out of the limits and jurisdiction of the government. It is in the memory of every one, that the King sent his requisitions to the colonies to raise men and money in the last war, which were readily complied with, by his most dutiful and loyal subjects, in the provinces: Wherefore was this, if the Parliament hath supreme legislative and taxative jurisdiction over them? And to put this matter beyond all doubt, and to shew that the colonies have right, not only to enjoy, but to defend themselves, and their liberties, against any and all (the parliament not excepted) that should be so stupid, or vile, as to invade them; hear the solemn declaration and warrant of their King, in their original constitutions: "And we do for us, our heirs and successors, give and grant unto, &c. and their successors, by these presents, that it shall and may be lawful to and for the chief command- ers, governors and officers of the said company for the time being, who shall be resident in the parts, &c. hereafter men- tioned, and others inhabiting there, by their leave, admittance, &c. from time to time, and at all times hereafter, for their special defence and safety, to assemble, martial array, and put in warlike posture, the inhabitants of the said colony, and commissionate, impower and authorise such person or persons as they shall think fit to lead and conduct the said inhabitants; and to encounter, expulse, repel and resist, by force of arms, as well by sea as by land; and also to kill, slay and destroy, by all fitting ways, enterprises and means whatsoever, all and every such person or persons, as shall at any time hereafter, attempt or enterprise the destruction, invasion, detriment or annoy- ance of the said inhabitants or plantation; and to use and exer- cise the law martial, &c. and to take or surprize, by all ways and means whatsoever, all and every such person or persons, with their ships, armour, ammunition, and other goods of such as shall in such hostile manner, invade, or attempt the defeating of the said plantation, or the hurt of the said com- pany and inhabitants." Thus, these liberties and priviledges are not only granted and confirmed, but a power is expressly given to the colonies to defend them to the utmost, against those who should invade or attempt to destroy them. And are the Americans chargeable with treason and rebellion, for yielding to the irresistable impulses of self-preservation, and acting under and in pursuance of the royal licence and authority of their king? It is certain that the colonies, in all their constitu- tions, were considered as being out of the jurisdiction of par- liament, from the provisions made in every one, to supply the want of such jurisdiction, by investing their several assemblies with supreme power of legislation; and that their kings ever considered and treated them as being so, until that fatal period when George Grenville, that monster of ministers, came into administration; and that the colonies so understood themselves to be.

From all which I think we may infer, with great clearness and certainty, that he that is king of Great-Britain, is, by the constitutions of the colonies, also king of the American colonies, bound to protect and govern them according to their several constitutions, and not to destroy them: and that the parliament hath no jurisdiction or power with respect to them; for the parliament consists of the three estates, the king, lords and commons, and was constituted for the government of that realm; and the king sustains a three-fold capacity, as king of Great-Britain, the first of the three estates in parliament, and as king of the American colonies, and according to the maxim of the English laws, *Quando duo jura concurrent in una & eadem persona, idem est, ac si essent in diversis*; when several rights or capacities meet and are vested in one and the same person, they remain entire, and as distinct as though they were vested in different persons. This right of sovereignty over the Americans, is derived from a different source from that of Great-Britain, viz. the constitutions of the colonies, extends to different objects, viz. the colonies, and is exercisable in a different manner, viz. according to their several constitutions. And what the king doth as king of Great-Britain, or as one of the estates in parliament, he doth not as king of the colonies; for if so, then all the judges and officers appointed in the realm of England, would be judges and officers in America; all the laws and taxes that receive the royal assent in parliament, would immediately be binding upon the Americans, unless expresly excepted; contrary to the united voice of all their princes, politicians and lawyers, which is, that even Ireland, which they hold as a conquered country, is not bound by acts of parliament, unless specially named. The Lords being the noble peers of that realm, set in parliament in right of their estates and dignity, their authority cannot extend beyond the limits of the kingdom of which they are peers. The House of Commons, act by a delegated authority, and can have no greater power than their constituents can give, and their constituents can give no greater than they have; and from whence, in the name of common sense, have the people of Great-Britain right of dominion over the persons, properties and liberties of the good people in America?

But some may object, that upon these principles, the colonies have an unlimited power of legislation, &c. within themselves,

contrary to an express clause in their constitutions, which restrains them from making laws, &c. contrary to the laws of the
realm of England.

These constitutions are to be considered, not only as the
stipulations of the sovereign and the particular colonies with
whom they are made, but also of the colonists among them-
selvs; although they are conceived wholly in the style and language of grants from the crown. And the language of the
clause referred to in the objection, is after this manner, "and
we do further of, &c. give and grant unto the said Governor
and Company, &c. that it shall and may be lawful for them,
&c. to erect and make all necessary and proper judicatories; to
hear and decide all matters and causes, &c. and to make, ordain and establish all manner of wholsome and reasonable
laws, statutes, ordinances, directions and instructions, not
contrary to the laws of this our realm of England."

This restraint to colony legislation, cannot be construed to
extend the jurisdiction of parliament; for if it could, it would
be repugnant to the grant, & void; for parliament might make
laws contrary to all the laws the colonies have or could make;
in this sense, it would be reserving a power that would devour
and destroy all the powers constituted and granted in the patents, &c.

Nor is it to be understood, that the colonies may not make
laws respecting their own people, which are contrary to laws in
England, concerning a similar matter; for instance, in England
the laws permit persons of certain rank and estate to play at
games; in the colonies all persons without distinction are prohibited playing at games. By the laws of this our realm, then is
not meant, any particular rules and regulations of law; but the
grounds, principles and spirit of the laws and constitution,
then existing in the realm of England, on which the whole
system of their laws were founded, by which dictated, and to
which they were conformed. As the constitutions of the colonies were founded on the same principles with that of England,
and the colonists entitled to like privileges with the natural
subjects of that realm, and referred to the great charter of English liberties, to learn the full extent and nature of their own:
Therefore it is stipulated and granted, that they may make all
reasonable laws, &c. not contrary, to what? To the genius of

the laws and civil constitution of this our realm of England; for such would likewise be contrary to the genius of their own governments. Between which and the English constitution there is such a similarity, that you cannot thwart the principles of one, without contradicting the spirit of the other; and the sword that pierces the sides of one, penetrates the bowels of the other. This restriction is limited to the laws or system of government then in being in and over that realm: and doth not extend to any civil constitutions that might afterwards be made; nor to any laws made, or that should be made there, to extend to the colonies, out of that realm; for this would, as hath been shewn, be repugnant to the grant; and further, such would not be the laws of that realm, but of the colonies. This clause therefore, instead of restraining the colonies under the power of parliament, doth demonstrate them to be distinct states, without and independent of the jurisdiction of parliament.

I am not insensible, that by act of parliament 7 and 8 Will. III. cap. 22. it is declared, that all laws, by laws, usuages and customs which shall be in practice in any of the plantations, repugnant to any law made, or to be made in England relative to the said plantations, shall be utterly void and of none effect. And by stat. 6 of Geo. III. cap. 12. It is further declared, that all his Majesties colonies and plantations in America, have been, are, and of right ought to be, subordinate to and dependant on the imperial crown and parliament of Great-Britain, who have full power and authority to make laws and statutes of sufficient validity, to bind the colonies and people of America, subjects of the crown of Great-Britain, in all cases whatsoever, with a number of other statutes of the present reign, founded on the same principles and of the same fatal tendency. By these statutes, the Americans are deprived of all authority, even to make a by-law; and of all their liberties and properties; by subjecting both to the arbitrary power and disposal of parliament, in all cases whatsoever. Let these statutes be executed upon the Americans; and what, in the name of wonder, I ask, what will they have left, that has even the shadow of power or privilege, natural, civil, or religious; that they will be able to exercise and enjoy? But let us examine the ground and authority of these acts that sound such a peal, the knell of American freedom.

It is not the parliament's declaring a thing to be so, that

makes it so, nor their enjoining a thing to be done, that makes it a duty to do it. Should the parliament, in the plenitude of their power, pass an act, that the four elements have been, are, and ought to be subordinate to, and dependant on the jurisdiction of parliament; and that they have full power, &c. to make laws of sufficient validity to bind them, in all cases whatsoever. And that there should be neither rain nor sunshine, seed time nor harvest, in all the continent of America, for three years and seven months; would the elements and the heavens be guilty of treason and rebellion, if they pursued their antient course: And are not the liberties of men, who are appointed lords of this lower creation, of more importance than those of the elements, and are they not equally sacred and inviolable?

The obligation of obedience to a law, arises wholly from the authority of the makers, over those on whom it is enjoined; so that if the Americans are naturally independant of the power of parliament, and by no concessions and civil constitutions of their own have submitted thereto, and put themselves under it; no acts of parliament can make them dependant. And if the parliament hath no right of dominion over the Americans; it follows that the Americans are under no obligation of obedience to its laws.

I cannot but remark upon the singular phraseology of this declaratory act of parliament, viz. that all his Majesty's colonies (not our colonies) have been, are, and of right ought to be subordinate to, and dependant on the imperial crown and parliament of Great-Britain, who have full power and authority to make laws and statutes of sufficient validity to bind the colonies and people in America, subjects of the crown of Great-Britain, in all cases whatsoever. What strange circumlocution of law language is used to express what they meant to conceal! What is the amount of this declaratory act? That the parliament has full power and authority to make laws, &c. to bind the colonies and people of America in all cases whatsoever? no, but to bind the colonies and people of America subjects of the crown of Great-Britain, viz. They have power to bind the subjects of the crown of Great Britain in America. Now if the colonies are not subjects of the crown of Great-Britain, viz. are not subjects of the King in virtue of his crown of that kingdom, then by their own declaration the parliament hath no right to bind them. And it is very evident from what has been said, that the King's right of sovereignty over the colonies is not derived from, or holden in virtue of his crown, as King of Great-Britain; but from the particular stipulations entered into with the colonies by their several constitutions; otherwise their constitutions would have been idle and unnecessary. Nor will it help the matter, should we for argument's sake, yield to them that the colonies were subjects of the crown of Great-Britain; then they would be entitled to the privileges of subjects, which is an exemption from legislation or taxation without their voice or consent. So that whether the colonies are or are not subjects of the crown of Great-Britain, the act is altogether unfounded.

But it may be objected to the colonies claim of exemption from the jurisdiction of parliament on account of their not being represented; that there are many persons of property, and large towns in England who do not vote in the election of representatives to parliament, yet are bound by its laws, &c. There is no borough, city, town, or shire in England, nor any man of competent estate and a subject of the kingdom, but what may have a voice in the election of representatives to parliament; if, therefore, some do wave a privilege which they might enjoy, their stupidity ought to be a warning, and not an example for the Americans to imitate: Nor doth it by any means follow, that because some are bound, who might and will not send representatives; that therefore, the parliament hath right to bind all, even those who cannot, if they would, be represented. Besides, every member of parliament, though chosen by one particular district, when elected and returned, serves for the whole realm; and no laws or taxes are made and imposed on such, but what equally affect those that make them, and their constituents. The case of the unrepresented Americans is directly the reverse; they cannot be represented, and the burthens laid on them proportionably alleviate the burthens of those that impose them, and their constituents.

Again, it may be objected, that several acts of parliament respecting America, have been acquiesced in, &c. Neither the parliament's making laws, nor the American's acquiescing therein, can create an authority to make them on one hand, nor an obligation to obey them on the other, though they may be considered as some evidence thereof. From the first settlement of the colonies, to the conclusion of the last war, no taxes, or duties have been claimed, or imposed by act of parliament in America, for the purpose of raising a revenue, unless the act respecting the post-office is considered as such. The first act that was made to extend to America, equally extended to Asia and Africa; and was made in the 12th of Charles II. merely for the regulation of trade; requiring all English goods to be shipped in English vessels, and navigated by English mariners. The 25th of the same reign produced the first act that imposed duties for any purpose in America, and the preamble declares it to be for the regulation of trade only; nor are the avails appropriated to any part of the revenue: Yet this produced an insurrection in Virginia, agents were sent to England on the account; and a declaration obtained from the King under his privy seal, dated April 19th, A. D. 1676 "That taxes ought not to be laid upon the proprietors and inhabitants of the colony, but by the common consent of the General Assembly." The other acts that respected the colonies, except the 7 and 8 of Will. III. antea, were for the regulation of trade only, until of late; the duties were never acquiesced in, were always murmered at, protested against, as being oppressive and unjust, and eluded as far as possible. And as the trade of the colonies was, of choice, principally with Great-Britain and the British Islands, many of those acts did not much affect them in their interest or inclination. If such an acquiescence may be construed a submission to acts of parliament; the nonuser of such power by parliament, for so long a time, may, with greater reason, be construed a relinquishment thereof. For the non user of a power, by those that are able to exercise such power, is greater evidence against the existence of it, than the non-resistence of thousands is for it, who are incapable of making resistance.

But it will be said that the post-office in America was by act of parliament and is for the express purpose of raising a revenue.

The post-office is a convenient and useful institution, and on that account, it hath been received and used in America, and not on account of the act of parliament; and derives all its authority, in America, from its being received and adopted there: As many of the rules of the Roman civil law, are received and adopted by universal consent in England, and are obligatory upon the people, not from the authority of the Roman

Emperors that ordained them, but from their own act in receiving and adopting them. Further, the act of parliament forbids all persons to carry or transport any letters, &c. by land or water, on pain of severe penalties, except the post-master or his deputies: And it is well known, that this part of the act was daily violated; yet no person was ever prosecuted: Which shews that the post-office in America was not such, as the parliament had enacted; but such as the universal consent and practice of the people there had made it; and also, how little deference is paid to acts of parliament in America.

From all the cases of pretended acquiescence to acts of parliament, nothing can be inferred favourable to the jurisdiction of parliament, for either it was for the interest of the Americans to comply with them, or it was not; if the former, then they complied, not from a principle of obedience to them; but from motives of interest and inclination; if the latter, then they demonstrate the incompetency of parliament to make laws for the Americans; who thro' ignorance, or some other principle, hath enjoined what is prejudicial. And no wise constitution would vest a power in any body of men, who, from their situation and circumstances, are and must be, necessarily incompetent for the proper exercise of it.

It may be objected, that all these charters and colony constitutions were made by and with the King, in his political capacity, as the supreme head of the kingdom; and that whatever he doth as such, is in virtue of authority derived from the kingdom; and for the use and benefit thereof, and not with and for the King only.

These constitutions, are either the compacts of both the king and kingdom of Great-Britain with the colonies; entered into by the King for himself, and in behalf of his kingdom, or they are the compacts of the King only.

If the former, then the kingdom of Great-Britain, as well as the King, is a party to them, bound and concluded by them; and can have no greater authority over the colonies, than is therein expressly stipulated, and in no other manner than is therein provided. For if the kingdom will take the benefit of the King's acts, it must in those respects, be likewise bound by them. And there is not the least colour of legislative authority in the colony constitutions, stipulated or reserved to the parliament, over the persons or properties of the Americans, except in one or two instances, which are altogether singular, and as absurd as singular, but full and compleat power of legislation is vested in the General Assemblies of the several colonies—subject only in some, to the royal dissent within a limited time; and to have the colony Assemblies, subject at the same time to the legislative power of Parliament, would be constituting an *imperium in imperio*, one supreme power within another, the height of political absurdity.

But if these constitutions, are the compacts of the King, only with the colonies, then the kingdom and parliament of Great-Britain have no power over them, more than they and their Assemblies have over the kingdom and parliament, for they are distinct sister states, neither having any power or authority over the other. And that these constitutions, were entered into and granted by the King for himself only, is evident, in that, no mention is made in them of the parliament, except as above, and in them the reservation is void, being against Magna Charta: Or of their being made by the King, in behalf of himself and kingdom; and this most certainly the King is capable of doing; for the King considered in his natural capacity as a man, is subject to all the frailties of human nature, hath sensations of pleasure and pain, which are his own, and may make contracts and be bound by them, although in his political capacity he is by way of eminence stiled perfect, &c.

In his political capacity he also hath certain prerogatives, royal rights and interests, which are his own, and not the kingdom's; and these he may alienate by gift or sale, &c.

Should France offer the King of Great-Britain the crown of that kingdom, and he accept it; could not France be subject to the King, without being subject to the kingdom of Great-Britain, and subordinate to the power of parliament? Upon these principles, should the King of England be elected Emperor of Germany, the British parliament, would legislate for the whole Germanic body. And the case would not be otherwise, with a people in a state of nature, that should make choice of the King of Great-Britain for their King, and he accept thereof, they would not thereby, elect the kingdom for their masters nor be subjected to its parliament. Thus, whether these constitutions are considered as the compacts of the King and kingdom of Great-Britain, or only of the King, the colonies are clearly out of the reach of the jurisdiction of parliament,—and it is evident that they were originally intended so to be, and all the advantages expected from them by Great-Britain, were their trade, which has far exceeded their most sanguine expectations. For these constitutions were not entered into and granted by the King in virtue of his being the King of Great-Britain; the King of France or Prussia might have done the same; or any individual, the Americans should have elected for their King. The force and authority of these constitutions, is not derived from any antecedent right in the crown of Great-Britain to grant them; but from the mutual agreements and stipulations contained in them, between the crown of Great-Britain and the colonies.

Further, it is objected, that the settlement of the crown is by act of parliament; and the colonies do acknowledge him to be their King, on whom the crown is thus settled, consequently in this they do recognize the power of parliament.

The colonies do and ever did acknowledge the power of parliament to settle and determine who hath right, and who shall wear the crown of Great-Britain; but it is by force of the constitutions of the colonies only, that he, who is thus crowned King of Great Britain, becomes King of the colonies. One designates the King of the colonies, and the other makes him so.

Lastly it is objected, that in all civil states it is necessary, there should some where be lodged a supreme power over the whole.

The truth of this objection will not be contested; but its application in the present argument is to be considered. If Great-Britain and America both constitute but one civil state, then it is necessary that there should be one supreme power, lodged either in Great-Britain or America, in such manner as is consistent with the liberties of the subjects. But if they are distinct states, then it is necessary, that there should be a supreme power lodged in each. The only thing then to be done is to prove, that Great-Britain and America are distinct states. And this point hath been already considered; so that little new can be said upon it. However it may be observed, that a civil state, is a country or body of people that are connected and united under one and the same constitution of civil government; by this the kingdoms and states in Germany and other parts of Europe are distinguished and known. Now there is no such civil constitution existing, as that of Great-Britain and America.

Great-Britain hath its civil constitution; the colonies have their's; and though, the spirit and principles of them are similar, yet the constitutions of the two countries are entirely distinct and several: The constitution of Great-Britain is not the constitution of the colonies, nor *vice versa*. They are two countries, three thousand miles distant from each other, inhabited by different people, under distinct constitutions of government, with different customs, laws and interests, both having one King. Now, if any can believe that Great-Britain and America are but one civil state, they must overthrow the doctrine of identity and diversity, confound all distinctions in nature, and believe that two is one and one is two. Further, they are and must be distinct states from the nature of their situation, and in order to their enjoying the privileges of their respective governments. And the constitutions of civil government ought to be erected on the foundation of reason and be conformable to the nature of things; nor is it difficult to conceive of two distinct countries, independent of each other, each having its own civil constitutions, laws, parliaments, courts, commerce and interest, united under one sovereign Prince. And would it be necessary that there should be in one of these states, a supreme power over the persons and properties of the other? If it would, then it follows, that it would be necessary in such case that the subjects of one should be slaves to the other, incapable of liberty or property. Are not Hanover and Saxony distinct states, both within the empire, and subordinate to the imperial crown of Germany? They are. And is not this the case of Great-Britain and America? Two distinct states, or countries under one sovereign Prince, both equally his subjects and incapable of being slaves? Each invested with plenary powers of government, in their several countries? This is really the situation of the colonies; and not to admit of a system of civil government, adapted to their situation, or to insist on the exercise of such powers over them, as are inconsistent with, and subversive of their natural and constitutional rights and liberties, is really pointing the controversy, not merely at the Americans, but at the great former and ruler of the universe, for making and situating them as they are. From all which it follows that the colonies are distinct states from that of Great-Britain; have and ought to have a supreme power of government lodged in them.

Thus, the question is reduced to a single point, either the parliament hath no such power over the persons and properties of the Americans as is claimed, or the Americans are all slaves. Slavery consists in being wholly under the power and controul of another, as to our actions and properties: And he that hath authority to restrain and controul my conduct in any instance, without my consent, hath in all. And he that hath right to take one penny of my property, without my consent, hath right to take all. For, deprive us of this barrier of our liberties and properties, our own consent; and there remains no security against tyranny and absolute despotism on one hand, and total abject, miserable slavery on the other. For power is entire and indivisible; and property is single and pointed as an atom. All is our's, and nothing can be taken from us, but by our consent; or nothing is our's, and all may be taken, without our consent. The right of dominion over the persons and properties of others, is not natural, but derived; and there are but two sources from whence it can be derived; from the almighty, who is the absolute proprietor of all, and from our own free consent. Why then wrangle we so long about a question so short and easy of decision? Why this mighty din of war, and garments roll'd in blood; the seas covered with fleets, the land with armies, and the nation rushing on swift destruction? Let the parliament shew their warrant, the diploma and patent of their power to rule over America, derived from either of the above fountains, and we will not contend; but if they cannot, wherefore do they contend with us? For even a culprit has right to challenge of the executioner, the warrant of his power, or refuse submission.

The question is not whether the king is to be obeyed or not, for the Americans, have ever recognized his authority as their rightful sovereign, and liege lord; have ever been ready, with their lives and fortunes, to support his crown and government, according to the constitutions of the nation; and now call upon him as their liege lord (whom he is bound to protect) for protection, on pain of their allegiance, against the army, levied by the British parliament, against his loyal and dutiful subjects in America.

Nor is the question Whether the Americans would be independent or not, unless the state they have ever enjoyed hath been such; for they ever have acknowledged themselves to be subjects of the king, subordinate to, and dependent on the crown, but not on the parliament of Great-Britain, unless any should think there is no medium between submission to parliament, and perfect independance.—But the question is, Whether the parliament of Great-Britain hath power over the persons and properties of the Americans, to bind the one, and dispose of the other at their pleasure? Hear the language of parliament in their acts disposing of the property of the Americans: "*We, your Majesty's dutiful subjects, the Commons of Great-Britain, in parliament assembled, have therefore resolved to give and grant unto your Majesty, the several rates and duties hereinafter mentioned, &c. in America.*"—Here the Commons in England are pluming themselves on their great liberality to their sovereign, with the property of the Americans, as though it was all their own. If the parliament have no such power as is claimed, their invading our rights, and in them the rights of the constitution, under pretence of authority; besieging and desolating our sea ports, employing dirty tools, whose sordid souls, like vermin, delight to riot on filth; to practice every artifice to seduce, that they may the easier destroy; with money tempting, with arms terrifying the inhabitants, to induce and compel a servile submission; is treason against the kingdom, of the deepest die, and blackest complexion: whereby the constitution, that firm foundation of the nation's peace, and pillar of government that supports the throne, is shaken to its very basis; the kingdom rent, and devided against itself; and those sons of thunder that should be the protectors of its rights, are become its destroyers. Nor will American freedom fall alone; Great-Britain's shakes, totters, and must tumble likewise, nor long survive the catastrophe: And the Americans resisting the measures, and defending against the force used to accomplish these dreadful events, and precipitate the nation into total, irreparable ruin and destruction, are deeds of the greatest loyalty to their king, and the constitution that supports him on the throne, and of fidelity to his government. For subjects to levy war against their king, is treason, but the king's levying war against his subjects, is a crime of royal magnitude, and wants a name. Should the king of France join with the enemies of his kingdom, and levy war against his subjects, would he notwithstanding, retain his royal authority over them, and they be incapable of defence against such an unnatural attack, without incurring the crime of treason and rebellion? If so, wo! to the inhabitants of kingdoms, for, by reason of their kings, the earth would be made desolate.

Let none be dismayed at the strength and power of our oppressors; nor at the horrors of war into which we are compelled, for the necessary defence of our rights. Can we expect the laurels, without entering the list? To be crowned without being tried? The fairest fruits are always most obnoxious to the birds of prey: English liberties, the boast and glory of the nation, the admiration of its friends, and envy of its foes; were obtained, sword in hand, from king John, by his free and spirited barons; and what rivers of blood have been shed, to maintain and defend them, against the encroachments of succeeding kings, to the time of the glorious revolution, is well known to all, acquainted with the English history. Such is the state of the world, that the way to freedom and glory, is a way of danger and conflict. The road to Canaan was through the desert and the deep; and the grave is the subterranean path to celestial bliss. And let it not be forgotten that those of Israel whose hearts failed them through fear of being destroyed by their enemies, and discouraged their brethren, were destroyed of their maker. Nor ought any to think, by joining themselves to the enemies of their country, they shall escape, however fair the promises, or great the reward; and though they should not meet with their deserts, from the hands of their injured countrymen: for the minister wants your assistance to destroy your fellows, only, that yourselves may be the easier destroyed; and when you have done his drudgery, you will become his prey. *Divide & impera, divide & distrue, divide & command, divide and destroy*, are maxims of deep policy, fabricated in a very old cabinet.

IV. I shall now proceed in the last place to consider this question in another light, viz. the equity of the demand made upon the colonies, and of the manner in which it is made. The ill policy of such measures, having in a most inimitable manner, been considered and exposed by those illustrious patriots, the Earl of Chatham, Burke, Barre, the Bishop of Asaph, &c. (whose names and memories no distance of place or time, will be able to obliterate from the grateful minds of the Americans) with such dignity of sentiment, energy and perspecuity of reason, such rectitude of intention, uncorruptness and candor of disposition, and with such force of elocution, as must have rendered them irresistable, only by the omnipotence of parliament.

Great-Britain can have no demands upon the old colonies, except for assistance afforded them against their enemies in war, and protection to their trade at sea; for the lands were neither acquired or settled at the expence of the crown. New York, indeed, was obtained by conquest from the Dutch, without much risk or loss; and was afterwards in the treaty at Breda, A. D. 1667, confirmed to the English in exchange for Surinam. Nor have those colonies since, been any expence to the crown, either for support of their governments, or inhabitants: And the Americans have had no enemies but what were equally the enemies of Great-Britain; nor been engaged in any wars, but what the nation was equally engaged in, except the wars with the Indians; which they carried on and maintained themselves. It will be necessary to state the advantages the Americans have been to Great-Britain, as well as those they have derived from thence, by assistance afforded in the wars, and by comparing, strike the ballance.

From the first settlement of the colonies, they have been almost continually engaged in a bloody and expensive, tho' successful war with the French and Indians, on their frontiers, until the reduction of Canada; whereby their settlements were extended; and by a rapid population, the number of inhabitants have been greatly encreased; and the trade to England proportionably augmented. In A. D. 1690, Sir William Phips raised an army in New-England, took Port Royal, or Annapolis, in Nova-Scotia, from the French; and reduced another settlement of considerable consequence, at the mouth of the river St. John's, on the Bay of Fundy, both which, king William ceded to the French at the peace of Riswick, A.D. 1697; and received an equivalent for them. In A. D. 1703, the beginning of Queen Ann's war, Annapolis was retaken, by the New-England people.

Afterwards Sir William Phips, with the New-England People, attempted the reduction of Canada, and was obliged to return, not by the arms of the enemy, but by the severity of the season coming on earlier than usual: However, he built a fort on the mouth of Pemaquid on the frontiers of the country, which reduced all the Indians, North West of Merimac river, under the crown of England. By these successes, Great-Britain was induced to engage in an expedition against Quebec. In A. D. 1711, Admiral Walker was sent to Boston, with a fleet, and some land forces; New-England furnished their quota of troops for the expedition; but by reason of the great fogs, and some mistake of the pilot's, part of the fleet was stove upon the rocks; eight hundred of the men lost, and the expedition rendered abortive. Annapolis, and all Nova-Scotia was confirmed to Great-Britain, at the peace of Utrecht, A. D. 1713; whereby all that country, its valuable fisheries, and trade, were added to the crown of Great-Britain. Not to mention the ineffectual, but costly expedition, formed by the New-England people against Canada, in A.D. 1740; and that against the Island of Cuba, at another time. On the 16th of June, A.D. 1745, the important fortress of Louisbourgh surrendered to Commodore Warren, and Mr. Pepperel; reduced by a long and perilous siege of forty-nine days (through the smiles of heaven) by the valour and intrepidity of American troops, assisted by Commodore Warren, with a small squadron in the harbour; by which, the command of the Newfoundland fishery, the gulph of St. Lawrence, the only pass by sea to Quebec, the capital of the French settlements in America, fell into the hands of the English, and which afterwards purchased the peace of Europe, and procured to the crown of England, in the peace of Aix Chappelle, sundry important places that had been taken. Thus, the Americans laboured, fought and toiled; and the Britons reaped the advantage. The noble exertions of the Americans, and the part they took in the last war; their laudable emulation to be foremost, in complying with the requisitions of their sovereign; their troops contending for stations of danger, as posts of distinction; esteeming their lives and their properties, an inconsiderable sacrifice, for the glory of their king, and the renown of his arms; and the large levies of men and money made by them, are fresh in every one's memory. The amazing advantages derived from the war in America, to the crown and kingdom of Great-Britain, is also well known. The whole eastern and northern country, the New-foundland fishery, trade, and navigation, a source of boundless wealth; the island of Cape-Breton, the extensive country of Canada and Louisiana, from the arctic pole, to the tropic of Cancer, with their train of fortresses, lakes, &c. the peltry and furr trade of that whole country, with the almost inexhaustable treasures of the Havanna; a harvest in which the Americans, with the Britons, bore the heat and burthen of the day; yet the Americans shared little or none of the fruit, except being delivered from troublesome neighbours, on their frontiers, and some individuals drawing a share in the plunder, at the Havanna. And what a mighty accession of weight and importance was this, to the crown of Great-Britain, in the scale of power, among the European states and princes! But why need I dwell upon these? At the conclusion of the last war, justice swayed the sceptre; and a righteous minister had the royal ear; the Americans were considered as creditors to the nation; and thousands of pounds were sent over to reimburse them. But Oh! the sad reverse of times, ministers and of measures!

In the next place, let me enquire, in respect to the protection afforded our trade at sea. Our trade, from inclination and choice, hath been principally with Great-Britain and the British isles, and like the trade in all cases, carried on between an infant country, in want of all kinds of manufactures, and an old, wealthy, manufacturing kingdom. Our's was of necessity and for consumption; their's for profit and advantage. They purchased of us our raw materials, and sold to us their wrought manufactures; both at their own price, and at their own ports. In this view of the matter, must it not be supposed, that the advantages of this trade to that kingdom, amply paid for its protection; and their motives to protect it were their own emolument and profit? But this will be more fully illustrated, when we consider, that the amount of the trade between Great-Britain, and the colonies, at a medium for three years, before it was interrupted by these unhappy disputes, is computed at about three millions, three hundred and eighty-five thousand pounds per annum: From which deduct a certain proportion, for raw materials, that are imported into England, which is comparatively inconsiderable; the remainder is a clear profit and gain to Great-Britain; and is divided between the public exchequer, and private coffers—for the whole cost of the raw materials, the duties on the importation of them, the manufacturer's labour, his living and his family's, his taxes upon his house, windows, salt, soap, candles, coal, &c. &c. &c. upon his eatables, his drinkables, and cloathing; those of his family, his apprentices and journeymen; and not only so, but also the taxes his shoemaker, weaver, and taylor paid, when working for him; the merchants profits, the charges of bailage, truckage, freight, insurance; and the duties upon the articles themselves, all go in to make up the price, and are paid by the American consumer. In this view of the matter, I believe I am within bounds to suppose, that the direct trade, (leaving out of the question the cercuitous trade by way of the West-Indies and other parts) neats a profit of three millions to Great-Britain: And near one half of that sum, is made up of taxes and duties, which are paid in England; whereby the public revenue is so much increased & eventually is actually paid by the Americans.

Can any suppose, that this is not an ample compensation, for all the protection afforded our trade at sea? What nation in Europe would not rejoice to receive our trade on these terms, and give us thousands for its purchase? But, upon supposition it is not sufficient, and that the colonies are indebted to them; ought they not to state the account, that the balance might be seen; and to make a demand of payment? And not without doing either, thrust their hands into our pockets; and rend from thence, not only what we owe them, but what they please: Not only what we ought to pay, but our whole property; nor that only, but our liberties too. And if asked wherefore this? the answer is, that the nation is in debt, and that we owe them. If we owe them, let them make it appear, and the colonies will pay them; that the nation is in debt, needs no proof; but for what? For expence in war, and for charges of government in time of peace? Could these have accumulated—the enormous sum of 145,000000, the national debt in A. D. 1766? Bribery and corruption, luxury and exorbitant pensions multiplied, might.

But it is time to close these enquiries; and what may we not expect, from what is threatened and already done, that is in the power of parliament to do?

Is not the King of Great-Britain, the visible head of the christian church in England? and by the Quebec bill, is he not, as amply constituted the head of the romish church in Canada? Have not the Americans, by the constitution of nature, as men, by the constitution of England, as Englishmen, and by the constitutions in America, as colonists; a right of exemption from all laws, that are made, and taxes that are imposed, without their voice and consent? And from other mode of trial, than by their peers of the vicinity?

And by the late acts of parliament, are not taxes and duties imposed, and laws enacted to bind them, not only without, but in which, they neither had nor could have any voice? And is not the whole government, of that ancient province of the Massachusetts, demolished at a blow, by an engine of tyranny, without being summoned, heard or tried? Are not strange and unusual methods for imprisonment, transportation and trial, introduced? Arbitrary tribunals erected, to decide in matters most interesting, without the intervention of a jury? In a word, are not all our rights and liberties, natural, religious and civil, made a mark for their arrows, and threatened to be laid in the dust? And to compleat our ruin, are not our harbours blocked up? our coasts lined with fleets? our country filled with armed troops? our towns sacked? inhabitants plundered? friends slaughtered? our pleasant places desolated with fire and sword? all announced rebels? our estates declared forfeit; and our blood eagerly panted for? When I think of Boston, that unhappy capital; what she once was, and the miserable captive state, to which she is now reduced, I am almost ready to adopt the plaintive strains of captive Israel concerning her: "By the rivers of Babylon there we set down, yea, we wept when we remembered Zion; we hanged our harps upon the willows, in the midst thereof, for there they that carried us captive and wasted us, required of us a song and mirth, saying, sing us one of the songs of Zion. How shall we sing the Lord's song in a strange land? if I forget thee Oh Jerusalem! let my right hand forget her cunning, if I do not remember thee, let my tongue cleave to the roof of my mouth; if I prefer not Jerusalem, above my chief joy. Remember O Lord! the children of Edom, in the day of Jerusalem, who said rase it, rase it, even to the foundation thereof."

What shall we say, is there any force in sacred compacts and national constitutions? any honour in crowned heads? any faith to be put in ministers, the nobles and great men of the nation? In a word, is there any such thing as truth and justice? Is there not a power above us? and that there is all nature declares; the vindicator of right and avenger of wrong. To him therefore we make our last appeal; and to the impartial world, to judge between Great-Britain and America.

These unheard of intolerable calamities, spring not of the dust, come not causeless, nor will they end fruitless. THEY call on the Americans for repentance towards their maker, and vengeance on their adversaries. And can it be a crime to resist? Is it not a duty we owe to our maker, to our country, to ourselves and to posterity? Does not the principle of self-preservation, which is implanted by the author of nature in the human breast, (to operate instantaneous as the lightning, resistless as the shafts of war, to ward off impending danger) urge us to the conflict; add wings to our feet, firmness and unanimity to our hearts, impenatrability to our battalions, and under the influence of its mighty author, will it not render successful and glorious American arms? But it may be said that the Americans have destroyed the tea of the East-India company, at Boston, which was a violation of private property, & ought to be paid for. That tea was sent on the same errand that Gage and his troops are; to effect by artifice what they are now attempting by force. I mention not Thomas Hutchinson, for his crimes here, and condign punishment hereafter, without repentance, must exceed all conception or description. Should the British parliament cause cargoes of wine, impregnated with poison, to be sent to America, with orders to have them dispersed amongst the inhabitants: and their servants, the miscreants of their power, should obstinately insist on doing it, the Americans must destroy the wines, which, by their baneful mixture would be justly obnoxious to destruction, or be destroyed by their poison.

My countrymen, we have every thing to fear, from the malignity, power and cunning of our adversaries. Yet, from the justness of our cause, the greatness of our numbers and resources, the unanimity of our hearts, cemented by interest and by perils; the bravery, and what's more, the desperateness of our spirits; who think not life worth saving, when all that is dear in life is gone, we have reason to be afraid of nothing. For your animation, hear the advice and lamentation of a French gentleman, Monsieur Mezeray, over the lost liberties of his country, to an English subject: "We had once in France, the same happiness and the same privileges, which you now have. Our laws were made by representatives of our own choosing; therefore our money was not taken from us, but granted by us. Our Kings, were then subject to the rules of law and reason. Now alas! we are miserable and all is lost. Think nothing Sir, too dear to maintain these precious advantages, if ever there should be occasion; venture your life and estate, rather than basely submit to that abject condition to which you see us reduced."

And for your encouragement, turn your eyes to the free states of Holland and Switzerland; and in them, as in a glass, see America struggling under intolerable oppressions; and with an intrepid, unconquerable spirit, overlooking all danger, bursting the bonds, and demolishing the engines of tyranny, emerging from a sea of calamities, rising superior to every obstacle; and overlooking in time the power and towering heights of their haughty oppressors.

Since then we are compelled to take up the sword, in the necessary defence of our country, our liberties and properties, ourselves and posterity: Let us gird on the harness, having our bosoms mailed, with firm defiance of every danger; and with fixed determined purpose, to part with our liberty only with our lives, engage in the conflict; and nobly play the man for our country, the cities and churches of him that transplanted and hitherto sustained them; thereby prove the truth of our descent, and demonstrate to the world, that the free irrepressable spirit, that inspired the breasts and animated the conduct of our brave fore-fathers; is not degenerated in us, their offspring. With fair pretences, they invite us to submit our necks to their yoke; but with unheard of cruelties and oppressions, they determine us, to prefer death to submission. Let none be disheartened from a prospect of the expence; though it should be to the half, or even the whole of our estates. Compared with the prize at stake, our liberty, the liberty of our country, of mankind, and of millions yet unborn, it would be lighter than the dust on the balance: For if we submit, adieu for ever; adieu to property, for liberty will be lost, our only capacity of acquiring and holding property.

And what shall I say, of the officers and soldiers of the British army, who are the appointed ministers of this vengeance on the Americans? against whom are they come forth, in hostile array? Strangers and foes to them and their nation? No, it is against their brethren, their fellows and companions, of their flesh and of their bone; members of the same nation; subjects of the same King; and entitled to the same or equal privileges; with kindred blood in their veins, and a pulse beating high for English liberties. And can their hearts be courageous, and their hands strong, when they level the shaft, or lift up the spear against those, with whom of late, side by side and shoulder to shoulder, in compacted battalions, they fought, bled, and conquered, in defence of the country, and the liberties, they are now sent to lay waste and destroy. I appeal to their sense of honour, their sentiments of justice, to their bowels of human-ity, those tender feelings of sympathy, these social passions, that possess and warm the human heart, and are the spring of all social and public virtues, and let their tongues utter the sentiments of their souls, and America will be justified, they being the judges.

Methinks I hear the King, retired with his hand upon his breast, in pensive solliloquy, saying to himself, who, and what am I? A King, that wears the crown, and sways the scepter of Great-Britain and America; and though a King, robed in roy-alty, yet I am a man, my power finite, my body mortal, and myself accountable to him, who raised me to this dignity, that I might be his minister for the people's good. But Oh! what tragic scenes do I behold? One part of my dominions aiming destruction against the other, plunging their swords in the bosoms, and imbruing their hands in the blood of their fellows and brethren. Is it possible, that Britons should become the foes and assassins of Britons, or their descendants? My throne totters, my loins tremble, my kingdom is divided and torn, my heart ready to fail, for the glory of my reign is departing. What can be the cause of these tremenduous convulsions, that threaten the dissolution of my kingdom? Do my subjects in America, refuse to resign their liberties and properties, to the disposal of my subjects in Great-Britain? And insist on holding and enjoying them as their unalienable rights? Well, what will be the mighty injury to my crown, or to the nation, in its wealth, strength, or honour, if America should enjoy its former freedom? What will be gained by reducing them to submission and slavery? lifeless carcases, a desolated country, millions in wealth, and millions in strength dashed at a blow. Mighty acquisition of loss. Should the attempt be pursued and fail, America will be lost, nay more, she will become Great-Britain's determined enemy. Have not my subjects in Great-Britain rights that are sacred and inviolable, and which they would not resign but with their lives? They have. Have not my subjects in America rights equally sacred, and of which they are and ought to be equally tenacious? They have. And are not those rights, for which they now so earnestly contend, of that kind? Certainly there is much in favour of their claim. What if they are mistaken? Ought they to atone for their mistake by rivers of blood, and the sacrifice of themselves, their country and their posterity? but what, my mind shudders and recoils at the thought, what, if the Americans are right? Oh heaven forgive! And all this ghastly ruin, is owing to the blunder of a minister, and the fatal errors adopted by parliament. Of whom will these rivers of blood be required? What can expiate such accumulated wrongs? and atone for such amazing devastations? I am sorely distressed, civil war rages within, foreign enemies threaten without, the commerce of my kingdom languisheth, manufacturers famish and fail, and discontentment is almost universal. What shall I do for the dignity of my crown, the peace of my dominions, and the safety of the nation? All is at risk. I have been deceived by my informers, misguided by my ministers, and by my own inattention to the sufferings, and dutiful petitions of my subjects, reduced all to the most dreadful hazard. For British troops cease to be glorious, in so inglorious a cause. Should their sea-ports, from Georgia to Nova-Scotia, be desolated with fire and sword, it would only consolidate their union, and render more impregnable their resistance in the interior country. Could we dry up their harbours, and bar every out-let to the sea, unless we had power to restrain the showers and the shines of heaven; and the fertility of the earth, they will possess inexhaustable resources. America must and will be free, their ancestors acquired it for them, my royal predecessors guaranteed it to them; it is theirs by purchase, it is theirs by the plighted faith of Kings; they are deserving of it; and with them it flourisheth, like a plant of generous kind, in its native soil, and the heavens are propitious to liberty. My legions must be recalled, the sword must be sheathed, the olive branch, the symbol of peace be held out; for it was never designed that Britons, invinsible by others, should contend with Britons or their descendants, in battle; and royal munificence be exerted, to alleviate the distresses, console the miseries, and repair the injuries, caused by the unhappy error, which let eternal darkness veil. Oh! may the future make reparation for the past, my crown flourish in the prosperity, liberty, and the happiness of all my dominions. Thus will my reign become glorious, my demise tranquil. But alas! where am I transported on the wings of groundless fancy? Repentance I fear is too late, for crimes so enormous; the injuries are irreparable, and America is irretrievably lost: the thunders I prepared, to lay her breathless at my feet, have discharged her of her allegiance, and driven her forever from my power.

APPENDIX.

THE preceeding pamphlet was wrote some time past, and not published sooner for want of paper: The author hath subjoined an appendix, containing some thoughts on government, and American independance.

To consider things rightly, is to consider them truly as they are, with all their relations and attending circumstances; to investigate truth, is the highest atchievement of reason; and to follow nature, the perfection of art. That which is conformable to axioms of immutable truth, founded in reason, and productive of general security and happiness to mankind, must in every sense, be denominated good.

Civil society, is allowed by all to be the greatest temperal blessing; and civil government is absolutely necessary to its subsistence; it is a temporary remedy, against the ill effects of general depravity; and because the introduction of moral evil has made it necessary; it is not therefore a necessary evil.

Liberty consists in a power of acting under the guidance and controul of reason: Licentiousness is acting under the influence of sensual passions, contrary to the dictates of reason; whilst we contend for the former, we ought to bear testimony against the latter: And whilst we point out arguments against the errors and abuses of government, we ought cautiously to distinguish between government and its abuses; to amputate the latter, without injuring the former, and not indifferently charge both; lest we raise an army of rebel spirits more dangerous and difficult to reduce, than all the legions of Britain.

Government originates (under God) from the people, as from its native source; centers in them, their good is its ultimate object; and operates by securing to them, the enjoyment of their natural rights and civil privileges; and as the mode of doing this, hath no prescribed form in nature, or revelation; mankind, at their option, have endeavoured it variously; and thereby given rise to the various forms of government subsisting in the world, as monarchy, aristocracy, democracy, &c. each of these have failed in their turns, through want of integrity, or discernment, or both in the administration; and have been alternately preferred or discarded by writers, not so much on account of their own excellence or defects, as of those who administered them. That form of government that is adapted to the genius and circumstances of the governed, affords them the greatest security, and places the authority of the governing most out of the reach of the former, to violate and contemn, their corruptions and abuses most within, to prevent and redress, is the best. A perfect model of civil government perfectly administered and obeyed, cannot be expected, but in a state of perfection, where it would be perfectly unnecessary. That government in ordinary is the best that is best administered.

Some begin their government with their political existence; it grows up with them; the great first principles thereof, are never altered while they continue a people, & become so incorporated with their being, that they have the force of natural, rather than political institutions. Others, after a century or two have occasion to alter and new model their old governments, or frame new ones: This is usually attended with much difficulty and great danger, requires an extensive knowledge of the genius, tempers, circumstances, situation, ancient customs, habits, laws and manners of the people; and great judgment and skill, to adapt new regulations to old usuages, so as to form a happy coalition. The British nation, at the time of forming their great charter (no matter how they became so) consisted of a King, nobility and commons: To connect the strength and wisdom of these, for the public weal, without infringing or endangering the rights of either, was their great object: And this was done in the constitution of parliament, so far as it concerned legislation and taxation. Its object therefore, was directly, political and civil liberty. All offices were in the gift of the crown; and the payment of them in the option of the people; The powers of government were so balanced, as to render all mutual restraints upon, and mutually restrained by each other. If the people have lost their liberties, suffered themselves to be bought and sold, like beasts of burden, the fault is theirs and their corrupters, and not the constitution's, which put in their power to have preserved them.

Thus, the principles were excellent, altho' the practice hath been most perverse. Amongst all the forms of civil government, none can be pronounced absolutely best, and only relatively so: For that which best suits one people would badly suit another, or the same, at a different period.

The strength and spring of every free government, is the virtue of the people; virtue grows on knowledge, and knowledge on education. Most nations have established a falshood for their first principle, viz. that their Kings are perfect; and the consequence of this, is a second, that gives them a licence to serve the devil with impunity, viz. that they can do no wrong: Then follows the most impious ascriptions of divine qualities and titles to him; and to compleat the image, the riches of the nation are lavished in the magnificence, costly equipage and dazzling splendors of their prince; thereby to build power on show; and like the *formido avium*, or scare crow, derive respect and obedience only from the passion of fear: A multitude of criminal laws, with severe penalties are necessary to support the authority of the rulers, and secure the obedience of the subjects; whilst the sovereign himself, is wholly insecure in the midst of his subjects, without a life guard. This is inverting the order of nature and of civil government; and leaving the necessary means of rendering mankind wise, virtuous and good. Rulers ought to know, and be known to their subjects, to be but men; and the punishment of their crimes, to be in proportion to their elevation in power. Half the sum, employed to diffuse general knowledge; by erecting public seminaries, with masters well furnished to teach children, not only common learning, but to instruct and impress on their young and tender minds, the principles of virtue and the rudiments of government, which would grow up with their growth, and derive strength from age; would be more effectual than all the brilliancy of a crown, or tortures of a rack; this is the only permanent foundation of a free government; this is laying the foundation in a constitution, not without or over, but within the subjects; love and not fear will become the spring of their obedience: the ruler be distinguished, only by his distinguished virtues, and know no good, separate from that of his subjects; and his authority be supported, more by the virtue of the people, than by the terror of his power. The only way to make men good subjects of a rational and free government, is to make them wise and virtuous; but such a government as this is utterly incompatible with the idea of slavery, because incompatible with a state of ignorance.

OF INDEPENDANCE.

IT is with states as it is with men, they have their infancy, their manhood and their decline: Nature hath its course in all, and never works in vain; when a people are ripe for any mighty change, means wont be wanting to effect it. From what providence hath done and is doing for us, we must learn, what is our duty to do; for we may only follow, where nature leads, and in this is infinite safety; from small, we are become great, from a few, many, from feeble, powerful, from poor, rich; nature has stored our country with all necessaries for subsistence in peace, and for defence in war; it has united our hearts, our interests and our councils, in the common cause.

Independance consists in being under obligation to acknowledge no superior power on earth. The King by withdrawing his protection and levying war upon us, has discharged us of our allegiance, and of all obligations to obedience: For protection and subjection are mutual, and cannot subsist apart: He having violated the compact on his part, we of course are released from ours; and on the same principles, if we owed any obedience to parliament (which we did not) we are wholly discharged of it. We are compelled to provide, not only for our own subsistence, but for defence against a powerful enemy: Our affections are weaned from Great-Britain, by similar means and almost as miraculously as the Israelites were from Egypt: These are facts, a surprising concurrence of incidents, equally out of our knowledge to have foreseen, or our power to have prevented, point us to some great event. Providence has furnished us with the means; the King, contrary to his design, hath discharged us of our allegiance and forced us from our dependance, and we are become necessarily independant, in order to preservation and subsistence, and this without our act or choice. And is it a crime to be, what we cant help but be? It is not from a rebellious spirit in the Americans, but unavoidable necessity, that we are become so: Like a timorous child that is able to walk but disinclined to attempt it, placed in the middle of a floor, must use his legs or fall; while the tender parent that placed him there, stands ready to save him, if likely to fall, *nam qui transtulit sustinet*, He that transplanted, upholds and sustains. All Europe, must gaze with wonder, approbation and applause; Great-Britain join in acquitting us; while the tyrant minister (Lord North) in his own bosom reads the sentence of his condemnation, for condemning us: to be where nature and providence hath placed us, is to be right, and to do what such a state points out and requires to be done, is duty. In this situation two objects of the greatest importance demand our attention, viz. defence and government; these we ought diligently to attend to and leave the event; and let those who begun the war, be first in the proposals of peace; those who have refused to hear others, when they prayed, pray without being heard. And since parliament will have our trade, only on terms incompatible with our liberty, permit them to have neither; welcome all nations to our ports and to a participation of our trade, and enter into alliance with none; thus, we may enjoy the commerce of all, without being concerned in the quarrels of any. Providence has furnished us with resources for defence; numbers to constitute armies, materials for constructing a navy, for making of powder, ball, cannon, mortars, arms, &c. and all kinds of ordnance and military stores. Our threatened situation demands, that we immediately take every precaution, and use all the means in our power for our preservation & defence, and with noble and valiant exertions, withstand and repel the attacks of tyranny. Nature hath placed the island of Great-Britain, and the continent of America so distant from each other, that it is impossible for them to be represented in one legislative body: The consequence is, that their distant situations are incompatible with their being subjects to one supreme legislature. Representation is the feet on which a free government stands, it ought therefore to be equal and full; maim and render partial the former, and it will infallibly mutilate the latter. The measures of government necessary to be adopted, at present, are the same, either for a temporary or a perpetual expedient.

The colonies have so long subsisted separate and independant of each other, enjoyed their particular forms of government, laws, customs and manners and particular rules for the regulation and distribution of property; that it will, doubtless, be thought expedient for each to retain its antient form of government, laws, &c. as far as possible; to have supreme legislative and executive powers of government over all causes, matters and things within its territorial limits, and to regulate its own internal police. Those whose Governors, or other officers, are taken off by the crown, to have them elected by the freemen, or appointed by their several assemblies; for which purpose particular constitutions to be framed, as they shall elect. That a certain number of delegates be annually elected by the freemen in each colony, to form a general council or congress, whose power to extend over all matters of common and general concernment: Such as making war and peace, sending and receiving ambassadors, general regulations respecting trade and maritime affairs; to decide all matters of controversy between colony and colony, relative to bounds and limits, &c. &c. of whom one to be chosen president, and to continue in office until another be chosen and sworn. And in matters so interesting, as that of making war and peace, to be a majority of at least two thirds, computed by colonies; and for carrying on a war to have power to levy troops and provide for their subsistence, &c. to have an explicit constitution, ascertaining the number of members the congress shall consist of, and that each colony shall send; containing regulations for convening, proroguing and adjourning; also granting, defining, and limiting the powers they are to have, exercise, &c. which constitution to be laid before the several assemblies, and by them acceded to and confirmed. By some such method the colonies may retain their independance of each other; and all their former usuages, laws, &c. and the wisdom and strength of each, be connected in general congress, for the security and defence of the whole.

To be reconciled to Great-Britain upon unjust terms, is to be reconciled to injustice, ruin and slavery; until they shall have condemned the measures that have been pursued against America, recalled their fleets and armies, exposed to the public eye, and condign punishment, the authors and advisers of the present unjust and cruel war; and have repaired the damage and expence caused thereby in America, and given up the claim of power in parliament, to dominion over us, they cannot expect that we will treat with them, about future connections. They have endeavoured, by all the arts of seduction, and of power, to destroy and enslave us; and now they have sent commissioners, under pretence of treating with the Americans. Accommodation is their ostensible, but we have reason to fear that to divide, corrupt and destroy is their real object: For with whom are they to treat? With the general Congress? No; it is said, with the several governors; all of whom, except one or two, live, and breath, and have their being, in the minister, and are mov'd by him like the puppets in the show, by the hand that pulls the wire, to which they are hung. They might as well have stayed at home, and treated with the minister. But it is said they are to treat with the several colonies. But how is this? unless they acknowledge their independence of parliament? The supreme legislature of a country only, hath power to treat and be treated with respecting war and peace. The act, 6th Geo. III. declares that the parliament of Great-Britain hath supreme power of legislation over the colonies; and to establish such power, the parliament is in war with America: The Commissioners therefore, cannot, consistent with their ideas of power, treat with any but the British parliament. By sending Commissioners to treat with us, they would acknowledge our power to make a treaty; which is predicable only of independence. Query then, whether those Commissioners are coming to treat for peace, with a mighty armament for war? In fine, that government, in which the people are subject to no laws, or taxes, but by their voice or consent; condemned by no sentence but by the verdict of their equals; where property is near equally distributed; crimes clearly defined and distinguished, & punishments duly proportioned to their nature and magnitude; and where the rising generation are universally instructed in the principles of virtue, and the rudiments of government; there civil liberty & general public felicity, will flourish in the greatest perfection.

FINIS.

[Thomas Paine], Common Sense; Addressed to the Inhabitants of America, . . . A New Edition, with Several Additions in the Body of the Work. To Which Is Added an Appendix; Together with an Address to the People Called Quakers. Philadelphia, 1776.

Most of the pamphleteers in the imperial debate were educated gentlemen who wrote for rational, enlightened, and restricted circles of genteel readers like themselves. They aimed to persuade or explain; their writings were often highly stylized, erudite, and filled with Latin quotations, classical allusions, and learned references to every conceivable figure in the heritage of Western culture, from Cicero and Plutarch to Montesquieu and Pufendorf. Like John Dickinson in his *Letters from a Farmer in Pennsylvania*, they delighted in citing authorities and displaying their scholarship, sometimes crowding their texts with footnotes.

Thomas Paine was a very different kind of writer. A former English corsetmaker, schoolmaster, and twice dismissed excise officer, he had arrived in America only in November 1774, at age thirty-seven full of rage at the ways the Old World had kept him down. Fourteen months later, in January 1776, he suddenly burst upon the New World with *Common Sense*. It was the most incendiary and popular pamphlet of the entire Revolutionary era, going through twenty-five editions in 1776 alone. The text that follows reproduces the second edition, significantly revised and expanded in response to early critics.

Paine was determined to reach a wide readership, especially among the middling sorts in the tavern and artisan centered worlds of the cities, and to do more than explain and persuade; he wanted to express feelings—even revulsions and visions—that the traditional conventions of writing tended to disparage. He refused to decorate his work with Latin quotations and scholarly references; instead, he relied on his readers knowing only the Bible and the *Book of Common Prayer*. He used simple, direct—some critics said coarse, even barnyard— imagery that could be understood by the unlearned. He wrote for ordinary people and forever changed the rules of rhetoric. After Independence had come, Edmund Randolph of Virginia reflected that *Common Sense* had "poured forth a style hitherto unknown on this side of the Atlantic, for the ease with which it insinuated itself into the hearts of the people who were unlearned, or of the learned, who were not callous to the feeling of man." It was, he concluded, a pamphlet "pregnant with the most captivating figures of speech," and because of it "the public sentiment, which a few weeks before had shuddered at the tremendous obstacles with which independence was environed, overleaped every barrier."

Although Paine's pamphlet did not create the idea of independence, it did express more boldly and passionately than any other writing what many Americans had already privately concluded. Paine dismissed the king, the remaining link to Great Britain, as "the Royal Brute" and called for American independence immediately. "The *time hath found us*," he declared. "The birthday of a new world is at hand."

COMMON SENSE;

ADDRESSED TO THE

INHABITANTS

OF

AMERICA,

On the following interesting

SUBJECTS.

I. Of the Origin and Design of Government in general, with concise Remarks on the English Constitution.

II. Of Monarchy and Hereditary Succession.

III. Thoughts on the present State of American Affairs.

IV. Of the present Ability of America, with some miscellaneous Reflections.

A NEW EDITION, with several Additions in the Body of the Work. To which is added an APPENDIX ; together with an Address to the People called QUAKERS.

N. B. The New Addition here given increases the Work upwards of one Third.

Man knows no Master save creating HEAVEN,
Or those whom Choice and common Good ordain.
THOMSON.

PHILADELPHIA PRINTED.
And SOLD by W. and T. BRADFORD.

INTRODUCTION.

PERHAPS the sentiments contained in the following pages, are not *yet* sufficiently fashionable to procure them general favor; a long habit of not thinking a thing *wrong*, gives it a superficial appearance of being *right*, and raises at first a formidable outcry in defence of custom. But the tumult soon subsides. Time makes more converts than reason.

As a long and violent abuse of power, is generally the Means of calling the right of it in question (and in Matters too which might never have been thought of, had not the Sufferers been aggravated into the inquiry) and as the King of England hath undertaken in his *own Right*, to support the Parliament in what he calls *Theirs*, and as the good people of this country are grievously oppressed by the combination, they have an undoubted privilege to inquire into the pretensions of both, and equally to reject the usurpation of either.

In the following sheets, the author hath studiously avoided every thing which is personal among ourselves. Compliments as well as censure to individuals make no part thereof. The wise, and the worthy, need not the triumph of a pamphlet; and those whose sentiments are injudicious, or unfriendly, will cease of themselves unless too much pains are bestowed upon their conversion.

The cause of America is in a great measure the cause of all mankind. Many circumstances hath, and will arise, which are not local, but universal, and through which the principles of all Lovers of Mankind are affected, and in the Event of which, their Affections are interested. The laying a Country desolate with Fire and Sword, declaring War against the natural rights of all Mankind, and extirpating the Defenders thereof from the Face of the Earth, is the Concern of every Man to whom Nature hath given the Power of feeling; of which Class, regardless of Party Censure, is the

AUTHOR.

P. S. The Publication of this new Edition hath been delayed, with a View of taking notice (had it been necessary) of any

Attempt to refute the Doctrine of Independance: As no Answer hath yet appeared, it is now presumed that none will, the Time needful for getting such a Performance ready for the Public being considerably past.

Who the Author of this Production is, is wholly unnecessary to the Public, as the Object for Attention is the *Doctrine itself*, not the *Man*. Yet it may not be unnecessary to say, That he is unconnected with any Party, and under no sort of Influence public or private, but the influence of reason and principle.

Philadelphia, February 14, 1776.

Common Sense.

OF THE ORIGIN AND DESIGN OF GOVERNMENT IN GENERAL. WITH CONCISE REMARKS ON THE ENGLISH CONSTITUTION.

SOME writers have so confounded society with government, as to leave little or no distinction between them; whereas they are not only different, but have different origins. Society is produced by our wants, and government by our wickedness; the former promotes our happiness *positively* by uniting our affections, the latter *negatively* by restraining our vices. The one encourages intercourse, the other creates distinctions. The first is a patron, the last a punisher.

Society in every state is a blessing, but government even in its best state is but a necessary evil; in its worst state an intolerable one; for when we suffer, or are exposed to the same miseries *by a government*, which we might expect in a country *without government*, our calamity is heightened by reflecting that we furnish the means by which we suffer. Government, like dress, is the badge of lost innocence; the palaces of kings are built on the ruins of the bowers of paradise. For were the impulses of conscience clear, uniform, and irresistably obeyed, man would need no other lawgiver; but that not being the case, he finds it necessary to surrender up a part of his property to furnish means for the protection of the rest; and this he is induced to do by the same prudence which in every other case advises him out of two evils to choose the least. *Wherefore*, security being the true design and end of government, it unanswerably follows that whatever *form* thereof appears most likely to ensure it to us, with the least expence and greatest benefit, is preferable to all others.

In order to gain a clear and just idea of the design and end of government, let us suppose a small number of persons settled in some sequestered part of the earth, unconnected with the rest, they will then represent the first peopling of any country, or of the world. In this state of natural liberty, society will be their first thought. A thousand motives will excite them thereto, the strength of one man is so unequal to his wants, and his mind so unfitted for perpetual solitude, that he is soon obliged to seek assistance and relief of another, who in his turn requires the same. Four or five united would be able to raise a tolerable dwelling in the midst of a wilderness, but *one* man might labour out the common period of life without accomplishing any thing; when he had felled his timber he could not remove it, nor erect it after it was removed; hunger in the mean time would urge him from his work, and every different want call him a different way. Disease, nay even misfortune would be death, for though neither might be mortal, yet either would disable him from living, and reduce him to a state in which he might rather be said to perish than to die.

Thus necessity, like a gravitating power, would soon form our newly arrived emigrants into society, the reciprocal blessings of which, would supersede, and render the obligations of law and government unnecessary while they remained perfectly just to each other; but as nothing but heaven is impregnable to vice, it will unavoidably happen, that in proportion as they surmount the first difficulties of emigration, which bound them together in a common cause, they will begin to relax in their duty and attachment to each other; and this remissness, will point out the necessity, of establishing some form of government to supply the defect of moral virtue.

Some convenient tree will afford them a State-House, under the branches of which, the whole colony may assemble to deliberate on public matters. It is more than probable that their first laws will have the title only of REGULATIONS, and be enforced by no other penalty than public disesteem. In this first parliament every man, by natural right, will have a seat.

But as the colony increases, the public concerns will increase likewise, and the distance at which the members may be separated, will render it too inconvenient for all of them to meet on every occasion as at first, when their number was small, their habitations near, and the public concerns few and trifling. This will point out the convenience of their consenting to leave the legislative part to be managed by a select number chosen from the whole body, who are supposed to have the same concerns at stake which those have who appointed them, and who will act in the same manner as the whole body would act were they present. If the colony continue increasing, it will

become necessary to augment the number of the representatives, and that the interest of every part of the colony may be
attended to, it will be found best to divide the whole into
convenient parts, each part sending its proper number; and
that the *elected* might never form to themselves an interest
separate from the *electors*, prudence will point out the propriety of having elections often; because as the *elected* might by
that means return and mix again with the general body of the
electors in a few months, their fidelity to the public will be
secured by the prudent reflexion of not making a rod for themselves. And as this frequent interchange will establish a common
interest with every part of the community, they will mutually
and naturally support each other, and on this (not on the unmeaning name of king) depends the *strength of government,
and the happiness of the governed.*

Here then is the origin and rise of government; namely, a
mode rendered necessary by the inability of moral virtue to
govern the world; here too is the design and end of government, viz. freedom and security. And however our eyes may be
dazzled with show, or our ears deceived by sound; however
prejudice may warp our wills, or interest darken our understanding, the simple voice of nature and of reason will say, it is
right.

I draw my idea of the form of government from a principle
in nature, which no art can overturn, viz. that the more simple
any thing is, the less liable it is to be disordered, and the easier
repaired when disordered; and with this maxim in view, I offer
a few remarks on the so much boasted constitution of England.
That it was noble for the dark and slavish times in which it was
erected, is granted. When the world was over run with tyranny
the least remove therefrom was a glorious rescue. But that it is
imperfect, subject to convulsions, and incapable of producing
what it seems to promise, is easily demonstrated.

Absolute governments (tho' the disgrace of human nature)
have this advantage with them, that they are simple; if the
people suffer, they know the head from which their suffering
springs, know likewise the remedy, and are not bewildered by
a variety of causes and cures. But the constitution of England
is so exceedingly complex, that the nation may suffer for years
together without being able to discover in which part the fault

lies, some will say in one and some in another, and every political physician will advise a different medicine.

I know it is difficult to get over local or long standing prejudices, yet if we will suffer ourselves to examine the component parts of the English constitution, we shall find them to be the base remains of two ancient tyrannies, compounded with some new republican materials.

First.—The remains of monarchical tyranny in the person of the king.

Secondly.—The remains of aristocratical tyranny in the persons of the peers.

Thirdly.—The new republican materials, in the persons of the commons, on whose virtue depends the freedom of England.

The two first, by being hereditary, are independent of the people; wherefore in a *constitutional sense* they contribute nothing towards the freedom of the state.

To say that the constitution of England is a *union* of three powers reciprocally *checking* each other, is farcical, either the words have no meaning, or they are flat contradictions.

To say that the commons is a check upon the king, presupposes two things.

First.—That the king is not to be trusted without being looked after, or in other words, that a thirst for absolute power is the natural disease of monarchy.

Secondly.—That the commons, by being appointed for that purpose, are either wiser or more worthy of confidence than the crown.

But as the same constitution which gives the commons a power to check the king by withholding the supplies, gives afterwards the king a power to check the commons, by empowering him to reject their other bills; it again supposes that the king is wiser than those whom it has already supposed to be wiser than him. A mere absurdity!

There is something exceedingly ridiculous in the composition of monarchy; it first excludes a man from the means of information, yet empowers him to act in cases where the highest judgment is required. The state of a king shuts him from the world, yet the business of a king requires him to know it thoroughly; wherefore the different parts, by unnaturally opposing and destroying each other, prove the whole character to be absurd and useless.

Some writers have explained the English constitution thus; the king, say they, is one, the people another; the peers are an house in behalf of the king; the commons in behalf of the people; but this hath all the distinctions of an house divided against itself; and though the expressions be pleasantly arranged, yet when examined they appear idle and ambiguous; and it will always happen, that the nicest construction that words are capable of, when applied to the description of some thing which either cannot exist, or is too incomprehensible to be within the compass of description, will be words of sound only, and though they may amuse the ear, they cannot inform the mind, for this explanation includes a previous question, viz. *How came the king by a power which the people are afraid to trust, and always obliged to check?* Such a power could not be the gift of a wise people, neither can any power, *which needs checking*, be from God; yet the provision, which the constitution makes, supposes such a power to exist.

But the provision is unequal to the task; the means either cannot or will not accomplish the end, and the whole affair is a felo de se; for as the greater weight will always carry up the less, and as all the wheels of a machine are put in motion by one, it only remains to know which power in the constitution has the most weight, for that will govern; and though the others, or a part of them, may clog, or, as the phrase is, check the rapidity of its motion, yet so long as they cannot stop it, their endeavors will be ineffectual; the first moving power will at last have its way, and what it wants in speed is supplied by time.

That the crown is this overbearing part in the English constitution needs not be mentioned, and that it derives its whole consequence merely from being the giver of places and pensions is self-evident, wherefore, though we have been wise enough to shut and lock a door against absolute monarchy, we at the same time have been foolish enough to put the crown in possession of the key.

The prejudice of Englishmen, in favour of their own government by king, lords and commons, arises as much or more from national pride than reason. Individuals are undoubtedly safer in England than in some other countries, but the *will* of the king is as much the *law* of the land in Britain as in France, with this difference, that instead of proceeding directly from his mouth, it is handed to the people under the more formidable shape of an act of parliament. For the fate of Charles the First, hath only made kings more subtle—not more just.

Wherefore, laying aside all national pride and prejudice in favour of modes and forms, the plain truth is, that *it is wholly owing to the constitution of the people, and not to the constitution of the government* that the crown is not as oppressive in England as in Turkey.

An inquiry into the *constitutional errors* in the English form of government is at this time highly necessary, for as we are never in a proper condition of doing justice to others, while we continue under the influence of some leading partiality, so neither are we capable of doing it to ourselves while we remain fettered by any obstinate prejudice. And as a man, who is attached to a prostitute, is unfitted to choose or judge of a wife, so any prepossession in favour of a rotten constitution of government will disable us from discerning a good one.

OF MONARCHY AND HEREDITARY SUCCESSION.

MANKIND being originally equals in the order of creation, the equality could only be destroyed by some subsequent circumstance; the distinctions of rich, and poor, may in a great measure be accounted for, and that without having recourse to the harsh ill sounding names of oppression and avarice. Oppression is often the *consequence*, but seldom or never the *means* of riches; and though avarice will preserve a man from being necessitously poor, it generally makes him too timorous to be wealthy.

But there is another and greater distinction for which no truly natural or religious reason can be assigned, and that is, the distinction of men into KINGS and SUBJECTS. Male and female are the distinctions of nature, good and bad the distinctions of heaven; but how a race of men came into the world so exalted above the rest, and distinguished like some new species, is worth enquiring into, and whether they are the means of happiness or of misery to mankind.

In the early ages of the world, according to the scripture chronology, there were no kings; the consequence of which was there were no wars; it is the pride of kings which throw mankind into confusion. Holland without a king hath enjoyed more peace for this last century than any of the monarchical governments in Europe. Antiquity favors the same remark; for the quiet and rural lives of the first patriarchs hath a happy something in them, which vanishes away when we come to the history of Jewish royalty.

Government by kings was first introduced into the world by the Heathens, from whom the children of Israel copied the custom. It was the most prosperous invention the Devil ever set on foot for the promotion of idolatry. The Heathens paid divine honors to their deceased kings, and the christian world hath improved on the plan by doing the same to their living ones. How impious is the title of sacred majesty applied to a worm, who in the midst of his splendor is crumbling into dust!

As the exalting one man so greatly above the rest cannot be justified on the equal rights of nature, so neither can it be defended on the authority of scripture; for the will of the Almighty, as declared by Gideon and the prophet Samuel, expressly disapproves of government by kings. All anti-monarchical parts of scripture have been very smoothly glossed over in monarchical governments, but they undoubtedly merit the attention of countries which have their governments yet to form. *"Render unto Cæsar the things which are Cæsar's"* is the scripture doctrine of courts, yet it is no support of monarchical government, for the Jews at that time were without a king, and in a state of vassalage to the Romans.

Near three thousand years passed away from the Mosaic account of the creation, till the Jews under a national delusion requested a king. Till then their form of government (except in extraordinary cases, where the Almighty interposed) was a kind of republic administred by a judge and the elders of the tribes. Kings they had none, and it was held sinful to acknowledge any being under that title but the Lord of Hosts. And when a man seriously reflects on the idolatrous homage which is paid to the persons of Kings, he need not wonder, that the Almighty ever jealous of his honor, should disapprove of a form of government which so impiously invades the prerogative of heaven.

Monarchy is ranked in scripture as one of the sins of the Jews, for which a curse in reserve is denounced against them. The history of that transaction is worth attending to.

The children of Israel being oppressed by the Midianites, Gideon marched against them with a small army, and victory, thro' the divine interposition, decided in his favour. The Jews elate with success, and attributing it to the generalship of Gideon, proposed making him a king, saying, *Rule thou over us, thou and thy son and thy son's son.* Here was temptation in its fullest extent; not a kingdom only, but an hereditary one, but Gideon in the piety of his soul replied, *I will not rule over you, neither shall my son rule over you.* THE LORD SHALL RULE OVER YOU. Words need not be more explicit; Gideon doth not *decline* the honor, but denieth their right to give it; neither doth he compliment them with invented declarations of his thanks, but in the positive stile of a prophet charges them with disaffection to their proper Sovereign, the King of heaven.

About one hundred and thirty years after this, they fell again into the same error. The hankering which the Jews had for the idolatrous customs of the Heathens, is something exceedingly unaccountable; but so it was, that laying hold of the misconduct of Samuel's two sons, who were entrusted with some secular concerns, they came in an abrupt and clamorous manner to Samuel, saying, *Behold thou art old, and thy sons walk not in thy ways, now make us a king to judge us like all the other nations.* And here we cannot but observe that their motives were bad, viz. that they might be *like* unto other nations, i. e. the Heathens, whereas their true glory laid in being as much *unlike* them as possible. *But the thing displeased Samuel when they said, Give us a king to judge us; and Samuel prayed unto the Lord, and the Lord said unto Samuel, Hearken unto the voice of the people in all that they say unto thee, for they have not rejected thee, but they have rejected me,* THAT I SHOULD NOT REIGN OVER THEM. *According to all the works which they have done since the day that I brought them up out of Egypt, even unto this day; wherewith they have forsaken me and served other Gods; so do they also unto thee. Now therefore hearken unto their voice, howbeit, protest solemnly unto them and shew them the manner of the king that shall reign over them,* i. e. not of any particular king, but the general manner of the kings of the earth, whom

Israel was so eagerly copying after. And notwithstanding the great distance of time and difference of manners, the character is still in fashion. *And Samuel told all the words of the Lord unto the people, that asked of him a king. And he said, This shall be the manner of the king that shall reign over you; he will take your sons and appoint them for himself, for his chariots, and to be his horsemen, and some shall run before his chariots* (this description agrees with the present mode of impressing men) *and he will appoint him captains over thousands and captains over fifties, and will set them to ear his ground and to reap his harvest, and to make his instruments of war, and instruments of his chariots; and he will take your daughters to be confectionaries, and to be cooks and to be bakers* (this describes the expence and luxury as well as the oppression of kings) *and he will take your fields and your olive yards, even the best of them, and give them to his servants; and he will take the tenth of your seed, and of your vineyards, and give them to his officers and to his servants* (by which we see that bribery, corruption and favoritism are the standing vices of kings) *and he will take the tenth of your men servants, and your maid servants, and your goodliest young men and your asses, and put them to his work; and he will take the tenth of your sheep, and ye shall be his servants, and ye shall cry out in that day because of your king which ye shall have chosen,* AND THE LORD WILL NOT HEAR YOU IN THAT DAY. This accounts for the continuation of monarchy; neither do the characters of the few good kings which have lived since, either sanctify the title, or blot out the sinfulness of the origin; the high encomium given of David takes no notice of him *officially as a king,* but only as a *man* after God's own heart. *Nevertheless the People refused to obey the voice of Samuel, and they said, Nay, but we will have a king over us, that we may be like all the nations, and that our king may judge us, and go out before us, and fight our battles.* Samuel continued to reason with them, but to no purpose; he set before them their ingratitude, but all would not avail; and seeing them fully bent on their folly, he cried out, *I will call unto the Lord, and he shall send thunder and rain* (which then was a punishment, being in the time of wheat harvest) *that ye may perceive and see that your wickedness is great which ye have done in the sight of the Lord,* IN ASKING YOU A KING. *So Samuel called unto the Lord, and the Lord sent thunder and rain that day, and all the people greatly feared the Lord and Samuel. And all the people said unto Samuel, Pray for thy servants unto the Lord thy God that we die not, for* WE HAVE ADDED UNTO OUR SINS THIS EVIL, TO ASK A KING. These portions of scripture are direct and positive. They admit of no equivocal construction. That the Almighty hath here entered his protest against monarchical government is true, or the scripture is false. And a man hath good reason to believe that there is as much of king-craft, as priest-craft, in withholding the scripture from the public in Popish countries. For monarchy in every instance is the Popery of government.

To the evil of monarchy we have added that of hereditary succession; and as the first is a degradation and lessening of ourselves, so the second, claimed as a matter of right, is an insult and an imposition on posterity. For all men being originally equals, no *one* by *birth* could have a right to set up his own family in perpetual preference to all others for ever, and though himself might deserve *some* decent degree of honors of his cotemporaries, yet his descendants might be far too unworthy to inherit them. One of the strongest *natural* proofs of the folly of hereditary right in kings, is, that nature disapproves it, otherwise she would not so frequently turn it into ridicule by giving mankind an *ass for a lion*.

Secondly, as no man at first could possess any other public honors than were bestowed upon him, so the givers of those honors could have no power to give away the right of posterity, and though they might say "We choose you for *our* head," they could not, without manifest injustice to their children, say "that your children and your childrens children shall reign over *ours* for ever." Because such an unwise, unjust, unnatural compact might (perhaps) in the next succession put them under the government of a rogue or a fool. Most wise men, in their private sentiments, have ever treated hereditary right with contempt; yet it is one of those evils, which when once established is not easily removed; many submit from fear, others from superstition, and the more powerful part shares with the king the plunder of the rest.

This is supposing the present race of kings in the world to have had an honorable origin; whereas it is more than probable, that could we take off the dark covering of antiquity, and trace them to their first rise, that we should find the first of them nothing better than the principal ruffian of some restless gang, whose savage manners or pre-eminence in subtility obtained him the title of chief among plunderers; and who by increasing in power, and extending his depredations, over-awed the quiet and defenceless to purchase their safety by frequent contributions. Yet his electors could have no idea of giving hereditary right to his descendants, because such a perpetual exclusion of themselves was incompatible with the free and unrestrained principles they professed to live by. Wherefore, hereditary succession in the early ages of monarchy could not take place as a matter of claim, but as something casual or complimental; but as few or no records were extant in those days, the traditionary history stuffed with fables, it was very easy, after the lapse of a few generations, to trump up some superstitious tale, conveniently timed, Mahomet like, to cram hereditary right down the throats of the vulgar. Perhaps the disorders which threatened, or seemed to threaten, on the decease of a leader and the choice of a new one (for elections among ruffians could not be very orderly) induced many at first to favor hereditary pretensions; by which means it happened, as it hath happened since, that what at first was submitted to as a convenience, was afterwards claimed as a right.

England, since the conquest, hath known some few good monarchs, but groaned beneath a much larger number of bad ones; yet no man in his senses can say that their claim under William the Conqueror is a very honorable one. A French bastard landing with an armed banditti, and establishing himself king of England against the consent of the natives, is in plain terms a very paltry rascally original.—It certainly hath no divinity in it. However, it is needless to spend much time in exposing the folly of hereditary right, if there are any so weak as to believe it, let them promiscuously worship the ass and lion, and welcome. I shall neither copy their humility, nor disturb their devotion.

Yet I should be glad to ask how they suppose kings came at first? The question admits but of three answers, viz. either by lot, by election, or by usurpation. If the first king was taken by lot, it establishes a precedent for the next, which excludes hereditary succession. Saul was by lot, yet the succession was not hereditary, neither does it appear from that transaction there was any intention it ever should. If the first king of any country was by election, that likewise establishes a precedent for the next; for to say, that the *right* of all future generations is taken away, by the act of the first electors, in their choice not only of a king, but of a family of kings for ever, hath no parrallel in or out of scripture but the doctrinc of original sin, which supposes the free will of all men lost in Adam; and from such comparison, and it will admit of no other, hereditary succession can derive no glory. For as in Adam all sinned, and as in the first electors all men obeyed; as in the one all mankind were subjected to Satan, and in the other to Sovereignty; as our innocence was lost in the first, and our authority in the last; and as both disable us from reassuming some former state and privilege, it unanswerably follows that original sin and hereditary succession are parrallels. Dishonorable rank! Inglorious connexion! Yet the most subtile sophist cannot produce a juster simile.

As to usurpation, no man will be so hardy as to defend it; and that William the Conqueror was an usurper is a fact not to be contradicted. The plain truth is, that the antiquity of English monarchy will not bear looking into.

But it is not so much the absurdity as the evil of hereditary succession which concerns mankind. Did it ensure a race of good and wise men it would have the seal of divine authority, but as it opens a door to the *foolish*, the *wicked*, and the *improper*, it hath in it the nature of oppression. Men who look upon themselves born to reign, and others to obey, soon grow insolent; selected from the rest of mankind their minds are early poisoned by importance; and the world they act in differs so materially from the world at large, that they have but little opportunity of knowing its true interests, and when they succeed to the government are frequently the most ignorant and unfit of any throughout the dominions.

Another evil which attends hereditary succession is, that the throne is subject to be possessed by 'a minor at any age; all which time the regency, acting under the cover of a king, have every opportunity and inducement to betray their trust. The same national misfortune happens, when a king worn out with age and infirmity, enters the last stage of human weakness. In both these cases the public becomes a prey to every miscreant, who can tamper successfully with the follies either of age or infancy.

The most plausible plea, which hath ever been offered in favour of hereditary succession, is, that it preserves a nation from civil wars; and were this true, it would be weighty; whereas, it is the most barefaced falsity ever imposed upon mankind. The whole history of England disowns the fact. Thirty kings and two minors have reigned in that distracted kingdom since the conquest, in which time there have been (including the Revolution) no less than eight civil wars and nineteen rebellions. Wherefore instead of making for peace, it makes against it, and destroys the very foundation it seems to stand on.

The contest for monarchy and succession, between the houses of York and Lancaster, laid England in a scene of blood for many years. Twelve pitched battles, besides skirmishes and sieges, were fought between Henry and Edward. Twice was Henry prisoner to Edward, who in his turn was prisoner to Henry. And so uncertain is the fate of war and the temper of a nation, when nothing but personal matters are the ground of a quarrel, that Henry was taken in triumph from a prison to a palace, and Edward obliged to fly from a palace to a foreign land; yet, as sudden transitions of temper are seldom lasting, Henry in his turn was driven from the throne, and Edward recalled to succeed him. The parliament always following the strongest side.

This contest began in the reign of Henry the Sixth, and was not entirely extinguished till Henry the Seventh, in whom the families were united. Including a period of 67 years, viz. from 1422 to 1489.

In short, monarchy and succession have laid (not this or that kingdom only) but the world in blood and ashes. 'Tis a form of government which the word of God bears testimony against, and blood will attend it.

If we inquire into the business of a king, we shall find that in some countries they have none; and after sauntering away their lives without pleasure to themselves or advantage to the nation, withdraw from the scene, and leave their successors to tread the same idle round. In absolute monarchies the whole weight of business, civil and military, lies on the king; the children of Israel in their request for a king, urged this plea "that he may judge us, and go out before us and fight our battles." But in countries where he is neither a judge nor a general, as in England, a man would be puzzled to know what *is* his business.

The nearer any government approaches to a republic the less business there is for a king. It is somewhat difficult to find a proper name for the government of England. Sir William Meredith calls it a republic; but in its present state it is unworthy of the name, because the corrupt influence of the crown, by having all the places in its disposal, hath so effectually swallowed up the power, and eaten out the virtue of the house of commons (the republican part in the constitution) that the government of England is nearly as monarchical as that of France or Spain. Men fall out with names without understanding them. For it is the republican and not the monarchical part of the constitution of England which Englishmen glory in, viz. the liberty of choosing an house of commons from out of their own body—and it is easy to see that when republican virtue fails, slavery ensues. Why is the constitution of England sickly, but because monarchy hath poisoned the republic, the crown hath engrossed the commons?

In England a king hath little more to do than to make war and give away places; which in plain terms, is to impoverish the nation and set it together by the ears. A pretty business indeed for a man to be allowed eight hundred thousand sterling a year for, and worshipped into the bargain! Of more worth is one honest man to society and in the sight of God, than all the crowned ruffians that ever lived.

THOUGHTS ON THE PRESENT STATE OF AMERICAN AFFAIRS.

In the following pages I offer nothing more than simple facts, plain arguments, and common sense; and have no other preliminaries to settle with the reader, than that he will divest himself of prejudice and prepossession, and suffer his reason and his feelings to determine for themselves; that he will put *on*, or rather that he will not put *off*, the true character of a man, and generously enlarge his views beyond the present day.

Volumes have been written on the subject of the struggle

between England and America. Men of all ranks have embarked in the controversy, from different motives, and with various designs; but all have been ineffectual, and the period of debate is closed. Arms, as the last resource, decide the contest; the appeal was the choice of the king, and the continent hath accepted the challenge.

It hath been reported of the late Mr. Pelham (who tho' an able minister was not without his faults) that on his being attacked in the house of commons, on the score, that his measures were only of a temporary kind, replied *"they will last my time."* Should a thought so fatal and unmanly possess the colonies in the present contest, the name of ancestors will be remembered by future generations with detestation.

The sun never shined on a cause of greater worth. 'Tis not the affair of a city, a country, a province, or a kingdom, but of a continent—of at least one eighth part of the habitable globe. 'Tis not the concern of a day, a year, or an age; posterity are virtually involved in the contest, and will be more or less affected, even to the end of time, by the proceedings now. Now is the seed time of continental union, faith and honor. The least fracture now will be like a name engraved with the point of a pin on the tender rind of a young oak; the wound will enlarge with the tree, and posterity read it in full grown characters.

By referring the matter from argument to arms, a new æra for politics is struck; a new method of thinking hath arisen. All plans, proposals, &c. prior to the nineteenth of April, *i. e.* to the commencement of hostilities, are like the almanacks of the last year; which, though proper then, are superceded and useless now. Whatever was advanced by the advocates on either side of the question then, terminated in one and the same point, viz. a union with Great-Britain; the only difference between the parties was the method of effecting it; the one proposing force, the other friendship; but it hath so far happened that the first hath failed, and the second hath withdrawn her influence.

As much hath been said of the advantages of reconciliation, which, like an agreeable dream, hath passed away and left us as we were, it is but right, that we should examine the contrary side of the argument, and inquire into some of the many material injuries which these colonies sustain, and always will sustain, by being connected with, and dependant on Great-Britain. To examine that connexion and dependance, on the principles of nature and common sense, to see what we have to trust to, if separated, and what we are to expect, if dependant.

I have heard it asserted by some, that as America hath flourished under her former connexion with Great-Britain, that the same connexion is necessary towards her future happiness, and will always have the same effect. Nothing can be more fallacious than this kind of argument. We may as well assert that because a child has thrived upon milk, that it is never to have meat, or that the first twenty years of our lives is to become a precedent for the next twenty. But even this is admitting more than is true, for I answer roundly, that America would have flourished as much, and probably much more, had no European power had any thing to do with her. The commerce, by which she hath enriched herself are the necessaries of life, and will always have a market while eating is the custom of Europe.

But she has protected us, say some. That she hath engrossed us is true, and defended the continent at our expence as well as her own is admitted, and she would have defended Turkey from the same motive, viz. the sake of trade and dominion.

Alas, we have been long led away by ancient prejudices, and made large sacrifices to superstition. We have boasted the protection of Great-Britain, without considering, that her motive was *interest* not *attachment*; that she did not protect us from *our enemies* on *our account*, but from *her enemies* on *her own account*, from those who had no quarrel with us on any *other account*, and who will always be our enemies on the *same account*. Let Britain wave her pretensions to the continent, or the continent throw off the dependance, and we should be at peace with France and Spain were they at war with Britain. The miseries of Hanover last war ought to warn us against connexions.

It hath lately been asserted in parliament, that the colonies have no relation to each other but through the parent country, *i. e.* that Pennsylvania and the Jerseys, and so on for the rest, are sister colonies by the way of England; this is certainly a very round-about way of proving relationship, but it is the nearest and only true way of proving enemyship, if I may so call it. France and Spain never were, nor perhaps ever will be our enemies as *Americans*, but as our being the *subjects of Great-Britain*.

But Britain is the parent country, say some. Then the more shame upon her conduct. Even brutes do not devour their young, nor savages make war upon their families; wherefore the assertion, if true, turns to her reproach; but it happens not to be true, or only partly so, and the phrase *parent* or *mother country* hath been jesuitically adopted by the king and his parasites, with a low papistical design of gaining an unfair bias on the credulous weakness of our minds. Europe, and not England, is the parent country of America. This new world hath been the asylum for the persecuted lovers of civil and religious liberty from *every part* of Europe. Hither have they fled, not from the tender embraces of the mother, but from the cruelty of the monster; and it is so far true of England, that the same tyranny which drove the first emigrants from home, pursues their descendants still.

In this extensive quarter of the globe, we forget the narrow limits of three hundred and sixty miles (the extent of England) and carry our friendship on a larger scale; we claim brotherhood with every European christian, and triumph in the generosity of the sentiment.

It is pleasant to observe by what regular gradations we surmount the force of local prejudice, as we enlarge our acquaintance with the world. A man born in any town in England divided into parishes, will naturally associate most with his fellow parishioners (because their interests in many cases will be common) and distinguish him by the name of *neighbour*; if he meet him but a few miles from home, he drops the narrow idea of a street, and salutes him by the name of *townsman*; if he travel out of the county, and meet him in any other, he forgets the minor divisions of street and town, and calls him *countryman*, i. e. *county-man*; but if in their foreign excursions they should associate in France or any other part of *Europe*, their local remembrance would be enlarged into that of *Englishmen*. And by a just parity of reasoning, all Europeans meeting in America, or any other quarter of the globe, are *countrymen*; for England, Holland, Germany, or Sweden, when compared with the whole, stand in the same places on the larger scale, which the divisions of street, town, and county do on the smaller ones; distinctions too limited for continental minds. Not one third of the inhabitants, even of this province, are of English descent. Wherefore I reprobate the phrase of parent or mother country applied to England only, as being false, selfish, narrow and ungenerous.

But admitting, that we were all of English descent, what does it amount to? Nothing. Britain, being now an open enemy, extinguishes every other name and title: And to say that reconciliation is our duty, is truly farcical. The first king of England, of the present line (William the Conqueror) was a Frenchman, and half the Peers of England are descendants from the same country; wherefore, by the same method of reasoning, England ought to be governed by France.

Much hath been said of the united strength of Britain and the colonies, that in conjunction they might bid defiance to the world. But this is mere presumption; the fate of war is uncertain, neither do the expressions mean any thing; for this continent would never suffer itself to be drained of inhabitants, to support the British arms in either Asia, Africa, or Europe.

Besides, what have we to do with setting the world at defiance? Our plan is commerce, and that, well attended to, will secure us the peace and friendship of all Europe; because, it is the interest of all Europe to have America a *free port*. Her trade will always be a protection, and her barrenness of gold and silver secure her from invaders.

I challenge the warmest advocate for reconciliation, to shew, a single advantage that this continent can reap, by being connected with Great Britain. I repeat the challenge, not a single advantage is derived. Our corn will fetch its price in any market in Europe, and our imported goods must be paid for buy them where we will.

But the injuries and disadvantages we sustain by that connection, are without number; and our duty to mankind at large, as well as to ourselves, instruct us to renounce the alliance: Because, any submission to, or dependance on Great-Britain, tends directly to involve this continent in European wars and quarrels; and sets us at variance with nations, who would otherwise seek our friendship, and against whom, we have neither anger nor complaint. As Europe is our market for trade, we ought to form no partial connection with any part of it. It is the true interest of America to steer clear of European contentions, which she never can do, while by her dependance on Britain, she is made the make-weight in the scale of British politics.

Europe is too thickly planted with kingdoms to be long at peace, and whenever a war breaks out between England and any foreign power, the trade of America goes to ruin, *because of her connection with Britain.* The next war may not turn out like the last, and should it not, the advocates for reconciliation now will be wishing for separation then, because, neutrality in that case, would be a safer convoy than a man of war. Every thing that is right or natural pleads for separation. The blood of the slain, the weeping voice of nature cries, 'TIS TIME TO PART. Even the distance at which the Almighty hath placed England and America, is a strong and natural proof, that the authority of the one, over the other, was never the design of Heaven. The time likewise at which the continent was discovered, adds weight to the argument, and the manner in which it was peopled encreases the force of it. The reformation was preceded by the discovery of America, as if the Almighty graciously meant to open a sanctuary to the persecuted in future years, when home should afford neither friendship nor safety.

The authority of Great-Britain over this continent, is a form of government, which sooner or later must have an end: And a serious mind can draw no true pleasure by looking forward, under the painful and positive conviction, that what he calls "the present constitution" is merely temporary. As parents, we can have no joy, knowing that *this government* is not sufficiently lasting to ensure any thing which we may bequeath to posterity: And by a plain method of argument, as we are running the next generation into debt, we ought to do the work of it, otherwise we use them meanly and pitifully. In order to discover the line of our duty rightly, we should take our children in our hand, and fix our station a few years farther into life; that eminence will present a prospect, which a few present fears and prejudices conceal from our sight.

Though I would carefully avoid giving unnecessary offence, yet I am inclined to believe, that all those who espouse the doctrine of reconciliation, may be included within the following descriptions. Interested men, who are not to be trusted; weak men, who *cannot* see; prejudiced men, who *will not* see;

and a certain set of moderate men, who think better of the European world than it deserves; and this last class, by an ill-judged deliberation, will be the cause of more calamities to this continent, than all the other three.

It is the good fortune of many to live distant from the scene of sorrow; the evil is not sufficiently brought to *their* doors to make *them* feel the precariousness with which all American property is possessed. But let our imaginations transport us for a few moments to Boston, that seat of wretchedness will teach us wisdom, and instruct us for ever to renounce a power in whom we can have no trust. The inhabitants of that unfortunate city, who but a few months ago were in ease and affluence, have now, no other alternative than to stay and starve, or turn out to beg. Endangered by the fire of their friends if they continue within the city, and plundered by the soldiery if they leave it. In their present condition they are prisoners without the hope of redemption, and in a general attack for their relief, they would be exposed to the fury of both armies.

Men of passive tempers look somewhat lightly over the offences of Britain, and, still hoping for the best, are apt to call out, *"Come, come, we shall be friends again, for all this."* But examine the passions and feelings of mankind, Bring the doctrine of reconciliation to the touchstone of nature, and then tell me, whether you can hereafter love, honour, and faithfully serve the power that hath carried fire and sword into your land? If you cannot do all these, then are you only deceiving yourselves, and by your delay bringing ruin upon posterity. Your future connection with Britain, whom you can neither love nor honour, will be forced and unnatural, and being formed only on the plan of present convenience, will in a little time fall into a relapse more wretched than the first. But if you say, you can still pass the violations over, then I ask, Hath your house been burnt? Hath your property been destroyed before your face? Are your wife and children destitute of a bed to lie on, or bread to live on? Have you lost a parent or a child by their hands, and yourself the ruined and wretched survivor? If you have not, then are you not a judge of those who have. But if you have, and still can shake hands with the murderers, then are you unworthy the name of husband, father, friend, or lover, and whatever may be your rank or title in life, you have the heart of a coward, and the spirit of a sycophant.

This is not inflaming or exaggerating matters, but trying them by those feelings and affections which nature justifies, and without which, we should be incapable of discharging the social duties of life, or enjoying the felicities of it. I mean not to exhibit horror for the purpose of provoking revenge, but to awaken us from fatal and unmanly slumbers, that we may pursue determinately some fixed object. It is not in the power of Britain or of Europe to conquer America, if she do not conquer herself by *delay* and *timidity*. The present winter is worth an age if rightly employed, but if lost or neglected, the whole continent will partake of the misfortune; and there is no punishment which that man will not deserve, be he who, or what, or where he will, that may be the means of sacrificing a season so precious and useful.

It is repugnant to reason, to the universal order of things, to all examples from former ages, to suppose, that this continent can longer remain subject to any external power. The most sanguine in Britain does not think so. The utmost stretch of human wisdom cannot, at this time, compass a plan short of separation, which can promise the continent even a year's security. Reconciliation is *now* a falacious dream. Nature hath deserted the connexion, and Art cannot supply her place. For, as Milton wisely expresses, "never can true reconcilement grow where wounds of deadly hate have pierced so deep."

Every quiet method for peace hath been ineffectual. Our prayers have been rejected with disdain; and only tended to convince us, that nothing flatters vanity, or confirms obstinacy in Kings more than repeated petitioning—and nothing hath contributed more than that very measure to make the Kings of Europe absolute: Witness Denmark and Sweden. Wherefore, since nothing but blows will do, for God's sake, let us come to a final separation, and not leave the next generation to be cutting throats, under the violated unmeaning names of parent and child.

To say, they will never attempt it again is idle and visionary, we thought so at the repeal of the stamp-act, yet a year or two undeceived us; as well may we suppose that nations, which have been once defeated, will never renew the quarrel.

As to government matters, it is not in the power of Britain to do this continent justice: The business of it will soon be too weighty, and intricate, to be managed with any tolerable degree of convenience, by a power, so distant from us, and so very ignorant of us; for if they cannot conquer us, they cannot govern us. To be always running three or four thousand miles with a tale or a petition, waiting four or five months for an answer, which when obtained requires five or six more to explain it in, will in a few years be looked upon as folly and childishness—There was a time when it was proper, and there is a proper time for it to cease.

Small islands not capable of protecting themselves, are the proper objects for kingdoms to take under their care; but there is something very absurd, in supposing a continent to be perpetually governed by an island. In no instance hath nature made the satellite larger than its primary planet, and as England and America, with respect to each other, reverses the common order of nature, it is evident they belong to different systems: England to Europe, America to itself.

I am not induced by motives of pride, party, or resentment to espouse the doctrine of separation and independance; I am clearly, positively, and conscientiously persuaded that it is the true interest of this continent to be so; that every thing short of *that* is mere patchwork, that it can afford no lasting felicity, —that it is leaving the sword to our children, and shrinking back at a time, when, a little more, a little farther, would have rendered this continent the glory of the earth.

As Britain hath not manifested the least inclination towards a compromise, we may be assured that no terms can be obtained worthy the acceptance of the continent, or any ways equal to the expence of blood and treasure we have been already put to.

The object, contended for, ought always to bear some just proportion to the expence. The removal of North, or the whole detestable junto, is a matter unworthy the millions we have expended. A temporary stoppage of trade, was an inconvenience, which would have sufficiently ballanced the repeal of all the acts complained of, had such repeals been obtained; but if the whole continent must take up arms, if every man must be a soldier, it is scarcely worth our while to fight against a contemptible ministry only. Dearly, dearly, do we pay for the repeal of the acts, if that is all we fight for; for in a just estimation, it is as great a folly to pay a Bunker-hill price for law, as for land. As I have always considered the independancy of this continent, as an event, which sooner or later must arrive, so from the late rapid progress of the continent to maturity, the event could not be far off. Wherefore, on the breaking out of hostilities, it was not worth the while to have disputed a matter, which time would have finally redressed, unless we meant to be in earnest; otherwise, it is like wasting an estate on a suit at law, to regulate the trespasses of a tenant, whose lease is just expiring. No man was a warmer wisher for reconciliation than myself, before the fatal nineteenth of April 1775,* but the moment the event of that day was made known, I rejected the hardened, sullen tempered Pharoah of England for ever; and disdain the wretch, that with the pretended title of FATHER OF HIS PEOPLE can unfeelingly hear of their slaughter, and composedly sleep with their blood upon his soul.

But admitting that matters were now made up, what would be the event? I answer, the ruin of the continent. And that for several reasons.

First. The powers of governing still remaining in the hands of the king, he will have a negative over the whole legislation of this continent. And as he hath shewn himself such an inveterate enemy to liberty, and discovered such a thirst for arbitrary power; is he, or is he not, a proper man to say to these colonies, *"You shall make no laws but what I please."* And is there any inhabitant in America so ignorant, as not to know, that according to what is called the *present constitution*, that this continent can make no laws but what the king gives leave to; and is there any man so unwise, as not to see, that (considering what has happened) he will suffer no law to be made here, but such as suit *his* purpose. We may be as effectually enslaved by the want of laws in America, as by submitting to laws made for us in England. After matters are made up (as it is called) can there be any doubt, but the whole power of the crown will be exerted, to keep this continent as low and humble as possible? Instead of going forward we shall go backward, or be perpetually

* Massacre at Lexington.

quarrelling or ridiculously petitioning.—We are already greater than the king wishes us to be, and will he not hereafter endeavour to make us less? To bring the matter to one point. Is the power who is jealous of our prosperity, a proper power to govern us? Whoever says *No* to this question is an *independant*, for independancy means no more, than, whether we shall make our own laws, or, whether the king, the greatest enemy this continent hath, or can have, shall tell us *"there shall be no laws but such as I like."*

But the king you will say has a negative in England; the people there can make no laws without his consent. In point of right and good order, there is something very ridiculous, that a youth of twenty-one (which hath often happened) shall say to several millions of people, older and wiser than himself, I forbid this or that act of yours to be law. But in this place I decline this sort of reply, though I will never cease to expose the absurdity of it, and only answer, that England being the King's residence, and America not so, makes quite another case. The king's negative *here* is ten times more dangerous and fatal than it can be in England, for *there* he will scarcely refuse his consent to a bill for putting England into as strong a state of defence as possible, and in America he would never suffer such a bill to be passed.

America is only a secondary object in the system of British politics, England consults the good of *this* country, no farther than it answers her *own* purpose. Wherefore, her own interest leads her to suppress the growth of *ours* in every case which doth not promote her advantage, or in the least interferes with it. A pretty state we should soon be in under such a second-hand government, considering what has happened! Men do not change from enemies to friends by the alteration of a name: And in order to shew that reconciliation *now* is a dangerous doctrine, I affirm, *that it would be policy in the king at this time, to repeal the acts for the sake of reinstating himself in the government of the provinces*; in order, that HE MAY ACCOMPLISH BY CRAFT AND SUBTILTY, IN THE LONG RUN, WHAT HE CANNOT DO BY FORCE AND VIOLENCE IN THE SHORT ONE. Reconciliation and ruin are nearly related.

Secondly. That as even the best terms, which we can expect to obtain, can amount to no more than a temporary expedient, or a kind of government by guardianship, which can last no longer than till the colonies come of age, so the general face and state of things, in the interim, will be unsettled and unpromising. Emigrants of property will not choose to come to a country whose form of government hangs but by a thread, and who is every day tottering on the brink of commotion and disturbance; and numbers of the present inhabitants would lay hold of the interval, to dispose of their effects, and quit the continent.

But the most powerful of all arguments, is, that nothing but independance, i. e. a continental form of government, can keep the peace of the continent and preserve it inviolate from civil wars. I dread the event of a reconciliation with Britain now, as it is more than probable, that it will be followed by a revolt somewhere or other, the consequences of which may be far more fatal than all the malice of Britain.

Thousands are already ruined by British barbarity; (thousands more will probably suffer the same fate). Those men have other feelings than us who have nothing suffered. All they *now* possess is liberty, what they before enjoyed is sacrificed to its service, and having nothing more to lose, they disdain submission. Besides, the general temper of the colonies, towards a British government, will be like that of a youth, who is nearly out of his time; they will care very little about her. And a government which cannot preserve the peace, is no government at all, and in that case we pay our money for nothing; and pray what is it that Britain can do, whose power will be wholly on paper, should a civil tumult break out the very day after reconciliation? I have heard some men say, many of whom I believe spoke without thinking, that they dreaded an independance, fearing that it would produce civil wars. It is but seldom that our first thoughts are truly correct, and that is the case here; for there are ten times more to dread from a patched up connexion than from independance. I make the sufferers case my own, and I protest, that were I driven from house and home, my property destroyed, and my circumstances ruined, that as a man, sensible of injuries, I could never relish the doctrine of reconciliation, or consider myself bound thereby.

The colonies have manifested such a spirit of good order and obedience to continental government, as is sufficient to make every reasonable person easy and happy on that head. No man can assign the least pretence for his fears, on any other grounds, than such as are truly childish and ridiculous, viz. that one colony will be striving for superiority over another.

Where there are no distinctions there can be no superiority, perfect equality affords no temptation. The republics of Europe are all (and we may say always) in peace. Holland and Swisserland are without wars, foreign or domestic: Monarchical governments, it is true, are never long at rest; the crown itself is a temptation to enterprizing ruffians at *home*; and that degree of pride and insolence ever attendant on regal authority, swells into a rupture with foreign powers, in instances, where a republican government, by being formed on more natural principles, would negociate the mistake.

If there is any true cause of fear respecting independance, it is because no plan is yet laid down. Men do not see their way out—Wherefore, as an opening into that business, I offer the following hints; at the same time modestly affirming, that I have no other opinion of them myself, than that they may be the means of giving rise to something better. Could the straggling thoughts of individuals be collected, they would frequently form materials for wise and able men to improve into useful matter.

Let the assemblies be annual, with a President only. The representation more equal. Their business wholly domestic, and subject to the authority of a Continental Congress.

Let each colony be divided into six, eight, or ten, convenient districts, each district to send a proper number of delegates to Congress, so that each colony send at least thirty. The whole number in Congress will be at least 390. Each Congress to sit   and to choose a president by the following method. When the delegates are met, let a colony be taken from the whole thirteen colonies by lot, after which, let the whole Congress choose (by ballot) a president from out of the delegates of *that* province. In the next Congress, let a colony be taken by lot from twelve only, omitting that colony from which the president was taken in the former Congress, and so proceeding on till the whole thirteen shall have had their proper rotation. And in order that nothing may pass into a law but what is satisfactorily just, not less than three fifths of the Congress to be called a majority.—He that will promote discord, under a government so equally formed as this, would have joined Lucifer in his revolt.

But as there is a peculiar delicacy, from whom, or in what manner, this business must first arise, and as it seems most agreeable and consistent that it should come from some intermediate body between the governed and the governors, that is, between the Congress and the people, let a CONTINENTAL CONFERENCE be held, in the following manner, and for the following purpose.

A committee of twenty-six members of Congress, viz. two for each colony. Two members from each House of Assembly, or Provincial Convention; and five representatives of the people at large, to be chosen in the capital city or town of each province, for, and in behalf of the whole province, by as many qualified voters as shall think proper to attend from all parts of the province for that purpose; or, if more convenient, the representatives may be chosen in two or three of the most populous parts thereof. In this conference, thus assembled, will be united, the two grand principles of business, *knowledge* and *power*. The members of Congress, Assemblies, or Conventions, by having had experience in national concerns, will be able and useful counsellors, and the whole, being impowered by the people, will have a truly legal authority.

The conferring members being met, let their business be to frame a CONTINENTAL CHARTER, or Charter of the United Colonies; (answering to what is called the Magna Charta of England) fixing the number and manner of choosing members of Congress, members of Assembly, with their date of sitting, and drawing the line of business and jurisdiction between them: (Always remembering, that our strength is continental, not provincial:) Securing freedom and property to all men, and above all things, the free exercise of religion, according to the dictates of conscience; with such other matter as is necessary for a charter to contain. Immediately after which, the said Conference to dissolve, and the bodies which shall be chosen comfortable to the said charter, to be the legislators and governors of this continent for the time being: Whose peace and happiness, may God preserve, Amen.

Should any body of men be hereafter delegated for this or some similar purpose, I offer them the following extracts from that wise observer on governments *Dragonetti*. "The science" says he "of the politician consists in fixing the true point of happiness and freedom. Those men would deserve the gratitude of ages, who should discover a mode of government that contained the greatest sum of individual happiness, with the least national expense. *Dragonetti on virtue and rewards*."

But where says some is the King of America? I'll tell you Friend, he reigns above, and doth not make havoc of mankind like the Royal Brute of Britain. Yet that we may not appear to be defective even in earthly honors, let a day be solemnly set apart for proclaiming the charter; let it be brought forth placed on the divine law, the word of God; let a crown be placed thereon, by which the world may know, that so far as we approve of monarchy, that in America THE LAW IS KING. For as in absolute governments the King is law, so in free countries the law *ought* to be King; and there ought to be no other. But lest any ill use should afterwards arise, let the crown at the conclusion of the ceremony be demolished, and scattered among the people whose right it is.

A government of our own is our natural right: And when a man seriously reflects on the precariousness of human affairs, he will become convinced, that it is infinitely wiser and safer, to form a constitution of our own in a cool deliberate manner, while we have it in our power, than to trust such an interesting event to time and chance. If we omit it now, some Massanello* may hereafter arise, who laying hold of popular disquietudes, may collect together the desperate and the discontented, and by assuming to themselves the powers of government, may sweep away the liberties of the continent like a deluge. Should the government of America return again into the hands of Britain, the tottering situation of things, will be a temptation for some desperate adventurer to try his fortune; and in such a case, what relief can Britain give? Ere she could hear the news,

---

* Thomas Anello, otherwise Massanello, a fisherman of Naples, who after spiriting up his countrymen in the public market place, against the oppression of the Spaniards, to whom the place was then subject, prompted them to revolt, and in the space of a day became King.

the fatal business might be done; and ourselves suffering like the wretched Britons under the oppression of the Conqueror. Ye that oppose independance now, ye know not what ye do; ye are opening a door to eternal tyranny, by keeping vacant the seat of government. There are thousands, and tens of thousands, who would think it glorious to expel from the continent, that barbarous and hellish power, which hath stirred up the Indians and Negroes to destroy us, the cruelty hath a double guilt, it is dealing brutally by us, and treacherously by them.

To talk of friendship with those in whom our reason forbids us to have faith, and our affections wounded through a thousand pores instruct us to detest, is madness and folly. Every day wears out the little remains of kindred between us and them, and can there be any reason to hope, that as the relationship expires, the affection will increase, or that we shall agree better, when we have ten times more and greater concerns to quarrel over than ever?

Ye that tell us of harmony and reconciliation, can ye restore to us the time that is past? Can ye give to prostitution its former innocence? Neither can ye reconcile Britain and America. The last cord now is broken, the people of England are presenting addresses against us. There are injuries which nature cannot forgive; she would cease to be nature if she did. As well can the lover forgive the ravisher of his mistress, as the continent forgive the murders of Britain. The Almighty hath implanted in us these unextinguishable feelings for good and wise purposes. They are the guardians of his image in our hearts. They distinguish us from the herd of common animals. The social compact would dissolve, and justice be extirpated from the earth, or have only a casual existence were we callous to the touches of affection. The robber, and the murderer, would often escape unpunished, did not the injuries which our tempers sustain, provoke us into justice.

O ye that love mankind! Ye that dare oppose, not only the tyranny, but the tyrant, stand forth! Every spot of the old world is overrun with oppression. Freedom hath been hunted round the globe. Asia, and Africa, have long expelled her.— Europe regards her like a stranger, and England hath given her warning to depart. O! receive the fugitive, and prepare in time an asylum for mankind.

OF THE PRESENT ABILITY OF AMERICA,
WITH SOME MISCELLANEOUS REFLEXIONS.

I HAVE never met with a man, either in England or America,
who hath not confessed his opinion, that a separation between
the countries, would take place one time or other: And there is
no instance, in which we have shewn less judgment, than in
endeavouring to describe, what we call, the ripeness or fitness
of the Continent for independance.

As all men allow the measure, and vary only in their opinion
of the time, let us, in order to remove mistakes, take a general
survey of things, and endeavour, if possible, to find out the
very time. But we need not go far, the inquiry ceases at once,
for, the *time hath found us.* The general concurrence, the glorious union of all things prove the fact.

It is not in numbers, but in unity, that our great strength
lies; yet our present numbers are sufficient to repel the force of
all the world. The Continent hath, at this time, the largest body
of armed and disciplined men of any power under Heaven; and
is just arrived at that pitch of strength, in which, no single colony is able to support itself, and the whole, when united, can
accomplish the matter, and either more, or, less than this, might
be fatal in its effects. Our land force is already sufficient, and as
to naval affairs, we cannot be insensible, that Britain would
never suffer an American man of war to be built, while the
continent remained in her hands. Wherefore, we should be no
forwarder an hundred years hence in that branch, than we are
now; but the truth is, we should be less so, because the timber
of the country is every day diminishing, and that, which will
remain at last, will be far off and difficult to procure.

Were the continent crowded with inhabitants, her sufferings
under the present circumstances would be intolerable. The
more sea port towns we had, the more should we have both to
defend and to loose. Our present numbers are so happily proportioned to our wants, that no man need be idle. The diminution of trade affords an army, and the necessities of an army
create a new trade.

Debts we have none; and whatever we may contract on this
account will serve as a glorious memento of our virtue. Can we
but leave posterity with a settled form of government, an

independant constitution of it's own, the purchase at any price will be cheap. But to expend millions for the sake of getting a few vile acts repealed, and routing the present ministry only, is unworthy the charge, and is using posterity with the utmost cruelty; because it is leaving them the great work to do, and a debt upon their backs, from which, they derive no advantage. Such a thought is unworthy a man of honor, and is the true characteristic of a narrow heart and a pedling politician.

The debt we may contract doth not deserve our regard if the work be but accomplished. No nation ought to be without a debt. A national debt is a national bond; and when it bears no interest, is in no case a grievance. Britain is oppressed with a debt of upwards of one hundred and forty millions sterling, for which she pays upwards of four millions interest. And as a compensation for her debt, she has a large navy; America is without a debt, and without a navy; yet for the twentieth part of the English national debt, could have a navy as large again. The navy of England is not worth, at this time, more than three millions and an half sterling.

The first and second editions of this pamphlet were published without the following calculations, which are now given as a proof that the above estimation of the navy is a just one. *See Entic's naval history, intro.* page 56.

The charge of building a ship of each rate, and furnishing her with masts, yards, sails and rigging, together with a proportion of eight months boatswain's and carpenter's sea-stores, as calculated by Mr. Burchett, Secretary to the navy.

		£.
For a ship of a 100 guns.	. . . .	35,553
90	. . . .	29,886
80	. . . .	23,638
70	. . . .	17,785
60	. . . .	14,197
50	. . . .	10,606
40	. . . .	7,558
30	. . . .	5,846
20	. . . .	3,710

And from hence it is easy to sum up the value, or cost rather, of the whole British navy, which in the year 1757, when it was at its greatest glory consisted of the following ships and guns.

Ships.	Guns.	Cost of one.	Cost of all.
6	100	35,553 *l.*	213,318 *l.*
12	90	29,886	358,632
12	80	23,638	283,656
43	70	17,785	764,755
35	60	14,197	496,895
40	50	10,606	424,240
45	40	7,558	340,110
58	20	3,710	215,180
85 Sloops, bombs, and fireships, one with another, at		2,000	170,000

Cost 3,266,786

Remains for guns 233,214

3,500,000

No country on the globe is so happily situated, or so internally capable of raising a fleet as America. Tar, timber, iron, and cordage are her natural produce. We need go abroad for nothing. Whereas the Dutch, who make large profits by hiring out their ships of war to the Spaniards and Portuguese, are obliged to import most of the materials they use. We ought to view the building a fleet as an article of commerce, it being the natural manufactory of this country. It is the best money we can lay out. A navy when finished is worth more than it cost. And is that nice point in national policy, in which commerce and protection are united. Let us build; if we want them not, we can sell; and by that means replace our paper currency with ready gold and silver.

In point of manning a fleet, people in general run into great errors; it is not necessary that one fourth part should be sailors. The Terrible privateer, Captain Death, stood the hottest engagement of any ship last war, yet had not twenty sailors on board, though her complement of men was upwards of two hundred. A few able and social sailors will soon instruct a sufficient number of active landmen in the common work of a ship.

Wherefore, we never can be more capable to begin on maritime matters than now, while our timber is standing, our fisheries blocked up, and our sailors and shipwrights out of employ. Men of war, of seventy and eighty guns were built forty years ago in New-England, and why not the same now? Ship-building is America's greatest pride, and in which, she will in time excel the whole world. The great empires of the east are mostly inland, and consequently excluded from the possibility of rivalling her. Africa is in a state of barbarism; and no power in Europe, hath either such an extent of coast, or such an internal supply of materials. Where nature hath given the one, she has withheld the other; to America only hath she been liberal of both. The vast empire of Russia is almost shut out from the sea; wherefore, her boundless forests, her tar, iron, and cordage are only articles of commerce.

In point of safety, ought we to be without a fleet? We are not the little people now, which we were sixty years ago; at that time we might have trusted our property in the streets, or fields rather; and slept securely without locks or bolts to our doors or windows. The case now is altered, and our methods of defence, ought to improve with our increase of property. A common pirate, twelve months ago, might have come up the Delaware, and laid the city of Philadelphia under instant contribution, for what sum he pleased; and the same might have happened to other places. Nay, any daring fellow, in a brig of fourteen or sixteen guns, might have robbed the whole Continent, and carried off half a million of money. These are circumstances which demand our attention, and point out the necessity of naval protection.

Some, perhaps, will say, that after we have made it up with Britain, she will protect us. Can we be so unwise as to mean, that she shall keep a navy in our harbours for that purpose? Common sense will tell us, that the power which hath endeavoured to subdue us, is of all others, the most improper to defend us. Conquest may be effected under the pretence of friendship; and ourselves, after a long and brave resistance, be at last cheated into slavery. And if her ships are not to be admitted into our harbours, I would ask, how is she to protect us? A navy three or four thousand miles off can be of little use, and on sudden emergencies, none at all. Wherefore, if we must hereafter protect ourselves, why not do it for ourselves? Why do it for another?

The English list of ships of war, is long and formidable, but not a tenth part of them are at any one time fit for service, numbers of them not in being; yet their names are pompously continued in the list, if only a plank be left of the ship: and not a fifth part, of such as are fit for service, can be spared on any one station at one time. The East, and West Indies, Mediterranean, Africa, and other parts over which Britain extends her claim, make large demands upon her navy. From a mixture of prejudice and inattention, we have contracted a false notion respecting the navy of England, and have talked as if we should have the whole of it to encounter at once, and for that reason, supposed, that we must have one as large; which not being instantly practicable, have been made use of by a set of disguised Tories to discourage our beginning thereon. Nothing can be farther from truth than this; for if America had only a twentieth part of the naval force of Britain, she would be by far an over match for her; because, as we neither have, nor claim any foreign dominion, our whole force would be employed on our own coast, where we should, in the long run, have two to one the advantage of those who had three or four thousand miles to sail over, before they could attack us, and the same distance to return in order to refit and recruit. And although Britain by her fleet, hath a check over our trade to Europe, we have as large a one over her trade to the West-Indies, which, by laying in the neighbourhood of the Continent, is entirely at its mercy.

Some method might be fallen on to keep up a naval force in time of peace, if we should not judge it necessary to support a constant navy. If premiums were to be given to merchants, to build and employ in their service, ships mounted with twenty, thirty, forty, or fifty guns, (the premiums to be in proportion to the loss of bulk to the merchants) fifty or sixty of those ships, with a few guard ships on constant duty, would keep up a sufficient navy, and that without burdening ourselves with the evil so loudly complained of in England, of suffering their fleet, in time of peace to lie rotting in the docks. To unite the sinews of commerce and defence is sound policy; for when our strength and our riches, play into each other's hand, we need fear no external enemy.

In almost every article of defence we abound. Hemp flourishes even to rankness, so that we need not want cordage. Our iron is superior to that of other countries. Our small arms equal to any in the world. Cannon we can cast at pleasure. Saltpetre and gunpowder we are every day producing. Our knowledge is hourly improving. Resolution is our inherent character, and courage hath never yet forsaken us. Wherefore, what is it that we want? Why is it that we hesitate? From Britain we can expect nothing but ruin. If she is once admitted to the government of America again, this Continent will not be worth living in. Jealousies will be always arising; insurrections will be constantly happening; and who will go forth to quell them? Who will venture his life to reduce his own countrymen to a foreign obedience? The difference between Pennsylvania and Connecticut, respecting some unlocated lands, shews the insignificance of a British government, and fully proves, that nothing but Continental authority can regulate Continental matters.

Another reason why the present time is preferable to all others, is, that the fewer our numbers are, the more land there is yet unoccupied, which instead of being lavished by the king on his worthless dependants, may be hereafter applied, not only to the discharge of the present debt, but to the constant support of government. No nation under heaven hath such an advantage as this.

The infant state of the Colonies, as it is called, so far from being against, is an argument in favor of independance. We are sufficiently numerous, and were we more so, we might be less united. It is a matter worthy of observation, that the more a country is peopled, the smaller their armies are. In military numbers, the ancients far exceeded the moderns: and the reason is evident, for trade being the consequence of population, men become too much absorbed thereby to attend to any thing else. Commerce diminishes the spirit, both of patriotism and military defence. And history sufficiently informs us, that the bravest atchievements were always accomplished in the non-age of a nation. With the increase of commerce, England hath lost its spirit. The city of London, notwithstanding its numbers, submits to continued insults with the patience of a coward. The more men have to lose, the less willing are they to venture. The rich are in general slaves to fear, and submit to courtly power with the trembling duplicity of a Spaniel.

Youth is the seed time of good habits, as well in nations as in individuals. It might be difficult, if not impossible, to form the Continent into one government half a century hence. The vast variety of interests, occasioned by an increase of trade and population, would create confusion. Colony would be against colony. Each being able might scorn each other's assistance: and while the proud and foolish gloried in their little distinctions, the wise would lament, that the union had not been formed before. Wherefore, the *present time* is the *true time* for establishing it. The intimacy which is contracted in infancy, and the friendship which is formed in misfortune, are, of all others, the most lasting and unalterable. Our present union is marked with both these characters: we are young, and we have been distressed; but our concord hath withstood our troubles, and fixes a memorable æra for posterity to glory in.

The present time, likewise, is that peculiar time, which never happens to a nation but once, *viz.* the time of forming itself into a government. Most nations have let slip the opportunity, and by that means have been compelled to receive laws from their conquerors, instead of making laws for themselves. First, they had a king, and then a form of government; whereas, the articles or charter of government, should be formed first, and men delegated to execute them afterward: but from the errors of other nations, let us learn wisdom, and lay hold of the present opportunity—*To begin government at the right end*.

When William the Conqueror subdued England, he gave them law at the point of the sword; and until we consent, that the seat of government, in America, be legally and authoritatively occupied, we shall be in danger of having it filled by some fortunate ruffian, who may treat us in the same manner, and then, where will be our freedom? where our property?

As to religion, I hold it to be the indispensible duty of all government, to protect all conscientious professors thereof, and I know of no other business which government hath to do therewith. Let a man throw aside that narrowness of soul, that selfishness of principle, which the niggards of all professions are so unwilling to part with, and he will be at once delivered of his fears on that head. Suspicion is the companion of mean souls, and the bane of all good society. For myself, I fully and conscientiously believe, that it is the will of the Almighty, that there should be diversity of religious opinions among us: It affords a larger field for our Christian kindness. Were we all of one way of thinking, our religious dispositions would want matter for probation; and on this liberal principle, I look on the various denominations among us, to be like children of the same family, differing only, in what is called, their Christian names.

In page 678, I threw out a few thoughts on the propriety of a Continental Charter, (for I only presume to offer hints, not plans) and in this place, I take the liberty of re-mentioning the subject, by observing, that a charter is to be understood as a bond of solemn obligation, which the whole enters into, to support the right of every separate part, whether of religion, personal freedom, or property. A firm bargain and a right reckoning make long friends.

In a former page I likewise mentioned the necessity of a large and equal representation; and there is no political matter which more deserves our attention. A small number of electors, or a small number of representatives, are equally dangerous. But if the number of the representatives be not only small, but unequal, the danger is increased. As an instance of this, I mention the following; when the Associators petition was before the House of Assembly of Pennsylvania; twenty-eight members only were present, all the Bucks county members, being eight, voted against it, and had seven of the Chester members done the same, this whole province had been governed by two counties only, and this danger it is always exposed to. The unwarrantable stretch likewise, which that house made in their last sitting, to gain an undue authority over the Delegates of that province, ought to warn the people at large, how they trust power out of their own hands. A set of instructions for the Delegates were put together, which in point of sense and business would have dishonored a schoolboy, and after being approved by a *few*, a *very few* without doors, were carried into the House, and there passed *in behalf of the whole colony*; whereas, did the whole colony know, with what ill-will that

House hath entered on some necessary public measures, they would not hesitate a moment to think them unworthy of such a trust.

Immediate necessity makes many things convenient, which if continued would grow into oppressions. Expedience and right are different things. When the calamities of America required a consultation, there was no method so ready, or at that time so proper, as to appoint persons from the several Houses of Assembly for that purpose; and the wisdom with which they have proceeded hath preserved this continent from ruin. But as it is more than probable that we shall never be without a Congress, every well wisher to good order, must own, that the mode for choosing members of that body, deserves consideration. And I put it as a question to those, who make a study of mankind, whether *representation and election* is not too great a power for one and the same body of men to possess? When we are planning for posterity, we ought to remember, that virtue is not hereditary.

It is from our enemies that we often gain excellent maxims, and are frequently surprised into reason by their mistakes. Mr. Cornwall (one of the Lords of the Treasury) treated the petition of the New-York Assembly with contempt, because *that* House, he said, consisted but of twenty-six members, which trifling number, he argued, could not with decency be put for the whole. We thank him for his involuntary honesty.*

To Conclude, however strange it may appear to some, or however unwilling they may be to think so, matters not, but many strong and striking reasons may be given, to shew, that nothing can settle our affairs so expeditiously as an open and determined declaration for independance. Some of which are,

First.—It is the custom of nations, when any two are at war, for some other powers, not engaged in the quarrel, to step in as mediators, and bring about the preliminaries of a peace: but while America calls herself the Subject of Great-Britain, no power, however well disposed she may be, can offer her mediation. Wherefore, in our present state we may quarrel on for ever.

---

* Those who would fully understand of what great consequence a large and equal representation is to a state, should read Burgh's political Disquisitions.

Secondly.—It is unreasonable to suppose, that France or Spain will give us any kind of assistance, if we mean only, to make use of that assistance for the purpose of repairing the breach, and strengthening the connection between Britain and America; because, those powers would be sufferers by the consequences.

Thirdly.—While we profess ourselves the subjects of Britain, we must, in the eye of foreign nations, be considered as rebels. The precedent is somewhat dangerous to *their peace*, for men to be in arms under the name of subjects; we, on the spot, can solve the paradox: but to unite resistance and subjection, requires an idea much too refined for common understanding.

Fourthly.—Were a manifesto to be published, and despatched to foreign courts, setting forth the miseries we have endured, and the peaceable methods we have ineffectually used for redress; declaring, at the same time, that not being able, any longer, to live happily or safely under the cruel disposition of the British court, we had been driven to the necessity of breaking off all connections with her; at the same time, assuring all such courts of our peaceable disposition towards them, and of our desire of entering into trade with them: Such a memorial would produce more good effects to this Continent, than if a ship were freighted with petitions to Britain.

Under our present denomination of British subjects, we can neither be received nor heard abroad: The custom of all courts is against us, and will be so, until, by an independance, we take rank with other nations.

These proceedings may at first appear strange and difficult; but, like all other steps which we have already passed over, will in a little time become familiar and agreeable; and, until an independance is declared, the Continent will feel itself like a man who continues putting off some unpleasant business from day to day, yet knows it must be done, hates to set about it, wishes it over, and is continually haunted with the thoughts of its necessity.

APPENDIX.

SINCE the publication of the first edition of this pamphlet, or rather, on the same day on which it came out, the King's Speech made its appearance in this city. Had the spirit of prophecy directed the birth of this production, it could not have brought it forth, at a more seasonable juncture, or a more necessary time. The bloody mindedness of the one, shew the necessity of pursuing the doctrine of the other. Men read by way of revenge. And the Speech, instead of terrifying, prepared a way for the manly principles of Independance.

Ceremony, and even, silence, from whatever motive they may arise, have a hurtful tendency, when they give the least degree of countenance to base and wicked performances; wherefore, if this maxim be admitted, it naturally follows, that the King's Speech, as being a piece of finished villany, deserved, and still deserves, a general execration both by the Congress and the people. Yet, as the domestic tranquillity of a nation, depends greatly, on the *chastity* of what may properly be called NATIONAL MANNERS, it is often better, to pass some things over in silent disdain, than to make use of such new methods of dislike, as might introduce the least innovation, on that guardian of our peace and safety. And, perhaps, it is chiefly owing to this prudent delicacy, that the King's Speech, hath not, before now, suffered a public execution. The Speech if it may be called one, is nothing better than a wilful audacious libel against the truth, the common good, and the existence of mankind; and is a formal and pompous method of offering up human sacrifices to the pride of tyrants. But this general massacre of mankind, is one of the privileges, and the certain consequence of Kings; for as nature knows them *not*, they know *not her*, and although they are beings of our *own* creating, they know not *us*, and are become the gods of their creators. The Speech hath one good quality, which is, that it is not calculated to deceive, neither can we, even if we would, be deceived by it. Brutality and tyranny appear on the face of it. It leaves us at no loss: And every line convinces, even in the moment of reading, that He, who hunts the woods for prey, the naked and untutored Indian, is less a Savage than the King of Britain.

Sir John Dalrymple, the putative father of a whining jesuitical piece, fallaciously called, "*The Address of the people of* ENGLAND *to the inhabitants of* AMERICA," hath, perhaps, from a vain supposition, that the people *here* were to be frightened at the pomp and description of a king, given, (though very unwisely on his part) the real character of the present one: "But," says this writer, "if you are inclined to pay compliments to an administration, which we do not complain of," (meaning the Marquis of Rockingham's at the repeal of the Stamp Act) "it is very unfair in you to withhold them from that prince, *by whose* NOD ALONE *they were permitted to do any thing.*" This is toryism with a witness! Here is idolatry even without a mask: And he who can calmly hear, and digest such doctrine, hath forfeited his claim to rationality—an apostate from the order of manhood; and ought to be considered—as one, who hath not only given up the proper dignity of man, but sunk himself beneath the rank of animals, and contemptibly crawls through the world like a worm.

However, it matters very little now, what the king of England either says or docs; he hath wickedly broken through every moral and human obligation, trampled nature and conscience beneath his feet; and by a steady and constitutional spirit of insolence and cruelty, procured for himself an universal hatred. It is *now* the interest of America to provide for herself. She hath already a large and young family, whom it is more her duty to take care of, than to be granting away her property, to support a power who is become a reproach to the names of men and christians—YE, whose office it is to watch over the morals of a nation, of whatsoever sect or denomination ye are of, as well as ye, who, are more immediately the guardians of the public liberty, if ye wish to preserve your native country uncontaminated by European corruption, ye must in secret wish a separation—But leaving the moral part to private reflection, I shall chiefly confine my farther remarks to the following heads.

First. That it is the interest of America to be separated from Britain.

Secondly. Which is the easiest and most practicable plan, RECONCILIATION or INDEPENDANCE? with some occasional remarks.

In support of the first, I could, if I judged it proper, produce the opinion of some of the ablest and most experienced men on this continent; and whose sentiments, on that head, are not yet publicly known. It is in reality a self-evident position: For no nation in a state of foreign dependance, limited in its commerce, and cramped and fettered in its legislative powers, can ever arrive at any material eminence. America doth not yet know what opulence is; and although the progress which she hath made stands unparalleled in the history of other nations, it is but childhood, compared with what she would be capable of arriving at, had she, as she ought to have, the legislative powers in her own hands. England is, at this time, proudly coveting what would do her no good, were she to accomplish it; and the Continent hesitating on a matter, which will be her final ruin if neglected. It is the commerce and not the conquest of America, by which England is to be benefited, and that would in a great measure continue, were the countries as independant of each other as France and Spain; because in many articles, neither can go to a better market. But it is the independance of this country on Britain or any other, which is now the main and only object worthy of contention, and which, like all other truths discovered by necessity, will appear clearer and stronger every day.

First. Because it will come to that one time or other.

Secondly. Because, the longer it is delayed the harder it will be to accomplish.

I have frequently amused myself both in public and private companies, with silently remarking, the specious errors of those who speak without reflecting. And among the many which I have heard, the following seems the most general, viz. that had this rupture happened forty or fifty years hence, instead of *now*, the Continent would have been more able to have shaken off the dependance. To which I reply, that our military ability, *at this time*, arises from the experience gained in the last war, and which in forty or fifty years time, would have been totally extinct. The Continent, would not, by that time, have had a General, or even a military officer left; and we, or those who may succeed us, would have been as ignorant of martial matters as the ancient Indians: And this single position, closely attended to, will unanswerably prove, that the present time is preferable to all others. The argument turns thus—at the conclusion of the last war, we had experience, but wanted numbers; and forty or fifty years hence, we should have numbers, without experience; wherefore, the proper point of time, must be some particular point between the two extremes, in which a sufficiency of the former remains, and a proper increase of the latter is obtained: And that point of time is the present time.

The reader will pardon this digression, as it does not properly come under the head I first set out with, and to which I again return by the following position, viz.

Should affairs be patched up with Britain, and she to remain the governing and sovereign power of America, (which, as matters are now circumstanced, is giving up the point intirely) we shall deprive ourselves of the very means of sinking the debt we have, or may contract. The value of the back lands which some of the provinces are clandestinely deprived of, by the unjust extention of the limits of Canada, valued only at five pounds sterling per hundred acres, amount to upwards of twenty-five millions, Pennsylvania currency; and the quit-rents at one penny sterling per acre, to two millions yearly.

It is by the sale of those lands that the debt may be sunk, without burthen to any, and the quit-rent reserved thereon, will always lessen, and in time, will wholly support the yearly expence of government. It matters not how long the debt is in paying, so that the lands when sold be applied to the discharge of it, and for the execution of which, the Congress for the time being, will be the continental trustees.

I proceed now to the second head, viz. Which is the easiest and most practicable plan, RECONCILIATION or INDEPENDANCE; with some occasional remarks.

He who takes nature for his guide is not easily beaten out of his argument, and on that ground, I answer *generally—That* INDEPENDANCE *being a* SINGLE SIMPLE LINE, *contained within ourselves; and reconciliation, a matter exceedingly perplexed and complicated, and in which, a treacherous capricious court is to interfere, gives the answer without a doubt.*

The present state of America is truly alarming to every man who is capable of reflexion. Without law, without government, without any other mode of power than what is founded on, and granted by courtesy. Held together by an unexampled concurrence of sentiment, which, is nevertheless subject to change, and which, every secret enemy is endeavouring to dissolve. Our present condition, is, Legislation without law; wisdom without a plan; a constitution without a name; and, what is strangely astonishing, perfect Independance contending for dependance. The instance is without a precedent; the case never existed before; and who can tell what may be the event? The property of no man is secure in the present unbraced system of things. The mind of the multitude is left at random, and seeing no fixed object before them, they pursue such as fancy or opinion starts. Nothing is criminal; there is no such thing as treason; wherefore, every one thinks himself at liberty to act as he pleases. The Tories dared not have assembled offensively, had they known that their lives, by that act, were forfeited to the laws of the state. A line of distinction should be drawn, between, English soldiers taken in battle, and inhabitants of America taken in arms. The first are prisoners, but the latter traitors. The one forfeits his liberty, the other his head.

Notwithstanding our wisdom, there is a visible feebleness in some of our proceedings which gives encouragement to dissentions. The Continental Belt is too losely buckled. And if something is not done in time, it will be too late to do any thing, and we shall fall into a state, in which, neither *Reconciliation* nor *Independance* will be practicable. The king and his worthless adherents are got at their old game of dividing the Continent, and there are not wanting among us, Printers, who will be busy in spreading specious falsehoods. The artful and hypocritical letter which appeared a few months ago in two of the New-York papers, and likewise in two others, is an evidence that there are men who want either judgment or honesty.

It is easy getting into holes and corners and talking of reconciliation: But do such men seriously consider, how difficult the task is, and how dangerous it may prove, should the Continent divide thereon. Do they take within their view, all the various orders of men whose situation and circumstances, as well as their own, are to be considered therein. Do they put themselves in the place of the sufferer whose *all* is *already* gone, and of the soldier, who hath quitted *all* for the defence of his country. If their ill judged moderation be suited to their own private situations *only*, regardless of others, the event will convince them, that "they are reckoning without their Host."

Put us, say some, on the footing we were on in sixty-three: To which I answer, the request is not *now* in the power of Britain to comply with, neither will she propose it; but if it were, and even should be granted, I ask, as a reasonable question, By what means is such a corrupt and faithless court to be kept to its engagements? Another parliament, nay, even the present, may hereafter repeal the obligation, on the pretence, of its being violently obtained, or unwisely granted; and in that case, Where is our redress?—No going to law with nations; cannon are the barristers of Crowns; and the sword, not of justice, but of war, decides the suit. To be on the footing of sixty-three, it is not sufficient, that the laws only be put on the same state, but, that our circumstances, likewise, be put on the same state; Our burnt and destroyed towns repaired or built up, our private losses made good, our public debts (contracted for defence) discharged; otherwise, we shall be millions worse than we were at that enviable period. Such a request, had it been complied with a year ago, would have won the heart and soul of the Continent—but now it is too late, "The Rubicon is passed."

Besides, the taking up arms, merely to enforce the repeal of a pecuniary law, seems as unwarrantable by the divine law, and as repugnant to human feelings, as the taking up arms to enforce obedience thereto. The object, on either side, doth not justify the means; for the lives of men are too valuable to be cast away on such trifles. It is the violence which is done and threatened to our persons; the destruction of our property by an armed force; the invasion of our country by fire and sword, which conscientiously qualifies the use of arms: And the instant, in which such a mode of defence became necessary, all subjection to Britain ought to have ceased; and the independancy of America, should have been considered, as dating its æra from, and published by, *the first musket that was fired against her.* This line is a line of consistency; neither drawn by caprice, nor extended by ambition; but produced by a chain of events, of which the colonies were not the authors.

I shall conclude these remarks, with the following timely and well intended hints. We ought to reflect, that there are three different ways, by which an independancy may hereafter be effected; and that *one* of those *three*, will one day or other, be the fate of America, viz. By the legal voice of the people in Congress; by a military power; or by a mob: It may not always happen that our soldiers are citizens, and the multitude a body of reasonable men; virtue, as I have already remarked, is not hereditary, neither is it perpetual. Should an independancy be brought about by the first of those means, we have every opportunity and every encouragement before us, to form the noblest purest constitution on the face of the earth. We have it in our power to begin the world over again. A situation, similar to the present, hath not happened since the days of Noah until now. The birthday of a new world is at hand, and a race of men, perhaps as numerous as all Europe contains, are to receive their portion of freedom from the event of a few months. The Reflexion is awful—and in this point of view, How trifling, how ridiculous, do the little, paltry cavellings, of a few weak or interested men appear, when weighed against the business of a world.

Should we neglect the present favorable and inviting period, and an Independance be hereafter effected by any other means, we must charge the consequence to ourselves, or to those rather, whose narrow and prejudiced souls, are habitually opposing the measure, without either inquiring or reflecting. There are reasons to be given in support of Independance, which men should rather privately think of, than be publicly told of. We ought not now to be debating whether we shall be independant or not, but, anxious to accomplish it on a firm, secure, and honorable basis, and uneasy rather that it is not yet began upon. Every day convinces us of its necessity. Even the Tories (if such beings yet remain among us) should, of all men, be the most solicitous to promote it; for, as the appointment of committees at first, protected them from popular rage, so, a wise and well established form of government, will be the only certain means of continuing it securely to them. *Wherefore*, if they have not virtue enough to be Whigs, they ought to have prudence enough to wish for Independance.

In short, Independance is the only Bond that can tye and keep us together. We shall then see our object, and our ears will be legally shut against the schemes of an intriguing, as well, as a cruel enemy. We shall then too, be on a proper footing, to treat with Britain; for there is reason to conclude, that the pride of that court, will be less hurt by treating with the American states for terms of peace, than with those, whom she denominates, "rebellious subjects," for terms of accommodation. It is our delaying it that encourages her to hope for conquest, and our backwardness tends only to prolong the war. As we have, without any good effect therefrom, withheld our trade to obtain a redress of our grievances, let us *now* try the alternative, by *independantly* redressing them ourselves, and then offering to open the trade. The mercantile and reasonable part in England, will be still with us; because, peace *with* trade, is preferable to war *without* it. And if this offer be not accepted, other courts may be applied to.

On these grounds I rest the matter. And as no offer hath yet been made to refute the doctrine contained in the former editions of this pamphlet, it is a negative proof, that either the doctrine cannot be refuted, or, that the party in favour of it are too numerous to be opposed. WHEREFORE, instead of gazing at each other with suspicious or doubtful curiosity, let each of us, hold out to his neighbour the hearty hand of friendship, and unite in drawing a line, which, like an act of oblivion shall bury in forgetfulness every former dissention. Let the names of Whig and Tory be extinct; and let none other be heard among us, than those of *a good citizen, an open and resolute friend, and a virtuous supporter of the* RIGHTS *of* MANKIND *and of the* FREE AND INDEPENDANT STATES OF AMERICA.

To the Representatives of the Religious Society of the People called Quakers, or to so many of them as were concerned in publishing a late piece, entitled "The ANCIENT TESTIMONY and PRINCIPLES of the People called QUAKERS renewed, with Respect to the KING and GOVERNMENT, and touching the COMMOTIONS now prevailing in these and other parts of AMERICA addressed to the PEOPLE IN GENERAL."

THE Writer of this, is one of those few, who never dishonors religion either by ridiculing, or cavilling at any denomination whatsoever. To God, and not to man, are all men accountable on the score of religion. Wherefore, this epistle is not so properly addressed to you as a religious, but as a political body, dabbling in matters, which the professed Quietude of your Principles instruct you not to meddle with.

As you have, without a proper authority for so doing, put yourselves in the place of the whole body of the Quakers, so, the writer of this, in order to be on an equal rank with yourselves, is under the necessity, of putting himself in the place of all those, who, approve the very writings and principles, against which, your testimony is directed: And he hath chosen this singular situation, in order, that you might discover in him that presumption of character which you cannot see in yourselves. For neither he nor you can have any claim or title to *Political Representation.*

When men have departed from the right way, it is no wonder that they stumble and fall. And it is evident from the manner in which ye have managed your testimony, that politics, (as a religious body of men) is not your proper Walk; for however well adapted it might appear to you, it is, nevertheless, a jumble of good and bad put unwisely together, and the conclusion drawn therefrom, both unnatural and unjust.

The two first pages, (and the whole doth not make four) we give you credit for, and expect the same civility from you, because the love and desire of peace is not confined to Quakerism, it is the *natural*, as well the religious wish of all denominations of men. And on this ground, as men laboring to establish an Independant Constitution of our own, do we exceed all others in our hope, end, and aim. *Our plan is peace for ever.* We are tired of contention with Britain, and can see no real end to it but in a final separation. We act consistently, because for the sake of introducing an endless and uninterrupted peace, do we bear the evils and burthens of the present day. We are endeavoring, and will steadily continue to endeavor, to separate and dissolve a connexion which hath already filled our land with blood; and which, while the name of it remains, will be the fatal cause of future mischiefs to both countries.

We fight neither for revenge nor conquest; neither from pride nor passion; we are not insulting the world with our fleets and armies, not ravaging the globe for plunder. Beneath the shade of our own vines are we attacked; in our own houses, and on our own lands, is the violence committed against us. We view our enemies in the character of Highwaymen and Housebreakers, and having no defence for ourselves in the civil law, are obliged to punish them by the military one, and apply the sword, in the very case, where you have before now, applied the halter—Perhaps we feel for the ruined and insulted sufferers in all and every part of the continent, with a degree of tenderness which hath not yet made it's way into some of your bosoms. But be ye sure that ye mistake not the cause and ground of your Testimony. Call not coldness of soul, religion; nor put the *Bigot* in the place of the *Christian*.

O ye partial ministers of your own acknowledged principles. If the bearing arms be sinful, the first going to war must be more so, by all the difference between wilful attack and un-avoidable defence. Wherefore, if ye really preach from con-science, and mean not to make a political hobby-horse of your religion, convince the world thereof, by proclaiming your doctrine to our enemies, *for they likewise bear* ARMS. Give us proof of your sincerity by publishing it at St. James's, to the commanders in chief at Boston, to the Admirals and Captains who are piratically ravaging our coasts, and to all the murder-ing miscreants who are acting in authority under HIM whom ye profess to serve. Had ye the honest soul of *Barclay** ye would preach repentance to *your* king; Ye would tell the Royal Wretch his sins, and warn him of eternal ruin. Ye would not spend your partial invectives against the injured and the insulted only, but, like faithful ministers, would cry aloud and *spare none*. Say not that ye are persecuted, neither endeavour to

---

* "Thou hast tasted of prosperity and adversity: thou knowest what it is to be banished thy native country, to be over-ruled as well as to rule, and set upon the throne; and being *oppressed* thou hast reason to know how *hateful* the *oppressor* is both to God and man: If after all these warnings and advertise-ments, thou dost not turn unto the Lord with all thy heart, but forget him who remembered thee in thy distress, and give up thyself to follow lust and vanity, surely great will be thy condemnation.—Against which snare, as well as the temptation of those who may or do feed thee, and prompt thee to evil, the most excellent and prevalent remedy will be, to apply thyself to that light of Christ which shineth in thy conscience, and which neither can, nor will flatter thee, nor suffer thee to be at ease in thy sins."

Barclay's Address to Charles II.

make us the authors of that reproach, which, ye are bringing upon yourselves; for we testify unto all men, that we do not complain against you because ye are *Quakers*, but because ye pretend to *be* and are NOT Quakers.

Alas! it seems by the particular tendency of some part of your testimony, and other parts of your conduct, as if, all sin was reduced to, and comprehended in, *the act of bearing arms*, and that by the *people only*. Ye appear to us, to have mistaken party for conscience; because, the general tenor of your actions wants uniformity: And it is exceedingly difficult to us to give credit to many of your pretended scruples; because, we see them made by the same men, who, in the very instant that they are exclaiming against the mammon of this world, are nevertheless, hunting after it with a step as steady as Time, and an appetite as keen as Death.

The quotation which ye have made from Proverbs, in the third page of your testimony, that, "when a man's ways please the Lord, he maketh even his enemies to be at peace with him"; is very unwisely chosen on your part; because, it amounts to a proof, that the king's ways (whom ye are so desirous of supporting) do *not* please the Lord, otherwise, his reign would be in peace.

I now proceed to the latter part of your testimony, and that, for which all the foregoing seems only an introduction, viz.

"It hath ever been our judgment and principle, since we were called to profess the light of Christ Jesus, manifested in our consciences unto this day, that the setting up and putting down kings and governments, is God's peculiar prerogative; for causes best known to himself: And that it is not our business to have any hand or contrivance therein; nor to be busy bodies above our station, much less to plot and contrive the ruin, or overturn of any of them, but to pray for the king, and safety of our nation, and good of all men: That we may live a peaceable and quiet life, in all godliness and honesty; *under the government which God is pleased to set over us*."—If these are *really* your principles why do ye not abide by them? Why do ye not leave that, which ye call God's Work, to be managed by himself? These very principles instruct you to wait with patience and humility, for the event of all public measures, and to receive *that event* as the divine will towards you. *Wherefore,* what occasion is there for your *political testimony* if you fully believe what it contains? And the very publishing it proves, that either, ye do not believe what ye profess, or have not virtue enough to practise what ye believe.

The principles of Quakerism have a direct tendency to make a man the quiet and inoffensive subject of any, and every government *which is set over him.* And if the setting up and putting down of kings and governments is God's peculiar prerogative, he most certainly will not be robbed thereof by us; wherefore, the principle itself leads you to approve of every thing, which ever happened, or may happen to kings as being his work. OLIVER CROMWELL thanks you. CHARLES, then, died not by the hands of man; and should the present Proud Imitator of him, come to the same untimely end, the writers and publishers of the Testimony, are bound, by the doctrine it contains, to applaud the fact. Kings are not taken away by miracles, neither are changes in governments brought about by any other means than such as are common and human; and such as we are now using. Even the dispersion of the Jews, though foretold by our Saviour, was effected by arms. Wherefore, as ye refuse to be the means on one side, ye ought not to be meddlers on the other; but to wait the issue in silence; and unless ye can produce divine authority, to prove, that the Almighty who hath created and placed this *new* world, at the greatest distance it could possibly stand, east and west, from every part of the old, doth, nevertheless, disapprove of its being independent of the corrupt and abandoned court of Britain, unless I say, ye can shew this, how can ye on the ground of your principles, justify the exciting and stirring up the people "firmly to unite in the *abhorrence* of all such *writings,* and *measures,* as evidence of desire and design to break off the *happy* connexion we have hitherto enjoyed, with the kingdom of Great-Britain, and our just and necessary subordination to the king, and those who are lawfully placed in authority under him." What a slap of the face is here! the men, who in the very paragraph before, have quietly and passively resigned up the ordering, altering, and disposal of kings and governments, into the hands of God, are now, recalling their principles, and putting in for a share of the business. Is it possible, that the conclusion, which is here justly quoted, can any ways follow from the doctrine laid down? The inconsistency is too glaring not to be seen; the absurdity too great not to be laughed at; and such as could only have been made by those, whose understandings were darkened by the narrow and crabby spirit of a dispairing political party; for ye are not to be considered as the whole body of the Quakers but only as a factional and fractional part thereof.

Here ends the examination of your testimony; (which I call upon no man to abhor, as ye have done, but only to read and judge of fairly;) to which I subjoin the following remark; "That the setting up and putting down of kings," most certainly mean, the making him a king, who is yet not so, and the making him no king who is already one. And pray what hath this to do in the present case? We neither mean to *set up* nor to *put down*, neither to *make* nor to *unmake*, but to have nothing to *do* with them. Wherefore, your testimony in whatever light it is viewed serves only to dishonor your judgement, and for many other reasons had better have been let alone than published.

First, Because it tends to the decrease and reproach of all religion whatever, and is of the utmost danger to society, to make it a party in political disputes.

Secondly, Because it exhibits a body of men, numbers of whom disavow the publishing political testimonies, as being concerned therein and approvers thereof.

Thirdly, Because it hath a tendency to undo that continental harmony and friendship which yourselves by your late liberal and charitable donations hath lent a hand to establish; and the preservation of which, is of the utmost consequence to us all.

And here without anger or resentment I bid you farewell. Sincerely wishing, that as men and christians, ye may always fully and uninterruptedly enjoy every civil and religious right; and be, in your turn, the means of securing it to others; but that the example which ye have unwisely set, of mingling religion with politics, *may be disavowed and reprobated by every inhabitant of* AMERICA.

FINIS.

[Charles Inglis], The True Interest of America Impartially Stated, in Certain Strictures on a Pamphlet Intitled Common Sense. Philadelphia, 1776.

Paine's inflammatory pamphlet quickly incited rejoinders from Tories and Whigs alike. One of the more sophisticated of the Tory responses was written by Charles Inglis, an Irish-born clergyman who served as the Anglican minister of Trinity Church in New York City from 1765 until the end of the Revolutionary War. Of course, Inglis, who professed to be a firm supporter of the Glorious Revolution of 1688 and "none of your *passive obedience and non-resistance men*," was a Tory only within the American context—that being the label given to all those who opposed the patriot cause.

Inglis was stunned by the passion that ran through Paine's pamphlet. The author seemed "everywhere transported with rage—a rage that knows no limits, and hurries him along, like an impetuous torrent." He was a "malignant spirit" full of "fire and fury" playing on the emotions and resentments of his readers and continually violating "the propriety of language." Paine's rage was shared by many common people—artisans, shopkeepers, traders, petty merchants—who were tired of being scorned and held in contempt by a monarchical and aristocratic world. Men such as James Otis, William Henry Drayton, or Moses Mather, all educated gentlemen who occupied established, elite positions within society, could never fully represent the fury and frenzy of these middling folk, but Paine could. Some of the more genteel resistance leaders became uneasy over the anger that Paine was stirring up, but because they themselves spoke in the name of the people they could not easily challenge his fiery language. Inglis felt no such restraint, and truly frightened by Paine's radical republicanism, he was free to denounce it.

Paine was indeed a radical Whig, someone who believed that society was benign—it unites our affections—and government was dangerous —it creates distinctions. Like Thomas Jefferson, whose ideas were remarkably similar, Paine trusted the common sense of ordinary people who, however lowly, possessed a moral or social capacity that tied each of them to others. This is what made both men democrats and advocates of minimal government. Like other radical Whigs, they believed that aggrandizing monarchs were responsible for the proliferation of war and disorder. In the spread of republicanism, and the creation of a world order shaped by commerce and not military alliances, they placed their hopes for a universal peace. This was the larger meaning of Paine's memorable phrase "a new era of politics is struck."

Charles Inglis would have none of these "*Utopian* systems." He fled to England in 1783, though he returned to the New World four years later to become the Anglican bishop of Nova Scotia.

THE TRUE

INTEREST of AMERICA

IMPARTIALLY STATED,

IN CERTAIN

STRICTURES

On a PAMPHLET INTITLED

COMMON SENSE.

By an AMERICAN.

" You have been told that we are feditious, impatient of go-
" vernment, and defirous of Independency. Be affured that
" thefe are not *Facts*, but *Calumnies*—Permit us to be as free as
" yourfelves, and we fhall ever efteem a union with you to be our
" *greateft glory* and our *greateft happinefs.*—Place us in the fame
" fituation we were at the clofe of the laft war, and our *former*
" *harmony* will be reftored."   CONTINENTAL CONGRESS'S
                              Addrefs to the People of Great-Britain.
  " Obtrectatio et liver pronis auribus accipiuntur." TACITUS.
            " ——Nihil eft, Antipho,
  " Quin mali narrando poffit depravarier." TERENCE.

PHILADELPHIA.

PRINTED AND SOLD BY JAMES HUMPHREYS, junr.
The Corner of Black-horfe Alley Front-ftreet

M,DCC,LXXVI.

TO ALL
SINCERE LOVERS
OF
PEACE AND TRUTH;
TO ALL WHO WISH FOR THE
HAPPINESS AND PROSPERITY
OF
A M E R I C A;
AND TO ALL THE
DISPASSIONATE, JUDICIOUS,
AND
R E A L   F R I E N D S
O F
CONSTITUTIONAL LIBERTY;
THE FOLLOWING STRICTURES
ARE HUMBLY INSCRIBED
BY   THE   AUTHOR.

PREFACE.

THE following pages contain an answer to one of the most artful, insidious and pernicious pamphlets I have ever met with. It is addressed to the passions of the populace, at a time when their passions are much inflamed. At such junctures, cool reason and judgment are too apt to sleep: The mind is easily imposed on, and the most violent measures will, *therefore*, be thought the most salutary. Positive assertions will pass for demonstration with many, rage for sincerity, and the most glaring absurdities and falshoods will be swallowed.

The author of COMMON SENSE, has availed himself of all these circumstances. Under the mask of friendship to America, in the present calamitous situation of affairs, he gives vent to his own private resentment and ambition, and recommends a scheme which must infallibly prove ruinous. He proposes that we should renounce our allegiance to our sovereign, break off all connection with Great-Britain, and set up an independent empire of the republican kind. Sensible that such a proposal must, even at this time, be shocking to the ears of Americans; he insinuates that the *novelty* of his sentiments is the only *obstacle* to their *success.*—that, "perhaps they are not yet sufficiently fashionable to procure them general favour; that a long habit of not thinking a thing wrong, gives it a superficial appearance of being right, and raises at first a formidable outcry in defence of custom."

In this he imitates all other enthusiasts and visionary assertors of paradoxes, who were conscious that the common feelings of mankind must revolt against their schemes: The author, however, though he did not intend it here, pays a compliment to the Americans; for this amounts to a confession, that amidst all their grievances, they still retain their allegiance and loyalty.

With the same view, I presume, to make his pamphlet go down the better, he prefixes the title of *Common Sense* to it— by a figure in rhetoric, which is called a *Catachresis*, that is, in plain English, an abuse of words. Under this title, he counteracts the clearest dictates of reason, truth, and common sense. Thus have I seen a book written by a popish bigot, entitled,

Mercy and Truth; or Charity maintained; in which the author very devoutly and charitably damns all heretics.

I find no *Common Sense* in this pamphlet, but much *uncommon* phrenzy. It is an outrageous insult on the common sense of Americans; an insidious attempt to poison their minds, and seduce them from their loyalty and truest interest. The principles of government laid down in it, are not only false, but too absurd to have ever entered the head of a crazy politician before. Even Hobbes would blush to own the author for a disciple. He unites the violence and rage of a republican, with all the enthusiasm and folly of a fanatic. If principles of truth and common sense, however, would not serve his scheme, he could not help that by any other method than by inventing such as *would*, and this he has done.

No person breathing, has a deeper sense of the present distresses of America, than I have—or would rejoice more to see them removed, and our liberties settled on a permanent, constitutional foundation. But this author's proposal, instead of removing our grievances, would aggravate them a thousand fold. The remedy is infinitely worse than the disease. It would be like cutting off a leg, because the toe happened to ache.

It is probable that this pamphlet, like others, will soon sink in oblivion—that the destructive plan it holds out, will speedily be forgotten, and vanish, like the baseless fabric of a vision; yet while any honest man is in danger of being seduced by it—whilst there is even a possibility that the dreadful evils it is calculated to produce should overtake us, I think it a duty which I owe to God, to my King and Country, to counteract, in this manner, the poison it contains. Nor do I think it less a duty thus to vindicate our honourable Congress, and my injured countrymen in general, from the duplicity and criminal insincerity with which this pamphlet virtually charges them.

The reader, however, must not expect that I should submit to the drudgery of returning a distinct answer to every part of a pamphlet, in which the lines in many places are out-numbered by falshoods: and where the author's malice and antipathy to monarchical government, misrepresent almost every thing relative to the subject. I have done, notwithstanding, what I conceive to be sufficient—I have developed his leading principles, and obviated such misrepresentations as are aptest to mislead the unwary. I have, moreover, shewn that this scheme is big with ruin to America—that it is contrary to the sentiments of the colonists, and that in a reconciliation with Great-Britain, on solid, constitutional principles, excluding all parliamentary taxation, the happiness and prosperity of this continent, are only to be sought or found.

I neither have nor can possibly have any interests separate from those of America—any object in view but her welfare. My fate is involved in her's. If she becomes a conquered country, or an independent republic, I can promise myself no advantage or emolument in either case; but must inevitably share with millions in the evils that will ensue. This I can declare, before the searcher of hearts, is the truth, the whole truth, and nothing but the truth. Can the author of *Common Sense* do the same? Can he truly and sincerely say, that he has no honour, power, or profit in view, should his darling republican scheme take place? If not, then he is an interested, prejudiced person, and very unfit to advise in this matter. We should be distrustful of his judgment, and on our guard against what he recommends.

The author calls himself an *Englishman*, but whether he is a native of *Old England* or *New England*, is a thing I neither know nor care about. I am only to know him by the features he hath here exhibited of himself, which are those of an avowed, violent Republican, utterly averse and unfriendly to the English constitution. He hath not prefixed his name to his pamphlet; neither shall I prefix mine to this. But as I fear his abilities just as little as I love his republican cause, I hereby pledge myself, that in case he should reply, and publish his name; I also, should I think it necessary to rejoin, shall publish my name. I honour genius wherever I meet with it; but detest its prostitution to bad purposes. The few faint glimmerings of it that are thinly scattered through this pamphlet, are but a poor compensation for its malevolent, pernicious design; and serve only to raise our indignation and abhorrence.

I hope the reader will distinguish—where there is a real difference—between this Republican's cause, and that of America. If not, and if he is not willing to listen calmly to truth, I advise him to stop here and lay down this pamphlet. But if the case be otherwise, I have only to beseech him, whilst perusing these STRICTURES, to remember that they were written to promote our reconciliation with a King and nation, whom, not long since, we sincerely loved and esteemed. The bitterest enmity I know, is that which subsists between those who were once friends, but have fallen out. On such occasions, and while our resentment is high, the advice which tends to gratify that resentment, may be the most welcome. But when our passions subside, our former affections will also return; and we shall then look upon him to be much more our friend who would calm our resentment, than him who would inflame it. From our former connection with Great Britain, we have already derived numberless advantages and benefits; from a closer union with her, on proper principles, we may derive still greater benefits in future. Duty, gratitude, interest, nay Providence, by its all-wise dispensations, loudly call on both countries to unite, and would join them together; and may infamy be the portion of that wretch who would put them asunder.

February 16, 1776.

STRICTURES *on the Author's Assertions concerning* "the Origin and Design of Government in general; and his Remarks on the English Constitution."

WRITERS on politics, like those on philosophy, are very apt to be warped by prejudice, and the systems they have previously adopted. They often draw general conclusions from particular premises, and form their judgement of human nature, not from a general view of mankind in their various situations; but from the conduct of a few individuals, and the particular state of things at the time they wrote. Whilst some of them pretend to delineate the true state of human nature, perhaps they only give us a disgusting picture of their own dark and gloomy minds. Moreover, those writers are charged with founding their principles, not on nature and fact, but on their own prejudices, on improbable suppositions and imaginary cases, which never had an existence. Hence that variety of visionary political fabrics that have been raised, contradictory to each other, and repugnant to common sense, and which will not bear the test of sober examination. Some of them indeed may do very well on paper; but can never be reduced to practice, unless a race of beings, very different from men, can be found for the purpose.

Whilst writers of this sort amuse themselves with *Utopian* systems, and go no further, they may be borne with, and pass without much censure. Their works may be read like other romances or fictions. But if they presume to loose the bands of society, and overturn governments that have been formed by the wisdom of ages, to make way for their own crude systems, and thereby entail misery and ruin upon millions; it is then absolutely necessary to examine those systems, point out their destructive tendency, and unmask the deceivers that propose them.

The author of a pamphlet, falsely and absurdly entitled COMMON SENSE, is not only chargeable with a large portion of the above defects, in common with other political system-makers, but also with the further design of rending the British empire asunder. To realize his beloved scheme of Independent Republicanism, he would persuade the colonists to renounce their allegiance to our true and lawful liege sovereign King GEORGE III—plunge themselves into a tedious, bloody, and most expensive war with Great Britain—and risque their lives, liberties and property on the dubious event of that war.

This is the principal object his pamphlet has in view; other things are only mentioned as conducive to that end. To prepare the reader for it—to take off that horror which every honest man and well-informed friend of America must naturally feel at a proposal so wicked and ruinous; he first treats of some other matters which he fashions to his purpose. He poisons the fountain that the stream may be rejected. With this design, he delivers his sentiments on government, the English constitution and monarchy. I shall now very briefly examine what he has offered on these subjects.

He tells us, that "some writers have confounded society with government;" and then supplies us with a distinction which is to set all right. He says, "Society is produced by our wants, and government by our wickedness." We may reasonably presume there are neither wants nor wickedness in Heaven. According to this doctrine then, there can be no society nor government there; and yet we are assured of the contrary.

This distinction is not only inaccurate, but it is also founded on false principles; and we might expect the reverse of both, when the errors of others are professedly corrected. Our wants do not produce society; nor are they the first or principal cause of it. Did this gentleman ever know of any one that was born out of society? Are we not by an act of Providence in our birth, made members of society? A state of society is the natural state of man; and by the constitution of his mind and frame he is fitted for it. Not only his wants and weakness require it, but his inclinations, his noblest faculties impel him to it; and the more perfect those faculties are, the better is he fitted for society. As nature has thus made us members of society, without any choice or will of ours; so, whatever happiness or perfection we are capable of, can only be attained in society.

This writer's account of the origin of government is equally exceptionable with that of the origin of society. I can no more assent to it than to Hobbes's notion,—"that mankind are naturally in a state of war, and that government is founded in superior power or force."

Since Providence hath formed us for society, and placed us in it from the time of our first existence, I am of Hooker's opinion,—"that society could not be without government, nor government without law," though mankind were ever so virtuous. For what is government, but the regulation of society by laws? It is well known to all who are conversant in history, that the different states, the different forms of government which have subsisted in the world, and of which we have any records, had their origin from a variety of causes peculiar to each. Of these I speak not, but of government in general, herein following my republican guide.

As we cannot doubt but the benevolent author of our being, wills our happiness in the state where he hath placed us, he surely wills also the means which lead to that end—those means are order and government. Thus far I hold, with the best republican writers on this subject, the divine right of government, whose end is the good of mankind; yet without appropriating that right to any particular form, exclusively of others. Were men as virtuous as angels; yet, if collected in large societies, there must be a variety of states and conditions among them; and wherever such societies are, government will be indispensibly necessary.

But not to enter deeply into this subject, which would be foreign to my design, I shall just observe, that man is a moral agent, and thereby fitted to be governed by laws:—He is born in society, whose ends cannot be obtained, but by subordination, order and the regulation of laws; and where these are, there is government. I conclude, therefore, that government is agreeable to the will of the Deity—that it has its origin in the nature and state of man—that in framing governments by mutual compact, men act according to the law of their nature, and dictates of reason, which thus point out the only effectual way to attain happiness and avoid evil. I draw my principles from nature and fact, without having recourse to system—the never failing refuge of weak minds, and of party writers.

Agreeable to the origin he assigns to government, our

author seems to think the only business of government is to *punish*; for, he says, that as society is a "patron," so government is "a punisher." But to think thus, betrays an equal ignorance of the principles of government, and of matter of fact. Numberless blessings flow from government, besides the security resulting from a restraint of vice by punishing the vicious. Were there no wickedness, there would probably be little occasion for penal laws; but are these the only laws enacted by government? The criminal law of any state makes but a small part of its general code. It is Livy, I think, who somewhere defines government to be, "The empire of laws, and not of men." According to this definition, the laws of our author's government, *produced by wickedness*, would exercise a most tyrannical sway—being designed only to *punish*, they would probably resemble the laws of Draco, which were said to be written in blood. Persons who entertain such notions of government, may be well calculated to form a sanguinary code of laws, and afterwards to execute them; for, as we may suppose their principles are congenial with their minds and disposition, doubtless they would feel very well inclined to inflict every kind of punishment without scruple.

To evince the truth of his assertion, that "Government is produced by wickedness," our author adds, "Government, like dress, is the badge of lost innocence; the palaces of Kings are built on the ruins of the bowers of Paradise." This is mighty *florid* —what pity that it has no solidity! Just so, say I—ploughing and sowing, like dress, are the badges of lost innocence: The farmer's cottage, barn, stable, and hog-house are built upon the ruins of the bowers of Paradise; I cannot see that this *pretty* sentence proves any thing but the author's enmity to Kings and monarchical governments: For if he would hereby shew the inexpediency of either, the same argument will equally shew the inexpediency of ploughing and sowing, of the farmer's cottage, barn, &c.

Having thus laid his foundation, the author proceeds to erect his superstructure; and I assure you, gentle reader, the one is perfectly suitable to the other. "In order to gain a clear and just idea of the design and end of government," says he, "let us suppose a small number of persons settled in some sequestered part of the earth, unconnected with the rest; they will represent the first peopling of any country, or of the world. In this state of natural liberty,"—well! what would they first do or think of? Why,—"society will be their first thought." This indeed might possibly happen, were we to suppose that these persons had dropped from the clouds, or sprung out of the earth, and could all speak the same language. On any other principle, the case here stated is utterly devoid of probability.

The author in this, follows the example of some other manufacturers of political systems, who fly to fiction, when matters of fact should be related: But as he has managed things, his fiction is contradictory and replete with absurdity. For he supposes that those persons "settled in some sequestered part of the earth," had emigrated—"that the first difficulties of emigration had bound them together;" and yet gravely tells us, "their first thought," when settled, "would be society!" I opine this thought would strike them, and had been practised long before.

But further: Amidst "a thousand motives that would excite them thereto," i. e. society, "one" among others, he says, would be that—"disease, nay even misfortune would be death; for altho' neither might be mortal, yet either would disable any individual from living, and reduce him to a state in which he might rather be said to perish than to die." Here, "disease, nay even misfortune" would be "death"; yet neither be "mortal"; yet still, either would "disable from living"; but this would only be "perishing" and not "dying"! here I give the author's own words—I did not make these contradictions and blunders, but found them.

It would be a waste of time to trace this gentleman's wonderful colony any further; which is so far from "representing the first peopling of any country," that I sincerely believe it represents the first peopling of no one country since the days of Adam; at least my memory does not furnish me with one parallel instance at present; and some parts of his scheme are destitute even of the faintest probability. It is very likely, however, that he had the first settlement of these British colonies in view, while thus helping us "to gain a clear and just idea of the design and end of government." Many circumstances favour his supposition; but there is not the least resemblance between them. The first British emigrants to America, were in a state of

Society before their emigration;—in England they jointly applied for grants of land here—they received grants, charters and instructions, which vested them with a legal title to those lands, and marked the outlines of those governments that were to be formed here. When those emigrants found themselves in America, they did not then first think of society; for they were in a state of society before, and the governments they erected here, were conformable to the plans they had previously received in England.

After finishing this goodly political edifice, the author is pleased to bestow some "remarks on the so much boasted constitution of England." He assures us—"he draws his idea of the form of government from a principle in nature which no art can overturn, viz. that the more simple any thing is, the less liable it is to be disordered, and the easier repaired when disordered; and with this maxim in view, he offers his remarks." But he instantly forgets his promise, and pays no regard to this maxim. Absolute monarchy is, past all doubt, the simplest form of government; yet this gentleman prefers democracy, which is infinitely more complex, and the most liable to disorders of any. The truth is, that this principle was ushered in, purely to contrast it with the complex nature of the English constitution, and thereby prejudice the reader against the latter. Let me add, that if, as he himself declares, "we are never in a proper condition of doing justice to others, while we continue under the influence of some leading partiality"; this partial, avowed republican, is one of the unfittest persons breathing to offer remarks on the English constitution. He cannot hold the scales of justice with an even hand.

"That the constitution of England was noble," says he, "for the dark and slavish times in which it was erected, is granted." This is condescending—it would be more so, had he informed us what "dark and slavish times" he refers to. The constitution of England, as it now stands, was fixed at the revolution, in 1688—an æra ever memorable in the fair annals of Liberty. It was then that the limits of royal prerogative on the one hand, and the liberties and privileges of the subject, on the other; were ascertained with precision. But certainly that was neither a "dark nor slavish time." It would not be worth while to contend with a man that could assert it. The lamp of science never shone brighter in any country than in Britain, nor did patriots of greater fame ever adorn the cause of freedom, than those who stood forth to assert her liberties, at that distinguished period. If our author means any time before that, it is impertinent to the purpose, nor am I concerned about it. What is it to us, what the constitution of England was two or three hundred or a thousand years ago? That constitution, as fixed at the revolution, as it *now* stands, is what we are interested in.

"But that it is imperfect," he continues, "subject to convulsions, and incapable of producing what it seems to promise, is easily demonstrated." If he will be pleased to inform me of any political constitution, of human contrivance, that was or is perfect, and not subject to convulsions, I shall be obliged to him, and readily give it the preference to that of England. But until he, or some other person does so, I shall continue in my present firm belief, that the constitution of England approaches the nearest to perfection—that it is productive of the greatest happiness and benefit to the subject, of any constitution on earth. Nor shall I hesitate to prefer it, in these respects, to any constitution that antiquity can boast of.

"But the constitution of England is so exceedingly complex, that the nation may suffer for years together, without being able to discover in which part the fault lies." These are matters that fall not within my line—I leave them to such *profound, eagle-eyed* politicians as our author. One thing is certain, that if any man is aggrieved, either in his person or property, he must soon know it; and in either case he has a speedy remedy by the constitution of England. The late legal decision in favour of Mr. Wilkes, (no favourite of the court or ministry)—respecting general warrants, evidently demonstrates the security enjoyed by an English subject, the equity and superior excellence of the British constitution. But what is the complexness of that constitution to us? The constitution of the colonies is very simple; each being administered by a governor, council and assembly. Let our liberties, property and trade be once secured on a firm constitutional bottom, and the complexness of the English constitution cannot in the least affect us.

Having hitherto skirmished only at a distance, our author prepares now for a nearer and more formidable attack on the

English constitution; such as seems to threaten it with total demolition. "By examining its component parts, he finds them to be the base remains of two ancient tyrannies, compounded with some new republican materials. 1st, The remains of monarchial tyranny in the person of the King. 2d, The remains of aristocratical tyranny in the persons of the Peers. 3d the new republican materials, in the persons of the Commons; the two former being hereditary, are independent of the people, and therefore in a constitutional sense contribute nothing towards the freedom of the state."

Here are several hard words; and as some readers may not well understand them, I shall beg leave to explain them. The learned reader will the more readily excuse me, as this method may best elucidate the subject before us, and develope this vile medly of jargon and misrepresentation.

It is, I think, generally admitted by political writers, that there is in every state, whatever its form of government may be, a supreme, absolute power. The distribution of this power is what constitutes the different forms of government; and that form is best, which most effectualy secures the greatest share of happiness to the whole. There are usually reckoned three forms of government, called *simple*, in opposition to those which are compounded of all three, or only two of the three. The first is Monarchy, when the supreme power of a state is lodged in one person. When this power is placed in the hands of a few, or small number of nobles, it is called an Aristocracy, which is the second form of simple government. The third is, where the sovereign power is lodged in the people at large, and this is called Democracy.

Each of these forms is subject to abuse, and often has been abused. The abuse of monarchy is called tyranny—The abuse of aristocracy is called oligarchy—The abuse of democracy is called anarchy; though the word tyranny may be applied to the abuse of any of them. Our republican author applies it to the two former, even when not abused; and through his whole pamphlet he makes no distinction between the right use and abuse of a thing. If he happens to dislike it, as in the case of monarchy, however restrained and calculated for the benefit of the subject, it is reprobated by the gross—it is nothing but *tyranny*.

It may not be improper to observe here, that monarchical

governments are best adapted to extensive dominions; popular governments to a small territory. It is also worthy of observation, that, although there have been, and still are many absolute monarchies; yet no government was ever purely aristocratical or democratical—owing probably to the unavoidable evils incident to each—or to the impracticableness of forming either. This is candidly owned by Harrington, a noted republican writer. "Though for discourse," says he, "politicians speak of pure aristocracy, and pure democracy, there is no such thing as either of these in nature or example." Algernon Sidney, another republican writer, acknowledges the same.*

As each of these simple forms would be attended with numberless inconveniences, it has been the opinion of the wisest men in every age, that a proper combination of the three, constitutes the best government. It is the peculiar, distinguishing glory of the English constitution, that it is a happy mixture of these; so tempered and balanced, that each is kept within its proper bounds, and the good of the whole thereby promoted.

For what is the constitution—that word so often used—so little understood—so much perverted? It is, as I conceive—*that assemblage of laws, customs and institutions which form the general system; according to which the several powers of the state are distributed, and their respective rights are secured to the different members of the community.* By impartially examining the component parts of the English constitution, it will be found, that the supreme power is distributed in the best manner to attain this important end—the security of their respective rights to all the members of the community. These parts are,—

I. The King; who has the executive power, and other prerogatives, which are all so ordered, so restrained within constitutional limits, as to prevent their being injurious. He can take no man's money, or property of any kind, without a law passed by the other branches of the legislature for that purpose. He can take no man's life, before the person has had a trial, and is condemned by his peers. He can deprive no man of his liberty, unless the person has violated the laws of the state. And this is what our *candid* republican calls the "base remains of monarchical tyranny."

* *See his works, page* 132.

II. The Peers; who are one branch of the legislature, and in some cases have a share in the judicial power. They have other privileges also, but all circumscribed so as to prevent injury to others. As these are chiefly hereditary, and are vested with large property, they are equally independent of the crown and people, and deeply interested in the welfare of the state. Hence they form a strong barrier against any encroachment from either of the other branches, and give stability to the constitution. These are what our *gentle* republican calls "the base remains of aristocratical tyranny."

III. The House of Commons; the members of which are chosen by the people; without whose consent, no money can be levied, nor law passed to bind the subject; and who are themselves, as well as others, bound by the laws that are enacted. These are what our author calls the "new republican materials." But why *new?* The House of Commons was not first formed at the Revolution. Its origin is hid in the remote depths of antiquity. It may be traced with certainty for near six hundred years back;—some, especially republican writers, trace it much further; although it may have undergone several variations before the revolution. Calling it *new*, therefore, is just of a piece with many other of our author's expressions.

The supreme power of the state is distributed among these three branches of the British legislature, in such a manner, that the constitution has almost all the advantages of each of the three simple forms of government, and scarcely any of their inconveniences. On preserving an equal poize in each of these branches, depends the good of the whole: No prudent man, therefore, no real friend of British Liberty, will ever wish to see any of them pass the constitutional limits; or attempt to throw power into any of them which would destroy the balance.

This is a plain, concise representation of the English constitution. It is sufficient to refute our Republican's misrepresentation of it, just as relating truth, in other cases, is a sufficient refutation of falshood. But lest he, or my reader, should think that I mean to skip over any thing that has the appearance of argument, I shall follow him a little further on this subject.

"To say, that the constitution of England is an union of three powers reciprocally checking each other is farcical," he tells us. This is a new and short method of confutation, such indeed as nothing can withstand. How happy is it for mankind, that this acute reasoner has not thought proper to employ it, in shewing the nullity of these reciprocal duties and obligations subsisting between husband and wife, parent and child, master and servant! They must all have infallibly vanished, and have been annihilated by a few *farcical* strokes of his pen! Yet so it happens, that the best and wisest men, the warmest advocates of liberty, have viewed this reciprocal check of the three branches of the legislature, not as "farcical, unmeaning or contradictory"; but as the most effectual method that human wisdom could devise to promote happiness and liberty.

Still, however, he insists,—that "to say the Commons are a check upon the King, presupposes two things. 1. That the King is not to be trusted without being looked after." I think no man should be trusted with uncontrouled power during life.— No, not even a *self-denying, humble* Republican. "Or that a thirst of absolute power is the natural disease of monarchy."— Not a jot more so than of republicanism. 2. That "the Commons by being appointed for that purpose, are either wiser or more worthy of confidence than the King. But as the same constitution which gives the Commons a power to check the King, gives afterwards the King a power to check the Commons; it again supposes that the King is wiser than those, whom it has already supposed to be wiser than him. A mere absurdity!"

There is, I confess, a palpable absurdity here; but it lies in our author's *suppositions* concerning what the constitution *supposes*; not in the mutual check which the King and Commons have upon each other. Is it not highly absurd to suppose, that a man, because he has a constitutional check upon others, must therefore be wiser than those others? A common constable has, in many cases, a check upon his fellow subjects; does it therefore follow that he must be wiser, or that the constitution *supposes* he is wiser than they?

The remaining part of this section is such miserable stuff, that it would only be flinging away time to *expose* it;—it is not worthy of *confutation*. It consists of declamation against the English constitution that would disgrace a school-boy. Some expressions, indeed, such as these, "That the English constitution is too incomprehensible to be within the compass of description,—"that no power can be from God that needs checking," with others of the same kind, seem to flow from insanity, and to be rather the effusions of a distempered brain, than the language of a person possessed of *common*, or any other, *sense*.

I shall conclude this head by referring my reader to the testimony of one of the best judges in subjects of this sort, and the greatest masters of jurisprudence, that any age has produced, in favour of the English constitution,—I mean the celebrated MONTESQUIEU. His testimony will out-weigh, with the judicious, the silly declamations of ten thousand such *Politicasters* as our republican author. The passage I allude to is in Book xi. Chap. 6. *Of the Spirit of Laws,*—though many others of the same kind are interspersed in that excellent work.

SECTION II.

STRICTURES on the Author's Sentiments, "*Of Monarchy and hereditary* Succession."

COME we now to our author's observations on "Monarchy and hereditary Succession." The last of these I shall say little about, for the following reasons. I have humility enough to think, that those illustrious patriots who settled the succession of the crown of England in the House of Hanover, soon after the revolution, knew full as much of the matter as I do,—or as even our author knows. What they did in this respect, I believe was right, and therefore acquiesce in it. Few, I imagine, will dissent from my opinion on this head, notwithstanding this author's objections. In the next place, the crudities here offered concerning hereditary succession, are not new, but borrowed from other writers.—Most of them may be found in a small treatise* written by one John Hall, a pensioner under Oliver Cromwell; and I have nothing to do with John Hall, but with the author of Common Sense. Hereditary monarchy

---

* *The Grounds and Reasons of Monarchy considered and exemplified in the Scotch Line, &c.* By JOHN HALL, *of* Gray's Inn. *Esquire; bound with* Harrington's *works.*

is infinitely preferable to elective, and more conducive to the welfare of mankind. In Poland we see a specimen of the misery and wretchedness to which elective monarchy exposes a nation.

But it will be proper to bestow a few minutes in examining what is here alledged concerning monarchy in general; against which this republican marshals a formidable host of arguments. The reader will remember, that monarchy may be either absolute; or mixed and combined with the other simple forms of government. Our author makes no distinction between these; and although all he says, and a thousand times more that might be said, were true with respect to the former; yet all this would not militate in the least against the mild and tempered monarchy of Great-Britain. Let us, however, attend to his arguments.

"In the early ages of the world, according to scripture chronology, there were no kings; the consequence of which was, there were no wars; it is the pride of kings which throws mankind into confusion. Holland without a king hath enjoyed more peace for this last century, than any of the monarchical governments in Europe." It were needless, at present, to determine how early kings began to reign; especially as we find by scripture chronology and scripture history, that there was murder, violence and war;—that "the earth was filled with violence."—long enough before we hear a syllable about kings,—I may say before there were any. Referring those disorders, therefore, to that origin, is unfair and untrue. Melchizedec is one of the first kings we read of; he lived in the times of patriarchal simplicity, and his character is respectable, being not only a king, but also "the priest of the most High God." This account of kings is very different from our author's.

The instance of Holland is injudiciously selected, to shew that states which have no kings, are therefore exempt from war. There has not been a general war in Europe for a century past, in which Holland was not deeply engaged; except the very last, and this was more owing to inability than any other cause. Every page almost of the history of the *Seven United Provinces*, is a refutation of our author's assertion. His insinuation, that states which have not kings, are exempt from, and not addicted to war, is equally groundless. Republics have been as much involved in wars as other states. The several republics of Greece inlisted under the banners of Sparta, on one side, or those of Athens on the other—both republics waged a most bloody war for thirty years together. And what is very remarkable, they were plunged into this war by Pericles, a popular Athenian, and celebrated speaker; who being impeached for *embezling the public money* and applying it to his *own private use*, took this terrible method to divert an enquiry. The war ended in the destruction of Athens. The single republic of Rome, made greater havoc of the human species, shed more blood, diffused more wretchedness and misery through the earth, and was guilty of more cruelty, oppression and tyranny, than perhaps any *three* monarchies that can be mentioned in the whole compass of ancient history. If a few small republics of modern date, have more respite from war than some monarchies, it is more owing, like their very existence, to their particular situations, the jealousy of neighbouring powers, and other similar circumstances, than to the nature of their government.

"Government by Kings," this writer tells us, "was first introduced by Heathens." And so, say I, was Greek and Latin—so was smoaking tobacco; and yet I can dip into Homer and Virgil, or enjoy my pipe, with great composure of conscience. The first hint of bleeding, in cases of sickness, is said to have been taken from the crocodile—of administring clysters, from the Ibis, an Egyptian bird. These seem to be of worse than heathen origin; yet mankind use them without scruple; and perhaps their discipline might not be amiss for our author, considering his state of mind. If a thing is good in itself, I conceive it to be a matter of very little moment, who it was that first introduced it. I am clearly of opinion also, that democracy, our author's favourite scheme of government, was of heathenish origin, as well as monarchy: And since he is so averse to any thing heathenish, I would beg leave to remind him, that falshood, deceit, and speaking evil of dignities, are heathenish crimes, and expressly forbidden by scripture.

But the worst is yet to come; for "government by Kings, was the most prosperous invention the devil ever set on foot for the promotion of idolatry. The heathens paid divine honours to their deceased Kings." If the devil was the author of this invention, for the purpose here alledged, then I aver he was mistaken in his forecast; or else he soon retained all the Heathen republics in his service, to promote the same end. For it is a most notorious, undeniable fact, that the ancient republics—Rome, Carthage, Athens, &c. were as infamous for every species of the grossest and most abominable idolatry, as any monarchies whatever. Let the Floralia of Rome, and human sacrifices offered at Carthage, to mention no other instances, serve as proofs of this. The truth is, that idolatry had spread its gloomy reign almost universally over the Heathen world. The form of government in any state, neither promoted nor retarded it any more than the shape of their shields, or the form of their wiskers. The purest system of religion, that Heathen antiquity can boast of, prevailed in Persia, where monarchy was established; the remains of which religion, are said to be preferred to this day among the inhabitants of Indostan.

But "Heathens paid divine honors to their deceased Kings." The more fools they, no doubt; however, they did the same to their deceased heroes, and benefactors in general, whether Kings or not, whether male or female. If this argument, therefore, is of any force against government by Kings, it is of equal force against any improvement in agriculture; against cleaning stables, and killing snakes; for Heathens paid divine honours to deceased persons for all those exploits. It is scarcely possible to return a grave answer to such sophistry; especially, when the author may, perhaps, care as little for the Bible, as he does for the Alcoran or Shasthah, only as it may serve his purpose.

From Heathenism, our author flies next to scripture for arguments against monarchy. Were I a parson I should be better qualified to deal with him in this way. However, as I am a sincere believer in divine revelation, I sometimes read the Scripture for instruction—nor am I ashamed to own it—Boyle, Locke, and Newton, did the same. I also have recourse sometimes to a few commentators, which the clergyman of the place where I live, hath recommended to me. Thus furnished, I shall venture to examine his scripture arguments. One consolation to me is, that he seems to be an equal adept in theology and jurisprudence.

"The will of the Almighty, as declared by Gideon and Samuel (says our republican) expresly disapproves of government by Kings." So it might on those particular occasions, and for some peculiar reasons; and yet our government by Kings at this time, may be as acceptable to the Almighty, as any other government. "All anti-monarchical parts of scripture (he continues) have been smoothly glossed over in monarchical governments." If so, our author has profited by the practice, and has greatly improved on it; for he has entirely slipt over (without giving even a *smooth gloss*) all the monarchical parts of Scripture, except one, which, I shall immediately consider; after assuring the reader, that I never have met with the anti-monarchical parts of Scripture. In the bible, I am sure they are not. The Jewish polity, in which the Almighty himself condescended to be King (and thence called a Theocracy) is rather in favour of monarchy than against it; though I am not clear, that any one species of regular government is more acceptable to the Deity now than another; whatever preference may be due to one above another, in point of expediency and benefit.

"Render unto Cæsar the things that are Cæsar's, is the Scripture doctrine of courts," says our author; and pray is it not Scripture doctrine in other places, as well as courts? Is it not the doctrine of Him who is the Saviour of men? The words are part of an answer which our Saviour returned to an insidious question that was proposed to him by some emissaries from the Pharisees, viz. Whether it was lawful to pay tribute to Cæsar, i. e. the Roman Emperor, or not? Judæa was at this time subject to the Romans. The Gaulonites, or Zealots, a sect or party so called, affirmed that the Jews, being God's people, should not acknowledge any other Lord, nor pay tribute to an heathen power—others affirmed the contrary—the determination was therefore put to Jesus, with design to ensnare him. His decision, which was for paying the tribute, was grounded on the then practice and established maxims of the Jews. They held, that wherever the money of any person, bearing his title and image, was current, the inhabitants thereby acknowledged that person for their sovereign. Since, therefore, the Jews owned this of Cæsar, by admitting his money, which bore his title and image, our Saviour told them, they should also pay him tribute. For he ordered the tribute money to be brought, and the Jews owning that it bore Cæsar's image and superscription, or title,—"Render, therefore (says he) to Cæsar the things that are Cæsars," i. e. since you acknowledge his sovereignty over you by admitting his coin, render to him the tribute which, on your own principles, is thereby due.

If this text has been applied to support monarchical government any further than to shew, that whatever is by custom, law, or otherwise, justly due to sovereigns, should be punctually paid, whether it be tribute, obedience, honour, &c.—if, I say, it has been applied to support monarchy any further than this, it must be by some person who understood it as little as our author; though not for the reason he assigns, and which in truth makes against himself.

But I hasten to the passages of Scripture, in which our republican author triumphs most; which, he says, "are direct and positive, and admit of no equivocal construction. That the Almighty has in them entered his protest against monarchical government, is true, or else the Scripture is false." On the contrary, I aver, that the Almighty has not there entered his protest against monarchical government, further than the Jews had departed from a former permission he had given them to chuse Kings, and that the Scripture is not false. Let us now see how a little common sense, reason and truth, will help to clear up the matter.

The passages alluded to by the author, are in 1 Sam. viii. where the Israelites assembled in a tumultuous manner, and desired Samuel to make them "a King, to judge them like all the nations;" which offended Samuel, and in some measure was displeasing to the Almighty. That simply desiring a King, could not be a crime, is undeniably evident; because the Almighty had long before expressly permitted it, had directed the mode of chusing a King, and prescribed the line of conduct the King should observe, when chosen. This is done in Deuteronomy xvii. 14–20; and I shall here lay a few of the passages before the reader.

"When thou art come into the land which the Lord thy God giveth thee, and shalt say, I will set a King over me, like as all the nations that are round about me; thou shalt in any wise set him King over thee whom the Lord thy God shall chuse: one from among thy brethren shalt thou set King over thee: thou mayest not set a stranger over thee which is not thy brother."

The Almighty then proceeds to give directions for the King's conduct, thus chosen; all, wisely suited to the Jewish state, both in a religious and political view. The King "was not to multiply horses;" to prevent any intercourse with Egypt, which supplied other nations with horses; and besides, cavalry was not suited to the hilly country of Judæa. The King was "not to multiply wives, that his heart turn not away;" as happened to Solomon when he disobeyed this precept: Nor "greatly multiply gold and silver to himself," which would introduce luxury and dissolution of manners.

The directions go on—"And it shall be when he, i. e. the King, sitteth upon the throne of his kingdom, that he shall write a copy of this law in a book, and it shall be with him, and he shall read therein all the days of his life: that he may learn to fear the Lord his God, to keep all the words of this law, and these statutes to do them: that his heart be not lifted up above his brethren, and that he turn not aside from the commandment—to the end that he may prolong his days in his kingdom; he and his children in the midst of Israel."

Now, after this, I leave the reader to judge, whether government by Kings could be displeasing to the Almighty; or, whether desiring a King, according to this permission, and these directions, could be a crime in the Israelites. It is impossible that either can be true. The crime of these people, therefore, when they desired a King of Samuel, "to judge them like all the nations," must be attributed to something else. And upon examination, we shall find, that their error lay in the *manner* of their asking a King—in the *principles* on which they acted—in a *disregard* of the venerable old prophet—but chiefly in a *neglect* of the *directions* above mentioned. This will appear evident from a bare recital of facts.

Samuel, by his faithful administration, had restored the purity of religion, and rescued the nation from the hostile attempts of their enemies. Debauched by prosperity, as too frequently happens, dazzled with the lustre of a splendid court, and desirous of its pomp, the people tumultuously assembled to desire a King, who would resemble the despotic Kings which surrounded them. They covered their real design with the pretext of Samuel's age and infirmities, and his sons irregularities, which was insulting the prophet's misfortunes. This is evidently implied in their own words, and in the sequel.

"Behold, (say they to Samuel) thou art old, and thy sons walk not in thy ways; now make us a King to judge us like all the nations." Hereby Samuel, who had faithfully served them, had been displaced; and such a despotic Prince as they desired, had destroyed the theocracy they were under. Accordingly, the Almighty tells Samuel, "They have not rejected thee, but they have rejected me, that I should not reign over them." i. e. It is not thee, so much as me, that they have rejected. Although Samuel was ungratefully treated; yet they still more wickedly neglected the directions given by the Almighty. Pride and ambition, stimulated them to seek a King, not such as the Almighty had directed them to chuse; but such as the nations had; and such as would overturn the theocracy. This was virtually rejecting the Almighty from being their King.

Samuel, however, was directed to hearken to the people; but at the same time to lay also before them, the nature of that monarchy they desired; a monarchy like those around them. The eastern nations, it is well known, were under despotic monarchs, the *manner* or nature of which, Samuel accordingly describes to the Israelites, to try, whether they would persist in their choice after hearing it. Kings of this sort would "take their sons and appoint them for himself, for his chariots, and to be his horsemen—he would take their daughter to be confectioners, and to be cooks, and to be bakers, &c. &c."

This whole passage is a description of the eastern despotic monarchs, which Samuel held up to the Israelites, with design to deter them from chusing such; and this is the passage which our author sets down, enriched with his own most *judicious* comments, to shew that God "entered his protest against monarchical government in general." Whereas, in truth, it is only an account of the then despotic monarchies of the East, which Samuel was directed to lay before the Israelites, that they might see how inconsistent such a monarchy was with their peculiar state and circumstances; and this again with design to divert them from chusing such.

Ambition and pride, however, got the better of duty and interest with the people—a case that happens but too frequently. They still insisted on having the King they had set their hearts on—"That we also, say they, may be like other nations." Hereby shewing the greatest blindness to their own happiness, which consisted in being unlike the other nations, by having God himself for their King; and such a Judge or King as would be his DEPUTY, not an absolute Prince. The Almighty at last condescended to their infirmities, and gave them a King: but as in the case of the ritual law, he tempered his justice with mercy. He gave them Saul, who proved a scourge; yet he ordered matters so that the general end of his dispensation to the Jews was not defeated. Saul's successor was "a man after his own heart," by a zealous attachment to, and punctual execution of, the Mosaic law in his regal character; and David again, in our author's phrase, "to the evil of monarchy, added that of hereditary succession;" which it seems, however, the Almighty did not disapprove of.

The reader is now left to determine freely, whether these passages make in the least against government by Kings; and whether this republican's perversion of them, either through real or affected ignorance, should have any weight to influence us against our sovereign. For my part, I think the case so plain, that I shall not bestow another word upon it; only to add the following reflections of a learned writer on the above transaction. "The secret spring of the people's conduct (says he) was the ambition of their leaders, who could live no longer without the splendor of a regal court—where every one of them might shine a distinguished officer of state. This it was that made their demand criminal; for their chusing regal, rather than aristocratical, vice-roys, was a thing plainly indulged to them by the law of Moses, Deuteronomy xvii. As therefore ambition only was in the view of the ringleaders, and no foolish fears for the state, or hopes of bettering the public administration, it is evident to all acquainted with the genius of this time and people, that compliance with their demand must have ended in the utter destruction of the Mosaic religion, as well as law." With this writer the most celebrated commentators on this passage agree.

Thus ambition set the Israelites on desiring a King; our republican author should reflect, whether the same principle does not actuate and lead him to reject his lawful sovereign.

The author of *Common Sense*, suspects, "there is as much King-craft as Priest-craft in witholding the Scripture from the public in Popish countries, for monarchy is the Popery of government." But is it not strange, that he himself should be guilty of the very crime he here charges upon others? Yet he does this by witholding from the reader every text that would develope the falshood of his own beloved scheme. This, I think, may be called *Republican*-craft; and let it hereafter be added to the two species of *craft* above mentioned. A man of candor would deal fairly, and give both sides of the question. Had there been another text in the bible that could be pressed into his service, besides what he has quoted, we may be sure he would have produced it, with his own *enlightened* comments. With his good leave, therefore, I shall now set down a few texts, which probably, he may call the "Scripture doctrine of monarchy;" but which are the words of inspired truth not-withstanding. I assure the reader further, that I am none of your *passive obedience and non-resistance men*. The principles on which the glorious Revolution in 1688 was brought about, constitute the articles of my political creed; and were it neces-sary, I could clearly evince, that these are perfectly conformable to the doctrines of scripture. To proceed then, like a parson, with my texts; referring in the margin, to the places in which they are contained, that the reader may consult them at his leisure.

"Destroy him not," says David to Abishai, when about to kill Saul, who was entirely in their power. "Destroy him not; for who can stretch forth his hand against the Lord's anointed, and be guiltless?"* "Curse not the King, no, not in thy thought,"† was the admonition of a wise, inspired preacher. Eternal wisdom is introduced, declaring, "By me Kings reign, and Princes decree justice."‡ The wise man's advice is, "My son, fear thou the Lord, and the King; and meddle not with them that are given to change."§ Kings are promised for "nurs-ing fathers" to the christian church.¶ The prophet Daniel declares of the Almighty—"He changeth the times and the

---

* 1 Sam, xxvi. 9.
† Eccles. x. 20.
‡ Prov. viii. 15.
§ Prov. xxiv. 21.
¶ Isaiah xlix. 23.

seasons: He removeth Kings, and setteth up Kings."* The same prophet says, "The most High ruleth in the kingdom of men, and giveth it to whomsoever he will."† These are a few of the many texts to be found in the Old Testament, which contradict our author's scheme. If we look into the New Testament, which properly contains the religion of christians, we find the same doctrine more explicitly inculcated.

"Let every soul be subject unto the higher powers," was Paul's direction to the Romans. "For their is no power but of God; the powers that be, are ordained of God."‡ I seem inclined to think that Paul did not believe with our author, that "Government by Kings, was the invention of the devil!" "I exhort," says the same apostle, in another place, "that first of all, supplications and prayers be made for all men; for Kings, and for all that are in authority; that we may lead a quiet and peaceable life in all godliness and honesty."§

Let us hear another apostle, namely, Peter. "Submit yourselves to every ordinance of man, for the Lord's sake; whether it be to the King, as supreme; or unto Governors, as unto them that are sent by him for the punishment of evil doers, and for the praise of them that do well. As free, and not using your liberty for a cloak of maliciousness, but as the servants of God. Love the brotherhood. Fear God. Honour the King."¶ In another part of his writings, I meet with this remarkable passage "The Lord knoweth how to deliver the godly—and to reserve the unjust unto the day of judgment, to be punished: But chiefly them which walk after the flesh, and despise government: Presumptuous are they, self-willed, they are not afraid to speak evil of dignities."** To the same purpose, another apostle, Jude, says,—"Likewise, these filthy dreamers, despise dominion, and speak evil of dignities. Yet Michael, the Arch-angel, when contending with the devil, he disputed about the body of Moses, durst not bring against him a railing accusation."

* Dan. i. 21.
† Dan. iv. 25.
‡ Rom. xiii.
§ 1 Tim. ii. 1, 2.
¶ 1 Peter ii. 13. 17.
** 2 Peter ii. 9, 10.

But said: "The Lord rebuke thee."* One would think that these apostles had spoken directly of our COMMON SENSE author, and meant to describe him, and such as him.

All these texts, besides many others of the same kind, I find in my bible. I must therefore renounce my bible, if I believe this republican. But I would not renounce the bible, which contains the words of eternal life, for any earthly consideration—no, not if this Gentleman were to assure me of being made Perpetual Dictator, Stadtholder, or Protector of his new Republic. I have taken the trouble to transcribe the above texts, however unusual the employment, merely to lay the plain truth, the genuine testimony of Scripture on this point; before such as might not be at the pains of examining it themselves; and might therefore be misled by our author. I confess, I felt both astonishment and indignation at his abuse of sacred writ. Had his principles, respecting monarchy, been good, had truth been their basis, certainly, this had not been necessary. But he is not the first *tempter* that would seduce others by the perversion of Scripture.

SECTION III.

STRICTURES on what the Author delivers as his "*Thoughts on the present State of American Affairs.*"

IF the person who was capable of so vile a prostitution of Scripture, as we have seen in the preceeding section, should equally prostitute the words, Reason, Argument, Common Sense, in this, it is not to be wondered at. That this is the case, will appear by a near examination. From the author's desultory way of writing, and want of method in delivering his thoughts, it is not easy to follow him,—however, I must do as well as I can.

In this section before me, this Gentleman unfolds his grand scheme of a revolt from the Crown of England, and setting up an independent republic in America. He leaves no method

* Jude, verses 8, 9.

untried, which the most experienced practitioner in the art of deceiving could invent, to persuade any people to a measure which was against their inclinations and interest, that was both disagreeable and destructive. He unsays in one place what he had said in another, if it happens to serve the present purpose; he cants and whines; he tries wit, raillery and declamation by turns. But his main attack is upon the passions of his readers, especially their pity and resentment,—the latter of which is too apt to be predominant in mankind. As for himself, he seems to be every where transported with rage—a rage that knows no limits, and hurries him along, like an impetuous torrent. Every thing that falls in with his own scheme, or that he happens to dislike, is represented in the most aggravated light, and with the most distorted features. Such a malignant spirit I have seldom met with in any composition. As often as I look into this section, I cannot forbear imagining to myself a guilty culprit, fresh reeking from the lashes of indignant justice, and raging against the hand that inflicted them. Yet I cannot persuade myself, that such fire and fury are genuine marks of patriotism. On the contrary, they rather indicate that some mortifying disappointment is rankling at heart; or that some tempting object of ambition is in view; or probably both. I always adopt the famous Bishop Berkeley's maxim in such cases,—"I see a man rage, rail and rave; I suspect his patriotism."

That these observations are justified by the author's own words, I shall now proceed to evince; and I doubt not but the candid reader will consider what I say in the sense it is meant— as directed against this republican's ruinous scheme of Independency. *This* and this *only*, is what I combat. My most ardent wish—next to future happiness—is, to see tranquillity restored to America—our Liberties, Property and Trade settled on a firm, generous and constitutional plan, so that neither of the former should be invaded, nor the latter impoliticly or unjustly restrained; that in consequence of this, a perfect Reconciliation with Great-Britain were effected, an union formed, by which both countries, supporting and supported by each other, might rise to eminence and glory, and be the admiration of mankind till time shall be no more. In such a plan, the real interest of America is indubitably to be sought; and could my influence avail, there would not be a dissenting voice in the colonies—all would unite as one man, and use every effort, to have such a plan speedily settled.

The author of Common Sense says, "He has no other preliminaries to settle with the reader, than that he would divest himself of prejudice and prepossession, and suffer his reasons and feelings to determine for themselves." I have no objection to these preliminaries. They are such as I myself would chuse to settle with the reader; provided his feelings are not those of rage and resentment, which are exceedingly improper to determine in matters of such moment. It is not improbable indeed, that every republican who is as prejudiced, interested, and vindictive as himself, will agree with him in all his extravagancies; and so perhaps they would, though an angel from Heaven were to assure them that they are wrong. But I am confident the readers of that stamp make but a very small number at present in America.

After observing, that "many writers have embarked in the present controversy, with various designs," he says, "they have all been ineffectual, and the period of debate is closed. Arms, as the last resource, decide the contest; the appeal was the choice of the King, and the continent accepted the challenge." That an appeal was made by the King to arms for the decision of this unhappy contest, on the 19th of April, the period our author fixes, is a matter in which I am not quite clear; but more of this presently. If such a challenge was accepted by the Americans, I am sure it was with great reluctance. They desired it not; although this writer, by his manner of expression, insinuates they did. But be these matters as they will, certain it is, that the period of debate did not then close. The challenge was not accepted so as to exclude an amicable accommodation. Since that time, the Honourable Continental Congress petitioned the King, and transmitted addresses to the inhabitants of Great-Britain and Ireland, to facilitate a reconciliation. Nor can I conceive it possible, that any one, unless some sanguinary wretch, who hopes to profit by our confusions, should wish to see the contest finally decided by arms.

"By referring the matter from argument to arms, a new æra of politics is struck—all plans, proposals, &c. prior to the 19th of April—are like the almanacks of last year; which, tho' proper then, are superceded and useless now." I shall not undertake to decide on the value of old almanacks, as I am not an almanack-maker—the author may know more of the matter. But he here takes for granted what should have been proved, viz. that the matter or contest was ultimately referred from argument to arms. If the sense of our Congress, and of the inhabitants of this continent at large, is any rule to judge by, all plans and proposals, even those prior to the 19th of April, are not useless. A free people, who have a just sense of their rights and liberties, are very justifiable in shewing they will not tamely give them up without a struggle. But no people, except some tribes of savages, who aim at the total extermination of their enemies, will ever lose sight of argument and negociation, to terminate such disputes. To insinuate the contrary of the Americans, is at once doing them the greatest injustice, and offering them the greatest insult. No people under Heaven are less sanguinary, or deserve such a character less.

Our author repeats the same sentiment elsewhere. "No man," says he, "was a warmer wisher for reconciliation than myself, before the fatal 19th of April, 1775; but the moment the event of that day was made known, I rejected the hardened, sullen tempered Pharaoh of England for ever; and disdain the wretch, that with the pretended title of father of his people, can unfeelingly hear of their slaughter, and composedly sleep with their blood upon his soul." This is the man, gentle reader, who declares, "he is not induced by motives of pride, party or resentment, to espouse the doctrine of separation and independence;" no, no; and if you will take his own word for it, he is by no means for "inflaming or exaggerating matters!" The reader must be sensible, that a person who can thus set truth and decency at defiance, and is regardless of even the appearance of consistency, has a great advantage over his antagonist.

That the expedition to Lexington was rash and ill-judged—that it was risking the peace of the continent, and wantonly involving fellow subjects in blood, for a most inconsiderable object—I shall most readily allow; and our author has my leave to load that expedition with all the reproaches he can invent. I disapprove the design of it as much as he—I lament its effects much more. And from whatever unhappy circumstances it arose, I am well assured, from the very best authority, that the King's orders to all his Commanders or Generals on this continent, were to act *only on the defensive*, and in support of the laws. Now, after giving such restraining orders, how the blood of those who were killed on either side, at the distance of 3000 miles from him, could be "on his soul" is utterly inconceivable. If this Republican, therefore, rejected his Sovereign, on account of the unforeseen blood-shed at Lexington, it was only because he had little attachment to him before; and this opportunity was only seized by the author to give vent to a disaffection which only slumbered before. Thus, by wilful slanders, to poison the minds of fellow subjects, and sow disaffection among them, which may be productive of general misery, is a crime of such complicated guilt, that none but men of the most abandoned profligate hearts, are capable of committing.

After all, it is impossible to assign any good reason, why a reconciliation with Great-Britain, which was so proper before the Lexington affair, should be so improper afterwards. Our author, indeed, in his usual way, dogmatically asserts it; but his assertions will not pass for proofs. If peace and reconciliation on constitutional grounds, and proper security for our several rights, were desirable and advantageous before the 19th of April, 1775, must they not have been equally so after the event of that unfortunate day? Let reason and common sense answer.

"But as so much has been said of the advantages of reconciliation," continues our author, "it is but right we should examine the contrary side of the argument, and inquire into the material injuries which the colonies sustain, and always will sustain by being connected with Great-Britain." He alledges, indeed, several evils which he supposes would attend that connection; but cautiously avoids any mention of the numberless evils and calamities which we must infallibly suffer by breaking it off. As in a former case, so in this also, I shall endeavour to supply his omission in due time.

"Some have asserted," he tells us, "that as America hath flourished under her former connection with Great-Britain, that the same connection is necessary towards her future happiness. Nothing can be more fallacious." He adds,—"We may as well assert, that because a child hath thrived upon milk, that it is never to have meat." However glib this quaint simile may run upon paper; or however convincing it may appear to shallow readers; yet, in truth, when examined, it contains a palpable impropriety, and is impertinent to the case before us. Great-Britain is figuratively called the Parent State of the colonies; their connection, therefore, may be properly compared to the *relation* subsisting between parent and child. But to compare our *connection* with Great-Britain to the *literal food* of a child, a thing different from, and not necessarily belonging to that *relation*, is manifestly absurd, and a violation of the propriety of language; as all who are judges of the nature of language must be sensible. The *relation* of parent and child ends not, when the latter has arrived to maturity, although the use of *milk* may be laid aside; and that relation may be still necessary to the happiness of both; the same may be truly affirmed of *connection* with Great-Britain. But if we must stretch the simile further, we find something analogous to the literal food of a child, it is the litteral support afforded by Great-Britain to the colonies, in their infant state *formerly*; and the administration of the colonies *now*, as well as the general laws of regulation she may make for us. As to any support now, in the above sense, it is confessed the colonies in general do not require it. With respect to the administration of the colonies, and regulating laws proper for them, these should certainly be varied, and adapted to our maturer state. The want of this is the true source of our present calamities; and the attainment of it, by a reconciliation and constitutional union with Great-Britain, is what every honest American should earnestly wish for. But the remedy proposed by our author, would resemble the conduct of a rash, froward stripling, who should call his mother a d–mn–d b—ch, swear he had no relation to her, and attempt to knock her down.

"But even this," subjoins our author, "is admitting more than is true, for I answer, roundly, that America would have flourished as much, and probably much more, had no European taken any notice of her. The commerce by which she hath enriched herself, are the necessaries of life, and will always have a market while eating is the custom of Europe." If no European power had taken any notice of America, that is to say, if none had been at the expence or trouble of discovering it, and settling colonies in it; there is great probability that

America had not flourished, but remained to this day as savage a wilderness as when Columbus or Cabot first described its coasts.—But to pass over this blunder. Let the reader only turn to any history of the settlement of the British colonies, and then judge what had been the condition of Virginia, the first colony, and latterly of Georgia and Nova-Scotia, if Great-Britain had not supported them. They must as infallibly have perished, as an infant without its proper food, had not Great-Britain afforded her aid and support; which have been more or less extended to the colonies in general. Even after they had surmounted their first difficulties, what had been their fate, had not Great-Britain protected them? It so happens that avarice, ambition and fighting, are customs of Europe as well as eating. This being the case, some other European power would indubitably have seized all these colonies, in their infant state, had not Great-Britain held out her protection.

And here much matter of grief is presented to this poor Gentleman. He pathetically laments, that—"Alas! we have been long led away by ancient prejudices, and made large sacrifices to superstition—not considering that the motive of Great-Britain in protecting us, was interest, not attachment;" and then he spins out a tedious, affected sentence of her "not protecting us from our enemies on our account, but from her enemies on her own account," &c. Supposing this were true, where is the harm? Great-Britain actually *did* protect us; and it is a matter of little moment to us, what her motives were. If she received benefit by it, so much the better. Mutual interest is the strongest bond of union between states, as the history of mankind testifies; and certainly that nation would act a most absurd, as well as wicked part, which lavished away its blood and treasure, without any prospect of national advantage in return. But I firmly believe, that his assertions on this head are as false, as they are ungenerous; and that Great-Britain, in protecting us, was actuated by motives of affection and attachment, as well as interest. The whole of her conduct to the colonies, till lately, evinces it—the Americans themselves have acknowledged it. Great-Britain, no doubt, derived many advantages from the colonies; but should we undervalue her protection on that account, or ascribe it to sordid motives only? It is every man's interest as well as duty to be honest;

would it, therefore, be candid, generous or true, to suppose, that every honest man is actuated by selfishness only?—But candour and truth are things that have nothing to do with the procedure of this dark republican, who aims at utterly effacing every trace of former affection and friendship between Great-Britain and the colonies; and like a fiend that delighted in human misery, would arm them with the most deadly, irreconcilable hatred against each other.

But he denies that Britain is the parent country of these colonies. He "reprobates the phrase, as being false, selfish, narrow and ungenerous.—Europe, (says he) and not England, is the parent country of the colonies." It is an observation of Epictetus, "That if a man will contradict the most evident truths, it will not be easy to find arguments wherewith to confute him—that the disposition to contradict such truths, proceeds from want of candor and modesty." He moreover adds—that when *some adventurous* spirits in his time, undertook to deny the plainest and most evident truths—"This denial was admired by the vulgar for strength of wit and great learning."

Whatever circumstances can denominate any country to be the parent state or country of colonies, may be truly predicated of England, with respect to these American colonies. They were discovered at the Expence of the English crown—first settled by English emigrants, and the governments erected here were formed on the model of the English government, as nearly as the state of things would admit. The colonists were deemed English subjects, and entitled to all the privileges of Englishmen. They were supported and protected at the expence of English blood and treasure. Emigrants, it is true, resorted here from other countries in great numbers; but these were not entitled to all the privileges of English subjects, till naturalized by an act of the English legislature, or some Assembly here; and the prodigious confluence of strangers into the colonies, is a proof of the mild and liberal spirit by which they were cherished and administered. If these particulars do not entitle England to the appellation of mother-country to these colonies, I know not what can; and these particulars cannot be predicated of any other country in Europe besides England.

The author tells us, however—"that the phrase parent or mother country, hath been jesuitically adopted by the King and his parasites, with a low papistical design of gaining an unfair bias on the credulous weakness of our minds." I conceive the present King, or his parasites, as he calls them, were not the first or only persons who adopted this phrase; and, therefore, it could not answer such a design. The phrase hath already been used, both here, and in Britain, since the first settlement of the colonies.

But this curious observation was introduced purely to insinuate the King is a papist; which has just as much truth in it, as to insinuate that he is a Mahometan or Gentoo; for there is not a firmer protestant in Great Britain, than his present Majesty. The insinuation might have some effect on the credulous weakness of some ignorant people, who have harboured such an opinion; and I have heard the Quebec-bill alledged as a proof of it, by which, they said, "popery was established in Canada, and the King had violated his coronation oath."

An examination of the Quebec bill, falls not within the compass of my design. It has undergone the scrutiny of much abler hands; some of which have affirmed, and others denied, that popery was thereby established. I dislike the bill, chiefly because it vests the Governor and his Council with exorbitant power. It is certain, however, that the popish clergy of Canada, complain of the bill, and think themselves in a worse situation by it, than the articles of capitulation and surrender left them. By its exempting such Canadians as come over to the protestant religion, from paying any ecclesiastical dues to their priests, it would seem, as if the bill was intended to diminish the number of papists. Be all this as it may, it is past any doubt, that the King did not in the least violate his coronation oath by assenting to that bill. This will evidently appear by inspecting the oath itself: and as the removal of mutual prejudices to facilitate a reconciliation, is my principal view; as the oath is short, and has been seen by few, I shall here insert it. The coronation oath is administered by one of the archbishops or bishops, in the following words and manner—

The archbishop shall say, Will you solemnly promise and swear, to govern the people of this kingdom of England, and the dominions thereunto belonging, according to the statutes in parliament agreed on, and the laws and customs of the same? *The King shall say*, I solemnly promise so to do.

The archbishop. Will you, to your power, cause law and justice, in mercy, to be executed in all your judgments? *King*. I will.

The archbishop. Will you to the utmost of your power, maintain the laws of God; the true profession of the gospel, and the protestant reformed religion, established by law? And will you preserve unto the bishops and clergy of this realm, and to the churches committed to their charge, all such rights and privileges, as by the law do or shall appertain unto them, or any of them? *King*. All this, I promise to do.

After this the King, laying his hand on the holy gospel, shall say, The things which I have here before promised, I will perform and keep: So help me God. *And then shall kiss the book*.

This is the coronation oath, and mode of administering it, as prescribed by law; and the reader must see that it has no more relation to the state of religion in Canada, a conquered province, than to the state of religion in Minorca, a conquered island, the inhabitants of which are papists, and enjoy as great, if not greater privileges than the Canadians.

"But admitting," continues our author, "that we were all of English descent, what does it amount to? Nothing. Britain being now an open enemy, extinguishes every other name and title; and to say that reconciliation is a duty, is truly farcical." Here the *farcical* argument meets me again; and what shall I say to it? I protest I do not understand it. I have searched for its meaning in vain; and have no hope of fathoming it, till the author is pleased to explain it.* But to the point in hand. If

---

* The author, elsewhere, recommends a manœuvre, to which I apprehend, the word *farcical* may be properly applied. After kindly offering a republican form of government, which he desires may be adopted in America, he introduces a person asking this question—"But where is the King of America?" and then returns this answer—"I'll tell you friend, he reigns above; and doth not make havock of mankind like the *Royal Brute* of Great-Britain." This *pretty flower*, with which he garnishes our Sovereign, seems to be culled rather from the *bowers* of *Billinsgate*, than those of *Paradise*, formerly mentioned. The reader cannot forbear seeing here the enthusiasm of *Fifth-monarchy* men, and their rudeness too. Strange that this Republican's rage should blind him so that he cannot see what every body else sees—that—
—"Want of decency is want of sense!"

what would promote our happiness and interest, to mention nothing else, be a duty, then reconciliation is our duty.

He elsewhere enlarges on this head. "Bring the doctrine of reconciliation," says he, "to the touch-stone of nature, and then tell me, whether you can hereafter love, honour and faithfully serve the power that carried fire and sword into your land!" All this, and a great deal more of the kind, can only proceed from a supposition of the author, that others are as vindictive and unforgiving as himself. When states go to war, mutual acts of hostility must necessarily ensue; and to think that no reconciliation should afterwards take place between them, is as contrary to every dictate of humanity and religion, as to think that a private person should never forgive a private injury, or be reconciled to him that offered it. I lament as much as any one, the blood that has been shed, and the devastation that has been made during this contest: But these have been comparatively small, if we consider the torrents of blood that have flowed, the wide-spread ruin that has attended the frequent destructive wars between England and Scotland; yet these nations are now happily united—they mutually love, honour, and faithfully serve each other.

The author refers us to the state of Boston, and paints the distresses of its inhabitants in the strongest colours, to stimulate the revenge of Americans, and banish every idea of reconciliation with Britain. I sincerely take part in the calamities of Boston, and other places that have suffered. I feel the most tender sympathetic pity for the distresses of their inhabitants. But how the shedding of more blood, or spreading equal devastation along the whole sea-coast of this continent—the

---

But to return. The *farcical* passage next follows—"Yet that we may not appear defective in earthly honours, let a day be solemnly set apart for proclaiming the [Continental] Charter; let it be brought forth placed on the divine law, the word of God; let a crown be placed thereon—But lest any ill use should afterwards arise, let the crown, at the conclusion of the ceremony, be demolished, and scattered among the people whose gift it is." I now submit it to the reader's better judgment, whether this whole ceremony is not highly *farcical*; especially as this Republican has given us the strongest suspicion that he has an *equal* regard for the word of God, and for Kings and monarchical government. If I am wrong in this conjecture, I utterly despair of success in finding out the meaning of this word.

inevitable consequences of not listening to reconciliation—
how these, I say, can alleviate the misfortunes of the people of
Boston, or any other sufferers, is what I am not able to see.

"Much hath been said," he tells us, "of the united strength
of Britain and the colonies; that in conjunction they might bid
defiance to the world: But this is a mere presumption; the fate
of war is uncertain—the next war may not turn out like the
last." But he chaunts quite another tune, when he would hold
up the advantages of a separation from Britain. In that case he
avers—" 'Tis not in the power of England, or of Europe to
conquer America—nay, our present numbers are sufficient to
repel the force of the whole world!"—This is only one sample
among a thousand, of the duplicity and contradiction which
run through his pamphlet.

After telling us, what is very true, that we have no business
to "set the world at defiance," he adds, as an inducement to
separate from Britain—"Our plan is commerce; and that well
attended to, will secure us the peace and friendship of Europe,
because it is the interest of Europe to have America a free port.
Her trade will always be a protection, and her barrenness of
gold and silver will secure her from invaders."—Yes, yes; no
doubt, if America were once to throw off her connection with
Britain, the golden age would be restored! The Millennial state
would commence. "Men would instantly beat their swords into
plough-shears, and their spears into pruning hooks. Nation
would not lift up sword against nation, nor learn war any more."
Such are the happy times our author promises us, if America
were an independent republic! But until he can give us some
assurance that may be relied on, that ambition, pride, avarice,
and all that dark train of passions which usually attend them,
will be extinguished in the human breast, and will no more exert
their baneful influence, I must beg leave to doubt the truth of
his assertions—I must question, whether we shall live in perpetual peace with Europe, or even with each other, after our
revolt from England.

The argument or reason he advances for it here, is contradicted by general experience and matter of fact. A flourishing
trade naturally increases wealth; and for this and other reasons,
as naturally leads to war. Carthage, Venice and Holland—all
commercial republics—were frequently engaged in bloody

wars, in the days of their prosperity. Nor is "barrenness of gold and silver" any security against war or invasions. Experience and fact are equally against this position. I never heard of the gold or silver mines of Flanders. The Low Countries are entirely barren of both; but they are remarkable for their fertility, good pasturage, manufactures, and formerly, for trade; Yet I may say, each field there is a field of blood, and has been the scene of some dreadful carnage. Great-Britain and France have few or no gold and silver mines; yet they have been theatres of bloody wars, as long as any record we have of either reaches. On the other hand, South America supplies half the globe with gold and silver; and yet, strange to tell, on our author's principles, no rival power has ever contended with Spain or Portugal for the dominion of South America! No invaders have attempted to dispossess them.

The truth is, that mines producing those metals are rather injurious than beneficial to any country. They unbrace the nerves of industry, induce sloth, and damp the spirit of commerce. Spain was one of the most flourishing, powerful monarchies in Europe, when this continent was discovered. Peru and Mexico then poured their immense treasures into her lap, and have been doing so ever since; yet Spain, ever since, has been on the decline, and is dwindled, notwithstanding her gold and silver, into a state, I may say, of insignificance. The country that abounds in fertile fields and luxuriant pasturage —that produces the necessaries of life in abundance—that furnishes the various materials for industry and art, and the articles for an extensive commerce; such a country, though barren of gold and silver, is the most inviting to ambition, the most exposed to invasions; and such a country is North-America.

But our author now waxes so exceedingly warm, and assumes so terrific an air, that I almost dread to approach him. "I challenge," says he, "the warmest advocate for reconciliation, to shew a single advantage that this country can reap by being connected with Great-Britain, I repeat the challenge, not a single advantage is derived."

The positive, dogmatical manner in which this challenge is repeated, reminds me of an observation made by the excellent Dr. Beattie, which applies, in the present case, as exactly, as if this blustering challenge had given rise to it. "In reading sceptical books," says the worthy Doctor, "I have often found, that the strength of the author's attachment to his paradox, is in proportion to its absurdity. If it deviates but a little from common opinion, he gives himself but little trouble about it; if it be inconsistent with universal belief, he condescends to argue the matter, and to bring what, with him, passes for a proof of it; if it be such as no man ever did or could believe, he is still more conceited of his proof and calls it demonstration, but if it is inconceivable, it is a wonder if he does not take it for granted." Our republican takes it for granted, that no advantage could result from our future connection with Great-Britain—a paradox which I think, must be utterly inconceivable to every other human understanding. Brimful, however, of this conceit, he throws down his gauntlet, and offers this challenge; leaving his readers to stare a convenient time, and to hesitate which they should admire most—the absurdity of taking this point for granted—or, the *fortitude of face* that could advance such a paradox.

I think it no difficult matter to point out many advantages which will certainly attend our reconciliation and connection with Great-Britain, on a firm, constitutional plan. I shall select a few of these; and that their importance may be more clearly discerned, I shall afterwards point out some of the evils which inevitably must attend our separating from Britain, and declaring for independency. On each article I shall study brevity.

1. By a reconciliation with Britain, a period would be put to the present calamitous war, by which so many lives have been lost, and so many more must be lost, if it continues. This alone is an advantage devoutly to be wished for. This author says— "The blood of the slain, the weeping voice of nature cries, 'Tis time to part." I think they cry just the reverse. The blood of the slain, the weeping voice of nature cries—It is time to be reconciled; it is time to lay aside those animosities which have pushed on Britons to shed the blood of Britons; it is high time that those who are connected by the endearing ties of religion, kindred and country, should resume their former friendship, and be united in the bond of mutual affection, as their interests are inseparably united.

2. By a Reconciliation with Great-Britain, Peace—that fairest offspring and gift of Heaven—will be restored. In one respect

Peace is like health; we do not sufficiently know its value but by its absence. What uneasiness and anxiety, what evils, has this short interruption of peace with the parent-state, brought on the whole British empire! Let every man only consult his feelings—I except my antagonist—and it will require no great force of rhetoric to convince him, that a removal of those evils, and a restoration of peace, would be a singular advantage and blessing.

3. Agriculture, commerce, and industry would resume their wonted vigor. At present, they languish and droop, both here and in Britain; and must continue to do so, while this unhappy contest remains unsettled.

4. By a connection with Great-Britain, our trade would still have the protection of the greatest naval power in the world. England has the advantage, in this respect, of every other state, whether of ancient or modern times. Her insular situation, her nurseries for seamen, the superiority of those seamen above others—these circumstances to mention no other, combine to make her the first maritime power in the universe—such exactly is the power whose protection we want for our commerce. To suppose, with our author, that we should have no war, were we to revolt from England, is too absurd to deserve a confutation. I could just as soon set about refuting the reveries of some brain-sick enthusiast. Past experience shews that Britain is able to defend our commerce, and our coasts; and we have no reason to doubt of her being able to do so for the future.

5. The protection of our trade, while connected with Britain, will not cost us a *fiftieth* part of what it must cost, were we ourselves to raise a naval force sufficient for the purpose.

6. Whilst connected with Great-Britain, we have a bounty on almost every article of exportation; and we may be better supplied with goods by her, than we could elsewhere. What our author says is true—"that our imported goods must be paid for, buy them where we will;" but we may buy them dearer, and of worse quality, in one place than another. The manufactures of Great-Britain confessedly surpass any in the world—particularly those in every kind of metal, which we want most; and no country can afford linens and woollens, of equal quality cheaper.

7. When a Reconciliation is effected, and things return into

the old channel, a few years of peace will restore every thing to its pristine state. Emigrants will flow in as usual from the different parts of Europe. Population will advance with the same rapid progress as formerly, and our lands will rise in value.

These advantages are not imaginary but real. They are such as we have already experienced; and such as we may derive from a connection with Great-Britain for ages to come. Each of these might easily be enlarged on, and others added to them; but I only mean to suggest a few hints to the reader.

Let us now, if you please, take a view of the other side of the question. Suppose we were to revolt from Great-Britain, declare ourselves Independent, and set up a Republic of our own—what would be the consequence?—I stand aghast at the prospect—my blood runs chill when I think of the calamities, the complicated evils that must ensue, and may be clearly foreseen—it is impossible for any man to foresee them all. Our author cautiously avoids saying any thing of the inconveniences that would attend a separation. He does not even suppose that any inconvenience would attend it. Let us only declare ourselves independent, break loose from Great-Britain, and according to him, a Paradisaical state will follow! But a prudent man will consider and weigh matters well before he consents to such a measure—when on the brink of such a dreadful precipice, he must necessarily recoil, and think of the consequences, before he advances a step forward. Supposing then we declared for Independency,—what would follow? I answer—

1. All our property throughout the continent would be unhinged; the greatest confusion, and most violent convulsions would take place. It would not be here, as it was in England at the Revolution in 1688. That revolution was not brought about by any defeazance or disannulling the right of succession. JAMES II, by abdicating the throne, left it vacant for the next in succession; accordingly his eldest daughter and her husband stept in. Every other matter went on in the usual, regular way; and the constitution, instead of being dissolved, was strengthened. But in case of our revolt, the old constitution would be totally subverted. The common bond that tied us together, and by which our property was secured, would be snapt asunder. It is not to be doubted but our Congress would endeavour to apply some remedy for those evils; but with all

deference to that respectable body, I do not apprehend that any remedy in their power would be adequate, at least for some time. I do not chuse to be more explicit; but I am able to support my opinion.

2. What a horrid situation would thousands be reduced to who have taken the oath of allegiance to the King; yet contrary to their oath, as well as inclination, must be compelled to renounce that allegiance, or abandon all their property in America! How many thousands more would be reduced to a similar situation; who, although they took not that oath, yet would think it inconsistent with their duty and a good conscience to renounce their Sovereign; I dare say these will appear trifling difficulties to our author; but whatever he may think, there are thousands and thousands who would sooner lose all they had in the world, nay life itself, than thus wound their conscience. A Declaration of Independency would infallibly disunite and divide the colonists.

3. By a Declaration for Independency, every avenue to an accommodation with Great-Britain would be closed; the sword only could then decide the quarrel; and the sword would not be sheathed till one had conquered the other.

The importance of these colonies to Britain need not be enlarged on, it is a thing so universally known. The greater their importance is to her, so much the more obstinate will her struggle be not to lose them. The independency of America would, in the end, deprive her of the West-Indies, shake her empire to the foundation, and reduce her to a state of the most mortifying insignificance. Great-Britain therefore must, for her own preservation, risk every thing, and exert her whole strength, to prevent such an event from taking place. This being the case—

4. Devastation and ruin must mark the progress of this war along the sea coast of America. Hitherto, Britain has not exerted her power. Her number of troops and ships of war here at present, is very little more than she judged expedient in time of peace—the former does not amount to 12,000 men—nor the latter to 40 ships, including frigates. Both she, and the colonies, hoped for and expected an accommodation; neither of them has lost sight of that desireable object. The seas have been open to our ships; and although some skirmishes have unfortunately happened, yet a ray of hope still cheared both

sides that, peace was not distant. But as soon as we declare for independency, every prospect of this kind must vanish. Ruthless war, with all its aggravated horrors, will ravage our once happy land—our sea-coasts and ports will be ruined, and our ships taken. Torrents of blood will be spilt, and thousands reduced to beggary and wretchedness.

This melancholy contest would last till one side conquered. Supposing Britain to be victorious; however high my opinion is of British Generosity, I should be exceedingly sorry to receive terms from her in the haughty tone of a conqueror. Or supposing such a failure of her manufactures, commerce and strength, that victory should incline to the side of America; yet who can say in that case, what extremities her sense of resentment and self-preservation will drive Great-Britain to? For my part, I should not in the least be surprized, if on such a prospect as the Independency of America, she would parcel out this continent to the different European Powers. Canada might be restored to France, Florida to Spain, with additions to each—other states also might come in for a portion. Let no man think this chimerical or improbable. The independency of America would be so fatal to Britain, that she would leave nothing in her power undone to prevent it. I believe as firmly as I do my own existence, that if every other method failed, she would try some such expedient as this, to disconcert our scheme of independency; and let any man figure to himself the situation of these British colonies, if only Canada were restored to France!

5. But supposing once more that we were able to cut off every regiment that Britain can spare or hire, and to destroy every ship she can send—that we could beat off any other European power that would presume to intrude upon this continent: Yet, a republican form of government would neither suit the genius of the people, nor the extent of America.

In nothing is the wisdom of a legislator more conspicuous than in adapting his form of government to the genius, manners, disposition and other circumstances of the people with whom he is concerned. If this important point is overlooked, confusion will ensue; his system will sink into neglect and ruin. Whatever check or barriers may be interposed, nature will always surmount them, and finally prevail. It was chiefly by attention to this circumstance, that Lycurgus and Solon were so much celebrated; and that their respective republics rose afterwards to such eminence, and acquired such stability.

The Americans are properly Britons. They have the manners, habits, and ideas of Britons; and have been accustomed to a similar form of government. But Britons never could bear the extremes, either of monarchy or republicanism. Some of their Kings have aimed at despotism; but always failed. Repeated efforts have been made towards democracy, and they equally failed. Once indeed republicanism triumphed over the constitution; the despotism of one person ensued; both were finally expelled. The inhabitants of Great-Britain were quite anxious for the restoration of *royalty* in 1660, as they were for its expulsion in 1642, and for some succeeding years. If we may judge of future events by past transactions, in similar circumstances, this would most probably be the case of America, were a republican form of government adopted in our present ferment. After much blood was shed, those confusions would terminate in the despotism of some one successful adventurer; and should the Americans be so fortunate as to emancipate themselves from that thraldom, perhaps the whole would end in a limited monarchy, after shedding as much more blood. Limited monarchy is the form of government which is most favourable to liberty—which is best adapted to the genius and temper of Britons; although here and there among us a crack-brained zealot for democracy or absolute monarchy, may be sometimes found.

Besides the unsuitableness of the republican form to the genius of the people, America is too extensive for it. That form may do well enough for a single city, or small territory; but would be utterly improper for such a continent as this. America is too unwieldy for the feeble, dilatory administration of democracy. Rome had the most extensive dominions of any ancient republic. But it should be remembered, that very soon after the spirit of conquest carried the Romans beyond the limits that were proportioned to their constitution, they fell under a despotic yoke. A very few years had elapsed from the time of their conquering Greece and first entering Asia, till the battle of Pharsalia, where Julius Cæsar put an end to the liberties of his country. Cæsar himself was the first who entirely

subdued the Gauls, though near neighbours, and that penetrated into Britain. Had it not been for the rivalship between
Sylla and Marius, who were a check upon each other, Rome
had surrendered her liberties before to one or other of those
tyrants. Holland is the most considerable republic in Europe,
at present; yet the small kingdom of Ireland is more than *twice*
as large as the *Seven United Provinces*. Holland, indeed, has
considerable colonies in the East and West Indies; but these
are under as rigid and arbitrary an administration as any colonies of France or Spain.

The author of *Common Sense*, in his abundant care and providence, lays before the public a sketch of the government he
would recommend. We thank him for his kindness; but dislike
his ware. It is patch-work, and would make *sad work* in America.
The principal outlines of this sketch seem to be taken from Mr.
Harrington's *Rota*, which was too romantic even for the times
of *Cromwell*. Our author has made such alterations as he conceived would adapt it to America. It is as much in the democratic
style as the *Rota*; and as improper for America, as the other was
for England. I may truly say of it, and its author, so far as he may
claim author-ship by it, what MONTESQUIEU said of Harrington
and his *Oceana*, of which the *Rota* is a kind of abridgment—"For
want of knowing the nature of real liberty, he busied himself in
pursuit of an imaginary one; and he built a Chalcedon, though
he had before his eyes a Byzantium." To make way for this
crude, wretched system, our author would destroy the best, the
most beautiful political fabric which the sun ever beheld!

6. In fine. Let us, for a moment, imagine that an American
republic is formed, every obstacle having been surmounted;
yet a very serious article still remains to be enquired into, viz.
the *expence* necessary to support it. It behoves those who have
any property, to think of this part of the business. As for our
author, it is more than probable he has nothing to lose; and
like others in the same predicament, is willing to trust to the
chapter of accidents and chances for something in the scram-
ble. He cannot lose; but may possibly gain. His own maxim is
certainly true—"The more men have to lose, the less willing
are they to venture;"* and *vice versa*, say I.

* *Common Sense*, page 71, 2d edition

It would be impossible to ascertain, with precision, the expence that would be necessary for the support of this New Republic. It would be very great undoubtedly—it would appear intolerable to the Americans, who have hitherto paid so few taxes. I shall just hint at a few articles.—

Our author asserts the necessity of our having a naval force when independent. It is granted—we could not be without one. The reader, however, will not expect that I should either adopt, or formally refute his hopeful scheme—viz. That merchant ships, armed, shall be employed for our defence—that is to say—That ships, when on trading voyages to Europe, Africa, the East or West Indies, or taking in their ladings at those places, shall defend the trade and coasts of America! "This, he says, would be uniting the sinews of commerce and defence, and making our strength and riches play into each others hands." The thought, I believe, is original, and the plan entirely his own—it might entitle him to a distinguished seat among the sage professors of *Laputa*, who, according to SWIFT, were employed in "extracting sun-beams out of cucumbers, calcining ice into gun-powder, and making fire malleable," and other such ingenious inventions.

This Gentleman thinks that, "50 or 60 ships, mounting 20, 30, 40, or 50 guns, with a few guard-ships, would keep up a sufficient navy." Let us take a medium of the first of those numbers, and suppose the American navy to consist partly of *fifty-five* ships, each mounting 50 guns. The precise cost of building a 50 gun ship in England, is £.14,355 sterl. Fifty-five such ships would cost £.789,525 sterling.

Besides these, it would be necessary to have some larger ships; not only to act as "guardships," but to make our navy respectable, and without which it could nor answer the intended purpose. Ships of 74 guns are reckoned the most serviceable; and the British navy has at this time no less than *forty-four* such, that could be fitted for actual service on the shortest notice; besides about *ten* more of the same sort, most of which could be got ready in a little time. The American navy would require at least *thirty* of these, and our harbours in the middle and southern colonies, would not conveniently admit larger ships. The cost of building a 74 gun ship in England, is exactly £.27,200 sterl. The cost of 30 such ships would be £716,000.

To the above ships it would be indispensibly necessary to add some frigates, which are very useful in scouring the seas, and for various kinds of business where larger ships would be unwieldy, and not answer so well. Frigates of 32 guns, and 20 guns, are reckoned the most serviceable. *Twelve* of each sort would be as few as our trade and coasts would require. The cost of building a 32 gun frigate is £.7480 sterl. Twelve such frigates would amount to £.89,760 sterl. The building a 20 gun frigate costs in England £.4370 sterling; twelve such frigates would amount to £.52,440 sterling.

Cannon, small-arms, ammunition, anchors, cables, &c. are all separate articles from that of building; and are so expensive, that a ship of war, when fitted for actual service, with six months pay and provisions, is generally reckoned to cost one thousand pounds sterling for every gun. But as it would be difficult to ascertain precisely the expence of these—or that of docks, arsenals, founderies, rope-walks, manufactories for sail-cloth, &c. &c. all which are necessary towards keeping up a regular navy, I shall not enter into a minute detail of them; but take them by the gross, and compute them at a third of the above cost. Considering the high price of labour in America, this computation will be deemed very moderate.

Let us now cast up those several articles of expence.

Expence of building 55 ships of 50 guns each . . . . . £.789,525
Ditto of building 30 ships of 74 guns each 716,000
Ditto of building 12 frigates of 32 guns 89,760
Ditto of building 12 frigates of 20 guns 52,440
                                         Total   £.1,647,725
One third of this for cannon and other
   articles above specified . . . . £.542,575
Whole cost of the navy. . . . . £.2,190,300

This number of ships, amounting to *one hundred and nine*, is a very moderate navy indeed for this continent. The British navy with which we are to contend, consists of *two hundred* and *twenty-four* ships, which may be fitted for sea on the shortest notice; and of these, *twenty-one* carry from 80 to 100 guns. On the British list are upwards of 300 ships, besides those building in the several dock-yards. The reader may rest assured that my intelligence in the preceding article of cost for constructing a navy, comes from the very best authority.

The annual expence is next to be considered. The certain, annual expence of a 50 gun ship in England, and for which provision is always made by government, is £.18,200 sterl.—that of a 74 gun ship, is £.33,800 sterl.—of a 32 gun frigate, £.11,440 sterl.—of a 20 gun frigate, £.8,320. This is allowed for wear and tear, victualling and wages. Repairs and expence of ammunition, are different articles; which, as they cannot be ascertained, I shall pass over. The certain annual expence of an American fleet, consisting of the above ships, would therefore be as follows—

Annual expence of 55 ships of 50 guns each . . . . £.1,001,000
Ditto of 30 ships of 74 guns 1,014,000
Ditto of 12 frigates of 32 guns 137,280
Ditto of 12 frigates of 20 guns 99,840
Total, £.2,252,120

It is not improbable that the American fleet might vary from this list, as to the number and size of the several ships, just as circumstances might require: Yet certain I am, that in case we became independent of England, a fleet *equal* in force to the above, and attended with *equal* expence, would be indespensibly necessary. If we are to have any foreign commerce, we must, like England, Holland, France, &c. keep ships of force in foreign parts, to protect that commerce; besides those which are necessary to defend our coasts, harbours, and trade near home.

Considering our extensive line of sea-coast, and our no less extensive frontiers, along which so many thousands of savages are settled, I think America, when independent, cannot keep less than 30 regiments of infantry in constant pay, each regiment consisting of 700 men; the whole amounting to 21,000 men. The small republic of Holland has an army of 40,000 men in time of peace. As matters are now circumstanced throughout Christendom, no state can preserve its independency without a standing army. The nation that would neglect to keep one, and a naval force, if it has any sea coast, must infallibly fall a prey to some of its ambitious and more vigilant neighbours.

The annual expence of an English regiment, consisting of 700 men, is nearly £.15,743 sterl: And the expence of raising, cloathing, and arming foot soldiers, is about £.6 a man; which will amount to £4,200 for a regiment of 700 men. Thus the annual expence of 30 regiments would be £.472,290 sterl; and the charge of raising, arming, &c. would be £.126,000 sterl. Moreover we should find it necessary to have some regiments of cavalry, to be distributed in or near the large towns and cities. Let us suppose six regiments to be raised of 300 men each. The annual expence of an English regiment of dragoons, of 300 men, is nearly £.16,187 sterl. The annual expence of six such regiments would be £.97,122 sterl; besides the charge of horses, arming, &c. which is computed at 30 guineas per man, and would amount to about £56,700 sterl.

Let us now cast up those several sums of annual expence.

Annual expence of the navy	£.2,252,120
Ditto of 30 regiments of infantry	472,290
Ditto of 6 regiments of cavalry.	97,122
Total expence, naval and military	£.2,821,532

The civil department still remains; and after considering it with as much exactness as the nature of the case will admit—after making an estimate of the salaries for Governors, Delegates, Judges, Ambassadors, Consuls, and that almost endless train of officers in various departments, which will be unavoidable, as soon as we become Independent, and which cost us nothing at present: The annual expence of America, when Independent, must greatly exceed THREE MILLIONS of pounds sterling—it will probably amount to three millions and an half. However, to avoid fractions, let it be stated at three millions—even this sum carries horror in the very idea of it; and yet many deluded people flatter themselves that they will pay no taxes, if we are once Independent! Supposing then that Canada, Nova-Scotia, and Florida were joined to the thirteen colonies now united, the number would be sixteen. The above sum equally divided among them would be £.187,500 sterl; which is nearly equal to 833,333 Spanish milled dollars, (reckoning a dollar at 4s. 6d. sterl.) *annual* expence to each colony. But it should be observed, that Rhode-Island is a small colony—that the three little counties of Newcastle, Kent and Sussex upon Delaware, are reckoned as a colony—that Nova-Scotia, Georgia and Florida are very young colonies: None of these therefore could possibly contribute an equal share with the older and larger colonies; the expence of the latter must, of course, be proportionably greater, to make up the deficiency: Supposing the inhabitants of all these colonies amount to *three millions* —and I am of opinion their number is not greater—each individual, man, woman, and child, black and white, would have *twenty shillings* sterling, i. e. above four Spanish dollars to pay *annually* for defraying the public expence. Or, taking every seventh person for a Taxable, which I think is near the usual proportion, and that this sum were to be paid by a Poll-tax, then every Taxable in the colonies must pay £.7 sterl. i. e. about 32 Spanish dollars *annually* for the public expence, over and above what he has paid in times past. In case of war or any extraordinary emergency, those taxes must rise proportionably.

Besides this annual expence, there is an immense sum for constructing a navy and raising an army—

For constructing a navy	£.2,190,300
For raising, arming, &c. 30 regim. of Infantry . .	126,000
For raising, arming, &c. 6 regim. of Cavalry . . .	56,700
Total,	£.2,373,000

This sum of two millions, three hundred and seventy-three thousand pounds sterling, joined to the sixteen millions of dollars, which I am informed the Honourable Congress has been obliged already to issue, besides as much more perhaps which they will find necessary to issue for the support of the war, if it continues, and the prodigious sums of paper currency which the several colonies have struck, and must hereafter strike; will make a load of debt, that must prove ruinous to this continent.

I have not knowingly exaggerated a single article in the above estimate; and were the trial made, I verily believe the expence would be found much greater. For I have formed this estimate according to the state of things in England; but it is well known that wages and the price of labour in general, are much higher in America than in England. Labour must necessarily be dear in every country where land is cheap, and large tracts of it unsettled, as is the case here. Hence an American regiment costs us *double* what a British regiment, of equal number, costs Britain. Were it proper to be explicit, and descend to particulars, I could evince this past all possibility of doubt; and I appeal for the truth of it to those gentlemen among us who are acquainted with these matters.

Where the money is to come from which will defray this enormous annual expence of *three millions*, sterling, and all those other debts, I know not; unless the author of *Common Sense*, or some other ingenious projector, can discover the *Philosopher's Stone*, by which iron and other base metals may be transmuted into gold. Certain I am, that our commerce and agriculture, the two principal sources of our wealth, will not support such an expence. The whole of our exports from the Thirteen United Colonies in the year 1769, amounted only to £.2,887,898 sterl.;* which is not so much, by near half a million, as our annual expence would be, were we Independent of Great-Britain. Those exports, with no inconsiderable part of the profits arising from them, it is well known, centered finally in Britain, to pay the merchants and manufacturers there for goods we had imported thence; and yet left us still in debt! What then must our situation be, or what the state of our trade, when oppressed with such a burthen of annual expence! When every article of commerce, every necessary of life, together with our lands, must be heavily taxed, to defray that expence!

Such is the load of debt and expence we should incur by this Writer's hopeful exchange of our connection with Great-Britain for Independency and Republicanism! And all this, after being exhausted by a tedious war, and perhaps our shipping and sea-ports destroyed! This is a very serious matter; which is obvious to every understanding, and which no sophistry can evade. All who have any prudence or common sense left, or any property to lose, will pause and consider well, before they

---

* See *Campbell's Political Survey of Great-Britain*, vol. 2.

plunge themselves into such a dreadful situation. How little do those who desire this situation, know what they are about, or what they desire.

Our author frequently refers us to Holland, as if that were the only land of liberty—crowned with every blessing, and exempt from every evil. But hear a little plain truth. The national debt of Holland is much greater, in proportion, than that of England. The taxes in Holland far exceed not only those in England, but even those in France, insomuch that a certain writer declares he scarcely knows any thing they have which has escaped taxation, "except the air they breathe". Nay more,—the people at large have no voice in chusing the members of their several Senates, as we have in chusing Representatives. The members of each Senate, upon any vacancy, elect new members; and the deputies from those Senates, constitute the *States General*. So that in fact, the people have no share in the government, as with us; "they have nothing to do but pay and grumble," as Lord Chesterfield observes. Yet this is the country our author holds up for imitation; and if we were to follow his advice, I have not the least doubt but we should soon resemble them in paying heavy taxes, as well as in every other matter.

But here it may be said—*That all the evils above specified, are more tolerable than slavery.* With this sentiment I sincerely agree —any hardships, however great, are preferable to slavery. But then I ask, is there no other alternative in the present case? Is there no choice left us but slavery, or those evils? I am confident there is; and that both may be equally avoided. Let us only shew a disposition to treat or negociate in earnest—let us fall upon some method to set a treaty or negociation with Great Britain on foot; and if once properly begun, there is a moral certainty that this unhappy dispute will be settled to the mutual satisfaction and interest of both countries. For my part, I have not the least doubt about it.

It would be improper and needless for me to enlarge on the particulars that should be adjusted at such a treaty. The maturest deliberation will be necessary on the occasion, as well as a generous regard to every part of the Empire, I shall just beg leave to suggest my opinion on a few points—I think America should insist, that the claim of parliamentary taxation be either explicitly relinquished; or else, such security given as the case will admit, and may be equivalent to a formal relinquishment, that this claim shall not be exerted. When this most important point is gained, America should consider, that there is a great difference between having her money wrested from her by others, and not giving any of it herself, when it is proper to give. While she is protected, and shares in the advantages resulting from being a part of the British Empire, she should contribute something for that protection and those advantages; and I never heard a sensible American deny this. Moreover, she should stipulate for such a freedom of trade as is consistent with the general welfare of the State; and that this interesting object be settled in such a manner as to preclude, as much as possible, any impolitic, or injurious infringements hereafter. All this may be easily done, if both sides are only disposed for peace; and there are many other particulars which would be exceedingly beneficial to America, and might be obtained, as they could not interfere with the interest of Great Britain or any other part of the empire. We have abundant proof of this as well as several good hints to proceed on, in the late concessions to Nova-Scotia from government.

But it may be asked—what probability is there that Britain will enter on such a treaty, or listen to proposals of this kind? Is she not preparing for war, and fitting out a formidable armament against the colonies? I answer—there is every reason to believe that she will enter on such a treaty, if it is desired; and that she will listen to reasonable proposals. It is her interest to do so. To hold these colonies by the sword only, were she ever so powerful, would be holding them by a very precarious, expensive tenure. Such a Union with the Colonies as will promote their interest equally with her's, is the only effectual way of attaching them to her. Is it reasonable to suppose that Great Britain does not see this? Or that she is not sensible of it? Besides, it has been openly and expressly declared in Parliament that *taxation is given up* by the Ministry; we are also assured that some very respectable names have been lately added to the advocates of America; and Commissioners have been appointed to treat with us. All these things are in our favour, and promise a prosperous issue to a negociation, if once begun. The British armament will not in the least impede a treaty.

Belligerent-Powers, when on the eve of peace, always make as vigorous preparations for war, as if there was no thoughts of peace. America also is preparing for war, which is no more than a prudent step. It need not prevent her from treating; and she may thereby obtain better terms.

But a Declaration for Independency on the part of America, would preclude treaty intirely; and could answer no good purpose. We actually have already every advantage of Independency, without its inconveniences. By a Declaration of Independency, we should instantly lose all assistance from our friends in England. It would stop their mouths; for were they to say any thing in our favour, they would be deemed rebels, and treated accordingly.

Our author is much elated with the prospect of foreign succour, if we once declare ourselves Independent; and from thence promiseth us mighty matters. This, no doubt, is intended to spirit up the desponding—all who might shrink at the thought of America encountering, singly and unsupported, the whole strength of Great-Britain. I believe in my conscience, that he is as much mistaken in this, as in any thing else; and that this expectation is delusive, vain and fallacious. My reasons are these, and I submit them to the readers judgement.

The only European power from which we can possibly receive assistance, is France. But France is now at peace with Great-Britain; and is it probable that France would interrupt that peace, and hazard a war with the power which lately reduced her so low, from a *disinterested* motive of aiding and protecting these Colonies? The fate of Corsica may teach us how *ready* European states are to act on *disinterested* motives, in such cases. France has now a pacific King; her finances are in a very ruinous state; both which circumstances will naturally tend to keep her quiet. If it be said—That the exclusive trade of America would be a sufficient inducement for France to engage on our side—I answer—That she never can have our exclusive trade, till the power of Great-Britain is totally annihilated. Now, supposing France were able to effect this—(a supposition not very probable)—yet the other European states are too jealous of her—too deeply interested in preserving a due ballance of power, which is a principal object in European politics, ever to suffer such an event to take place.

It is well known that some of the French and Spanish Colonists, not long since, offered to put themselves under the protection of England, and declare themselves Independent of France and Spain; but England rejected both offers. The example would be rather dangerous to states that have colonies—to none could it be more so than to France and Spain, who have so many and such extensive colonies. "The practice of courts are as much against us" in this, as in the instance our author mentions. Can any one imagine, that because we declared ourselves Independent of England, France would *therefore* consider us as really Independent! And before England had acquiesced, or made any effort worth mentioning to reduce us? Or can any one be so weak as to think, that France would run the risque of a war with England, unless she (France) were sure of some extraordinary advantage by it, in having the colonies under her *immediate jurisdiction?* If England will not protect us for our trade, surely France will not.

But I have some *facts* to alledge further on this head, which will have great weight with all sober, dispassionate persons. As for those who give themselves up to passion and prejudice, they are scarcely capable of judging. Like men who are drawn in and whirled about, by some impetuous vortex, they have lost the proper command of themselves.

The several European states who have colonies on this continent, or the adjacent islands, are exceedingly jealous of those colonies, lest they should aspire to independency. He must be totally ignorant of the state of things in Europe who is not sensible of this. The great distance of America from Europe contributes to raise that jealousy; and it is heightened by our growing strength and importance, and our enterprizing spirit. Hence it was that France lately sent such a number of regular troops to Martinico; and disarmed all the inhabitants, to whom the defence of that island was chiefly committed formerly. The professed reason for disarming the inhabitants was to prevent their joining the North Americans in their contest with Great-Britain. This information comes from a gentleman who was then at Martinico, and lately arrived on this continent. The inhabitants of the French West-Indies, it is probable, would willingly join us, and shake off the despotic yoke under which they groan; but this disposition in them will only serve to alarm France the more, and induce the latter to oppose, rather than assist us.

Discountenancing *our* independency by France, would only be such a return as Britain will naturally expect, and most probably receive, for a similar conduct in her to the French inhabitants of Hispaniola. Not long after the conclusion of the late war, those inhabitants were driven by the most glaring oppression, to take up arms. The French Governor applied for assistance to the English Admiral, then on the West-India station. Several ships were sent immediately by the latter, with the promise of more, if necessary. The insurrection was quelled by the Governor's insidiously drawing the leaders of the insurrection into a treaty, and then making prisoners of them—a circumstance not very inviting to place much faith in French promises or generosity.

The King of Denmark's late proclamation, in which he declares, that *the estates of such of his subjects as shall join the Americans, will be forfeited,* is a further proof of the disposition of European powers, who have settlements in America.

Let any man calmly reflect on these particulars; and then judge whether it is probable that France or any other European state that has possessions on this quarter of the globe, will contribute to erect an independent empire in America; especially when it is considered, that this new empire, from its proximity, must, sooner or later, infallibly swallow up those possessions. I am firmly of opinion, that our Declaration of Independency will have an effect directly contrary to what our author suggests, and what some warm people expect. I think it infinitely more likely that it will produce a coalition or treaty between the several European nations, who have settlements in America, to guarantee and secure their respective settlements to each other; than that any of these nations will co-operate with our design, and thereby lend a hand to injure themselves.

Nay, further; I can whisper a secret to the author of *Common Sense*, provided he will let it go no further—which is—That France and Spain have *actually made an offer of their assistance* to Great-Britain, in the present contest with the Colonies. This intelligence comes from such authority as would remove all doubt about the matter, even from our zealous Republican, were I at liberty to mention that authority.

Indeed were France ever so willing and able to assist us, the experiment would be imprudent in us, and hazardous to the highest degree. There is scarcely an instance recorded in history of Foreigners being called in to assist in domestic quarrels, that it did not prove ruinous to those that sought their aid. The ancient Britons invited the Saxons to assist them against the Picts—the Picts were subdued; and the Britons enslaved. One instance more I cannot forbear mentioning. The Etolians and other Greek states called in the Romans to assist them against Philip of Macedon, one of Alexander's Successors. Philip was reduced; and the Roman yoke was imposed on the Grecian states. Sensible of their error, when it was too late, and anxious for deliverance from the Romans, the Etolians applied for Aid to Antiochus, who then possessed the remains of Alexander's Asiatic Dominions. The Romans now employed Philip to subdue Antiochus and the Etolians, as before they had employed the Etolians to subdue Philip. The Roman yoke was more confirmed and made heavier. Were we to call in France on this occasion; and should our united force succeed against Britain, something similar to this would probably follow.

I have heard the case of Holland's revolt from Spain, and Queen Elizabeth's affording aid to the former, mentioned as parallel to ours. But instead of being parallel, the cases differ in every circumstance. Elizabeth, embarrassed greatly by Roman Catholics at home, was then at war with Philip IId. of Spain—a cruel, gloomy tyrant, who had lately introduced the inquisition into the low countries, where hundreds of his protestant subjects were sacrificed by that bloody court. This was the real cause of the Dutch revolt; though civil matters partly mingled with it. Elizabeth by assisting the Dutch, served two important purposes. One was to protect the protestants who were every where threatned with destruction. The other was, to distress her implacable enemy, who aimed at no less than the utter ruin of her religion, crown and kingdom. The Dutch states offered Elizabeth the sovereignty of their country; but she refused it, having no design of that sort. It is more than probable the French King would not be so disinterested, modest and self-denying as Elizabeth was, were we to make him the like offer. Such was the case of Holland; yet some have been so silly as to compare our present case with that of the Dutch.

Consider this matter as you will, view the Declaration of Independency in what light you please; the ruin of America must be the inevitable consequence. Our author's earnestness and zeal therefore, that we should declare ourselves Independent, serves only to prove that he himself is desperate; and that he would gladly bring this whole continent into the same situation.

But our author repeatedly tells us—"That to expend so many millions for the sake of getting a few vile acts repealed, is unworthy of the charge." Now to pass over the gross insult here offered to the Continental Congress, who had this important object principally in view, in the spirited measures they have taken: I answer—That if five times as many millions had been expended, America would be an immense gainer, provided those acts are repealed, and her liberties, property, and trade, are settled on a firm basis, by a Constitutional Union with Great-Britain. Were that measure once effected, the peace and prosperity of this continent would be as immutably and certainly secure as any thing in this world can. We should be the happiest people in the world. The Americans have fully evinced, to the conviction of the most incredulous, that they have an high sense of their liberties, and sufficient spirit to vindicate those liberties. Their numbers, strength, and importance, will be daily increasing; these will command respect from Great-Britain, and insure to them a mild and equitable treatment from her. She will not hereafter be over anxious to contend, or come to blows with them. This I think is clear to demonstration; and hence we may learn to set a proper value on the rant which this author throws out, as if America would be perpetually embroiled with England hereafter, unless we declare for independency.

For my part, I look upon this pamphlet to be the most injurious, in every respect, to America, of any that has appeared since these troubles began. Its natural and necessary tendency is, to produce jealousy, dissention and disunion among us. The Continental Congress, the several Provincial Congresses and Assemblies, have all unanimously and in the strongest terms, disclaimed every idea of Independency. They have repeatedly declared their abhorrence of such a step; they have as often declared their firm attachment to our Sovereign and the Parent State. They have declared that placing them in the same situation that they were at the close of the last war, was their only object; that when this was done, by repealing the obnoxious acts, our former harmony and friendship would be restored. I appeal to the reader whether all this has not been done from one end of the continent to the other.

Yet here steps forth a writer, who avers with as much assurance as if he had the whole continent at his back, and ready to support his asseverations—That Independency is our duty and interest—That it was folly and rashness to go to the expence we have been at for sake of repealing those obnoxious acts; and moreover, loads with the most opprobrious terms, that Sovereign and Nation to which we had declared our attachment! In what light can this be viewed in Britain? Must it not weaken the influence of our friends—strengthen the hands of the ministry—and give weight to every thing our enemies have said to our disadvantage? Must it not induce people to suspect our candour—that all our declarations were insincere, fallacious —intended only to amuse and deceive?—It is as much to vindicate my injured countrymen from this disgrace, which they deserve not, as to oppose the destructive project of Independency, that I appear on this occasion—a project which is as *new* as it is destructive.

I have now considered every thing in this Incendiary's pamphlet, that deserves notice. If some things are passed over, it is not because they are unanswerable; but because they are not worthy of an answer. I have on purpose omitted every subject, the discussion of which might tend to raise jealousy among the colonists; such as religion, the claims of some colonies on others, besides many more of the same kind. But it was more difficult to avoid speaking of these, than to point out what prolific sources of animosity, bitterness and bloody contests they must infallibly prove, were America to become independent. The whole is freely submitted to the reader's candid, dispassionate judgment.

The Author of *Common Sense* may probably call me "a disguised tory, a prejudiced man," or what in his estimation "will be productive of more calamities to this continent than all others—a moderate man." But I am too conscious of the sincerity of my own heart, and of the rectitude of my intentions, to pay any regard to whatever he is pleased to call me. Who indeed would be ambitious of his approbation, when he expressly reprobates Moderation—that offspring of true wisdom and sound judgment? The welfare of America is what I wish for above any earthly thing. I am fully, firmly and conscientiously persuaded, that our author's scheme of Independency and Republicanism, is big with ruin—with inevitable ruin to America. Against this scheme therefore, which totally changes the ground we set out on, as an honest man, as a friend to human nature, I must and will bear testimony.

Let the spirit, design and motives which are undeniably evident in our respective pamphlets, decide which should be attended to most.

The author of *Common Sense* is a violent stickler for Democracy or Republicanism only—every other species of government is reprobated by him as tyrannical: *I* plead for that constitution which has been formed by the wisdom of ages—is the admiration of mankind—is best adapted to the genius of Britons, and is most friendly to liberty.

He takes pleasure in aggravating every circumstance of our unhappy dispute—would inspire others with the same rage that instigates himself, and would set his fellow subjects to cutting each others throats. *I* would most gladly, were it in my power, draw a veil of eternal oblivion over any errors which Great Britain or the colonies may have fallen into—I would willingly persuade them to mutual harmony and union; since on these their mutual happiness and interest depend.

He is evidently goaded on by ambition and resentment, to seek for the gratification of those passions in an independent republic here; which would reduce America to the same desperate state with himself: *I* have no interest to serve but what is common to my countrymen—but what every American of property is concerned in equally with me.

He places himself at the head of a party; and spurns from him with the utmost contempt and indignation, all who will not enlist under his banner: *I* am of no party, but so far as the welfare of America is aimed at; and I believe there are many who aim at this in every party. I have not learnt to pace with such intire acquiescence in the trammels of any party, as not to desert it, the moment it deserts the interest of my country.

He recommends a new, untried romantic scheme, at which

we would at first have shuddered—which is big with inevitable ruin, and is the last stage of political phrenzy. *I* am for pursuing the same object, and acting on the same principles and plan with which we set out, when this contest began, and of whose success there is a moral certainty.

This, as far as I can know or see, is the true state of our case—let Heaven and Earth judge between us.

America is far from being yet in a desperate situation. I am confident she may obtain honourable and advantagious terms from Great Britain. A few years of peace will soon retrieve all her losses. She will rapidly advance to a state of maturity, whereby she may not only repay the parent state amply for all past benefits; but also lay under the greatest obligations. America, till very lately, has been the happiest country in the universe. Blest with all that nature could bestow with the profusest bounty, she enjoyed besides, more liberty, greater privileges than any other land. How painful is it to reflect on these things, and to look forward to the gloomy prospects now before us! But it is not too late to hope that matters may mend. By prudent management her former happiness may again return; and continue to encrease for ages to come, in a union with the parent state.

However distant humanity may wish the period; yet, in the rotation of human affairs, a period may arrive, when, (both countries being prepared for it) some terrible disaster, some dreadful convulsion in Great Britain, may transfer the seat of empire to this western hemisphere—where the British constitution, like the Phœnix from its parent's ashes, shall rise with youthful vigour and shine with redoubled splendor.

But if America should now mistake her real interest—if her sons, infatuated with romantic notions of conquest and empire, ere things are ripe, should adopt this republican's scheme: They will infallibly destroy this smiling prospect. They will dismember this happy country—make it a scene of blood and slaughter, and entail wretchedness and misery on millions yet unborn.

Quod Deus a nobis procul avertat.

FINIS.

[Thomas Hutchinson], Strictures upon the Declaration of the Congress at Philadelphia; in a Letter to a Noble Lord, &c. London, 1776.

The Second Continental Congress met in Philadelphia in May 1775. In spite of the outbreak of fighting, Congress continued to seek some kind of reconciliation with Great Britain. In July, at the urging of John Dickinson, Congress approved the Olive Branch Petition, which vowed loyalty to the king and humbly asked him to break with the "artful and cruel" ministers whom the Congress blamed for the oppressive measures enacted in his name. At the same time the Congress issued a Declaration of the Causes and Necessities of Taking Up Arms (largely written by Dickinson and Thomas Jefferson) which denied that Americans had any "ambitious design of separating from Great Britain, and establishing independent states." The king ignored the Olive Branch Petition and in August 1775 proclaimed the colonies to be in open rebellion. In October he publicly accused them of aiming at independence; two months later the British government had declared all American shipping liable to seizure by British warships. By early 1776 most members of the Continental Congress were committed to independence; it took just a few more months to convince the reluctant delegates from the Middle Colonies to join in a formal Declaration of Independence. The debate was over, and swords rather than pens now would have to decide whether that independence could be sustained.

To Thomas Hutchinson goes the last word. In June 1773, letters that he had written to London in the winter of 1768–69 fell into patriot hands and were published. In them, Hutchinson, who was then lieutenant governor, had urged that stern measures, including "an abridgment of what are called English liberties," were needed in America to maintain the colonies' dependence on Great Britain. If nothing were done, "or nothing more than some declaratory acts or resolves," he had warned, "*it is all over with us*. The friends . . . of anarchy will be afraid of nothing, be it ever so extravagant." Confirmed in their suspicions of a conspiracy against their liberty, members of the Massachusetts House of Representatives petitioned the Crown to recall the governor, and he in turn asked the ministry for permission to sail to London to defend himself. In June 1774 Hutchinson left for England, never to return.

Receiving a copy of the Declaration of Independence in August 1776, Hutchinson was at once determined to counter this "most infamous Paper" full of "a great number of Pretended tyrannical deeds of the King." Because some of the charges in the Declaration were directed specifically at him and his colony, he had a personal as well as a political motivation to refute the Declaration's "false and frivolous reasons" for America's rebellion. Deeply attached both to Massachusetts and to the empire, Hutchinson rejected as false the basic premise of the Declaration, that the colonists were "one *distinct people*." In an important sense the entire imperial debate could be said to have turned on this crucial question—whether or not the Americans were a distinct people.

STRICTURES

UPON THE

DECLARATION

OF THE

CONGRESS at PHILADELPHIA;

In a LETTER to a NOBLE LORD, &c.

LONDON:

PRINTED IN THE YEAR 1776.

A Letter to a Noble Lord, &c.

MY LORD,

THE last time I had the honour of being in your Lordships company, you observed that you was utterly at a loss to what facts many parts of the Declaration of Independence published by the Philadelphia Congress referred, and that you wished they had been more particularly mentioned, that you might better judge of the grievances, alledged as special causes of the separation of the Colonies from the other parts of the Empire. This hint from your Lordship induced me to attempt a few Strictures upon the Declaration. Upon my first reading it, I thought there would have been more policy in leaving the World altogether ignorant of the motives to this Rebellion, than in offering such false and frivolous reasons in support of it; and I flatter myself, that before I have finished this letter, your Lordship will be of the same mind. But I beg leave, first to make a few remarks upon its rise and progress.

I have often heard men, (who I believe were free from party influence) express their wishes, that the claims of the Colonies to an exemption from the authority of Parliament in imposing Taxes had been conceded; because they had no doubts that America would have submitted in all other cases; and so this unhappy Rebellion, which has already proved fatal to many hundreds of the Subjects of the Empire, and probably will to many thousands more, might have been prevented.

The Acts for imposing Duties and Taxes may have accelerated the Rebellion, and if this could have been foreseen, perhaps, it might have been good policy to have omitted or deferred them; but I am of opinion, that if no Taxes or Duties had been laid upon the Colonies, other pretences would have been found for exception to the authority of Parliament. The body of the people in the Colonies, I know, were easy and quiet. They felt no burdens. They were attached, indeed, in every Colony to their own particular Constitutions, but the Supremacy of Parliament over the whole gave them no concern. They had been happy under it for an hundred years past: They feared no imaginary evils for an hundred years to come. But there were men in each of the principal Colonies, who had

Independence in view, before any of those Taxes were laid, or proposed, which have since been the ostensible cause of resisting the execution of Acts of Parliament. Those men have conducted the Rebellion in the several stages of it, until they have removed the constitutional powers of Government in each Colony, and have assumed to themselves, with others, a supreme authority over the whole.

Their designs of Independence began soon after the reduction of Canada, relying upon the future cession of it by treaty. They could have no other pretence to a claim of Independence, and they made no other at first, than what they called the natural rights of mankind, to chuse their own forms of Government, and to change them when they please. This, they were soon convinced, would not be sufficient to draw the people from their attachment to constitutions under which they had so long been easy and happy: Some grievances, real or imaginary, were therefore necessary. They were so far from holding Acts for laying Duties to be unconstitutional, and, as has been since alledged, meer nullities, that in Massachuset's Bay the General Assembly, about the year 1762, ordered an Action to be brought against the Officers of the Customs, for charges made in the Court of Admiralty, which had caused a diminution of the part of forfeitures to the Province, by virtue of what is called the Sugar Act, passed in the sixth year of George the Second. Surely they would not deny the authority of Parliament to lay the Duty, while they were suing for their part of the penalty for the non-payment of it.

Their first attempt, was against the Courts of Admiralty, which they pronounced unconstitutional, whose judgments, as well as jurisdiction, they endeavoured to bring into examen before the Courts of Common Law, and a Jury chosen from among the people: About the same time, a strong opposition was formed against Writs of Assistants, granted to the Officers of the Customs by the Supreme Courts, and this opposition finally prevailed in all the Colonies, except two or three, against, and in defiance of, an Act of Parliament which required the supreme Courts to grant these writs.

It does not, however, appear that there was any regular plan formed for attaining to Independence, any further than that every fresh incident which could be made to serve the purpose, by alienating the affections of the Colonies from the Kingdom, should be improved accordingly. One of these incidents happened in the year 1764. This was the Act of Parliament for granting certain duties on goods in the British Colonies, for the support of Government, &c. At the same time a proposal was made in Parliament, to lay a stamp duty upon certain writings in the Colonies; but this was deferred until the next Session, that the Agents of the Colonies might notify the several Assemblies in order to their proposing any way, to them more eligible, for raising a sum for the same purpose with that intended by a stamp duty. The Colony of Massachuset's Bay was more affected by the Act for granting duties, than any other Colony. More molasses, the principal article from which any duty could arise, was distilled into spirits in that Colony than in all the rest. The Assembly of Massachuset's Bay, therefore, was the first that took any publick notice of the Act, and the first which ever took exception to the right of Parliament to impose Duties or Taxes on the Colonies, whilst they had no representatives in the House of Commons. This they did in a letter to their Agent in the summer of 1764, which they took care to print and publish before it was possible for him to receive it. And in this letter they recommend to him a pamphlet, wrote by one of their members, in which there are proposals for admitting representatives from the Colonies to sit in the House of Commons.

I have this special reason, my Lord, for taking notice of this Act of the Massachuset's Assembly; that though an American representation is thrown out as an expedient which might obviate the objections to Taxes upon the Colonies, yet it was only intended to amuse the authority in England; and as soon as it was known to have its advocates here, it was renounced by the Colonies, and even by the Assembly of the Colony which first proposed it, as utterly impracticable. In every stage of the Revolt, the same disposition has always appeared. No precise, unequivocal terms of submission to the authority of Parliament in any case, have ever been offered by any Assembly. A concession has only produced a further demand, and I verily believe if every thing had been granted short of absolute Independence, they would not have been contented; for this was the object from the beginning. One of the most noted among the American clergy, prophesied eight years ago, that within eight years from that time, the Colonies would be formed into three distinct independent Republics, Northern, Middle and Southern. I could give your Lordship many irrefragable proofs of this determined design, but I reserve them for a future letter, the subject of which shall be the rise and progress of the Rebellion in each of the Colonies.

Soon after the intention of raising monies in America for the purpose of a revenue was known, the promoters of Independence, and Revolt, settled certain principles of polity, such as they thought would be best adapted to their purpose.

"The authority of Parliament over the Colonists ceased upon their leaving the Kingdom. Every degree of subjection is therefore voluntary, and ought to continue no longer than the authority shall be for the public good.

"If there had been no express *compact* by charters, or implied by submitting to be governed under Royal Commissions, the Colonists would be under no obligations to acknowledge the King of Great Britain as their Sovereign, and this obligation must cease when he shall cease to perform his part of the conditions of the compact.

"As every Colony, by charter or by Royal Commissions, was constituted with special legislative powers to raise monies by Taxes, Duties, &c. no monies ought to be raised from the inhabitants, by any other powers than the several respective legislatures.

"As the Colonies were settled by encouragement from, and some at great expence of, the Kingdom, and principally for commercial purposes, subjection to *necessary* and *reasonable* Acts for regulating commerce ought to be specially acknowledged.

"Other Acts to be submitted to, or not, as they may, or may not, be for the benefit of the Colonies."

These principles of Government in Colonies must soon work an Independence.

To carry them to effect, Confederacies were formed by the chiefs of the revolters in each Colony; and Conventions were held by Delegates when judged necessary: Subjects for controversy in opposition to Government were fought for in each of the Colonies, to irritate and inflame the minds of the people, and dispose them to revolt: Dissentions and commotions in any Colony, were cherished and increased, as furnishing proper matter to work upon: For the same purpose, fictitious letters were published, as having been received from England, informing of the designs of ministry, and even of Bills being before the Parliament for introducing into the Colonies arbitrary Government, heavy Taxes and other cruel oppressions: Every legal measure for suppressing illicit trade was represented as illegal and grievous; and the people were called upon to resist it: A correspondence was carried on with persons in England, promoters of the revolt, whose intelligence and advice from time to time were of great use: Persons in England of superior rank and characters, but in opposition to the measures of administration, were courted and deceived, by false professions; and the real intentions of the revolters were concealed: The tumults, riots, contempt and defiance of law in England, were urged to encourage and justify the like disorders in the Colonies, and to annihilate the powers of Government there.

Many thousands of people who were before good and loyal subjects, have been deluded, and by degrees induced to rebel against the best of Princes, and the mildest of Governments.

Governors, and other servants of the Crown, and Officers of Government, with such as adhered to them, have been removed and banished under pretence of their being the instruments of promoting ministerial tyranny and arbitrary power; and finally the people have subjected themselves to the most cruel oppressions of fifty or sixty Despots.

It will cause greater prolixity to analize the various parts of this Declaration, than to recite the whole. I will therefore present it to your Lordship's view in distinct paragraphs, with my remarks, in order as the paragraphs are published:

In Congress, July 4, 1776.

A Declaration by the Representatives of the United States of America in General Congress assembled.

When in the course of human events it becomes necessary for one People to dissolve the political bands which have connected them with another, and to assume among the Powers of the earth, the separate and equal station to which the laws of nature and of nature's God entitle them, a decent respect to the opinions of mankind requires that they should declare the causes which impel them to the separation.

We hold these truths to be self evident—That all men are created equal, that they are endowed by their Creator with certain unalienable rights, that among these are life, liberty and the pursuit of happiness, that to secure these rights, governments are instituted among men, deriving their just powers from the consent of the governed; and whenever any form of government becomes destructive of these ends, it is the right of the people to alter or abolish it, and to institute new government, laying its foundation on such principles, and organizing its powers in such form as to them shall seem most likely to effect their safety and happiness. Prudence indeed will dictate that governments long established, should not be changed for light and transient causes; and accordingly all experience hath shewn that mankind are more disposed to suffer while evils are sufferable, than to right themselves by abolishing the forms to which they are accustomed. But when a long train of abuses and usurpations pursuing invariably the same object, evinces a design to reduce them under absolute despotism, it is their right, it is their duty to throw off such government, and to provide new guards for their future security. Such has been the patient sufferance of these Colonies, and such is now the necessity which constrains them to alter their former systems of Government. The history of the present King of Great Britain is a history of repeated injuries and usurpations, all having its direct object, the establishment of an absolute tyranny over these States. To prove this, let facts be submitted to a candid world.

They begin, my Lord, with a false hypothesis, That the Colonies are one *distinct people*, and the kingdom another, connected by *political* bands. The Colonies, *politically* considered, never were a *distinct* people from the kingdom. There never has been but one *political* band, and that was just the same before the first Colonists emigrated as it has been ever since, the Supreme Legislative Authority, which hath essential right, and is indispensably bound to keep all parts of the Empire entire, until there may be a separation consistent with the general good of the Empire, of which good, from the nature of government, this authority must be the sole judge. I should therefore be impertinent, if I attempted to shew in what case *whole people* may be justified in rising up in oppugnation to the powers of government, altering or abolishing them, and substituting, in whole or in part, new powers in their stead; or in what sense all men are created equal; or how far life, liberty, and the *pursuit of happiness* may be said to be unalienable; only I could wish to ask the Delegates of Maryland, Virginia, and the Carolinas, how their Constituents justify the depriving more than an hundred thousand Africans of their rights to liberty, and *the pursuit of happiness*, and in some degree to their lives, if these rights are so absolutely unalienable; nor shall I attempt to confute the absurd notions of government, or to expose the equivocal or inconclusive expressions contained in this Declaration; but rather to shew the false representation made of the facts which are alledged to be the evidence of injuries and usurpations, and the special motives to Rebellion. There are many of them, with design, left obscure; for as soon as they are developed, instead of justifying, they rather aggravate the criminality of this Revolt.

The first in order, *He has refused his assent to laws the most wholesome and necessary for the public good*; is of so general a nature, that it is not possible to conjecture to what laws or to what Colonies it refers. I remember no laws which any Colony has been restrained from passing, so as to cause any complaint of grievance, except those for issuing a fraudulent paper-currency, and making it a legal tender; but this is a restraint which for many years past has been laid on Assemblies by an act of Parliament, since which such laws cannot have been offered to the King for his allowance. I therefore believe this to be a general charge, without any particulars to support it; fit enough to be placed at the head of a list of imaginary grievances.

The laws of England are or ought to be the laws of its Colonies. To prevent a deviation further than the local circumstances of any Colony may make necessary, all Colony laws are to be laid before the King; and if disallowed, they then become of no force. Rhode-Island, and Connecticut, claim by Charters, an exemption from this rule, and as their laws are never presented to the King, they are out of the question. Now if the King is to approve of all laws, or which is the same thing, of all which the people judge for the public good, for we are to presume they pass no other, this reserve in all Charters and

Commissions is futile. This charge is still more inexcusable, because I am well informed, the disallowance of Colony laws has been much more frequent in preceding reigns, than in the present.

He has forbidden his Governors to pass laws of immediate and pressing importance, unless suspended in their operation till his assent should be obtained, and when so suspended, he has utterly neglected to attend them.

Laws, my Lord, are in force in the Colonies, as soon as a Governor has given his assent, and remain in force until the King's disallowance is signified. Some laws may have their full effect before the King's pleasure can be known. Some may injuriously affect the property of the subject; and some may be prejudicial to the prerogative of the Crown, and to the trade, manufactures and shipping of the kingdom. Governors have been instructed, long before the present or the last reign, not to consent to such laws, unless with a clause suspending their operations until the pleasure of the King shall be known. I am sure your Lordship will think that nothing is more reasonable. In Massachuset's Bay, the Assembly would never pass a law with a suspending clause. To pass laws which must have their whole operation, or which must cause some irreparable mischief before the King's pleasure can be known, would be an usurpation of the People upon the Royal Prerogative: To cause the operation of such laws to be suspended until the King can signify his pleasure by force of instructions, similar to what has been given in all former Reigns, can never be charged as an usurpation upon the rights of the People.

I dare say, my Lord, that if there has ever been an instance of any laws lying longer than necessary before the King's pleasure has been signified, it has been owing to inattention in some of the servants of the Crown, and that upon proper application any grievance would have been immediately redressed.

He has refused to pass other laws for accommodation of large districts of People, unless those People would relinquish the rights of representation in the legislature, a right inestimable *to them, and formidable to tyrants only.*

We shall find, my Lord, that Massachuset's Bay is more concerned in this Declaration than any other Colony. This article respects that Colony alone. By its charter, a legislature is constituted: The Governor is appointed by the King.—The Council, consisting of twenty-eight members, were appointed, in the first instance, by the King, but afterwards are to be elected annually by the two Houses—The House of Representatives is to consist of two members elected annually by each town, but the number of the House is nevertheless made subject to future regulations by acts of the General Assembly. Besides the Council, the Civil Officers of the Government are also to be annually elected by the two Houses. It appeared in a course of years, that by multiplying towns, the House of Representatives had increased to double the number of which it consisted at first. Their importance in all elections was increased in proportion; for the number of the Council continued the same as at first. To prevent further deviation from the spirit of the Charter, an instruction was then first given to the Governors, not to consent to laws for making new towns so as to increase the number of the House, unless there should be a clause in the law to suspend its operation, until the King signifies his pleasure upon it. But here, my Lord, lies the most shameful falsity of this article. No Governor ever refused to consent to a law for making a new town, even without a suspending clause, if provision was made that the inhabitants of the new town should continue to join with the old, or with any other town contiguous or near to it, in the choice of Representatives; so that there never was the least intention to deprive a single inhabitant of the right of being represented; and, in fact, such provision has ever been made, except where the inhabitants of the new town chose to forego the right, which we must suppose they did not think *inestimable*, rather than pay the wages of their Representatives. This has been the case in several instances, and it is notorious that the Assembly of that Province have made it their practice, from year to year, to lay fines on their towns for not chusing Representatives. This is a wilful misrepresentation made for the sake of the brutal insult at the close of the article.

He has called together legislative bodies at places unusual, uncomfortable, and distant from the depository of their public records, for the sole purpose of fatiguing them into a compliance with his measures.

To the same Colony this article also has respect. Your Lordship must remember the riotous, violent opposition to Government in the Town of Boston, which alarmed the whole Kingdom, in the year 1768. Four Regiments of the King's forces were ordered to that Town, to be aiding to the Civil Magistrate in restoring and preserving peace and order. The House of Representatives, which was then sitting in the Town, remonstrated to the Governor against posting Troops there, as being an invasion of their rights. He thought proper to adjourn them to Cambridge, where the House had frequently sat at their own desire, when they had been alarmed with fear of the small pox in Boston; the place therefore was not unusual. The public rooms of the College, were convenient for the Assembly to sit in, and the private houses of the Inhabitants for the Members to lodge in; it therefore was not *uncomfortable*. It was within four miles of the Town of Boston, and less *distant* than any other Town fit for the purpose.

When this step, taken by the Governor, was known in England, it was approved, and conditional instructions were given to continue the Assembly at Cambridge. The House of Representatives raised the most frivolous objections against the authority of the Governor to remove the Assemby from Boston, but proceeded, nevertheless, to the business of the Session as they used to do. In the next Session, without any new cause, the Assembly refused to do any business unless removed to Boston. This was making themselves judges of the place, and by the same reason, of the time of holding the Assembly, instead of the Governor, who thereupon was instructed not to remove them to Boston, so long as they continued to deny his authority to carry them to any other place.

They *fatigued* the Governor by adjourning from day to day, and refusing to do business one Session after another, while he gave his constant attendance to no purpose; and this they make the King's *fatiguing* them to compel them to comply with his measures.

A brief narrative of this unimportant dispute between an American Governor and his Assembly, needs an apology to your Lordship; how ridiculous then do those men make themselves, who offer it to the world as a ground to justify Rebellion?

He has dissolved Representatives Houses repeatedly for opposing with manly firmness his Invasions on the Rights of the People.

Contentions between Governors and their Assemblies have caused dissolutions of such Assemblies, I suppose, in all the Colonies, in former as well as later times. I recollect but one instance of the dissolution of an Assembly by special order from the King, and that was in Massachuset's Bay. In 1768, the House of Representatives passed a vote or resolve, in prosecution of the plan of Independence, incompatible with the subordination of the Colonies to the supreme authority of the Empire; and directed their Speaker to send a copy of it in circular letters to the Assemblies of the other Colonies, inviting them to avow the principles of the resolve, and to join in supporting them. No Government can long subsist, which admits of combinations of the subordinate powers against the supreme. This proceeding was therefore, justly deemed highly unwarrantable; and indeed it was the beginning of that unlawful confederacy, which has gone on until it has caused at least a temporary Revolt of all the Colonies which joined in it.

The Governor was instructed to require the House of Representatives, in their next Session to rescind or disavow this resolve, and if they refused, to dissolve them, as the only way to prevent their prosecuting the plan of Rebellion. They delayed a definitive answer, and he indulged them, until they had finished all the business of the Province, and then appeared this *manly firmness* in a rude answer and a peremptory refusal to comply with the King's demand. Thus, my Lord, the regular use of the prerogative in suppressing a begun Revolt, is urged as a grievance to justify the Revolt.

He has refused for a long time after such dissolutions to cause others to be erected whereby the legislative powers, incapable of annihilation, have returned to the people at large for their exercise; the state remaining in the mean time exposed to all the dangers of invasions from without and convulsions within.

This is connected with the last preceding article, and must relate to the same Colony only; for no other ever presumed, until the year 1774, when the general dissolution of the established government in all the Colonies was taking place, to convene an Assembly, without the Governor, by the meer act of the People.

In less than three months after the Governor had dissolved the Assembly of Massachuset's Bay, the town of Boston, the first mover in all affairs of this nature, applied to him to call another Assembly. The Governor thought he was the judge of the proper time for calling an Assembly, and refused. The town, without delay, chose their former members, whom they called a *Committee*, instead of Representatives; and they sent circular letters to all the other towns in the Province inviting them to chuse *Committees* also; and all these *Committees* met in what they called a *Convention*, and chose the Speaker of the last house their *Chairman*. Here was a House of Representatives in every thing but name; and they were proceeding upon business in the town of Boston, but were interrupted by the arrival of two or three regiments, and a spirited message from the Governor, and in two or three days returned to their homes.

This vacation of three months was the *long time* the people waited before they exercised their unalienable powers; the *Invasions from without* were the arrival or expectation of three or four regiments sent by the King to aid the Civil Magistrate in preserving the peace; and the *Convulsions within* were the tumults, riots and acts of violence which this Convention was called, not to suppress but to encourage.

He has endeavoured to prevent the population of these States; for that purpose obstructing the laws for naturalization of foreigners, refusing to pass others to encourage their migration hither, and raising the conditions of new appropriations of lands.

By this and the next article, we have a short relief from the Province of Massachuset's Bay. I cannot conceive that the subjects in the Colonies would have had any cause of complaint if there never had been any encouragement given to foreigners to settle among them; and it was an act of meer favour to the Colonies which admitted foreigners to a claim of naturalization after a residence of seven years. How has the King obstructed the operation of this act? In no other way than by refusing his assent to colony acts for further encouragement. Nothing can be more regular and constitutional. Shall any other than the supreme authority of the Empire judge upon what terms foreigners may be admitted to the privilege of natural born subjects? Parliament alone may pass acts for this purpose. If there had been further conditions annexed to the grants of unappropriated lands, than have ever yet been, or even a total restriction of such grants when the danger of Revolt was foreseen, it might have been a prudent measure; it certainly was justifiable, and nobody has any right to complain.

He has obstructed the administration of justice by refusing his assent to laws for establishing judiciary powers.

I was, my Lord, somewhat at a loss, upon first reading this article, to what transaction or to what Colony it could refer. I soon found, that the Colony must be North Carolina; and that the transaction, referred to, is a reproach upon the Colony, which the Congress have most wickedly perverted to cast reproach upon the King.

In most, if not all, of the Colonies, laws have passed to enable creditors to attach the effects of absent or absconding debtors; and to oblige the trustees of such debtors to disclose upon oath the effects in their hands; and also all persons indebted to them to disclose the debts. Whatever these laws may have been in their original intention, they have proved most iniquitous in their operation. The creditors, who first come to the knowledge of any effects, seize them to the exclusion even of the other creditors in the Colony; and the creditors in England, or at the greatest distance, stand still a worse chance. I have known in some Colonies, instances of attachments of the effects of bankrupts in England, which by force of these laws have been made, by the American creditors, to the full satisfaction of their debts, when the creditors in England have received a few shillings only in the pound. This frustrates our own bankrupt laws. I believe they have never had any equitable bankrupt laws in any Colony, of any duration: In New York, they have done more towards them than in any other Colony.

These laws for attachments in most of the Colonies were temporary. The Governors were very properly instructed not to consent to the revival of them, or not without a suspending clause. In North Carolina, the law for attachments was tacked to, or was part of, the same law which established their Courts of Justice. The Governor, as he ought to have done if he had received no instruction, refused a bill for reviving the law, because the provision for attachments was part of it: The Assembly refused to pass the bill without the provision, and in this way determined they would have no Courts of Justice, unless they were such as should be bound to support these iniquitous attachments, peculiarly injurious to British and other distant creditors, and very unequal to the creditors within the Colony.

All this was fully known to the Congress, who, notwithstanding, have most falsely represented the regular use of the prerogative to prevent injustice, as an obstruction to the administration of justice.

He has made Judges dependent on his will alone for the tenure of their offices, and the amount and payment of their salaries.

The Americans claim a right to the English constitution and laws, as they stood when the Colonies were planted. The Judges of England were then dependent on the Crown for their continuance in office, as well as for their salaries. The Judges in America, except in the Charter-Colonies, have always been dependent on the Crown for their continuance in office; and, in some Colonies, the salaries of the Chief Justice, and sometimes of the other Judges, have been paid by the Crown, and the Colonies have considered it as an act of favour shewn them.

There has been a change in the constitution of England in respect of the tenure of the office of the Judges. How does this give a claim to America? It will be said, the reason in both cases is the same. This will not be allowed, and until the King shall judge it so, there can be no room for exception to his retaining his prerogative.

And for the salaries, they are *fixed* and do not depend upon the behaviour of the Judges, nor have there ever been any instances of salaries being with-held. If the Assemblies in the Colonies would have *fixed* the like salaries on their Judges, no provision would ever have been made by the Crown; it being immaterial by whom the salary is paid, provided the payment be made sure and certain.

This is a complaint against the King, for not makeing a change in the constitution of the Colonies, though there is not so much as a pretence that there has been the least grievance felt in any Colony for want of this change; nor has there been any complaint even of danger, in any Colony, except Massachuset's Bay.

He has erected a Multitude of new offices and sent hither Swarms of officers, to harrass our people and eat out their subsistence.

I know of no new offices erected in America in the present reign, except those of the Commissioners of the Customs and their dependents. Five Commissioners were appointed, and four Surveyors General dismissed; perhaps fifteen or twenty clerks and under officers were necessary for this board more than the Surveyors had occasion for before: Land and tide waiters, weighers &c. were known officers before; the Surveyors used to encrease or lessen the number as the King's service required, and the Commissioners have done no more. Thirty or forty additional officers in the whole Continent, are the *Swarms* which eat out the subsistence of the boasted number of three millions of people.

Cases had often happened in America, which Surveyors General had not authority to decide. The American merchants complained of being obliged to apply to the Commissioners of the Customs in London. The distance caused long delay, as well as extraordinary charge. A Board in America, was intended to remove the cause of these complaints, as well as to keep the inferior officers of the Customs to their duty. But no powers were given to this Board more than the Commissioners in London had before; and none but illicit traders ever had any reason to complain of grievances; and they of no other than of being better watched than they had ever been before. At this time, the authority of Parliament to pass Acts for regulating commerce was acknowledged, but every measure for carrying such Acts into execution was pronounced an injury, and usurpation, and all the effects prevented.

He has kept among us, in times of peace, standing armies, without the consent of our legislatures.

This is too nugatory to deserve any remark. He has kept no armies among them without the consent of the Supreme Legislature. It is begging the question, to suppose that this authority was not sufficient without the aid of their own Legislatures.

He has affected to render the Military independent of, and superior to, the Civil Power.

When the subordinate Civil Powers of the Empire became Aiders of the people in acts of Rebellion, the King, as well he might, has employed the Military Power to reduce those rebellious Civil Powers to their constitutional subjection to the Supreme Civil Power. In no other sense has he ever *affected* to render the Military independent of, and superior to, the Civil Power.

He has combined with others to subject us to a jurisdiction foreign to our Constitution and unacknowledged by our Laws; giving his assent to their pretended Acts of Legislation.

This is a strange way of defining the part which the Kings of England take in conjunction with the Lords and Commons in passing Acts of Parliament. But why is our present Sovereign to be distinguished from all his predecessors since Charles the Second? Even the Republic which they affect to copy after, and Oliver, their favourite, because an Usurper, *combined* against them also. And then, how can a jurisdiction submitted to for more than a century be *foreign* to their constitution? And is it not the grossest prevarication to say this jurisdiction is *unacknowledged* by their laws, when all Acts of Parliament which respect them, have at all times been their rule of law in all their judicial proceedings? If this is not enough; their own subordinate legislatures have repeatedly in addresses, and resolves, in the most express terms *acknowledged* the supremacy of Parliament; and so late as 1764, before the conductors of this Rebellion had settled their plan, the House of Representatives of the leading Colony made a public declaration in an address to their Governor, that, although they humbly apprehended they might propose their objections, to the late Act of Parliament for granting certain duties in the British Colonies and Plantations in America, yet they at the same time, *acknowledged* that it was their duty to yield obedience to it while it continued unrepealed.

If the jurisdiction of Parliament is foreign to their Constitution, what need of specifying instances, in which they have been subjected to it? Every Act must be an usurpation and injury. They must then be mentioned, my Lord, to shew, hypothetically, that even if Parliament had jurisdiction, such Acts would be a partial and injurious use of it. I will consider them, to know whether they are so or not.

For quartering large bodies of armed troops among us.

When troops were employed in America, in the last reign, to protect the Colonies against French invasion, it was necessary to provide against mutiny and desertion, and to secure proper quarters. Temporary Acts of Parliament were passed for that purpose, and submitted to in the Colonies. Upon the peace, raised ideas took place in the Colonies, of their own importance, and caused a reluctance against Parliamentary authority, and an opposition to the Acts for quartering troops, not because the provision made was in itself unjust or unequal, but because they were Acts of a Parliament whose authority was denied. The provision was as similar to that in England as the state of the Colonies would admit.

For protecting them by a mock trial from punishment, for any murder which they should commit on the Inhabitants of these States.

It is beyond human wisdom to form a system of laws so perfect as to be adapted to all cases. It is happy for a state, that there can be an interposition of legislative power in those cases, where an adherence to established rules would cause injustice. To try men before a biassed and pre-determined Jury would be *a mock trial*. To prevent this, the Act of Parliament, complained of, was passed. Surely, if in any case Parliament may interpose and alter the general rule of law, it may in this. America has not been distinguished from other parts of the Empire. Indeed, the removal of trials for the sake of unprejudiced disinterested Juries, is altogether consistent with the spirit of our laws, and the practice of courts in changing the venue from one county to another.

For cutting off our trade with all parts of the world.

Certainly, my Lord, this could not be a *cause* of Revolt. The Colonies had revolted from the Supreme Authority, to which, by their constitutions, they were subject, before the Act passed. A Congress had assumed an authority over the whole, and had rebelliously prohibited all commerce with the rest of the Empire. This act, therefore, will be considered by the *candid world*, as a proof of the reluctance in government against what is the dernier resort in every state, and as a milder measure to bring the Colonies to a re-union with the rest of the Empire.

For imposing taxes on us without our consent.

How often has your Lordship heard it said, that the Americans are willing to submit to the authority of Parliament in all cases except that of taxes? Here we have a declaration made to the world of the causes which have impelled to a separation. We are to presume that it contains all which they that publish it are able to say in support of a separation, and that if any one cause was distinguished from another, special notice would be taken of it. That of taxes seems to have been in danger of being forgot. It comes in late, and in as slight a manner as is possible. And, I know, my Lord, that these men, in the early days of their opposition to Parliament, have acknowledged that they pitched upon this subject of taxes, because it was most alarming to the people, every man perceiving immediately that he is personally affected by it; and it has, therefore, in all communities, always been a subject more dangerous to government than any other, to make innovation in; but as their friends in England had fell in with the idea that Parliament could have no right to tax them because not represented, they thought it best it should be believed they were willing to submit to other acts of legislation until this point of taxes could be gained; owning at the same time, that they could find no fundamentals in the English Constitution, which made representation more necessary in acts for taxes, than acts for any other purpose; and that the world must have a mean opinion of their understanding, if they should rebel rather than pay a duty of three-pence *per* pound on tea, and yet be content to submit to an act which restrained them from making a nail to shoe their own horses. Some of them, my Lord, imagine they are as well acquainted with the nature of government, and with the constitution and history of England, as many of their partisans in the kingdom; and they will sometimes laugh at the doctrine of fundamentals from which even Parliament itself can never deviate; and they say it has been often held and denied merely to serve the cause of party, and that it must be so until these unalterable fundamentals shall be ascertained; that the great Patriots in the reign of King Charles the Second, Lord Russell, Hampden, Maynard, &c. whose memories they reverence, declared their opinions, that there were no bounds to the power of Parliament by any fundamentals whatever, and that even the hereditary succession to the Crown might be, as it since has been, altered by Act of Parliament; whereas they who call themselves Patriots in the present day have held it to be a fundamental, that there can be no taxation without representation, and that Parliament cannot alter it.

But as this doctrine was held by their friends, and was of service to their cause until they were prepared for a total independence, they appeared to approve it: As they have now no further occasion for it, they take no more notice of an act for imposing taxes than of many other acts; for a distinction in the authority of Parliament in any particular case, cannot serve their claim to a general exemption, which they are now preparing to assert.

For depriving us, in many cases, of the benefit of a trial by jury.

Offences against the Excise Laws, and against one or more late Acts of Trade, are determined without a Jury in England. It appears by the law-books of some of the Colonies, that offences against their Laws of Excise, and some other Laws, are also determined without a Jury; and civil actions, under a sum limited, are determined by a Justice of Peace. I recollect no cases in which trials by Juries are taken away in America, by Acts of Parliament, except such as are tried in the Courts of Admiralty, and these are either for breaches of the Acts of trade, or trespasses upon the King's woods. I take no notice of the Stamp Act, because it was repealed soon after it was designed to take place.

I am sorry, my Lord, that I am obliged to say, there could not be impartial trials by Juries in either of these cases. All regulation of commerce must cease, and the King must be deprived of all the trees reserved for the Royal Navy, if no trials can be had but by Jury. The necessity of the case justified the departure from the general rule; and in the reign of King William the Third, jurisdiction, in both these cases, was given to the Admiralty by Acts of Parliament; and it has ever since been part of the constitution of the Colonies; and it may be said, to the honour of those Courts, that there have been very few instances of complaint of injury from their decrees. Strange! that in the reign of King George the Third, this jurisdiction should suddenly become an usurpation and ground of Revolt.

For transporting us beyond seas to be tried for pretended offences.

I know of no Act, but that of the 12th of the present reign, to prevent the setting fire to his Majesty's Ships, Docks, Arsenals, &c. to which this article can refer.—But are these *pretended* offences?

By an Act of Parliament made in the 35th year of King Henry the Eighth, all treasons committed in any parts without the realm, may be tried in any county of England; and in the reign of Queen Anne, persons were condemned in England for offences against this Act in America; but the Act does not comprehend felonies.

The offences against the last Act are made felony; and as it is most likely they should be committed in times of faction and party-rage, the Act leaves it in the power of the Crown to order the trial of any offence committed without the realm, either in the Colony, Island, Fort, where it may be committed, or in any County within the Realm.

An opinion prevailed in America, that this Act was occasioned by the burning the King's Schooner, Gaspee, by people in the Colony of Rhode Island; but the Act had passed before that fact was committed, though it was not generally known in America, until some months after. The neglect of effectual inquiry into that offence, by the authority in Rhode Island Colony, shews that the Act was necessary; but when it passed, there does not appear to have been any special view to America, more than to the forts and settlements in Europe, Asia, or Africa.

For abolishing the free system of English laws in a neighbouring province, establishing therein an arbitrary Government and enlarging its boundaries, so as to render it at once an example and fit instrument for introducing it into their Colonies.

It would be impertinent to make any remarks upon the general fitness of the Quebec Act for the purposes for which it passed, seeing your Lordship has so lately fully considered and given your voice in it.

But what, my Lord, have the American Colonies to do with it? There are four New England Colonies: In two of them, both Governor and Council are annually elected by the body of the people; in a third, the Council is annually elected by the Assembly; in the fourth, both Governor and Council are appointed by the Crown: The three Charter Governments, for near a century past, have never felt, nor had any reason to fear, any change in their constitutions, from the example of the fourth. Just as much reason have the Colonies in general to fear a change in their several constitutions, no two of which are alike, from the example of Quebec.

With as little reason may they complain of the enlargement of the boundaries of Quebec. It was time to include the ungranted territory of America in some jurisdiction or other, to prevent further encroachments upon it. What claim could any of the Colonies have to a territory beyond their own limits? No other security against an improper settlement of this country could have been made equally judicious and unexceptionable. This exception is therefore utterly impertinent, and seems to proceed from disappointment in a scheme for engrossing the greatest part of this ungranted territory.

For taking away our Charters, abolishing our most valuable laws, altering fundamentally the forms of our Governments.

For suspending our own legislatures and declaring themselves vested with power, to legislate for us in all cases whatsoever.

These two articles are so much of the same nature, that I consider them together. There has been no Colony Charter altered except that of Massachuset's Bay, and that in no respect, that I recollect, except that the appointment and power of the Council are made to conform to that of the Council of the other Royal Governments, and the laws which relate to grand and petit juries are made to conform to the general laws of the Realm.

The only instance of the suspension of any legislative power is that of the Province of New York, for refusing to comply with an Act of Parliament for quartering the King's troops posted there for its protection and defence against the French and Indian enemies.

The exceptions, heretofore, have rather been to the authority of Parliament to revoke, or alter Charters, or legislative powers once granted and established, than to the injurious or oppressive use of the authority upon these occasions.

When parties run high, the most absurd doctrines if a little disguised, are easily received and embraced. Thus, because in the Reign of Charles the First, resistance to Taxes imposed by the authority of the *King alone* was justifiable, and the contrary doctrine having taken the names of *Passive Obedience and Non-Resistance*, those terms became odious; therefore in the Reign of George the Third, resistance to Taxes imposed, by the *King, Lords and Commons*, upon America while not represented in Parliament, is justifiable also; and the contrary doctrine is branded with the odious terms of *Passive Obedience and Non-Resistance*; as if the latter case were analogous to the former. And because in the Reign of Charles the Second and James the Second, Royal Charters were deemed *sacred* and not to be revoked or altered at the will and pleasure of the *King alone*; therefore in the Reign of George the Third, they are *sacred* also and not to be revoked nor altered by the authority of *Parliament*.

The common people who, relying upon the authority of others, confound cases together which are so essentially different, may be excused; but what excuse, my Lord, can be made for those men, in England as well as in America, who, by such fallacies, have misguided the people and provoked them to rebellion?

He has abdicated Government here, by declaring us out of his protection and waging War against us.

He has plundered our Seas, ravaged our Coasts, burnt our Towns and destroyed the Lives of our People.

He is at this time, transporting large Armies of foreign mercenaries to compleat the works of death, desolation and tyranny, already begun with circumstances of cruelty and perfidy scarcely parallelled in the most barbarous ages, and totally unworthy the head of a civilized Nation.

He has constrained our fellow Citizens, taken captive on the high Seas, to bear arms against their Country, to become the executioners of their Friends and Brethren, or to fall themselves by their hands.

He has excited domestick insurrections amongst us and has endeavoured to bring on the Inhabitants of our frontiers the merciless Indian Savages, whose known rule of warfare, is an undistinguished destruction of all ages, sexes and conditions.

These, my Lord, would be weighty charges from a *loyal and dutiful* people against an *unprovoked* Sovereign: They are more than the people of England pretended to bring against King James the Second, in order to justify the Revolution. Never was there an instance of more consummate effrontery. The Acts of a *justly incensed* Sovereign for suppressing a most *unnatural, unprovoked* Rebellion, are here assigned as the *causes* of this Rebellion. It is immaterial whether they are true or false. They are all short of the penalty of the laws which had been violated. Before the date of any one of them, the Colonists had as effectually renounced their allegiance by their deeds as they have since done by their words. They had displaced the civil and military officers appointed by the King's authority and set up others in their stead. They had new modelled their civil governments, and appointed a general government, independent of the King, over the whole. They had taken up arms, and made a public declaration of their resolution to defend themselves, against the forces employed to support his legal authority over them. To subjects, who had forfeited their lives by acts of Rebellion, every act of the Sovereign against them, which falls short of the forfeiture, is an act of favour. A most ungrateful return has been made for this favour. It has been improved to strengthen and confirm the Rebellion against him.

In every stage of these oppressions, we have petitioned for redress in the most humble terms; our repeated petitions have been answered only by repeated injury.

What these oppressions were your Lordship has seen, for we may falsly conclude, that every thing appears in this Declaration, which can give colour to this horrid Rebellion, so that these men can never complain of being condemned without a full hearing.

But does your Lordship recollect any petitions in the several stages of these pretended oppressions? Has there ever been a petition to the King

—To give his Assent to these wholesome and necessary Laws to which he had refused it?

—To allow his Governors to pass laws without a suspending clause, or without the people's relinquishing the right of Representation?

—To withdraw his instructions for calling legislative bodies at unusual, uncomfortable and distant places?

—To allow Assemblies, which had been dissolved by his order, to meet again?

—To pass laws to encourage the migration of foreigners?

—To consent to the establishment of judiciary Powers?

—To suffer Judges to be independent for the continuance of their offices and salaries?

—To vacate or disannul new erected offices?

—To withdraw his troops *in times of peace*, until it appeared that the reason for it was to give a free course to Rebellion?

And yet these, my Lord, are all the oppressions pretended to have been received from the King except those *in combination* with the two Houses of Parliament; and they are all either grossly misrepresented, or so trivial and insignificant as to have been of no general notoriety in the time of them, or mere contests between Governors and Assemblies, so light and transient, as to have been presently forgot. All the petitions we have heard of, have been against Acts of the Supreme Legislature; and in all of them something has been inserted, or something has been done previous to them, with design to prevent their being received.

They have petitioned for the repeal of a law, because Parliament had no right to pass it. The receiving and granting the prayer of such petition, would have been considered as a renunciation of right; and from a renunciation in one instance, would have been inferred a claim to renunciation in all other instances. The repealing, or refraining from enacting any particular laws, or relieving from any kind of service, while a due submission to the laws in general shall be continued, and suitable return be made of other services, seems to be all which the Supreme Authority may grant, or the people or any part of them, require. If any thing, my Lord, short of Independence was the redress sought for, all has been granted which has been prayed for, and could be granted.

A Prince, whose character is thus marked, by every act which defines the tyrant, is unfit to be the ruler of a free people.

Indignant resentment must seize the breast of every loyal subject. A tyrant, in modern language, means, not merely an absolute and arbitrary, but a cruel, merciless Sovereign. Have these men given an instance of any one Act in which the King has exceeded the just Powers of the Crown as limited by the English Constitution? Has he ever departed from known established laws, and substituted his own will as the rule of his actions? Has there ever been a Prince by whom subjects in rebellion, have been treated with less severity, or with longer forbearance?

Nor have we been wanting in attention to our British Brethren. We have warned them from time to time of attempts by their legislature, to extend an unwarrantable jurisdiction over us. We have reminded them of the circumstances of our emigration and settlement here. We have appealed to their native justice and magnanimity, and we have conjured them by the ties of our common kindred to disavow those usurpations which would inev-

itably interrupt our connections and correspondence. They too have been deaf to the voice of justice and consanguinity. We must therefore acquiesce in the necessity which denounces our separation and hold them as we hold the rest of mankind, Enemies in War, in Peace, Friends.

We therefore, the Representatives of the United States of America, in General Congress assembled, appealing to the Supreme Judge of the World, for the rectitude of our intentions, do in the name and by the authority of the good People of these Colonies, solemnly publish and declare, That these United Colonies, are, and ought to be, Free and Independent States, and that they are absolved from all allegiance to the British Crown, and that all political connection between them and the State of Great Britain, is and ought to be totally dissolved, and that as free and Independent States they have full power to levy War, conclude Peace, contract Alliances, establish Commerce, and to do all other Acts and things which Independent States may of right do. And for the support of this Declaration, with a firm reliance on the protection of Divine Providence, we mutually pledge to each other, our Lives, our Fortunes and our sacred Honour. Signed by order and in behalf of the Congress.

JOHN HANCOCK, President

They have, my Lord, in their late address to the people of Great Britain, fully avowed these principles of Independence, by declaring they will pay no obedience to the laws of the Supreme Legislature, they have also pretended, that these laws were the mandates or edicts of the Ministers, not the acts of a constitutional legislative power, and have endeavoured to persuade such as they called their British Brethren, to justify the Rebellion begun in America; and from thence they expected a general convulsion in the Kingdom, and that measures to compel a submission would in this way be obstructed. These expectations failing, after they had gone too far in acts of Rebellion to hope for impunity, they were under the *necessity* of a separation, and of involving themselves, and all over whom they had usurped authority, in the distresses and horrors of war against that power from which they revolted, and against all who continued in their subjection and fidelity to it.

Gratitude, I am sensible, is seldom to be found in a community, but so sudden a revolt from the rest of the Empire, which had incurred so immense a debt, and with which it remains burdened, for the protection and defence of the Colonies, and at their most importunate request, is an instance of ingratitude no where to be parallelled.

Suffer me, my Lord, before I close this Letter, to observe, that though the professed reason for publishing the Declaration was a decent respect to the opinions of mankind, yet the real design was to reconcile the people of America to that Independence, which always before, they had been made to believe was not intended. This design has too well succeeded. The people have not observed the fallacy in reasoning from the *whole* to *part*; nor the absurdity of making the *governed* to be *governors*. From a disposition to receive willingly complaints against Rulers, facts misrepresented have passed without examining. Discerning men have concealed their sentiments, because under the present *free* government in America, no man may, by writing or speaking, contradict any part of this Declaration, without being deemed an enemy to his country, and exposed to the rage and fury of the populace.

I have the honour to be,
My LORD,
Your Lordship's most humble,
And most obedient servant.

To the Right Honourable ⎫
   the E—— of —— ⎭

London, October, 15*th*. 1776.

A Chronology of the First British Empire

<table>
<tr>
<td>1497</td>
<td>Sponsored by the English king, Henry VII (r. 1485–1509), Venetian Giovanni Caboto (John Cabot) sails across the North Atlantic and makes landfall in eastern Canada. Cabot's discovery of this "newe founde lande" becomes the basis for English claims to all of North America.</td>
</tr>
<tr>
<td>1533</td>
<td>Amid the controversy with Rome over his divorce from Catherine of Aragon, Henry VIII (1509–47) effects passage in Parliament of an Act in Restraint of Appeals, which declares "that this realm of England is an empire, and so hath been accepted in the world, governed by one supreme head and King having the dignity and royal estate of the imperial crown of the same, unto whom a body politic, compact of all sorts and degrees of people divided in terms and by names of spirituality and temporality, be bounded and owe to bear next to God a natural and humble obedience." Henry's eventual break with Rome and the subsequent flowering of Protestantism in England during the short reign of his son, Edward VI (1547–53), will introduce a religious dimension to England's long struggle for empire with Europe's Catholic powers, France and Spain.</td>
</tr>
<tr>
<td>1541</td>
<td>Henry VIII is declared King of Ireland by the Irish Parliament, a body that represents the island's minority population of Anglo-Norman descent, those living within the Pale, a swath of territory in the east that encompasses Dublin. For much of the remainder of the century the Tudor monarchs will attempt to subdue the rest of Ireland through various colonization efforts and military adventures, developing strategies and ideologies that will inform English colonization in the New World.</td>
</tr>
<tr>
<td>1559</td>
<td>England loses Calais, the last vestige of its dynastic claims on the Continent.</td>
</tr>
<tr>
<td>1562</td>
<td>With backing from London merchants and the court of Queen Elizabeth I (1558–1603), John Hawkins makes the first of three voyages carrying enslaved people from Africa to Spanish America. When this trade is halted by the Spanish, Hawkins, Francis Drake, and other seafarers turn to</td>
</tr>
</table>

privateering expeditions against Spain's New World possessions.

1565   Spain establishes the first permanent European settlement in North America at St. Augustine in Florida.

1584   Walter Raleigh receives a royal patent from the queen for the exploration and settlement of North America. His principal venture, a settlement at Roanoke Island in North Carolina's Outer Banks, ends in failure.

1588   The successful defense of the kingdom against a major invasion force (the Spanish Armada) boosts English pride and confidence on the world stage.

1600   The East India Company, a joint-stock venture, is formed by a group of London merchants in an effort to break Portugal's monopoly on trade with Asia.

1603   With the death of Elizabeth, her cousin, James VI of Scotland, succeeds to the English throne as James I (1603–25). The first of the Stuart monarchs tries to unite the two mostly Protestant kingdoms—one presbyterian and the other episcopal—but meets with resistance from the English Parliament, notwithstanding his assurance that his motivation "in seeking union is only to advance the greatness of your empire seated here in England." Despite Parliament's concerns, James styles himself King of Great Britain.

1604   Confronted with a nearly bankrupt government in England after years of war with Spain, James concludes a peace and announces a ban on privateering, a pivot that frees resources for renewed attempts to establish overseas plantations.

1605   A group of English Catholics, disappointed by the failure of the new king (whose wife is Catholic) to relax legal and political restrictions on followers of the old faith, conspires to blow up the Houses of Parliament when James is present to open the session. The so-called Gunpowder Plot is discovered before it can be put into effect and Guy Fawkes and his fellow conspirators are arrested, tried, and executed. November 5, the day the plot is uncovered, is proclaimed "the joyful day of deliverance" by an act of Parliament and "Guy Fawkes Day," as it will become known, is long commemorated throughout the empire as a reminder of the nefarious specter of "popery."

1606   Under a royal patent North American settlement rights are granted to two joint-stock companies made up of merchants and investors, one based in London, the other in Plymouth, which are to be governed by a council in London appointed by the king. The charter states that subjects who emigrate to or are born in a colony "shall have and enjoy all Liberties, Franchises and Immunities . . . as if they had been abiding and born within this our Realm of England," a principle that will be echoed in subsequent colonial charters.

1607   An expedition sent by the London Company establishes the first permanent English settlement in North America, on Jamestown Island, in Virginia.

1608   Samuel de Champlain establishes a settlement at Quebec, the genesis of what will be the colony of New France. Essentially a series of trading posts for the fur trade, New France grows slowly along the St. Lawrence River, its success dependent on good relations with the region's native inhabitants. English merchants establish the first trading post or "factory" in India.

1609   In the wake of a long conflict with the Gaelic chieftains of Ireland (the Nine Years' War), James initiates a program encouraging Protestants from England and Scotland to establish plantations, organized principally through guilds and corporations, on confiscated Catholic land in Ulster.

1612   England establishes permanent settlement on Bermuda and the island is later incorporated under the Virginia Company's charter. In Virginia, John Rolfe begins to experiment with the cultivation of tobacco, a labor-intensive crop that will quickly become the colony's staple commodity.

1619   After imposing increasingly harsh legal codes in response to persistent starvation and disorder in Virginia, the Company promises to reform the colony and reaffirms the settlers' claims to the rights of Englishmen, including a representative assembly. The first General Assembly of Virginia accordingly meets at Jamestown in July. The Company also grants a community of English Separatists living in Leiden (the Pilgrims) permission to settle in the northern part of its Virginia claim. In August, Dutch slave traders sell twenty Africans—the first known to have reached English America—into servitude at Jamestown. By the end of the century over half a million unfree people will have crossed the Atlantic to the English colonies, including 350,000 African slaves and 200,000 indentured servants.

1620   The Pilgrims land on Cape Cod and decide to establish a colony at Plymouth, beyond the Virginia Company's northern boundary. Outside any organized jurisdiction, the settlers enter into a formal agreement, the Mayflower Compact, which serves as the basis for the colony's government. Plymouth remains autonomous until absorbed into Massachusetts in 1691.

1621   Sir Edwin Sandys, one of the founders of the Virginia Company and chair of a parliamentary committee investigating England's flagging trade and bullion scarcity, proposes a bill to establish a monopoly for Virginia tobacco in the English market. Jealously guarding his prerogative powers, the king announces his opposition to the measure, as he will another seeking to regulate access to colonial fisheries, insisting that the administration of overseas plantations is not subject to parliamentary oversight because the colonies are not annexed to the Crown, that is, they are not part of the realm of England, but rather the personal property of the monarch.

1622   John Mason and Ferdinando Gorges receive royal grants to the territory between the Merrimack and Sagadahoc (Kennebec) rivers, and settlement begins along the Piscataqua River, the site of present-day Portsmouth, New Hampshire, the following year. These and other settlements further north along the Maine coast will fall into the orbit of the Massachusetts Bay Colony government.

1623   In Indonesia, ten English traders are put to death by authorities of the Dutch East India Company, which has established control of the Spice Islands. The incident strengthens the Dutch hold on the region, and encourages the English to focus instead on India.

1624   Virginia becomes a royal colony after a commission appointed by the king dissolves the Company for chronic mismanagement. The Dutch West India Company establishes the New Netherland colony, with settlements along the Hudson River. Like New France, it grows slowly. The first permanent English settlement in the Caribbean is established on St. Kitts. Nearly a score of additional settlements will follow, though many are subsequently destroyed by the Spanish, who claim all the Caribbean. In addition to St. Kitts, the most successful English colonies in the region are Barbados (1627), Nevis (1628), Montserrat and Antigua (1632), the Bahamas (1647), and Jamaica (conquered from Spain in 1655). Of the more than 200,000 English who migrate to the New World between 1630 and 1660, more than half travel to these small West Indian colonies, where the lucrative sugar trade promises fast wealth to those who can survive the harsh conditions and unhealthful climate.

1625   With the death of James I, his son becomes Charles I (1625–49). The new king presides over a deteriorating economy, as English trade suffers from the disruption of Continental markets resulting from the Thirty Years' War, and a fractured English Church; religious non-conformists (Puritans) who believe the national church to be insufficiently reformed resist the imposition of uniformity in worship and vestments by an increasingly active episcopacy under the leadership of Charles's advisor William Laud, who will become the archbishop of Canterbury in 1633.

1628   Having failed in the early years of his reign to secure sufficient funds to support the army from Parliament, Charles resorts to martial law and the forcible quartering of troops in private homes. These and other actions provoke Parliament to issue the Petition of Right, which seeks to define the proper limits on prerogative. Edward Coke, the petition's principal architect, observes that "the prerogative is like a river without which men cannot live, but if it swell too high it may lose its own channel." Charles accepts the petition in exchange for much-needed subsidies.

1629   Initially conceived as a commercial venture, the Massachusetts Bay Company is chartered by the king and granted rights to an area north of the Plymouth colony. Led by John Winthrop, a majority group of the company's shareholders determine to use the grant to create a refuge for Puritans facing persecution in England. Charles dissolves Parliament in the wake of recurring conflicts over his financial and religious policies. He will not call another for eleven years, a period that will become known as the "Personal Rule."

1630   Large groups of migrants, most of them Puritans, establish
            settlements at Boston and ten other sites in the Massachu-
            setts Bay Colony. By 1641, some 20,000 men, women,
            and children will have made the crossing, in what will be-
            come known as the Great Migration. Leading the first
            wave, John Winthrop brings with him the Company's charter
            —which is missing the standard clause requiring adminis-
            trative meetings to be held in England—affording him and
            the Company's other leaders considerable latitude in set-
            ting up their holy commonwealth. The charter's provision
            for a General Court of shareholders, responsible for elect-
            ing a governor and a board of assistants, serves as the basis
            for what becomes by 1644 the colony's bicameral repre-
            sentative assembly.

1632   In a move away from joint-stock ventures as the principal
            mode of overseas colonization, Charles grants Cecilius
            Calvert, 2nd Baron Baltimore, a royal charter to found a
            colony in a large tract of land north of the Potomac River.
            Under the terms of the grant, Baltimore, as Lord Propri-
            etor, is exempt from royal taxation and granted the power
            to appoint all sheriffs and judges and to create a local no-
            bility. Settlement in the new colony of Maryland, named
            for the queen consort, Henrietta Maria, and conceived in
            part as a refuge for English Catholics, begins two years
            later.

1635   Expelled from Massachusetts, Roger Williams, a Puritan
            minister with Separatist leanings, relocates to the south,
            where on land purchased from Narragansett Indians he
            founds a colony called Providence Plantation. Other settle-
            ments by those seeking freedom of worship are founded
            along Narragansett Bay, and in 1644 Williams secures a
            parliamentary patent uniting the towns into a single col-
            ony.

1635–37   Dissatisfied with church government in the Bay Colony
            and seeking economic opportunities in the fertile Con-
            necticut River Valley, groups of Puritans move to the
            southwest, establishing the Saybrook, Connecticut, and
            New Haven colonies. Saybrook will merge with the larger
            Connecticut colony in 1644, New Haven in 1664. Among
            the financial devices Charles exploits to raise revenues
            during the Personal Rule is "ship money," a traditional
            rate charged to the gentry in coastal counties for naval

defense in times of emergency, now extended to those in inland communities in times of peace. Several gentlemen resist this novelty, which they say opens the door for the king to tax his people at his pleasure and without their consent. Among them is John Hampden, a wealthy member of Parliament who forces the case to trial before King's Bench. Hampden loses the decision, but the case proves a Pyrrhic victory for the king, who suffers badly in popular opinion.

1638   The Swedish West India Company establishes a series of fur trading posts along the lower Delaware River, genesis of the short-lived colony of New Sweden, which will be annexed by the more powerful New Netherland colony in 1655.

1639–40   In need of money to pay the English army he has dispatched to Scotland to impose religious conformity on his northern kingdom (the First Bishops' War), Charles summons and then promptly dissolves the so-called Short Parliament, because it will not appropriate funds without major restrictions on his prerogative powers. When Scottish forces overrun northern England (the Second Bishops' War), Charles summons the so-called Long Parliament into session. It will sit for the better part of a decade and contains a vocal Puritan bloc that quickly moves to impeach the king's advisors, including Archbishop Laud, and launch a legislative campaign against prerogative monarchy.

1641   Rebellion breaks out in Ireland, as the Catholic majority there seeks to capitalize on the disorder in England. Massachusetts leaders promulgate a legal code, the Body of Liberties, which guarantees freedom of speech, jury trials, and the right to counsel, among other provisions.

1642   The English Civil War begins when Charles, unable to dissolve a defiant Parliament, raises his standard against parliamentary forces.

1643   Royalist forces in Ireland reach a truce with Catholic insurgents, releasing manpower to fight the parliamentary army in England. For its part, Parliament enters into an alliance with the Scots. Massachusetts, Plymouth, Connecticut, and New Haven form a military alliance called the United Colonies of New England, or the New England Confederation, in order to combat threats from Dutch and Indian communities bordering their settlements.

1645–46   Parliament reforms its army, removing it from the control of county elites. The officer corps of the resulting "New Model Army," including second in command Oliver Cromwell, is more uniformly Puritan in outlook. After a series of military defeats, Charles surrenders to a Scottish army and is eventually transferred to Parliament's custody.

1648   Cromwell conclusively defeats a resurgent Scottish-Royalist army. In London, he directs officers of the New Model Army to prevent some 180 members of Parliament from taking their seats, and arrest forty more. The resultant staunchly Puritan "Rump Parliament" proceeds to abolish the monarchy, calling it "unnecessary, burdensome, and dangerous to the liberty, safety and public interest of the people." The House of Lords is similarly abolished soon thereafter and England is declared a "Commonwealth and Free State" under the rule of a unicameral Parliament, with the government entrusted to a Council of State chaired by Cromwell.

1649   Charles is charged with high treason and put on trial. Found guilty, he is beheaded on January 30. Cromwell launches a retributive assault on Ireland. Large numbers of Royalist officers and sympathizers go into exile; many of the aristocratic families who will come to dominate Virginia trace their foundation in America to this Cavalier exodus.

1651   In exchange for guarantees of religious tolerance to the Scots, the eldest son of Charles I is crowned King of Scotland. Charles II leads an army into England to recover his father's throne, but is defeated by Cromwell and goes into exile abroad. The Rump Parliament passes the first of what will become known as Navigation Acts; it stipulates that no goods may be imported into "this Commonwealth of England, or into Ireland, or any lands, islands, plantations, or territories to this Commonwealth belonging, or in their possession," except on English ships or on ships of the country where the commodity being transported was grown or produced. Though the act is neutral in its language, it is evidently aimed at the Dutch and their extensive carrying trade and it further polarizes relations between the two countries, whose far-flung traders compete for markets around the globe. (The resulting Anglo-

Dutch War of 1652–54 is the first of several naval conflicts which will be fought between the two states before century's end.) Parliament justifies its regulation of the colonies' trade with a muscular assertion of its authority: "Colonies and Plantations, which were planted at the Cost, and settled by the People, and by Authority of this Nation, which are and ought to be subordinate to, and dependent upon England; and hath ever since the Planting thereof been, and ought to be subject to such Laws, Orders and Regulations as are or shall be made by the Parliament of England."

1653   Cromwell declares himself Lord Protector of the Commonwealth, assuming powers akin to a monarch.

1658   On his death Cromwell is succeeded by his son Richard, but financial crisis cripples the Commonwealth. Negotiations begin for the restoration of the Stuart dynasty.

1660   Charles II (1649–85) is officially restored to the English throne on May 29. The Restoration Parliament re-enacts the Navigation Act of 1651, and goes further, enumerating certain colonial commodities, including sugar, tobacco, and cotton, which must be shipped directly to England. The Crown's administration of colonial affairs is delegated to the newly created secretary of state for the Southern Department, whose portfolio also includes southern England, Wales, Ireland, and southern Europe.

1663   Parliament passes another Navigation Act providing administrative machinery to enforce the existing trade regulations. The Company of Royal Adventurers Trading to Africa (renamed the Royal African Company in 1672) is chartered by Charles and granted a monopoly on trade with that continent. The Company acquires slaves in Africa in return for cloths and other manufactured goods from England and exchanges them in the West Indies and the American colonies for sugar, tobacco, and other staples for sale in the English market, a circuit that becomes known as the Atlantic triangular trade. Charles also makes a grant of a large swath of land between Virginia and Spanish Florida to a group of eight courtiers, including Anthony Ashley Cooper, later the Earl of Shaftsbury. These Lords Proprietors name their colony Carolina in honor of the king and offer fifty-acre grants to attract settlers. In 1669 Shaftsbury's secretary, John Locke, drafts the Fundamental Constitutions of Carolina, an intricate charter mixing liberal and quasi-feudal elements that bears little resemblance to the highly competitive, slave-based society that will develop. The king also grants a liberal charter to the colony of Rhode Island and the Providence Plantations, including provision for an elected governor. New France is made a royal province by Louis XIV, who takes measures to stimulate migration to the sparsely populated colony.

1664   Amid rising hostilities which will lead to the Second Anglo-Dutch War (1665–67), an English naval force conquers New Netherland. Charles II names his brother James, the Duke of York, proprietor of the new province, which is renamed New York. Though provision is made in the new colony's charter for a representative assembly, the proprietor will not call one into being until 1682; of all the Restoration colonies New York will come closest to realizing the proprietors' ideal of a hierarchical, feudalistic society in which they could profit from settlers' rents. The southern section of the grant includes the territories that will become the colonies of New Jersey and Delaware, which James will re-grant to various proprietors. New Jersey will be divided into two halves in 1676: West Jersey will be settled predominantly by Quakers, East Jersey by Anglicans and Scotch Presbyterians. The three counties of the Delaware region will be governed by a deputy from New York until 1682, when they will be absorbed into Pennsylvania.

1670   A group of English merchants and investors forms the Hudson's Bay Company and the Crown grants it a monopoly on the fur trade in the Hudson Bay watershed, comprising much of present-day Canada.

1672   Concerned about smuggling, especially of tobacco, Parliament passes a third Navigation Act, this time requiring a bond on enumerated articles brought into England.

1673   Aimed at Catholics and Nonconformists, the Test Act imposes legal penalties on public officials who refuse to swear an oath of allegiance recognizing the monarch as the head of the Church of England and to subscribe to a declaration denying the Catholic doctrine of transubstantiation. The Duke of York resigns his post as lord high admiral rather than swear the oath, thereby publicly revealing his conversion to Catholicism, which has occurred some years earlier.

1674   In keeping with the Restoration policy of placing military men as colonial governors, the Duke of York appoints Edmund Andros, a distinguished veteran of the Dutch wars, to be governor of New York. By 1680 more than 60 percent of American colonists are subject to such "governors general."

1676   As settlement in Virginia presses westward and meets stiffening resistance from the region's Indians, who have twice before, in 1622 and 1644, launched major uprisings threatening the existence of the colony, a group of up-country settlers led by Nathaniel Bacon demand a policy of armed expansion from the colony's leadership in the east. Unable to command the votes of the colonial assembly (the House of Burgesses) at Jamestown, Bacon and his followers—newly established planters with relatively small holdings, and indentured servants, both white and black—stage a coup and force the royal governor, William Berkeley, to flee. Bacon's Rebellion does not long outlast its namesake, who succumbs to dysentery within a month of putting the colonial capitol to torch, and the planter elite promptly reestablishes control. But the episode is emblematic of a persistent friction between backcountry settlers and coastal power centers, often involving relations with Indians, which will recur in many colonies throughout the colonial period.

1679   Exasperated by resistance to royal authority in Puritan Massachusetts, where the Navigation Acts are largely ignored, Charles II carves out a new royal colony, New Hampshire, from its territory. The province of Maine will remain part of Massachusetts until 1820.

1679–81   Mounting fears about Catholics at court, stoked by the so-called Popish Plot to kill the king a year earlier, provoke a parliamentary inquiry that reveals compromising correspondence between the Duke of York's secretary and the French court. Charles II dissolves the Parliament and calls a new election, the first since 1661. At the same time the expiration of the Licensing Act unleashes a torrent of propagandistic literature on a scale unseen since the early 1640s. In this heated atmosphere two political coalitions —each given their lasting name by their adversaries—take shape: Whigs (the term was originally applied to Scottish rebels) favor a bill to formally exclude the Duke of York from the succession; Tories (Irish brigands) defend royal prerogative and warn against a repeat of the disorders of the Civil War. After the election Charles II quickly dissolves the new parliament, which again favors exclusion, and summons a third, this time to meet in Oxford, away from the Whig power center in London. Finally, Charles II secures a secret subsidy from Louis XIV of France that frees him from financial dependence on Parliament, and he once more dissolves the body, ending the Exclusion Crisis.

1681   Repaying a debt owed to Penn's father, Charles grants to William Penn the last large unallocated tract of American territory at his disposal. Penn, sole proprietor of the new colony of Pennsylvania, is a Quaker, a member of one of the more radical sects born amid the tumult of the Civil War. Penn's First Frame of Government (1682) establishes civil liberties, an elected assembly, and an appointed governor representing the proprietor. With its guarantees of religious liberty and easy access to land, Pennsylvania will attract large numbers of migrants from Europe, including some 100,000 Germans by 1775. Penn grants the three Lower Counties (Delaware) their own assembly in 1704.

1684   In an effort to exercise greater control over Massachusetts, the Crown issues a *quo warranto* writ for its 1629 charter, and dispatches commissioners to ensure compliance. Massachusetts becomes a royal colony, though the incumbent governor and General Court continue to govern until 1686.

1685   With the death of Charles II, who converts to Catholicism on his deathbed, his brother, the Duke of York, ascends to the throne as James II (1685–89). Charles's illegitimate son, James Scott, the Duke of Monmouth, a Protestant, challenges his uncle for the throne. His West Country rebellion is put down at the battle of Sedgemoor and he is executed for treason. In the ensuing "Bloody Assizes" presided over by George Jeffreys, lord chief justice of the King's Bench, scores of Monmouth's followers are tried and executed and some eight hundred are transported to Barbados.

1686–88   Continuing the project of streamlining the administration of the colonies begun under his brother, James II consolidates the territories of Connecticut, Rhode Island,

Plymouth, Massachusetts, and New Hampshire into the Dominion of New England and appoints Edmund Andros as its governor. In 1688, New York and East and West Jersey are added to the territory, which Andros governs from Boston, where the introduction of Anglicanism, together with the governor's arbitrary manner, makes the Dominion intensely unpopular.

1688–89   Popular opinion in England is inflamed when James II's second wife, Mary of Modena, also a Catholic, gives birth to a son. The child raises the specter of a Catholic succession and is denounced as a fraud. Whig leaders who favor the succession of James's eldest daughter, Mary, a Protestant and wife of the Dutch prince William of Orange, leader of the Protestant coalition arrayed against the forces of Louis XIV, appeal to the couple to claim the throne. On November 5 (Guy Fawkes Day) William lands a large multinational force at Torbay in the southwest of England, and as English nobles and officers defect to his standard, James II flees into exile in France. William III (1689–1702) and Mary II (1689–94) are proclaimed joint monarchs on February 13, 1689. (The following month James II lands in Ireland with a large French army, and quickly secures control of most of the island.) The Glorious Revolution, as it is called, imposes new limitations on the monarchy: Parliament enacts a Bill of Rights that prohibits the keeping of a standing army or the levying of taxes without its consent and defines the terms of the royal succession, definitively excluding Catholics from the throne.

The Revolution also spawns a series of "rebellions" in the American colonies, where popular leaders capitalize on the instability to overthrow colonial structures that had been established under the Stuarts, especially the Dominion of New England, or that are associated with Catholicism, as is the proprietary government of Maryland. Connecticut and Rhode Island are restored to the status they had prior to the Dominion and New Hampshire, New York, and New Jersey are reconstituted as royal colonies. Ascension to the English throne greatly strengthens William's hand in his contest with France as England and Scotland join the League of Augsburg in opposition to Louis XIV and become embroiled in the Nine Years' War (1688–97). The conflict is known as King William's War in North America, the first of several that will be fought over the next seventy years between the English colonies, especially in New England, and New France and its Indian allies.

1690   William defeats James at the battle of the Boyne in Ireland in July, and in a little over a year completes the re-conquest of the island. The Irish Parliament introduces a comprehensive series of penal laws that will effectively bar Catholics from public life throughout the eighteenth century.

1691   Massachusetts and Maryland are granted new royal charters. In royal colonies the form of government is established by the royal governor's commission from the king. This generally provides for a legislature composed of a council appointed by the Crown and an elected assembly or house of representatives that, together with the governor (who wields a veto), is empowered to make laws for the colony, with the stipulation that any such laws may be nullified by the Crown if found contrary to those of England.

1696   Administration of the colonies, previously the domain of ad hoc committees of the Privy Council, is formalized with William's appointment of the Lords Commissioners of Trade and Foreign Plantations, an eight-member committee commonly known as the Board of Trade. Among other functions, the Board funnels information received from the colonies to the secretary of the Southern Department and relays his instructions to the colonial governors.

1698   A year after English weavers, dyers, and linen drapers, threatened by its importation of Indian cloth, attacked the East India Company's London headquarters, and amid growing criticism of the Company's monopoly from English merchants, Parliament establishes a new East India Company to rival the existing one. It also ends the monopoly of the Royal African Company, greatly expanding the slave trade. French settlements are established near the mouth of the Mississippi, reinforcing France's claim to the vast territory of Louisiana, which extends to Canada in an arc around the English colonies.

1700   Between 377,000 and 397,000 individuals have emigrated from the British Isles to America over the course of the seventeenth century, the overwhelming majority from England and Wales. In the first eighty years of the eighteenth century 270,000 more will make the crossing.

Seventy percent of these emigrants will come from Scotland and Ireland.

1701   In the Act of Settlement, Parliament makes provision for succession in the event of the deaths of William and his heir presumptive, Princess Anne, both of whom are childless. (Queen Mary died in 1694.) The crown will revert to the nearest Protestant claimant, in this case Sophia, Elector of Hanover, twelfth child of Elizabeth, daughter of James I and wife of Frederick V, the Elector Palatine.

1702   With the death of William III, his sister-in-law Anne (1702–14), the last of the Stuarts, assumes the throne. After a brief interlude war resumes among the European powers, this time over control of the Spanish throne. The War of the Spanish Succession (1701–14) reignites conflict in North America, where it is known as Queen Anne's War (1702–13).

1704–5 The Scottish Parliament passes the Act of Security, stipulating that it will not accept the Hanoverian succession unless Scotland's constitutional, economic, and religious liberties are secured. The English Parliament retaliates with the Aliens Act, which categorizes Scots as foreign nationals and bars them from trade in England or its colonies. Troubled, however, by the looming threat of rebellion in Scotland, where the Stuarts retain popular support, especially in the Highlands, the English include a suspending clause in the Aliens Act to be triggered if the Scottish Parliament appoints commissioners to treat for union between the two kingdoms.

1707   The Act of Union formally combines England and Scotland into Great Britain, guaranteeing the Hanoverian succession over the unified realm. The Scottish Parliament is dissolved, but the Scots receive forty-five seats in the House of Commons and sixteen in the House of Lords in the British Parliament at Westminster. The Scots also gain legal access to the empire's extensive overseas markets and Scottish merchants will figure prominently in Britain's colonial trade, especially in the tobacco-growing colonies in America.

1709   The rival East India Companies are consolidated into the United East India Company, which receives a grant of £3 million from the Crown.

1710   Parliament incorporates the existing colonial postal ser-
            vices within that of Great Britain and Ireland.

1713   The Treaty of Utrecht, ending the War of the Spanish Suc-
            cession, confirms Spanish authority in South America and
            awards Great Britain the asiento, an exclusive thirty-year
            contract to supply slaves to the Spanish colonies. The mo-
            nopoly is in turn granted to the South Sea Company, a
            joint-stock venture, in exchange for its taking on govern-
            ment debt accumulated during the war. Under the terms
            of the treaty Britain also gains Gibraltar and Minorca from
            Spain, greatly enhancing its naval position in the Mediter-
            ranean, and Acadia (present-day New Brunswick and Nova
            Scotia excepting Cape Breton Island) and Newfoundland
            from France, strengthening its control of the valuable
            North Atlantic fishing banks.

1714   Queen Anne dies on August 1. Sophia of Hanover having
            died in the spring, Sophia's eldest son becomes George I
            (1714–27), King of Great Britain and Ireland. The new
            king, who does not speak English, retains his title as Elec-
            tor of Hanover and will spend much of his reign in the
            German territory. The shift of power embodied by Parlia-
            ment's control of the royal succession accelerates a transi-
            tion, begun with the Glorious Revolution, to a cabinet-style
            government, in which crown authority is controlled by a
            group of ministers which must maintain majority support
            in Parliament to be effective. At the same time the royal
            negative, the prerogative right to refuse assent to parlia-
            mentary measures, falls into disuse.

1715   Having engineered the succession, Whigs win a convinc-
            ing victory in parliamentary elections over the Tories, who
            object to the deviation from hereditary rule. Whigs will
            remain politically ascendant for the next fifty years, as To-
            ries are marginalized at the Hanoverian court. In Scotland,
            embittered supporters of the deposed Stuarts (Jacobites)
            rise in an ill-fated and underfunded rebellion in support of
            James II's son James Francis Edward Stuart, "The Old
            Pretender" to his Whig detractors. Maryland reverts to
            proprietary control when Benedict Calvert, 4th Baron
            Baltimore, converts to Protestantism.

1718   The Transportation Act allows for penal transportation to
            British colonies. Some 50,000 convicts will be brought to
            America by 1775. Large-scale migration of Scots and

Irish-born Presbyterians from Ulster to America also begins. As many as 200,000 Scots-Irish will cross the Atlantic by 1775, more than two-thirds of those in the decade from 1765 to 1775; most will pass through colonial ports and into the hinterlands, especially the backcountries of Pennsylvania, Virginia, and the Carolinas.

1720　　In order to settle a constitutional dispute provoked by jurisdictional claims made by the Irish House of Lords, Parliament passes an "Act for the better securing the Dependency of the Kingdom of Ireland upon the Crown of Great Britain," sometimes called the Irish Declaratory Act, asserting its "full power and authority to make laws and statutes of sufficient validity to bind the Kingdom and people of Ireland." Bolstered by rumors of the vast riches to be had in overseas trade and by the implied endorsement of the government, which continues to exchange debt for company stock, shares in the South Sea Company soar to more than ten times their initial value. When investor confidence in the Company begins to wane in July and a sell-off begins, the stock quickly plummets in value, and the South Sea Bubble bursts.

1721　　Parliamentary investigations of the Bubble lead to impeachment or resignation of several cabinet ministers and Robert Walpole assumes the post of chancellor of the Exchequer. He emerges as a driving force in the cabinet, and from his leadership position in the House of Commons, he will control the government for the next twenty years, effectively inaugurating the position of prime minister.

1727　　George II (1727–60) succeeds to the throne on the death of his father. Walpole remains in the premiership and extends the Whig ministry's control over Parliament through the use of crown patronage.

1729　　Indian wars in the province of Carolina having exposed divisions between the colony's northern and southern sections and the weakness of proprietary rule in both, the Crown buys out the Proprietors' heirs and creates the separate royal colonies of North Carolina and South Carolina.

1732　　Parliament grants a twenty-one-year charter to a group of trustees led by James Oglethorpe to found a colony between South Carolina and Spanish Florida. Conceived in part as a refuge for debtors, and established with an idealistic legal code that bans slavery and alcohol, the new colony of Georgia does not attract settlers and is eventually converted to a royal colony in 1752.

1733   In an effort to establish a monopoly within the empire for the sugar cane growers of Britain's West Indian colonies, Parliament passes the Molasses Act, imposing a prohibitory tax of six pence per gallon on all foreign molasses entering British America. But because the British West Indies produce far too little molasses to meet the demand on the American mainland, where it is distilled into rum, the act is widely flouted by smuggling.

1740   Parliament passes the Plantation or Naturalization Act, stipulating that foreign-born Protestants residing in any of the American colonies for a period of seven years who swear allegiance to the king and to "the true faith of a Christian . . . should be deemed, adjudged, and taken to be his Majesty's natural born subjects of this kingdom."

1744–48 During King George's War, the North American theater of the War of Austrian Succession (1740–48), New England forces capture the French fortress at Louisbourg on Cape Breton Island. Subsequent attempts to organize an inter-colonial invasion of Canada fail, and frontier settlements from Maine to New York face depredations from the French and their Indian allies. The Treaty of Aix-la-Chapelle ending the war returns Louisbourg to the French in exchange for concessions in India, angering American colonists. The Earl of Halifax assumes the presidency of the Board of Trade, and will exercise a steady hand on colonial affairs until his resignation in 1761.

1745–46 From the Jacobite stronghold of the Scottish Highlands, Charles Edward Stuart, grandson of James II, mounts an invasion of England that advances as far as Derby before turning back for want of support from the French. His forces are finally defeated at Culloden in the Highlands, and the fractious region is subjected to harsh reprisals that effectively end the Jacobite threat for good.

1750   In an influential, widely reprinted sermon entitled *A Discourse Concerning Unlimited Submission*, Boston minister Jonathan Mayhew uses the occasion of the anniversary of the execution of Charles I (who has become memorialized as a martyr in the Church of England) to make the case for resistance "made in defence of the natural and legal rights of the people, against the unnatural and illegal encroachments of arbitrary power."

1751   Responding to protests from English merchants who object to the use of public bills of credit issued by the colonial assemblies in New England to pay private debts, Parliament passes an act prohibiting the use of such bills as legal tender and restricting further such currency emissions.

1754   Competing claims by Virginia, Pennsylvania, and France to the Ohio River Valley, which is also contested by various Indian tribes, spark a conflict that ignites the French and Indian War (1754–63), the last of the North American colonial wars between Britain and France. Delegates from seven colonies north of Virginia meet in Albany to lay plans for collective defense. The delegates endorse a Plan of Union proposed by Benjamin Franklin of Pennsylvania and Thomas Hutchinson of Massachusetts which would create an intercolonial Grand Council to regulate Indian affairs, resolve territorial disputes between colonies, and provide for coordinated military action. The Grand Council would be empowered to requisition funds from the colonies according to an agreed-upon formula to fulfill its aims. The Albany Plan of Union comes to naught when the colonial assemblies reject or ignore it, and look instead to the British government to take the lead in the management of the conflict, which in 1756 will expand into the global Seven Years' War.

1755   British influence in the Ohio Valley suffers a major setback when, on July 9, a large force of British regulars and colonial volunteers under General Edward Braddock are ambushed by French and Indian forces near Fort Duquesne and routed. Other expeditions against French fortresses at Niagara and Crown Point are also unsuccessful. Only in Nova Scotia are key French posts taken, precipitating the forced expulsion of some five to seven thousand French Canadians (Acadians) who refuse to swear an oath of allegiance.

1757   Although Anglo-Americans outnumber the population of New France by more than twenty to one, French forces under commander in chief Louis Joseph Montcalm maintain the offensive initiative, and friction hinders a coordinated response from the British colonies. Franklin, who as a leader in the Pennsylvania Assembly has been pressing for the revocation of the Penn family's proprietary exemption from land taxes, accepts the Assembly's nomination to serve as its agent in London. He will remain in England for most of the next eighteen years, eventually serving as agent for Georgia, New Jersey, and Massachusetts as well as Pennsylvania, which he will seek to have converted into a royal colony. William Pitt, as secretary of state for the Southern Department, assumes a leading role in the Whig ministry of the Duke of Newcastle, directing the war effort ("I know that I can save this country and that no one else can"). Newcastle had previously served for twenty-four years in the Southern Department and he and Pitt share a conviction that the key to victory in North America is the effective mobilization of colonial soldiers. Pitt proposes to reimburse colonial governments for the cost of raising and maintaining provincial troops.

1758   The colonies muster 21,000 troops in response to Pitt's offer, enabling new commander in chief General Jeffery Amherst to mount successful attacks against Fort Duquesne, renamed Fort Pitt (Pittsburgh), and Louisbourg, turning the tide of the conflict in North America. In Virginia, in order to relieve taxpayers in the wake of droughts which have led to short crops, the House of Burgesses passes the second of the so-called Twopenny Acts, temporary measures permitting the commutation of payments to the colony's established Anglican clergy at a rate of two pence per pound of tobacco, the traditional medium of exchange. Because these acts are designed to deal with an exigent situation, they do not contain the standard suspending clause required under the colony's charter, which stipulates that all acts are in abeyance until approved by the Crown. The colony's Anglican ministers appeal to London for redress.

1759   Anglo-American forces drive the French from northern New York in a campaign that culminates in the capture of the fortress city of Quebec on September 18. This triumph, coupled with decisive British victories on land and sea in Europe, prompts many in the empire to christen this the Annus Mirabilis. On August 10, after hearings before the Board of Trade, the Privy Council disallows the Twopenny Acts (which in any case have already expired) and reprimands Virginia's royal governor for having signed the 1758 measure. This doctrinaire interpretation of the charter is viewed by many Americans as a threat to their traditional self-government of internal affairs. The Council at the same time declines to award the ministers back pay for the period the law was in effect, opening the way for a series of lawsuits in Virginia known as the Parsons' Cause, in which Patrick Henry will rise to prominence.

1760   In southern India, forces of the British East India Company score a victory over those of the French, opening the way to its control of the region. Organized French resistance in North America ends with the British capture of Montreal on September 8 and Detroit on September 15. George II dies suddenly on October 25 and is succeeded by his twenty-two-year-old grandson, George III (1760–1820), whose father, Frederick, Prince of Wales, had died in 1751. The new king, the first of the Hanoverians to speak English as his primary language, resolves to take a more active leadership role than either of his predecessors.

1761   In February, in arguments before the Massachusetts Superior Court, presided over by Chief Justice Thomas Hutchinson, Boston lawyer James Otis challenges the constitutionality of general writs of assistance (search warrants) which, in furtherance of the Navigation Acts, authorize customs officers to search any ship or building they suspect contains contraband goods, and to demand the assistance of local law enforcement in conducting the searches. After the death of George II, Massachusetts customs officials had petitioned the court to renew their writs, which expire six months following the death of the sovereign in whose name they are issued. Otis, the advocate general of the Boston vice-admiralty court, has resigned his position in order to appear before the superior court on behalf of Boston merchants challenging the petition. Otis loses the case, but of his impassioned attack on what he considers arbitrary power, John Adams, who is present in the courtroom, later recalls: "Then and there the child Independence was born." In March, George III installs his longtime tutor John Stuart, 3rd Earl of Bute, a Scotsman and a Tory, as secretary of state for the Northern Department. The king is determined on peace, and Pitt, under pressure to conclude negotiations contrary to his desire to

further Britain's gains by declaring war on Spain, resigns in
October.

1762   Having stated the year before that he would oppose "any
        alteration, that may be proposed of the present Constitu-
        tion, or receiv'd usage and practice, with regard either to
        Scotland, Ireland, or our Settlements in America," New-
        castle falls out with Bute and resigns in May and Bute be-
        comes the prime minister. Despite long-standing English
        antipathy for standing armies, the king and his new advi-
        sors make provisions for the maintenance of a peacetime
        army in North America, concluding that only such a force
        can preserve order among the many restive parts of the
        now greatly expanded empire. The annual cost of main-
        taining ten regiments in North America is more than
        £300,000. This, coupled with the reimbursement to the
        colonial assemblies of their war-related expenses, inflames
        opinion against Americans among taxpayers in Britain,
        where hopes for a peace dividend evaporate in the face
        of a national debt that has nearly doubled in less than a
        decade.

1763   As negotiations proceed toward a formal end to the Seven
        Years' War, the British press debates the merits of retaining
        the rich sugar islands of Guadeloupe and Martinique cap-
        tured from the French, and returning Canada to the
        French, but the government finally decides to relinquish
        the islands. The Treaty of Paris, signed on February 10,
        formalizes British control of the North American conti-
        nent from the Gulf of Mexico to Hudson Bay. Fearing that
        this uncontested hegemony will accelerate colonial en-
        croachment on their lands, and angered by their treatment
        at the hands of General Amherst, Indians in the Ohio
        Valley rise up in May under the leadership of an Ottawa
        leader and destroy all British posts in the region except
        Fort Pitt and Detroit. Confronted with Pontiac's Rebel-
        lion, as this uprising becomes known, as well as a welter of
        conflicting and competing colonial claims to western
        lands, George III issues on October 7 a proclamation bar-
        ring colonial settlement beyond, roughly, the Appalachian
        ridge line. The proclamation also establishes royal colonies
        in Quebec and East and West Florida, which the Crown
        hopes will serve as alternative sites for expansion. Mean-
        while, Bute's decision to retire in April in the face of

vehement attacks from the press, much of it, like John Wilkes's scandalous newspaper *North Briton*, fueled by anti-Scot bigotry, elevates George Grenville, First Lord of the Treasury, to the premiership. Grenville faces an early confidence vote when opposition forces led by Newcastle and Pitt challenge the Crown's use of general warrants to silence the press criticism, but prevails, largely owing to the support of the Scottish bloc in Parliament.

1764   In January, an armed group of Pennsylvania frontiersmen, known as the Paxton Boys, march to Philadelphia to remonstrate against the colonial government, which they feel has been inattentive to their security amid the ongoing hostilities related to Pontiac's Rebellion. In London, on March 9, Grenville proposes a revision of the 1733 Molasses Act to make it more productive of revenue. The rationale for the proposed bill is made clear in its text: "it is just and necessary, that a revenue be raised, in your Majesty's said dominions in America, for defraying the expenses of defending, protecting, and securing the same." At the same time Grenville introduces complicated new regulations designed to further combat smuggling by funneling colonial trade to or through British ports and by creating a vice-admiralty court in Halifax, Nova Scotia, where customs violators can be prosecuted without obstruction from sympathetic colonial juries. In his remarks Grenville suggests the possibility of a further revenue measure, a stamp tax. Parliament passes the American Revenue Act, better known as the Sugar Act, on April 5. Parliament also passes a Currency Act extending the provisions of the 1751 act (which in the interest of harmony the British government had not enforced during the war) to the colonies south of New England. By year's end, petitions protesting Parliament's actions are endorsed by the assemblies of Massachusetts, Rhode Island, Connecticut, New York, Pennsylvania, Virginia, North Carolina, and South Carolina.

1765   By forestalling to the next parliamentary session action on a stamp tax—which, rather than regulating trade through an *external* duty, will impose an *internal* tax on the paper used in the colonies for newspapers, almanacs, pamphlets, broadsides, and legal and commercial documents—Grenville intends to provide the colonies an opportunity to suggest alternative measures for raising revenues to defray the costs of maintaining British forces in North America. However, no official requests are made to the colonial assemblies or to the colonial governors, through the Board of Trade or otherwise, and no alternatives are forthcoming. At a last-minute meeting on February 2 with Grenville, four colonial agents, including Franklin, present petitions from their assemblies protesting the proposed measure, but the House of Commons, in keeping with its traditional practice, refuses to hear appeals related to a money bill. The ministry presses ahead with the measure in the Commons, insisting, in the words of a government spokesperson, on "the important point it establishes, the right of Parliament to lay an internal tax on the colonies. We wonder here that it was ever doubted. There is not a single member of Parliament that will dispute it." By a large majority the Commons passes the Stamp Act on February 27; it receives the royal assent on March 22 and is scheduled to go into effect on November 1. On May 15, Parliament passes the Quartering Act, requiring colonial assemblies, in the absence of barracks, to provide for the billeting of His Majesty's troops in private buildings, taverns, and inns at the colonies' expense.

News of the Stamp Act's passage reaches America in April and the Virginia House of Burgesses on May 30 adopts a series of resolves introduced by Patrick Henry, among them "that the Taxation of the People by themselves, or by Persons chosen by themselves to represent them . . . is the distinguishing Characteristick of *British* Freedom." On June 8, the Massachusetts House of Representatives issues a circular letter to the other colonial assemblies calling upon them to send delegates to a congress in New York "to consider of a general and united, dutiful, loyal and humble, Representation of their Condition to His Majesty and the Parliament; and to implore Relief." Popular protests against the Stamp Act occur throughout the colonies during the summer. In Boston—where active opponents of the Stamp Act will adopt the name "Sons of Liberty" by the end of the year—mobs loot the homes of Andrew Oliver, a prominent merchant who had been appointed stamp distributor for Massachusetts, on August 14, and of Lieutenant Governor Thomas Hutchinson (Oliver's brother-in-law) on August 26. Similar actions follow in other colonial ports, and by the end of October all but two of the stamp distributors, those for North Carolina and Georgia, resign in the face of intimidation and violence. The holdouts will not give way until November and January respectively, but the act is essentially nullified before the date it is scheduled to take effect. The Stamp Act Congress, comprising twenty-seven delegates from nine colonies, meets in New York's City Hall, October 7–25, and issues a Declaration of the Rights and Grievances of the Colonies calling for repeal.

1766   The Grenville ministry having been dismissed in July 1765 for reasons unrelated to the American controversy, the new administration of Lord Rockingham engineers repeal of the Stamp Act on March 18; at the same time Parliament passes the Declaratory Act, which asserts its authority to legislate for the colonies "in all cases whatsoever." On June 6, in a bid to further calm tensions, Parliament passes a Revenue Act, further reducing the duty on molasses from three pence per gallon to just one. In July, Pitt, whose health is poor and who no longer commands a large following in the Commons, assumes the premiership once more when Rockingham is dismissed, again for reasons unrelated to the colonial dispute. Pitt is elevated to the peerage as the Earl of Chatham, and governs from the House of Lords. In New York, in defiance of the Quartering Act, the Assembly refuses to fully fund a request for provisions submitted by General Thomas Gage, commander of British forces in North America, who maintains his headquarters in New York City. Chatham alienates many in his cabinet when he launches an investigation into the financial management of the East India Company and calls for the transferal to the Crown of its territorial holdings in India, which have grown extensive. Before he can implement his plan, Chatham's gout forces him to retire to Bath in December.

1767   In the absence of strong leadership from Chatham, Charles Townshend, chancellor of the Exchequer, emerges as the driving force in the ministry. On May 13, seizing on the distinction between internal and external taxation that has emerged from the Stamp Act controversy, he proposes duties on lead, glass, paper, tea, and other goods imported into the colonies. The ministry also proposes the New

York Restraining Act, suspending the New York Assembly until it complies with the Quartering Act. After negotiations with the East India Company (of which Townshend is a shareholder), the ministry also proposes the Indemnity Act, which lowers taxes on Company tea imported to England and allows a drawback on the export of tea to Ireland and the British colonies in America in exchange for an annual payment to the Exchequer and the right to retain its territory in India. To streamline enforcement of the new duties, the ministry further proposes to establish a board of customs commissioners to be based in Boston, where resistance to customs regulations is most pronounced, along with three new admiralty courts in Philadelphia, Charleston, and Boston, to supplement the one previously established in Halifax. Passed by the House of Commons on July 2, the Townshend Acts renew tensions in America. In June, on receiving news of the proposed suspension, the New York Assembly quickly passes an act fulfilling the terms of the Quartering Act. Townshend dies on September 4 and is replaced by Frederick North (called Lord North as a courtesy title).

1768   On February 11, the Massachusetts House of Representatives adopts a petition, written by Samuel Adams, protesting the Townshend Acts. After the protest is circulated to the other colonial assemblies, Massachusetts governor Francis Bernard dissolves the General Court, prompting further popular unrest. In response to the mounting crisis, the British government creates a third secretary of state responsible specifically for colonial administration. The Earl of Hillsborough, a hardliner on American affairs who had been president of the Board of Trade, assumes the post and quickly runs afoul of colonial leaders with his imperious response to the Massachusetts Circular Letter. Demonstrations in Boston in March lead the harried customs commissioners to request that troops be sent to Boston to maintain order. Contrary to Hillsborough's orders, the Massachusetts House—by a vote of 92–17, enshrining the number 92 in patriot political discourse—refuses to rescind its resolutions, and several other colonial assemblies issue similar statements. In May the British warship *Romney* arrives in Boston. Further harassment of customs officials follows the seizure in June of John Hancock's sloop *Liberty* on suspicion of smuggling. In late summer, merchants in Boston and New York adopt agreements to cease importing most goods from Britain until the Townshend duties are repealed. The first British troops land in Boston on October 1.

1769   Debate on American affairs resumes in the House of Commons as the ministry successfully moves a motion for an address to the king pledging the nation to support all measures necessary "to maintain entire and inviolate the supreme authority of the Legislature of Great Britain over every part of the British empire." Premised on the idea that the disorder in Massachusetts has been produced by a small number of rabble-rousers, among the measures contemplated is the extension to the colonies of a treason law from the reign of Henry VIII, enabling the Crown to bring the ringleaders to England for trial. The idea is never implemented, but it nonetheless provokes considerable anger in America. In February merchants in Philadelphia adopt a non-importation agreement similar to those in Boston and New York. Other colonies follow suit, and in May the Virginia House of Burgesses passes resolves again denying Parliament's right to tax colonies. When the royal governor promptly dissolves the House, the Burgesses reconvene at a nearby tavern and adopt non-importation. British manufacturers and traders begin to agitate for repeal of the Townshend duties. Hillsborough sends a circular letter to the colonial governors in May announcing that the cabinet has decided to propose repeal of the duties in the next session of Parliament.

1770   Long-simmering tensions in Boston erupt when on March 5 British soldiers under Captain Thomas Preston open fire on an angry, taunting crowd, killing five Boston residents. In the aftermath, facing the prospect of what he calls a "general insurrection" among Bostonians, Massachusetts's acting governor Thomas Hutchinson arranges to have British troops removed to Castle William in Boston Harbor to avoid further clashes. On April 12 Parliament votes to repeal most of the Townshend duties, retaining only the duty on tea, which the cabinet of Lord North, who has succeeded to head of the Treasury and prime minister in January, preserves by a five-to-four vote in order to maintain the principle of parliamentary sovereignty. In late autumn, John Adams leads the defense at the trials of Captain Preston and eight of his soldiers charged in the "Boston Massacre." Preston and his men are acquitted save for two, who are convicted of manslaughter and branded on the thumb. Repeal of the Townshend duties results in the collapse of the non-importation movement in the colonies and a general easing of tensions with the mother country.

1771   As the imperial controversy absorbs the major port cities in the colonies, persistent frictions on the frontier flare in the contested borderlands between New York and New Hampshire, where the Green Mountain Boys have become a de facto government, and in western North Carolina, where bands of self-appointed "Regulators" disrupt the mechanisms of a provincial government they believe to be corrupt and unconcerned with their interests. The Regulator Movement culminates on May 16 at the battle of Alamance, when the royal governor and twelve hundred militia defeat a force of two thousand poorly organized Regulators.

1772   On June 9, citizens of Providence burn the *Gaspee*, a British revenue schooner, when it runs aground in Narragansett Bay. A special royal commission is appointed to investigate the incident but cannot gather the names of anyone to punish. In his June 22 judgment in the *Somersett* case, Lord Mansfield, chief justice of the King's Bench, rules that no positive law in England permits a slave-owner to forcibly send a slave overseas. Interpretation of his decision by other judges will make slavery legally unenforceable in Britain, eventually resulting in de facto emancipation there. While the case has no effect as a matter of law in the colonies, it does complicate the recurrent American appeals to natural liberty and the rights of Englishmen in their dispute with Parliament. In July, in one of his last acts as secretary of state for the Colonies, Hillsborough issues an order that the salaries of the judges of the Massachusetts Superior Court be paid by the Crown, instead of the General Court, an inflammatory move designed to insulate the judges from the influence of popular opinion.

1773   In March, the Virginia House of Burgesses elects a standing Committee of Correspondence to communicate and coordinate with other assemblies. Other colonial legislatures follow suit over the course of the year. With the East India Company approaching insolvency, Parliament in May passes the Regulating Act, establishing a new governing structure for the Company, and the Tea Act, granting it a monopoly on the sale of tea in the colonies. The first of three ships carrying East India Company tea arrives in Boston on November 28. Duty is payable upon off-loading, which must by law be accomplished within twenty days of docking, but which Boston mobs prevent. Governor Hutchinson refuses entreaties to allow the ships to depart with their cargo, which defuses similar situations in other colonial ports, and as the deadline approaches a large crowd boards the ships on December 16 and dumps 342 chests of tea, worth an estimated £10,000, into the harbor.

1774   News of the destruction of the East India Company's tea reaches London on January 19. In response to the Boston Tea Party, Parliament passes four measures that become known as the Coercive Acts, but which American patriots will call the Intolerable Acts. The Boston Port Act closes Boston's harbor, effective June 1, until "peace and obedience to the laws" are restored in the town and its people pay for the destroyed tea. The Massachusetts Government Act abrogates Massachusetts's 1691 royal charter by removing power of appointing the governor's council from the elected assembly and giving it to the king. It also gives the royal governor power to appoint (or nominate, for the king's assent) all provincial judges and sheriffs, makes the sheriffs responsible for choosing jury panels, and severely restricts town meetings. The Administration of Justice Act allows trials of those accused of committing capital crimes while enforcing the law or collecting revenue to be removed to Britain or Nova Scotia. The Quartering Act allows quartering of troops in occupied dwellings throughout the colonies. (The Quebec Act, which establishes civil government for Quebec without an elected legislature, grants the Roman Catholic Church the right to collect tithes, and potentially extends the province's borders to the Mississippi and Ohio rivers, is viewed as a hostile measure by many colonists, and comes to be regarded as one of the Intolerable Acts.) General Thomas Gage, commander in chief of British forces in North America, is commissioned as royal governor of Massachusetts and arrives in Boston on May 13; British troops begin landing in the city in mid-June. Unable to enforce the law outside of Boston, Gage begins fortifying the city on September 3.

The Coercive Acts electrify public opinion in America, and calls for an intercolonial congress to propose common measures of resistance are made in Providence, Philadelphia, New York, and Williamsburg, Virginia, in May. The First Continental Congress opens in Philadelphia on September 5 and is eventually attended by fifty-six delegates. On September 17 it endorses the Suffolk County Resolves, recently adopted by a convention in Massachusetts, which declare that no obedience is due the Coercive Acts and advocate measures of resistance, including the formation of a provincial congress, nonpayment of taxes, the boycott of British goods, and weekly militia training. On October 14 Congress adopts a series of declarations and resolves that denounce the Coercive Acts and Quebec Act as "impolitic, unjust, and cruel, as well as unconstitutional"; call for the repeal of several other laws passed since 1763; protest the dissolution of elected assemblies and the royal appointment of colonial councils; and condemn the keeping of a standing army in the colonies in peacetime, without the consent of colonial legislatures, as "against law." Congress votes on October 18 to create the Continental Association, modeled on the Virginia Association formed in early August. Its articles pledge the colonies to discontinue the slave trade and cease importing goods from Great Britain, Ireland, and the East and West Indies after December 1, 1774; to cease consuming British goods after March 1, 1775; and, if necessary, to cease all exports (excluding rice) to Britain, Ireland, and the West Indies after September 10, 1775. The Association is to be enforced by elected town, city, and county committees, which will punish violators by publicity and boycott. After preparing addresses to the British people and to the king, Congress calls on the people of the colonies to elect deputies to provincial congresses, which in turn will elect delegates to a second congress, called for May 10, 1775. Congress adjourns October 26. By the end of the year, provincial congresses or conventions have been formed in eight colonies.

1775   On February 9 Parliament declares Massachusetts to be in rebellion. The House of Commons endorses on February 27 a conciliatory proposal by the North ministry, under which Parliament would refrain from laying revenue taxes upon the colonies if the colonial assemblies agree to levy their own taxes to support imperial defense. General Gage receives orders from the ministry on April 14 (written January 27 but not dispatched until March 13) directing him to use force against the Massachusetts rebels. The Revolutionary War begins when a British force attempts to destroy military supplies at Concord, leading to fighting with militia at Lexington, Concord, and along the road back to Boston on April 19. Massachusetts forces thereafter begin a siege of Boston.

The Second Continental Congress meets in Philadelphia on May 10, with representatives from every state except Georgia present. The Massachusetts Provincial Congress asks Congress for advice on establishing a government during the conflict with Great Britain. Congress responds on June 9 by recommending that the colony elect a new assembly and council to govern itself until the Crown agrees to abide by the 1691 charter (the new Massachusetts legislature meets in late July, with the council serving as the executive). Congress votes on June 14 to form a Continental army. John Adams nominates Virginia delegate George Washington as its commander, and he is unanimously approved on June 15, just two days before the battle of Bunker Hill is fought at Charlestown, Massachusetts (Washington assumes command in Cambridge, Massachusetts, on July 3). To finance the army, Congress votes on June 22 to issue $2 million in paper money not backed by specie and pledges that the "12 Confederated Colonies" will redeem the issue.

On July 5 Congress approves the Olive Branch Petition, a conciliatory message to George III drafted by John Dickinson, and on July 6 adopts the Declaration of the Causes and Necessities of Taking Up Arms, drafted by Thomas Jefferson and rewritten by Dickinson. The Declaration disavows any intention to establish American independence, but asserts that colonists are "resolved to die freemen rather than to live slaves" and states that "foreign assistance is undoubtedly attainable" for the colonial cause. Congress appoints commissioners to negotiate with Indians on July 19; establishes a post office department headed by Benjamin Franklin on July 26; and rejects Lord North's proposal for conciliation on July 31, before adjourning on August 2. George III rejects the Olive Branch Petition and on August 23 proclaims the American colonies to be in rebellion (news which reaches Congress on November 9).

Congress begins organizing a navy in October, appoints on November 29 a five-member Committee of Correspondence to establish contact with foreign supporters (which becomes the Committee for Foreign Affairs on April 17, 1777), and on December 6 disavows allegiance to Parliament. British rule continues to collapse throughout the thirteen colonies in the autumn and winter. George III signs the Prohibitory Act on December 23, closing off commerce with America and making American ships and crews subject to seizure by the Royal Navy.

1776   Congress votes on March 3 to send Silas Deane to Europe to buy military supplies. The British garrison evacuates Boston on March 17 and sails to Nova Scotia. South Carolina's Provincial Congress adopts a plan of government on March 26. Congress opens American ports to all nations except Britain on April 6. North Carolina's Provincial Congress authorizes its delegates on April 12 to vote in Congress for independence, while reserving for North Carolina the "sole and exclusive right" of forming its own constitution and laws.

At the urging of his foreign minister the Comte de Vergennes, Louis XVI of France authorizes clandestine support of the American insurgents on May 2. (After his arrival in Paris on July 7, Silas Deane will work with Vergennes and Pierre de Beaumarchais in arranging covert shipments of arms, supplies, and money, an effort soon joined in by Spain.) Rhode Island's legislature disavows allegiance to George III on May 4. Under the leadership of John Adams and Richard Henry Lee, Congress recommends on May 10 that each of the "United Colonies" form a government and on May 15 calls for royal authority in the colonies to be "totally suppressed." On May 15 the Virginia convention (successor to the convention called by the assembly after its dissolution by Lord Dunmore in 1774) instructs its delegates in Congress to propose a declaration of independence and the formation of a confederation; it also appoints a committee to prepare a declaration of rights and constitution for Virginia. Following these instructions, Richard Henry Lee submits a resolution in Congress on June 7, declaring that "these United Colonies are, and of right ought to be, free and independent States," urging the formation of foreign alliances, and recommending the preparation and transmission of "a plan of confederation" to the colonies for their approval. John Dickinson, James Wilson, Robert R. Livingston, and others argue that an immediate declaration of independence would be premature. Congress postpones decision and refers the resolution on independence to a committee of five (Franklin, John Adams, Livingston, Jefferson, and Roger Sherman) on June 11; Jefferson begins drafting a declaration. On June 12 a resolution to form an American confederation is submitted to a committee of thirteen, consisting of one representative from each colony; its chairman, John Dickinson, begins drafting a confederation plan. On July 1 Congress resumes debate on Lee's independence resolution and approves it on July 2, severing all political ties with Great Britain. After revising Jefferson's draft (changes include the deletion of a passage condemning the slave trade), Congress adopts the Declaration of Independence on July 4.

The Revolutionary War, which with the addition of France, Spain, and the Dutch Republic as belligerents becomes the global War of American Independence, lasts eight years and costs the British at least £80 million. Over its course some 60,000 Loyalists leave America and resettle in other parts of the empire, taking roughly 15,000 slaves with them. In the Treaty of Paris, which formally ends the war in 1783, Great Britain recognizes the independence of the United States with borders extending north to the Great Lakes, west to the Mississippi, and south to the 31st parallel. In doing so it acknowledges the loss of a million square miles of its empire and the allegiance of over two and a half million subjects.

Biographical Notes

JOHN ADAMS (October 30, 1735–July 4, 1826) Born Braintree, Massachusetts, the son of a farmer. Graduated from Harvard College in 1755 and admitted to the Massachusetts bar in 1758. Married Abigail Smith in 1764. Moved to Boston in 1768, where he successfully defended John Hancock against a smuggling charge that year. Elected to represent Boston in the Massachusetts House of Representatives in 1770. With Josiah Quincy, successfully defended British soldiers in October–November 1770 against murder charges in the controversial "Boston Massacre" trials. Wrote speeches related to the imperial crisis on behalf of the Massachusetts House of Representatives as part of an exchange of views with the colony's governor, Thomas Hutchinson, January–March 1773, later published as a pamphlet. Elected to the First Continental Congress in 1774; served on various committees. Elected to Massachusetts provincial congress and published, January–April 1775, twelve essays signed "Novanglus" in the *Boston Gazette*, written in response to Tory views of Daniel Leonard ("Massachusettensis"). Served in the Second Continental Congress, 1775–78. Went to France as a diplomatic commissioner in 1778 and returned in 1779. Served in Europe as a peace commissioner and as an envoy to Holland, 1780–84. Appointed by Congress as the first American minister to Great Britain in 1785 and served until 1788. Returned to the United States and became vice president in the Washington administration, 1789–97. Elected president as a Federalist in 1796, with Thomas Jefferson becoming vice president. Served one term, 1797–1801; defeated for reelection by Jefferson. Retired to his farm in Quincy, Massachusetts, where he died.

EBENEZER BALDWIN (July 3, 1745–October 1, 1776) Born in Norwich, Connecticut, the son of a farmer and land speculator. Educated for the ministry at Yale College, 1759–63. Taught at an academy in Hatfield, Massachusetts, before returning to Yale as a tutor in 1766. Ordained by the First Church of Danbury Connecticut in 1770. Became active in effort to end slavery in Connecticut, publishing abolitionist essays with Jonathan Edwards Jr. in the *Connecticut Journal and New-Haven Post-Boy*. Represented the General Association of Connecticut's Congregational churches at the General Convention of Presbyterian and Congregational clergy at Elizabethtown, New Jersey, in September 1774, where he preached the opening sermon. In December, his essay "Stating the Heavy Grievances the Colonies

Labour Under from Several Late Acts of the British Parliament" was published as an appendix to a sermon by Samuel Sherwood, a clerical colleague. In August 1776 he accompanied a number of his parishioners to join in the defense of New York, acting as their chaplain, and there contracted a contagious disease. Died in Danbury.

HENRY BARRY (1750–November 2, 1822) Entered the army in 1762; commissioned as an ensign in the 52nd Regiment of Foot in 1768 and transferred to Quebec, where he was promoted to lieutenant in 1772. Regiment was posted to Boston in 1774, where Barry published *The Strictures on the Friendly Address Examined*. Regiment fought in the battle of Bunker Hill, June 17, 1775. Promoted to captain in 1770. During southern campaign, 1780–81, served as aide-de-camp and private secretary to Lord Rawdon, afterwards Marquis of Hastings, distinguishing himself by the quality of his military dispatches. Captured at the battle of Eutaw Springs, September 5, 1781, and exchanged the following March. Served in India, 1782–92; promoted to major in 1783, regimental major in 1789, lieutenant-colonel in 1790, and colonel in 1793, the year he left the army. Died in Bath, Somerset.

JONATHAN BOUCHER (March 12, 1738–April 27, 1804) Born in Blencogo, Cumberland, the son of an Anglican minister. Migrated to Virginia in 1759 to become a private tutor to the children of a Port Royal merchant. Sailed to England in 1762 seeking ordination. Returned to Virginia, where in 1763 he established himself as rector at St. Mary's parish, in Caroline County, becoming a tobacco planter and operating a small school. Tutored George Washington's stepson Jackie Custis, 1768–73. In 1770 he moved to fashionable St. Anne parish in Maryland, where he established friendship with Maryland governor Robert Eden and became an outspoken defender of the Anglican establishment. May have written *A Letter from a Virginian* in 1774. On July 20, 1775, designated a day of prayer and fasting by the Continental Congress, he preached a defiant sermon on the religious duty of obedience to the magistrate (i.e., the Crown). Fled from his home in August and sailed to England in September. Curate at Paddington, 1776–85, and Epsom, 1785–1804. Wrote memoir, *Reminiscences of an American Loyalist*, not published until 1925. Died in Epsom, Surrey.

EDMUND BURKE (1729?–July 9, 1797) Born in Dublin, Ireland, the son of a lawyer. Mother's family was Catholic; father, a Protestant, may have been a convert from Catholicism. Educated at a Quaker school and Trinity College. Moved to London to study law at the Middle Temple, but abandoned legal career. Published *A Vindication of Natural Society* (1756) and *A Philosophical Enquiry into the Origin of our Ideas of the Sublime and Beautiful* (1757); the latter, especially, garnered praise in England and abroad. Also in 1757, published, with William Burke, a fellow Irishman and possible relation, *An Account of the European Settlements in America*. Beginning in 1758, edited and made extensive contributions to a new periodical, *The Annual Register*, with which he remained associated for three decades. Appointed private secretary to Lord Rockingham, the prime minister, in 1765, and elected to Parliament from Wendover in 1766 (later represented Bristol, 1774–80, and Malton, 1780–94). Distinguished himself with his oratory as leader of the opposition to the North government in the House of Commons. Published political pamphlets critical of administration policy at home and in the American colonies: *Thoughts on the Cause of the Present Discontents* (1770), *On American Taxation* (1774), *On Moving His Resolutions for Conciliation with the Colonies* (1775), and *A Letter . . . to the Sheriffs of Bristol, on the Affairs of America* (1777). Launched efforts to reform the Irish penal code and the administration of the East India Company, especially seeking the ouster of Warren Hastings, governor-general of Bengal. Expressed revulsion for the French Revolution and the natural rights theory that inspired it in a series of works including *Reflections on the Revolution in France* (1790), *An Appeal from the New to the Old Whigs* (1791), and *Two Letters on a Regicide Peace* (1796). Died at Gregories, his estate in Beaconsfield, Buckinghamshire.

THOMAS BRADBURY CHANDLER (April 26, 1726–June 17, 1790) Born in Woodstock, Connecticut, the son of a wealthy farmer. Graduated from Yale College in 1745 and taught school in Elizabethtown, New Jersey, while studying for the ministry. Traveled to England in 1751 to be ordained, returning to Elizabethtown as missionary for the Society for the Propagation of the Gospel in Foreign Parts and as rector of St. John's Anglican Church. Awarded divinity degree from Oxford in 1766. Published *An Appeal in Behalf of the Church of England in America* (1767) calling for the establishment of an American episcopacy; it sparked a pamphlet war with Presbyterian and Congregationalist writers who feared that an American bishop would lead to the establishment of the Church of England in America. Published three pamphlets related to the imperial crisis in 1774: *The American Querist: or, Some Questions Proposed Relative to the Present Disputes between Great-Britain and her American Colonies*; *A Friendly Address to All Reasonable Americans, on the Subject of our Political Confusions*; and *What Think Ye of the Congress Now? Or, An Enquiry, How Far the Americans are Bound to Abide by, and Execute the Decisions of, the Late-Congress*. Moved to England in May 1775. Returned

to the United States in 1785, and resumed rectorship. Died in Elizabethtown.

WILLIAM HENRY DRAYTON (September 1742–September 3, 1779)
Born at Drayton Hall, family estate in St. Andrew's parish, South
Carolina, the son of a wealthy planter. Maternal grandfather was the
colony's long-serving lieutenant governor, William Bull. Sent to England in 1753 for his education; attended Westminster School and
Balliol College, Oxford, but father, angry over his profligate spending,
forced him to return to South Carolina in 1763 before receiving a
degree. Elected to the South Carolina Assembly in 1765. Opposed
colonial resistance to Stamp Act and Townshend Acts and lost seat in
1768. The following year, writing as "Freeman" (though his authorship was widely known), published criticism of the non-importation
movement in a series of articles in the *South Carolina Gazette*. Facing
unpopularity and diminished prospects at home, sailed to England in
1770. There he collected his Freeman essays for publication and was
rewarded by the Crown with an appointment to the South Carolina
council in 1771; sought additional crown appointments without success. Finally named an associate justice by his uncle in 1774, filling a
temporary vacancy. Published *A Letter from Freeman of South-Carolina,
to the Deputies of North-America* (1774), signaling his change of heart
about the colonial cause. Member of South Carolina's first provincial congress, 1775, and president of the second in 1776. Named first
chief justice under the new state constitution. Delegate to the Continental Congress, 1778–79. Contracted typhus in Philadelphia, where
he died.

JOSEPH GALLOWAY (c. 1731–August 29, 1803) Born in West River,
Ann Arundel County, Maryland, the son of a wealthy landowner.
Studied law and began to practice in Philadelphia in 1747. Renounced
Quaker faith in order to marry Grace Growden, an Episcopalian and
the daughter of an influential member of the Pennsylvania Assembly.
Elected to the assembly in 1756, but lost his seat in 1764, along with
friend Benjamin Franklin, after leading attempt to have the colony's
proprietary charter revoked in favor of a royal government. Regained
seat in 1765, defeating John Dickinson, the leader of the proprietary
party in the assembly, and served as speaker, 1766–75. Vice-president
of the American Philosophical Society, 1769–75. Delegate to the First
Continental Congress in 1774, where he proposed a plan, rejected by
the Congress, for an imperial legislature and written constitution.
Published *A Candid Examination of the Mutual Claims of Great-
Britain, and the Colonies: with a Plan of Accommodation, on Constitutional Principles* (1775) which, as the title suggests, included the Plan
of Union he had proposed to the Congress. Declined to serve in the

Second Continental Congress and in December 1776 sought the protection of the British army, serving as superintendent-general for the maintenance of peace in occupied Philadelphia. Evacuated with other loyalists to New York in June 1778. Banned from returning to Pennsylvania by the assembly after being convicted in absentia of treason; family property in Pennsylvania worth some £40,000 confiscated by the state. Relocated family to London, where he published numerous pamphlets advocating for loyalists and criticizing the British war effort. Died in Watford, Hertfordshire.

THOMAS HUTCHINSON (September 9, 1711–June 3, 1780) Born in Boston, Massachusetts, the son of a wealthy merchant. Graduated from Harvard College in 1727 and entered into business. Elected to the Massachusetts House of Representatives in 1737, serving as its speaker, 1746–48. Elected to the governor's council in 1749. With Benjamin Franklin, proposed plan for colonial union at Albany in 1754. Appointed lieutenant governor in 1758 and chief justice of the Massachusetts Superior Court in 1760; the latter appointment, made by new governor Francis Bernard, earned the enmity of James Otis the elder, leader of the colony's popular party, who had been promised the post by the previous governor. Upheld the use of writs of assistance (search warrants) to combat smuggling in case argued by James Otis Jr. His house was sacked on August 26, 1765, by an angry Boston crowd protesting the Stamp Act. Named acting governor in 1769 before officially assuming the position in 1771. Entered into extended colloquy with the Massachusetts legislature about the imperial crisis, January–March 1773, later published as a pamphlet. Purloined copies of letters to London officials written in 1768–69, in which the then lieutenant governor recommended policies to restore order in the colony, published in June 1773, lead to calls for his removal. In December 1773, withheld clearance to leave Boston Harbor from ships bearing taxed East India Company tea, precipitating crisis that resulted in the Boston Tea Party. Resigned post in May 1774 and sailed to England to lobby against the Coercive Acts. Awarded honorary degree from Oxford, July 4, 1776. *Strictures upon the Declaration of the Congress at Philadelphia; in a Letter to a Noble Lord, &c.*, privately published in the autumn of 1776. Wrote highly regarded three-volume *History of the Colony of Massachusetts-Bay*; the first two volumes were published in Boston in 1764 and 1767, the third posthumously in London in 1828. Died in London.

CHARLES INGLIS (1734–February 24, 1816) Born in Glencolumb-kille, Donegal, the son of a Church of Ireland curate. Education interrupted by death of father in 1745. Emigrated to Philadelphia in 1754, and taught school in Lancaster, 1755–58. Sailed to England for ordination and returned to Dover, Delaware, as missionary for the Society for the Propagation of the Gospel in Foreign Parts. Assistant at Trinity Church in New York City, 1765–77, before becoming rector, 1777–83. Received divinity degrees from Oxford in 1770 and 1777. Published *The Deceiver Unmasked; or, Loyalty and Interest United: In Answer to a Pamphlet entitled Common Sense* in New York in March 1776, but all copies were destroyed by a mob. Published revised version of the pamphlet, *The True Interest of America Impartially Stated*, in Philadelphia shortly after. Became British army chaplain during the occupation of New York, and was attained for treason by the state of New York in 1779. Returned to England in 1783. Appointed first colonial bishop of Nova Scotia, and later became bishop of Quebec, New Brunswick, and Newfoundland. Died at Clermont, his home near Aylesford, Nova Scotia.

THOMAS JEFFERSON (April 13, 1743–July 4, 1826) Born at Shadwell, Goochland (now Albemarle) County, Virginia, son of a landowner and surveyor. Educated at the College of William and Mary. Admitted to the Virginia bar in 1767. Served in Virginia Assembly, 1769–74. His *Summary View of the Rights of British America* was published in 1774. Delegate to the Continental Congress, 1775–76; drafted the Declaration of Independence. Served in Virginia Assembly, 1776–79, and as governor of Virginia, 1779–81. Delegate to the Continental Congress, 1783–84. Replaced Benjamin Franklin as American minister to France, 1785–89, establishing his residence in Paris, where he had printed a private edition of *Notes on the State of Virginia* in 1785. Appointed secretary of state by George Washington and held office from March 1790 until December 1793, during which time political alignments in Congress began to take on the character of parties, with Jefferson widely viewed as leader of the opposition to the Federalist policies of the Washington administration. The "Republican" candidate for president in 1796, he finished second in the electoral voting to John Adams and served as vice president, 1797–1801. He drafted the Kentucky Resolutions opposing the Alien and Sedition Acts in 1798. In the electoral ballot of 1800 he tied with fellow Republican Aaron Burr and was elected president by the House of Representatives; he won reelection in 1804, defeating Federalist candidate Charles Cotesworth Pinckney, and served as the third president of the United States, 1801–9. Founded University of Virginia. Died at Monticello, his estate near Charlottesville.

SAMUEL JOHNSON (September 18, 1709–December 13, 1784) Born in Lichfield, Staffordshire, the son of a bookseller. Survived childhood illnesses, including scrofula, that left his vision and hearing impaired; was also subject to recurring episodes of depression. Attended

Pembroke College, Oxford, 1728–29, but financial constraints prevented his completion of a degree. Moved to Birmingham, where he taught school and began writing. Moved to London in 1737 and began contributing to *The Gentleman's Magazine* the following year. Initiated major lexicographic project in 1746; *A Dictionary of the English Language* published in 1755, to great acclaim. Published *The Rambler*, a twice-weekly periodical, 1750–52. Received royal pension in 1762. At the behest of the government, published pamphlets highly critical of the claims of the American colonists: *The Patriot* (1774), *Taxation No Tyranny* (1775), *Hypocrisy Unmasked, or, A Short Inquiry into the Religious Complaints of Our American Colonies* (1776). Major works include *The History of Rasselas, Prince of Abissinia* (1759), an edition of Shakespeare (1765), and *The Lives of the Most Eminent English Poets* (1779–81). Died in London. Subject of perhaps the most celebrated biography in the English language, *The Life of Samuel Johnson, LL.D.*, published by longtime associate James Boswell in 1791.

CHARLES LEE (January 26, 1732–October 2, 1782) Born in Dernhall, Cheshire, the son of an army officer. Educated in Switzerland, where he learned Greek and Latin and four other languages. Commissioned in 1746, an ensign in father's regiment, the 55th (later renamed 44th) Foot, then stationed in Ireland. Promoted to lieutenant in 1751. Served with regiment in North America during the Seven Years' War. Returned to England in 1760, and lobbied for the retention of Canada. Appointed major in the 103rd regiment in 1761, and fought against Spain in Portugal, 1762–63. Much aggrieved at being retired at half-pay from the army, joined the service of the Polish king, Stanislaus Augustus, as aide-de-camp. Fought against the Turks in 1769, fell ill, and while recuperating in Italy engaged in a duel in which he killed his opponent but lost two fingers. After finally securing promotion to lieutenant-colonel in the British army, he moved to America, where he embraced the patriot cause, publishing two pamphlets in 1775 in which he encouraged confidence in the fighting potential of colonial militia. Appointed second major-general in the Continental Army on June 17, 1775, and resigned British commission. Led defense of Charleston, South Carolina, before assuming command of a wing of Washington's force in the campaign in New York and New Jersey. Captured by British dragoons in December 1776, he grew disenchanted with the American cause during sixteen-month captivity. Exchanged in April 1778 and resumed command, but remained dubious about the quality of his soldiers, an attitude which led to his failure at the battle of Monmouth, where he retreated contrary to orders. Dismissed from the battlefield by Washington for breach of duty, he demanded a court martial, which resulted in a one-year suspension. Congress voted to discharge him permanently in 1780. Died in Philadelphia.

PHILIP LIVINGSTON (January 15, 1716–June 12, 1778) Born at Livingston Manor in Albany, New York, the son of a merchant and landed proprietor. Educated at Yale College. Moved to New York City where he amassed a fortune provisioning and privateering during the Anglo-French wars. Led or contributed to the founding of a number of civic and philanthropic endeavors, including King's College (now Columbia University, established 1754), the New York Society Library (1754), the New York Chamber of Commerce (1768), and the New York Hospital (1771). Elected to the New York Assembly, 1758. Delegate to the Stamp Act Congress, 1765. Elected speaker of the assembly in 1768, but voted out the following year. Elected to the First Continental Congress, 1774, and published that year *The Other Side of the Question, or, A Defense of the Liberties of North-America*. Signed the Declaration of Independence. Died in York, Pennsylvania, where Congress was then sitting.

MOSES MATHER (February 23, 1719–September 21, 1806) Born in Lyme, Connecticut, the son of a militia captain. Graduated from Yale College in 1739. Ordained in the Congregational church at Darien, Connecticut, in 1744 and served as its pastor for the remainder of his life. Published *America's Appeal to the Impartial World* in 1775. An outspoken patriot, he was twice imprisoned, in 1779 and in 1781, by British raiding parties from nearby New York. Awarded a divinity degree from the College of New Jersey (now Princeton) in 1791. Died in Darien.

THOMAS PAINE (January 29, 1737–June 8, 1809) Born in Thetford, Norfolk, the son of a corset maker. Worked in the excise service, 1762–65 and 1768–74. Immigrated to Philadelphia in November 1774 and began writing for newspapers and magazines. Published widely read pamphlet *Common Sense*, advocating independence from Britain and republican government, on January 10, 1776. Served with Pennsylvania militia in New Jersey, July–December 1776. Published pamphlet *The American Crisis, Number 1* on December 19, 1776. Wrote a further twelve numbers of *The Crisis*, 1777–83, along with many other political articles and pamphlets. Went to France with John Laurens in 1781 on mission to secure additional French aid. Returned to England in 1787 to work on his design for a wrought-iron bridge. Published *Rights of Man* (1791–92), a defense of the French Revolution. Served as a member of the French National Convention, 1792–93. Arrested by the Jacobins and imprisoned in Paris, December 1793–

November 1794. Published *The Age of Reason* (1794–95), a deistic attack on biblical religion. Returned to the United States in 1802 and continued to write for the press until his death in New York City.

SAMUEL SEABURY (November 30, 1729–February 25, 1796) Born in Groton, Connecticut, the son of a missionary of the Society for the Propagation of the Gospel in Foreign Parts. Graduated from Yale College in 1748 and pursued medical studies (considered useful for missionaries) at University of Edinburgh before being ordained in 1753. Returned to America and served in series of rectorships before settling in Westchester, New York. Became an ardent advocate for an American episcopacy and, in pamphlets written as "A. W. Farmer," an outspoken defender of crown authority over the colonies. Briefly imprisoned by revolutionary forces in Connecticut in 1775 on suspicion of being the author of the farmer pamphlets, he was released and served as chaplain to the King's forces in New York City during the war. Invited in 1783 to become the first Protestant bishop in the new United States by a group of Connecticut clergymen, but because consecration as a bishop in the Anglican church required an oath of allegiance to the Crown, which as an American citizen he could not take, he secured consecration from Scottish bishops, and was installed as bishop of Connecticut at a ceremony in Aberdeen in 1784. Settled in New London, where he died after a particularly exhausting diocesan tour.

JAMES WILSON (September 14, 1742–August 21, 1798) Born in Caskardy, Fifeshire, Scotland, the son of a farmer. Studied on scholarship at the University of St. Andrews, 1757–61, and then entered university's divinity school before being forced to leave school after his father's death in 1762. Moved to Edinburgh to learn bookkeeping and merchant accounting. Emigrated to America in the fall of 1765 and was hired as a Latin tutor at the College of Philadelphia (now University of Pennsylvania) that winter. Read law with John Dickinson in 1766, and was admitted to the bar in Reading, Pennsylvania, where he began to practice in 1767. Moved to Carlisle, Pennsylvania, in 1770, where an advantageous marriage and prospering practice enabled him to begin lifelong engagement with land speculation. In 1774, became head of committee of correspondence and was elected to first provincial convention in Philadelphia. Published that year *Considerations on the Nature and Extent of the Legislative Authority of the British Parliament* (written in 1768). Served in the Second Continental Congress, 1775–77. Initially favored delay of vote on independence in 1776, but was one of the three out of seven delegates from Pennsylvania who voted for it on July 2. Opposed the Pennsylvania state constitution of 1776 and was not reelected to the Continental Congress by the assembly in 1777. Moved to Philadelphia after the British evacuated the city in 1778 and defended Tories in court, developing new legal concept of treason. Defended his house against angry mob in 1779. Helped Robert Morris, superintendent of Continental finances, establish the Bank of North America, becoming its attorney. Served in Continental Congress, 1783–87. Elected to American Philosophical Society in 1786. Delegate from Pennsylvania to the Constitutional Convention of 1787, where he was one of the most influential members, and to the Pennsylvania ratifying convention, where he led the Federalist forces for ratification. Primary architect of new Pennsylvania state constitution, drafted in convention, 1789–90. Served as associate justice of the U.S. Supreme Court, 1789–98. Over-extension of land speculation led to his arrest for debt in 1797. Released on bail, he died in disgrace in Edenton, North Carolina.

Note on the Texts

This volume, the second of a two-volume set, collects twenty pamphlets from the polemical contest that resulted from and in many significant ways contributed to the escalation of tensions between Great Britain and its North American colonies in the period from 1773 to 1776. During these crucial years a political debate that had in the 1760s been focused on questions of representation and consent deepened into a controversy over the nature of sovereignty in the British Empire. The pamphlets gathered here were written both by Americans and Britons, though the increasingly interconnected character of the empire in this period can make such distinctions misleading. Englishman Thomas Paine had been resident in the colonies for only fourteen months when he wrote the most influential expression of the "American" position during the debate, while Massachusetts governor Thomas Hutchinson, who articulated the "British" position as forcefully as any writer, had deep ancestral roots in the colonies. The fluidity of these categories emerges from the debate itself, indeed it became the central issue to be resolved: Were Americans and Britons one people, one nation, or not?

These texts were part of a lively transatlantic discourse in which pamphlets published in Boston or Philadelphia soon appeared in London and were quickly reprinted, and vice versa, triggering further rounds of pamphleteering. Printers and booksellers, often themselves political partisans, played a crucial role in this rapid-fire exchange by preparing the works for publication, advertising them in newspapers, distributing them to subscribers and other book buyers, and posting copies to vendors in other locales. Though print runs for political pamphlets could be relatively small, often as few as five hundred copies, their reach was multiplied many times over by being made available in coffeehouses, clubs, and other gathering places and by extensive republication in part or in full in newspapers and periodical digests. The circulation of pamphlets built and reinforced ties among like-minded readers in the different colonies, encouraging the coalescence of shared convictions about the imperial relationship and exposing the ideological fissures that were ultimately to upend the traditional structures of authority in the colonies and break the imperial bonds.

What follows is a brief account of the publication history of each of the pamphlets collected here, along with some details about its reception and influence. These works ranged from as few as fourteen to as many as 126 pages in length. Normally published in either octavo or quarto format, they varied from roughly 7 to 8¾ inches in height, resulting in shapes that were rectangular if octavo or, if quarto, somewhat more square. Two bibliographies by Thomas Randolph Adams (1921–2008), the longtime librarian of the John Carter Brown Library at Brown University, are indispensable guides to this literature: *American Independence: The Growth of an Idea: A Bibliographical Study of the American Political Pamphlets Printed Between 1764 and 1776 Dealing with the Dispute Between Great Britain and Her Colonies* (Providence, RI: Brown University Press, 1965) and *The American Controversy: A Bibliographical Study of the British Pamphlets About the American Disputes, 1764–1783* (2 vols., Providence, RI: Brown University Press, 1980).

20: *The Speeches of His Excellency Governor Hutchinson* . . . (1773)

The seven speeches collected in this pamphlet—three by Massachusetts governor Thomas Hutchinson, two by a committee of the Governor's Council, and two by a committee of the House of Representatives (though principally written by nonmember John Adams)— were delivered during a special session of the Massachusetts legislature convened by the governor to address the controversy arising from the publication in November 1772 of the *Votes and Proceedings* of the Boston town meeting, the so-called Boston pamphlet (Pamphlet 19 in the companion to this volume). Hutchinson opened the session on January 6, 1773, with a speech that was printed five days later in the *Massachusetts Gazette and the Boston Weekly News-Letter*. The Council responded on January 25 and the House on January 26, in speeches subsequently printed in the *Massachusetts Gazette* on January 28 and February 1. Hutchinson initiated the second round of debate on February 16 (printed in the *Massachusetts Gazette*, February 22), with replies coming from the Council on February 25 (printed in the *Massachusetts Gazette* on March 1) and the House on March 2, before he closed the debate with a final speech on March 6 and dismissed the legislature; these last two speeches were printed in the *Massachusetts Gazette* on March 8. Before it was prorogued, the House voted to have the entire exchange published in pamphlet form, contracting with the Boston printers Benjamin Edes and John Gill, proprietors since 1755 of the *Boston Gazette and Country Journal*, the organ of the patriot movement in Massachusetts, to produce seven hundred copies for its members and for town clerks throughout the colony, and one hundred for the Council. This volume prints the complete text of the 126-page pamphlet that Edes and Gill produced.

21: [Thomas Jefferson], *A Summary View of the Rights of British America* (1774)

On May 24, 1774, shortly after news of the Boston Port Act reached Williamsburg, the Virginia House of Burgesses passed a resolution cowritten by Thomas Jefferson calling for a day of fasting and prayer on June 1, the date the act was to be put into effect. When Lord Dunmore, the royal governor, promptly dissolved the House for this show of intercolonial solidarity, eighty-nine legislators reconvened at the nearby Raleigh Tavern. There they adopted a non-importation association, proposed a meeting of colonial representatives to address the crisis, and called for a Virginia convention to meet on August 1. Illness prevented Jefferson from attending that convention, but he had prepared a statement of principles for the delegates it would elect for the Continental Congress scheduled to convene in Philadelphia in the early fall, and he sent a copy to his cousin, Peyton Randolph, who had been speaker of the House of Burgesses and who resumed a leadership role in the Convention. Randolph's nephew Edmund Randolph, who became the first attorney general of the United States, recorded a picture of the reception of Jefferson's views in Williamsburg, recalling

> the applause bestowed on most of them, when they were read to a large company at the house of Peyton Randolph, to whom they were addressed. Of all, the approbation was not equal. From the celebrated letters of the Pennsylvania Farmer [Pamphlet 11 in the companion to this volume] we had been instructed to bow to the external taxation of parliament, as resulting from our migration, and a necessary dependence on the mother country. But this composition of Mr. Jefferson, shook this conceded principle, although it had been confirmed by a still more celebrated pamphlet, written by Daniel Dulany of Maryland, and cited by Lord Chatham, as a text book of American rights [Pamphlet 7]. The young ascended with Mr. Jefferson to the source of those rights; the old required time for consideration, before they could tread this lofty ground.

In the end, though the Convention considered Jefferson's instructions, it chose to adopt milder terms. (Jefferson observed many years later that "tamer sentiments were preferred, and I believe, wisely preferred; the leap I proposed being too long as yet for the mass of our citizens.") However, some sympathetic individual or individuals forwarded his resolves to Clementina Rind, Williamsburg's only female printer (her husband, William, with whom she had published the *Virginia Gazette* since 1766, had died in 1773), who issued it as a twenty-three-page pamphlet sometime in early August. Patrick

Henry and perhaps others in the Virginia delegation to the Congress brought copies of the pamphlet with them to Philadelphia, where it was reprinted by John Dunlap, publisher of the *Pennsylvania Packet, or the General Advertiser*; it was advertised for sale in the September 5 edition of Dunlap's paper. Copies also found their way to London, where *A Summary View* was twice reprinted by George Kearsley in late autumn. (Kearsley had a history of publishing radical works; in 1763 he had been arrested for issuing copies of John Wilkes's *North Briton* No. 45.) The London editions featured an address "To the King," signed by "Tribunus," which is believed to have been the work of Arthur Lee, a member of the famous Virginia clan who was then practicing law in London. It opens in dramatic fashion:

> THERE is not a man of thought, in the whole nation, who does not espouse bad measures from bad principles, but is justly alarmed, and seriously anxious, for the common good. Affairs of such magnitude now employ the public attention, as seem to involve in them the *fate* of EMPIRE. The times are big with great events. What will be the consequence, it is not in human sagacity to foretel. But if the same system be pursued, which for a long time hath employed the attention of your Majesty's ministers, they ought to tremble for their heads.

This edition was the subject of brief notices in the major London periodicals, including the November 1774 issue of *The Critical Review, or Annals of Literature*, a generally Tory publication that had been edited by Tobias Smollett from 1756 to 1763. There it was dryly characterized as "An expostulation with his majesty respecting the right of taxing America; a right which the author considers as inherent in the colonies, and not constitutionally pertaining to the British parliament."

A Summary View helped to establish Jefferson's reputation beyond Virginia, and it made him something of a celebrity when he arrived in Philadelphia in June 1775 for the Second Continental Congress. As the delegates were assembling, Samuel Ward of Rhode Island wrote home that "yesterday the famous Mr. Jefferson a Delegate from Virginia in the Room of Mr. Randolph arrived, I have not been in Company with him yet, he looks like a very sensible, spirited, fine Fellow and by the Pamphlet which he wrote last Summer he certainly is one." In his "Autobiography," John Adams attributed Jefferson's appointment to the committee for drafting a declaration of independence to the regard with which the *Summary View* was held: "Mr. Jefferson had the reputation of a masterly pen; he had been chosen a delegate in Virginia, in consequence of a very handsome public paper which he had written for the House of Burgesses, which had given him the character of a fine writer." As indicated in the Notes to the present volume, Jefferson made alterations and annotations to two copies of the pamphlet, but evidently never communicated these to a printer, since no revised edition is known to exist. This volume prints the complete text of the Clementina Rind edition.

22: [James Wilson], *Considerations on . . . the Legislative Authority of the British Parliament* (1774)

Though written in 1768, this essay was not published until 1774, when it was issued in Philadelphia as a forty-page pamphlet by the father-son firm of William and Thomas Bradford, publishers of the *Pennsylvania Journal*; it was advertised for sale in the September 28 edition of the *Journal* and seems to have exercised some influence on the then-sitting First Continental Congress. Largely on the strength of this publication, Wilson was elected to represent Pennsylvania in the Second Continental Congress, where, notwithstanding the radical nature of this pamphlet, he emerged as a leading conservative. (In this regard he was similar to fellow Pennsylvanian John Dickinson, in whose law office he had clerked.) The *Considerations* was advertised as "This Day published" in the October 20, 1774, edition of *Rivington's New-York Gazetteer*, where it was attributed to "the celebrated Dr. B. FRANKLIN." In that issue publisher James Rivington also presented a lengthy excerpt from the pamphlet, with another following in the next week's edition. (Though the second installment ended with "(To Be Continued)," Rivington abandoned the serialization there.) Copies of these issues of the *Gazetteer* made their way across the Atlantic, where they caught the eye of English pamphleteer (and dean of the cathedral at Gloucester) Josiah Tucker. In his January 1775 pamphlet, *Tract V. The Respective Pleas and Arguments of the Mother Country and of the Colonies, Distinctly Set Forth*, Tucker cited the *Considerations*—which following Rivington he ascribed to Franklin —as proof that no compromise was possible with the Americans. Tucker had evidently not seen the December 1 edition of the *Gazetteer*, which included an anonymous letter from Philadelphia, dated November 30, 1774, disabusing Rivington and his readers on the authorship of the pamphlet:

> Mr. RIVINGTON,
> You have been mis-informed in attributing to Dr. Benjamin Franklin, the piece entitled, Considerations on the Nature and Extent of the legislative Authority of the British Parliament, over the American Colonies —His political principles are quite different, that Gentleman always acknowledged that Great-Britain had a right to regulate our trade.— The real author of that performance is Mr. Wilson, of this province, a native of Scotland, and a warm Patriot.

This volume prints the complete text of the Bradford and Bradford edition.

23: [William Henry Drayton], *A Letter from Freeman of South-Carolina* **(1774)**

In 1769, as Americans mobilized in opposition to the Townshend duties, William Henry Drayton, a former South Carolina assemblyman writing under the pseudonym "Freeman," published letters in the *South Carolina Gazette* highly critical of the non-importation movement, which he objected to as coercive and disruptive of proper social order. The negative response to these letters contributed to his decision to travel to England, where he had been educated, in order to reestablish his career. There he published *The Letters of Freeman* in 1771 and was awarded a seat on the South Carolina council. In August 1774, once more enmeshed in South Carolina politics, Drayton revived his controversial nom de plume, this time for the vigorous forty-seven-page defense of the patriot cause collected here. He sent copies of this pamphlet, which was printed by Peter Timothy, the publisher of the *South Carolina Gazette*, to various members of the Congress and to Lord North and other administration officials in England, so that "they might see the State of Affairs in & the sentiments of America." This volume publishes the complete text of the Timothy edition.

24: *Some Fugitive Thoughts on a Letter Signed Freeman* **(1774)**

If Drayton's pamphlet did much to restore his good name among South Carolina patriots—Henry Laurens, who had been highly critical of Drayton, conceded that the pamphlet was "not a bad thing & coming from a proselyte a good one"—it greatly antagonized the colony's official power structure, including the governor, William Bull, who also happened to be Drayton's uncle. Bull, writing to the Earl of Dartmouth, pronounced that the *Letter* was "replete with sentiments so derogatory to the Royal Prerogative, the Authority of Parliament and the long established Constitution of Government in America, that it cannot fail to excite indignation." One such outraged reader was "A Backsettler," whose identity is unknown, but whose high dudgeon in *Some Fugitive Thoughts* suggests that he may have been one of the placemen that Drayton pointedly attacks in the *Letter*. This volume prints the complete text of "Backsettler"'s thirty-six-page pamphlet. No publisher is indicated on the title page.

25: [Jonathan Boucher?], *A Letter from a Virginian* **(1774)**

This anonymous twenty-nine-page pamphlet, which like Drayton's is framed as an address to the members of the Congress, was published in the summer of 1774. Neither printer nor place of publication is indicated on the title page. Charles R. Hildeburn, in *A Century of Printing: The Issues of the Press in Pennsylvania 1685–1784* (1886), attributed its production to the Philadelphia printer Henry Miller (the Hessian-born Johann Heinrich Müller). However, based on the pamphlet's distinctive type ornaments, Thomas R. Adams identified the printer as Hugh Gaine, the publisher of the *New-York Gazette and the Weekly Mercury*. Authorship of this pamphlet has often been attributed to Jonathan Boucher, though in his memoir *Reminiscences of an American Loyalist* (first published in 1925) Boucher makes no mention of the work. The pamphlet was reprinted in Boston by the Tory firm of John Hicks and Nathaniel Mills, publishers of the *Massachusetts Gazette, and the Boston Post-Boy and Advertiser*, and advertised in the September 1, 1774, edition of the *Massachusetts Gazette and the Boston Weekly News-Letter*. Hicks and Mills followed with a second edition before the year was out. A London edition was published in November by John Wilkie, treasurer of the London Stationers' Company and publisher of the *London Chronicle*. It was briefly noticed in the Whig *Monthly Review, or Literary Journal* for December: "Our Virginian appears to have made an effort to dissuade the members of the Congress from adopting the non-importation and non-exportation agreements; but as they have disregarded his arguments, and as his performance contains nothing new or important to the people of Great Britain, we think the republication of it here was unseasonable." *The Critical Review* was equally succinct, but predictably more enthusiastic: "The author of this Letter, in a warm and sensible address, exhorts the delegates to conduct their deliberations with coolness and discretion, on the important occasion of their assembly, which, according as the measures they proposed were prudent or pernicious, might terminate either in a salutary accommodation with Great Britain, or in the ruin of America. He particularly advises them to preserve their minds from being heated with the spirit of party, or misled by false representations. The Letter recommends prudent and moderate measures from all arguments which can be suggested by a regard to the interests of both countries." The present volume prints the complete text of the first edition.

26: [Samuel Seabury], *The Congress Canvassed* (1774)

Westchester minister Samuel Seabury first assumed the pseudonym "A. W. Farmer" (short for A Westchester Farmer) in *Free Thoughts on the Proceedings of the Continental Congress*, which was completed on November 16, 1774, and published by James Rivington, who advertised it for sale in the November 24 issue of *Rivington's Gazette*. (This pamphlet was answered by a young Alexander Hamilton, still a student at King's College [now Columbia], in *A Full Vindication of the Measures of the Congress*, also published by Rivington.) "A. W. Farmer" returned in short order with the twenty-seven-page *The Congress Canvassed*, which was completed on November 28. Again published by Rivington, it was advertised in the December 15 edition of *Rivington's Gazette*. (Seabury refers to Hamilton's pamphlet in the postscript, and the two exchanged another round of pamphlets that winter.) *The Congress Canvassed* was reprinted in London in late January 1775 by the London firm of William Richardson and Leonard Urquhart. *The Critical Review* for February praised it as "judicious and animated," adding that "we sincerely wish that the Americans would pay that attention which is due to the sensible admonitions of this sagacious and prudent writer."

Meanwhile New York and Connecticut patriots were much exercised with trying to uncover the identity of the Westchester Farmer. Without a flesh-and-bone author to prosecute, they ceremonially tarred and feathered or burned copies of his pamphlets. Finally, Seabury came under suspicion, and on November 19, 1775, he was abducted and carried to New Haven. There, as he recounted a year later in a letter to officials of the Society for the Propagation of the Gospel in Foreign Parts, he was accused of writing pamphlets "against the Liberties of America." "If I would have disavowed these publications," he recalled, "I should have been set at liberty in a few days; but as I refused to declare whether I were, or were not, the author, they kept me." Confronted with Seabury's formidable intransigence, his captors let him go after six weeks. He served as a chaplain to the British army during the war and in 1784 become the first bishop of the American Episcopal Church. It appears to have been Jonathan Boucher who first identified "A. W. Farmer" as Seabury in his 1797 work, *A View of the Causes and Consequences of the American Revolution*: "whilst the revolt was still in its infancy, he wrote several seasonable pieces, adapted to the capacities of the people, under the assumed character of a farmer. They were generally acknowledged to have done much good." The authorship question was conclusively settled with the discovery of a detailed undated memorial addressed by Seabury to the Society's commissioners, which was published in *The Magazine of American History* in 1882. In it he specifically claimed the "A. W. Farmer" pamphlets and offered further detail as to their genesis:

> when it was evident from continual publications in Newspapers, & from the uniting of all the jarring interests of the Independents [Congregationalists] & Presbyterians from Massachusetts bay to Georgia; under Grand committees & Synods that some mischievous scheme was meditated against the Church of England & the British government in

America your memorialist did enter into an agreement with the Revd. Dr. T. B. Ch—— [Thomas Bradbury Chandler, author of Pamphlet 27] then of Eliz. Town New Jersey & with the Revd. Dr. Inglis [Charles Inglis, author of Pamphlet 37] the present Rector of Trinity Church in the City of New York, to watch all publications either in Newspapers or pamphlets, & to obviate the evil influence of such as appeared to have a bad tendency by the speediest answers.

This volume prints the complete text of the Rivington edition of *The Congress Canvassed*.

27: [Thomas Bradbury Chandler], *A Friendly Address to All Reasonable Americans* (1774)

Pursuant to the agreement described by Samuel Seabury above, Thomas Bradbury Chandler entered the pamphlet debate in the late summer of 1774 with *The American Querist: or, Some Questions Proposed Relative to the Present Disputes between Great-Britain and her American Colonies*, published by Rivington. It was soon reprinted, again by Rivington, this time with a provocative note on the title page:

> ☞ This pamphlet, on the 8th Day of September last, was, in full Conclave of the Sons of Liberty in New-York, committed to the Flames by the Hands of their Common Executioner; as it contains some Queries they cannot, and others they will not answer!

Chandler followed up *The American Querist* with the fifty-five-page *Friendly Address*, which was published sometime in early November and advertised in the November 17 edition of *Rivington's Gazette*. The *Massachusetts Gazette and the Boston Weekly News-Letter* for the same date announced that *A Friendly Address* was "In press and speedily will be published" by the Boston firm of Hicks and Mills. By year's end, or shortly thereafter, Richardson and Urquhart issued an edition in London and another followed in Dublin early in 1775. *The Monthly Review*'s notice from its January 1775 issue repeated what was then the most common assumption about the authorship of the pamphlet:

> This performance is ascribed to Dr. [Myles] Cooper, president of King's College in New York; and probably very opposite opinions will be entertained of its merit by different individuals. The Author, whoever he may be, has employed considerable art, and some abilities, in holding forth an alarming representation of the distress and carnage likely to ensue in America from a contention with Great Britain, and in an endeavor to excite jealousies, divisions, and animosities between the several colonies and religious sects on the continent: and for this laudable purpose he addresses first the members of the church of England,

and then the Quakers, Baptists, Germans, Dutch, &c. in succession, representing it as the aim of the Presbyterians of New England to exterminate all other religious sects in America.

The Critical Review, also for January, found "this Address a cool and rational expostulation with the Americans, respecting the supreme power of the British parliament over our colonies." For its part, the *London Magazine: or, Gentleman's Monthly Intelligencer* concluded that "this pretended American is very friendly to Government, and inimical to his brethren. However, they may profit by some of his hints, though they chuse not to follow his advice in becoming subject to the will of parliament, where they are not represented, in all cases whatsoever. They would then have reason to adopt our author's cries, in prospect of a civil war — 'O all pitying heaven! preserve me! preserve my friends! preserve my country!'" The present volume prints the complete text of the Rivington edition of *A Friendly Address*.

28: [Philip Livingston], *The Other Side of the Question* (1774)

Chandler's *Friendly Address* triggered a mini-debate that played out over three pamphlets (numbers 28, 30, and 31 in the present volume) in the winter of 1774–5. The first of these, this anonymous twenty-nine-page riposte, whose true authorship seems never to have been much in doubt, was published by the tireless Rivington sometime in early December. It was advertised in the December 8 edition of *Rivington's Gazette* and the January 5, 1775, edition of the *Massachusetts Gazette and the Boston Weekly News-Letter*. Though the pamphlet was advertised for sale by Richardson and Urquhart in the February 10 edition of the *London Gazetteer*, no copies of a London edition have been found; it is likely that Richardson and Urquhart were selling imported copies of the New York edition. *The Critical Review* for February professed to be "glad to find that, amidst the general discontent which prevails among the partizans for America, some of her advocates have yet so much good humour left, as to reply to their opponents in a strain of pleasantry. The author of the present defence has had recourse to this method; but the arguments of the writer whom he criticizes were too *reasonable* to be totally invalidated." The present volume prints the complete text of the Rivington edition.

29: Ebenezer Baldwin, "An Appendix, Stating the Heavy Grievances the Colonies Labour Under" (1774)

Ebenezer Baldwin of Danbury and Samuel Sherwood of Fairfield were two of Connecticut's more prominent Congregationalist ministers. They had been among eight clergymen selected to represent the Consociated Churches of Connecticut at a convention with New

York and Pennsylvania Presbyterians in Elizabethtown, New Jersey, in September 1774. (Baldwin was chosen to preach the sermon opening this Grand Convention on September 21, and Sherwood was named its chairman.) It was not uncommon for clerical colleagues to join their works for publication in this period; sometimes publishers combined or collected works on their own initiative in an attempt to reduce costs or broaden appeal. In this case it is not known precisely how, in late December 1774, Baldwin's essay came to be attached to Sherwood's sermon, and the two issued together in one ninety-one-page pamphlet by the brothers Thomas and Samuel Green, publishers of the *Connecticut Journal and New-Haven Post-Boy* and members of the third generation of a family of printers who owned and operated most of the presses in the colony. The Greens advertised the book as "just published" in the January 4, 1775, edition of their paper. The present volume prints the complete text of Baldwin's "Appendix" from the Green and Green edition of Sherwood's *A Sermon, Containing, Scriptural Instructions to Civil Rulers, and All Free-Born Subjects.*

30: [Charles Lee], *Strictures on . . . a "Friendly Address to All Reasonable Americans . . ."* (1775)

As with Livingston's *Other Side of the Question*, the authorship of this anonymous fifteen-page rejoinder to Chandler's *Friendly Address* appears to have been widely known or surmised at the time of its publication in late November or early December 1774. Though he nowhere names his antagonist, Charles Lee seems to have written the pamphlet under the assumption that Cooper was the author of the *Friendly Address.* At least, as is clear in the text, he was convinced that his opponent was an Anglican churchman. The *Strictures* was published by the Bradfords in Philadelphia and advertised in the *Pennsylvania Journal* for November 30, 1774. Reprints soon followed in Boston (advertised January 5, 1775), Newport (January 9), Providence (January 21), and, evidence suggests, New York, though no copies are known to exist. It was also reprinted in several southern newspapers, including the *South Carolina Gazette* (December 26), the *South Carolina Gazette and Country Journal* (January 10), and Williamsburg's two newspapers, both called the *Virginia Gazette* (January 26 and February 3). A sixteen-page second edition, featuring a preface ("Advertisement") by Silas Deane ("a Gentleman in Connecticut"), was issued in New London by Timothy Green, a brother of Thomas and Samuel Green. This volume prints the complete text of that edition. The text of the *Strictures* in the second edition is identical to that of the first, with the exception of sixteen minor variations in spelling and punctuation.

31: [Henry Barry], *The Strictures on the Friendly Address Examined*
(1775)

On January 30, 1775, the Boston minister John Eliot sent a copy of
this anonymous, fourteen-page pamphlet, a response to Lee's *Strictures*, to his friend Jeremy Belknap, pastor of the Congregational
church in Dover, New Hampshire, identifying its author as Lieutenant Henry Barry of the 52nd Regiment, stationed in Boston. It had
been published that month, possibly by the young Tory printer John
Howe. Soon after, in New York, Rivington issued Barry's and Lee's
works together in a twenty-five-page pamphlet entitled *The General,
Attacked by a Subaltern*. This volume prints the complete text of the
Boston edition of Barry's *Strictures*.

32: [Joseph Galloway], *A Candid Examination of the Mutual Claims of
Great-Britain, and the Colonies* (1775)

Joseph Galloway and John Dickinson had been leaders of opposing
factions in the Pennsylvania Assembly for more than a decade when
they were selected as delegates to the First Continental Congress,
where Dickinson led the successful effort to quash Galloway's proposal for an American assembly subordinate to Parliament. After the
Congress closed, Galloway spent some weeks in New York before
returning to his estate in Bucks County in early December. There,
in a January 14, 1775, letter to his friend Samuel Verplanck of New
York, Galloway gave vent to his feelings about the Congress's proceedings:

> I totally disagree with them in all, and think they have not taken one
> foot of that ground which they should have taken. When I went to the
> Assembly and found that they had approved of the measures of the Con-
> gress so fully, and had appointed me one of the Delegates at the next,
> I very explicitly told them, that I entirely disapproved of them. I did so
> in Congress and continued yet of the same opinion and that I might
> not appear to undertake the Execution of measures which my judge-
> ment and conscience disapproved I could not serve them as a Delegate
> at the ensuing Congress.

It was in this spirit that he sat down to compose his pamphlet, which
was published by Rivington in a sixty-two-page edition in late February. Galloway revealed his authorship of the *Candid Examination*,
and explained his rationale for writing it, in another letter to Verplanck, this one dated February 14. Verplanck, as so many politically
engaged individuals did during this period, had sent Galloway copies
of the latest offerings from the press, and these likely included those
by Seabury and Chandler:

I should be greatly defective in that Friendship which I entertain for you, should I omit to inform you in Confidence, that you will see my sentiments more at Large in a Pamphlet now in the Press in New York. . . . I thank you for the Pamphlets. They are well wrote, and will be of great service. They have produced a happy effect in this Province. I wish more of them had been for sale in Philadelphia and advertised in our Papers. Many complain they cannot procure them, and yet I think they all have capital Defects. They assert a necessity of a Supreme Legislative Authority, but do not prove it to the comprehension of common Readers. They do not show the rights of the American Subject or even acknowledge that we have any. They do not own that we have any Grievance and consequently nothing is pointed out as a Constitutional Remedy, and therefor they all leave the mind of the inquisitive Reader totally unsatisfied, which perceiving something very essential to their Freedom & Happiness wanting, in their present situation, become bewildered on the subject and are thence led to condemn the Performance.

Galloway sought to address this lack of a "Constitutional Remedy" by including in the *Candid Examination* the plan for union he had proposed to the Congress. This, in turn, prompted Dickinson and Charles Thomson, secretary to the Congress, to publish in the *Pennsylvania Journal* for March 8, 1775, an anonymous letter "To the Author of a Pamphlet, entitled 'A Candid Examination of the mutual Claims of Great Britain and her colonies,'" defending Congress's rejection of Galloway's plan and decrying his pamphlet. "You have no doubt seen the answer to the 'Candid Examination,'" Galloway wrote to Verplanck on April 1. "It is the production of a fortnight Labour of the Pennsylvania Farmer and his old Assistant Charles Thomson. From the little approbation it met with here, I should not have thought it worthy of a Reply, But it gave me an opportunity of explaining some Principles of the Pamphlet more fully—And besides I thought the vanity and Ignorance of the Authors ought to be exposed. I have therefor sent to Mr. Rivington a reply, which I hope he will publish with all convenient Speed." Galloway was not disappointed: his *Reply* was offered for sale in the April 6 edition of *Rivington's Gazette*. The following month the *Candid Examination* was advertised by Richardson and Urquhart as "Just Received from Mr. Rivington of New York" in the *London Gazetteer* for May 1. British Whigs were skeptical of the work and the motives behind it. *The Monthly Review* for June attributed Galloway's publication to frustrated ambition:

This pamphlet (imported from New York) has been advertised as the production of Mr. Galloway, one of the Delegates (for Pennsylvania) in the late American congress; and we have otherwise sufficient authority not only to ascribe it to that gentleman, but to consider it as the effect of illiberal motives and unworthy passions. In this we are warranted, not only by facts of general notoriety, but by many indiscreet expressions in the pamphlet itself.

As some extenuation however, of Mr. Galloway's misconduct, it may be proper to remark that he was sent to the late Congress under impressions of disgust at the loss of his former popularity, and of envy for the applause bestowed on his rival antagonist Mr. Dickenson. And being emulous of popular fame, he proposed a plan . . . [for] an American House of Commons . . . [that] was not approved by the Congress; some of whom thought it too great an innovation to be admitted by Parliament, and others were apprehensive (with how much reason we pretend not to determine) that the execution of it might be dangerous to the freedom of America.

Even before the *Candid Examination* was published, Galloway had sent copies of his rejected plan of union to key figures in the mother country, including Benjamin Franklin, his longtime ally in the Pennsylvania Assembly, who at Galloway's request dutifully shared it with Lord Chatham and other officials. On February 25, 1775, in a friendly but frank letter to Galloway, Franklin revealed his principal objection to his friend's plan, and in doing so exposed the increasingly calcified nature of the imperial controversy: "when I consider the extream Corruption prevalent among all Orders of Men in this old rotten State, and the glorious publick Virtue so predominant in our rising Country, I cannot but apprehend more Mischief than Benefit from a closer Union." On April 17, 1775, Samuel Wharton, a Pennsylvania merchant in England to secure official support for a land company he had established with a group that included Franklin, wrote to his famous partner to express his frustration with Galloway's decision to publish the *Candid Examination*:

I am realy grieved at the Publication of Mr. Galloway's extraordinary Pamphlet. Our great Friends in both Houses are extremely angry at it, and express themselves in most resentful Terms against the Author; While the Courtiers rejoice at that Part of the Pamphlet, which represents our Divisions and Controversys as to Boundaries and Modes of Religion, our Incompetency to resist the Power of this Country, And the undecided State of the Congress, for several Weeks, As to what realy were the *Rights* of America; Yet the Courtiers at the same Time treat with ineffable Contempt the Plan of Union proposed, and which they say, by *not* being adopted, offended the Authors Pride, and has been the happy Means of their being satisfactorily *confirmed* in their Ideas of the Weakness and Division of the Colonies; and that by Perseverance, They shall unquestionably obtain a perfect Submission. Mr.

Pope, you remember, has wisely said [in the *Essay on Man*] "How shall
We reason but from what We know", On which, I shall only make this
short Observation, that if our Friend Mr. Galloway had *properly known*
The real Plans of this arbitrary Administration, He would never, I am
persuaded, have committed Himself, in the very indiscreet Manner,
that He had done.

Galloway's two pamphlets were collected in a 116-page edition issued
in London in 1780, testimony to the lingering appeal for some of the
idea of an empire restored. By then Galloway was in exile in England,
convicted of high treason in absentia by the same Pennsylvania Assembly he had led as speaker. This volume prints the complete text of
the Rivington edition of the *Candid Examination*.

33: [Samuel Johnson], *Taxation No Tyranny* (1775)

Samuel Johnson wrote a half dozen pamphlets dealing in part or in
full with the American controversy, but none more famous than this
ninety-one-page work issued in March 1775 by the prominent London publishers William Strahan and Thomas Cadell. Commissioned
on behalf of the North government by Sir Grey Cooper, the secretary
of the Treasury, the pamphlet was designed to rebut the *Extracts from
the Votes and Proceedings of the American Continental Congress*, the
pamphlet that publicized the Congress's Declarations and Resolves,
widely referred to as the American "Bill of Rights." To Johnson's cha-
grin, the government watered down some of the most vitriolic passages in *Taxation No Tyranny*, but it retains a contemptuous tone that
reflected the administration's hardening attitude toward the colonies.

Publication notices were many and spirited, and suggested little
mystery about the pamphlet's authorship. The lengthy review in *The
Gentleman's Magazine* for March began by noting that "common
fame attributes the merit of this performance to the celebrated Dr.
Johnson, and every page of it confirms the truth of the report. That
gentleman has been charged, in his former political productions, with
writing by compulsion; in this it is plain he has written from the heart."
After quoting Johnson's assertion that "an English individual may by
the supreme authority be deprived of liberty, and a Colony divested
of its powers, for reasons of which that authority is the only judge,"
the reviewer parenthetically observed that "it is somewhere said, that,
in whatever shape the Fiend appears, he never fails to show his
cloven foot. If these positions are admitted, we have profited little by
the boasted revolution; and the British nation have shifted sovereigns
to very little purpose, if only to change their names." *The Monthly
Review*, also for March, opened its long notice on a charitable note:
"Human powers and human knowledge are circumscribed within

such narrow limits, that no individual can excell in all undertakings.—The writer to whom we ascribe the work before us, has on other occasions by the right application of his talents merited a large share of public approbation; and if his present effort has less claim to applause, it is not because his abilities have been impaired, but because they have been misapplied." It concluded more ominously, though, noting that if the British were to lose the colonies, "we shall have abundant cause to reprobate those measures and principles for which our Author is a zealous, if not a successful advocate." Johnson's status as a royal pensioner left him open to the charge that he was prostituting himself, and in this vein *The London Magazine* minced no words, calling his pamphlet "An abortion of corruption, impregnated by Jacobitism. Administration seem to have no compassion on their pensioner Dr. Johnson. This is another hasty production of his in their favor, and possibly may procure another addition to his pension." Johnson, for his part, remained proud of the pamphlet, and on at least three occasions he contracted with Strahan to produce additional copies, more than two thousand in all. The present volume prints the complete text of the first Strahan and Cadell edition.

34: *An Answer to a Pamphlet, Entitled Taxation No Tyranny* (1775)

Johnson's pamphlet provoked numerous responses in kind, including this sixty-three-page anonymous effort published in April 1775 by the London bookseller and journalist John Almon (a protégé of Lord Temple and confidant of John Wilkes), which appeared first in excerpted form in the *London Chronicle*, April 1–4. It was reviewed with three other rejoinders in *The London Magazine* for May: "The above four pamphlets are well written, and sufficiently expose the venality of the pen they attack, and the weakness of the pensioner's arguments against American constitutional liberty, notwithstanding the harmony of his periods." *The Gentleman's Magazine* for April called it "one of those masterly productions of the press that seldom appear but on great occasions." What set the *Answer* apart, from this reviewer's perspective, was its author's exposure of "the fallacy of the doctor's fundamental position . . . , and the disingenuity of his reasoning upon it." "It is wished," the reviewer concluded, "that this pamphlet may be universally read before the measures of government are carried to the extreme." The present volume prints the complete text of the Almon edition.

35: Edmund Burke, *The Speech . . . on Moving His Resolutions for Conciliation* (1775)

Published on May 22, 1775, by the London bookseller James Dodsley, this sixty-five-page pamphlet presented the full text of Burke's several-hour-long speech before the House of Commons on March 22, 1775. It was the second major speech of Burke's to be published in 1775, joining his *Speech on American Taxation*, which had been issued in January. *The Critical Review* for June was grudging in its admiration: "Whatever opinions may be entertained of the plan of accommodation proposed by Mr. Burke, it will, we doubt not, be acknowledged, that, amidst the sallies of imagination, natural to this gentleman, the present Speech displays greater ingenuity of argument, and more extensive reflection, than any of his former rhetorical productions." *The Gentleman's Magazine* for August opined that "Mr. Burke may fail to convince, but he never fails to charm." Two more editions appeared from Dodsley within a month, and in short order it was reprinted in Dublin as well. The *Speech* reached America first in the form of extracts published in the *Virginia Gazette* on August 10. The first full American edition, a seventy-six-page pamphlet published by Rivington in September, was advertised for sale in *Rivington's Gazette* on September 23 and in the *Pennsylvania Journal* on September 20. Because the American edition is the one that many Americans would have read, its text is printed in the present volume. It is substantially similar to that of the first edition, though Burke's nine resolutions are run before the text of the speech itself, while in the first edition they appear after the speech.

The New York edition deviates from the first edition in its use of capital letters, italics, and footnotes, and in some cases in its punctuation. It also includes a significant typesetting error on its eighteenth page involving the transposition of several lines of type, which has been corrected here by comparison against the first edition. So too have a number of other errors likely to impair comprehension. Most are minor, but some are worthy of note: 533.25, "importance" replaces "impotence"; 539.19, "£6,022,132" [the correct total] replaces "£6,024,171"; 539.23, ":—and this is a matter for meditation." deleted after "within this century."; 540.8, "seventeen" replaces "sixteen"; 541.4, "time" replaces "day"; 544.6 "your" replaces "our"; 546.36, "is a refinement on the principle of resistance; it is the dissidence of dissent; and the protestantism of the protestant religion. This religion, under a variety of denominations, agreeing in nothing but in the communion of the spirit of liberty, is predominant in most of the Northern provinces;" deleted after "in our northern colonies;"; 547.1, "strain" replaces "stream"; 548.7, "makes" replaces "marks"; 548.24, "martial" replaces "mercurial"; 549.9–10, "Circassia" replaces "Curdistan"; 549.31, "that produced" replaces "which produce"; 549.33, "desired," deleted after "might be"; 549.40, "it!" replaces "it?"; 568.14, "ever" deleted after "hardly"; 574.3, "formerly" replaces "formally"; 577.34, "office and" deleted after "their"; 581.8, "being" added after "from"; 582.17, "portion" replaces "proportion"; 584.15, "will" replaces "must"; and 587.31, "can" deleted after "they." Other alterations to the text have been preserved.

With the exception of Paine's *Common Sense*, Burke's *Speech on Conciliation*, as it is generally known, enjoyed an afterlife unrivaled among the pamphlets of the American Revolution. It was regularly reprinted throughout the nineteenth century and into the twentieth for use as a textbook in oratory and rhetoric classes, once a universal component of secondary education. One such American textbook from 1900 suggested that "it is a matter of agreement among teachers of English that Burke's *Speech on Conciliation* should be studied, not as an *end* in itself, nor simply to acquire a knowledge of it, but as a *means* toward certain definite training of the student." How definite the training was may be gleaned by the questions for the student that were keyed to nearly every phrase of the speech, as for instance: "*Unity of spirit*. Has not Burke here seized upon an immutable principle, which is that of every artistic creation, as well as that upon which a confederation like the United States reposes?"

36: [Moses Mather], *America's Appeal to the Impartial World* (1775)

This volume prints the complete text of this anonymous seventy-two-page pamphlet, which was published in the early spring of 1775 by Ebenezer Watson in Hartford, and advertised for sale in the April 3 edition of Watson's paper, the *Connecticut Courant*. Mather's authorship was suggested by Charles Evans in the fifth volume of *American Bibliography*, published in 1909, and accepted by Adams.

37: [Thomas Paine], *Common Sense* (1776)

Thomas Paine's *Common Sense* went through twenty-five editions in 1776 alone, with tens of thousands of copies sold, the scale and scope of its publication in many ways as revolutionary as its content. It appeared first on January 10, 1776, in a seventy-nine-page edition from the Philadelphia printer Robert Bell. Attributed simply "to an Englishman," the first printing of perhaps a thousand copies sold so well that Bell immediately issued a second edition without consulting the author, and more editions followed. A disgruntled Paine then engaged with William and Thomas Bradford to produce an expanded edition, first issued on February 14; demand was by now so great that the Bradfords subcontracted the presswork to two local printers, each of whom produced three thousand copies. Fueled in part by the competition between Bell and the Bradfords, a total of sixteen editions were issued in Philadelphia, including one in German, and nine more appeared quickly in other colonial towns, from Andover, Massachusetts, to Charlestown, South Carolina. Amid this swirl of publicity, with newspapers scrambling to run excerpts in their pages, the pamphlet's authorship did not long remain a mystery. But before Paine's name became public, his celebrated work was attributed to a range of prominent American patriots, even such unlikely candidates as John Adams.

The first British edition of *Common Sense* was issued by John Almon in London in May, a reprint of the Bradfords' expanded edition, and others followed in Newcastle-upon-Tyne, Edinburgh, and Dublin, as well as a French-language edition from Rotterdam. *The Monthly Review* for June took care to inform its readers that "the American editions of this pamphlet (one of which is now before us) contain, in different parts, such reflections on the king and government of Great Britain as could not have been printed here without considerable hazard: and therefore, in Mr. Almon's impression frequent chasms occur: some of these are, however, so short, and the words omitted are so obvious, that the defects may be easily supplied." (Perhaps to further insulate himself, Almon also issued *Common Sense* in conjunction with one of its many rejoinders, an American pamphlet called *Plain Truth*.) Newspapers recorded the spread of Paine's work throughout the empire. *The Gentleman's Magazine, and Historical Chronicle* for August reprinted an extract from the *Jamaica Gazette*: "A pamphlet has been circulated here under the title of 'Common Sense,' which was sent hither from America. It is written with great virulence against the English administration; and its design is to stir up the Colonists to assert their independency on the mother-country. There are many false assertions in it." Paine himself would later estimate that 150,000 copies were sold in 1776, a claim that has been uncritically repeated by many historians. Even if this number is exaggerated, the reach and influence of *Common Sense* is hard to overstate. The present volume prints the complete text of the Bradford and Bradford expanded edition.

38: [Charles Inglis], *The True Interest of America Impartially Stated* (1776)

Common Sense triggered numerous rejoinders, which appeared in newspapers and pamphlets throughout the fateful spring and summer of 1776. Perhaps the most forceful came from Charles Inglis, the third (with Thomas Bradbury Chandler and Samuel Seabury) of the troika of Anglican ministers committed to pushing back in print against patriot pamphlets. His pamphlet was first published in New York in March under the title *The Deceiver Unmasked; or, Loyalty and Interest United: In Answer to a Pamphlet entitled Common Sense*. No copies of this edition are extant, and its existence is known only because of a letter Inglis attached to a copy of the second edition which he sent to an English correspondent. It described a harrowing scene: "This Pamphlet was first printed at New York, in March 1776; & when advertised for Sale, the whole impression seized & burned by the Sons of Liberty. The Author, with much Trouble & no less Hazard, conveyed a Copy to Philadelphia, after expunging some Passages that gave greatest offence, softening others, inserting a few adapted to the Spirit of the Times, & altering the Title Page." Now called *The True Interest of America Impartially Stated*, Inglis's pamphlet was published in a seventy-one-page edition by the loyalist Philadelphia printer James Humphreys Jr. in May. A second edition was advertised for sale on July 1 in the *Pennsylvania Packet*, but no others followed. Before the year was over Humphreys fled the city, not to return until the British occupied it a year later. The present volume prints the complete text of the first Humphreys edition.

39: [Thomas Hutchinson], *Strictures upon the Declaration of the Congress* (1776)

News of the Declaration of Independence reached London on August 10, 1776, and the text of the Declaration was soon published in a number of newspapers, including the *London Chronicle* for August 15–17. Framed as a "Letter to a Noble Lord" dated October 13, 1776, Thomas Hutchinson's point-by-point refutation of the Declaration's claims and arguments was anonymously published sometime in November. The present volume prints the complete text of this edition. Hutchinson sent copies of his *Strictures* to a number of important people, including George III. His inscription in the copy presented to the king reads: "Governor Hutchinson, being prompted by zeal for your Majesty's service, and a desire to expose, and as far as may be to frustrate, the very criminal designs of the leaders of your Majesty's deluded unhappy American subjects, has wrote, and caused to be printed a small Pamphlet, which he begs leave to lay at your Majesty's feet, humbly entreating your Majesty's forgiveness of this presumption." The *Strictures* were republished in full by Almon in 1777 in *The Remembrancer; or, Impartial Repository of Public Events . . . For the Year 1776* under the heading "*The following* Strictures, *&c. having been privately circulated among a few persons, they are sent to you to be given to the public at large.*"

This volume presents the texts of the editions chosen for inclusion here without change, except in the following respects. Typographical errors have been corrected, and errata listed in the original sources have been incorporated. Instances of inverted letters, a common error in typesetting during this period, have been silently corrected.

The use of quotation marks to begin every line of a quoted passage, a convention of the time, has been dispensed with, though the inclusion of the identification of the speaker within the quotation marks, also conventional, has been retained. In those instances where a sentence clearly ends, but without terminal punctuation, a period has been added. Footnote symbols, which in the eighteenth century often preceded the text or quotation being noted, have been moved to conform to modern usage. Spelling, punctuation, capitalization, and italicization are often expressive features, and they have not been altered, even when inconsistent or irregular. Each pamphlet reflects the style of its author and publisher, and no effort has been made to standardize their use of italics for proper names and large and small capitals for emphasis. With the exception of facsimile title pages, this edition does not attempt to reproduce nontextual features of typographical design or such features of eighteenth-century typography as the long "s". The following is a list of typographical errors corrected in this edition, cited by page and line number: 16.20, Earls Barons; 19.1, together, so; 19.38, Excellenny; 22.2, same in; 31.3, to understood; 31.11, it shall; 33.15, are Resiant; 33.40, Parliament. We; 36.2–3, the (Governor); 36.24, transacts it; 39.40, Dutch. And; 45.16, Queen her; 54.28, of of; 58.34, Authoriy,; 63.16, meey; 63.29, Servies; 66.8, is holden; 66.11–12, follows, that; 71.38, Declarations; 73.2, Ebablishment; 73.19–20, ploclaimed; 75.31, so, for; 94.38, c.11. 25; 96.38, 5. G. 270.; 103.7, Westminister; 115.11, advanges, 117.20, good.; 119.32, 24 Officers; 119.35, RAIPIN.; 136.8, Viginia.; 141.18, Besies; 141.39, beformentioned; 142.37, suject; 145.1, INDEPDANT; 145.7, enterfering; 156.26, representarion; 159.11, Englnd,; 163.12, of of a; 164.38, C. 31.; 166.20, he "will; 169.7, the the; 173.16, midddle; 177.13, words."—; 180.16, go the; 197.11, Least; 197.13, to to those; 201.24, Forty *Abany*; 201.28, least; 202.13, Inhabitabitants; 206.28, least; 207.31, mentioned.".; 227.2, humilitaing; 231.9, inverate; 232.28, thcm. Do; 242.17, particalar; 246.40, committes; 251.9, manœuvre; 275.16, taken; 288.10, puting; 299.14, not,; 307.29, procceeedings,; 313.14, but in; 323.14, influence, if; 324.25, and and; 341.3, step; 341.27, comformable; 354.13, resolve; 360.18, here; 361.21, and and; 363.3, follows; 363.39, jury, If; 367.29, roit; 367.33, goverment; 368.40, *vol*,; 370.35, adventrous; 372.5, Robberties; 374.6, be. I; 383.23–24, distinquished.; 385.2, AMERCA.; 387.6, evidently absurd; 387.20, *Ships, then*; 388.7, author. But; 388.37, Heros. In; 389.17, tremendious; 390.2, is he; 391.11, themseves; 391.37, irrestable; 392.30, cannot; 393.2, soldiers; 393.17, Taking therefore,; 394.6, rotine; 394.19, instances, that; 394.20, country; 394.35, of; 395.24, scabbard,; 395.25, symtoms; 396.3, Athen,; 396.3, subjucated; 421.39, governtment.; 430.31, authority;

432.37, of of; 435.10–11, *opposition*"; 435.15, military?; 439.9, fredom; 444.6, us, The; 448.7, indepence; 449.35, follwoing; 475.22, nor; 511.24, ligitiousness; 515.9, it it; 517.19, undutiful.; 518.9, before?; 520.19, words, an; 523.14, tradionary; 534.10–11, insignificance for judging; 537.1, of which; 542.7, value of their last harvest;; 542.18, acquisitions, for; 543.17, America gentlemen say is; 544.30, as ardent; 545.16, otherwise, on; 545.17, elequent; 545.24, parchments to blind; 546.17, as no; 548.24, people more; 550.22, oporose; 551.24, averted; 551.30, by thus; 552.18, plans to; 553.8, restraint, they; 555.33, pliticians; 555.34–35, alterative; 556.16, bodies entrusted; 559.1–2, consideration, I; 561.20, countergaurd; 563.1, profund; 564.24, times were; 567.30, Chester civilized; 574.37–38, to acquisition.; 587.5, enenies; 587.20, losened;; 600.32, parliamant's; 603.24, to he; 603.27, they they; 610.16, membes; 612.22, England,"; 615.33, Whefore; 627.6, ame sl,; 627.24, decisions,?; 629.32, minister,; 631.27–28, the capital of the capital of; 632.18, a a ; 632.33, thier; 635.17, ward of; 636.11, precicious; 636.17, strugglig; 636.24, defence or; 640.19, in; 646.20, Commissiners; 664.16, parellels.; 673.17, things to; 677.18, fate) Those; 701.19, *likwise*; 710.11, enthusiam; 712.6, whech; 715.3, in founded; 715.23, angles;; 720.31, aubused; 721.10, Algernos; 725.4, nation,; 726.11, nnd; 728.34, whereever; 728.40, superspription,; 733.26, guiltless?*; 737.29, peried; 743.33–34, faciliate; 744.17, is has; 745.33, least; 748.6, If; 748.11–12 and 18, parodox; 754.36, again.; 755.31–32, purpose,; 756.4, well,; 759.19, Incase; 761.28, avoided?; 761.32, certainly; 765.22, professions; 770.33, infalibly; 797.25, supending.

Notes

In the notes below, the reference numbers denote page and line of this volume (the line count includes headings, but not rule lines). No note is made for material included in the eleventh edition of *Merriam-Webster's Collegiate Dictionary*, except for certain cases where common words and terms have specific historical meanings or inflections. Biblical quotations and allusions are keyed to the King James Version; references to Shakespeare to *The Riverside Shakespeare*, ed. G. Blackmore Evans (Boston: Houghton Mifflin, 1974). For further historical background and references to other studies, see Bernard Bailyn, *The Ideological Origins of the American Revolution* (Cambridge, MA: The Belknap Press of Harvard University Press, 1967); Bailyn, *The Ordeal of Thomas Hutchinson* (Cambridge, MA: The Belknap Press of Harvard University Press, 1974); Jack P. Greene, *The Constitutional Origins of the American Revolution* (New York: Cambridge University Press, 2010); Merrill Jensen, *The Founding of a Nation: A History of the American Revolution, 1763–1776* (New York: Oxford University Press, 1968); Pauline Maier, *From Resistance to Revolution: Colonial Radicals and the Development of American Opposition to Britain, 1765–1776* (New York: W. W. Norton & Company, 1972, 1991); Robert Middlekauff, *The Glorious Cause: The American Revolution, 1763–1789* (New York: Oxford University Press, 1982); and Gordon S. Wood, *The American Revolution: A History* (New York: Modern Library, 2002).

INTRODUCTION

xvii.28–29   John Dickinson's . . . *in Pennsylvania*] Pamphlet 11 in the companion to this volume, *The American Revolution: Writings from the Pamphlet Debate 1764–1772*.

xviii.3–4   "every kind of Filth,"] One such victim was merchant Nathaniel Rogers, a nephew of Thomas Hutchinson, whose house was twice "besmeared" before "principles of self-preservation," as he recalled it, finally led him to accede to the will of the Boston crowd.

xviii.15   "contrary to . . . Commerce."] From a May 13, 1769, circular letter from Hillsborough to the colonial governors.

xviii.38–40   "as a mark . . . the Colonies."] North's March 5, 1770, remarks made announcing the motion for partial repeal of the Townshend duties were described the next day in a letter, quoted here, from William Samuel Johnson,

Connecticut's agent in London, to Jonathan Trumbull, the colony and later state governor (1769–84).

xix.35   "Boston Pamphlet,"] Pamphlet 19 in the companion to this volume.

xx.20–25   "This is . . . an Epocha in History."] Diary entry, December 17, 1773, from Gordon S. Wood, ed., *John Adams: Revolutionary Writings 1755–1775* (New York: The Library of America, 2011), 286.

xx.35–36   "that we are in . . . vigour."] As recorded in *The Parliamentary History of England from the Earliest Period to 1803* (London, 1813), XVII, 1171.

xxi.23–25   "dangerous to . . . all America."] From Article 10 of the Suffolk Resolves, September 8, 1774.

20: SPEECHES OF GOVERNOR HUTCHINSON WITH ANSWERS FROM THE MASSACHUSETTS GENERAL ASSEMBLY

2.11   1769 *Remarks.*] Pamphlet 17 in the companion to this volume.

6.10–14   "when a Nation . . . its ancient Possessions."] From Emmerich de Vattel, *Le droit des gens; ou, Principes de la loi naturelle, Appliqués à la conduite et aux affaires des nations et des souverains* (1758; *The Law of Nations; or, Principles of the Law of Nature, Applied to the Conduct and Affairs of Nations and Sovereigns*, London, 1759), Bk. I, ch. xviii, sect. 210.

7.10–11   a Number of Inhabitants . . . Towns in the Province] In 1768, Boston had convened an assembly of representatives from nearly a hundred towns of the colony without the authorization of the royal governor, Francis Bernard. In the summer of 1772, Boston continued its defiance by requesting that the provincial legislature be called into session. When the governor, now Hutchinson, responded that convening the legislature was the executive's prerogative, Samuel Adams (1722–1803) proposed that Boston establish a committee of correspondence asking the other towns to communicate their sense of American rights. Boston published its report in the "Boston Pamphlet"; half the towns in the colony responded in short order, forming their own committees of correspondence and echoing Boston's claim that officials in Britain were plotting to enslave Americans.

12.30   *his Majesty's Council*] The council was the middle branch in the colonial governments, corresponding to the House of Lords in England's mixed constitution. In the other royal colonies the councils were appointed by the Crown, but in Massachusetts the members of the council were elected annually by both houses of the legislature, that is, by the entire General Court, with the governor's consent—a difference that many British officials believed made the Massachusetts council too susceptible to popular pressure.

14.20–26   in a former ministry . . . rejected accordingly] A reference to the Grenville ministry (April 1763–July 1765) which, in the eyes of many colonists and their supporters in Parliament, had been disingenuous in its interactions with colonial agents in the year between its first announcement of a proposed stamp tax on the colonies and the passage of the Stamp Act in March 1765, professing an openness to counterproposals belied by its actions. In a February 15, 1765, speech in the House of Commons, Henry Seymour Conway (1721–1795), Member for Thetford, protested Parliament's refusal to even hear the American petitions, recalling that at the "last Session of Parliament we came to a Resolution, that it might be proper to Tax the Americans; at that Time, it was thrown out.—I am sure I understood it so, that the Intention of this Resolution was, to give the Americans Time to represent their Inability, or to suggest the Propriety of a less burthensome Tax than the Stamp Duty: This time has been given; the Representations are come from the Colonies; and shall we shut our Ears against that Information, which, with an Affectation of Candour, we allotted sufficient Time to reach us?" After urging the House not to use the prohibition of petitions against money bills ("What is this Rule?") as a pretext for ignoring American concerns, Conway asked "from whom, unless from themselves, are we to learn the Circumstances of the Colonies, and the fatal Consequences that may attend the imposing of this Tax"?

16.17   The Statute of the 34th of Edward I] Citations to parliamentary statutes are made with an abbreviation that designates the year of the reign, or regnal year, in which the measure was passed, in this case 1297. *De Tallagio non Concedendo* (Latin: On not allowing tallage, or royal taxes), a secondary charter of obscure origins that confirmed and reinforced the Magna Carta, was not formally recognized as a statute of Parliament until it was cited prominently as such in the 1628 Petition of Right (see Chronology).

17.18   which established its Constitution] Although the seventeenth-century charters that the Crown had granted to individuals and groups to settle colonies had been documents that *created* power, by the 1760s in the eyes of most colonists they had become defensive documents that *limited* power, in effect, rudimentary written constitutions. Viewing the colonial charters in this way, Americans naturally turned to written constitutions when organizing their newly independent states in 1776.

18.40–19.1   "Letters Patent must be . . . together,"] A well-known legal maxim, recorded in these same words in *A Law Grammar; or, Rudiments of the Law* (London, 1744) by legal scholar and literary critic Giles Jacob (1686–1744). Jacob, in turn, cites Sir Edward Coke, *The First Part of the Institutes of the Laws of England* (first published London, 1628).

24.2–5   *Mr.* Adams . . . *Col.* Stockbridge] The House committee charged with replying to the governor's speech included House clerk Samuel Adams, John Hancock (1737–1793), and John Bacon (1738–1820), all of Boston; Jerathmiel (or Jerathmeel) Bowers (d. 1795?) of Swansea; Joseph Hawley (1723–1788) of Northampton; Richard Derby Jr. (1712–1783) of Salem; William Phillips (1722–1804) of Boston; Ebenezer Thayer Jr. (1721–1794) of Braintree; and David Stockbridge of Hanover. It was Hawley, dissatisfied with the committee's first draft of the reply, who insisted on bringing John Adams

(1735–1826) in to consult on the effort. Although he was not currently a member of the House, Adams's legal expertise was especially desired for the portions of the reply dealing with the constitutional nature of the empire and the colonies' position in it. He, Bowers, and Phillips were elected by the House to serve on the council in May 1773, shortly after the conclusion of the debate recorded in this pamphlet. All three were vetoed by Hutchinson, though the governor consented to the election of Hancock and four others who, he said, "were of the same sentiments with the others; yet had they been rejected also, there would not have been a quorum."

24.27–31   "have, ever had . . . in all Cases whatever,"] Quoting from the Declaratory Act of 1766.

24.31–32   another Revenue Act was made] The Revenue Act of 1767, one of the Townshend Acts.

26.10–11   a Right which . . . by the Pope] In 1493 Pope Alexander VI issued a series of bulls designating all lands to the east of a pole-to-pole line running 100 leagues west of the Azores to Portugal, and all lands to the west of the line to Spain.

26.31   Attainder of Sir Walter] With the accession of King James I to the English throne in 1603, Walter Raleigh was accused of treason and condemned to the Tower of London, where he lived for most of the rest of his life, until he was beheaded in 1618.

28.14   *Imperium in Imperio*] Latin: government within a government. Writers on all sides of the imperial debate subscribed to the conventional wisdom that it was impossible to have more than one locus of sovereignty within a single political entity. Overcoming this fundamental assumption of eighteenth-century political science was one of the greatest achievements of the Revolutionary generation in America.

28.19   But further to show . . .] This is one of the passages that shows the influence of Edward Bancroft's *Remarks*, which also presents the statements of James I and Charles I quoted here.

29.5–7   an Act . . . sent it there by Lord Colpepper] One of the three measures drafted by the Privy Council that Thomas, Lord Culpeper (1635–1689), brought with him to Virginia when he assumed the governorship in person in 1680. (Culpeper had been appointed to the post in 1677, but like most governors of the Old Dominion had been content to be an absentee until being pressured by the Crown to make the transit.) The other two offered a free and general pardon after Bacon's Rebellion (see Chronology for 1676) and provided for a more generous naturalization process. The clause quoted here is found in all three acts. A similar argument to that made by the committee here is made in Richard Bland, *An Inquiry into the Rights of the British Colonies* (Williamsburg, 1766), Pamphlet 8 in the companion to this volume.

29.17   the old Charter] The Virginia Company was issued three charters, the first in April 1609, the second in May 1609, and the third in March 1612. The last of these was revoked in May 1624, when the Crown assumed direct control of the colony.

30.11–12   *Quod ab initio . . .* said *Grotius.*] Bancroft had presented this excerpt (in Latin) from book 3 of Hugo Grotius's *De Jure Belli ac Pacis* (1625; *The Laws of War and Peace*, 1654) in his *Remarks.* Grotius (1583–1645) was a Dutch jurist whose work contributed to the development of international law. Many subsequent English translations of *De Jure Belli ac Pacis* were entitled *The Rights of War and Peace.*

30.17–20   The celebrated Author . . . at Pleasure."] Vattel, *The Law of Nations*, Bk. II, ch. xvii, sect. 265.

31.5–8   If, says an eminent Lawyer, . . . like Liberties."] Sir Henry Finch (c. 1558–1625), *Law, or, A Discourse Thereof; in Four Books* (1627), Bk. I, ch. iv, sect. 99. Finch's Law, as this work was popularly known, was the most important exposition of the common law prior to the publication of William Blackstone's *Commentaries on the Laws of England* in 1765.

31:10   the first Charter to this Colony] The Massachusetts Bay Charter of 1629.

33.29–31   Appeals from the Courts . . . the House of Lords] The House of Lords functioned as the kingdom's highest appellate court during this period.

34.9   some Parts of your own History] The passages quoted in this paragraph are from the first volume of Hutchinson's *History of the Colony of Massachusetts-Bay, from the First Settlement Thereof in 1628, until . . . 1691,* which was published in Boston in 1764. The second volume, which took the history to 1750, was published in 1767. A second edition of the full work appeared in London in 1768.

34.25   quoted in the Margin] That is, in a footnote.

35.7–15   "They apprehended . . . strictly attended."] In the *History* Hutchinson quotes from an October 2, 1678, letter from the Massachusetts General Court to Charles II, forwarded through the colony's agents William Stoughton and Peter Bulkley.

35.26–27   your Excellency's Collection . . . lately published.] Hutchinson, *A Collection of Original Papers Relative to the History of the Colony of Massachusetts-Bay* (Boston, 1769). The English colonial administrator Edward Randolph (1632–1703) was a much hated figure in Massachusetts for his role in abrogating the original charter in 1684.

36.23   Mr. Neal's History of New-England] Daniel Neal, *The History of New-England Containing an Impartial Account of the Civil and Ecclesiastical Affairs . . . to the Year of our Lord, 1700* (2 vols., London, 1720).

36.25   the present Charter] The Massachusetts Charter of 1691.

37.35   says the same Author] Vattel. The passage that follows is from *The Law of Nations*, Bk. I, ch. iii, sect. 34.

38.27–31   "seeing just Cause . . . *beyond their Reach*."] Hutchinson's *History* reproduced in an appendix the Massachusetts General Court's 1651 petition to Parliament, quoted here. The "then Bishop" referred to is William Laud, archbishop of Canterbury, 1633–45.

44.27   anonimous Pamphlet] Bancroft's *Remarks*.

45.13–14   *as of our Manor of East Greenwich*] This royal estate, located some four miles below London Bridge, was conventionally referred to in legal documents of the era, including in most of the colonial charters, which stipulated that the colony in question is to be held of the king of England "as of the Manor of East Greenwich in the County of Kent, in free and common soccage and not *in capite* or by knight's service." This formula dates to the middle of the sixteenth century, when the manor was the principal royal residence, and its use in the colonial charters indicated the extent to which crown officials viewed American lands as simply an extension of English soil.

45.30   your System] That is, the structure of your argument.

45.39   the Council at Plimouth in Devon] See Chronology for 1606.

46.27   one of the Secretaries of State declared] Sir George Calvert (1579–1632), a Stuart courtier who served as a secretary of state from 1619 to 1625 (when he became the 1st Baron Baltimore), was likely expressing more than his own personal opinion when he told Parliament that it "was not fit to make any laws here for those countries, which were not as yet annexed to the crown."

47.9   Ship Money] See Chronology for 1635–37.

47.22   Sir Edward Coke] Coke (1552–1634) was the most prominent English jurist of his age and an architect of the 1628 Petition of Right. His defense of the common law in the face of Stuart claims of royal prerogative made him a hero for eighteenth-century Whigs, for whom his four-part *Institutes of the Laws of England* was an essential, oft-cited resource.

49.12   that high Court] A vestigial designation for Parliament, reflecting its medieval origins.

49.37   I believe has never been said] Coke, in his comments on Dr. Bonham's Case (1610), had in fact maintained that "in many Cases, the Common Law will controll Acts of Parliament, and sometimes adjudge them to be utterly void." *The Eighth Part of the Reports of Sir Edward Coke, Kt.* (London, 1727), 118.

50.2   Wales and Calais] Wales had been conquered by England by the end of the thirteenth century, but was not represented in Parliament until 1535. The French port of Calais was an English possession from 1347 until 1558, but enjoyed representation in Parliament for only the last twenty-two years of that period.

50.4   Guernsey, Jersey, Alderney, &c.] The Channel Islands were part of the Duchy of Normandy when its duke, William, following his conquest of England in 1066, became William I. They remain a self-governing possession of the English Crown, owing allegiance to the monarch in his or her capacity as the Duke of Normandy.

50.20–24   "being Feudatory . . . Jurisdiction at Home."] The "very great Authority" was William Murray, Lord Mansfield (1705–1793), Chief Justice of the King's Bench, and the passage quoted is from his decision in the 1759 case *Rex* v. *Cowle*, as recorded in Sir James Burrow, comp., *Reports of Cases Adjudged in the Court of King's Bench* (5 vols., London, 1766), II, 851. The "Counties Palatine" refers to Chester and Durham, which were established in the eleventh century as semi-autonomous buffer states on the western (Welsh) and northern (Scottish) borders of England. Chester maintained its own parliament until it was absorbed into England and granted representation at Westminster in 1543. Durham gained permanent representation in Parliament in 1675. The Latin *jura regalia* means royal rights, or rights held by others similar in nature to royal rights.

50.34–35   the Statute of 7th and 8th] An Act for Preventing Frauds and Regulating Abuses in the Plantation Trade, also known as the Plantation Trade Act of 1695.

50.36–37   Mr. Dummer . . . Defence of the Charter] Jeremiah Dummer (1681–1739), Harvard 1699, was agent in London for Massachusetts, 1710–21, and Connecticut, 1712–30, and author of *A Defence of the New-England Charters* (London, 1721), which John Adams considered "one of our most classical American productions."

52.27   the King's Commissioners] In 1664, in an effort to reaffirm his control over the colonies, Charles II sent four commissioners to New England to investigate the governments there, settle boundary disputes, secure compliance with the Navigation Acts, and enlist the colonies' aid in the war against the Dutch. Massachusetts refused to comply fully with the commissioners' mandate that all Christians of orthodox belief be admitted to membership in the colony's churches, and three of the four commissioners recommended the revocation of its charter.

53.16   memorable Order of 1642] In which the Long Parliament exempted English or colonial vessels with goods to or from England from any customs imposed either there or in New England, stipulating that the act was to remain in effect until Parliament ordered otherwise.

55.11   *Act of Parliament made in the 15th Year*] An Act for the Encouragement of Trade, better known as the Navigation Act of 1663. (Though Charles II was in exile until 1660, his regnal years are measured from the date of the execution of his father in 1649.)

55.20   an Act of Parliament had passed in 1741] Public land banks were established in many colonies in the eighteenth century (South Carolina had the first in 1712, nine other colonies followed suit by 1737) as a means of infusing liquidity into specie-starved colonial economies. The banks loaned paper money to individuals who put up collateral in the form of real estate. The Crown generally viewed such measures unfavorably and in 1720, chastened by the experience of the South Sea Bubble (see Chronology), it instructed royal governors to suspend the operation of land banks pending review in the Privy Council, though many continued to function until 1740. Massachusetts investors established a short-lived private land bank in 1741, only to have it invalidated by the law referred to here, An Act for Restraining and Preventing Several Unwarrantable Schemes and Undertakings in His Majesty's Colonies and Plantations in America.

55.28–29 an Act of Parliament made in the first Year of Queen Ann] The demise of the Crown Act of 1702, the second measure passed under the new monarch. It remains in effect for England and Wales.

55.34 Governor Dudley] Massachusetts-born Joseph Dudley (1647–1720) was governor of the colony from 1702 to 1715.

61.9–12 Mr. Hancock, . . . Capt. Gardner] Though not included on the committee roster for the House's second reply to the governor, Samuel Adams continued to play a shaping role, as did his cousin, nonmember John Adams. The rest of the committee was made up of returning members Hancock and Phillips, now joined by Nathaniel Gorham (1738–1796) of Charlestown, Abraham Fuller (1720–1794) of Newton, Jonathan Greenleaf (1723–1807) of Newburyport, William Heath (1737–1814) of Roxbury, Stephen Nye (1720–1810) of Sandwich, Jonathan Brown (1724–1797), and Thomas Gardner of Cambridge (1724–1775, from wounds suffered at the battle of Bunker Hill).

62.21–24 "a State of perpetual . . . extremely defective."] This quotation combines a number of phrases from the first volume of The History of the Reign of the Emperor Charles V (3 vols., London, 1769), by the popular Scottish historian William Robertson (1721–1793). An edition of this work was published in Philadelphia in 1770.

62.24–63.6 "A Constitution so . . . eradicated its Principles.] This section in particular reveals the influence of John Adams, as the quotations in this paragraph were drawn from his Dissertation on the Canon and Feudal Law, a four-part series published in the Boston Gazette, May–October 1765, and later collected in book form in London in 1768. The first of the quotes here paraphrases the opening passage of the essay "Introduction of the Feudal Law into Scotland" by Scottish philosopher and jurist Henry Home, Lord Kames (1692–1782). Adams's personal library included the third edition of Kames's Essays upon Several Subjects Concerning British Antiquities (Edinburgh, 1761). The second is from Jean-Jacques Rousseau, A Treatise on the Social Contract (London, 1764), Bk. III, ch. xv. Both are used by Adams in the closing paragraph of the second installment of the *Dissertation*, while the remainder of this paragraph paraphrases portions of the first installment.

63.15–16 "in Reality a meer Fiction of our English Tenures."] Blackstone, *Commentaries on the Laws of England*, Bk. II, ch. iv. This seminal work was first published in four volumes, 1765–69, by the Clarendon Press at Oxford University.

63.34–35 "The Lord was . . . over all his Feudatories,"] Ibid.

65.1–5 "there being no Precedent . . . the Law of Nations."] These remarks by Sir Edwin Sandys (1561–1629) in re Calvin's Case (1608), also known as the Case of the Postnati or the Case of the Union Between Scotland and England, which established that a subject of James VI of Scotland, born after he had become James I of England, was entitled to English rights, were taken from *Cases Collect & Report per Sir Fra. Moore Chavelier, Serjeant del Ley* (London, 1688), a legal compendium conventionally referred to as Moore's Reports. This reference is another indicator of John Adams's authorship of the House's reply. Reflecting on the debate with the governor four decades after the fact, Adams recalled that "Mr. Hutchinson really made a meagre figure in that dispute. He had waded beyond his depth. He had wholly misunderstood the legal doctrine of allegiance. . . . I had quoted largely from a law authority which no man in Massachusetts, at that time, had ever read. Hutchinson and all his law counsels were in fault; they could catch no scent. They dared not deny it, lest the book should be produced to their confusion. It was humorous enough to see how Hutchinson wriggled to evade it. He found nothing better to say than that it was 'the artificial reasoning of Lord Coke.' The book was Moore's Reports. The owner of it, for alas! master, it was borrowed, was a buyer, but not a reader, of books. It had been Mr. Gridley's [Jeremiah Gridley (1702–1767), one of the leading lawyers of Boston and a mentor to Adams]." Adams to William Tudor, March 8, 1817.

65.23–24 as quoted by a very able Lawyer in this Country] Referring to James Otis's *The Rights of the British Colonies Asserted and Proved* (Boston, 1764), Pamphlet 3 in the companion to this volume, where the same passages from Pufendorf and Grotius appear.

65.40–66.3 "If a King go . . . *his Laws are confined*."] From Moore's *Reports*.

66.28–37 "Every Subject is . . . detestable Consequents."] From *The Seventh Part of the Reports of Sir Edward Coke, Kt.* (1608).

66.37–39 The Judges of England, . . . declared] The remaining quotations in this paragraph are from Moore's *Reports*.

69.11 The Account published by Sir Fernando Gorges] *A Briefe Narration of the Originall Undertakings of the Advancement of Plantations into the Parts of America* (London, 1658).

70.4–5 that excellent Defence] See note 50.36–37.

70.19–22   "the Laws of England . . . in Parliament."] Under its original
charter, the Massachusetts Bay Colony had enjoyed a remarkably free hand,
and was under no legal obligation even to transmit its laws to England for
review. This had begun to change by the 1670s, when Edward Randolph and
other imperial officials, irritated by the colony's refusal to obey the Navigation
Acts, administer proper oaths, and afford toleration to Episcopalians, and by
its unauthorized purchase of Maine, determined on review that many of the
colony's acts were repugnant to the laws of England and threatened revocation of the charter. In 1678, in an attempt to achieve compliance with the
Navigation Acts without acknowledging Parliament's right to legislate for
the colony, the Massachusetts House issued through their agents in London
the defiant statement quoted from here while passing a law adopting "the said
acts of navigation and trade" under its own authority.

70.29–35   "It seems reasonable . . . within the Realm."] From Dummer's
Defence.

71.18–19   a Letter of Mr. *Stoughton*] Massachusetts agent William Stoughton's December 1, 1677, letter is reproduced in Hutchinson's *History*.

73.15   There had been a Revolution here as well] See Chronology for 1688–
89.

73.24   as a learned Author observes] Possibly referring to Bancroft's *Remarks*, in which a similar point is made. See page 713 in the companion to this
volume.

74.39–40   this Province pass'd an Act] An Act for the More Speedy Finishing
of the Land-Bank or Manufactory Scheme. See note 55.20.

75.7   a learned Writer on the Laws of Nature] Vattel.

75.24–37   "The lawful Power . . . before consented."] These passages from
Bk. I, sect. 10 of *The Lawes of Ecclesiastical Polity* (1594), an influential work
by the English theologian Richard Hooker (1554?–1600), appear as a footnote
in ch. xi, 134 sect. of the second of John Locke's *Two Treatises of Government*
(1689).

82.11   Burrow's Reports] See note 50.20–24.

21: [THOMAS JEFFERSON], A SUMMARY VIEW OF THE RIGHTS

88.6   Cicero de Of. L. 1, C. 34.] Cicero, *De Officiis* (On Duties), Bk. I, ch.
xxxiv.

91.37   their Saxon ancestors] So taken was Jefferson with the Saxon origins
of English liberties that in his 1776 proposal for revising the laws of Virginia
he suggested that the state return to "that happy system of our ancestors, the
wisest and most perfect ever yet devised by the wit of man, as it stood before
the 8th century." Jefferson's thinking about the Saxon inheritance may have
been influenced by an anonymous pamphlet written in defense of Parliament's

right to tax the American colonies entitled *An Historical Essay on the English Constitution* (London, 1771). Long thought to be the work of Allan Ramsay (author of Pamphlet 12 in the companion to this volume), this pamphlet is now attributed to a Yorkshireman named Obadiah Hulme.

92.18 Not a shilling] Jefferson made alterations to his personal copy of the pamphlet, which will be indicated in the notes that follow. He changed this phrase to "No shilling."

92.28 Portugal, and] Struck out in Jefferson's copy.

93.24 parted] Altered to "parceled" in Jefferson's copy.

93.25 followers of their fortunes,*] In Jefferson's copy the footnote referred to here is struck out and the following substituted: "in 1621 Nova Scotia was granted by James I. to Sir Wm. Alexander. in 1632 Maryland was granted by Charles I. to Ld Baltimore. in 1664 New York was granted by Charles II. to the Duke of York, so also was New Jersey which the D. of York conveied again to Ld. Berkeley & Sir George Carteret. so also were the Delaware counties which the same Duke conveyed again to Wm. Penn. in 1665 the country including North & South Carolina, Georgia & the Floridas was granted by Charles II. to the E. of Clarendon, Sir John Coleton, & Sir William Berkley. in 1681 Pennsylvania was granted by Charles II. to William Penn." In the footnote as printed, "14. C. 2" refers to 1663, the fourteenth year of the reign of Charles II.

93.26 were] Altered to "was" in Jefferson's copy.

94.37 Cape Finesterre] Cape Finisterre, the northern- and westernmost point in Spain, was often used in British trade regulations as a line of demarcation between northern European and Mediterranean markets or customs zones, the latter including Spain and Portugal.

94.38–39 12. c. 2. c. 18. . . . 6. G. 2. c. 13.] In addition to regnal years, citations to parliamentary statutes like the ones Jefferson makes here also designate the chapter, a sequential ordering of public acts passed in a given parliamentary session. Thus 12 c. 2 c. 18. refers to the Navigation Act of 1660, the eighteenth act of Parliament in the twelfth year of the reign of Charles II. The other acts listed here are the Navigation Acts of 1663 and 1672; the Plantation Trade Act of 1695, passed in a session that extended from the seventh to the eighth year of the reign of William and Mary; the Woollen Act of 1699; an unspecified act passed during the reign of Queen Anne, any one of several setting duties on imports and exports; and the Molasses Act of 1733.

95.38 5. G. 2.] The Hat Act of 1732.

95.39 23. G. 2. c. 29.] The Iron Act of 1750.

96.22–24 accommodating his majesty's ministers and favourites with . . . easy office.] Jefferson refers disparagingly to the Post Office Act of 1710. He had at this point yet to make the acquaintance of Benjamin Franklin, deputy postmaster general for the colonies from 1753 to 1774.

96.38   5. G. 2. c. 7.] An Act for the More Easy Recovery of Debts in His Majesty's Plantations and Colonies in America (1732).

97.19–20   the reign] Changed to "his reign" in Jefferson's copy.

97.26–27   the common feelings] Changed to simply "the feelings" in Jefferson's copy.

97.34   4. G. 3. c. 15.] The Sugar Act of 1764.

97.35   5. G. 3. c. 12.] The Stamp Act of 1765.

97.36   6. G. 3. c. 12.] The Declaratory Act of 1766.

97.37   7. G. 3.] The Revenue Act of 1767.

97.38   7. G. 3. c. 59.] The New York Suspending Act of 1767, terminating all legislative functions of the New York Assembly until it fully complied with all the requirements of the Quartering Act of 1765.

98.12   hold] Altered to "withhold" in Jefferson's copy.

98.31   New England] Altered to "Massachusetts" in Jefferson's copy.

99.14–15   knighthood] In a note on a manuscript copy of the *Summary View*, Jefferson wrote "alluding to the knighting of Sir Francis Bernard." Francis Bernard was royal governor of Massachusetts Bay from 1760 to 1769, and for many American colonists he symbolized much that was wrong with the governance of the British Empire. He is the author of Pamphlet 2 in the companion to this volume.

99.22   subsistence by its charities.] Boston was the beneficiary of a massive outpouring of support from other communities in Massachusetts and beyond in the wake of the closure of its port. Donations came from as far away as Savannah, Georgia, which sent sixty-three barrels of rice and £122 sterling, with the message that "there are many among us, who sincerely espouse the great cause contended for by you; & who ardently wish that the noble stand you have made in defense of these rights, which as men, and British subjects we are entitled to, may be crowned with success."

100.38   14. G. 3.] The Dockyards, &c. Protection Act of 1772 made arson in the king's naval yards punishable by death. It remains so, statutorily, even after the abolition of the death penalty in the United Kingdom in 1965.

101.20   modestly declined the exercise] Though under the English constitution the assent of the monarch was required for an act to become law, no ruler had vetoed any parliamentary legislation since 1708. The same forbearance did not apply to the acts of the colonial legislatures, however, which were regularly set aside by royal governors or crown officials in England.

102.2   African] Altered to "British" in Jefferson's copy.

102.3–4   this infamous practice.] Jefferson is here objecting to the slave trade.

not to slavery itself. By the 1740s the bulk of the growth in Virginia's slave population was coming from natural reproduction, and further importation was increasingly seen as superfluous, if not dangerous.

102.27–28   his majesty's] Struck, and "the" substituted in Jefferson's copy.

103.6   Tresilian] Sir Robert Tresilian (d. 1388), Chief Justice of the King's Bench.

103.11–13   Since the establishment . . . at the glorious revolution] In Jefferson's copy these clauses are changed to "Since the reign of the second William however, under whom the British constitution, was settled . . ."

103.19   constitution] In a note on his manuscript copy, Jefferson wrote "Since this period the king has several times dissolved the parliament a few weeks before its expiration, merely as an assertion of right." And "On further inquiry I find two instances of dissolutions before the Parliament would, of itself, have been at an end: viz., the Parliament called to meet August 24, 1698, was dissolved by King William, December 19, 1700, and a new one called, to meet November 11, 1701, which was also dissolved November 30, 1701."

104.13   proper] Another note to Jefferson's manuscript copy: "insert 'and the frame of government thus dissolved should the people take upon them to lay the throne of your majesty prostrate, or to discontinue their connection with the British empire, none will be so bold as to decide against the right of the efficacy of such avulsion.'"

105.15   farmers] Struck, and "laborers" substituted in Jefferson's copy.

106.25–26   expressly made the civil subordinate to the military.] Most dramatically by installing Thomas Gage, commander of the British army in America, as governor of Massachusetts.

107.25   and] Struck, and "on" substituted in Jefferson's copy.

22: [JAMES WILSON], ON LEGISLATIVE AUTHORITY

109.27–28   "that our provincial . . . authorities in our colonies."] From "Novanglus No. VII," March 6, 1775, in *John Adams: Revolutionary Writings 1755–1775*, 512.

109.38–39   "from the necessity . . . of both countries."] From the Declaration and Resolves of the First Continental Congress, October 14, 1774.

113.15   such a Line does not exist] Just as the Massachusetts House committee had, Wilson accepted the logic of the English doctrine of sovereignty—that Parliament's power could not be divided, that it was impossible to have an *imperio in imperium*. In this way a British argument in favor of parliamentary supremacy was, in the context of the pamphlet debate traced here, being transformed by the colonists into a rationale for defiance. But independence did not resolve the problem of sovereignty for Americans. During the debate over ratification of the new federal Constitution in 1787–88, anti-federalists immediately revived the issue, asking where the supreme final law-making authority would rest in the new government. Since sovereignty could not be divided, they warned that the new federal government would sooner or later assume all power to itself. Much as the colonists had in the imperial debate, supporters of the Constitution struggled to answer this charge, trying to divide what seemed indivisible. Finally Wilson offered a simple but extraordinary solution. Unlike some of his fellow Federalists, he did not try to deny the doctrine of sovereignty; instead he reconceived it, relocating ultimate authority in the people at large. For Wilson the people were not just the source of all political legitimacy, which every good Whig believed, but in fact the final supreme lawmaking authority in America. This breakthrough helped to justify a host of American constitutional innovations, including federalism, the distinction between a constitution and legislation, judicial review, constitutional conventions, the process of ratification, and the presence of popular representation throughout all the institutions of government. It also provided the theoretical foundation for later initiatives designed to foster direct democracy, including the primaries, referendums, processes of recall, and ballot initiatives.

116.14–17   "That there is . . . sovereignty reside:"] From the first volume of Blackstone's *Commentaries*. Despite Blackstone's endorsement of the sovereignty of Parliament, the *Commentaries* were immediately popular in the colonies and became a bible for American lawyers in the late eighteenth century.

117.35   BURL.] This footnote offers a paraphrase from the second volume of *The Principles of Natural and Politic Law* (2 vols., London, 1747–50) by Swiss legal and political theorist Jean-Jacques Burlamaqui (1694–1748), an influential work that was translated into six languages and often cited by American writers.

117.38   Dissert. on parties.] *A Dissertation upon Parties: In Several Letters to Caleb D'Anvers, Esq.* (London, 1735) by Henry St. John, Lord Bolingbroke (1678–1751), Tory politician and theorist whose works were widely read in America. The nineteen letters that comprise the *Dissertation* were first published, 1733–34, in *The Craftsman*, an anti-Walpole periodical Bolingbroke produced with William Pulteney (1684–1764).

118.21–22   says Montisquieu] Montesquieu's *The Spirit of the Laws*, first translated into English in 1750, was one of the most influential works of political theory in both the French- and English-speaking worlds of the eighteenth century. Wilson quotes here from Bk. II, ch. ii.

118.28–29   of the last consequence] Today we would say of the first consequence.

118.32   2. WILLIAM's reports.] William Peere Williams, ed., *Reports of Cases Argued and Determined in the High Court of Chancery* (2 vols., London, 1740).

118.33   4. Institute.] Sir Edward Coke, *The Fourth Part of the Institutes of the Laws of England* (1644).

118.35–36   Lord RAYMOND's reports.] *Reports of Cases Argued and Adjudged in the Court of King's Bench and Common Pleas* (London, 1732), by Robert Raymond (1673–1733), Lord Chief Justice of the King's Bench.

119.32   2. Geo. 2. c. 24.] An Act for the More Effectual Prevention of Corrupt Practices at Parliamentary Elections (1728).

119.35   RAPIN] Paul de Rapin-Thoyras, *Histoire D'Angleterre* (10 vols., 1723–27), translated to English as *The History of England, as well Ecclesiastical as Civil* (15 vols., 1728–32).

120.21–23   All such officers . . . the House of Commons.] Per a provision of the 1701 Act of Settlement.

121.15   especially in great emergencies] Many of Wilson's readers would have perceived here an allusion to William Pitt, who had become a national hero during the Seven Years' War, guiding the British war effort as leader of the House of Commons.

122.29   that called by King Charles I, in the year 1640] The so-called Long Parliament decided that it could be dissolved only by a vote of its members, and thus continued to sit until it was purged by Cromwell in 1648; it was restored in 1658 in order to legalize the Restoration of Charles II and its own final dissolution.

123.39   The Earls of Clarendon and Southampton.] Edward Hyde, 1st Earl of Clarendon (1609–1674), and Thomas Wriothesley, 4th Earl of Southampton (1607–1667), English statesmen who were important in making possible the peaceful restoration of Charles II in 1660.

124.8   the Statute 6. W. and M. c. 2.] The Triennial Act of 1694, which determined that Parliament would meet annually and hold elections for a new Parliament at least every three years. The resultant frequent electioneering and political instability led to the Septennial Act of 1716, changing the electoral requirement to at least every seven years. Most royal governors in the colonies were under no such restrictions, and some kept pliant legislatures sitting for many years without elections. This abuse resulted in nearly all the new Revolutionary state constitutions drafted in 1776 requiring annual elections of their houses of representatives.

126.35   Bacon's Abridgment] Matthew Bacon, *A New Abridgment of the Law* (5 vols., London, 1736).

126.36   "per communitatem . . . concess."] Latin: "granted by the community of honest Englishmen." The passage is from the fourth volume of Coke's *Institutes*.

128.38–40   It is self-evident . . . derive from them.] From a 1716 speech against the Septennial Act by Tory M.P. William Shippen (1673–1743), as recorded in volume six of *The History and Proceedings of the House of Commons from the Restoration to the Preset Time* (14 vols., London, 1742).

131.11 as my Lord Bacon says] Francis Bacon, *The Proficience and Advancement of Learning, Divine and Human* (1605), Bk. II, ch. xxiii, sect. 49.

132.11–12 *Gascoigne*, and *Guienne.*"] The provinces of Gascony and Guyenne in the southwest of France were under the suzerainty of the kings of England from the twelfth through the mid-fifteenth centuries.

132.37 4. Modern Reports. . . . Calvin's case.] *Modern Reports: Being a Collection of Several Cases Argued and Adjudged in the Court of King and Queen's Bench, in the Second . . . Seventh Year of King William* (4 vols., London, 1757), IV, 225, and *The Seventh Part of the Reports of Sir Edward Coke, Kt.* (London, 1727), which includes a lengthy discussion of Calvin's Case (see note 65.1–5).

134.39 SALKELD's reports, 411. Modern Reports, 215.] In *Blankard* v. *Galdy* (1694) the court ruled that the municipal laws of England do not extend to Jamaica: "the laws by which the people were governed before the conquest of the island, do bind them till new laws are given, and Acts of Parliament made here since the conquest do not bind them unless they are particularly named." Wilson cites descriptions of the case in *Modern Reports* and *Reports of Cases Adjudged in the Court of King's Bench* (2 vols., London, 1717), a posthumously published edition of the casebook of William Salkeld (1671–1715), chief justice of the Great Sessions for the counties of Carmarthen, Cardigan, and Pembroke.

135.15–16 Lord Chief Justice Holt] Sir John Holt (1642–1710) had been instrumental in creating the legal framework of the Glorious Revolution and was rewarded with appointment as chief justice in 1689.

135.23–24 another was determined] *Smith* v. *Brown and Cooper* (c. 1705), in which Holt ruled that trover (a common law action for the recovery of personal property illegally withheld) was not available to the plaintiff, who sought to collect £20 owed on the sale of an African slave to the defendants in England. Holt's pronouncement came in the form of advice to the unsuccessful plaintiff: "As soon as a Negro comes into England, he becomes free; and one may be a Villein in England, but not a Slave: You should have averred in the Declaration, that the Sale of the Negro was in Virginia, and by the laws of that Country Negroes are saleable; for the Laws of England do not extend to Virginia."

136.27 Foster's Crown Law] *A Report of Some Proceedings on the Commission for the Trial of Rebels in the Year 1746, . . . and of Other Crown Cases* (1762), compiled by Sir Michael Foster (1689–1763), judge of the King's Bench.

140.39 Bacon's works] "The Argument of Sir Francis Bacon, Knight, His Majesty's Solicitor General, in the Case of the Post-Nati of Scotland, in the Exchequer Chamber and all the Judges of England" in volume four of *The Works of Francis Bacon* (London, 1740).

142.37–40 duplex et reciprocum . . . in se duplex legamen.] Latin: "a double and reciprocal bond. Because just as the subject is bound to obey the king so the king is bound to protect the subject. Rightly therefore are kings called 'Lieges' from 'ligo, to bind or tie,' because the double tie holds them in it."

143.28   the privilege of naturalization] Wilson here advances an argument that would be turned against Americans after independence, when seamen claiming American citizenship were impressed into the British navy on the theory that allegiance to the British Crown was indefeasible.

23: [WILLIAM HENRY DRAYTON], A LETTER FROM FREEMAN

147.19–23   "with men who never were . . . able statesmen."] From a September 16, 1769, letter to the *South Carolina Gazette*.

151.14   an anonymous letter] Addressed "To my noble Friends of the Lower-House of Parliament," this letter was reproduced in the first volume of John Rushworth, ed., *Historical Collections of Private Passages of State, Weighty Matters in Law, Remarkable Proceedings in Five Parliaments* (8 vols., London, 1721).

151.37–38   as an independent . . . ought to act] As a member of the South Carolina Council, the "middle branch" between the people and the governor, Drayton needed to establish his patriotic credentials at the outset.

152.5–6   *Junius*] Pseudonym of an unknown British writer who contributed a series of sixty-nine letters to the London *Public Advertiser* from January 21, 1769, to January 21, 1772. This popular series was highly critical of the ministry; the letter addressed to Lord Bedford quoted from here was number xxiii and appeared on September 19, 1769.

152.22   popular measures in the year 1769] Reference to the gift of £1,500 that the assembly of South Carolina sent that year to the Society of the Gentlemen Supporters of the Bill of Rights, a London organization formed to pay the legal debts of John Wilkes (1725–1797), the radical Whig firebrand who was embroiled in controversy with the government for publishing libels against King George III. Drayton's public objection to the gift was nothing compared to the anger expressed by the British government. The resultant Wilkes Fund controversy eventually brought all legislative business in the colony to a halt.

153.11   *influenced* by disgust] Drayton here attempts to dispel the idea that his political shift was triggered by frustrated ambition. When John Murray, an assistant justice of the South Carolina judiciary, was killed in a duel, Drayton offered to fill the position on an interim basis, even though he knew that a lawyer from Britain of "proper rank and character" would soon replace him.

154.4–5   the Acts of a whole Session,*] The retributive measures of the so-called Merciless Parliament of 1388 (the eleventh year of Richard II's reign), passed at the expense of the king's favorites in the wake of conflict between Richard and a group of courtiers known as the Lords Appellant, were subsequently annulled by the Parliament of Shrewsbury (1398).

154.26   the Sovereign at Constantinople] For eighteenth-century Anglo-Americans and Europeans the Ottoman Empire epitomized absolutism.

154.33   *Reis Effendi!*] A senior official in the administration of the Ottoman Empire.

154.37   31 Henry] Referring to an act, passed in 1539, during the reign of Henry VIII, that established a mechanism by which royal proclamations, when signed by twelve councilors, would have the force of law "as though they were made by act of parliament"; it proved impractical and unnecessary and was repealed in 1547.

155.3   *multis minatur, uni qui injuriam facit.*] Latin: attributed to Publilius Syrus, a Roman aphorist of the first century B.C., meaning He who does an injury to one, threatens many.

155.10–11   the Lord Keeper to Charles the First on a similar occasion] On June 6, 1628, Charles I came to the House of Lords to address the Petition of Right and was greeted by Thomas Coventry (1578–1640), Lord Keeper of the Great Seal, with the words Drayton quotes here, which he likely drew from the eighth volume of *The Parliamentary or Constitutional History of England* (24 vols., London, 1751–61).

156.3–4   dernier resort] The court of last resort.

156.6   a tenure dangerous to the liberty] In 1701 Parliament passed the Act of Settlement which, among other things, declared that judges would no longer serve *durante bene placito* ("as long as it pleases" the prince) but rather *quamdiu se bene gesserint* ("as long as they conduct themselves properly"), that is, with a life tenure. But this aspect of the revolutionary settlement was explicitly denied to the colonies in 1761 when the Privy Council instructed royal governors to desist from issuing judicial commissions that were not revocable at the pleasure of the king, a move that provoked considerable protest from Americans who feared that it would compromise the ability of their judges to act independently of crown control. Parliament went further with the Townshend Acts of 1767, levying new colonial duties with the proceeds to be used to pay the salaries of colonial governors and judges, which were traditionally granted by the colonial assemblies.

157.39   2 Inst. Proem.] The introduction to Coke's *Second Institutes*.

157.40   7 Parl. Hist.] To substantiate this point Drayton cites here a 1627 speech by Coke recorded in the seventh volume of *The Parliamentary or Constitutional History of England*, as well as three statutes. The first, from the twentieth year of reign of Henry VI, he drew from John Maynard, ed., *Year Books, or, Reports in the Following Reigns* . . . (11 vols., London, 1679–80). The last, from the twenty-fifth year of Charles II, concerned the representation of Durham in Parliament (see note 50.20–24).

160.11   laches] Negligence; in law, an unreasonable delay in pursuing a right or claim.

161.39–40   *res ardua*] Latin: literally hard things, here serious matters.

162.23–24 he had never eat commons at the Temple] That is, Lowndes had never studied law at one of the Inns of Court in London (Inner Temple, Middle Temple, Lincoln's Inn, and Gray's Inn).

164.38 7. Rep.] The seventh volume of Coke's *Reports*.

165.39 Finch] See note 31.5–8.

167.18 a Petition] The famous Petition of Right, outlining the liberties of subjects that the king was prohibited from violating.

167.36 Rambler.] *The Rambler*, a twice-weekly periodical published from 1750 to 1752, with 208 articles by Samuel Johnson.

169.8 the case of General Gansel] On August 23, 1773, London bailiff John Hyde and four associates attempted to arrest William Gansel for a debt of £134. When they entered the Craven Street apartment house where Gansel lodged, a ruckus ensued in the stairwell and the general, fearful of unknown assailants below, locked himself in an upstairs room. When Hyde attempted to force entry, Gansel fired his pistol twice before being subdued. He was tried at the Old Bailey on September 8 and acquitted of "felonious shooting." In the prepared statement he read in his own defense, the general cited Blackstone's well-known assertion from the *Commentaries*: "For every man's house is looked upon by the law to be his castle of defence and asylum, wherein he should suffer no violence."

171.11 Locke and Hooker] See note 75.24–37.

171.23 to be called out of American families] The weakness in most colonies of the Governor's Council was much lamented by royal bureaucrats. It flowed in part from the absence in America of an aristocracy that was clearly distinguishable from other colonial elites.

172.36 16 Car. 1, c. 10.] The Habeas Corpus Act of 1640.

172.40 2 Hawk. P. C. 2.] *A Treatise of the Pleas of the Crown* (2 vols., 1716–21) by English serjeant-at-law William Hawkins (1673–1746).

174.15 to deprive them of the power of hearing appeals] In the Irish Declaratory Act of 1720, Parliament expressly denied to that kingdom's House of Lords the same kind of appellate function as exercised by the British peers.

174.38 VAUGH.] Edward Vaughan, ed., *The Reports and Arguments of the Learned Judge, Sir John Vaughan, Kt., Late Chief Justice of the Court of Common-Pleas* (London, 1677).

175.18 *eo instanti*] Latin: upon the instant.

176.34–35 *Bracton* says, . . . *de jure potest*] Henry of Bracton (1210–1268), English jurist and author of *De Legibus et Consuetudinibus Angliae* (On the Laws and Customs of England). Coke cites this line, which may be translated "The king can do nothing but what he can do lawfully," in the *Second Institutes*.

176.38   Carolina Charter] See Chronology for 1663.

177.39   6 Anne, C. 37.] The 1707 Act for the Encouragement of Trade to America. Among other things this act was understood as prohibiting impressment in the colonies.

179.16   the liberties of Ireland and America] Ireland became a touchstone for many writers in the imperial debate, its constitutional relationship to Great Britain seen as similar in many respects to that of the North American colonies.

179.33   Brehon law of Ireland.] An indigenous legal system of Celtic origin, operative in Ireland before the English conquest.

179.39   2 Pryn. Rec. 85.] William Prynne (1600–1669), *An Exact Abridgement of the Records in the Tower of London* (1657).

180.39   6 Geo. I. c. 5] The Irish Declaratory Act of 1720.

181.39   2 Ric. III. 12.] A reference to the *Merchants of Waterford Case* (1484), in Year Book 2 Richard III, 12, plea 26, which Drayton likely drew from *The Twelfth Part of the Reports of Sir Edward Coke, Kt.* (1658).

182.30–31   *Populum laté regem*] Latin: "A people of extensive empire." Cf. Virgil, *The Aeneid*, I.21.

183.17   Runningmede] Runnymede, where according to custom the Magna Carta was sealed.

24: SOME FUGITIVE THOUGHTS ON FREEMAN

185.7–9   "full of the most . . . his Majesty's subjects."] Thomas Irving (1738?–1800), quoted here, was an energetic and efficient imperial administrator. He served a controversial stint in Boston, 1767–71, as inspector general of import and exports for North America, before relocating in early 1774 to South Carolina, where he was receiver general and sat on the governor's council. Within a year he had run afoul of the colony's popular party and "for his health" he was "advized to try the sea air." He soon fled to the Bahamas, only to be captured when American forces seized Nassau in May 1776.

185.13–14   "eyes of the discontented," . . . unwearied diligence."] Bull to the Earl of Dartmouth, August 31, 1774.

185.17–18   "settle the Affair . . . a Gentleman's Weapon,"] Drayton published his account of this affair in the September 17, 1774, edition of the *South Carolina Gazette*.

189.28   *simplex vel unus, compositus vel idem*] Latin: one or the other, or both together.

191.20   *Foro Cæli*] Latin: heavenly forum.

191.35   the executive Magistrate] James I.

193.16   the Duke of *Buckingham*] George Villiers, 1st Duke of Buckingham (1592–1628), a favorite of James I. Widely unpopular, he was assassinated in 1628. For the bill referred to here, see Chronology for 1621.

193.37   Commons Journal, 1622.] The Journal of the Commons, a record of debate that began to be kept in 1547 and from which extracts were regularly published.

193.38   The King's Secretary, and Mr. G—.] Secretary of State George Calvert (see note 46.27) was proprietor of the colony of Avalon (Newfoundland). John Guy (d. 1629), English merchant adventurer and the first proprietary governor of Newfoundland.

193.39   Sir Edward Sackville's Speech] Sackville (1590–1652), who became the 4th Earl of Dorset in 1624, sat in the Commons, 1621–22, where he was one of the leaders of the popular party.

195.27–28   the Nicks of *Seven* and *Eleven*] A reference to Drayton's notorious gambling.

195.35   *Hudibras*] A mock-heroic poem written by Samuel Butler (1613–1680), published in three parts between 1663 and 1678. The author quotes from part III, canto i, lines 1221–24.

198.23   *George Fox*] Fox (1624–1691), a radical missionary and founder of the Society of Friends (Quakers), often preached the apocalypse.

199.5   *pro causis*] Latin: for this reason.

200.12–13   the Marquis of *Rockingham*] Charles Watson-Wentworth, 2nd Marquess of Rockingham (1730–1782), was prime minister from July 1765 to July 1766.

201.17   *Elsenburgh*] The precise location of Fort Elfsborg, in Elsinboro Township, New Jersey, is not known.

201.18   an *Englishman*] Henry Hudson.

201.25–26   a Colony on the Banks of the *Connecticut* River.] The Dutch were the first Europeans to explore what they christened the Versche (Fresh) River in 1614, establishing trading posts as far north as the site of present-day Hartford.

202.30–31   the 12th *Charles* the Second] The Tenures Abolition Act of 1660, which the author refers to as the *Soccage-Act* at 204.3.

202.36   *Charta de Foresta*] A complementary charter (1217) to the Magna Charter, so named because it dealt with rights related to the use of royal forests.

203.6   *Ton*] French: form or mode.

203.31–32   *speculum Justitiæ*] Latin: mirror of justice.

207.2–3 the Chief Justice's Argument] Thomas Knox Gordon (1728–1796) was chief justice of South Carolina from 1771 to 1776, when he would be replaced by Drayton. On September 21, 1774, he and fellow justice Charles Mathews Coslett (c. 1741–1776), appointed 1772, filed a remonstrance with the lieutenant governor complaining that Drayton's pamphlet represented "them as men totally unfit for the offices they hold."

211.1–5 three Assistant-Judges, . . . Mr. Justice *Fewtrell*] The rest of the South Carolina high court consisted of Edward Savage, John Murray, and John Fewtrell, all appointed in 1771.

211.39 Vide Observations on Lord *Ferrers's* Trial] Lawrence Shirley, 4th Earl Ferrers (1720–1760), who in 1760 shot and killed the steward of his estates; he was tried and found guilty by the House of Lords and was hanged. An account of the trial was quickly published.

212.10 *Rawlins Lowndes*] Lowndes (1721–1800) would be elected governor of the state of South Carolina in 1778.

212.20 *sub ficto nomine*] Latin: under a false name.

213.13–15 *Frange, miser,* . . . *imagine macra.*] Juvenal, *Satires*, VII.27, translation by John Dryden.

25: [JONATHAN BOUCHER?], A LETTER FROM A VIRGINIAN

222.32–33 a Gregory, or a Venner] Two figures, like Charles I and Oliver Cromwell, meant to define opposing extremes: Pope Gregory XV, whose 1623 exchange of letters with Charles concerning the latter's proposed marriage to the Spanish Infanta—in which the then Prince of Wales expressed his desire that "as we all confess one undivided Trinity and one Christ crucified, we may be banded together unanimously into one faith"—was published as a pamphlet in 1729; and Thomas Venner, a wine cooper who had emigrated to New England in 1637 and returned to London in 1651, joining the radical republican underground of the Interregnum. He led the Fifth Monarchy Men, a millenarian Puritan sect that rose in rebellion in the name of "King Jesus" in 1657 and again in 1661, when he was executed.

226.4 pernicious Maxims of a Polish Diet] From the mid-seventeenth into the eighteenth century any one of the nobles in the Polish legislature could exercise his *liberum veto*, blocking any legislative measure whatsoever. This need for unanimity created no end of legislative confusion.

230.9 every Post-Day shews us a Precedent] More than once during the debates over the Stamp Act and Townshend duties, supporters of the British administration pointed to the 1710 act establishing a postal system for the colonies as evidence of Americans' prior acceptance of Parliament's authority to tax them. This was a false analogy for most Americans, including Benjamin Franklin, deputy postmaster general for the colonies from 1753 to 1774: "The Post-Office, say the Grenvillians, is, in Effect, a Tax upon America, which they have never complained of. The advancing of so frivolous an Apology for their Injustice and Oppression, shews the Difficulty they find in patching up an indefensible Cause. They might as well have drawn a Defence of their Policy from the establishing of Tolls at Turnpikes. Will any Man of common Sense attempt to force a Comparison between a Regulation evidently for the Benefit of the Colonies, and of our Merchants trading with them, and whose Effect is a saving of Money to the Colonists, and a Scheme, whose declared Intention is, to take from them their Property, and to increase the Revenue at their Expence, and contrary to their Inclination?" (From "The Colonist's Advocate: III," printed in *The Public Advertiser* [London], January 11, 1770.)

232.27–28 "i. e. The Consent of the Majority, . . . by them."] Locke, *Second Treatise*, ch. xi, sect. 140.

233.15–16 more than one rich Province, that refused to comply] The colonies as a whole had spent £2,568,248 on military operations during the Seven Years' War, according to a January 1766 Board of Trade report, for which Parliament had reimbursed them £1,068,769. There was, as Boucher suggests, a significant range in contributions from the individual colonies: Massachusetts, with the highest expenses, £818,000, received the largest reimbursement, £351,994; Maryland (£39,000) and Georgia (£1,820) received none. Maryland, the colony he likely has in mind here, had been comparatively backward in the war effort because of a lengthy dispute between the colony's House of Delegates and Council over the proper method of supporting paper emissions. Numerous attempts to fund appropriations with a tax on licenses for ordinaries (taverns) were stymied, resulting in modest total war expenditures far less than Pennsylvania's or Virginia's.

234.21–22 a Philip the Second, a Katharine of Medicis] Philip II (1527–1598), king of Spain who waged a long, brutal, and ultimately unsuccessful effort to put down a rebellion in the Spanish Netherlands; and Catherine de Medici (1519–1589), who as regent for her young son, Charles IX of France, was held responsible for the St Bartholomew's Day massacre of 1572 in which thousands of French Protestants (Huguenots) were killed.

26: [SAMUEL SEABURY], THE CONGRESS CANVASSED

238.8–9 "A democratical despotism," . . . contradiction in terms."] From "Novanglus No. V," February 20, 1775, in *John Adams: Revolutionary Writings 1755–1775*, 469.

239.13 *A.W. Farmer*] A Westchester farmer.

239.17 Cicer. contra Rullum.] Cicero, *De Lege Agraria Contra Rullum* Against the Agrarian Law of Rullus), 64 B.C.

243.12–13 Look into their addresses] On October 21, 1774, the Congress approved separate statements to the people of Great Britain (prepared by John Jay) and the North American colonies, and on October 26 a similar address to the people of Quebec (John Dickinson). These were quickly published as pamphlets in Philadelphia, the one to Quebec in both French and German editions (two thousand copies of the French edition were printed for distribution in Canada). The letter to the people of Great Britain was reprinted in London and Coventry in January 1775. All three letters were also published in a collected edition entitled *Extracts from the Votes and Proceedings of the American Continental Congress.* Widely republished on both sides of the Atlantic, this pamphlet included the Congress's Declaration and Resolves, which were often referred to (either proudly or contemptuously, depending on the writer's loyalties) as the American "bill of rights."

243.32   those gentlemen who were delegated from your city.] Six towns in five New York counties formed committees to nominate and select delegates for the Congress. In New York City, merchants and mechanics formed separate committees in May that were soon merged into a single body of fifty-one individuals. Other committees were formed in Suffolk, Orange, King, Albany, Westchester, and Dutchess counties in June and July. On July 4, the Committee of 51 in New York selected five delegates (James Duane, John Jay, Philip Livingston, Isaac Low, and John Alsop) who were gradually confirmed by popular committees in Albany, Westchester, and Dutchess counties. William Floyd (Suffolk Co.), Simon Boerum (King's Co.), John Herring (Orange Co.), and Henry Wisner (Orange Co.) rounded out the New York delegation.

244.3–4   the names of every Delegate . . . one only excepted] The Declaration and Resolves was undersigned for New York by Low, Alsop, Jay, Duane, Floyd, Wisner, and Boerum.

244.35–36   the legal Treasurer of the province] Abraham Lott (1726–1794), who continued to be the object of public scorn in 1785, when the New York state assembly passed an act "to more effectually compel Abraham Lott, late Treasurer of the Colony of New York, to account to the Treasurer of this State for such sums of money as the said Abraham Lott has received while he was Treasurer of the said Colony, and for which he has not accounted."

246.5–6   Captain *Chambers*] On April 22, 1774, the merchant ship *London*, James Chambers, captain, arrived in New York bearing eighteen quarter-chests of East India Company tea. Confronted at the wharf by a committee of concerned citizens, who had been tipped off by another captain with whom Chambers had communicated offshore, Chambers confessed to having the tea but said he planned to sell it on his own account. The committee let the gathering crowd decide how to proceed, and in short order a group of bystanders boarded the vessel and dumped the tea. Chambers fled amid the confusion, abandoning his ship and personal possessions.

249.9–10   their letter to his Excellency General Gage] Dated October 10, 1774, and also reproduced in the *Extracts from the Votes and Proceedings of the American Continental Congress.*

250.2–3   Mr. ——, I forget his name] Paul Revere (1734–1818), Boston silver-smith who acted as courier between the Massachusetts Committee of Safety and the Congress in Philadelphia. Revere made two circuits while the Congress sat: the first in September to deliver the Suffolk Resolves to the Congress and the second in October to disseminate the Declaration and Resolves.

250.9–10 Like the country people in the fable] One of Aesop's Fables, notably employed in Horace's *Ars Poetica*: "Pompous Exordiums studiously forbear; / Nor, like the Bard of old, thus wound the Ear— / Of Priam's Fortunes, and his Wars, I'll sing— / What will such ostentatious Boasting bring? / By the judicious Reader left with Scorn, / The Mountain labours, and a Mouse is born!" Translation from William Popple, *Horace's Art of Poetry Translated* (London, 1753).

250.26 patoo-patoos] Bludgeons, as described in James Cook's account of his South Sea voyages, first published in 1773.

250.34–35 a report was spread . . . attacked the town.] See the headnote to Pamphlet 27.

252.32 the *Association*] Adopted on October 18, 1774, the Continental Association pledged the colonies to discontinue the slave trade and cease importing goods from Great Britain, Ireland, and the East and West Indies after December 1, 1774, to cease consuming British goods after March 1, 1775, and, if necessary, to cease all exports (excluding rice) to Britain, Ireland, and the West Indies after September 10, 1775. To enforce these regulations the Association requested that committees of safety be elected in every county, city, and town to "observe the conduct of all persons touching the association," publicize in the newspapers the violators as "enemies of American liberty," and "break off all dealings" with them. The articles of the Association further urged the colonies to "encourage frugality, economy, and industry" and "discourage every species of extravagance and dissipation" and threatened any colony that did not observe the agreement with economic boycotts.

254.40 an old neglected book] Cf. Revelation 13:17.

256.27 from Dan to Beersheba] A common expression in the Hebrew Scriptures, indicating the extent of the settled areas of the Tribes of Israel.

257.4 the *Saints shall inherit the earth?*] Seabury plays here on Massachusetts's Puritan heritage.

258.33 Jack's hanging bout, in the history of John Bull] In *The History of John Bull* (1712), by Dr. John Arbuthnot (1667–1735), the allegorical work that introduced the blunt and honest character who came to symbolize Britain, Jack (who represented Scottish Presbyterianism) is convinced by his friends that the only way to escape justice for past misdeeds against John Bull, for which he is soon to be executed, is to hang himself first.

268.1–2 *Free Thoughts*] *Free Thoughts, on the Proceedings of the Continental Congress, Held at Philadelphia*, which Seabury had published shortly before *The Congress Canvassed*.

268.10–11 "and his *wit* ridiculed,"] The title page of Hamilton's *A Full Vindication of the Measures of Congress, from the Calumnies of their Enemies; in Answer to a Letter, under the Signature of A.W. Farmer*, included the following claim: "Whereby His *Sophistry* is exposed, his *Cavils* confuted, his *Artifices* detected, and his *Wit* ridiculed." Samuel Johnson's *Dictionary of the English Language* (1755) defines *ridicule* as "wit of that species that provokes laughter," offering two usage illustrations from Pope and one from Swift.

27: [THOMAS BRADBURY CHANDLER], A FRIENDLY ADDRESS

270.4–5 "little real cause."] From "Massachusettensis [Daniel Leonard] No. V," January 9, 1775, in *John Adams: Revolutionary Writings 1755–1775*, 360.

271.17 Am I *therefore* . . . I tell you the Truth?] Galatians 4:16.

273.3 (says an excellent English Writer)] Robert Lowth, *A Sermon Preached at the Assizes Holden at Durham, August 15, 1764* (London, 1764). This work was also published in the October 1764 issue of *The Monthly Review, or Literary Journal*.

273.38–274.2 "Only *take heed to thyself*, . . . all the days of thy life."] Deuteronomy 4:9.

274.31–32 *subject to the higher powers*, . . . *for conscience's sake.*] Romans 13:1, 5.

277.31–33 "If Parliament . . . our whole property;"] A very loose paraphrase of Locke, *Second Treatise*, ch. xi, sect. 140.

283.30–31 the words of the justly celebrated Dr. BLACKSTONE] From a footnote in the introduction to section 4 of the first volume of the *Commentaries*.

284.17 "in the midst of a crooked and perverse generation"] Philippians 2:15.

286.36–40 *The Justice and Policy* . . . reprinted by Mr. RIVINGTON.] The first of these two anonymous pamphlets is attributed to William Knox (author of Pamphlet 16 in the companion to this volume); it was published in London in the early summer of 1774 and was reprinted in New York by Hugh Gaine (1726–1807), printer for the province and publisher of the *New York Gazette; and the Weekly Mercury*. The second, *A Letter to the Earl of Chatham, on the Quebec Bill*, was published in London about the same time as the first and is attributed to Sir William Meredith (c. 1725–1790), a Rockingham Whig. It was reprinted in New York by James Rivington (1724–1802), publisher of the *New-York Gazetteer*.

287.37–288.3 "For rulers . . . that doth evil."] Romans 13:3–4.

288.14 *the fox in the fable*] "The Fox without a Tail," one of Aesop's Fables.

288.23 *de Lana Caprina*] Latin: literally, about goat's wool; that is, something trivial, not germane.

290.11–13   messages that passed . . . the address of the assembly of *Virginia*] Chandler was likely led to these examples by William Knox's *The Controversy between Great Britain and Her Colonies Reviewed; . . . and the Nature of Their Connection with, and Dependence on, Great Britain, Shewn, upon the Evidence of Historical Facts and Authentic Records* (London, 1769), Pamphlet 16 in the companion to this volume. Among the "authentic records" included in the latter portion of the pamphlet (which is not reproduced in the present edition) are extracts of three messages from the Massachusetts House of Representatives to William Shirley (1694–1771), royal governor of the colony, 1741–49, 1753–56. In the communication dated October 30, 1754, the House confessed that "we apprehend it *impossible, in the present distressing circumstances of the province, to maintain a force necessary for the defence of so extensive a frontier; and therefore we must humbly rely on his majesty's paternal goodness*." Also included was the Virginia Assembly's 1754 address to the king, in which the Burgesses warn of France's building forts in the Ohio country while admitting that their provision of £10,000 toward the defense of the region, "*though not sufficient to answer all the ends for which it is designed, is the utmost that your people under their present circumstances are able to bear.* We therefore most humbly beseech your majesty, *to extend your royal beneficence* to us your loyal subjects, that we may be enabled effectually to defeat the *unjust and pernicious designs* of your enemies." The italics are Knox's.

292.22   father BAXTER] Richard Baxter (1615–1691), an influential Puritan pastor and theologian and author of numerous works, including *The Saints Everlasting Rest, or, A Treatise of the Blessed State of the Saints in the Enjoyment of God in Heaven* (1650).

292.44   GREY's *answer to* NEAL.] Zachary Grey, *An Impartial Examination . . . of Mr. Daniel Neal's History of the Puritans* (4 vols., London, 1733–39). For Neal see note 36.23. Grey in particular objected to Neal's sympathetic portrait of the Puritan regicides in the English Civil War.

293.5   PROTECTOR] Chandler's choice of words here identifies the people of Massachusetts with the Puritan revolutionaries of the Interregnum.

293.10   Mr. SCOT] The identity of this harassed merchant is not known.

293.14   the King's *General* and *Governor*] Thomas Gage's remarks to Joseph Warren, president of the Boston Committee of Correspondence, appeared in the same dispatch from Boston that recounted Mr. Scot's fate.

293.23–24   the ANABAPTISTS *of* MUNSTER] Perhaps the most famous example of the excesses of the radical Reformation was the short-lived (1534–35) Anabaptist commune at Münster, in Westphalia. Under the leadership of the charismatic Dutch "prophet" Jan Matthys and his disciple John of Leiden, the German city was transformed into a volatile "New Jerusalem" where ecstatic visions abounded—one of John of Leiden's led to the institution of polygamy —and Catholics and Lutherans who refused to be rebaptized were driven into exile or forced to undergo the procedure in the public marketplace.

293.38–39   *We have no part in* DAVID, . . . O ISRAEL.] 2 Samuel 20:1.

293.40   Mr. GAINE's *Mercury*] The *New York Gazette*. See note 286.36–40.

294.34   Ex illo fluere, . . . spes danaum.] From Virgil, *The Aeneid*, II.169–70: "From that time the hopes of the Danaans ebbed and, backward stealing, receded." Translation from H. Rushton Fairclough, *Virgil: Eclogues, Georgics, Aeneid I–IV* (Cambridge: Harvard University Press, 1935).

295.16 17   the battle of *Edge-Hill*] The first pitched battle in the English Civil War, fought between the king's army and the parliamentary forces on October 23, 1642.

295.18–19   HAVOC . . . *the dogs of war*] Cf. *Julius Caesar*, III.i.273.

297.3–4   good subjects of the town of *Rye*] Rivington opened the October 13, 1774, edition of the *New-York Gazetteer* with a letter, dated September 24, he had received from "the freeholders and inhabitants of Rye, in the county of Westchester, being much concerned with the unhappy situation of public affairs think it our duty to our King and country to declare, that we have not been concerned in any resolutions entered into, or measures taken, with regard to the disputes at present subsisting with the mother country; we also testify our dislike to many hot and furious proceedings, in consequence of said disputes, which we think are more likely to ruin this once happy country, than remove grievances, if any there are."

297.13–14   the *Resolves* from *Georgia*] A group of Georgia patriots meeting in Tondee's Tavern in Savannah on August 10, 1774, issued a set of resolves declaring the Coercive Acts to be unconstitutional and voicing support for their sister colonies. The meeting was unable to reach agreement on sending delegates to the First Continental Congress, however.

297.37–298.2   "O! that they were *wise*, . . . their LATTER END!"] Deuteronomy 32:29.

306.29   *Nemo repente fit turpissimus*] Juvenal, *Satires*, II.83.

307.15   *dissent*] Another jab at "Puritan" Massachusetts, where, Chandler implies, only the royal government prevents Dissenters (i.e., those who abjure the Church of England) from erecting an oppressive theocracy.

308.38–39   Mr. MORTON, . . . *New-England's Memorial.*] Nathaniel Morton (1613–1685), secretary of the Plymouth Colony (serving under his uncle Governor William Bradford) and author of the 1669 history mentioned here.

309.10   Three *Homilies* on *Obedience*, and six against *Rebellion*] The First Book of Homilies for use in the Church of England was published in 1547. A second collection was published in 1562, and then expanded in 1571.

309.11–14   They are also taught to pray in the Litany, . . . solemn office i provided] Both of these are found in the Book of Common Prayer, which Chandler quotes from in the lines following.

311.10–12   *whips, . . . scorpions*] Cf. 1 Kings 12:11.

28: [PHILIP LIVINGSTON], THE OTHER SIDE OF THE QUESTION

315.12–13   "the greatest deference to . . . the British parliament."] From a September 11, 1764, address by the New York Assembly to Lieutenant Governor Cadwallader Colden.

315.23   "in Trade"] Adams's comments are from his diary, August 22–23, 1774.

319.32   my Master James] Rivington, publisher of both the Chandler and Livingston pamphlets.

321.15   "excellent writer,"] See note 273.3.

322.10   Vicar of Bray] A byword for political expediency and hypocrisy, from a popular eighteenth-century satirical song of the same name about a clergyman who stays in office by changing his principles.

322.32   honest Sir Toby] Sir Toby Belch, comic character in Shakespeare's *Twelfth Night*.

324.12–15   Our basest beggars, . . . Man's life is cheap as beast's.] *King Lear*, II.iv.264–67.

324.25   the eighth and ninth pages] Corresponding to pages 276–78 in the current edition.

326.23   Jack O'Lanthorn] A will-o'-the-wisp or delusion.

327.37–38   The King can do no wrong.] A maxim expressed most famously in the eighteenth century in Blackstone's *Commentaries*.

328.12–13   If, to his share . . . you forgive them all.] A play on Pope, *The Rape of the Lock*, lines 17–18: "If to her share some Female Errors fall, / Look on her Face, and you'll forget 'em all."

329.10–12   A true State . . . of the Massachusetts-Bay, &c.] This pamphlet, published in London in May 1774, was written by Arthur Lee (1740–1792), agent for Massachusetts and future U.S. envoy to France, Spain, and Prussia, from material furnished by Franklin.

329.19–20   because—*it was a Money Bill*] See note 14.20–26.

330.1   A vessel also was seized] In May 1768, customs commissioners in Boston used a perjured statement from a customs inspector to seize John Hancock's ship *Liberty* for failure to pay £700 in duties on £3,000 worth of Madeira wine. The commissioners then imposed a penalty of triple charges on the wine, for a total fine many times greater than the taxes allegedly evaded. The seizure itself was greeted with angry protests in Boston, resulting in customs officials being harassed and government property being destroyed. This in turn led to the decision to send British troops to Boston in September.

330.7–8   a royal martyr had done so before him.] Having failed in the early years of his reign to secure sufficient funds to support the army from Parliament, Charles I turned to martial law and the forcible quartering of troops in private homes. This was one of the actions that triggered the Petition of Right of 1628.

330.14–15 shot three brace by way of starting the covey.] A reference to the "Boston Massacre" of March 5, 1770, in which five Bostonians were killed and several others were wounded. Livingston appears to be using the Old Style date here (see note 615.4).

330.18 Judge Oliver's narration] Peter Oliver (1713–1791), judge of the Massachusetts Superior Court who sat during the Boston Massacre trials. Livingston appears to be referring to his charge to the jury, which was reprinted in newspapers after the trials, and in which Oliver pointedly suggested to the jury that the central question to consider was whether the crowd, which he calls "riotous," was an "unlawful assembly." Oliver became lieutenant-governor when Hutchison was appointed governor in 1770, and later wrote a lively Tory account of the Revolution that remained unpublished until 1961.

333.15–23 Merciful Heaven! . . . makes the Angels weep.] *Measure for Measure*, II.ii.114–22.

333.28–29 to enter the alleys of Billingsgate.] That is, to descend into coarse and abusive language, from the London ward that was home to the city's fish market. According to *A Classical Dictionary of the Vulgar Tongue* (1785), "Billingsgate is the market where the fish women assemble to purchase fish, and where in their dealings and disputes, they are somewhat apt to leave decency and good manners a little on the left hand."

340.10 if thy member offendeth . . . cast it away.] Cf. Matthew 5:30.

340.26 the northern colonies] That is, the North American continental colonies, as distinct from those in the British West Indies.

29: EBENEZER BALDWIN, STATING THE HEAVY GRIEVANCES

343.37–344.5 "declaimers on both sides . . . insanity of *head*."] From a letter published in the January 21, 1768, edition of *The Gazetteer and New Daily Advertiser* of London.

345.25–26 *Sit Denique . . . De Republica sentiat.*] From Cicero's first *Oration against Cataline*, sect. xiii: "Let it be finally inscribed upon the forehead of every man what he feels about the commonwealth."

345.27 *Patria mihi mea vita multo est Carior.*] Ibid., sect. xi: "My country, which is much dearer to me than my life."

350.12 Sir *Edmund Andross*] English officer and colonial administrator (1637–1714) who held a number of positions in America, including governor of the Dominion of New-England, 1686–89, which annulled several colonial

charters and sought to create a more authoritarian and centralized government over the colonies of New England, New York, and the Jerseys. This post
ended with Andro's arrest at the hands of Boston leaders emboldened by news
of the Glorious Revolution in the mother country.

351.26–28 two expensive expeditions . . . proved unsuccessful.] New
Englanders twice tried and failed to take Port Royal, capital of the French
province of Acadia: first, in May 1690, during King William's War, under the
leadership of Massachusetts governor Sir William Phips (1651–95), and then
again in May 1707, during Queen Anne's War, under Massachusetts governor
Joseph Dudley.

351.29–30 the important fortress of Louisbourg] See Chronology for 1744–
48.

351.40 they refunded to them] Massachusetts was reimbursed for £183,649
spent on the expedition to Cape Breton.

354.26–27 to pass the castle] That is, clearance to sail past Fort William on
Castle Island, which guarded the entrance to Boston's inner harbor.

354.31–32 At New-York also . . . in the like manner.] See note 246.5–6.

362.7 *Josiah Quincy, junr.*] Quincy Jr., (1744–1775), John Adams's co-
counsel, defending the soldiers involved in the Boston Massacre, had published this pamphlet in Boston in May 1774 and shortly after sailed to England
to argue the patriot cause. Illness cut his trip short, and he died of tuberculosis
on board ship returning to Boston in April 1775.

366.24–25 bestowing those places on them or their friends.] Americans came
to believe that by granting crown places and offices of profit to members of
Parliament (or their associates and family members), the monarch was corrupting the legislature and bending it to his will. This fear lay behind the pro
hibition of members of the executive department from simultaneously holding
office in the legislature in all the Revolutionary state constitutions of 1776, a
separation of powers that foreclosed the development of the kind of parliamentary cabinet system of government that had emerged in England. In the United
Kingdom today the Crown's ministers must be members of Parliament.

374.21–22 Remember how . . . from Haman's cursed devices.] As related
in the biblical book of Esther.

374.32 Rider's History of England] William Rider, *A New History of England*
50 vols., London, 1761–64). The poet was Edmund Waller (1606–1687), who
was something of a prodigy, having been elected to Parliament at the age of
sixteen. The bishops were Richard Neile (1562–1640), archbishop of York, and
Lancelot Andrewes (1555–1626), the scholar who oversaw the translation of the
King James Bible.

375.1–2 *The king's heart . . . whithersoever he will.*] Proverbs 21:1.

30: [CHARLES LEE], STRICTURES ON THE FRIENDLY ADDRESS

381.13   "Let's canvaſs Him in his broad Cardinal's Hat."] Deducing his opponent was a clergyman, Lee makes a play on *1 Henry VI*, I.iii.36, where the Duke of Gloucester confronts the Bishop of Winchester in similar fashion. To canvass is to toss in a canvas sheet, to belabor.

383.3   a profligate, venal printer] Rivington.

386.38   the distractions in Poland] In 1772, Poland was partitioned among three powers, Prussia, Austria, and Russia, with a rump state remaining.

387.39   Massie's Estimates] British political economist Joseph Massie (d. 1784) wrote many statistical works on trade and other economic issues.

388.35   Wolfe] General James Wolfe's capture of Quebec in 1759 was instrumental in bringing the Seven Years' War to an end. His death from wounds suffered in the attack, which came only after he knew victory had been achieved, made him a hero throughout the British empire.

389.26–27   they would be an addition to this continent] One estimate suggests that a sixth of the thirty thousand German soldiers who came to America remained after the war, many doubtless enticed by the Congress's promise of fifty-acre land grants to any who would desert.

389.32   the empire] The Holy Roman Empire, an elective monarchy in which the emperor was chosen by a small group of German princes known as the Electors. The last such election had occurred on March 27, 1764, in Frankfurt and one of the nine electors was George III, King of Great Britain and Elector of Hanover. The convention that Lee refers to was one of the reforms that accompanied the election of Joseph II of Austria as the King of the Romans, or heir to the throne.

390.12–13   St. Stephen's Chapel] The royal chapel in the old palace at Westminster, meeting place of the House of Commons from 1547 to 1834, when it was destroyed by fire.

390.32–33   Mr. Justice Sewall, . . . Brigadier Ruggles] Jonathan Sewell (1729–1796), last attorney-general of Massachusetts Bay Colony; Charles Paxton (1708–1788), customs official in Boston; Timothy Ruggles (1711–1793) one of the Massachusetts mandamus councilors appointed by General Gage in 1774. All three men did indeed become Loyalists.

391.7–8   *In hoc signo vinces*] Latin: By this sign you will conquer. An allusion to the battlefield apparition thought to have triggered the Roman emperor Constantine's conversion to Christianity.

392.23   The corpse . . . General Monkton] Robert Monckton (1726–1782) commanded British forces to a series of victories in Nova Scotia during the Seven Years' War. Lee uses a now obsolete spelling of *corps*.

392.29   conquest of Martinico] Captured by Britain in 1759 and 1762 respectively, the valuable West Indian islands of Guadeloupe and Martinique were restored to France in the Treaty of Paris (1763) in exchange for the cessation of its claims in North America.

394.34–35   "more sinned against or sinning?"] Cf. *King Lear*, III.ii.59.

394.37   one Gentleman of high rank] Probably General John Burgoyne (1722–1792), British army officer, member of Parliament, and playwright. He had been Lee's superior officer in Portugal and attempted to use Lee as a conduit for negotiations with the Americans in Boston in 1775.

395.15–16   The Grislers . . . and Straffords of England] Various agents of tyranny, from the Whig perspective: Albrecht Gessler, legendary tormentor of fifteenth-century Swiss folk hero William Tell; Cardinal de Granvelle (1517–1586), Spanish courtier and member of the council of state for the Low Countries in the last years before the Dutch rebellion; William Laud, as Archbishop of Canterbury, and Sir Thomas Wentworth, 1st Earl of Strafford (1593–1641), as lord-deputy of Ireland, were principal architects of the repressive policies of the Personal Rule of Charles I.

395.20   Barnards] Referring to Francis Bernard (see note 99.14–15).

31: [HENRY BARRY], THE STRICTURES EXAMINED

397.27–31   "The respect and control . . . since the 19th of April."] From an August 20, 1775, letter from Burgoyne to Lord George Germain, soon to replace Dartmouth as secretary of state for the colonies.

399.11   Ne quid falſi . . . veri non audeat.] Cicero *De Oratore*, II.xv.62: "[Who does not recognize that the first law of history is that] we shall never dare to say what is false; the second that we shall never fear to say what is true."

401.24–25   the noble author of the Characteristics] Arthur Ashley Cooper, 3rd Earl of Shaftesbury (1611–1713), English politician and philosopher, and author of *Characteristicks of Men, Manners, Opinions, Times* (1711), which had a profound influence on English ideas of cultivation and politeness.

402.15   Fontenoy] Major battle fought May 11, 1745, in Flanders during the War of the Austrian Succession, in which a large allied army composed of British, Dutch, Hanoverian, and Austrian troops was defeated by the French.

402.40   General Pepperrell] Sir William Pepperrell (1696–1759), Maine (Massachusetts) merchant and soldier who organized, financed, and led the New England expedition of 1745 that captured the French fort of Louisbourg during King George's War.

403.28   "baneful smile"] Cf. lines 80–82 of "The Bard: A Pindaric Ode," a 1757 poem by Thomas Gray: "Close by the regal chair / Fell Thirst and Famine scowl / A baleful smile upon their baffled guest."

404.37   recommended by Marshal Saxe] Maurice, Count of Saxony (1696–1750), was an accomplished military strategist who served in several different armies before becoming a marshal in the French army, which he led to victory in the battle of Fontenoy. Saxe was the author of an important work on the art of war, *Mes Rêveries* (1732).

406.10 Minden] The battle of Minden, fought in Prussia on August 1, 1759, in which an Anglo-German force defeated a French army. Along with Wolfe's almost simultaneous triumph at Quebec, the victory at Minden helped to convince the French to end the war.

406.16 two Generals] Three British generals had been dispatched to Boston in the spring of 1775: Burgoyne, Henry Clinton (1730–1795), and William Howe (1729–1814). Howe had overall command and he and Burgoyne were the oldest and most experienced; they are likely the two generals referred to here.

407.3 the Moro] After a month-long siege in July 1762 the nearly impregnable Morro castle, which guarded the harbor of the Spanish stronghold of Havana, fell to a well-coordinated British assault involving mines.

407.4 Arcot] In 1751, forces of the British East India Company seized Arcot in southern India and then successfully defended it through a two-month siege by French and Indian forces.

407.17–20 "for the safety of the kingdom, . . . balance of power in Europe."] From 1732 to 1866, with only a few exceptions, this language was used in the annual Mutiny Bill to justify the maintenance of a standing army.

407.28 laughed at the decree of the Aulic Council] In 1552, Philip, the Landgrave of Hesse, Prince Maurice (or Moritz) of Saxony, and other Lutheran princes formed the Protestant League of Saxony despite proscriptions from Charles V, the Habsburg ruler of the Holy Roman Empire, and the Aulic Council, one of the empire's two high courts.

32: [JOSEPH GALLOWAY], A CANDID EXAMINATION

411.18 "it almost a perfect Plan."] As recorded by John Adams in his diary, September 28, 1774.

417.5 Tully gives us this definition] Marcus Tullius Cicero, that is, in *De Re Publica*, Bk. I, sect. 39. Galloway appears to have taken his translation from Burlamaqui's *Principles of Natural and Politic Law* (see note 117.35).

417.9 Mr. Locke tells us] In the *Second Treatise*, ch. xi, sect. 134.

417.13 And in another place, he says] Ibid., ch. xiii, sect. 149.

417.15–17 The judicious Burlamaqui, . . . declares] In three passages that Galloway paraphrases from *The Principles of Natural and Politic Law*, Bk. I, ch. vi, sect. 4, and ch. xix, sects. 1–2.

417.40 *Acherley*, in his treatise on the Britannic constitution] Roger Acherley (1665–1740), English lawyer and author of *The Britannic Constitution: or the Fundamental Form of Government in Britain* (1727), ch. II, sect. xix.

419.26   Mr. Locke tells us] In the *Second Treatise*, ch. xiii, sect. 151.

421.37   Sebastian Cabot] Born c. 1474 in Venice, Sebastiano Caboto may have accompanied his father Giovanni on the latter's 1497 voyage of discovery.

424.15   the opinion of Mr. *Locke*] From the *Second Treatise*, ch. viii, sect. 120.

426.6   says the judicious Burlamaqui] In *The Principles of Natural and Politic Law*, Bk. I, ch. iv, sect. 4.

426.10   the words of Mr. Locke] From the *Second Treatise*, ch. xiii, sect. 151.

426.16   And in another place] Ibid., ch. xi., sect. 134.

427.28–30   we can discover no exemption, . . . save one.] Maryland's 1632 charter expressly exempted the colony from "any Impositions, Customs, or other Taxations, Quotas, or Contributions whatsoever."

428.35–36   the learned Pufendorf tells us] Samuel von Pufendorf (1632–1694) in *De Jure Naturae et Gentium* (1672; *Of the Law of Nature and Nations*, 1703), Bk. VII, ch. iii, sect. 22.

429.10   Mr. Locke says] In the *Second Treatise*, ch. xiii, sects. 150, 151.

429.19   in the latter part of his treatise] Chapter xix.

431.11–16   "That the colonies . . . *used and accustomed*."] The fourth resolution in the Congress's Declaration and Resolves of October 14, 1774.

432.29–40   "But from the necessity . . . of its *respective members*."] Ibid.

434.25   the only constitutional plan] That is, Galloway's own, presented on pages 450–51 in this volume.

435.7–11   "the late acts . . . *in their opposition*."] One of the supplemental resolves included in the *Extracts from the Votes and Proceedings of the American Continental Congress*.

439.16–17   in capite] Latin: literally, in chief; in feudal law, holding land immediately of the king or lord.

444.10–11   The commissioners . . . at Albany] See Chronology for 1754. Galloway's plan borrows much from the Albany Plan of Union, which had been crafted by his friend Franklin.

444.38–39   Message from . . . Massachusetts Bay, in 1754.] Cf. note 290.11.

445.40–446.1   a dangerous enemy within their own bowels] A reference to the large slave population in the southern colonies.

449.10–11   expunged from the minutes] Congressional secretary Charles Thomson did not enter the plan in the body's journal. In an anonymous letter to the *Pennsylvania Journal* (March 8, 1775), Thomson asserted that the plan had been omitted because a majority of the delegates were "of opinion that the inserting of it on their Journal would be disgraceful and injurious [and that] they unquestionably had a right to reject it."

450.16   in the following proportions] Galloway left blank spaces for these. In the Albany Plan of Union, the proportions were "Massachusetts-Bay 7, New Hampshire 2, Connecticut 5, Rhode-Island 2, New-York 4, New-Jerseys 3, Pensilvania 6, Maryland 4, Virginia 7, North-Carolina 4, South-Carolina 4."

33: [SAMUEL JOHNSON], TAXATION NO TYRANNY

459.13–16   "long before indulged . . . short of hanging."] James Boswell, *The Life of Samuel Johnson, LL.D.* (2 vols., London, 1791), I, 458.

459.29–32   "the first thing . . . if it stood alone."] From an April 20, 1775, diary entry of Dr. John Campbell, as published in *Johnsoniana: Anecdotes of the Late Samuel Johnson, LL.D.* (London, 1884), 248.

463.7   gratuitous] In the sense of "asserted without proof," the second definition in Johnson's *Dictionary*.

463.27   their lawful sovereign] Referring not just to the king, but to the king-in-parliament, the supreme legislative authority of the empire.

464.35   another friend of the Americans] Lord Chatham, who had urged the recall of the troops from Boston in a January 20, 1775, speech in the House of Lords, highlighting the commercial importance of the colonies and praising the Americans for their "glorious spirit of Whiggism."

465.15–16   every quarter of a century doubles their numbers.] An estimate popularized by Benjamin Franklin in "Observations Concerning the Increase of Mankind, Peopling of Countries, &c.," an essay written in 1751 and first published in 1754 as an appendix to another pamphlet. Franklin included the essay in the fourth edition of his *Experiments and Observations on Electricity* (London, 1769), assuring it a broad circulation and wide influence, including on the work of the political economist Thomas Malthus.

466.13   The traders of *Birmingham*] While other English commercial centers were petitioning Parliament for conciliation with the colonies, merchants in Birmingham publicly attested on January 25, 1775, that they were "apprehensive that any relaxation in the execution of the late laws respecting the colonies of Great Britain will ultimately tend to the injury of the commerce of [this Town and neighbourhood." Their petition was published in the January 3 edition of the *London Chronicle*.

466.21–22   the great actor of patriotism] Lord Chatham.

466.33–35   *The removal of the people . . . important in its consequences.*] This is the first of several quotations in the pamphlet from the *Extracts from the Votes and Proceedings of the American Continental Congress*.

467.13   *profuse with bliss, and pregnant with delight.*] A line describing

"Liberty, thou Goddess Heav'nly bright" from Joseph Addison's *A Letter from Italy, to the Right Honorable Charles, Lord Halifax* (London, 1709), a short pamphlet presenting two poems.

467.38 the states assembled] That is, the estates assembled: monarch, peers, and people.

468.30 Fontenelle] The French essayist Bernard le Bovier de Fontenelle (1657–1757) made this quip in *Entretiens sur la pluralité des mondes* (1686, *Conversations on the Plurality of Worlds*, 1687), a lively work designed to make the latest scientific findings (for instance the Copernican model of the universe) accessible for a popular audience.

471.16–17 Stukeley of London] English mercenary Thomas Stukeley (c. 1525–1578), whose adventurous life fighting in various lands, including France, Ireland, and Morocco, was chronicled in several works, among them Thomas Fuller, *The History of the Worthies of England* (1662): "he blushed not to tell queen Elizabeth, 'that he preferred rather to be sovereign of a mole-hill, than the highest subject to the greatest king in Christendom;' adding, moreover, 'that he was assured he should be a prince before his death.'"

473.17 as a member to the body] Eighteenth-century writers favored physical or medical analogies when writing about the body politic. States were thought to have life cycles like the human body, and as such to be subject to disease, corruption, and even death. The demise of the classical republics of antiquity was an important object lesson in this regard. Just as bleeding and other purgative cures were designed to maintain the human body's equilibrium, so political science was dedicated to the search for balance in the body politic.

474.37–39 *in a free state . . . his own government.*] Montesquieu, *Spirit of the Laws*, Bk. XI, ch. 6, described in the Congress's Address to the Inhabitants of Quebec as a maxim "sanctified by the authority of a name which all Europe reveres."

476.4–6 *That they are entitled . . . without their consent.*] The first resolution in the Congress's Declaration and Resolves of October 14, 1774.

477.9 a knight or burgess] Designations for members of the House of Commons representing, respectively, a county or a borough.

477.26 Doris amara suam non intermisceat undam.] From Virgil, *Eclogues*, X.5: "[If, when thou glidest beneath Sicilian waves,] thou woulds't not have briny Doris blend her stream with thine, [begin!]" Translation from Fairclough, *Virgil: Eclogues, Georgics, Aeneid I–IV*. The Latin poets sometimes invoked Doris, wife of the sea-god Nereus, when referring to the sea.

477.28 *ubi imperator, ibi Roma.*] Latin: where the emperor is, there is Rome.

478.4 *professed*] This was changed to *possessed* in subsequent editions.

478.30 Mr. Cushing.] Thomas Cushing (1725–1788), Massachusetts politician and member of the First Continental Congress. Cushing was a lukewarm patriot, but because he was speaker of the Massachusetts House of Representatives his name was affixed to many documents protesting British policies, and officials in London mistook him for a ringleader among the American radicals.

479.12 a cess] In Johnson's *Dictionary*, "a levy made upon the inhabitants of a place, rated according to their property."

479.35–36 Dr. Tucker has shewn] Josiah Tucker (1713–1799), Dean of Gloucester, in *Four Tracts, Together with Two Sermons, on Political and Commercial Subjects* (Gloucester, 1774).

479.39–40 Davenant, . . . against Molyneux] Charles Davenant, LL.D. (1656–1714), English politician and economist and author of *An Essay on the Probable Methods of Making the People Gainers in the Balance of Trade* (1699), a rebuttal to *The Case of Ireland Being Bound by Acts of Parliament in England Stated* (1698), by Irish patriot and philosopher William Molyneux (1656–1698).

480.36 the *Old Member* who has written an *Appeal*] *An Appeal to the Justice and Interests of the People of Great Britain, in the Present Disputes with America. By an old Member of Parliament* (London, 1774), an anonymous pamphlet by Virginia-born Arthur Lee (who was never a member of Parliament).

481.17–18 6 Geo. I. chap. 5.] The Irish Declaratory Act of 1720.

484.10 They have published an address to the inhabitants of Quebec] See note 243.12–13.

484.39 Mr. Mauduit] Israel Mauduit (1708–1787), political pamphleteer and brother of former Massachusetts agent Jasper Mauduit. His most recent contribution to the imperial debate was the anonymous pamphlet *A Short View of the History of the Colony of Massachusetts Bay, with Respect to Their Original Charter and Constitution* (London, 1768).

485.18–19 An Italian philosopher] Johnson may have in mind Machiavelli, who wrote in *The Prince* (1537) that "mankind in general form their judgment rather from appearances than realities: all men have eyes, but not many have the gift of penetration."

487.31 the Pactolus of America] Referring to the river in Phrygia (Turkey) rich in gold deposits resulting, according to Greek mythology, from King Midas having bathed in it in order to divest himself of his golden touch.

488.16–17 some master . . . of political electricity] A playful reference to Franklin.

488.27–29 the Scythians . . . by their slaves.] As recounted by Herodotus in his *History*, Scythian warriors returned to their native country after twenty-eight years on the hoof to discover that they were unwelcome in their own homes, their wives having married their slaves in their absence.

490.13–14 a larger part . . . than any other county.] Cornwall was divided into far more boroughs than any other county of comparable size, resulting in an outsized return of forty-four members to the House of Commons. For comparison, all of Scotland had forty-five members and the densely populated northern counties of Durham, Northumberland, and York together had only forty-two.

491.12–13 poisoned with the copper of your own kitchens.] Observing that "Copper Utensils are now employed in almost every Kitchen in the Kingdom," an anonymous pamphlet entitled *Serious Reflections on the Manifold Dangers Attending the Use of Copper Vessels* (London, 1755) warned that "these Utensils, from the very nature of the Metal, throw out a poisonous Matter, more or less, which mixing with our Food, renders it in a greater or lesser degree pernicious."

491.15–16 St. Michael's Mount] Similar in appearance to Mont Saint-Michel in Normandy, a steep and rocky island crowned by a medieval church, located in a tidal flat off the Cornish coastal town of Marazion.

491.37–39 If we do not withhold . . . they will cross the Atlantick and enslave us.] Johnson here misunderstands or purposefully misrepresents a point made in the Congress's open letter to the people of Great Britain, in which the Americans warn their fellow subjects that once the king's ministers have "our lives and property in their power, they may with the greater facility enslave you."

492.2–3 the cranes . . . pygmies] An allusion to an ancient Greek fable in which the legendary diminutive tribe did battle with aggressive birds.

492.4 The Great Orator] Either Lord Chatham or Edmund Burke, each of whom delivered addresses in Parliament in the early months of 1775 about the threat to domestic liberty posed by administration policies supported by "the garrison of *King's men*" (as Burke described it in his 1770 pamphlet *Thoughts on the Cause of the Present Discontents*), though neither suggested, as Johnson implies, that the threat to English liberties might somehow come from America.

492.11–12 the learned author of the *Reflections on Learning*] Thomas Baker (1656–1740), English antiquarian and author of *Reflections upon Learning: Wherein is Shewn the Insufficiency Thereof* (London, 1699).

492.17 a female patriot] Catherine Macaulay (1731–1791), English historian and political activist ("a great republican," Johnson called her) who clashed with Johnson in print and in person. Much to Johnson's annoyance, in her 1775 *Address to the People of England, Scotland and Ireland, on the Present Important Crisis of Affairs*, she repeatedly addressed her readers as "my friends and fellow-citizens."

493.29 ninety thousand men.] John Wilkes made this claim in a speech to the House of Commons that was published soon after in the London *Public Advertiser* for February 10, 1775.

494.1   The Dean of Gloucester has proposed] See note 479.35–36. Tucker
did indeed assert that Britain would be better off if the American colonies
became independent, largely on the basis of an anti-mercantilist theory that
British trade would flourish once the restrictions imposed by imperial regulations were lifted: "it is Freedom, and not Confinement, or Monopoly, which
increases Trade."

494.3   whistle them down the wind.] Cf. *Othello*, III.iii.266–67.

496.19   Sit Thomas Brown predicted] In "A Prophecy Concerning Several
Nations" published in *Certain Miscellany Tracts* (1683), from which the quotation is drawn. Browne (1605–1682) was a physician best known for his 1643
apologia *Religio Medici*.

496.33   an oath of abjuration.] Of the kind that British office-holders were
made to swear, forswearing allegiance to the deposed Stuarts.

34: AN ANSWER TO TAXATION NO TYRANNY

497.35–498.1   "a state of the most . . . UPON THEM."] From Dickinson's
Letters from a Farmer in Pennsylvania, Pamphlet 11 in the companion to this
volume.

498.4–6   "the colonists are by the law . . . because he is black?"] From
Otis's *The Rights of the British Colonies Asserted and Proved*, Pamphlet 3.

505.30   year book] The collected law reports of medieval England, regularly
published from 1268 to 1535.

507.5   declining, or decayed boroughs.] The chaotic nature of representation in the House of Commons was coming under increasing criticism during this period. Some of the constituencies of the House of Commons were
large, with thousands of voters, but others were small and more or less in the
hands of a single great landowner. Many of the electoral districts had few voters, and some so-called rotten boroughs had no inhabitants at all. One town
Dunwich, continued to send representatives to Parliament even though it had
long since slipped into the North Sea. All the while new burgeoning cities
like Manchester and Birmingham sent no representatives at all. Because the
hodgepodge of representation, the product of centuries of history, benefited
the aristocratic ruling elites, it remained unchanged.

507.11   without *residing* on the spot.] The medieval English Parliament did
have residential requirements for its members, but by the eighteenth century
those requirements had long since fallen away, and do not exist even today. By
contrast the American colonists insisted on representatives being residents of
their electoral districts.

508.9   burgage tenure] A tenure under which a property of the king or a lord
in a town or city was held in return for service or rent.

508.14–16   property is the universal constituent . . . Honorary freeman

There were property qualifications for both the officeholders and the electors of the House of Commons. Since property alone created the independence that Englishmen most valued in politics, men who lacked it, and were therefore beholden to others, were denied the suffrage. The status of honorary freeman, a municipal or guild honorific that involved the grant of voting rights absent traditional property or residence requirements, originated in the seventeenth century, but its use in the eighteenth century to tip the scale in local elections became another object of concern for reform-minded Britons.

508.34–35   sitting by the act of the crown merely] The peers of the realm sat in the House of Lords by virtue of their peerage, not their property. This was why the Lords could not introduce money bills, only the Commons could.

511.15–16   Mr. Greenville] George Grenville, prime minister from April 1763 to July 1765.

516.7–8   an acknowledged Financier] Grenville led the government as chancellor of the Exchequer.

520.18   your 24th page] Page 471 in this volume.

520.37   your 60th page] Page 485 in this volume.

523.12   a Saturnalia of cruelty] This kind of overheated language well reflected the anger and anxiety with which slaveholders reacted to suggestions like Johnson's. Such emotions reached a pitch in November 1775 when Earl Murray, 4th Earl of Dunmore (1732–1809), the last royal governor of Virginia, issued a proclamation declaring that all servants and slaves able and willing to bear arms who deserted their masters to fight on the side of "his Majesty" would be granted their freedom. By early 1776 some eight hundred enslaved men had escaped to Dunmore's standard, bringing with them at least as many women and children, in an exodus notably free of the kind of violent retribution foreseen here.

523.25   whither do you rush?] Cf. Virgil, *The Aeneid*, V.742.

523.31   tumour] Affected grandeur; bombast.

5: EDMUND BURKE, SPEECH ON CONCILIATION

525.31–33   "metaphysical distinctions" . . . discussed with safety"] From the *Speech of Edmund Burke, Esq. on American Taxation, April 19, 1774* (London, 1775).

530.8   the several acts] Detailed on pages 575–76 in this volume.

531.2   the Chair] Fletcher Norton, 1st Baron Grantley (1716–1789), speaker of the House from 1770 to 1780, was generally supportive of the government's handling of the American crisis. On February 10, 1775, he told the Commons that "levying war against the King is treason; so is endeavouring to wrest the sword out of the hands of the executive power." Norton had been reelected as speaker on the first day of the current session, November 29, 1774.

531.8–9   the grand Penal Bill] Better known as the New England Restraining Act, this measure had been debated in the Commons on March 6, 1775, and overwhelmingly passed two days later by a vote of 215 to 61. "As the Americans had refused to trade with this kingdom," Lord North said in proposing the bill, it is "but just that we should not suffer them to trade with any other nation."

532.8–9   by every wind of fashionable doctrine.] Cf. Ephesians 4:14.

532.39   Mr. Rose Fuller.] English politician (1708–1777) and a member of the House of Commons from 1756 to 1777; his motion to repeal the tea duty, brought on April 19, 1774, had been the occasion for Burke's speech on American taxation.

534.25–26   shadowy boundaries] Cf. Pope, *Essay on Man*, II.205–10.

534.30–31   *former unsuspecting confidence . . . in the mother country*] Cf. the conclusion of the fifth of the *Letters from a Farmer in Pennsylvania* (Pamphlet 11), found on page 432 in the companion to this volume.

535.3   pruriency of curious ears.] Cf. 2 Timothy 4:3. The phrase "itching ears" in the English is *prurientes auribus* in the Latin.

535.6   the noble Lord in the blue riband.*] Lord North wore this badge of the Knights of the Garter, very rare for anyone in the House of Commons. His Conciliatory Proposal, described in the footnote, was the carrot that was supposed to balance the stick of the Restraining Acts. It refused to recognize the Continental Congress as the collective voice of the colonies, and instead was a clear attempt to foster divisions among them. As such, it had no prospect of a positive reception in the colonies and was emphatically rejected by the Second Continental Congress.

535.18–19   the menacing front of our address] Parliament approved an address to the king on February 7, 1775, that pronounced Massachusetts to be in a state of rebellion and pledged "our fixed resolution, at the hazard of our lives and properties, to stand by your Majesty" in defense of "the just rights of your Majesty and the two Houses of Parliament."

536.21   peace with honour] An echo of the phrase *otium cum dignitate* from Cicero's *Oratio Pro Sestio* (In Defense of Publius Sestius, 62 B.C.).

537.31–32   *minima*] Invoking the law maxim, *De minimus non curat lex*: The law does not concern itself with trifling matters.

538.7   a distinguished person] On March 16, 1775, merchant Richard Glover (1712–1785) appeared before the Commons (at "the bar" beyond which non-members could not pass) to support the petition of the West Indian planters concerning the colonists' non-importation agreement, "praying the House to take into their most serious consideration that great political system of the Colonies heretofore so very beneficial to the Mother Country and her dependencies, and adopt such measures as to them shall seem meet to prevent the evils with which the petitioners are threatened, and to preserve the intercourse between the West India islands and the Northern Colonies." Burke's estimation of Glover as "one of the first literary characters of his age," made largely on the strength of his epic poem *Leonidas* (a paean to liberty first published in nine books in 1737 and expanded to twelve in 1770), is not shared by many literary scholars today.

38.31 Davenant] Charles Davenant was inspector general of imports and exports from 1705 until his death and the author of many works on English trade. See for example note 479.39–40.

40.23 Lord Bathurst] Allen Bathurst, 1st Earl of Bathurst (1684–1775), a political opponent of Robert Walpole and friend to many eighteenth-century literary figures. In 1771 his son Henry was raised to the peerage as Baron Apsley and became Lord High Chancellor.

40.25–26 *acta parentum . . . cognoscere virtus*] From Virgil, *Eclogues*, IV.26–27: "thou canst read of [the glories of heroes and] thy father's deeds, and canst know what valour is . . ." Translation from Fairclough, *Virgil: Eclogues, Georgics, Aeneid I–IV.*

40.30–31 in the fourth generation, . . . the House of Brunswick] George III, third of the kings of the House of Hanover (rulers also of the Duchy of Brunswick-Lunëburg), had succeeded to the throne on the death of his grandfather, George II, in 1760, because his father had died in 1751.

41.6 taste of death] Cf. Matthew 16:28.

41.17–18 if he lives to see nothing . . . cloud the setting of his day!] On September 16, 1775, less than six months after this speech was given, Bathurst died at the age of ninety-one.

42.13 a Roman charity] Burke here invokes the exemplary story, related in different versions by Festus and Pliny, of a Roman daughter (Pero) secretly breastfeeding her father (Cimon) who had been sentenced to death by starvation; this scene of filial piety was depicted by many artists in the seventeenth and eighteenth centuries.

42.30 the frozen serpent of the South.] The Hydrus, a small constellation within the Antarctic circle.

45.8–9 every nation has formed . . . the criterion of their happiness.] Cf. Oliver Goldsmith, *The Traveller, or a Prospect of Society* (London, 1764), lines 8–96: "Hence every state, to one lov'd blessing prone, / Conforms and models life to that alone. / Each to the favorite happiness attends, / And spurns the plan that aims at other ends."

46.9 popular in an high degree, some are merely popular] That is, all had popularly elected assemblies, some had councils elected by those assemblies (rather than appointed by the Crown), and some, like Rhode Island and Connecticut, were wholly democratic ("merely popular"), electing even the governor.

547.18–19   as broad and general as the air] Cf. *Macbeth*, III.iv.22.

547.28–29   such in our days were the Poles] The inequality of Polish society was notorious. In a 1772 essay (*Considérations sur le gouvernement de la Pologne*) Rousseau famously described the Polish nation as being "composed of three orders: the nobles, who are everything; the burghers, who are nothing, and the peasants, who are less than nothing."

548.6–11   General Gage makes out . . . your capital penal constitutions. Gage had reported to Parliament that Boston convened its town meeting without his permission, a violation of the Massachusetts Government Act. When he pointed this out to the Bostonians, Gage was informed that the town meeting was only the continuation of a previously adjourned session. "By such means," the exasperated governor replied, "you may keep your meeting alive these ten years." When he brought the matter before the newly installed "Mandamus Council," which he presumed would back him up, Gage was told that "it is a point of law, and should be referred to Crown lawyers."

548.15   my honourable and learned friend*] Edward Thurlow (1731–1806), Tory Member for Tamworth and an ardent supporter of the government in the American crisis, had been appointed attorney general in 1771. He was the first to respond when Burke concluded his speech.

548.21   *Abeunt studia in mores.*] From Ovid, *Heroides*, XV.83: "Practices zealously pursued become traits."

549.3   "So far shalt thou go, and no farther."] Cf. Job 38:11.

549.24–25   grown with the growth] Cf. Pope, *Essay on Man*, II.136.

550.1   with all its imperfections on its head.] Cf. *Hamlet*, I.v.79.

550.33   Lord Dunmore] Fearful of being taking hostage by restive Virginians in the wake of his dissolution of the House of Burgesses and seizure of gunpowder from Williamsburg's magazine, Lord Dunmore abandoned the colonial capital on June 8, 1775, for the safety of a British man-of-war, from whence he issued his famous proclamation (see note 523.12) in November. The Burgesses took his flight for an abdication, established themselves as a convention, and created a Committee of Safety to function as an executive.

553.18   "increase and multiply."] Genesis 1:28, by way of Milton, *Paradise Lost*, X.730.

553.20–21   by an express charter] Cf. Psalm 115:16.

554.15   *Spoliatis arma supersunt.*] Juvenal, *Satires*, VIII.124: "The plundered still have recourse to arms."

554.21–22   your speech would betray you.] Cf. Matthew 26:73.

555.30–31   "Ye Gods, . . . make two lovers happy!"] From *Peri Bathous, or, Of the Art of Sinking in Poetry* (1727), one of a collection of satirical pieces by "Martinus Scriblerus," the literary creation of Alexander Pope, Jonathan Swift, and John Arbuthnot, members of the Scriblerus Club.

556.14   Coke insulted one excellent individual] At Sir Walter Raleigh's trial in November 1603, Coke, as attorney general, used every insult he could conceive of to convict Raleigh in a weak case, calling him a "most vile and execrable traitor," a "monster" with "an English face but a Spanish heart," a "damnable atheist," and the worst "viper" that ever lived.

556.34   *ex vi termini*] Latin: from the force of the term.

558.1–2   nor have any steps been taken . . . of any individual offender] Such steps would be taken less than a month after Burke spoke these words, when on April 18, 1775, Gage dispatched nearly a thousand troops to Lexington and Concord in an attempt to apprehend Samuel Adams and John Hancock and seize a stockpile of arms and powder.

559.17–18   *great Serbonian bog, . . . where whole armies have sunk.*] Milton, *Paradise Lost*, II.592–94.

559.35   unity of spirit] Cf. Ephesians 4:3.

560.39   Mr. Rice.] George Rice (1724?–1779), member of Parliament from Carmarthenshire in Wales, was no friend of the Americans. On April 19, 1774, in response to Rose Fuller's motion to repeal the tea duty, Rice said he could not "submit to anything which tends to an appearance of a doubt of the supremacy of this country. This cannot be a proper moment for our entering on this consideration. The Americans have ever advanced in demands as we have yielded to their complaints. Taxation and supremacy must go together. I must say the Americans do not rest their complaints merely on taxation; they like no control at all . . . I wish for no new tax, but that which remains must not be given up."

561.27   the pamphlet] Josiah Tucker's *Four Tracts* (see note 494.1).

563.6–7   of the Austrian family] The Habsburgs, who ruled Spain from 1516 to 1700.

563.11   they had not chosen the most perfect standard.] Spain reached the apex of its power during the long reign (1556–98) of Philip II, yet he was best known in the Anglo-American world for his inability to suppress the Dutch rebellion and for the failure of the Spanish Armada in 1588. Spain also suffered a series of bankruptcies under his rule.

563.33–34   to all Ireland.] That is, to the great majority of the island that was beyond the Pale, the coastal district surrounding Dublin inhabited by English settlers.

563.36–37   Sir John Davis shews] John Davies (1569–1626), English lawyer and politician who became attorney-general for Ireland, in *Discoverie of the True Causes Why Ireland was Never Entirely Subdued, nor Brought Under Obedience of the Crown of England, Until the Beginning of His Majesty's Happy Reign* (1612).

564.39   Lords Marchers] Originally appointed by William the Conqueror, barons exercising semi-autonomous authority over the border areas (Marches) between England and Wales.

565.32   rid] Rode.

566.20–25   *Simul alba . . . Unda recumbit.*] From Horace, *Odes*, I.xii.27–32: "[Shall I also praise *Hercules*, and the Sons of *Leda*, *Castor* and *Pollux*; the first famous for excelling in Horse-Course; the other famous for his Actions on foot:] Whose white or lucky Star, as soon as it shineth again to the Mariners, the troubled Waves *being stormy before*, flow from the Rocks, the Winds fall, *are quiet*, and the Clouds fly away, and the Waves before threatening, *being boisterous*, become calm and smooth. (For so *these Gods* have willed it.)" (David Watson, *The Odes, Epodes, and Carmen Seculare of Horace, Translated into English Prose* [2 vols., London, 1712], I, 54.)

568.10–11   Judge Barrington's account of North Wales] Daines Barrington (1727–1800), English lawyer and judge of Great Sessions for North Wales.

568.32–33   *Opposuit natura.*] "Opposed by nature." Juvenal, *Satires*, X.152, referring to Hannibal's passage over the Alps. Burke was much too invested in the status quo to have conceded an American presence in Parliament, which would likely have forced an overhaul of the whole hodgepodge of representation and weakened the strength of his party, the Rockingham Whigs.

568.38–39   the arm of public benevolence is not shortened] Cf. Isaiah 59.1.

568.40   What nature has disjoined] Echoing language from Matthew 19:6.

569.9–10   the rude swain . . . clouted shoon.] Cf. Milton, *Comus*, lines 633–34.

570.9   The second is like unto the first] Cf. Matthew 22:39.

570.23–24   *Non meus hic . . . abnormis sapiens.*] Horace, *Satires*, II.ii.2–3: "[*Come*, learn *with me*, my Friends, what, and how great, Virtue is, to live frugally:] (for this Discourse I *now deliver* is none of mine, but what Ofellus inculcated; a *plain* Country-man, wise without the Rules of Art, and *of* strong Sense.)" Translation from *The Satires, Epistles, and Art of Poetry of Horace, Translated into English Prose* (London, 1743).

570.28–29   It would be a profanation . . . the sacred altar of peace.] An allusion to Exodus 20:25.

570.35–36   not to be wise beyond what was written] Cf. 1 Corinthians 4:6.

570.36–37   the form of sound words] Cf. 2 Timothy 1:13.

571.20   the sixth of George II?] The Molasses Act of 1733. As Burke suggests, the Sugar Act of 1764 reduced the 1733 act's prohibitory duty of six pence per gallon of molasses, which had been universally evaded, to three pence, which it was believed would bring the cost of legitimate trade in line with that of illicit smuggling, and thereby generate revenue.

571.25   which Lord Hillsborough tells you] See note xviii.15.

572.12–13   Those who . . . deny this right] Referring principally to Grenville, about whom Burke observed in his *Speech on American Taxation*: "He was of opinion, which he has declared in this House an hundred times, that the Colonies could not legally grant any revenue to the Crown; and that infinite mischiefs would be the consequences of such a power."

575.38   *An Act for granting certain duties*] The Revenue Act of 1767, establishing what became known as the Townshend duties.

576.7   *An Act to discontinue*] The Boston Port Act of 1774, one of the Coercive Acts.

576.13–14   *An Act for the impartial administration of justice*] The Administration of Justice Act of 1774, another of the Coercive Acts.

576.19   *An Act for the better regulating the government*] The Massachusetts Government Act of 1774, another of the Coercive Acts.

576.22–23   *An Act for the trial of treasons*] The Treason Act of 1543, which stated that acts of treason committed outside of the realm could be tried in England.

576.26–28   it was passed, . . . than it ought.] After limited debate, the Boston Port Act was hurriedly passed on March 31, 1774, without a division in the Commons (that is, by a decisive voice vote) and by a unanimous vote in the Lords.

576.30   the restraining bill] See note 531.8–9.

576.40–577.1   the Crown has far less power . . . than it enjoyed in the latter] Connecticut and Rhode Island were charter colonies that elected their own governors, as opposed to Massachusetts, a royal colony with a crown-appointed governor.

577.14–16   The act for bringing persons . . . the probable duration] The Administration of Justice Act was scheduled to take effect on June 1, 1774, "and be and continue in force for and during the term of *three years*."

580.7   the immediate jewel of his soul.] Cf. *Othello*, III.iii.156.

580.8   a great house is apt to make slaves haughty] Cf. Juvenal, *Satires*, V.66.

580.21   the cords of man.] Cf. Hosea 11:4.

580.23   Aristotle, . . . cautions us] In the *Nicomachean Ethics*, Bk. I, ch. 3.

581.22   proposition of the noble Lord] See note 535.6.

581.34–35   *Experimentum in corpore vili*] Latin, usually *Fiat experimentum in corpore vili*: Let experiment be made on a worthless body.

584.9   extent] A writ issued against the body or property of a debtor.

584.18–19   the worst revenue, . . . in the world.] In the final decades of its existence during this period, the Holy Roman Empire was widely seen as a failing state, its delicate internal balance increasingly unsettled by the emerging powers of Prussia and Austria.

585.25   *Posita luditor arca.*] Juvenal, *Satires*, I.90: "[And when did vice with growth so rank prevail? / Or av'rice wanton in so fair a gale? / When has the gambling spirit run so high?] / Whole fortunes hang suspended on a dye: / [They play, their strong-box not their purses nigh!]" Translation from *The Satires of Juvenal, Translated into English Verse* (2 vols., London, 1785).

586.18   "Ease would retract . . . violent and void."] Cf. Milton, *Paradise Lost*, IV.96.

586.20–21   the immense, ever-growing, eternal debt] Cf. ibid., IV.52.

587.12–13   light as air, . . . links of iron.] Cf. *Othello*, III.iii.322, and *Julius Caesar*, I.iii.94.

587.15   grapple to you] Cf. *Hamlet*, I.iii.62.

587.31–32   This is the commodity of price] Cf. Matthew 13:46.

588.35   *Sursum corda!*] Latin: Lift up your hearts! The opening phrase of the Eucharistic liturgy in many Christian churches.

588.38   high calling] Cf. Philippians 3:14.

589.5   (*quod felix faustumque sit*)] Latin: may it be happy and prosperous.

589.13   the previous question was put] What is commonly called a vote of cloture today. Supported only by the Rockingham Whigs, Burke's resolutions were soundly rejected by the House of Commons, all but one going down without a division.

36: [MOSES MATHER], AMERICA'S APPEAL

591.19   "black regiment"] Oliver used this phrase in a letter published in the *Boston Weekly News-Letter*, January 11, 1776, and again in his *Origin and Progress of the American Rebellion* (see note 330.18).

591.26   "the *Christian* Sparta."] Samuel Adams to John Scollay, December 30, 1780. Adams wrote these words in a mood of despair over the stubborn persistence of luxury ("Pomp & Parade") in the new republic: "I love the People of Boston. I once thought, that City would be the *Christian* Sparta. But alas! Will men never be free! They will be free no longer than while they remain virtuous."

598.38–40 Most justly then did a celebrated French writer, . . . say] Montesquieu, in *Considération sur les causes de la grandeur des Romains, et de leur décadence* (1734, Considerations on the Causes of the Greatness of the Romans and their Decline), ch. viii.

599.20 Lord Cook] Coke.

600.37 triers] Lawyers.

601.21–22 says Dr. Blackstone] The quote that follows is from the *Commentaries on the Laws of England*, vol. III, ch. xxiii.

602.17 says the above cited author] Ibid., vol. I, ch. i.

602.36–37 *nam qui sentit onus, sentire debet commodum*] A maxim of contract law dating at least to the fifteenth century, often cited by Coke and other English jurists.

603.14 *causa sine qua non*] Latin: indispensable condition.

604.3–4 like St. Pauls] The apostle Paul claims Roman citizenship numerous times in Acts of the Apostles, specifically insisting (Acts 22:28) that it was bestowed on him through birth.

604.35–36 natural allegiance is universal and perpetual] See note 143.28.

605.9 enter into religion] That is, the monastic life.

607.18 Lord Delaware] Sir Thomas West, Lord De La Warr (1577–1618), became a member of the London Virginia Company in 1609 and the following year was appointed the first governor and captain-general of Virginia. He arrived in Virginia with three ships and 150 settlers on June 8, 1610, intercepting the surviving colonists at Jamestown just as they were attempting to abandon the site.

607.18–21 Thus Virginia, . . . vindicating the rights of Americans.] Because Virginia was by far the largest, richest, and most populous of the colonies, New Englanders like Mather recognized that its support was crucial to the success of the patriot cause. They also needed to combat the idea, often put forward by the British government, that independence was purely a New England scheme. This helps explain why in June 1775, Virginian George Washington was unanimously chosen to take command of the "New England army" laying siege to Boston, and why it was crucial in June 1776 that Virginian Richard Henry Lee be the one to put forward the resolution for independence in the Second Continental Congress.

607.40–608.1 says an English historian] William Guthrie (1708?–1771) in *A New Geographical, Historical, and Commercial Grammar; and Present State of the Several Kingdoms of the World* (3rd ed., London, 1771). Guthrie was Scottish, not English.

609.7–8 could the British parliament alter . . . the constitution] By the eighteenth century, this was precisely what Parliament could do. As Blackstone pointed out, in England there could be no distinction between the "constitution or frame of government" and "the system of laws." All were of a piece: every act of Parliament was part of the constitution and all law, both customary and statutory, was thus constitutional. "Therefore," concluded the eighteenth-century English philosopher William Paley, "the terms *constitutional* and *unconstitutional*, mean *legal* and *illegal*." This was of course strikingly different from what Americans came to believe.

609.23 *nam ex nihilo nihil gignitur*] Latin: for nothing is produced from nothing.

610.39–611.10 "We do, for us, . . . in any wise notwithstanding."] The first of three passages Mather quotes from the Connecticut Charter of 1662 (also 611.12–29 and 612.14–22).

612.38 the manor of East-Greenwich] See note 45.13–14.

613.13 the words of the English historian] Guthrie, again from *A New Geographical, Historical, and Commercial Grammar*.

614.28 an act was framed and sent over] See note 29.5–7.

614.36–39 "that is was unnecessary, . . . in matters relating to them."] See Chronology for 1621.

615.4 1683-4] This is an instance of double dating arising from Parliament's act of 1750 abandoning the old Julian calendar, which had marked the new year on March 25 (Annunciation Day), in favor of the new Gregorian calendar, the calendar in use today. To avoid confusion, both the "Old Style" and "New Style" years were often used in English and colonial records for dates falling between the new and old New Year. So, in this case, the date is March 8, 1684.

615.21 L. Jenkins] Sir Leoline Jenkins (1623–1685), secretary of state, 1680-84.

615.40–616.22 "And we do for us, . . . the said company and inhabitants." More from the Connecticut Charter of 1662.

618.9–16 "and we do further . . . our realm of England."] Ibid.

618.28–29 in the colonies all persons . . . are prohibited playing at games. All the *New England* colonies, that is, a vestige of their Puritan origins. The other colonies, especially Virginia and the Carolinas, were noticeably more lax about games. James I's Declaration of Sports (1617), which clarified which leisure activities were permissible on Sundays, had been provoked by Puritan efforts to impose their more restrictive sabbatarianism on the English gentry.

619.17–18 7 and 8 Will. III. cap. 22.] See note 50.34–35.

619.22 stat. 6 of Geo. III cap. 12.] The Declaratory Act of 1766.

622.6 the 12th of Charles II.] The Navigation Act of 1660.

622.12–13   this produced an insurrection in Virginia] Bacon's Rebellion (see Chronology for 1676).

623.40   except in one or two instances] With the Pennsylvania Charter of 1681 Charles II granted to William Penn and his heirs "the Customes and Subsidies" arising from trade with the province, "Saveing unto us, our heirs and Successors, such impositions and Customes, as by Act of Parliament are and shall be appointed."

627.24–25   garments roll'd in blood] Cf. Isaiah 9:5.

628.31–32   those suns of thunder] Jesus bestows this appellation on James and John, the sons of Zebedee, in Mark 3:17, elsewhere admonishing them for their intemperate zeal—they have asked him to empower them to rain fire down on the Samaritans—by reminding them that "the Son of man is not come to destroy men's lives, but to save *them*" (Luke 9:56).

630.3   Barre, the Bishop of Asaph] Isaac Barré (1726–1802), Irish-born politician who consistently supported Chatham on the American question; he is supposed to have first called the American patriots "Sons of Liberty." Jonathan Shipley (1714–1788), Bishop of St. Asaph, 1769–88, was the only prelate who supported the American cause in Parliament. He published a pamphlet in protest of the Coercive Acts in which he wrote, "I look upon North America as the only great nursery of freemen left on the face of the earth."

631.1   Sir William Phips] See note 351.26–28.

631.9   Admiral Walker] The force commanded by Hovenden Walker (1656?–1728) consisted of ten ships of the line and about thirty transports, carrying some five thousand troops. Dismissed from the service after the failure of the expedition on Quebec, he eventually became a planter in South Carolina.

631.19–20   against Canada, in A.D. 1740; and . . . Cuba] Operations undertaken as part of the War of Jenkins' Ear, a conflict between Britain and Spain that began in 1739 and became subsumed into the larger War of the Austrian Succession. The assault on Havana was prelude to a protracted and ultimately unsuccessful siege of Cartagena.

631.21–22   Commodore Warren, and Mr. Pepperel] Sir Peter Warren (1703?–1752) commanded a relatively small fleet of one ship of the line and three frigates in the expedition to Cape Breton. He was made a rear-admiral for his role in the successful siege of Louisbourg. For Pepperrell see note 402.40.

631.31   the peace of Aix Chappelle] See Chronology for 1744–48.

632.18–20   a righteous minister . . . to reimburse them.] William Pitt was especially esteemed in America for his role in organizing the reimbursement of colonial expenses from the Seven Years' War (see note 233.15–16).

634.29–40   "By the rivers of Babylon . . . the foundation thereof."] Psalm 137:1–7.

636.3–4   hear the advice . . . Monsieur Mezeray] The original source for the quote that follows was an anonymous 1692 pamphlet entitled *Some Considerations about the Most Proper Way of Raising Money in the Present Conjuncture*, whose author claimed the words were "said to me at Paris ten years ago, by the great Historian" François Eudes de Mézeray (1610–1683). The pamphlet was republished in the three-volume *Collection of State Tracts, Publish'd on Occasion of the Late Revolution in 1688, and During the Reign of King William III* (London, 1705–7), and the remarks were quoted in another anonymous work, *The Groans of Britons at the Gloomy Prospect of the Present Precarious State of their Liberties and Properties* (London, 1743). Either of these may have been Mather's source.

636.16   Holland and Switzerland] Two examples—savored by eighteenth-century Whigs, especially in America—of small federated states which had successfully asserted themselves against powerful and despotic adversaries (Habsburg Spain and Austria).

637.1   dust on the balance] Cf. Isaiah 40:15.

642.28   grow up with their growth] See note 549.24–25.

644.3   *nam qui transtulit sustinet*] Motto of the state of Connecticut.

646.3–4   they have sent commissioners] In an October 26, 1775, speech to Parliament the king promised to commission "certain Persons on the Spot" to grant pardons and to receive the "Submission of any Province or Colony" that wished "to return to its Allegiance." Lord North was concerned that even this minimal gesture of conciliation would be opposed by hardline supporters of the ministry. Ultimately, the Crown empowered General William Howe and his brother Admiral Lord Richard Howe, newly appointed commander of British land and naval forces in North America, to act as peace commissioners as well as military leaders—contradictory roles that proved difficult to reconcile. On September 11, 1776, after the huge British expeditionary force successfully occupied New York and its environs, Admiral Lord Howe met congressional peace delegation that included John Adams, Benjamin Franklin, and Edward Rutledge at Billup Manor on Staten Island, but negotiations came to naught, as Howe refused to recognize American independence.

37: [THOMAS PAINE], COMMON SENSE

647.36   Edmund Randolph of Virginia reflected] In a history of the Revolution in Virginia that the former U.S. attorney general and secretary of state wrote in retirement, 1809–13.

649.19–20   Man knows . . . and common Good ordain.] James Thomson *Liberty: A Poem* (1736), IV.636–37. This four-part epic poem, which traces the course of liberty from ancient Greece and Rome to the Glorious Revolution appealed to patriots because of its passionate protests against corruption.

651.28–29   laying a Country desolate with Fire and Sword] Cf. Ezekiel 30:6–8

653.7–8   Society is produced by our wants, and government by our wickedness] This view, common among Anglo-American radicals in the late eighteenth century, assumed that government interfered with the natural flow of benevolence among human beings, primarily through the manipulation of patronage of various sorts—filling offices, granting monopolies, conferring titles. By doing so it created distinctions and inequality that would not otherwise have arisen, obscuring the fact that all people, however lowly, possessed a natural social sense and an innate desire to get along with their fellow human beings. These assumptions lay behind the belief in minimal government shared by Whig radicals like Paine and Jefferson.

655.25–26   the more simple any thing is] This notion was rejected by many patriot readers of Paine's pamphlet, including John Adams, who was deeply committed to the idea of mixed government expressed by the British constitution. For Adams it was only the ministry's ability to corrupt Parliament that had upset the balance in the British system. Paine's emphasis on simple democracy greatly influenced the writing of the controversial Pennsylvania constitution of 1776, which, unlike the other state constitutions drafted that year, dispensed with both an upper house and a single executive.

657.6–7   an house divided against itself] Cf. Mark 3:25.

659.21   Gideon and the prophet Samuel] Judges 6–8, especially 8:22–23; I Samuel 8:5–20, 12:17–19.

659.25–26   *"Render unto Cæsar the things which are Cæsar's"*] Matthew 22:21; Mark 12:17; Luke 20:25.

660.8 12   *Rule thou over us, . . . rule over you.*] Judges 8:22–23.

661.29   a *man* after God's own heart.] Acts 13:22.

662.23   *ass for a lion*] Reference to Aesop's fable of the ass trying to overawe his fellow animals by wearing a lion's skin.

662.29–30   "that your children . . . for ever."] Cf. Ezekiel 37:25.

666.7–8   Sir William Meredith calls it a republic] A long-serving member of Parliament, and one of the Rockingham Whigs, Meredith (c. 1725–1790) called "our present constitution" a republic in an exchange of letters with a constituent published in the May 1773 issue of *The Gentleman's Magazine.*

667.7   the late Mr. Pelham] Henry Pelham (c. 1695–1754), first lord of the Treasury (prime minister) and chancellor of the Exchequer from 1743 until his death. He was the younger brother of the Duke of Newcastle, who succeeded him in the premiership.

668.32–33   The miseries of Hanover] The German electorate was overrun and occupied by a French army in 1757, with consequences so devastating some Hanoverian ministers considered severing the dynastic ties with the British monarchs.

668.34–35   the colonies have no relation . . . but through the parent coun-
try] There was some truth to this assertion. More of the delegates to the
Continental Congress in 1774 had been to London than had previously been
to Philadelphia, then the largest city in America.

670.2–3   Not one third . . . of English descent.] Paine is exaggerating.
Modern estimates suggest that about 60 percent of the white population of
the British colonies was of English descent, followed by 14 percent Scots and
Scots-Irish. Those of African descent made up about 20 percent of the total
population. Germans are thought to have constituted a third of Pennsylvania's
population, but less than 9 percent of the white population of the colonies as
a whole.

670.21   Our plan is commerce] Radical Whigs believed that commerce, especially as practiced by republics, could act as a peaceful means of tying nations
together and preventing war, which they thought was principally caused by
monarchical rivalries.

673.25   as Milton wisely expresses] Albeit in Satan's voice, in *Paradise Lost*,
IV.98–99.

673.32   Witness Denmark and Sweden.] Anglo-American Whigs often pointed
to these two countries as case studies of once free states that had succumbed
to absolutism. Their principal sources were *An Account of Denmark, as it was
in the Year 1692* by Robert Lord Viscount Molesworth (1656–1725), which was
first published in 1694 and appeared in its sixth edition in 1752, and Voltaire's
L'Histoire de Charles XII (1731, *The History of Charles XII, King of Sweden*, 1732).

675.3   a Bunker-hill price] A high price for little gain. The British suffered
fifteen hundred casualties in their Pyrrhic victory in the battle of Bunker Hill
(June 17, 1775), making it one of the costliest engagements of the entire war.

676.13   a youth of twenty-one] George III was actually twenty-two when he
became king in 1760.

677.23–24   a youth, . . . out of his time] That is, a youth whose period of
indenture is nearly over.

678.31   A space was left here in each of the first three editions, an indication,
perhaps, of Paine's uncertainty or flexibility with regard to the duration of
congressional sessions.

680.8   *Dragonetti on virtue and rewards."*] Giacinto Dragonetti (1738–1818)
Trattato delle virtù e dei premi (1765, *A Treatise on Virtues and Rewards*
1769).

680.36   Thomas Anello, otherwise Massanello] Masaniello's six-day insurrection (July 1647) against Naples's Habsburg rulers ended with his assassination
by agents of the viceroy; within two years it was dramatized in an anonymous
English play, *The Rebellion of Naples, or The Tragedy of Massanello Commonly
so Called.*

681.8–9   stirred up the Indians] Another reference to Lord Dunmore, royal governor of Virginia, who, in addition to his overture to the colony's slaves (see note 523.12), attempted to enlist Indians from the northwest frontier as allies against the American patriots.

683.23   *Entic's naval history*] John Entick, *A New Naval History: or, Compleat View of the British Marine* (London, 1757).

683.27   as calculated by Mr. Burchett, Secretary to the navy.] Josiah Burchett (1666?–1746), secretary of the Admiralty, 1698–1742, and author of *A Complete History of the Most Remarkable Transactions at Sea . . . in Five Books* (London, 1720).

684.12   bombs] Small naval vessels used for shore bombardment.

684.33   The Terrible privateer, Captain Death] Captain William Death commanded the privateer *Terrible*, 26 guns, in its engagement with the French privateer *Vengeance*, 36 guns, at the western entrance to the English Channel on December 27, 1756. After a battle lasting three hours, Captain Death was fatally wounded and the *Terrible* surrendered. Paine later wrote in *Rights of Man* that he had briefly enlisted on board the *Terrible*.

687.16–17   The difference between Pennsylvania and Connecticut] Royal charters granted to Connecticut colonists in 1662 and to William Penn in 1681 resulted in conflicting territorial jurisdiction over the Wyoming Valley in present-day northeastern Pennsylvania. In 1769, Connecticut settlers began moving into the valley, and in 1774–75 the Connecticut colonial government organized the region as a township, and then as a separate county, of Connecticut. After Pennsylvania militia unsuccessfully attempted to drive the Connecticut settlers from the valley late in 1775, the Continental Congress mediated an agreement allowing the settlers to remain for the duration of hostilities with Britain. A commission appointed by the Congress awarded permanent jurisdiction to Pennsylvania in 1782.

687.33   the ancients far exceeded the moderns] Such comparisons were commonplace in the seventeenth and eighteenth centuries, when the question of the relative superiority or inferiority of antiquity to the present had an urgency difficult to recapture today.

689.26   Associators petition] A committee of privates serving in the Military Association (the Pennsylvania militia) submitted two petitions to the assembly in October 1775. The first called for the adoption of a law making militia service compulsory for all freemen; the second asserted that it would not violate liberty of conscience to levy fines on Quakers who refused to serve. On November 17, 1775, the assembly divided 14–14 on the question of requiring twenty days of compulsory militia drill a year. The speaker cast the deciding vote in the affirmative, and on November 25 the assembly passed a militia law that levied fines on "Non-Associators."

689.30–31   this whole province had been governed by two counties only]

Because the western counties of Pennsylvania were grossly underrepresented in the colonial assembly, the eastern counties of Bucks and Chester possessed a disproportionate amount of power. The underrepresentation of the west had contributed to the Paxton Boys uprising in 1764 (see Chronology).

690.20–22   Mr. Cornwall . . . New-York Assembly with contempt] Charles Wolfran Cornwall (1735–1789) was a junior lord of the Treasury in the North government, 1774–80, and then speaker of the House of Commons, 1780–89. In early 1775 the New York Assembly had adopted a remonstrance to the House of Commons that protested several parliamentary measures. The Commons debated the petition on May 15, 1775—with Cornwall arguing that "it was contrary to every idea of the supremacy of Parliament to receive a paper in which the Legislative rights of Parliament were denied"—before declining to receive it by a vote of 186–67.

690.39   Burgh's political Disquisitions.] James Burgh (1714–1775), Whig writer whose three-volume *Political Disquisitions* (London, 1774; Philadelphia, 1775), criticizing the structure of government in Great Britain, was widely influential in the American colonies. Burgh treats the problem of unequal representation in Parliament in Vol. I, Bk. ii.

692.3–4   the same day . . . the King's Speech] On January 10, 1776, copies of the speech delivered by George III at the opening of Parliament on October 26, 1775, reached Philadelphia. In it the king condemned the "desperate Conspiracy" of American rebels who were bent on independence and promised "to put a speedy End to these Disorders by the most decisive Exertions."

693.3   Sir John Dalrymple] Scottish judge (1726–1810) and author of *The Address of the People of Great-Britain to the Inhabitants of America* (London, 1775), which attempted to intimidate Americans with such warnings as "Your Destruction is inevitable." Dalrymple suggested that all the imperial difficulties were caused by lawyers, men "who gain by uncertainty and disorder," against whom the colonists had to be especially on their guard, for "there is no region on earth in which the people are so much oppressed by the extortions of Lawyers, as in many parts of America."

696.29–31   The artful and hypocritical letter . . . New-York papers] An extract from a letter "from a Gentleman in London, to his friend in this city, dated July 26, 1775," appeared in *Rivington's New-York Gazetteer* on October 12, 1775, and was reprinted in Gaine's *New-York Gazette and the Weekly Mercury* the following week. The letter described the North ministry as sincerely pursuing reconciliation with the colonists and urged Americans to negotiate a settlement with Britain that recognized parliamentary supremacy over the colonies. A reply printed in the *New York Journal* on November 14, 1775, attributed the letter to Dr. Myles Cooper (1737–1785), a Loyalist clergyman who had served as president of King's College in New York from 1763 until May 1775, when he fled the city.

697.3   "they are reckoning without their Host."] A once common phrase meaning to enter upon an enterprise without knowing the cost, or, more simply, to be imprudent.

699.29   *a late piece*] The Quaker address, written by John Pemberton (1727–1795), clerk of the Monthly Meeting of Philadelphia, and dated January 20, 1776, was published in the *Pennsylvania Ledger* on January 27.

701.1   the shade of our own vines] Evoking a recurring image from the Hebrew Scriptures; cf. Micah 4:4, 1 Kings 4:25, 2 Kings 18:31, Isaiah 36:16.

701.41   *Barclay's Address to Charles II.*] This address served as the introduction to *An Apology for the True Christian Divinity: Being an Explanation and Vindication of the Principles and Doctrines of the People called Quakers* by Scottish Quaker Robert Barclay (1648–1690). Originally published in Latin as *Theologiæ Verè Christianæ Apologia* in 1676 and released in English in 1678, this work was issued in what was billed as "the Ninth Edition in English" in Philadelphia in 1775.

703.19–20   the dispersion . . . foretold by our Savior] Luke 21:24.

38: [CHARLES INGLIS], THE TRUE INTEREST OF AMERICA

707.17   "Obtrectatio . . . accipiuntur."] Tacitus, *Historiæ*, Bk. I, ch. i: "Spleen and calumny are devoured with a greedy ear." (Craufurd Tait Ramage, *Beautiful Thoughts from Latin Authors* [Liverpool, 1864], 390.)

707.18–19   "——Nihil eſt, Antipho, . . . depravarier."] Terence, *Phormio*, IV.iv.15–16: "There is nothing, Antipho, but by telling may be made to appear the worse." (Samuel Patrick, *Terence's Comedies, Translated into English Prose* [2 vols., Dublin, 1810], II, 196.)

710.1   *Mercy and Truth; or Charity maintained*] A 1634 treatise by Jesuit Matthias Wilson (1580–1666), writing as Edward Knott. The Oxford theologian William Chillingworth (1602–1644) replied to it with the very popular *The Religion of Protestants* (1638). Inglis likely encountered Wilson's pamphlet in Chillingworth's oft-reprinted *Works*, where it was reproduced in full.

710.24   the baseless fabric of a vision] Cf. *The Tempest*, IV.iv.151.

712.16–17   "join them together; . . . put them asunder.] Cf. Mark 10:9.

715.2   Hobbes's notion] The quote that follows distills chapter 13 of *Leviathan* (1651).

715.6–7   Hooker's opinion] Richard Hooker, *Of Ecclesiastical Polity*, Bk. I, sect. 10.

716.10   It is Livy, I think] Harrington attributed such an assertion to Livy and Aristotle in *The Commonwealth of Oceana*, Bk. I, ch. ii.

716.15   Draco] Athenian lawgiver whose code (621 B.C.) was proverbially harsh, hence draconian.

719.29–30   The late legal decision in favour of Mr. Wilkes] The government
had prosecuted John Wilkes for seditious libel in 1763, but because the general warrant was poorly drawn and because Wilkes as a member of Parliament
claimed parliamentary privilege, the case had been thrown out.

721.7   candidly owned by Harrington] In *The Commonwealth of Oceana*,
Bk. I.

721.10–11   Algernon Sidney, . . . acknowledges the same.*] Algernon Sidney (1623–1683), an influential republican theorist executed for treason against
the government of Charles II. The text of his then-unpublished *Discourses
Concerning Government*—which Inglis refers to here—was used as evidence
of his treason. Published posthumously in 1698, the work became very important to eighteenth-century radical Whigs.

721.19   For what is the constitution] Inglis here offers the traditional English
definition of a constitution as the accretion of all laws and acts of government,
both customary and statutory. In his *Rights of Man* (London, 1791), Paine
would clarify for the world the new American definition, emphasizing two
central departures from the English model. First, a constitution is material,
"not a thing in name only, but in fact. It has not an ideal, but a real existence; and wherever it cannot be produced in a visible form, there is none." It
was, in short, a written document that could be picked up and read, like
the Bible. Second, a constitution is foundational, "a thing *antecedent* to a
government, and a government is only the creature of a constitution. The
constitution of a country is not the act of its government, but of the people
constituting a government."

724.30   one John Hall] English poet and pamphleteer (1627–1656) who
wrote a number of works on education and politics, including *The Grounds
and Reasons of Monarchy, Considered and Exemplified out of the Scottish History*
(Edinburgh, 1651).

725.2   In Poland we see a specimen] Contemporary observers attributed the
weakness that left Poland subject to the will of its neighbors (see note 386.38)
to the chronic internecine struggle for the throne by Polish nobles.

725.24–25   "the earth was filled with violence"] Genesis 6:11.

726.35   speaking evil of dignities] Cf. 2 Peter 2:10, an important text for
eighteenth-century conservatives. Since political authority rested on the social
status of the officeholders, any writing that brought that status into question
was punishable under the common law of seditious libel. The truthfulness of
such writing was generally understood to be immaterial; indeed it actually aggravated the offense. The Federalist Sedition Act of 1798 liberalized the law at
the federal level by allowing truth to be a defense of statements about public
officials. Today, as a result of the Supreme Court's decision in *New York Time
Co. v. Sullivan* (1964), even false and untrue statements about public officials
are allowed as long as no malice was intended.

727.7 Floraria of Rome] In 238 B.C. a temple was built in Rome to honor Flora, goddess of flowers and blossoming plants, who became the object of an annual celebration, April 28–May 3, involving games (*ludi Florales*) and farces and mimes known for their licentiousness.

727.23 for Heathens paid divine honours] There follow allusions to myths associated with Hercules.

732.20 reflections of a learned writer] William Warburton (1698–1779), English churchman and critic who was Bishop of Gloucester from 1759 to his death; among many works, he wrote *The Divine Legation of Moses Demonstrated, on the Principles of a Religious Deist* (2 vols., London 1738), which Inglis paraphrases.

736.23 the famous Bishop Berkeley's maxim] Inglis refers to the thirty-ninth of the *Maxims concerning Patriotism* (Dublin, 1750), by Irish philosopher George Berkeley (1685–1753).

742.13–20 "That if a man . . . and great learning."] From Bk. I, ch. 5 of the *Discourses* of Epictetus (A.D. 101).

743.12 Gentoo] An English term, from the Portuguese *gentio* (cf. "gentile"), or non-Muslim Indians, or Hindus.

744.38 *Fifth-monarchy* men] See note 222.32–33.

744.41 "Want of decency is want of sense!"] An oft-quoted line from *An Essay on Translated Verse* (1684) by Irish poet Wentworth Dillon, 4th Earl of Roscommon (1633–1685). Franklin criticizes the verse in the first part of his *Autobiography*.

746.23 The Millennial state] The thousand-year reign of Christ preceding the final judgment, as foretold in Revelation 20:1–6.

746.24–26 "Men would . . . nor learn war any more."] Cf. Isaiah 2:4.

747.38–39 an observation . . . Dr. Beattie] James Beattie (1735–1803), Scottish poet, philosopher, and author of *An Essay on the Nature and Immutability of Truth; in Opposition to Sophistry and Scepticism* (Edinburgh, 1770), from which Inglis quotes. This work, an answer to David Hume, was much celebrated and resulted in an introduction to the king, a pension, and a degree of LL.D. from Oxford.

750.33–34 his eldest daughter and her husband stept in.] That is, Mary and her husband William of Orange, who became William III.

753.1 Lycurgus and Solon] Lawgivers of Sparta and Athens.

753.38–39 the battle of Pharsalia] Decisive battle in central Greece on August 9, 48 B.C., in which Julius Caesar defeated Pompey and effectively ended the republic.

754.3 Sylla and Marius] Lucius Cornelius Sulla (c. 138–78 B.C.), the general who was the last leader, before Julius Caesar, to hold the title of dictator of the Roman Republic. His chief rival for power was the consul Gaius Marius (c. 157–86 B.C.).

754.15–16   Mr. Harrington's *Rota*] In 1659 James Harrington helped form a club called the Rota to implement the commonwealth designed in his *Oceana*.

754.21   what MONTESQUIEU said of Harrington] In his *Spirit of the Laws*, Bk. xi, ch. 6.

754.34–35   the chapter of accidents] An idiomatic expression for unforeseen events or chance. The Roman laws were divided into books, and each book into chapters. The chapter of accidents concerned delicts (torts) involving neither malicious intent nor negligence, but simple happenstance.

754.39   *Common Sense*, page 71] Page 688 in this volume.

755.18–19   according to SWIFT,] Cf. *Gulliver's Travels*, part II, ch. 5. This passage would later be employed by Federalists to ridicule what they took to be the fanciful utopianism of Jefferson and his followers.

759.1   Spanish milled dollars] So called because of their milled or patterned edges, designed to prevent shaving. Also called pieces of eight, these were valid as currency in the United States until the late 1850s.

760.19   in the year 1769] Inglis has chosen a year when American boycotts in protest of the Townshend duties had significantly reduced total exports.

760.39   See *Campbell's Political Survey*] John Campbell (1708–1775), *A Political Survey of Britain: Being a Series of Reflections on the Situation, Lands, Inhabitants, Revenues, Colonies, and Commerce of this Island* (2 vols., London, 1774)

761.9–10   a certain writer declares] William Guthrie (see note 607.40–608.1)

761.18–19   Lord Chesterfield observes.] In "Some Account of the Government of the Republic of the United Provinces," collected in the fourth volume of *Letters Written by the Late Right Honourable Philip Dormer Stanhope, Earl of Chesterfield, to His Son . . . Together with Several Other Miscellaneous Pieces on Various Subjects* (4 vols., London, 1774).

762.21   late concessions to Nova-Scotia] Britain granted Nova Scotia an elected assembly in 1758—the first of its kind in Canada—in part in an attempt to lure settlers north from New England.

762.35   *taxation is given up* by the Ministry] Referring to North's Conciliatory Resolution (see note 535.6), which called for voluntary contributions in place of mandated taxes.

763.28   The fate of Corsica] Corsica struggled for decades to free itself from Genoese rule, only to be conquered by France after Genoa sold its claim to the island to the French crown in 1768.

765.16   The King of Denmark's late proclamation] This edict, issued by

Christian VII, King of Denmark and Norway, on October 4, 1775, specifically prohibited the exportation of arms and ammunition to the American colonies.

769.37–38   pace . . . in the trammels] An idiomatic expression for following heedlessly.

770.36   Quod Deus a nobis procul avertat.] Latin: God forbid that we turn away from him.

39: [THOMAS HUTCHINSON], STRICTURES UPON THE DECLARATION

771.27–28   fell into patriot hands and were published.] Specifically, Benjamin Franklin's hands. In December 1772 the colonial agent had received the letters—communiqués between Hutchinson and Thomas Whately and other officials in London—from an anonymous source and circulated them under the condition that they not be made public. He sent copies to Massachusetts, where they were published as a pamphlet in Boston in June 1773. An uproar ensued on both sides of the Atlantic: the Massachusetts House called for Hutchinson's immediate recall and the British government determined to discover who had purloined the letters. William Whately, the brother of the now deceased Thomas Whately, accused William Temple, another imperial official, resulting in a duel in which Whately was injured. When a second challenge was issued, in December 1773, Franklin was moved to step forward and admit his part in the affair. As a result of the scandal, Franklin was publicly reprimanded by Parliament and dismissed as postmaster general.

772.2–4   "most infamous . . . deeds of the King."] Hutchinson to Philip Yorke, 2nd Earl of Hardwicke, August 10, 1776 (the day news of the American declaration reached London). Hardwicke (1720–1790) was a privy councilor who supported the Rockingham Whigs. He became one of Hutchinson's closest correspondents after the exiled former governor arrived in England and is the Noble Lord to whom this pamphlet is addressed.

777.20–21   a letter to their Agent in the summer of 1764] A memorial written by Boston representative James Otis and presented to the Massachusetts House of Representatives, which in turn sent it to Jasper Mauduit, the colony's agent in London, 1762–65. It is included as an appendix in Otis's *The Rights of the British Colonists Asserted and Proved* (Boston, 1764), Pamphlet 3 in the companion to this volume. This is the pamphlet Hutchinson refers to in the next sentence.

778.1–2   One of the most noted . . . American clergy] Possibly the Reverend Samuel Cooper, Congregational minister of the liberal Brattle Street Church and the leading patriot clergyman in Boston. His older brother, William Cooper, was the town clerk of Boston and one of the organizers of the Sons of Liberty.

781.5   *pursuit of happiness*] Hutchinson responds here to one of Jefferson's most notable innovations in the Declaration. "Life, Liberty, and Property" was a familiar phrase in the Anglo-American world, its origins traceable to Locke's *Second Treatise* (ch. ix, sect. 131): "Men . . . enter into society . . . with an intention in every one the better to preserve himself, his liberty and property." "Liberty and Property" became a political slogan of the Glorious Revolution, one so associated with Whigs that by 1713 the opposition was heard to protest "No Liberty and Property Men!"

783.16 not to consent . . . making new towns] In 1767 the Privy Council, fearful of "too great an increase of the number and influence of the representative body, and . . . a disproportion to the other branches of the legislature," forbade governors from approving any bill that altered the apportionment of representatives in the colonial assemblies.

785.18 The Governor] Francis Bernard, Hutchinson's predecessor as Massachusetts governor.

787.8 the Colony must be North Carolina] In its bills to fund and regulate procedures for the colony's superior court the North Carolina Assembly had traditionally allowed for the attachment of nonresidents' property in prosecutions for debt, and in some cases the property of English debtors who had never resided in the colony had been attached. In 1770 the Board of Trade objected to this practice as a violation of the common law, insisting that cases involving British debtors should be tried in British courts. Three years later, as a result of the Board's refusal to assent to bills containing this provision, the assembly refused to fund the superior courts, causing a paralysis of the colony's legal system that ended only with independence.

788.8 *He has made Judges dependent on his will*] See note 156.6.

790.3 *He has combined with others*] This was indeed, as Hutchinson observes, "a strange way" of characterizing the English constitution. Though it had been acts of Parliament which had provoked the American crisis, the Congress was scrupulous in not mentioning Parliament in the Declaration of Independence. Since 1774 the colonists had contended that they had no constitutional relationship whatsoever with Parliament, and were therefore tied only to the Crown. By the summer of 1776, from the American perspective, that was the sole constitutional connection left to sever.

790.27 it was their duty to yield obedience] In 1764 many of the colonies, including Massachusetts, opposed the Sugar Act as an unwise and crippling regulation of trade without challenging the constitutional right of Parliament to enact it.

791.24 *For cutting off our trade*] Referring to Parliament's Restraining Acts (1775) closing the Newfoundland fisheries and forbidding Americans from trading outside of the empire. Worried about the need to encourage the Loyalists in America, Hutchinson had lobbied unsuccessfully to lessen the harshness of these acts.

792.30–31   Russell, Hampden, Maynard] Three Whig icons: Lord William
Russell (1639–1683), who supported the exclusion of the Catholic Duke of
York from the throne and was executed for treason against the Crown; John
Hampden (1594–1643), who famously resisted Charles I's attempts to im-
pose taxes (ship money) without Parliament's consent; and Sir John Maynard
(1604–1690), who had been one of the parliamentary prosecutors of both
Strafford and Laud (see note 395.15–16).

793.22   trees reserved for the Royal Navy] In 1711, 1722, and 1729, Parliament passed acts forbidding the colonists from cutting down large pine trees
that were to be used for masts for the Royal Navy. The colonists resented these
acts, often evaded them, and, as in New Hampshire in 1772, sometimes rioted
in protest.

Index

This book is set in 10 point ITC Galliard Pro, a
face designed for digital composition by Matthew Carter
and based on the sixteenth-century face Granjon. The paper
is acid-free lightweight opaque and meets the requirements
for permanence of the American National Standards Institute.
The binding material is Brillianta, a woven rayon cloth made
by Van Heek–Scholco Textielfabrieken, Holland.
Composition by Dedicated Book Services. Printing and
binding by Edwards Brothers Malloy, Ann Arbor.
Designed by Bruce Campbell.

THE LIBRARY OF AMERICA SERIES

The Library of America fosters appreciation and pride in America's literary heritage by publishing, and keeping permanently in print, authoritative editions of America's best and most significant writing. An independent nonprofit organization, it was founded in 1979 with seed funding from the National Endowment for the Humanities and the Ford Foundation.

To subscribe to the series or to order individual copies, please visit www.loa.org or call (800) 964-5778.

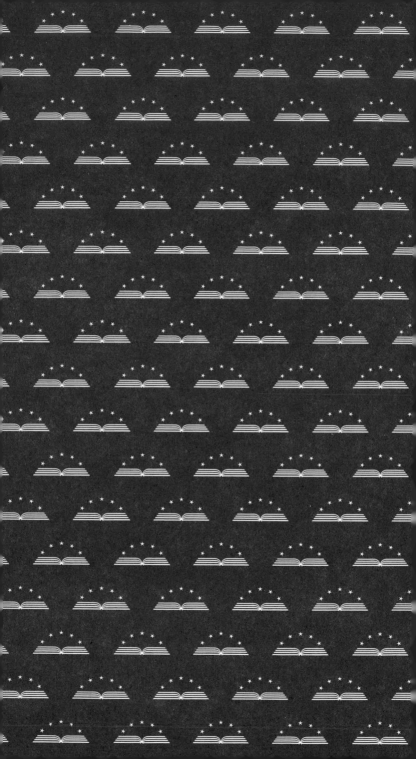